Frommer's®

Maui

with Molokai and Lanai

D0927303

Here's what the critics say about Frommer's:

"Amazingly easy to use. Very portable, very complete."
—*Booklist*

♦

"The only mainstream guide to list specific prices. The Walter Cronkite of guidebooks—with all that implies."
—*Travel & Leisure*

♦

"Complete, concise, and filled with useful information."
—*New York Daily News*

♦

"Hotel information is close to encyclopedic."
—*Des Moines Sunday Register*

Other Great Guides for Your Trip:

Frommer's Hawaii

Frommer's Hawaii from $60 a Day

Frommer's Honolulu, Waikiki & Oahu

The Complete Idiot's Travel Guide to Hawaii

Frommer's® 99

Maui

with Molokai and Lanai

**by Jeanette Foster
& Jocelyn Fujii**

MACMILLAN • USA

ABOUT THE AUTHORS

A resident of the Big Island, **Jeanette Foster** has skied the slopes of Mauna Kea—during a Fourth of July ski meet, no less—and scuba dived with manta rays off the Kona Coast. A prolific writer widely published in travel, sports, and adventure magazines, she's also a contributing editor to *Hawaii* magazine.

Kauai-born **Jocelyn Fujii,** a resident of Honolulu, is one of Hawaii's leading journalists. She has authored *Under the Hula Moon: Living in Hawaii* and *The Best of Hawaii,* as well as articles for the *New York Times, National Geographic Traveler, Islands, Condé Nast Traveler, Travel Holiday,* and other national and international publications.

In addition to this guide, Jeanette and Jocelyn also co-authored *Frommer's Hawaii, Frommer's Hawaii from $60 a Day,* and *Frommer's Honolulu, Waikiki & Oahu.*

MACMILLAN TRAVEL

A Simon & Schuster Macmillan Company
1633 Broadway
New York, NY 10019

Find us online at **www.frommers.com**

ISBN 0-02-862242-1
ISSN 1076-2817

Editor: Leslie Shen
Production Editor: Michael Thomas
Photo Editor: Richard Fox
Design by Michele Laseau
Digital Cartography by Roberta Stockwell and Ortelius Design
Page Creation by Tammy Ahrens, John Bitter, and Jerry Cole

SPECIAL SALES

Contents

List of Maps

An Invitation to the Reader

In researching this book, we discovered many wonderful places—hotels, restaurants, shops, and more. We're sure you'll find others. Please tell us about them so that we can share the information with your fellow travelers in upcoming editions. If you were disappointed with a recommendation, we'd love to know that, too. Please write to:

Frommer's Maui '99
Macmillan Travel
1633 Broadway
New York, NY 10019

An Additional Note

Please be advised that travel information is subject to change at any time—and this is especially true of prices. We therefore suggest that you write or call ahead for confirmation when making your travel plans. The authors, editors, and publisher cannot be held responsible for the experiences of readers while traveling. Your safety is important to us, however, so we encourage you to stay alert and be aware of your surroundings. Keep a close eye on cameras, purses, and wallets, all favorite targets of thieves and pickpockets.

What the Symbols Mean

✪ Frommer's Favorites
Hotels, restaurants, attractions, and entertainment you should not miss.

The following abbreviations are used for credit cards:

AE	American Express	EURO	Eurocard
CB	Carte Blanche	JCB	Japan Credit Bank
DC	Diners Club	MC	MasterCard
DISC	Discover	V	Visa
ER	EnRoute		

Find Frommer's Online

Arthur Frommer's Outspoken Encyclopedia of Travel (www.frommers.com) offers more than 6,000 pages of up-to-the-minute travel information—including the latest bargains and candid, personal articles updated daily by Arthur Frommer himself. No other Web site offers such comprehensive and timely coverage of the world of travel.

The Best of Maui

by Jeanette Foster & Jocelyn Fujii

Maui, also called the Valley Isle, is but a small dot in the vast Pacific Ocean, but it offers visitors dreamlike—even surreal—experiences: floating weightless in a rainbowed sea of tropical fish, standing atop a 10,000-foot volcano watching the muted colors of dawn etch the sky, listening to the symphony of raindrops in a bamboo forest, breathing the salt-filled ocean air.

From around the globe, travelers are drawn to the island of Maui, each in search of a unique encounter. Some come to experience the "real" Hawaii; some anticipate heart-pounding adventure; some seek the relaxing and healing powers of this sacred place; and some are drawn by the indescribable, unexplainable concept of the aloha spirit, where harmony and love prevail.

This book is designed to help you find the paradise of your dreams. We have compiled everything you need to enjoy the islands of Maui, Molokai, and Lanai. For readers who are too excited to page through all the way, this chapter highlights what we consider the very best and the very finest this paradise has to offer.

1 The Best Beaches

Maui has all kinds of beaches: white-sand coves with waving palm trees, black-sand bays with thundering surf, wide stretches of pebbled bays that make primitive music as the waves roll in, even beaches with volcanic red sand. You'll discover beaches for swimming, for snorkeling and diving, for surfing and windsurfing, for fishing, and for simply sitting and staring. Below is a list of our favorites.

- **Kapalua Beach:** On an island of many great beaches, this one takes the prize. A golden crescent with swaying palms protected from strong winds and currents by two outstretched lava-rock promontories, Kapalua has calm waters that are perfect for snorkeling, swimming, and kayaking. Even though it borders the Kapalua Bay Hotel, the beach is long enough for everyone to enjoy. Facilities include showers, rest rooms, and lifeguards. See chapter 8.
- **D. T. Fleming Beach Park:** This quiet, out-of-the-way beach cove, located north of the Ritz-Carlton Hotel, starts at the 16th hole of the Kapalua golf course (Makaluapuna Point) and rolls around to the sea cliffs on the other side. Ironwood trees provide

The Hawaiian Islands

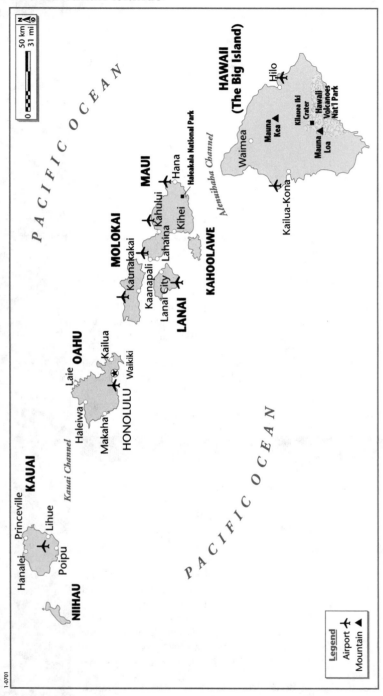

shade on the land side. Offshore, a shallow sandbar extends out to the edge of the surf. Generally, the waters are good for swimming and snorkeling, but sometimes, off near the sea cliffs, the waves build enough for bodyboarders and surfers to get a few good rides in. See chapter 8.

- **Kaanapali Beach:** Four-mile-long Kaanapali stands out as one of Maui's best beaches, with grainy gold sand as far as the eye can see. Most of the beach parallels the sea channel, and a paved beach walk links hotels and condos, open-air restaurants, and the Whalers Village shopping center. Summertime swimming is excellent. The best snorkeling is around Black Rock, in front of the Sheraton; the water is clear, calm, and populated with multitudes of tropical fish. See chapter 8.

- **Wailea Beach:** Named after Lea, the Hawaiian goddess of canoe makers, Wailea is the best gold-sand, crescent-shaped beach on Maui's sunbaked southwestern coast. One of five beaches within Wailea Resort, Wailea is big, wide, and protected on both sides by black lava points. It serves as the front yard for the Four Seasons Wailea and the Grand Wailea Resort Hotel & Spa, respectively Maui's most elegant and outrageous hotels. From the beach, the view out to sea is magni-ficent, framed by neighboring Kahoolawe and Lanai and the tiny crescent of Molokini, probably the most popular snorkel spot in these parts. The clear waters tumble to shore in waves just the right size for gentle riding, with or without a board. From shore, you can see Pacific humpback whales in season (December through April), as well as unreal sunsets nightly. See chapter 8.

- **Makena Beach:** On the southern end of Maui's resort coast, development falls off dramatically, leaving a wild, dry countryside punctuated by green kiawe trees. The wide, palm-fringed crescent of golden sand is set between two black lava points and bounded by big sand dunes topped by a grassy knoll. Makena can be perfect for swimming when it's flat and placid, but it can also offer excellent bodysurfing when the waves come rolling in. Or, if you prefer, it can be a place of serenity, with vistas of Molokini Crater and Kahoolawe off in the distance. See chapter 8.

- **Hamoa Beach, Hana:** This half moon–shaped, gray-sand beach (a mix of coral and lava) in a truly tropical setting is a favorite among sunbathers, snorkelers, and bodysurfers in Hana. The 100-foot-wide beach is three football fields long and sits below 30-foot black lava sea cliffs. An unprotected beach open to the ocean, Hamoa is often swept by powerful rip currents. Surf breaks offshore and rolls ashore, making it a popular surfing and bodysurfing area. The calm left side is best for snorkeling in the summer. See chapter 8.

- **Waianapanapa State Park:** The 120 acres of this state park offer 12 cabins, a caretaker's residence, a picnic area, a shoreline hiking trail, and, best of all, a black-sand beach (it's actually small black pebbles). Swimming is generally unsafe, though, due to strong waves breaking offshore, which roll into the beach unchecked, and strong rip currents. But it's a great spot for picnicking, hiking along the shore, and just sitting and relaxing. See chapter 8.

2 The Best Maui Experiences

There are hundreds of wonderful things to see and do on the Valley Isle, but we've narrowed the list down to a few "best of the best" that offer a unique "Maui experience."

- **Greet the Rising Sun Atop Haleakala:** Bundle up in warm clothing, fill a thermos full of hot java, and drive up to the summit to watch the sky turn from inky black to muted charcoal as a small sliver of orange forms on the horizon. Something about standing at 10,000 feet, breathing in the rarefied air, and watching the first rays of light streak across the sky makes this a mystical experience of the first magnitude. See chapter 8.

- **Swim in a Rainbowed Sea:** Don mask, fins, and snorkel, and explore the magical world beneath the surface, where kaleidoscopic clouds of tropical fish flutter by exotic corals; a sea turtle might even come over to check you out. Molokini is everyone's favorite snorkeling destination, but the shores of Maui are lined with magical spots as well. Can't swim? No problem: hop on the **Atlantis Submarine** (☎ **800/548-6262**) for a plunge beneath the waves without getting wet. See chapter 8.

- **Hunt for Whales on Land:** No need to shell out megabucks to go to out to sea in search of humpback whales—you can watch these majestic mammals breach and spy hop from shore. One of the best places is scenic McGregor Point, located at mile marker 9 along Honoapiilani Highway, just outside of Maalaea in South Maui. The humpbacks arrive as early as November, but the majority travel through Maui's waters from mid-December to mid-April, with a few stragglers hanging around until May. See chapter 8.

- **Relax and Watch the Windsurfers:** Sit on a grassy bluff or stretch out on the sandy beach at Hookipa, and watch the world's top-ranked windsurfers twirling and dancing on the wind and waves like colorful butterflies. World championship contests are held at Hookipa, which is known around the world as one of the greatest windsurfing spots on the planet. See chapters 8 and 9.

- **Experience Maui's History:** Wander the historic streets of the old whaling town of Lahaina, where the 1800s are alive and well thanks to the efforts of the Lahaina Restoration Society. Drive the scenic Kahekili Highway, where the preserved village of Kahakuloa looks much as it did a century ago. Stand in awe at Piilanihale, Hawaii's largest *heiau* (temple). It's located just outside Hana, where two generations of Maui *alii* (royalty) built it to honor the god of war. See chapter 9.

- **Drive through a Tropical Rain Forest:** The Hana Highway is not just a "drive" but an adventure: stop along the way to plunge into icy mountain ponds filled by cascading waterfalls; gaze upon vistas of waves pummeling soaring ocean cliffs; absorb the sound of the wind through a bamboo forest; inhale the sweet aroma of blooming ginger; and take a walk back in time, catching a glimpse of what Hawaii looked like before concrete condos and fast-food joints washed ashore. See chapter 9.

- **Explore a Different Hawaii—Upcountry Maui:** On the slopes of Haleakala, cowboys, farmers, ranchers, and other country people make their homes in serene, neighborly communities like Makawao, Kula, and Ulupalakua—worlds away from the bustling beach resorts. Acres of onions, lettuce, tomatoes, carrots, cabbage, and flowers cover the hillsides. Maui's only winery is located here, offering the perfect place for a picnic and a chance to sample the tropical varieties of paradise. See chapter 9.

- **Zoom over to the Island of Lanai for a Day:** From Lahaina, take **Trilogy Excursion**'s snorkel cruise to Lanai (☎ **800/874-2666**), or take the **Expeditions Lahaina/Lanai Passenger Ferry** over and rent a four-wheel-drive jeep on Lanai from **Red Rover** (☎ **808/565-7722**), a two-for-one island experience. You board in Lahaina Harbor and admire Maui from offshore, then get off at

Lanai and see a glimpse of life on that nearly private plantation-turned-luxury-enclave. Go snorkeling in Lanai's clear waters, tour the tiny former plantation island, and catch the last ferry home. See chapter 13.

3 The Best of Natural Maui

Mother Nature pulled out all the stops when she went to work on Maui. Simply put, this is Hawaii at its finest.

- **Volcanoes:** Maui was conceived by two volcanoes: Puu Kukui, in the West Maui Mountains, and Haleakala, in the east, which flowed together to create the island. Don't miss an opportunity to see **Haleakala National Park.** A bird's-eye view into this long-dormant volcanic crater—big enough to contain the island of Manhattan!—is more than just staring at a big hole in the ground. You'll see other-worldly swirls of burnt-red, orange, brown, and black cinders; Haleakala's own mini-mountain range; lava tubes; hiking trails; cabins; and camping areas. See chapters 8 and 9.
- **Waterfalls:** Rushing waterfalls thundering downward into sparkling freshwater pools—they're some of Maui's most beautiful natural wonders. The Hana Highway offers numerous viewing opportunities and chances to stop for swims at the deep pools. At the end of the road you'll find **Oheo Gulch** (also known as the Seven Sacred Pools), some of the most dramatic and accessible waterfalls in the islands. See chapter 9.
- **Gardens:** The islands radiate the sweet smell of flowers. For a glimpse of Hawaii's spectacular range of tropical flora, we suggest spending an afternoon at one of Maui's lush gardens. At **Kula Botanical Garden,** you can take a leisurely self-guided stroll through more than 700 native and exotic plants, including orchids, proteas, and bromeliads. In Hana, numerous gardens display everything from tropical natives to exotics from around the globe. See chapter 9.
- **Marine Life Conservation Areas:** These preservation areas, submerged in a Neptunian underworld, possess a sensual serenity that's unmatched in the world above the waves. Four underwater parks are spread across Maui County: Honolua-Mokuleia Marine Life Conservation District and Ahihi-Kinau Natural Area Reserve, both off the shores of Maui (see chapters 8 and 9); Molokini Marine Life Conservation District, off Maui's southwest coast (see chapter 8); and Manele-Hulopoe Marine Life Conservation District, on Lanai (see chapter 13). Be sure to take your snorkel to at least one of these wonderful places.
- **Garden of the Gods:** Out on the north shore of the island of Lanai lies the ultimate rock garden: a rugged, barren, beautiful place full of rocks strewn by volcanic forces and shaped by the elements into an infinite variety of shapes and colors—brilliant reds, oranges, ochres, and yellows. Scientists explain how these boulders got here with phrases like "ongoing post-erosional event"; the ancient Hawaiians, however, considered this desolate, windswept place an entirely supernatural phenomenon. Natural badlands or mystical garden? Take a four-wheel-drive trip out here and see for yourself. See chapter 13.

4 The Best Island Adventures

Branch out while you're in Maui; do something you wouldn't normally do—after all, you're on vacation. Below are a list of adventures we highly recommend. They might be a bit pricey, but these splurges are worth every penny.

- **Fly over the Remote West Maui Mountains:** Your helicopter streaks low over razor-thin cliffs, then flutters past sparkling waterfalls and down into the canyons and valleys of the inaccessible West Maui Mountains—it's like flying in your dreams, except there's so much beauty to absorb that it all goes by in a rush. You'll never want to stop flying over this spectacular, surreal landscape—and it's the only way to see the dazzling beauty of the prehistoric area of Maui. See chapter 8.

- **See the Stars from Inside a Volcanic Crater:** Driving up to see the sunrise is a trip you'll never forget, but to *really* experience Haleakala, plan to hike in and spend the night. To get a feel for why the ancient Hawaiians considered this one of the most sacred places on the island, you simply have to wander into the heart of the dormant volcano, where you'll find some 27 miles of hiking trails, two camping sites, and three cabins. See chapter 8.

- **Explore a Lava Tube:** Most people come to Maui to get outdoors and soak up some Hawaiian sunshine, not to go underground and traipse through cold, dark lava tubes. But if you're into cave exploration or you're looking for an offbeat adventure, **Island Spelunkers** (☎ 808/248-7308) offers a geology lesson you will not forget: hiking into the subterranean passages of a huge, extinct lava tube with 40-foot ceilings. See chapter 8.

- **Try Scuba Diving:** You're in love with snorkeling and the chance to view the underwater world, but it's just not enough—you want to get closer and see even more. Take an introductory scuba dive; after a brief lesson on how to use the diving equipment, you will be down swimming with the tropical fish and eyeball to eyeball with other marine critters. See chapter 8.

- **Hike to a Waterfall:** There are waterfalls and there are waterfalls, but the hike to the magnificent 400-foot Waimoku Falls, in Oheo Gulch outside of Hana, is worth the long drive and the uphill hike. The falls are surrounded by lush green ferns and endemic orchids, and you can even make a pit stop at the pool at the top of Makahiku Falls on the way. See chapter 8.

- **Skim over the Ocean in a Kayak:** Glide silently over the water, hearing only the sound of your paddle dipping beneath the surface. This is the way the early Hawaiians traveled along the coastline. You'll be eye-level and up-close-and-personal with the ocean and the coastline, exploring areas you can't get to any other way. Venture out on your own, or go with an experienced guide—either way, you won't be sorry. See chapter 8.

- **Take a Drive on the Wild Side:** Mother Nature's wild side, that is—on the Kahekili Highway on Maui's northeast coast. This back-to-nature experience will take you past ancient Hawaiian heiau; along steep ravines; and by rolling pastures, tumbling waterfalls, exploding blowholes, crashing surf, and jagged lava coastlines. You'll wander through the tiny Hawaiian village of Kahakuloa and around the "head" of Maui to the Marine Life Conservation Area of Honolua-Mokuleia and on to the resort of Kapalua. You'll be telling the story of this adventure for years. See chapter 9.

- **Ride a Mule to Kalaupapa:** Even if you have only 1 day to spend on Molokai, spend it on a mule. The **Molokai Mule Ride** (☎ 800/567-7550) trek from "topside" Molokai to the Kalaupapa National Historic Park, Father Damien's world-famous leper colony, is a once-in-a-lifetime adventure. The cliffs are taller than 300-story skyscrapers—but Buzzy Sproat's mules go up and down the narrow 2.9-mile trail daily, rain or shine, without ever losing a rider or mount on 26 switchbacks. From 1,600 feet on the nearly perpendicular ridge, the sure-footed mules step down the muddy trail, pausing often to calculate their next move. See chapter 12.

5 The Best Snorkeling & Diving Sites

An entirely different Hawaii greets anyone with a face mask, snorkel, and fins. Under the sea, you'll find schools of brilliant tropical fish, lumbering green sea turtles, quick-moving game fish, slack-jawed moray eels, and prehistoric-looking coral. It's a kaleidoscope of color and wonder.

- **Molokini:** Shaped like a crescent moon that fell from the sky, this islet's shallow concave side serves as a sheltering backstop against sea currents for tiny tropical fish; on its opposite side is a deep-water cliff inhabited by spiny lobsters, moray eels, and white-tipped sharks. Neophyte snorkelers report to the concave side; experienced scuba divers, the other. Either way, the clear water and abundant marine life make this islet off the Makena coast one of Maui's most popular dive spots. See chapter 8.
- **Ahihi-Kinau Natural Preserve:** You can't miss in Ahihi Bay, a 2,000-acre State Natural Area Reserve in the lee of Cape Kinau, on Maui's rugged south coast, where Haleakala spilled red-hot lava that ran to the sea in 1790. Fishing is strictly *kapu* (forbidden) here, and the fish know it; they're everywhere in this series of rocky coves and black-lava tide pools. The black, barren, lunar-like land stands in stark contrast to the green-blue water, which is home to a sparkling mosaic of tropical fish, making for excellent snorkeling. Scuba divers might want to check out **La Perouse Pinnacle** in the middle of La Perouse Bay, where a pinnacle rises from the 60-foot bottom to about 10 feet below the surface. Clouds of damsel and trigger fish will greet you on the surface. Divers can approach even the timid bird wrasse. See chapter 8.
- **Black Rock:** This spot, located on the Kaanapali Beach just off the Sheraton Maui Resort, is excellent for beginner snorkelers during the day and for scuba divers at night. Schools of fish congregate at the base of the rock and are so used to snorkelers that they go about their business as if no one were around. If you take the time to look closely at the crannies of the rock, you'll find lion fish in fairly shallow water. At night, lobsters, Spanish dancers, and eels come out. See chapter 8.
- **Hawaiian Reef:** Scuba divers love this area off the Kihei-Wailea coast because it hosts a good cross-section of topography and marine life typical of Hawaiian waters. Diving to depths of 85 feet, you'll see everything from lava formations and coral reef to sand and rubble, plus a diverse range of both shallow and deep-water creatures. See chapter 8.
- **Third Tank:** Scuba divers looking for a photo opportunity will find it at this artificial reef, located off Makena Beach at 80 feet. This World War II tank acts like a fish magnet: because it's the only large solid object in the area, any fish or invertebrate looking for a safe home comes here. Surrounding the tank is a cloak of schooling snapper and goat fish just waiting for a photographer with a wide-angle lens. For its small size, the Third Tank is loaded with more marine life per square inch than any site off Maui. See chapter 8.
- **Olowalu:** When the wind is blowing and the waves are crashing everywhere else, Olowalu, the small area 5 miles south of Lahaina, can be a scene of total calm—perfect for snorkeling and diving. You'll find a good snorkeling area around the 14-mile marker. You might have to swim about 50 to 75 feet; when you get to

the large field of finger coral in 10 to 15 feet of water, you're there. You'll see a turtle-cleaning station here, where turtles line up to have small cleaner wrasses pick small parasites off. This is also a good spot to see crown-of-thorns starfish, puffer fish, and lots of juvenile fish. Occasionally, manta rays have been spotted here. See chapter 9.

6 The Best Golf Courses

Some people come to Maui solely to play golf: you're out in the sunshine, the views are spectacular, and you're even getting a little exercise. For those who think that a golf course is a golf course, be it in Arizona or Hawaii, you haven't seen the 16th hole at the Kapalua Golf Course, where the velvet green grass stands out against the black lava rock shoreline and the azure ocean in the background. Golf in Hawaii is not just a sport, but a sensual experience.

- **Kapalua Resort Courses** (☎ 808/669-8044): Kapalua is probably the best nationally known golf resort in Hawaii, due to the Lincoln Mercury Kapalua International played here each November. The Bay Course and the Village Course are vintage Arnold Palmer designs, whereas the new Plantation Course is a strong Ben Crenshaw/Bill Coore design. All are sited on Maui's windswept northwestern shore, at the rolling foothills of Puu Kukui, the summit of the West Maui Mountains. See chapter 8.
- **Kaanapali Courses** (☎ 808/661-3691): All golfers, from high handicappers to near-pros, will love these two challenging courses. The **North Course** (originally called the Royal Lahaina Golf Course) is a true Robert Trent Jones design: an abundance of wide bunkers; several long, stretched-out tees; and the largest, most contoured greens on Maui. The **South Course** is an Arthur Jack Snyder design; although shorter than the North Course, it does require more accuracy on the narrow, hilly fairways. Just like its sister course, it has a water hazard on its final hole, so don't tally up your score card until the final putt is sunk. See chapter 8.
- **Wailea Courses** (☎ 808/879-2966): On the sunbaked south shore of Maui stands Wailea Resort, *the* hot spot for golf in the islands. You'll find great golf at these three resort courses: the Blue course is an Arthur Jack Snyder design, and the Emerald and Gold courses are both by Robert Trent Jones, Jr. All boast outstanding views of the Pacific and the mid-Hawaiian Islands. See chapter 8.
- **Makena Courses** (☎ 808/879-3344): Here you'll find 36 holes by "Mr. Hawaii Golf"—Robert Trent Jones, Jr.—at his best. Add to that spectacular views: Molokini islet looms in the background, humpback whales gambol offshore in the winter, and the tropical sunsets are spectacular. This is golf not to be missed. The **South Course** has magnificent views (bring your camera) and is kinder to golfers who haven't played for a while. The **North Course** is more difficult but also more spectacular. The 13th hole, located part way up the mountain, has a view that makes most golfers stop and stare. The next hole is even more memorable: a 200-foot drop between tee and green. See chapter 8.
- **The Lanai Courses** (☎ 808/565-GOLF): For quality and seclusion, nothing in Hawaii can touch Lanai's two golf resort offerings. The Ted Robinson and Greg Norman–designed **Experience at Koele** and **The Challenge at Manele,** a wonderful Jack Nicklaus effort with ocean views from every hole, both rate among Hawaii's best courses. Both are tremendous fun to play, with the Experience featuring the par-four 8th hole, which drops some 150 yards from

tee to fairway, and the Challenge boasting the par-three 12th, which plays from one cliff side to another over a Pacific inlet—one of the most stunning holes in Hawaii. See chapter 13.

7 The Best Luxury Hotels & Resorts

Maui has built its reputation as a luxury destination by offering breathtakingly beautiful locations for its top resorts, the most exquisite service, and a knack for knowing just how to create your dream vacation. At the following resorts, no detail—no matter how small—is overlooked.

- **Ritz-Carlton Kapalua** (☎ **800/262-8440**): With its great location, style, and loads of hospitality, this is the best Ritz anywhere. Situated on the coast below the picturesque West Maui Mountains, this grand, breezy hotel overlooks the Pacific and Molokai across the channel. The natural setting, on an old coastal pineapple plantation, is the picture of tranquillity. The service is legendary; the golf courses are daunting; and the nearby beaches are perfect for snorkeling, diving, and just relaxing. See chapter 6.

- **Sheraton Maui** (☎ **800/STAY-ITT**): Offering the best location on Kaanapali Beach, the most recent renovations, and a great "hassle free" place to stay, the Sheraton Maui is our pick of Kaanapali hotels. This is the place for travelers who just want to arrive, have everything ready for them, and get on with their vacation (Sheraton has a "no hassle" check-in: the valet takes you and your luggage straight to your room, which means no time wasted standing in line at registration). The first hotel to be built in Kaanapali (in 1963), the grand dame reopened in April 1997 after a 2-year, $160 million complete reconstruction (all of the original building was demolished). See chapter 6.

- **Four Seasons Resort Wailea** (☎ **800/334-MAUI**): This is the ultimate beach hotel for latter-day royals, offering excellent cuisine, spacious rooms, gracious service, and Wailea Beach—one of Maui's best gold-sand beaches, right outside the front door. Every room has at least a partial ocean view from a private lanai. The luxury suites are as big as some Honolulu condos, and full of marble and deluxe appointments. Since Four Seasons lured chef George Mavrothalassitis away from the Halekulani, the hotel's cuisine has vastly improved. See chapter 6.

- **Grand Wailea Resort Hotel & Spa** (☎ **800/888-6100**): Grand is right—in fact, this place borders on the grandiose—but after all, you're on vacation, and you might as well treat yourself to some fantasy. No money was spared here: some $600 million went into creating this mega-resort with 10,000 tropical plants in the lobby; an intricate pool system with not only pools, slides, waterfalls, and rapids, but also a water-powered elevator to take you to the top; a floating New England–style wedding chapel; and nothing but ocean-view rooms, outfitted with all the amenities you could ask for. And it's all crowned with $30 million worth of original art, much of it created expressly for the hotel by Hawaii artists and sculptors. There's also a fantastic beach in the front yard. See chapter 6.

- **Renaissance Wailea Beach Resort** (☎ **800/9-WAILEA**): This is the kind of place for visitors craving the luxury of a Wailea hotel in a smaller, more intimate setting. Located on 15 acres of rolling lawn and tropical gardens, this resort has the feel of a small boutique hotel. Maybe it's the U-shaped design, or the spacious rooms, or the series of small coves and beaches on the property; whatever the reason, it just doesn't feel crowded here. See chapter 6.

- **Hotel Hana-Maui** (☎800/321-HANA): Shangri-la Hawaiian style: 66 acres rolling down to the sea in the remote Hawaiian village of Hana, complete with wellness center, two swimming pools, and access to one of the best beaches in Hana. Since it was built in 1946, Hotel Hana-Maui has been the "getaway" luxury destination for celebrities from around the globe (Princess Di slept here). See chapter 6.
- **The Lodge at Koele** (☎800/321-4666): For old-world luxury in an old pineapple plantation town, come to The Lodge on the island of Lanai. There's nothing else in Hawaii like it: an extravagant inland hotel set amid a misty grove of pines far from any beach. It's like visiting Emile DeBeque's rubber plantation house in the Hollywood film classic *South Pacific*. With giant stone fireplaces, stuffed furniture, and lavishly chintzed rooms, the decor is reminiscent of an English country lodge, with the same sense of serenity that accompanies a rural atmosphere. If sun, sand, and surf don't top your list of requirements, this sophisticated retreat is the perfect choice. And you can always catch the free shuttle down to Manele Bay for a dip with the spinner dolphins. See chapter 13.

8 The Best Moderately Priced Hotels & Condos

You don't have to take out a second mortgage to stay in Maui; choose from one of many excellent, affordable accommodations. Here's a sampling of our favorites.

- **Napili Bay** (☎888/661-7200): One of Maui's best-kept secrets (until now, that is), this intimate two-story condo complex is located right on half-mile-long white-sand Napili Beach. The beach here is so beautiful that people staying at the much-more-expensive resort down the street frequently haul all their beach paraphernalia here to set up for the day. The compact studio apartments, which have everything you need, start at just $58—unbelievable! See chapter 6.
- **Lahaina Inn** (☎800/669-3444): If the romance of historic Lahaina catches your fancy, a stay here will really complete the experience. Built in 1938 as a general store, it has been restored as a charming, Victorian antique–filled inn right in the heart of town. Downstairs you'll find one of Hawaii's most popular storefront bistros, David Paul's Lahaina Grill. See chapter 6.
- **Aston Maui Islander** (☎800/367-5226): This wooden complex isn't on the beach, but it is on a quiet side street (a rarity in Lahaina) and within walking distance to restaurants, shops, attractions, and, yes, the beach (it's just 3 blocks away). All of the good-sized rooms, decorated in a tropical-island style, are comfortable and quiet. These units are one of Lahaina's great buys—especially those with kitchenettes. The entire complex is spread across 10 landscaped acres and includes tennis courts (with night lights until 10pm), pool, sundeck, barbecue, and picnic area. See chapter 6.
- **Plantation Inn** (☎800/433-6815): Attention, romantic couples: You need look no further. This charming inn looks like it's been here 100 years or more, but looks can be deceiving. The Victorian-style hotel is actually of 1990s vintage—an artful deception. The rooms are romantic to the max, tastefully done with period furniture, hardwood floors, stained glass, ceiling fans, and four-poster canopy beds. The rooms wrap around the large pool and deck; also on site are a spa and an elegant pavilion lounge, where breakfast is served. See chapter 6.
- **Aston Maui Lu Resort** (☎800/92-ASTON): At the quieter, northern end of Kihei, the Polynesian-style Maui Lu offers a nostalgic Old Hawaii atmosphere on its 28 green acres by the sea. The rooms are big and airy, with beach units right

on the sand; they definitely don't make them like this anymore. The rest of the resort is across the road and up on a rise, situated around a swimming pool in the shape of the island of Maui. See chapter 6.

- **Punahoa Beach Apartments** (☎ 800/564-4380): This small oceanside Kihei condo is hidden on a quiet side street; the grassy lawn out front rolls about 50 feet down to the beach. You'll find great snorkeling just offshore and a popular surfing spot next door, with shopping and restaurants all within walking distance. Every well-decorated unit features a lanai with fabulous ocean views. See chapter 6.

9 The Best Bed-and-Breakfasts

"Bed-and-breakfast" on Maui can mean anything from a traditional inn, where guests sit down to a formal breakfast each morning, to essentially a vacation rental, where breakfast fixings can be found in the refrigerator. Choices range from a historic inn to a charming old converted cattle ranch. Below are our favorites.

- **Old Wailuku Inn at Ulupono** (☎ 800/305-4899): Located in Historic Wailuku, this restored, 1924 former plantation manager's home is the place to stay if you're looking for a night in the old Hawaii of the 1920s. The guest rooms are wide and spacious, with exotic ohia wood floors and traditional Hawaiian quilts. The morning meal is a full gourmet breakfast served on the enclosed back lanai, or on a tray delivered to your room if you prefer. See chapter 6.

- **Guest House** (☎ 800/621-8942): This is one of the great bed-and-breakfast deals in Lahaina: a charming inn offering more amenities than the expensive Kaanapali hotels just down the road. The spacious home features floor-to-ceiling windows, parquet floors, and a large swimming pool. Guest rooms have quiet lanais and romantic hot tubs. Breakfasts are a gourmet affair. See chapter 6.

- **What a Wonderful World B&B** (☎ 808/879-9103): One of Kihei's best B&Bs offers a great central location in town—just a half mile to Kamaole II Beach Park, 5 minutes from Wailea Golf Courses, and convenient to shopping and restaurants. All rooms boast cooking facilities, individual entrances, private baths, and private phones. A family-style breakfast (eggs Benedict, Alaskan waffles, skillet eggs with mushroom sauce, fruit blintzes, and more) is served on the lanai, which has views of white-sand beaches, the West Maui Mountains, and Haleakala. See chapter 6.

- **Makena Landing** (☎ 808/879-6286): This gem, one of the island's best B&Bs, offers a fabulous location (right on the ocean at Makena Landing); incredible views (sunsets to die for); and some of the best swimming, snorkeling, diving, and shoreline fishing just outside your bedroom. To complete the picture, add private entrances, full kitchens, and the nicest hosts you'll ever meet. See chapter 6.

- **Huelo Point Flower Farm** (☎ 808/572-1850): Here's a little Eden by the sea in remote Huelo, situated on a spectacular 300-foot sea cliff near a waterfall stream. Celebs like Ann Margret, Woody Harrelson, and Roger Clinton, to name a few, are drawn to the 2-acre estate, which overlooks Waipio Bay and contains two guest cottages, a guest house, and a main house, all available for rent. Facilities include a swimming pool and an oceanfront hot tub. Homemade scones, tree-ripened papayas, and fresh-roasted coffee are available to start your day, and you're welcome to pick fruit, vegetables, and flowers from the extensive garden. See chapter 6.

- **Olinda Country Cottage & Inn** (☎800/932-3435): Breathe the crisp, clean air of Olinda at this charming B&B, located on an 8½-acre protea farm on the slopes of Haleakala and surrounded by 35,000 acres of ranch lands (with miles of great hiking). The 5,000-square-foot Tudor mansion, refurbished and outfitted with priceless antiques, has large windows with incredible panoramic views of all of Maui. In addition to the guest rooms in the country house, two cozy cottages and a romantic country suite are also available. See chapter 6.
- **Silver Cloud Ranch** (☎800/532-1111): Old Hawaii lives on at Silver Cloud Ranch, founded in 1902 by a sailor who jumped ship when he got to Maui. Located in Kula at 2,800 feet, the former working cattle spread offers a commanding view of four islands and features antique-filled guest rooms, quaint studios, and even a romantic honeymooners' cottage. See chapter 6.
- **Ekena** (☎808/248-7047): Situated on 8½ acres in the hills above Hana, this Hawaiian-style wooden pole house, with 360-degree views of the coastline, the ocean, and Hana's verdant rain forest, is perfect for those in search of a quiet, peaceful vacation. Inside, the elegantly furnished home features floor-to-ceiling sliding glass doors and a fully equipped kitchen; outside, hiking trails into the rain forest start right on the property. Beaches, waterfalls, and pools are mere minutes away. See chapter 6.
- **Hamoa Bay Bungalow** (☎808/248-7884): This enchanting retreat sits on 4 verdant acres within walking distance of Hamoa Beach, just outside Hana. The romantic, 600-square-foot Balinese-style cottage has a full kitchen and hot tub. This very private place is perfect for honeymooners—even the tropical breakfast of fruit, yogurt, and muffins is left out daily to eat at your leisure. See chapter 6.

10 The Best Culinary Experiences

Maui is the quintessence of dining, a haven for foodies, one feast after another in a string of commendable restaurants curling around its west and south shores. No one has done a count, but there are arguably more good restaurants per capita on this island than on any other in Hawaii. Here are some of our favorites, in all price ranges, from a sandwich shop in Makawao to the toniest room on the south Maui shore.

- **A Pacific Cafe Maui** (Kihei; ☎808/879-0069): Jean-Marie Josselin's pan-seared mahimahi with garlic and sesame, pan-seared scallops, tiger-eye sushi tempura, and roster of daily specialties are only part of the reason diners flock to this Kihei magnet. One never knows what to expect from this energetic chef, only that it will be good. Soups, salads, fish, lamb, tenderloin, and specialty meats in exquisite reductions—the offerings are always an adventure into the freshest resources of the region. See chapter 7.
- **A Saigon Cafe** (Wailuku; ☎808/243-9560): Jennifer Nguyen's unmarked dining room in an odd corner of town is always packed, a tribute to her clean, crisp Vietnamese cuisine—and the Maui grapevine. Grab a round of rice paper and wrap your own Vietnamese "burrito" of tofu, noodles, and vegetables. Lemongrass shrimp, curries, and the Nhung Dam, the Vietnamese version of fondue, are among the solid hits. See chapter 7.
- **Café 'O Lei** (Makawao; ☎808/573-9065): A hot new arrival on the Makawao scene, this tiny outdoor cafe is putting the upcountry town on the culinary map. What Casanova is to nightlife, Café 'O Lei is to lunch: reliable, exciting, tirelessly creative, and always satisfying. Makawao merchants come daily for the Asian

salad, the quinoa salad, and the breathtaking sandwich of fresh Maui vegetables marinated and grilled, served on focaccia with goat cheese. Served on hand-painted ceramic dinnerware, on a narrow terrace cooled by mountain breezes, the meal is a totally uplifting experience. See chapter 7.

- **David Paul's Lahaina Grill** (Lahaina; ☎ **808/667-5117**): It's a tough call on this island, but most people choose David Paul's as their favorite Maui eatery. No one seems to tire of his kalua duck, Kona coffee–roasted rack of lamb, or tequila shrimp. We love the Kula salad, eggplant napoleon, and lobster risotto, along with his marvelous presentations of fresh Maui produce. The menu changes often, but thank goodness the room doesn't; its pressed-tin ceilings and 1890s decor continue to satisfy. See chapter 7.

- **Hula Grill** (Kaanapali; ☎ **808/667-6636**): You can wander straight off the beach into this Whalers Village restaurant, where you'll be met by the welcoming embrace of Peter Merriman's firecracker mahimahi, crab and corn cakes, ahi poke rolls, and, at lunch, down-home sandwiches and salads. During the day, watch sailboats bob on the horizon; at night, flickering torchlight warms the koa walls and Hawaiian canoes. Hula Grill is not intimate—in fact, it's big and bustling—but it's a happy, upbeat place to enjoy top-notch island cookery with a storybook view. See chapter 7.

- **Pauwela Cafe** (Haiku; ☎ **808/575-9242**): Out in the boonies of east Maui, in the industrial sailboard-manufacturing center of the Islands, Becky and Chris Speere serve sandwiches, salads, and inexpensive island cuisine with culinary finesse. The kalua turkey sandwich is the best, but the black-bean chili comes close. It's a long drive out for breakfast, but the eggs chilaquile (layers of tortilla, beans, chiles, and cheese, topped with egg custard) are a handsome reward. See chapter 7.

- **Prince Court** (Makena; ☎ **808/874-1111**): The guava-glazed shredded baby back ribs are brilliant, and so is the seafood-poi risotto. A new culinary generation at the Maui Prince has infused this Maui institution with heightened creativity and dining pleasure. At Sunday brunch, you can enjoy the view; at night, the cuisine sparkles. See chapter 7.

- **Roy's Kahana Bar & Grill/Roy's Nicolina Restaurant** (Kahana; ☎ **808/ 669-6999**): It's odd that they're right next to each other, have the same menu, and are both so successful. Roy Yamaguchi has perfected his Euro-Asian cookery and snap-to service so that people get what they expect. The staples: fresh fish (eight or nine choices), rack of lamb, roast chicken—and dozens of specials on the daily changing menu. A new feature: lanai dining at Roy's Nicolina. See chapter 7.

- **Seasons** (Wailea; ☎ **808/874-8000**): Leave it to George Mavrothalassitis to create a temple of fine dining—again. With Halekulani's La Mer long behind him, he has established in this ethereal seaside room a quietly powerful dining experience that marries the best of Provence, Hawaii, the ocean, the soil, and the seasons. His signature dishes—rock salt–crusted *onaga* (ruby snapper) and whole *kumu* (goatfish) filled with watercress—and our personal favorites—fresh mashed Molokai sweet potatoes with French vanilla, seared yellowfin tuna—are reason enough for a Seasons splurge. And the room: like Mavro's creations, it takes your breath away. See chapter 7.

11 The Best of Maui for Kids

Maui isn't just for adults—there are plenty of activities to keep the *keiki* (kids), as well as the kids at heart, busy.

A Night to Remember: Maui's Top Luau

Despite its imminent move (in mid-May 1998) to a larger 2-acre spot up the street, the **Old Lahaina Luau** (☎ **800/248-5828** or 808/667-1998) promises more, not less, of those qualities we've come to love in its many years at 505 Front St. Its authenticity, intimacy, hospitality, cultural integrity, and sheer romantic beauty have made this Maui's top luau and one of our two favorites in the state, often sold out a week or two in advance. Old Lahaina Luau's staff, location, cultural and educational acuity, and quality of food and entertainment make it a luau to which visitors return time and time again.

The luau's new location will be on the shoreline at 1251 Front St., oceanside of the Lahaina Cannery, with views of Molokai and Lanai, and, at night, a twinkling, wide-angle view of the Kaanpalai skyline. The luau will grow from its former size of 275 people to 400 a night. We've come to associate the luau's previously small size with its wonderful intimacy, so naturally, questions have arisen about the possible loss of this feature with the increase in size. The owners, who started the luau 12 years ago, intend to retain the same level of service by creating mini-luaus within the complex, each with its own separate buffet hale, a thatched structure with sides open to the views (and all connections tied with coconut sennit!). The nine thatched buildings, four buffet hales, tiered amphitheater seating, highly trained staff, and same service philosophy should add up to a socko luau experience.

Extensive lava-rock walls throughout the complex add to the flavor of old Hawaii. The showstopper of the old luau—the Hawaiian maiden who emerges from the darkness in a torchlit canoe heading for shore—is no longer possible because of the rocky beach. We can, however, count on the same dramatic presence of the ocean, and of outrigger canoes afloat, to evoke images of the Polynesian migration and the intrepid navigators who sailed to Hawaii's shores.

As guests await dinner, pupu platters of sweet potato, pipikaula, haupia, and other Hawaiian foods will offer a preview of the Hawaiian buffet. The imu ceremony, the heart of the feast, will have a luxury the old luau lacked: space, and plenty of it. Staging, too, has been thoughtfully planned. The placement of the stage allows the audience to face the ocean and the sunset, with hidden underground dressing rooms allowing the dancers dramatic entrances and exits. When the dancing begins, it will encompass both Tahitian and Hawaiian styles, including ancient hula and an intelligent narrative on its rocky course of survival into modern times. Flickering torches, surreal sunsets, old milo and coconut trees, cultural sensitivity, romance, and genuine hospitality—these are the elements we can count on with the Old Lahaina Luau.

Shows during the summer start at 6pm; in winter, at 5:30pm. Tickets are $65 for adults, $30 for children; AE, MC, V are accepted.

- **Plunge Underwater on a Submarine Ride:** Take the whole family down into the shallow coastal waters off Lahaina in a real sub, care of **Atlantis Submarines** (☎ 800/548-6262). You'll see plenty of fish—and maybe even a shark! The kids will love it, and you'll stay dry the entire time. See chapter 9.
- **Ride a Real Sugarcane Train:** Small kids love this ride, as do train buffs of all ages. A steam engine pulls open passenger cars of the **Lahaina/Kaanapali and Pacific Railroad** (☎ 808/661-0089) on a 30-minute, 12-mile round-trip through sugarcane fields between Lahaina and Kaanapali while the conductor

sings and calls out the landmarks. Along the way, you can see Molokai, Lanai, and the backside of Kaanapali. See chapter 9.

- **Search for Stars:** After sunset, when the stars over Kaanapali shine big and bright, amateur astronomers can probe the Milky Way, see the rings of Saturn's and Jupiter's moons, and scan the Sea of Tranquillity in a 60-minute star search on the world's first recreational computer-driven telescope. Not just for kids, this cosmic adventure takes place every night on the rooftop at **Hyatt Regency Maui** (☎ **808/661-1234**). See chapter 9.

- **Roll with In-Line Skating:** Bring your own skates and roll, glide, and skid around the free, newly constructed rink in Kihei's Kalama Park. It's open daylight hours, with the occasional Maui In-Line Hockey Association game scheduled. For information, call ☎ **808/874-4860.** See chapter 9.

- **See Sharks, Stingrays, and Starfish:** Hawaii's largest aquarium, **Maui Ocean Center** (☎ **808/875-1962**), is home to a wide range of sea critters—from tiger sharks to tiny starfish—that are sure to fascinate kids of all ages. At this 5-acre facility in Maalaea, visitors can take a virtual walk from the beach down to the ocean depths via the three dozen tanks, countless exhibits, and 100-foot-long, 600,000-gallon main oceanarium. See chapter 9.

- **See the World from a Dragonfly's Point of View:** Kids will think this is too much fun to be educational. Don a face mask and get the dizzying perspective of what a dragonfly sees as it flies over a mountain stream, or watch the tiny *oopu* fish climb up a stream at the **Hawaii Nature Center** (☎ **808/244-6500**) in beautiful Iao Valley, where you'll find some 30 hands-on, interactive exhibits and displays of Hawaii's natural history. See chapter 9.

12 The Best Shopping

What does one do on Maui when it's too late for a Haleakala sunrise, not quite happy hour, and not sunny enough for the beach? Go shopping. Shops and galleries throughout central Maui and the south and west shores offer gifts to go, finds for collectors, practical beach wear, arts, crafts, serious pamperings, and silly indulgences.

- **Bailey House Gift Shop** (Wailuku; ☎ **808/244-3920**): You can travel Hawaii and peruse its past with the assemblage of made-in-Hawaii items at this museum gift shop. Tropical preserves, Hawaiian music, pareus, prints by esteemed Hawaii artists, cookbooks, hatbands, and magnificent wood bowls reflect a sense of authority, a discerning standard of selection. Unequaled for Hawaiian treasures on Maui. See chapter 10.

- **Brown-Kobayashi** (Wailuku; ☎ **808/242-0804**): At this quiet, tasteful, and elegantly Asian shop, the selection of antiques and collectibles changes constantly but reflects an unwavering sense of gracious living. There are old and new European and Hawaiian objects, from koa furniture (which disappear fast) to Hawaiian ephemera to lacquerware, Bakelite jewelry, Peking glass beads, and a few priceless pieces of antique ivory. Every square inch a treasure trove. See chapter 10.

- **Gallery Ltd.** (Lahaina; ☎ **808/661-0696**): Its low-key entrance is easy to miss on busy Front Street, but inside, a world of pearls, antiques, and netsuke unfolds in quiet splendor. Jade carvings, snuff bottles, scrolls, screens, and ropes of pearls from Japan and the South Seas are some of the special features of this 2-story gallery. See chapter 10.

- **Hui No'eau Visual Arts Center** (Makawao; ☎808/572-6560): Half the experience is the center itself, one of Maui's historic treasures: a strikingly designed 1917 kamaaina estate on 9 acres; two of Maui's largest hybrid Cook and Norfolk pines; and an art center with classes, exhibitions, and demonstrations. The gift shop is as memorable as the rest of it. You'll find one-of-a-kind works by local artists, from prints to jewelry and pottery. See chapter 10.
- **Ki'i Gallery** (Kahului, ☎808/871-4557; and Wailea, ☎808/871-4557): The Kahului shop focuses on South Pacific pearls, handmade jewelry and hand-turned wooden bowls, and marvelous gift items and works of art, including studio glass, a Ki'i specialty. The Wailea gallery is a gleaming corner space of museum-quality glass and wood vessels—just a few pieces, but big in size, spirit, and impact. See chapter 10.
- **Ola's** (Makawao; ☎808/573-1334): Imaginative, bright, and impeccably tasteful, the selection represents the work of more than 100 artists from Hawaii and the mainland. Ola's celebrates craftsmanship at its finest, from studio glass to wood turning, painting, porcelain, fabrics, and jewelry. See chapter 10.
- **Old Daze** (Kihei; ☎808/875-7566): What fun to browse this eclectic collection of Hawaiian collectibles and 19th-century Americana. Chockablock with collections of Depression glass, old washboards, county-fair souvenir plates, head vases, and assorted memorabilia, it's a riotous celebration of the old days. See chapter 10.
- **Summerhouse** (Kahului; ☎808/871-1320): Bright and sassy tropical wear, and the jewelry and accessories to go with them, are a cut above at Summerhouse. T-shirts are tailored and in day-to-evening colors, while dresses are good for both the office and a party. See chapter 10.
- **Viewpoints Gallery** (Makawao; ☎808/572-5979): We love this airy, well-designed gallery and its helpful staff, which complement the fine Maui art: paintings, sculpture, jewelry, prints, woods, and glass. This is Maui's only fine-arts cooperative, showcasing the work of dozens of local artists. See chapter 10.
- **Village Galleries** (Kapalua, ☎808/669-1800; and Lahaina, ☎808/661-4402): Maui's oldest galleries have maintained high standards and the respect of a public that is increasingly impatient with clichéd Maui art. The three galleries exhibit the finest contemporary Maui artists in all media, with a discerning selection of handcrafted jewelry. In Lahaina, the new contemporary gallery has a larger selection of jewelry, ceramics, glass, and gift items, as well as paintings and prints. See chapter 10.

Introducing the Valley Isle

2

by Jeanette Foster

Maui is the only island in the Hawaiian chain named after a god—well, actually a demigod (half man, half god). Hawaiian legends are filled with the escapades of Maui, who had a reputation as a trickster. In one story, Maui is credited with causing the birth of the Hawaiian Islands when he threw his "magic" fish hook down to the ocean floor and pulled the islands up from the bottom of the sea. Another legend tells how Maui lassoed the sun to make it travel more slowly across the sky—so that his mother could more easily dry her clothes. Maui's status as the only island to carry the name of a deity seems fitting, considering its reputation as the perfect tropical paradise, or as Hawaiians say, "Maui no ka oi" (Maui is the best).

Maui sits in the midst of a remote fleet of islands, isolated from the nearest land mass by some 2,500 miles. At the extreme end of the inhabited Hawaiian Islands is Kauai, which has been worn by 7 million years' worth of wind, waves, and erosion into a paradise ringed with sandy beaches. At the other end of the chain is the Big Island of Hawaii, just over a million years old, with a dramatic volcano that is still erupting.

Maui's origins place it somewhere between these two extremes. At one time, Maui, Molokai, and Lanai most likely composed one land mass, but today Molokai and Lanai are two satellite islands just off Maui's coast. The 728.8-square-mile island is the result of the marriage of two volcanoes, the 5,778-foot-high Puu Kukui and the 10,000-foot-high Haleakala, which spilled enough lava between them to create a valley—thus inspiring the island's nickname, Valley Isle. Thanks to this unusual makeup, Maui offers a diversity of natural landscapes: the beachside communities from Kapalua along the coast through Kaanapali-Lahaina, stretching down to Maalaea-Kihei and on to Wailea; the central plains of

Impressions

For me, its balmy airs are always blowing, its summer seas flashing in the sun, the pulsing of its surf beat is in my ears. . . . [Hawaii is] the loveliest fleet of islands anchored in any ocean.

—Mark Twain (1866)

Wailuku-Kahului; the lush breadbasket of Upcountry; the tropical rain forest of the Hana coast; and the arid desert from Kaupo to Makena.

A visit to Maui combines the best elements of the Hawaiian experience: the island boasts more sandy swimming beaches than even Kauai; it offers the resorts, shopping, and dining of urban Waikiki and Honolulu on Oahu, but in a more rural, laid-back atmosphere; and it has its own majestic volcano, which scientists say is dormant, or just resting, until its next eruption.

Indeed, there's no place quite like this sun-drenched mid-Pacific island, so remote from any continent yet visited by nearly 2.5 million guests a year. They come from the far corners of the globe seeking relaxation under the tropical sun, exotic adventures, and a taste of the much-touted way of life embodied by the aloha spirit.

1 Maui Today

Following the U.S. overthrow of the Hawaiian monarchy in 1893, the first years of the 20th century saw Maui in a state of confusion. Island life was thrown into upheaval with a massive influx of immigrants, drawn to Maui by the sugar and pineapple plantations. World War II and a series of postwar labor-union skirmishes created still more conflict on the island, and as soon as that settled down, a new change emerged: the rapid increase in the number of visitors to this sleepy, agrarian community, which found itself suddenly designated the "in" place to visit.

The islanders spent the 1970s trying to adjust not only to this sudden influx of visitors, but also to the fact that the visitors liked what they saw and wanted to stay. Seemingly overnight, a massive building campaign began, with condominiums mushrooming along the coastline. By the 1980s, the furious pace of building had slowed, but the new visitors to the island were no longer content to just sit on the beach: they wanted snorkeling and sailing trips, bike rides down Haleakala, and guided tours to Hana. A new industry developed to service these action-oriented vacationers.

In the 1990s, Hawaii's state economy went into a tailspin following a series of events: first, the Gulf War severely curtailed air travel to the island; then, Hurricane Iniki slammed into Kauai, crippling its infrastructure; and finally, sugarcane companies across the state began shutting down, laying off thousands of workers.

However, Maui seemed to be the only place able to weather this turbulent economic storm. As the rest of the state struggled with the stormy economy, the outlook remained sunny and clear on Maui.

What did Maui have that the other islands didn't? According to experts, the farsightedness to build up the island's name recognition in the fickle tourism industry, coupled with a diversified economy. Not only had Maui started planning "destination resort areas" in the 1960s, with Kaanapali the first planned resort area outside of Waikiki, but the island's tourism industry also knew that a reputation for the ability to deliver was the key calling card to success. Or as one expert put it: "Maui has been unbelievably successful at name recognition. You'd be hard-pressed to find someone in the U.S. or Canada over 20 years old who has not heard of Maui."

Impressions

If paradise consists solely of beauty, then these islands were the fairest that man ever invaded, for the land and sea were beautiful and the climate was congenial.

—James A. Michener, *Hawaii*

> **?   Did You Know?**
>
> - Maui has more miles of swimming beaches than any of the other Hawaiian islands.
> - Haleakala is the largest dormant volcano in the world, rising some 30,000 feet from the ocean floor.
> - Maui has the largest heiau in the state, Piilanihale, in Hana.
> - Maui has the only paved road in the world that goes from sea level to 10,000 feet in just 37 miles.
> - Haleakala Crater is so big that the entire island of Manhattan could easily fit inside it.
> - Kamehameha chose Lahaina as the capital of Hawaii after he united all the islands.
> - Puu Kukui, the highest point in the West Maui Mountains, gets some 40 feet (500 inches) of rain a year.
> - The lowest temperature ever recorded in Hawaii was atop Haleakala, when the thermometer dropped to 11° in 1961

In addition, Maui did not put all its eggs into the visitor-industry basket. Instead, island leaders continued to nurture Maui's agricultural roots, but instead of wooing giant agribusiness, they courted small niche farming: organic farmers, the flower industry, herb growers. The island also branched out into various high-tech fields, including the rapidly growing Internet industry. It's no coincidence that just as the World Wide Web was starting to become a household word, Maui's visitor industry—from tiny, two-bedroom B&Bs to megaresorts—had one of the highest rates of Web sites per capita in the United States.

On the eve of the 21st century, the island of Maui finds itself mellowing. It has seen centuries of change since Captain Cook first cruised by. The island, once populated only by Hawaiians, is today home to a diverse mix of Asians, Pacific Islanders, Caucasians, and African Americans. The population has had to learn lessons in balance: how to nurture the visitor industry without destroying the very product that visitors come to see.

2 Life & Language

Plantations brought so many different people to Hawaii that the state is now a rainbow of ethnic groups. No one group is a majority; everyone's a minority. Living here are Caucasians, African Americans, American Indians, Eskimos, Aleuts, Japanese, Chinese, Filipinos, Koreans, Tahitians, Asian Indians, Vietnamese, Hawaiians, Guamanians, Samoans, Tongans, and other Asian and Pacific Islanders. Add to that a few Canadians, Dutch, English, French, German, Irish, Italians, Portuguese, Scottish, Puerto Ricans, and Spanish.

More than a century ago, W. Somerset Maugham noted: "All these strange people live close to each other, with different languages and different thoughts; they believe in different gods and they have different values; two passions alone they share: love and hunger." More recently, noted travel journalist Jan Morris said of Hawaii's population: "Half the world's races seem to be represented and interbred here, and between them they have created an improbable microcosm of human society as a whole."

In combination, it's a remarkable potpourri. Many people seem to retain an element of the traditions of their homeland. Some Japanese Americans of Hawaii, even three and four generations removed from the homeland, are more traditional than the Japanese of Tokyo. And the same is true of many Chinese, Koreans, Filipinos, and the rest of the 25 or so ethnic groups that make Hawaii a kind of living museum of various Asian and Pacific cultures.

THE HAWAIIAN LANGUAGE

Almost everyone here speaks English, so except for pronouncing place names, you should have no trouble communicating in Hawaii. Many folks in Hawaii now speak Hawaiian, for the ancient language is making a comeback. Everybody who visits Hawaii, in fact, will hear the words *aloha* and *mahalo* (thank you). If you've just arrived, you're a *malihini*. Someone who's been here a long time is a *kamaaina*. When you finish a job or your meal, you are *pau* (over). On Friday it's *pau hana* (work over). When you go *pau hana,* you put *pupus* in your mouth (that's Hawaii's version of hors d'oeuvres).

The Hawaiian alphabet, created by the New England missionaries, has only 12 letters—the 5 regular vowels (*a, e, i, o,* and *u*) and 7 consonants (*h, k, l, m, n, p,* and *w*). The vowels are pronounced in the Roman fashion, that is, *ah, ay, ee, oh,* and *oo* (as in "too")—not *ay, ee, eye, oh,* and *you,* as they are in English. For example, *huhu* is pronounced *who-who.* Almost all vowels are sounded separately, although some are pronounced together, as in *Kalakaua: Kah lah cow ah.*

WHAT *HAOLE* MEANS   When Hawaiians first saw Western visitors, they called the pale-skinned, frail men haole because they looked so out of breath. In Hawaiian, *ha* means breath, *ole* means an absence of what precedes it. In other words, a lifeless-looking person.

Today, the term *haole* is generally a synonym for *Caucasian* or *foreigner* and is used casually without intending any disrespect. However, if uttered by an angry stranger who adds certain adjectives like *stupid* or *dumb,* the term *haole* can be construed as a mild racial slur.

SOME HAWAIIAN WORDS   Here are some basic Hawaiian words that you'll often hear in Hawaii and see throughout this book. For a more complete list of Hawaiian words, point your Internet browser to www.volcanoalley.com/lang.html.

akamai   smart
alii   Hawaiian royalty
aloha   greeting or farewell
ewa   in the direction of Ewa, an Oahu town; generally meaning west ("drive ewa 5 miles")
halau   school
hale   house or building
heiau   Hawaiian temple or place of worship
hui   a club, assembly
kahuna   priest or expert
kamaaina   old-timer
kapa   tapa, bark cloth
kapu   taboo, forbidden
keiki   child
lanai   porch or verandah
lomilomi   massage
mahalo   thank you

makai   a direction, toward the sea
malihini   stranger, newcomer
mana   spirit power
mauka   a direction, toward the mountains
muumuu   loose-fitting gown or dress
nene   official state bird, a goose
ono   delicious
pali   cliff
wiki   quick

PIDGIN: 'EH FO'REAL, BRAH

If you venture beyond the tourist areas, you might hear another local tongue: pidgin English. A conglomeration of slang and words from the Hawaiian language, pidgin was developed by sugar planters as a method to communicate with their Chinese laborers in the 1800s. Today it's used by people who grew up in Hawaii to talk with their peers.

"Broke da mouth" (tastes really good) is the favorite pidgin phrase; "'Eh fo'real, brah" means "It's true, brother." You might be invited to hear an elder "talk story" (relating myths and memories), or to enjoy local treats like "shave ice" (a tropical snow cone) and "crack seed" (highly seasoned preserved fruit). But since pidgin is really the province of the locals, your visit to Hawaii is likely to pass without your hearing much pidgin at all.

3 A Taste of Hawaii

by Jocelyn Fujii

A decade ago, visitors could expect to find frozen mahimahi beurre blanc with frozen or canned vegetables as the premium dish on a fine-dining menu in Hawaii. But not anymore. It's a whole new world in Hawaii's restaurant kitchens.

THE NEW GUARD: HAWAII REGIONAL CUISINE

Since the mid-eighties, when Hawaii Regional Cuisine ignited a culinary revo-lution, Hawaii has elevated its standing on the global Epicurean map to bona fide star status. Fresh ideas and sophisticated menus have made the islands a culinary destination, applauded and emulated nationwide. (In a tip of the toque to island tradition, "ahi"—a word ubiquitous in Hawaii—has replaced "tuna" on many chic New York menus.) And options have proliferated at all levels of the local dining spectrum: waves of new Asian residents have planted the food traditions of their homelands in the fertile soil of Hawaii, resulting in unforgettable taste treats true to their Thai, Vietnamese, Japanese, Chinese, and Indo-Pacific roots. Like the peoples of Hawaii, traditions are mixed and matched—and when combined with the bountiful, fresh harvests from sea and land for which Hawaii is known, these ethnic and culinary traditions take on renewed vigor and a cross-cultural, uniquely Hawaiian quality.

This is good news for the eager palate. From the very haute to the informal neighborhood gathering place, from the totally eclectic to the purely Japanese to the multiethnic plate lunch, dining in Hawaii is one great culinary joyride.

Today, you can expect to encounter Indonesian sates, Polynesian imu-baked foods, and guava-smoked meats in sophisticated presentations in the finest dining rooms in the state. If there's pasta or risotto or rack of lamb on the menu, it could be nori (seaweed) linguine with opihi (limpet sauce), or risotto with local seafood served in taro cups, or a rack of lamb in cabernet and hoisin sauce (fermented

Ahi, Ono & Opakapaka: A Hawaiian Seafood Primer

The fresh seafood in Hawaii has been described as the best in the world. In the pivotal book *The New Cuisine of Hawaii*, by Janice Wald Henderson, acclaimed chef Nobuyuki Matsuhisa (chef-owner of Matsuhisa in Beverly Hills and Nobu in Manhattan and London) writes, "As a chef who specializes in fresh seafood, I am in awe of the quality of Hawaii's fish; it is unparalleled anywhere else in the world." And why not? Without a doubt, the islands' surrounding waters, the waters of the remote northwestern Hawaiian Islands, and a growing aquaculture industry are fertile grounds for this most important of Hawaii's food resources.

The reputable restaurants in Hawaii buy fresh fish daily at predawn auctions or from local fishermen. Some chefs even spear-fish their ingredients themselves. "Still wiggling" is the ultimate term for freshness in Hawaii. The fish can then be grilled over *kiawe* (mesquite) or prepared in innumerable ways.

Although most menus include the Western description for the fresh fish used, most often the local nomenclature is listed, turning dinner for the uninitiated into a confusing, quasi-foreign experience. To help familiarize you with the menu language of Hawaii, here's a basic glossary of island fish:

Ahi　Yellowfin or bigeye tuna, important for its use in sashimi and poke, at sushi bars, and in Hawaii Regional Cuisine.

Aku　Skipjack tuna, heavily utilized by local families in home cooking and poke.

Ehu　Red snapper, delicate and sumptuous, yet lesser known than opakapaka (see below).

Hapuupuu　Grouper, a sea bass whose use is expanding from ethnic to nonethnic restaurants.

Hebi　Spearfish, mildly flavored and frequently featured as the "catch of the day" in upscale restaurants.

soybean, garlic, and spices), or with macadamia nuts and coconut. Watch for ponzu sauce too; it's lemony and zesty, much more flavorful than the soy sauce it resembles, and a welcome new staple on local menus.

While in Hawaii, you'll encounter many labels that embrace the fundamentals of HRC (Hawaii Regional Cuisine) and the sophistication, informality, and nostalgia it encompasses. Euro-Asian, Pacific Rim, Pacific Edge, Euro-Pacific, fusion cuisine, Hapa cuisine—by whatever name, Hawaii Regional Cuisine has evolved as Hawaii's singular cooking style, what some say is this country's current gastronomic, as well as geographic, frontier. It highlights the fresh seafood and produce of Hawaii's rich waters and volcanic soil, the cultural traditions of Hawaii's ethnic groups, and the skills of well-trained chefs. Culinary artists such as Roy Yamaguchi (Roy's on Oahu, Maui, and Kauai), Peter Merriman (Merriman's on the Big Island and Hula Grill on Maui), George Mavrothalassitis (Four Seasons Resort Wailea), and Jean-Marie Josselin (A Pacific Cafe on Kauai, Maui, and Oahu) broke ranks with their European predecessors to forge new ground in the 50th state. Some of Hawaii's most prominent chefs, such as David Paul (David Paul's Lahaina Grill and the new David Paul's Diamond Head Grill), were not original HRC members but have forged ahead to form their own strong culinary identities.

Fresh ingredients are foremost, and farmers and fishermen work together to provide steady supplies of just-harvested seafood, seaweed, fern shoots, vine-ripened

Kajiki   Pacific blue marlin, also called *au,* with a firm flesh and high fat content that make it a plausible substitute for tuna in some raw fish dishes, and as a grilled item on menus.

Kumu   Goatfish, a luxury item on Chinese and upscale menus, served en papillote or steamed whole, Oriental style, with sesame oil, scallions, ginger, and garlic.

Mahimahi   Dolphin fish (the game fish, not the mammal) or dorado, a classic sweet, white-fleshed fish requiring vigilance among purists because it is often disguised as fresh when it's actually "fresh frozen"—a big difference.

Monchong   Bigscale or sickle pomfret, an exotic, tasty fish, scarce but gaining a higher profile on Hawaiian Island menus.

Nairagi   Striped marlin, also called *au;* good as sashimi and in poke, and often substituted for ahi in raw fish products.

Onaga   Ruby snapper, a luxury fish, versatile, moist, and flaky; top-of-the-line.

Ono   Wahoo, firmer and drier than the snappers, often served grilled and in sandwiches.

Opah   Moonfish, rich and fatty, versatile; cooked, raw, smoked, and broiled.

Opakapaka   Pink snapper, light, flaky, and luxurious, suited for sashimi, poaching, sautéing, and baking; the best-known upscale fish.

Papio   Jack trevally, light, firm, and flavorful, and favored in island cookery.

Shutome   Broadbill swordfish, of beeflike texture and rich flavor.

Tombo   Albacore tuna, with a high fat content, suitable for grilling and sautéing.

Uhu   Parrot fish, most often encountered steamed, Chinese style.

Uku   Gray snapper of clear, pale-pink flesh, delicately flavored and moist.

Ulua   Large jack trevally, firm-fleshed and versatile.

tomatoes, goat cheese, lamb, herbs, taro, gourmet lettuces, and countless harvests from land and sea that wind up in myriad forms on ever-changing menus, prepared in Asian and Western culinary styles. Exotic fruits introduced by recent Southeast Asian immigrants, such as sapodilla, soursop, and rambutan, are beginning to appear regularly in Chinatown markets. Aquacultured seafood, from seaweed to salmon to lobster, is a staple on many menus. Additionally, fresh-fruit salsas and sauces (mango, litchi, papaya, pineapple, guava), ginger-sesame-wasabi flavorings, corn cakes with sake sauces, tamarind and fish sauces, coconut-chili accents, tropical-fruit vinaigrettes, and other local and newly arrived seasonings from Southeast Asia and the Pacific impart unique qualities to the preparations.

Here's a sampling of what you can expect to find on a Hawaii Regional menu: seared Hawaiian fish with lilikoi shrimp butter; taro-crab cakes; Molokai sweet-potato or breadfruit vichyssoise; Ka'u orange sauce and Kahua Ranch lamb; fern shoots from Waipio Valley; Hawaiian bouillabaisse with fresh snapper, Kona crab, and fresh aquacultured shrimp; blackened ahi summer rolls; and gourmet Waimanalo greens, picked that day. With menus that often change daily, and the unquenchable appetites that the leading chefs have for cooking on the edge, the possibilities for once-in-a-lifetime dining adventures are more available than ever in Hawaii.

PLATE LUNCHES & MORE: LOCAL FOOD

At the other end of the spectrum is the cuisine of the hoi polloi, the vast and endearing world of "local food." By that we mean plate lunches and poke, shave ice and saimin, bento lunches and manapua—cultural hybrids all.

Reflecting a polyglot population of many styles and ethnicities, Hawaii's idiosyncratic dining scene is eminently inclusive. Consider Surfer Chic: barefoot in the sand, in a swimsuit, chowing down on a plate lunch ordered from a lunch wagon, consisting of fried mahimahi, "two scoops rice," macaroni salad, and a few leaves of green, typically julienned cabbage. (Generally, teriyaki beef or shoyu chicken are options.) Heavy gravy is often the condiment of choice, accompanied by a soft drink in a paper cup. Like saimin—the local version of noodles in broth topped with scrambled egg, green onions, and, sometimes, pork—the plate lunch is Hawaii's version of high camp.

Because this is Hawaii, at least a few licks of *poi*—the Hawaiian staple of cooked, pounded taro—and the other examples of indigenous cuisine are de rigueur, if not at a corny luau, then at least in a Hawaiian plate lunch. The native samplers include foods from before and after Western contact, such as *lau lau* (pork, chicken, or fish steamed in ti leaves), *kalua* pork (pork cooked in a Polynesian underground oven known here as an *imu*), *lomi* salmon (salted salmon with tomatoes and green onions), squid *luau* (octopus cooked in coconut milk and taro tops), *poke* (cubed raw fish seasoned with onions and seaweed, and the occasional sprinkling of roasted *kukui* nuts), *haupia* (creamy coconut pudding), and *kulolo* (steamed pudding of coconut, brown sugar, and taro).

Bento, another popular choice for the dine-and-dash set, is also available throughout Hawaii. The compact, boxed assortment of picnic fare usually consists of neatly arranged sections of rice; pickled vegetables; and fried chicken, beef, or pork. Increasingly, however, the bento is becoming more streamlined and health-conscious, as in macrobiotic bento lunches or vegetarian brown-rice bentos. A derivative of the modest lunch box for Japanese immigrants who once labored in the sugar and pineapple fields, bentos are dispensed ubiquitously throughout Hawaii, from department stores like Daiei and Shirokiya (bento bonanzas) to corner delis and supermarkets.

Also from the plantations come *manapua*, a bready, doughy round with tasty fillings of sweetened pork or sweet beans. In the old days, the Chinese "manapua man" would make his rounds with bamboo containers balanced on a rod over his shoulders. Today you'll find white or whole-wheat manapua containing chicken, vegetables, curry, and other savory fillings.

The daintier Chinese delicacy, dim sum, is made of translucent wrappers filled with fresh seafood, pork hash, and vegetables, served for breakfast and lunch in Chinatown restaurants. The Hong Kong–style dumplings are ordered fresh and hot from bamboo steamers from invariably brusque servers who move their carts from table to table. Much like hailing a taxi in Manhattan, you have to be quick and loud for dim sum.

TASTY TREATS: SHAVE ICE & MALASSADAS

For dessert or a snack, the prevailing choice is shave ice, the Island version of a snow cone. Particularly on hot, humid days, long lines gather for the rainbow-colored cones heaped with finely shaved ice and topped with sweet tropical syrups. (The sweet-sour *li hing mui* flavor is a current rage.) The fast-melting mounds requiring prompt, efficient consumption are quite the local summer ritual for those with a sweet tooth. Aficionados order shave ice with ice cream and sweetened adzuki beans plopped in the middle.

You might also encounter *malassadas,* the Portuguese version of a doughnut, and if you do, it's best to eat them immediately. A leftover malassada has all the appeal of a heavy, lumpen cold doughnut. When fresh and hot, however, as at school carnivals (where they attract the longest lines) or at bakeries and roadside stands, the sugary, yeasty doughnut-without-a-hole is enjoyed by many as one of the enduring legacies of the Portuguese in Hawaii.

PINEAPPLES, PAPAYAS & OTHER FRESH ISLAND FRUITS

Lanai isn't growing pineapples commercially anymore, but low-acid, white-fleshed, wondrously sweet Hawaiian Sugar Loaf pineapples are being commercially grown, on a small scale, on Kauai as well as the Big Island. That is just one of the developments in a rapidly changing agricultural scene in Hawaii, where the litchi-like Southeast Asian *rambutan;* the *longan* (Chinese dragon's-eye litchis); 80-pound Indian jackfruits; the starfruit; the luscious, custardy mangosteen; and the usual mangoes, papayas, guava, and *lilikoi* (passion fruit) make up the dazzling parade of fresh Island fruits that come and go with the seasons.

Papayas, bananas, and pineapples grow year-round, but pineapples are always sweetest, juiciest, and most yellow in the summer. Although new papaya hybrids are making their way into the marketplace, the classic bests include the fleshy, firm-textured Kahuku papayas, the queen of them all; the Big Island's sweet Kapoho and Puna papayas; and the fragile, juicy, and reddish-orange Sunrise papayas from Kauai. Those who have transferred their allegiance from Puna to Sunrise claim they're sweeter, juicier, and more elegant than all others. Also called strawberry papayas, the Sunrise variety is easily misjudged and often served overripe; delicate inside and out, these papayas are easily bruised and fragile in texture, yet robust in flavor. Apple bananas are smaller, firmer, and tarter than the standard, and they are a local specialty that flourish throughout the Islands.

Litchis and mangoes are long-awaited summer fruit. Mangoes begin appearing in late spring or early summer and can be found at roadside fruit stands, markets, and health-food stores (where the high prices might shock you). My favorite is the white pirie—rare and resinous, fiberless, and so sweet and juicy it makes the high-profile Hayden seem prosaic. A popular newcomer is the Rapoza mango, only a few years in the Islands yet already earning raves for its sweetness, resilience, and fiberless, 2-pound fruit.

Watermelons are a summer hit and a signature of Molokai and Oahu. The state of Hawaii, which consumes more watermelons per capita than any other in the union, also produces topnotch fruit for its loyal clientele. Kahuku watermelons, available in the summer months, give the popular Molokai variety a run for its money. Juicy, fleshy, and sweet, Kahuku watermelons are now grown primarily in Waialua on Oahu's north shore, while production of the Molokai variety has expanded to central Oahu. Most markets sell these bulging orbs of refreshment throughout summer and early fall.

In the competitive world of oranges, the Kau Gold navel oranges from the southern Big Island put Sunkist to shame. Grown in the volcanic soil and sunny conditions of the South Point region (the southernmost point in the United States), the "Ugly Orange" is brown, rough, and anything but pretty. But the browner and uglier they are, the sweeter and juicier they are. Because the thin-skinned oranges are tree-ripened, they're fleshy and heavy with liquid, and they will spoil you for life.

Although these oranges have traditionally been a winter fruit, they're appearing more abundantly year-round.

4 The Natural World: An Environmental Guide to Maui

Born of violent volcanic eruptions from deep beneath the ocean's surface, the first Hawaiian islands emerged about 70 million years ago—more than 200 million years after the major continental land masses formed. Two thousand miles from the nearest continent, Mother Nature's fury began to carve beauty from barren rock. Untiring volcanoes spewed forth curtains of fire that cooled into stone, while severe tropical storms, some with hurricane-force winds, battered and blasted the cooling lava rock into a series of shapes. Ferocious earthquakes flattened, shattered, and reshaped the islands into precipitous valleys, jagged cliffs, and recumbent flatlands. Monstrous surf and gigantic tidal waves rearranged and polished the lands above and below the reaches of the tide.

It took millions upon millions of years for nature to chisel the familiar form of Maui's majestic Haleakala peak, to create the waterfalls on Molokai's northern side, to shape the reefs of Hulopoe Bay on Lanai, and to establish the lush rain forests of the Hana coastline. The result is an island-chain-within-a-chain like no other on the planet—a tropical dream of a landscape, rich in unique flora and fauna and surrounded by a vibrant underwater world, that will haunt your memory forever.

THE ISLAND LANDSCAPES

Maui is more than just palm trees and white-sand beaches. The island contains a wide range of climate and topography, from high mountaintops to lava-rock beaches, verdant rain forests to arid deserts, fertile farming areas to swamps. Each island in Maui County has its own particular climate and topography.

MAUI   When two volcanoes—Puu Kukui, in the West Maui Mountains, and 10,000-foot Haleakala, in the east—flowed together about a million years ago, the event gave the Valley Isle of Maui a range of climates from arid desert to tropical rain forest. The 728-square-mile island is the only place in the world where you can drive from sea level to 10,000 feet in just 37 miles, passing through tropical beaches, sugar and pineapple plantations, and rolling grassy hills; past the timber line; and up to the lunar-like surface of the top of Haleakala. In addition to 33 miles of public beaches on the south and west shores, Maui is home to the arid dry lands of Kihei, the swampy bogs of the West Maui Mountains, the rain forest of Hana, and the desert of Kaupo.

KAHOOLAWE   Just 7 miles southwest of Maui lies Kahoolawe, the smallest of the main Hawaiian islands. This arid island has some beautiful white-sand beaches and a unique topography: years of overgrazing by ranchers coupled with the island's use as a bombing target by the U.S. military from 1945 to 1994 caused the fairly flat island to lose most of its topsoil. Native Hawaiians, who recently reclaimed the island from the federal government, are attempting to restore, reforest, and replant the island. Access to Kahoolawe is restricted.

LANAI   This small, kidney bean–shaped island—only 13 miles wide by 17 miles long—rises out of the ocean like the shell of a turtle, with cliffs on the west side that rise to a high point of 3,370 feet. Lanai slopes down to sea level on the east and south sides; the only town on the island, Lanai City, sits at 1,600 feet. The high point of the island is covered with Norfolk pines and is usually shrouded in clouds, whereas the arid beaches survive on minimal rainfall. One area in particular stands out: the Garden of the Gods, just 7 miles from Lanai City. Here, oddly strewn boulders lie in the amber- and ochre-colored dirt, and bizarre stone formations dot the landscape. The ancient Hawaiians formed romantic legends explaining the enigma, but modern-day scientists are still debating this mystery.

MOLOKAI   Roughly the shape of Manhattan, Molokai is 37 miles long and 10 miles wide, with a thumb protruding from the north shore. The north shore begins on the west, with miles of white-sand beaches that fringe a desert-like landscape. The protruding thumb—the Kalaupapa Peninsula—is cut off by a fence of cliffs, some 2,000 feet tall, that line the remainder of the north side. Molokai can be divided into two areas: the dry west end, where the high point is 1,381 feet; and the rainy, tropical east and north ends, where the high point is Mount Kamakou, at 4,970 feet.

THE FLORA OF MAUI

Maui radiates the sweet smell of flowers, lush vegetation, and exotic plant life. Some of the more memorable plants and flowers found in the islands include:

African Tulip Tree   Even from afar, you can see the flaming red flowers on these large trees, which can grow to be more than 50 feet tall. Children in Hawaii love them because the buds hold water—they use the flowers as water pistols.

Angel's Trumpet   This small tree can grow up to 20 feet tall, with an abundance of large (up to 10 inches in diameter) pendants—white or pink flowers that resemble, well, trumpets. The Hawaiians call them *nana-honua,* which means "earth gazing." The flowers, which bloom continually from early spring to late fall, have a musky scent. However, beware: All parts of the plant are poisonous and contain a strong narcotic.

Anthurium   One of Hawaii's most popular cut flowers, anthuriums originally came from the tropical Americas and the Caribbean islands. There are more than 550 species, but the most popular in Hawaii are the heart-shaped red, orange, pink, white, and even purple flowers with a tail-like spathe (green, orange, pink, red, white, purple, and combinations thereof). Look for the heart-shaped green leaves in shaded areas. These exotic plants have no scent but will last several weeks as cut flowers.

Bird of Paradise   This native of Africa has become something of a trademark of Hawaii. The plants are easily recognizable by the orange and blue flowers nestled in gray-green bracts, looking somewhat like birds in flight.

Bougainvillea   Originally from Brazil and named for the 18th-century French explorer Louis Antoine de Bougainville, these colorful, tissue-thin bracts (ranging in color from majestic purple to fiery orange) hide tiny white flowers.

Bromeliads   The pineapple plant is the best-known bromeliad. Native to tropical South America and the islands of the Caribbean, bromeliads comprise more than 1,400 species. "Bromes," as they are affectionately called, are generally spiky plants ranging in size from a few inches to several feet in diameter. They're popular not only for their unusual foliage but also for their strange and wonderful flowers, which range from colorful spikes to delicate blossoms resembling orchids. Bromeliads are widely used in landscaping and as interior decoration, especially in resort areas.

Coffee   Hawaii is the only state that commercially produces coffee. Coffee is an evergreen shrub with shiny, waxy, dark-green, pointed leaves. The flower is a small, fragrant white blossom that develops into half-inch berries that turn bright red when ripe. Look for coffee plants in Kaanapali on Maui and in Kualapuu on Molokai.

Gingers   Some of the most fragrant flowers in Hawaii are white and yellow gingers, which the Hawaiians call *'awapuhi-ke'oke'o* and *'awapuhi-melemele*. Usually found in clumps, and growing 4 to 7 feet tall in areas blessed by rain, these sweet-smelling, 3-inch-wide flowers are composed of three dainty petal-like stamens and three long, thin petals. Both white and yellow gingers are so prolific that many people assume that they are native to Hawaii; actually, they were introduced in the 19th century from the Indonesia-Malaysia area. Look for white and yellow ginger from late spring to fall. If you see them on the side of the road (especially on the Hana Highway), stop and pick a few blossoms—your car will be filled with a divine fragrance for the rest of the day. The only downside is that, once picked, the flowers will live only briefly.

Other members of the ginger family frequently seen in Hawaii (there are some 700 species) include red, shell, and torch gingers. Red ginger consists of tall, green stalks with foot-long red "flower heads." The red "petals" are actually bracts; inch-long white flowers are protected by the bracts and can be seen if you look down into the red head. Red ginger (*'awapuhi-'ula'ula* in Hawaiian), which does not share the heavenly smell of white ginger, will last a week or longer when cut. Look for red ginger from spring through late fall. Cool, wet mountain forests are ideal conditions for shell ginger; Hawaiians call this variety *'awapuhi-luheluhe,* which means "drooping" ginger. These plants, natives of India and Burma, have pearly white, clam shell–like blossoms, and they bloom from spring to fall.

Perhaps the most exotic gingers are the red or pink torch gingers. Cultivated in Malaysia as seasoning (the young flower shoots are used in curries), torch ginger rises directly out of the ground; the flower stalks, which are about 5 to 8 inches in length, resemble the fire of a lighted torch. The Hawaiians call this plant, one of the few gingers that can bloom year-round, *'awapuhi-ko'oko'o,* or "walking-stick" ginger.

Heliconias   Some 80 species of the colorful heliconia family came to Hawaii from the Caribbean and Central and South America. The bright yellow, red, green, and orange bracts overlap and appear to unfold like origami birds. The most obvious heliconia to spot is the lobster claw, which resembles a string of boiled crustacean pincers—the brilliant crimson bracts alternate on the stem. Another prolific heliconia is the parrot's beak. Growing to about hip height, the parrot's beak is composed of bright-orange flower bracts with black tips, not unlike the beak of a parrot. Look for parrot's beak in the spring and summer, when it blooms in profusion.

Hibiscus   One variety of this year-round blossom, the yellow hibiscus, is the official state flower. The 4- to 6-inch hibiscus flowers come in a range of colors, from lily white to lipstick red. The flowers resemble crepe paper, with stamens and pistils protruding spirelike from the center. Hibiscus hedges can grow up to 15 feet tall. Once plucked, the flowers wither quickly.

Jacaranda   Beginning around March and sometimes lasting until early May, these huge, lacy-leafed trees metamorphose into large clusters of spectacular lavender-blue sprays. The bell-shaped flowers drop quickly, leaving a majestic purple carpet beneath the tree.

Night-Blooming Cereus Look along rock walls for this spectacular night-blooming flower. Originally from Central America, this vinelike member of the cactus family has green scalloped edges, and it produces foot-long white flowers that open as darkness falls and wither as the sun rises. The plant also bears a red fruit that is edible.

Orchids To many minds, nothing says Hawaii more than orchids. The orchid family is the largest in the entire plant kingdom; orchids are found in most parts of the world. Some species are native to Hawaii, but because they're inconspicuous in most places, people might overlook them. The most widely grown orchids—and the major source of flowers for leis and garnish for tropical libations—are the vanda orchids. The vandas used in Hawaii's commercial flower industry are generally lavender or white, but they grow in a rainbow of colors, shapes, and sizes. The orchids used for corsages are the large, delicate cattleya; the ones used in floral arrangements—you'll probably see them in your hotel lobby—are usually dendrobiums.

Plumeria Also known as frangipani, this sweet-smelling, five-petal flower, found in clusters on trees, is the most popular choice of lei makers. The Singapore plumeria has five creamy-white petals, with a touch of yellow in the center. Another popular variety, ruba—with flowers from soft pink to flaming red—is also used in leis. When picking plumeria, be careful of the sap from the flower, because it is poisonous and can stain clothes.

Protea Originally from South Africa, this unusual plant comes in more than 40 varieties. Proteas are shrubs that bloom into a range of flower types. Different species of proteas range from those resembling pincushions to a species that looks just like a bouquet of feathers. Proteas are long-lasting cut flowers; once dried, they will last for years.

FRUIT TREES

Banana Edible bananas are among the oldest of the world's food crops. By the time Europeans arrived in the islands, the Hawaiians had more than 40 types of bananas planted. Most banana plants have long green leaves hanging from the tree, with the flower giving way to fruit in clusters.

Breadfruit A large tree—over 60 feet tall—with broad, sculpted, dark-green leaves, the famous breadfruit produces a round, head-size green fruit that is a staple in diets of all Polynesians. When roasted or baked, the whitish-yellow meat tastes somewhat like a sweet potato.

Litchi This evergreen tree, which can grow to well over 30 feet across, originated in China. Small flowers grow into panicles about a foot long in June and July. The round, red-skinned fruit appears shortly afterward.

Macadamia A transplant from Australia, macadamia nuts have become a commercial crop in recent decades. The large trees—up to 60 feet tall—bear a hard-shelled nut encased in a leathery husk, which splits open and dries when ripe.

Mango From Indonesia and Malaysia comes the delicious mango, a fruit with peachlike flesh. Mango season usually begins in the spring and lasts through the summer, depending on the variety. The trees can grow to more than 100 feet tall. The tiny reddish flowers give way to a green fruit that turns red-yellow when ripe. Some people enjoy unripe mangoes, either thinly sliced or in chutney, a traditional Indian preparation. The mango sap can cause a skin rash on some people.

Papaya   One of the sweetest of all tropical fruits, the pear-shaped papayas turn yellow or reddish pink when ripe. They are found at the base of the large, scalloped-shaped leaves on a pedestal-like, nonbranched tree whose trunk is hollow. Papayas ripen year-round.

OTHER TREES & PLANTS

Among the world's largest trees, **banyans** have branches that grow out and away from the trunk, forming descending roots that grow down to the ground to feed and form additional trunks, making the tree very stable during tropical storms. The banyan in the courtyard next to the old Court House in Lahaina is an excellent example of a spreading banyan—it covers two-thirds of an acre.

Monkeypod trees are among Hawaii's most majestic trees; they grow more than 80 feet tall and 100 feet across. Seen near older homes and in parks, monkeypod trees have leaves that drop in February and March. The wood from the tree is a favorite of woodworking artisans.

One very uncommon and unusual plant—in fact seen only on the Big Island and in the Haleakala Crater on Maui—is the **silversword**. Once a year, this rare relative of the sunflower family blooms between July and September. More like a pinecone in appearance than a sunflower, the silversword in bloom is a fountain of red-petaled, daisy-like flowers that turn silver soon after blooming.

Around pools, near streams, and in neatly planted fields, you'll see the green heart-shaped leaves of **taro,** whose dense roots are a staple of all Polynesians. The ancient Hawaiians pounded the roots into poi. Originally from Sri Lanka, taro not only is a food crop, but also is grown as an ornamental.

One not so rare-and-unusual plant is **marijuana,** or *pakalolo*—"crazy weed" as the Hawaiians call it—which is grown throughout the islands. You probably won't see it as you drive along the roads, but if you go hiking, you might glimpse the feathery green leaves with tight clusters of buds. Despite years of police effort to eradicate the plant, the illegal industry continues. Don't be tempted to pick a few buds, because the purveyors of this nefarious industry don't take kindly to poaching.

THE FAUNA OF MAUI

When the first Polynesians arrived in Hawaii between A.D. 500 and A.D. 800, scientists say they found some 67 varieties of endemic Hawaiian birds, a third of which are now believed to be extinct. What's even more astonishing is what they didn't find—there were no reptiles, amphibians, mosquitoes, lice, or fleas, not even a cockroach.

There were only two endemic mammals: the **hoary bat** and the **monk seal.** The small bat, called *ope'ape'a,* must have accidentally blown to Hawaii at some point, from either North or South America. It can still be seen today on its early evening forays.

The Hawaiian monk seal, a relative of warm-water seals found in the Caribbean and Mediterranean, was nearly slaughtered into extinction for its skin and oil during the 19th century. These seals have recently experienced a minor population explosion, forcing relocation of some males from their protected homes in the islets north of the main Hawaiian Islands. Periodically, these endangered animals turn up at various beaches throughout the state. They are protected under federal law by the Marine Mammals Protection Act. If you're fortunate enough to see a monk seal, just look; don't disturb one of Hawaii's living treasures.

The first Polynesians brought a few animals from home: dogs, pigs, and chickens (all were for eating). A stowaway on board the Polynesian sailing canoes was the rat. All four animals are still found in the Hawaiian wild today.

BIRDS

More species of native birds have become extinct in Hawaii in the past 200 years than anywhere else on the planet. Of the 67 native species, 23 are extinct, 29 are endangered, and 1 is threatened. Even the Hawaiian crow, *'alala,* is threatened.

The *a'eo,* or Hawaiian stilt, a 16-inch-long bird with a black head, a black coat, a white underside, and long pink legs, can be found in protected wetlands like the Kanaha Wild Life Sanctuary (where it shares its natural habitat with the Hawaiian coot) and the Kealia Pond.

Endemic to the islands, the **nene** is Hawaii's state bird. It is currently being brought back from the brink of extinction through captive breeding and by strenuous protection laws. A relative of the Canada goose, the nene stands about 2 feet high and has a black head and yellow cheek, a buff neck with deep furrows, a grayish-brown body, and clawed feet. It gets its name from its two-syllable, high nasal call, "nay-nay." The approximately 500 nenes in existence can be seen at Haleakala National Park.

The Hawaiian short-eared owl, **pueo,** which grows to about 12 to 17 inches in size, can be seen at dawn and dusk when it goes hunting for rodents. These black-billed, brown-and-white birds were highly regarded by Hawaiians; according to legend, spotting a pueo is a good omen.

OTHER LAND FAUNA

Geckos   These harmless, soft-skinned, insect-eating lizards come equipped with suction pads on their feet, enabling them to climb walls and windows to reach tasty insects like mosquitoes and cockroaches. You'll see them on windows outside a lighted room at night or hear their cheerful chirp.

Mongooses   The mongoose was a mistake in Hawaii. It was brought here in the 19th century to counteract the ever-growing rat problem. But rats are nocturnal creatures, sleeping during the day and wandering out at night. Mongooses, however, are day creatures. Instead of getting rid of the rat problem, the mongooses eat bird eggs, contributing to the destruction of the native bird population in Hawaii.

Snakes   Thanks to strict measures to keep snakes out of the state, Hawaii has but one tiny earthworm-like snake. On the island of Guam, the brown tree snake has obliterated most of the bird population. Officials in Hawaii are well aware of this danger and are committed to preventing snakes from entering the state.

SEALIFE

Approximately 680 species of fish are known to inhabit the waters around the Hawaiian Islands. Of those, approximately 450 species stay close to the reef and inshore areas.

CORAL   The reefs surrounding Hawaii are made up of various coral and algae. The living coral grows through sunlight that feeds a specialized algae, called zooxanthellae, which in turn allows the development of the coral's calcareous skeleton. The reefs, which take thousands of years to develop, attract and support fish and crustaceans, which use them for food, habitat, mating, and raising their young. Mother Nature can batter the fragile reefs with a strong storm or large waves, but humans—through seemingly innocuous acts such as touching the coral—have proven far more destructive.

The corals most frequently seen around Maui are hard, rocklike formations named for their familiar shapes: antler, cauliflower, finger, plate, and razor coral. Wire coral looks just like its name—a randomly bent wire growing straight out of the reef. Some corals appear soft, such as tube coral, which can be found in the ceilings of caves. Black coral, which resembles winter-bare trees or shrubs, is found at depths of over 100 feet.

REEF FISH   Of the approximately 450 reef fish, about 27% are native to Hawaii and are found nowhere else on the planet. This might seem surprising for a string of isolated islands, 2,000 miles from the nearest land mass. But as the Hawaiian Islands were born from erupting volcanoes, evolving over millions of years, ocean currents—mainly from Southeast Asia—carried the larvae of thousands of marine animals and plants to Hawaii's reef. Of those, approximately 100 species not only adapted, but thrived.

Some species are much bigger and more plentiful than their Pacific cousins, and many developed unique characteristics. Some, like the lemon or milletseed butterfly fish, are not only particular to Hawaii but also unique within their larger, world-wide family in their specialized schooling and feeding behaviors. Another surprising thing about Hawaii endemics is how common some of the native fish are; you can see the saddleback wrasse, for instance, on virtually any snorkeling excursion or dive in Hawaiian waters.

You're likely to spot one or more of the following reef fish while underwater. **Angel fish,** often mistaken for butterfly fish, can be distinguished by the spine, located low on the gill plate. Angel fish are very shy; several species live in colonies close to coral for protection.

Blennys are small, elongated fish, ranging from 2 to 10 inches long, with the majority in the 3- to 4-inch range. Blennys are so small that they can live in tide pools; you might have a hard time spotting one.

Butterfly fish, among the most colorful of the reef fish, are usually seen in pairs (scientists believe they mate for life), and they appear to spend most of their day feeding. There are 22 species of butterfly fish, of which 3 (blue-stripe, lemon or milletseed, and multiband or pebbled butterfly fish) are endemic. Most butterfly fish have a dark band through the eye and a spot near the tail resembling an eye, meant to confuse their predators (the moray eel loves to lunch on butterfly fish).

Moray and conger **eels** are the common eels seen in Hawaii. Morays are usually docile unless provoked, or if there is food or an injured fish around. Unfortunately, some morays have been fed by divers and—being intelligent creatures—associate divers with food; thus, they can become aggressive. But most morays like to keep to themselves, hidden in their hole or crevice. Whereas morays might look menacing, conger eels look downright happy, with big lips and pectoral fins (situated so that they look like big ears) that give them the appearance of a perpetually smiling face. Conger eels have crushing teeth so that they can feed on crustaceans; in fact, since they're sloppy eaters, they usually live with shrimp and crabs who feed off the crumbs they leave.

One of the largest and most colorful of the reef fish, the **parrot fish** can grow up to 40 inches long. Parrot fish are easy to spot—their front teeth are fused together, protruding like buck teeth and resembling a parrot's beak. These unique teeth allow them to feed by scraping algae from rocks and coral. The rocks and coral pass through the parrot fish's system, resulting in fine sand. In fact, most of the white sand found in Hawaii is parrot-fish waste; one large parrot fish can produce a ton of sand a year. Hawaiian native parrot-fish species include yellowbar, regal, and spectacled.

Scorpion fish are what scientists call "ambush predators." They hide under camouflaged exteriors and ambush their prey when they come along. Several sport a venomous dorsal spine. These fish don't have a gas bladder, so when they stop swimming, they sink—that's why you usually find them "resting" on ledges and on the ocean bottom. Although these fish are not aggressive, an inattentive snorkeler or diver could feel the effects of those venomous spines—so be very careful where you put your hands and feet in the water.

Surgeon fish, sometimes called tang, get their name from the scalpel-like spines located on each side of their bodies near the base of their tails. Some surgeon fish have a rigid spine; others have the ability to fold their spine against their body until it's needed for defense purposes. Some surgeon fish, like the brightly colored yellow tang, are boldly colored. Others are adorned in more conservative shades of gray, brown, or black. The only endemic surgeon fish—and the most abundant in Hawaiian waters—is the convict tang (*manini* in Hawaiian), a pale white fish with vertical black stripes (like a convict's uniform).

Wrasses are a very diverse family of fish, ranging in size from 2 to 15 inches. Several wrasses are brilliantly colored and change their colors through aging and sexual dimorphism (sex changing). Wrasses have the ability to change gender with maturation, from female (when young) to male. Several wrasses are endemic to Hawaii: the Hawaiian cleaner, shortnose, belted, and gray (or old woman).

GAME FISH Fishers have a huge variety to choose from in Hawaii, from pan-sized snapper to nearly 1-ton marlin. Hawaii is known around the globe as *the* place for big game fish—marlin, swordfish, and tuna—but its waters are also great for catching other offshore fish, such as mahimahi, rainbow runner, and wahoo; coastal fish, such as barracuda and scad; bottom fish, such as snappers, sea bass, and amberjack; and inshore fish, such as trevally and bonefish.

Six kinds of **billfish** are found in the offshore waters around the islands: Pacific blue marlin, black marlin, sailfish, broadbill swordfish, striped marlin, and shortbill spearfish. Hawaii billfish range in size from the 20-pound shortbill spearfish and striped marlin to an 1,805-pound Pacific blue marlin, the largest marlin ever caught on rod and reel anywhere in the world. **Tuna** ranges in size from small (a pound or less) mackerel tuna used as bait (Hawaiians call them *oioi*) to 250-pound yellowfin ahi tuna. Other species of tuna found in Hawaii are bigeye, albacore, kawakawa, and skipjack.

Some of the best eating fish are also found in offshore waters: **mahimahi** (also known as dolphin fish or dorado) in the 20- to 70-pound range, **rainbow runner** (*kamanu*) from 15 to 30 pounds, and **wahoo** (*ono*) from 15 to 80 pounds. Shoreline fishermen are always on the lookout for **trevally** (the state record for giant trevally is 191 lb.), **bonefish, ladyfish, threadfin, leatherfish,** and **goatfish.** Bottom fishermen pursue a range of **snappers**—red, pink, gray, and others—as well as **sea bass** (the state record is a whopping 563 lbs.) and **amberjack,** which weigh up to 100 pounds.

WHALES The most popular visitors to Hawaii come every year around November and stay until springtime (April or so), when they return to their summer home in Alaska. Humpback whales—some as big as a city bus and weighing many tons—migrate to the warm, protected Hawaiian waters in the winter to mate and calve.

You can take whale-watching cruises that will let you observe these magnificent leviathans close up, or you can spot their signature spouts of water from shore as they expel water off in the distance. Humpbacks grow to up to 45 feet long, so when they breach (propel their entire body out of the water) or even wave a fluke, you can see it for miles.

Humpbacks are among the biggest whales found in Hawaiian waters, but other whales—like pilot, sperm, false killer, melon-headed, pygmy killer, and beaked whales—can be seen year-round. These whales usually travel in pods of 20 to 40 animals and are very social, interacting with each other on the surface.

SHARKS Yes, Virginia, there are sharks in Hawaii, but more than likely you won't see a shark unless you specifically go looking for one. The ancient Hawaiians had great respect for these animals and believed that some sharks were reincarnated relatives who had returned to assist them.

About 40 species of shark inhabit the waters surrounding Hawaii. They range from the totally harmless whale shark (at 60 feet, the world's largest fish), which has no teeth and is so docile that it frequently lets divers ride on its back, to the not-so-docile, infamous—and extremely uncommon—great white shark. The most common sharks seen in Hawaii are white-tip reef sharks, gray reef sharks (about 5 ft. long), and black-tip reef sharks (about 6 ft. long). Since records have been kept, starting in 1779, there have been only about 100 shark attacks in Hawaii, of which 40% have been fatal. The biggest number of attacks occurred after someone fell into the ocean from the shore or from a boat. In these cases, the sharks probably attacked after the person was dead.

General rules for avoiding sharks are: Don't swim at sunrise or sunset, or where the water is murky due to stream runoff—sharks might mistake you for one of their usual meals. And don't swim where there are bloody fish in the water—sharks become aggressive around blood.

MAUI'S ECOSYSTEM PROBLEMS

Maui might be paradise, but even paradise has its problems. The biggest threat facing Maui's natural environment is human intrusion—simply put, too many people want to experience paradise firsthand. From the magnificent underwater world to the breathtaking rain forest, the presence of people isn't always benign, no matter how cautious or environmentally aware they might be.

MARINE LIFE Hawaii's beautiful and abundant marine life has attracted so many visitors that they threaten to overwhelm it. A great example of this over-enthusiasm is Molokini, a small crater off the coast of Maui. In the 1970s, residents made the area a conservation district to protect the unique aquarium-like atmosphere of the waters inside the arms of the crater. Unfortunately, once it was protected, everyone wanted to go there just to see what was worth special protection. Twenty-five years ago, one or two small six-passenger boats made the trip once a day to Molokini; today, it is not uncommon to sight 20 or more boats, each carrying 20 to 49 passengers, moored inside the tiny crater. One tour operator has claimed that on some days, it's so crowded that you can actually see a slick of suntan oil floating on the surface of the water.

People who fall in love with the colorful tropical fish and want to see them all the time back home are also thought to be impacting the health of Hawaii's reefs. The growth in home, office, and decor aquariums has risen dramatically in the past 20 years. As a result, more and more reef fish collectors are taking a growing number of reef fish from Hawaiian waters.

The reefs themselves have faced increasing ecological problems over the years. Runoff of soil and chemicals from construction, agriculture, erosion, and even heavy storms can blanket and choke a reef, which needs sunlight to survive. The intrusion of foreign elements—like breaks in sewage lines—can cause problems for Hawaii's reef. Human contact with the reef can upset the ecosystem as well. Coral, the basis of the reef system, is very fragile; snorkelers and divers grabbing on to coral can break off pieces that took decades to form. Feeding the fish can also upset the balance of the ecosystem (not to mention upsetting the digestive systems of the fish). One glass-bottom boat operator reported that divers fed an eel for years, considering it their "pet" eel. One day the eel decided that he wanted more than just the food being offered and bit the diver's fingers. Divers and snorkelers report that in areas where the fish are fed, the fish have become more aggressive; clouds of reef fish—normally shy—surround divers, demanding to be fed.

FLORA   One of Hawaii's most fragile environments is the rain forest. Any intrusion—from a hiker carrying seeds on his shoes to the rooting of wild boars— can upset the delicate balance in these complete ecosystems. In recent years, development has moved closer and closer to the rain forest.

FAUNA   The biggest impact on the fauna in Hawaii is the decimation of native birds by feral animals, which have destroyed the birds' habitats, and by mongooses that have eaten the birds' eggs and young. Government officials are vigilant about snakes because of the potential damage tree snakes can do to the remaining birdlife.

3 Planning a Trip to Maui

by Jeanette Foster

Maui has so many places to explore, things to do, sights to see—it can be bewildering to plan your trip with so much vying for your attention. Where to start? That's where we come in. In the pages that follow, we've compiled everything you need to know to plan your ideal trip to Maui: information on airlines, seasons, a calendar of events, how to make camping reservations, and much more (even how to get married in the islands).

If possible, fly directly to Maui; doing so can save you a 2-hour layover in Honolulu and another plane ride. If you're headed for Molokai or Lanai, you'll have to connect through Honolulu.

Remember that the planning process can be part of the excitement of your trip. So, in addition to reading this guide, you should try to spend some time either looking at sites on the Internet (we've included Web site addresses throughout this book) or calling and writing for brochures. We fully believe that searching out the best bargains and planning your dream vacation to Hawaii should be half the fun.

1 Visitor Information & Money

VISITOR INFORMATION

For information about traveling in Maui, contact the **Maui Visitors Bureau,** 1727 Wili Pa Loop, Wailuku, HI 96793 (☎ **800/525-MAUI** or 808/244-3530; fax 808/244-1337; www.visitmaui.com).

There are also a few regional tourist boards that can help you out. The **Kaanapali Beach Resort Association** is at 2530 Kekaa Dr., Suite 1-B, Kaanapali-Lahaina, HI 96761 (☎ **800/245-9229** or 808/661-3271; fax 808/661-9431; www.maui.net/~kbra; e-mail kbra@maui.net). The **Wailea Destination Association** is at 3750 Wailea Alanui Dr., Wailea, HI 96753 (☎ **800/78 ALOHA** or 808/879-4258; fax 808/874-5044).

The state agency responsible for tourism is the **Hawaii Visitors and Convention Bureau** (HVCB), Suite 801, Waikiki Business Plaza, 2270 Kalakaua Ave., Honolulu, HI 96815 (☎ **800/ GO-HAWAII** or 808/923-1811; www.gohawaii.com). The HVCB also has a U.S. mainland office at 180 Montgomery St., Suite 2360, San Francisco, CA 94104 (☎ **800/353-5846**). All other HVCB offices on the mainland have been closed due to budget constraints.

If you want information about working and living in Hawaii, contact **The Chamber of Commerce of Hawaii,** 1132 Bishop St., Suite 200, Honolulu, HI 96815 (☎ **808/545-4300**).

INFORMATION ON MAUI'S PARKS

NATIONAL PARKS   Both Maui and Molokai have one national park each: **Haleakala National Park,** P.O. Box 369, Makawao, HI 96768 (☎ 808/572-9306; www.nps.gov/hale); and **Kalaupapa National Historical Park,** P.O. Box 2222, Kalaupapa, HI 96742 (☎ 808/567-6802; www.nps.gov/kala). For more information, see "Hiking & Camping" in chapters 8 and 12.

STATE PARKS   To find out more about state parks on Maui and Molokai, contact the **Hawaii State Department of Land and Natural Resources,** 54 S. High St., Wailuku, HI 96793 (☎ 808/984-8109; www.hawaii.gov), which provides information on hiking and camping, and will send you free topographic trail maps on request.

COUNTY PARKS   For information on Maui County Parks, contact **Maui County Parks and Recreation,** 1580-C Kaahumanu Ave., Wailuku, HI 96793 (☎ 808/243-7380; www.mauimapp.com).

MAUI ON THE NET

Maui may be part of the world's most remote inhabited island group, but more than 200 Internet sites now originate from the state of Hawaii, making it one of the most "wired" places in the country. You can preview the islands, visit or book a hotel room, get the weather report, order Maui-grown coffee or exotic tropical flowers, check on surf conditions, see Maui's beaches, and much more. Many Maui B&Bs are now on the Internet as well; we've included their site URLs in the accommodations listings in chapter 6.

Here are some useful links to Hawaii:
- **Hawaii Visitors & Convention Bureau:** www.gohawaii.com
- **Hawaii State Vacation Planner:** www.hshawaii.com
- **Hawaii State Tourism Office:** www.hawaii.gov/tourism/
- **Travel and Visitor Information:** www.planet-hawaii.com/travel
- **Maui information:** www.maui.net
- **Maui Visitors Bureau:** www.visitmaui.com
- **Kaanapali Beach Resort Association:** www.maui.net/kbra
- **Molokai information:** www.molokai.com
- **Hawaii Yellow Pages:** www.surfhi.com
- **Weather information:** www.weather.com/weather/us/states/Hawaii.html or www.cnn.com/WEATHER/cities/us.hawaii.html

MONEY

Hawaii pioneered the use of automatic teller machines (ATMs) more than 2 decades ago, and now they're everywhere. You'll find them at most banks, in supermarkets, at Long's Drug stores, and in some resorts and shopping centers like Whaler's Village in Kaanapali. It's actually cheaper and faster to get cash from an ATM than to fuss with traveler's checks, and credit cards are accepted just about everywhere. To find the ATM location nearest you, call ☎ **800/424-7787** for the **Cirrus** network or ☎ **800/843-7587** for the **Plus** system. You can also locate Cirrus ATMs on the web at **www.mastercard.com** and Plus ATMs at **www.visa.com.**

Although the U.S. dollar is the coin of the realm in Hawaii, you can easily exchange most major foreign currencies (see "Money" in chapter 4).

2 When to Go

The majority of visitors don't come to Maui when the weather's best in the islands; rather, they come when it's at its worst everywhere else. Thus, the **high season**—when prices are up and resorts are booked to capacity—generally runs from mid-December through March or mid-April. The last 2 weeks of December in particular are the prime time for travel to Hawaii; if you're planning a holiday trip, make your reservations as early as possible, count on holiday crowds, and expect to pay top dollar for accommodations and airfare.

The **off-seasons,** when the best bargain rates are available, are spring (from mid-April to mid-June) and fall (from September to mid-December)—a paradox, since weather-wise, these are the best seasons in Maui. If you're looking to save money, or if you just want to avoid the crowds, this is the time to visit. Hotel rates tend to be significantly lower during these off-seasons. Airfares also tend to be lower—again, sometimes substantially—and good packages and special deals are often available.

Note: If you plan to come to Maui between the last week in April and mid-May, be sure to book your accommodations, interisland air reservations, and car rental in advance. In Japan, the last week of April is called "Golden Week," because three Japanese holidays take place one after the other; the Hawaiian Islands are especially busy with Japanese tourists during this time.

Due to the large number of families traveling in **summer** (June through August), you won't get the fantastic bargains of spring and fall. However, you'll still do much better on packages, airfare, and accommodations than you will in the winter months.

CLIMATE   Since Maui lies at the edge of the tropical zone, it technically has only two seasons, both of them warm. The dry season corresponds to summer, and the rainy season generally runs during the winter from November to March. It rains every day somewhere in the islands at any time of the year, but the rainy season can cause "gray" weather and spoil your tanning opportunities. Fortunately, it seldom rains for more than 3 days straight.

The **year-round temperature** usually varies no more than 15°F, but it depends on where you are. Maui is like a ship in that it has leeward and windward sides. The **leeward** sides (the west and south) usually are hot and dry, whereas the **windward** sides (east and north) generally are cooler and moist. When you want arid, sunbaked, desert-like weather, go leeward. When you want lush, often wet, jungle-like weather, go windward. Your best bet for total year-round sun are the Kihei-Wailea and Lahaina-Kapalua coasts.

Maui is also full of **microclimates,** thanks to its interior valleys, coastal plains, and mountain peaks. If you travel into the mountains, it can change from summer to winter in a matter of hours, since it's cooler the higher up you go. In other words, if the weather doesn't suit you, go to the other side of the island—or head into the hills.

HOLIDAYS   When Hawaii observes holidays, especially those over a long weekend, travel between the islands increases, interisland airline seats are fully booked, rental cars are at a premium, and hotels and restaurants are busier than usual.

Federal, state, and county government offices are closed on all federal holidays: January 1 (New Year's Day); third Monday in January (Martin Luther King, Jr., Day); third Monday in February (Presidents' Day, Washington's Birthday); last Monday in May (Memorial Day); July 4 (Independence Day); first Monday in September (Labor Day); second Monday in October (Columbus Day); November 11 (Veteran's Day); fourth Thursday in November (Thanksgiving Day); and December 25 (Christmas).

State and county offices also are closed on local holidays, including Prince Kuhio Day (March 26), honoring the birthday of Hawaii's first delegate to the U.S. Congress; King Kamehameha Day (June 11), a statewide holiday commemorating Kamehameha the Great, who united the islands and ruled from 1795 to 1819; and Admission Day (third Friday in August), which honors Hawaii's admission as the 50th state in the United States on August 21, 1959.

Other special days celebrated by many people in Hawaii but that do not involve the closing of federal, state, or county offices are Chinese New Year (in January or February), Girl's Day (March 3), Buddha's Birthday (April 8), Father Damien's Day (April 15), Boy's Day (May 5), Samoan Flag Day (in August), Aloha Week (in September or October), and Pearl Harbor Day (December 7).

MAUI CALENDAR OF EVENTS

Please note that, as with any schedule of upcoming events, the following information is subject to change; always confirm the details before you plan your schedule around an event. For a complete and up-to-date list of events throughout the islands, point your Internet browser to www.hawaiian.net/~mahalo/calendar/current.html.

January

- **PGA Kapalua Mercedes Championship,** Kapalua Resort, Maui. Top PGA golfers compete for $1 million. Call ☎ **808/669-0244.** First weekend in January.
- **Hula Bowl Football All-Star Classic,** War Memorial Stadium, Maui. An annual all-star football classic featuring America's top college players. Call ☎ **808/947-4141.** Second week in January.
- **Maui Pro Surf Meet,** Hookipa Beach and Honolua Bay, Maui. The top professional surfers from around the globe compete for some $40,000 in prize money. Call ☎ **808/575-9264.** Mid-January.
- **Celebration of Whales,** Four Seasons Resort, Wailea, Maui. Cetacean experts host discussions, whale-watching excursions, entertainment, social functions, and art exhibits. Call ☎ **808/847-8000.** Last weekend in January.
- ✪ **Ka Molokai Makahiki,** Kaunakakai Town Baseball Park, Mitchell Pauole Center, Kaunakakai, Molokai. Makahiki, a traditional time of peace in ancient Hawaii, is re-created with performances by Hawaiian music groups and hula halau (dance troupes), ancient Hawaiian games and sporting competition, and Hawaiian crafts and food. A wonderful chance to experience the Hawaii of yesteryear. Call ☎ **800/800-6367** or 808/553-3876. Late January.

February

- ✪ **Chinese New Year,** Wo Hing Temple, Front Street, Lahaina, Maui. The Chinese New Year is ushered in with a lion dance, food booths, Chinese calligraphy, firecrackers, and other activities. Call ☎ **808/667-9175.**

March

- **Maui Marathon,** Kahului to Kaanapali, Maui. For nearly 3 decades, runners have lined up at the Maui Mall before daybreak and headed off for Kaanapali, some 26.2 miles across the island. Call ☎ **808/871-6441.**
- **St. Patrick's Day Parade,** Kaanapali Parkway, Kaanapali Resort, Maui. Everyone becomes Irish for a day when this hometown parade makes its way through the Kaanapali Resort area. Call ☎ **808/661-3271.** March 17.
- **East Maui Taro Festival,** Hana, Maui. Here's your chance to taste taro in its many different preparations, from poi to chips. Also on hand are Hawaiian exhibits, demonstrations, and food booths. Call ☎ **808/248-8211.** Usually the last weekend in March.
- **Queen Kaahumanu Festival,** Kaahuman Center, Kahului, Maui. A day of celebration for Kamehameha's first wife, with Hawaiian exhibits, entertainment, games, and storytelling. Call ☎ **808/877-3369.**
- **Prince Kuhio Celebration.** Various festivals throughout the state commemorate the birth of Jonah Kuhio Kalanianaole, born March 26, 1871. He might have been one of Hawaii's kings, if not for the U.S. overthrow of the monarchy and Hawaii's annexation to the United States. Prince Kuhio was elected to Congress in 1902. Molokai has a daylong event; call ☎ **808/553-5215.** End of March.
- ✪ **Annual Ritz-Carlton Kapalua Celebration of the Arts,** Ritz-Carlton Kapalua, Maui. Contemporary and traditional artists give hands-on lessons. Call ☎ **808/669-6200.** End of March or early April.
- **Molokai Hawaiian Paniolo Heritage Rodeo,** Molokai Rodeo Arena, Maunaloa, Molokai. A celebration of Hawaii's *paniolo* (cowboy) heritage. Call ☎ **808/552-2791.**

April

- **Buddha Day,** Lahaina Jodo Mission, Lahaina, Maui. This historic mission holds a flower-festival pageant honoring the birth of Buddha. Call ☎ **808/661-4303.** April 6.
- **Polo Season,** Olinda Polo Field, Makawao, Maui. Most weekends throughout the summer feature a polo match played by Hawaii's top players, often joined by famous international players. Call ☎ **808/572-7326.**
- **Molokai Earth Day,** Mitchell Pauole Center, Kaunakakai, Molokai. A daylong event honoring the natural resources and beauty of the island of Molokai. Call ☎ **808/553-5236.** Mid-April.
- **Da Kine Hawaiian Pro Am Windsurfing,** Hookipa Beach Park, Maui. The top competitors from around the globe flock to the world-famous windsurfing beach for this annual competition. Call ☎ **808/575-9264.**
- ✪ **Maui County Agricultural Trade Show and Sampling,** Ulupalakua Ranch and Tedeschi Winery, Ulupalakua, Maui. The name might be long and cumbersome, but this event is hot, hot, hot. Local product exhibits and sampling, food booths, and live entertainment. Call ☎ **808/875-0457** for this year's schedule.

May

- ✪ **Annual Lei Day Celebration.** May Day is Lei Day in Hawaii, celebrated with lei-making contests, pageantry, arts and crafts, and concerts throughout the islands. Call ☎ **808/244-3550** for Maui events. May 1.
- **Molokai Kayak Challenge,** Molokai to Oahu. Kayakers race 38 grueling miles from Kaluakoi Resort on Molokai to Hawaii Kai's Koko Marina. Call ☎ **808/537-8660.** Mid-May.

❂ **Molokai Ka Hula Piko,** Papohaku Beach Park, Kaluakoi, Molokai. A daylong celebration of the creation of hula on the island where it was born, featuring performances by hula halau, musicians, and singers from across the state. Hawaiian crafts, including quilting, woodworking, feather work, and deer-horn scrimshaw, will be demonstrated. Hawaiian food, including Molokai specialties, will also be available. Call ☎ **800/800-6367** or 808/553-3876.

• **Outrigger Canoe Season,** all islands. From May to September, nearly every weekend, canoe paddlers across the state will participate in outrigger canoe races. Call ☎ **808/961-5797.**

• **In Celebration of Canoes, A Street Festival,** Front Street, Lahaina, Maui. Daylong events with food booths, music, parades, cultural demonstrations, and more, all in celebration of the Hawaiian canoe. Call ☎ **808/667-9175.**

• **Maui Music Festival,** Kapalua Resort, Maui. Weekend of events featuring the top musicians in the state. Call ☎ **808/661-3271.**

June

❂ **King Kamehameha Celebration,** statewide. It's a state holiday with a massive floral parade, *hoolaulea* (party), and much more. Call ☎ **808/667-9175** for Maui events and ☎ **808/552-2791** for Molokai events. First weekend in June.

❂ **Earth Maui,** Kapalua Resort, Kapalua, Maui. A weeklong series of events to encourage appreciation of Maui's natural environment, plus hiking and snorkeling trips. Call ☎ **800/527-2582** or 808/669-0244 for this year's schedule of events.

• **Cowhorse Classic,** Molokai Rodeo Arena, Maunaloa, Molokai. The island's cowboys celebrate Hawaii's paniolo heritage. Call ☎ **808/552-2791.**

July

• **Pineapple Festival,** Lanai City, Lanai. Some of Hawaii's best musicians participate in Lanai's liveliest event, celebrating the golden fruit with everything from fishing tournaments to pineapple cooking contests, food and craft booths, water activities, and demonstrations by well-known chefs. Call ☎ **808/565-7600.**

• **Makawao Parade and Rodeo,** Makawao, Maui. The annual parade and rodeo event has been taking place in this upcountry cowboy town for generations. Call ☎ **808/572-9565** or 808/572-2076 for this year's date.

❂ **Hoolaulea O Ke Kai—A Molokai Sea Fest,** Kaunakakai, Molokai. Canoe races, windsurfing competition, Hawaiian music, and foods at this daylong celebration of the sea. Call ☎ **800/800-6367** or 808/553-3876 for this year's date and schedule.

❂ **Kapalua Wine Symposium,** Kapalua, Maui. Famous wine and food experts and oenophiles gather at the Ritz-Carlton and Kapalua Bay hotels for formal tastings, panel discussions, and samplings of new releases. Call ☎ **800/669-0244** for this year's dates and schedule.

August

• **Maui Onion Festival,** Whaler's Village, Kaanapali, Maui. Everything you ever wanted to know about the sweetest onions in the world. Food, entertainment, tasting, and Maui Onion Cook-Off. Call ☎ **808/661-4567.** First week in August.

• **Admissions Day,** all islands. Hawaii became the 50th state on August 21, 1959, so the state takes a holiday; all state-related facilities will be closed. Third Friday in August.

• **Molokai Museum and Cultural Center Annual Music Festival,** Meyer Sugar Mill and Museum Grounds, Kalae, Molokai. An outdoor music festival featuring top Hawaiian musicians. Call ☎ **808/567-6436.** Saturday following Admissions Day.

September

○ **Aloha Festivals,** various locations statewide. Parades and other events celebrate Hawaiian culture. Call ☎ **800/852-7690,** 808/545-1771, or 808/885-8086 for a schedule of events.

○ **Great Molokai Mule Drag and Hoolaulea,** Kaunakakai, Molokai. As part of the Aloha Festivals celebration on Molokai, the local residents honor the importance of the mule to the island's heritage with a mule race (which is sometimes a mule-dragging contest) down the main street of Kaunakakai. Call ☎ **800/800-6367** or 808/553-3876.

• **Run to the Sun,** Paia to Haleakala, Maui. The world's top ultra-marathoners make the journey from sea level to the top of 10,000-foot Haleakala, some 37 miles. Call ☎ **808/871-6441.**

• **Maui Writer's Conference,** Grand Wailea Resort, Wailea, Maui. Workshops, lectures, and panel discussions with writers, agents, and publishers. Call ☎ **808/ 879-0061.** Labor Day Weekend.

• **A Taste of Lahaina,** Lahaina Civic Center, Maui. Some 20,000 people show up to sample 35 signature entrees of Maui's premier chefs during the weekend-long festival, which includes cooking demonstrations, wine tastings, and live entertainment. Call ☎ **808/667-9175** or send an e-mail to acton@maui.net. Usually mid-September.

• **Na Wahine O Ke Kai,** Molokai to Waikiki. A women's 40.8-mile outrigger canoe race from Molokai to Oahu. Departs from Hale O Lono, Molokai, and finishes at Duke Kahanamoku Beach, Hilton Hawaiian Village, Waikiki. Call ☎ **808/262-7567.** End of September.

October

• **Hawaii's Winter Baseball,** island-wide. The season starts in early October and runs through mid-December, as the four teams compete: West Oahu CaneFires (Hans L'Orange Park in Waipahu), Maui Stingrays (Iron Maehara Baseball Stadium in Wailuku), Honolulu Sharks (UH Rainbow Stadium, in Honolulu), and the Hilo Stars (Dr. Francis Wong Stadium in Hilo). Call ☎ **808/242-2950.**

• **Maui County Fair,** War Memorial Complex, Wailuku, Maui. The oldest county fair in Hawaii features a parade, amusement rides, live entertainment, and exhibits. Call ☎ **808/875-0457.** Early October.

○ **Aloha Classic World Wavesailing Championship,** Hookipa Beach, Maui. The top windsurfers in the world gather for this final event in the Pro Boardsailing World Tour. If you're on Maui, don't miss it—it's spectacular to watch. Call ☎ **808/575-9151.**

• **Molokai Hoe,** Molokai to Oahu. The season's biggest canoe race, this men's 40.8-mile outrigger contest crosses the channel from Molokai to finish at Fort DeRussy Beach in Waikiki. Call ☎ **808/261-6615.** Mid-October.

○ **Halloween in Lahaina,** Maui. There's Carnival in Rio, Mardi Gras in New Orleans, and Halloween in Lahaina. Come to this giant costume party (some 20,000 people show up) on the streets of Lahaina; Front Street is closed off for the party. It'll be the greatest memory of your trip. Call ☎ **808/667-9175.**

November

• **Hawaii International Film Festival,** various locations on Maui. A cinema festival with a cross-cultural spin, featuring filmmakers from Asia, the Pacific Islands, and the United States. Call ☎ **808/528-FILM** or point your browser to www.hiff.org. Mid-November.

- **Molokai Ranch Rodeo and Great Molokai Stew Cookoff,** Molokai Rodeo Arena, Maunaloa, Molokai. The island's cowboys celebrate Hawaii's paniolo heritage. Call ☎ **800/800-6367** or 808/552-2681.

December

- **Festival of Lights,** island-wide. Festivities include parades and tree-lighting ceremonies. Call ☎ **808/667-9175** on Maui and 808/567-6361 on Molokai. Early December.

3 What to Pack

Maui is very informal. You'll get by with shorts, T-shirts, and tennis shoes at most attractions and restaurants; a casual dress or a polo shirt and khakis is fine even in the most expensive places. Dinner jackets are required only at a very few resorts, such as the Lodge at Koele on Lanai, and they'll cordially provide a jacket if you don't bring your own.

So bring T-shirts, shorts, long pants, a couple of bathing suits, a long-sleeved cover-up (to throw on at the beach when you've had enough sun for the day), tennis shoes, rubber water shoes or flip-flops, and hiking shoes and several pairs of good socks if you plan to do any hiking.

The tropical sun poses the greatest threat to anyone who ventures into the great outdoors, so be sure to bring **sun protection:** a good pair of sunglasses, plenty of strong sunscreen, a light hat (like a baseball cap or a sun visor), binoculars (if you have them), and a canteen or water bottle if you'll be hiking—you'll easily dehydrate on the trail in the tropic heat, so figure on carrying 2 liters of water per day on any hike. Campers should bring water purification tablets or devices. Also see "Staying Healthy: Protecting Yourself Against Natural Hazards," below.

Don't bother overstuffing your suitcase with 2 whole weeks' worth of shorts and T-shirts: Maui has **laundry facilities** everywhere. If your accommodation doesn't have a washer and dryer or laundry service, there will most likely be a Laundromat nearby. The only exception to this is Hana; the tiny town has no Laundromat, so either check with the place you're staying beforehand, or do a load of laundry before you arrive.

One last thing: **It really can get cold in Hawaii.** If you plan to see the sunrise from the top of Haleakala, bring a warm jacket—40°F upcountry temperatures, even in summer when it's 80°F at the beach, are not uncommon. It's always a good idea to bring at least a windbreaker, a sweater, or a light jacket. And be sure to toss some rain gear into your suitcase if you'll be in Maui from November to March.

4 The Active Vacation Planner

If you want nothing more from the islands than a fabulous beach and a perfectly mixed Mai Tai, we have what you're looking for—some of the most spectacular beaches (not to mention the best Mai Tais) in the world. But Maui's wealth of natural wonders is hard to resist; the year-round tropical climate and spectacular scenery tend to inspire even the most committed desk jockeys and couch potatoes to get outside and explore.

You can have some of the greatest outdoor adventures on earth in Maui. From snorkeling with schools of kaleidoscopic fish to hiking into lush rain forests that hint at what Eden must have been like, the islands offer something for everyone, no matter what your age or ability. And best of all, enjoying the great outdoors doesn't have to cost a fortune—in fact, it can be the least expensive fun you've had in years.

Safety Tip

Be sure to see the section directly following this one, "Staying Healthy: Protecting Yourself Against Natural Hazards," before setting out on any adventure; it includes useful information on hiking, camping, and ocean safety. Even if you just plan to lie on the beach, be sure to check out the box called "Don't Get Burned: Smart Tanning Tips" on page 48 to learn how to protect yourself against the sun's harmful rays—a must for *everyone* in Hawaii.

PREPARING FOR YOUR ACTIVE VACATION

If you have your own snorkel gear or other water-sports equipment, by all means bring it if you can. However, if you don't have it, don't fret; everything you'll need is available for rent in the islands. We discuss all kinds of places to rent or buy gear in chapter 8.

SETTING OUT ON YOUR OWN VS. USING AN OUTFITTER

There are two ways to go: Plan all the details before you go and schlep your gear 2,500 miles across the Pacific, or go with an outfitter or a guide and let the guide worry about the details.

Experienced outdoors enthusiasts can follow their nose to coastal camp-grounds or even trek into the rain forest on their own, but in Maui it's often preferable to go with a local guide, who is familiar with the local conditions at both sea level and summit peaks, knows the land and its flora and fauna in detail, and has all the gear you'll need. It's also good to go with a guide if time is an issue. It takes time to research and plan an outdoor adventure; if you really want to see native birds, for instance, an experienced guide will take you directly to the best areas for sightings. And many forests and valleys in the interior of the islands are either on private property or in wilderness preserves that are accessible only on guided tours. If you go with a guide, plan on spending at least $100 a day per person; we recommend the best local outfitters and tour-guide operators in chapter 8.

But if you have the time, already own the gear, and love doing the research and planning, try exploring on your own. Chapter 8 discusses the best spots to set out on your own, from the best offshore snorkel and dive spots to great daylong hikes, as well as the federal, state, and county agencies that can help you with hikes on public property; we also list references for spotting birds, plants, and sea life. We recommend that you always use the resources available and inquire about weather, trail or surf conditions, water availability, and other conditions before you take off on your adventure.

For hikers, a great alternative to hiring a private guide are the guided hikes offered by the **Nature Conservancy of Hawaii,** 1116 Smith St., Honolulu, HI 96817 (☎ 808/537-4508 on Oahu; 808/573-4147 on Maui; 808/553-5236 or 808/524-0779 on Molokai), and the **Hawaii Chapter of the Sierra Club,** P.O. Box 2577, Honolulu, HI 96803 (☎ 808/573-4147 on Maui). Both organizations offer guided hikes on preserves and special places during the year, as well as 1- to 7-day work trips to restore habitats and trails and root out invasive plants like banana poka, New Zealand flax, non-native gorse, and wild ginger. It might not sound like a dream vacation to everyone, but it's a chance to see the "real" Hawaii—including wilderness areas that are ordinarily off-limits.

All Nature Conservancy hikes are free. However, you must reserve a spot for yourself, and a deposit is required for guided hikes to ensure that you'll show up; your deposit is refunded once you do. The hikes are generally offered once a month

Using Activities Desks to Book Your Island Fun

If you want to go out with an outfitter or a guide—especially if you're interested in an activity that requires an outfitter or a guide, such as horseback riding, whale watching, or sportfishing—and you'd like to save some money, you might want to consider booking your activity through a discount activities center or activities desk. These agents—whose sole business it is to act as a clearinghouse for activities, much like a consolidator functions as a discount clearinghouse for airline tickets—can often get you a better price than you'd get by booking an activity directly with the outfitter.

Discount activities centers will, in effect, split their commission with you, giving themselves a smaller commission to get your business—and passing, on average, a 10% discount on to you. In addition to saving you money, good activities centers should be able to help you find, say, the snorkel cruise that's right for you, or the luau that's most suitable for both you *and* the kids. But it's in the activities agent's best interest to sign you up with outfitters from which they earn the most commission; some agents have no qualms about booking you into any activity if it means an extra buck for them. If an agent tries to push a particular outfitter or activity too hard, be skeptical. Conversely, they'll try to steer you away from outfitters that don't offer big commissions. For example, Trilogy, the company that offers Maui's most popular snorkel cruises to Lanai (and the only one with rights to land at Lanai's Hulupoe Beach), offers only minimal commissions to agents and does not allow agents to offer any discounts at all; as a result, most activities desks you speak to on Maui will automatically try to steer you away from Trilogy if you say you want to book it.

Another important word of warning: Be careful to avoid those activity centers offering discounts as fronts for timeshare sales presentations. Using a free snorkel cruise or luau tickets as bait, they'll suck you into a 90-minute presentation—and try to get you to buy into a Hawaii timeshare in the process. Not only will they try to sell you a big white elephant you never wanted in the first place, but—since their business is timeshares, not activities—they also won't be as interested, or as knowledgeable, about which activities might be right for you. These shady deals seem to be particularly rampant on Maui. Just do yourself a favor and avoid them altogether.

On Maui, we recommend **Tom Barefoot's Cashback Tours,** at Dolphin Shopping Center, 2395 S. Kihei Rd., Kihei (☎ **808/879-4100**), and 834 Front St., Lahaina (☎ **808/661-8889**). Tom offers a 10% discount on all tours, activities, and adventures when you pay in cash or with traveler's checks. If you pay with credit card or personal check, he'll give you a 7% discount. The two showrooms are loaded with pictures and maps of all the activities the company books. We found Tom's to be very reliable and honest.

on Maui, Molokai, and Lanai (call the Oahu office for reservations). There's also no charge for the trips to restore habitats. Write for a schedule of guided hikes and other programs.

The Sierra Club offers weekly hikes on Maui. Hikes are led by certified Sierra Club volunteers and are classified as easy, moderate, or strenuous. These half-day or all-day affairs cost $1 for Sierra Club members, $3 for nonmembers (bring exact change). For a copy of their newsletter, which lists all outings and trail repair work, send $2 to the address above.

OUTDOOR ETIQUETTE

Act locally, think globally, and carry out what you carry in. Find a rubbish container for all your litter (including cigarette butts; it's *very* bad form to throw them out of your car window). Observe kapu and "no trespassing" signs. Don't climb on ancient Hawaiian heiau walls and temples or carry home rocks, all of which belong to the Hawaiian Volcano Goddess Pele. Some say it's just a silly superstition or coincidence, but each year the National and State Park Services get boxes of lava rocks in the mail, sent back to Hawaii by visitors who have experienced unusually bad luck.

5 Staying Healthy: Protecting Yourself Against Natural Hazards

Maui is one of the healthiest places in the world to visit. People who live here have a longer life expectancy than anywhere else in the United States (74 years for men and 78 years for women). However, there are some hazards you should be aware of so that, if necessary, you can take the necessary steps to prevent them from blooming into full-scale problems.

ON LAND

As in any tropical climate, there are lots of bugs in Hawaii. Most of them won't harm you; however, three insects—mosquitoes, centipedes, and scorpions—do sting, and they can cause anything from mild annoyance to severe swelling and pain.

MOSQUITOES These pesky insects aren't native to Hawaii, but arrived as larvae stowed away in the water barrels on the ship *Wellington* in 1826. There's not a whole lot you can do about them, but be sure to apply commercial repellent to keep them off you, burn mosquito punk or citronella candles to keep them out of your area, or apply sting-stopping ointments (available at any drugstore) after they've struck to ease the itching and swelling. Most bites disappear in anywhere from a few hours to a few days.

CENTIPEDES These segmented insects with a jillion legs come in two varieties: 6- to 8-inch-long brown ones and the smaller 2- to 3-inch-long blue guys; both can really pack a wallop with their sting. Centipedes are generally found in damp, wet places, like under wood piles or compost heaps. Wearing closed-toe shoes can help prevent stings if you happen to accidentally unearth one. If you're stung, reaction can range from something similar to a mild bee sting to severe pain; apply ice at once to prevent swelling. See a doctor if there is extreme pain, swelling, nausea, or any other severe reaction.

SCORPIONS Rarely seen, scorpions are found in arid, warm regions; their stings can be serious. Campers in dry areas should always check their boots before putting them on, and shake out sleeping bags and bed rolls. Symptoms of scorpion stings include shortness of breath, hives, swelling, and nausea. In the unlikely event that you're stung, apply diluted household ammonia and cold compresses to the area of the sting and seek medical attention immediately.

HIKING SAFETY

In addition to taking the appropriate cautions regarding Maui's bug population (see above), hikers should always let someone know where they're heading, when they're going, and when they plan to return; too many hikers get lost in Hawaii because they don't inform others of their basic plans.

Impressions

Thousands have daily lined the wharves to witness the carpenter, Mr. Dibble, in his novel suit of India-rubber with a glass helmet disappear beneath the surface of the water. . . .

—1840 Honolulu newspaper article

Always check weather conditions with the **National Weather Service** (☎ **808/877-5111**) before you go. Hike with a pal, never alone. Wear hiking boots, a sun hat, clothes to protect from sun and scratches, and high-SPF sunscreen on all exposed areas of skin. Take water. Stay on the trail. Watch your step. It's easy to slip off precipitous trails and into steep canyons, with often disastrous—even fatal—results. Incapacitated hikers are often plucked to safety by fire and rescue squads, who must use helicopters to gain access to remote sites. Many experienced hikers and boaters today pack a cellular phone in case of emergency; just call ☎ **911.**

VOG

The volcanic haze dubbed "vog" is caused by gases released when molten lava—from the continuous eruption of the volcano on the flank of Kilauea on the Big Island—pours into the ocean. This hazy air, which looks like urban smog, limits viewing from scenic vistas and plays havoc with photographers trying to get clear panoramic shots. Some people claim that long-term exposure to vog has even caused bronchial ailments.

There actually is a "vog" season in Hawaii: the fall and winter months, when the trade winds that blow the fumes out to sea die down. The vog is felt not only on the Big Island but as far away as Maui and Oahu.

OCEAN SAFETY

Because most people coming to Hawaii are unfamiliar with the ocean environment, they are often unaware of the natural hazards that it holds. But with just a few precautions, your ocean experience can be a safe and happy one.

An excellent book to get is *All Stings Considered: First Aid and Medical Treatment of Hawaii's Marine Injuries* (University of Hawaii Press, 1997), by Craig Thomas (an emergency medicine doctor) and Susan Scott (a registered nurse). These avid water people have put together the authoritative book on first aid for Hawaii's marine injuries.

SEASICKNESS   The waters in Hawaii can range from calm as glass to downright frightening (in storm conditions), and they usually fall somewhere in between; in general, expect rougher conditions in winter than in summer.

Some 90% of the population tends toward seasickness. If you've never been out on a boat or if you've gotten seasick in the past, you might want to heed the following suggestions:

• The day before you go out on the boat, avoid alcohol; caffeine; citrus and other acidic juices; and greasy, spicy, or hard-to-digest foods.
• Get a good night's sleep the night before.
• Take or use whatever seasickness prevention works best for you—medication, an acupressure wrist band, ginger-root tea or capsules, or any combination—*before* you board; once you set sail, it's generally too late.

Don't Get Burned: Smart Tanning Tips

For years, the best souvenir to bring back from Hawaii was a golden tan—especially in mid-winter. Oh, the look of green-eyed envy from your friends as your bronzed glow silently told the world that you'd just returned from Hawaii!

Tanning just ain't what it used to be. Nowadays, it can kill you—especially if, in your quest for a tan, you get burned instead.

Strong words, but supported by reality: Hawaii's Caucasian population has a higher incidence of deadly skin cancer, malignant melanoma, than anywhere else in the country. But no one is safe from the sun's harmful rays: people of all skin types and races can burn when exposed to the sun too long.

To ensure that your vacation won't be ruined by a painful, throbbing sunburn (especially in your first few days), here are some helpful tips on how to tan safely and painlessly:

- **Wear a strong sunscreen at all times.** Use a sunscreen with a sun-protection factor (SPF) of 15 or higher; people with light complexion should use 30. The SPF rating works this way: a fair-skinned person, without any sun protection, can burn in 10 minutes in the sun; a sunscreen with an SPF of 30 will give its wearer 10 minutes of protection from the sun (the time before you burn) times 30 (the SPF), or 300 minutes (5 hours) of protection.

  Apply sunscreen as soon as you get out of the shower in the morning, and at least 30 minutes before you're exposed to the sun.

- **And use lots of it.** Margaret Tucker, chief of genetic epidemiology at the National Cancer Institute, says "a little dab will *not* do ya." You need a table-spoon of lotion per limb; slather it on and rub it in. No matter what the box says—even if the sunscreen is waterproof—reapply it every 2 hours and immediately after swimming.

- **Read the labels.** To avoid developing allergies to sunscreens, New York University dermatologist Robert Friedman suggests avoiding any sunscreens that contain para-aminobenzoic acid (PABA). The American Academy of Dermatology suggests looking for sunscreens with zinc oxide, talc, or titanium dioxide, because they reduce the risk of developing skin allergies.

- While you're on the boat, stay as low and as near the center of the boat as possible. Avoid the fumes (especially if it's a diesel boat); stay out in the fresh air and watch the horizon. Do not read.
- If you start to feel queasy, drink clear fluids like water, and eat something bland, such as a soda cracker.

STINGS The most common stings in Hawaii come from jellyfish, particularly Portuguese man-of-war and box jellyfish. Since the poisons they inject are very different, you need to treat each sting differently.

Portuguese Man-of-War A bluish-purple floating bubble with a long tail, the Portuguese man-of-war causes some 6,500 stings a year on Oahu alone. Stings, although painful and a nuisance, are rarely harmful; fewer than one in a thousand requires medical treatment. The best prevention is to watch for these floating bubbles as you snorkel (look for the hanging tentacles below the surface); get out of the water if anyone near you spots these jellyfish.

- **Wear a hat and sunglasses.** The hat should have a minimum 4-inch-wide brim (all the way around, to cover not only your face but also the sensitive back of your neck). Make sure that your sunglasses have UV filters to protect your corneas from getting sunburned and to prevent cataracts. To avoid the irritation of sunscreen dripping into your eyes, use a waxy sunscreen stick (available just about everywhere in Hawaii) to draw half-circles above your eyebrows.
- **Don't rely on a T-shirt for protection.** Believe it or not, that T-shirt you put over your bathing suit has an SPF of only 6. Either wear special UV-protective clothing or lather on a high-SPF sunscreen.
- **Avoid being in the sun between 9am and 3pm.** Seek the shade during these peak hours. Remember that a beach umbrella is not protection enough from the sun's harmful UV rays; in fact, with the reflection from the water, the sand, and even the sidewalk, some 85% of the ultraviolet rays are still bombarding you.
- **Protect children from the sun, and keep infants out of the sun altogether.** Infants under 6 months should not be in the sun at all. Older babies need zinc oxide to protect their fragile skin, and children should be slathered with sunscreen every hour. The burns that children get today predict what their future will be with skin cancer tomorrow.

If you start to turn red, **get out of the sun.** Contrary to popular belief, you don't have to turn red to tan; if your skin is red, it's burned—and that's serious. The redness from a burn might not show until 2 to 8 hours after you get out of the sun, and the full force of that burn might not appear for 24 to 36 hours. During that time, you can look forward to pain, itching, and peeling. The best **remedy** for a sunburn is to get out of the sun immediately and stay out of the sun until all the redness is gone. Aloe vera (straight from the plant or from a commercial preparation), cool compresses, cold baths, and anesthetic benzocaine might also help with the pain of sunburn.

If you've decided to get a head start on your tan by using a self-tanning lotion that dyes your skin a darker shade, remember that this will not protect you from the sun. You'll still need to generously apply sunscreen when you go out.

Reactions to stings range from mild burning and reddening to severe welts and blisters. *All Stings Considered* recommends the following treatment: first, pick off any visible tentacles with a gloved hand, a stick, or anything handy; rinse the sting with salt or fresh water; and apply ice to prevent swelling and to help control pain.

Hawaii folklore advises using vinegar, meat tenderizer, baking soda, papain, or alcohol, or even urinating on the wound. Studies have shown that these remedies might actually cause further damage. Why did people swear by these folk remedies for so many years? Probably because most Portuguese man-of-war stings will disappear by themselves within 15 to 20 minutes if you do nothing to treat them. Still, be sure to see a doctor if pain persists or if a rash or other symptoms develop.

Box Jellyfish   These transparent, square-shaped bell jellyfish are nearly impossible to see in the water. Fortunately, they seem to follow a monthly cycle: 8 to 10 days after the full moon, they appear in the waters on the leeward side of the island and hang around for about 3 days. Also, they seem to sting more in the morning hours, when they're on or near the surface. The best prevention is to get out of the water.

Stings range from no visible marks to red hivelike welts, blisters, and pain (a burning sensation) lasting from 10 minutes to 8 hours. *All Stings Considered* recommends the following course of treatment: first prevent undischarged nematocysts still on the skin from discharging, and then treat the sting. Nematocysts are the stinging structures inside the thin, threadlike tentacles of the jellyfish; to prevent them from discharging, don't touch them. To treat the sting, first pour regular household vinegar on it; this might not relieve the pain, but it will stop additional burning. Do not rub the area with anything. Then pick off any vinegar-soaked tentacles with a stick. For pain, apply an ice pack. Seek additional medical treatment if you experience shortness of breath, weakness, palpitations, muscle cramps, or any other severe symptoms.

Again, Hawaiian folklore recommends using meat tenderizer, baking soda, papaya, commercial sprays, alcohol, or even urine on the sting, but studies have shown that these applications can make the injury worse. Most box jellyfish stings will disappear by themselves without treatment.

PUNCTURES   Most sea-related punctures come from stepping on or brushing against the needle-like spines of sea urchins (known locally as *wana*). Be careful when you're in the water; don't put your foot down (even if you have booties or fins on) if you cannot clearly see the bottom. Waves can push you into wana in a surge zone in shallow water (the wana's spines can even puncture a wet suit).

A sea urchin sting can result in burning, aching, swelling, and discoloration (black or purple) around the area where the spines have broken off. The best thing to do is to pull any protruding spines out. The body will absorb the spines within 24 hours to 3 weeks, or the remainder of the spines will work themselves out.

Again, contrary to popular wisdom, do not urinate or pour vinegar on the embedded spines—this will not help.

CUTS   All cuts obtained in the marine environment must be taken seriously, because the high level of bacteria present can quickly cause the cut to become infected. The most common cuts are from corals. Contrary to popular belief, coral cannot grow inside your body; however, bacteria can—and very often does—grow inside a cut. The best way to prevent cuts is to wear a wet suit, gloves, and reef shoes. Never, under any circumstances, should you touch a coral head; not only can you get cut, but you can also damage a living organism that took decades to grow.

The symptoms of a coral cut can range from a slight scratch to severe welts and blisters. *All Stings Considered* recommends gently pulling the edges of the skin open and removing any embedded coral or grains of sand with tweezers, or rinsing well with fresh water. Next, scrub the cut well with fresh water. Never use ocean water to clean a cut, because it can be loaded with bacteria. Urinating on the cut will also make it worse. If the wound is bleeding, press a clean cloth against it until it stops. If bleeding continues or the edges of the injury are jagged or gaping, seek medical treatment.

6 Getting Married on Maui

Whatever your dreams and your budget, Maui is a great place for a wedding. Not only does the entire island exude romance and natural beauty, but after the ceremony, you're only a few steps away from the perfect honeymoon. And your family, friends, and members of your wedding party will most likely be delighted—you've given all of them the perfect excuse for their own island vacations.

Just being on this spectacular island takes the pressure down a notch or two and promotes a feeling of celebration. Many couples who were married long ago come to Maui to renew their vows, enjoy a second honeymoon, and rediscover the loving spirit that brought them together the first time.

Couples can get married, or remarried, in historic Hawaiian churches, on the beach, under a waterfall in a rain forest, on horseback in a pasture with an ocean view, in a lush tropical garden, on a sailboat, on a lava flow, on top of a volcano, on a deserted islet, underwater with a school of brilliant-colored fish for witnesses, barefoot on the beach at sunset and draped in fragrant leis, or in full regalia on formal parade from chapel to luxury hotel.

It happens every day of the year in Hawaii, where more than 20,000 marriages are performed each year. Nearly half (44.6%) of the couples married here are from somewhere else. This booming business has spawned dozens of companies that can help you organize a long-distance event and stage an unforgettable wedding, Hawaiian style or your style (see "Using a Wedding Planner," below). However, you can also plan your own island wedding, even from afar, and not spend a fortune doing it.

THE PAPERWORK

The state of Hawaii has some very minimal procedures for obtaining a marriage license. The first thing you should do is contact the **Marriage License Office,** State Department of Health Building, 54 S. High St., Wailuku, HI 96793 (☎ 808/984-8210; www.hawaii.gov), which is open Monday through Friday from 8am to 4pm, except holidays. The staff will mail you a brochure, *Getting Married,* and direct you to the marriage licensing agent closest to where you'll be staying on Maui.

Upon arrival in Maui, the prospective bride and groom must go together to the marriage licensing agent to get a license. A license costs $25 and is good for 30 days; if you don't have the ceremony within the time allotted, you'll have to pay another $25 for another license. The only requirements for a marriage license are that both parties are 15 years of age or older (couples 15 to 17 years must have proof of age, written consent of both parents, and the written approval of the judge of the family court) and are not more closely related than first cousins. That's it.

Contrary to some reports from the media, gay couples cannot marry in Hawaii. Although the state courts ruled a few years ago that the State of Hawaii had to show a compelling reason why it wouldn't issue a marriage license to gay couples, the issue is still being decided in the courts and will be brought before Hawaii's voters in November 1998. Until the issue is decided, the state will not issue marriage licenses to same-sex couples.

PLANNING THE WEDDING
DOING IT YOURSELF

The marriage licensing agents, which range from the Governor's satellite office to private individuals, are usually friendly, helpful people who can steer you to a nondenominational minister or marriage performer who's licensed by the state of Hawaii to perform the ceremony. These marriage performers are great sources of information for budget weddings. They usually know great places to have the ceremony free or for a nominal fee.

If you don't want to use a wedding planner (see below) but want to make arrangements before you arrive in Maui, our best advice is to get a copy of the daily newspaper, the *Maui News,* P.O. Box 550, Wailuku, HI 96793 (☎ 808/244-7691).

The Welcoming Lei

Nothing makes you feel more welcome, or more like you're in paradise, than a lei. The stunning tropical beauty of the delicate garland, the deliciously sweet fragrance of the blossoms, the sensual way the flowers curl softly around your neck . . . there's no doubt about it: getting lei'd in Hawaii is a sensuous experience.

Leis are much more than just a decorative necklace of flowers; they're also one of the nicest ways to say hello, good-bye, congratulations, I salute you, my sympathies are with you, or I love you. The custom of lei giving can be traced back to Hawaii's very roots: according to chants, the first lei was given by Hiiaka, the sister of the volcano goddess Pele, who presented Pele with a lei of lehua blossoms on a beach in Puna.

During ancient times, leis given to *alii* (royalty) were accompanied by a bow, since it was *kapu* (forbidden) for a commoner to raise his arms higher than the king's head. The presentation of a kiss with a lei didn't come about until World War II; it's generally attributed to an entertainer who kissed an officer on a dare, then quickly presented him with her lei, saying it was an old Hawaiian custom. It wasn't then, but it sure caught on fast.

Lei making is a tropical art form. All leis are fashioned by hand in a variety of traditional patterns; some are sewn of hundreds of tiny blooms or shells, or bits of ferns and leaves. Some are twisted, some braided, some strung; all are presented with love. Every island has its own lei of the land, so to speak—a special flower lei. On Oahu, the choice is *ilima,* a small orange flower. Big Islanders prefer the *lehua,* a large delicate red puff. Maui likes the *lokelani,* a small rose. On Kauai, it's the *mokihana,* a fragrant green vine and berry. Molokai prefers the *kukui,* the white blossom of a candlenut tree. Lanai's lei is made of *kaunaoa,* a bright yellow moss, and Niihau utilizes its abundant seashells to make leis that were once prized by royalty and are now worth a small fortune.

Leis are available at the Kahului Airport, from florists, and even at supermarkets.

Leis are the perfect symbol for Hawaii: they're given in the moment, their fragrance and beauty are enjoyed in the moment, and when they fade, their spirit of aloha lives on. Welcome to Hawaii!

People willing and qualified to conduct weddings advertise in the classifieds. They're great sources of information, because they know the best places to have the ceremony and can recommend caterers, florists, and everything else you'll need.

USING A WEDDING PLANNER

Wedding planners—many of whom are marriage licensing agents themselves—can arrange everything for you, from a small, private, outdoor affair to a full-blown formal ceremony in a tropical setting. They charge anywhere from $450 to a small fortune—it all depends on what you want. Planners on Maui include **A Wedding Made in Paradise,** P.O. Box 986, Kihei, HI 96753 (☎ 800/453-3440 or 808/879-3444; fax 808/874-12278, www.wedinparadise.com; e-mail wedmaui@ maui.net); **A Dream Wedding: Maui Style,** 143 Dickenson St., Suite 201, Lahaina, HI 96761 (☎ 800/743-2777; fax 808/667-2042; www. visitmaui.com; e-mail dreamwed@maui.net); **A Romantic Maui Wedding,** P.O. Box 307, Kihei, HI 96752 (☎ 800/808-4144 or 808/874-6441; fax 808/

879-5525; www.justmauied.com; e-mail sandy@justmauied.com); **Dolphin Dreams Weddings,** P.O. Box 10546, Lahaina, HI 96761 (☎ 800/793-2WED or 808/661-8535; www.visitmaui.com; e-mail dolphin@maui.net); and **Weddings the Maui Way,** 2718 Iolani St., Pukalani, HI 96768 (☎ 800/291-0110 or 808/572-7898; www.visitmaui.com; e-mail married@maui.net).

7   Tips for Travelers with Special Needs

FOR TRAVELERS WITH DISABILITIES

Travelers with disabilities are made to feel very welcome in Maui. Hotels are usually equipped with wheelchair-accessible rooms, and tour companies provide many special services. **The Commission on Persons with Disabilities,** 919 Ala Moana Blvd., Suite 101, Honolulu, HI 96814 (☎ **808/586-8121**), and the **Hawaii Center for Independent Living,** 414 Kauwili St., Suite 102, Honolulu, HI 96817 (☎ **808/522-5400;** fax 808/586-8129; www.hawaii.gov/health/cpd_indx.htm; e-mail cpdppp@aloha.net), can provide information and send you a copy of the *Aloha Guide to Accessibility* ($15).

A World of Options, a 658-page book of resources for travelers with disabilities, covers everything from biking trips to scuba outfitters. It costs $45 and is available from **Mobility International USA,** P.O. Box 10767, Eugene, OR 97440 (☎ **541/343-1284,** voice and TDD; www.miusa.org).

For travelers with disabilities who want to do their own driving, hand-controlled cars can be rented from **Avis** (☎ **800/331-1212**) and **Hertz** (☎ **800/654-3131**). The number of hand-controlled cars in Maui is limited, so be sure to book well in advance. Hawaii recognizes other states' windshield placards indicating that the driver of the car has a disability; these can give you access to specially marked handicapped parking spaces, so be sure to bring yours with you.

Vision-impaired travelers who use a Seeing Eye dog can now travel to Maui without the hassle of quarantine. A recent court decision ruled that visitors with Seeing Eye dogs need only to present documentation that the dog has had rabies shots and that the dog is a trained Seeing Eye dog in order to bypass quarantine. Previously, all dogs and cats in Hawaii had to spend 4 months in quarantine, since Hawaii is rabies-free (quarantine has been reduced to 1 month, Seeing Eye dogs exempted). For more information, contact the **Animal Quarantine Facility** (☎ **808/483-7171;** www.hawaii.gov).

FOR SENIORS

Discounts for seniors are available at almost all of Maui's major attractions, and occasionally at hotels and restaurants. Always inquire when making hotel reservations. Members of the **American Association of Retired Persons** (AARP), 601 E St. NW, Washington, DC 20049 (☎ **800/424-3410** or 202/434-2277), are usually eligible for such discounts; AARP also puts together organized tour packages at moderate rates through the AARP Travel Service. The **National Council of Senior Citizens,** 8403 Colesville Dr., Suite 1200, Silver Spring, MD 20910 (☎ **301/578-8800**), is a nonprofit advocacy organization with a travel program that entitles members ($29.95 to join) to hotel, condominium, and car-rental discounts, as well as a 24-hour emergency alert service for accident, injury, or illness.

Some great, low-cost trips to Hawaii are offered to people 55 and older through **Elderhostel,** 75 Federal St., Boston, MA 02110 (☎ **617/426-8056;** www.elderhostel.org; e-mail cadyg@elderhostel.org), a nonprofit group that offers travel and study programs around the world. Trips are usually unbelievably cheap and include moderate accommodations and meals in one low package price. You can obtain a complete catalog of offerings by writing to Elderhostel, P.O. Box 1959, Wakefield, MA 01880-5959.

If you're planning to visit Haleakala National Park, you can save sightseeing dollars if you're 62 or older by picking up a **Golden Age Passport** from any national park, recreation area, or monument. This lifetime pass has a one-time fee of $10 and provides free admission to all of the parks in the system, plus a 50% savings on camping and recreation fees. You can pick one up at any park entrance; be sure to have proof of your age with you.

FOR GAYS & LESBIANS

Hawaii is known for its acceptance of all groups. Most accommodations greet gay and lesbian visitors like any other travelers—with aloha.

To get a sense of the local gay and lesbian community, contact Lifestyle Publishing, Inc., publishers of the monthly magazine *Island Lifestyle,* P.O. Box 11840, Honolulu, HI 96828 (☎ **808/737-6400;** fax 808/735-8825; www.islandlifestyle.com; e-mail editor@islandlifestyle.com). The gay and lesbian magazine presents alternative news, arts, entertainment, and happenings in Hawaii; to have a copy sent to you, enclose $5.

For more information on gay and lesbian groups on Maui, contact **Both Sides Now,** P.O. Box 5042, Kahului, HI 96732 (☎ **808/244-4566**).

For the latest information on the gay marriage issue, contact the **Hawaii Marriage Project** (☎ **808/532-9000;** www.xq.com/hermp/).

TRAVEL AGENCIES   **Pacific Ocean Holidays,** P.O. Box 88245, Honolulu, HI 96830 (☎ **800/735-6600** or 808/923-2400; http://gayhawaii.com), offers vacation packages that feature gay-owned and gay-friendly lodgings. It also publishes the *Pocket Guide to Hawaii: A Guide for Gay Visitors & Kamaaina,* a list of gay-owned and gay-friendly businesses throughout the islands. Send $5 for a copy (mail order only; no phone orders, please), or access the online version on the agency's Web site; you can even book your entire Hawaii vacation online.

FOR FAMILIES

Hawaii is paradise for children: beaches to run on, water to splash in, unusual sights to see, and a host of new foods to taste. Be sure to check out the "Family-Friendly Accommodations" box in chapter 6 and the "Especially for Kids" box in chapter 9 for information and ideas for families.

The larger hotels and resorts have supervised programs for children and can refer you to qualified baby-sitters. You can also contact **People Attentive to Children** (PATCH), which can refer you to individuals who have taken their training courses on child care; call ☎ **808/242-9232.**

8 Getting There & Getting Around

For additional advice on getting to and around Maui, see chapter 5.

ARRIVING IN THE ISLANDS

Three airlines fly directly from the mainland to Maui: **United Airlines** (☎ 800/241-6522; www.ual.com) offers one flight a day nonstop to Maui from San Francisco, and one from Los Angeles; **Hawaiian Airlines** (☎ 800/367-5320;

www.hawaiianair.com) has several daily direct flights from San Francisco and Los Angeles with a stopover in Honolulu (but no plane change); and **Delta Airlines** (☎ 800/221-1212 www.delta-air.com) offers direct flights from San Francisco and Los Angeles. The other carriers fly to Honolulu, where you'll have to pick up an interisland flight to Maui. Both **Aloha Airlines** (☎ 800/367-5250; www.alohaair.com) and **Hawaiian Airlines** (☎ 800/367-5320) offer jet service from Honolulu. See "Interisland Flights," below, and "Arriving," in chapter 5, for details.

For information on airlines serving Hawaii from places other than the U.S. mainland, see chapter 4, "For Foreign Visitors."

AGRICULTURAL SCREENING AT THE AIRPORTS   All baggage and passengers bound for the mainland must be screened by agricultural officials before boarding. This takes a little time, but it isn't a problem unless you happen to be carrying a football-sized local avocado home to Aunt Emma. Officials will confiscate fresh avocados, bananas, mangoes, and many other kinds of local produce in the name of fruit-fly control. Pineapples, coconuts, and papayas inspected and certified for export, boxed flowers, leis without seeds, and processed foods (macadamia nuts, coffee, jams, dried fruit, and the like) will pass. Call federal or state agricultural officials before leaving for the airport if you're not sure about your trophy.

INTERISLAND FLIGHTS

Don't expect to jump a ferry between any of the Hawaiian islands. Today, everyone island-hops by plane. In fact, almost every 20 minutes of every day from just before sunrise to well after sunset (usually around 8pm), a plane takes off or lands at the Kahului Airport on the interisland shuttle service. If you miss a flight, don't worry; they're like buses—another one will be along real soon.

Aloha Airlines (☎ 800/367-5250 or 808/244-9071; www.alohaair.com) is the state's largest provider of interisland air transport service. It offers 180 regularly scheduled daily jet flights throughout Hawaii, utilizing an all-jet fleet of Boeing 737 aircraft. Aloha's sibling company, **Island Air** (☎ 800/323-3345 or 808/ 484-2222), operates deHavilland DASH-8 and DASH-6 turboprop aircraft and serves Hawaii's small interisland airports on Maui, Molokai, and Lanai.

Hawaiian Airlines (☎ 800/367-5320 or 808/871-6132; www.hawaiianair.com; e-mail webmaster@hawaiianair.com), Hawaii's first interisland airline (which also flies daily to Hawaii from the West Coast; see above), has carried more than 100 million passengers to and around the state. It's one of the world's safest airlines, having never had a fatal incident since it began operations in 1929.

MULTI-ISLAND PASSES   At press time, the standard interisland fare on both islands was $86. However, both airlines offer multiple-flight deals that you might want to consider.

Aloha Airlines   Nonresidents of Hawaii can purchase Aloha's **Visitor Seven-Day Island Pass.** For just $315 per person, including tax, you get unlimited travel on Aloha and Island Air for 7 consecutive days; Aloha also offers a 1-month version for $999.

If you're traveling for more than a week but less than a month, you can buy a **Coupon Book** for $309, which contains six blank tickets that you can use—for yourself or any other traveler—any time within 1 year of purchase. This is probably the best deal going if you're island-hopping two or three times in the course of your stay.

Travel Deals for Net Surfers

It's possible to get some great deals on airfare, hotels, and car rentals via the Internet. Grab your mouse and start surfing before you hit the real waves in Hawaii—you could save a bundle on your trip. The Web sites we've highlighted below are worth checking out, especially since all services are free.

Microsoft Expedia (www.expedia.com) The best part of this multipurpose travel site is the Fare Tracker: you fill out a form on the screen indicating your interest in cheap flights to Hawaii from your hometown, and Microsoft Expedia will e-mail you the best airfare deals each week. The site's Travel Agent will steer you to bargains on hotels and car rentals; you can book everything, including flights, right online. This site is useful even after you're booked: before you go, log on to Expedia for oodles of up-to-date travel information, including weather reports and foreign exchange rates.

Preview Travel (www.reservations.com and www.vacations.com) Another useful travel site, Reservations.com has a Best Fare Finder, which will search the Apollo computer reservations system for the three lowest fares for any route on any days of the year. Say you want to go from Chicago to Honolulu and back between December 6 and December 13. Just fill out the form on the screen with times, dates, and destinations, and within minutes, Preview will show you the best deals. If you find an airfare you like, you can book your ticket right online— you can even reserve hotels and car rentals on this site. If you're in the preplanning stage, head to Preview's Vacations.com site, where you can check out the latest package deals for Hawaii and other destinations around the world by clicking on Hot Deals.

Travelocity (www.travelocity.com) This is one of the best travel sites out there. In addition to its Personal Fare Watcher, which notifies you via e-mail of the lowest airfares for up to five different destinations, Travelocity will track the three lowest fares for any routes on any dates in minutes. You can book a flight right then and there, and if you need a rental car or hotel, Travelocity will find you the best deal via the SABRE computer reservations system (a huge database used by travel agents worldwide). Click on Last Minute Deals for the latest travel bargains, including a link to H.O.T. Coupons (**www.hotcoupons.com**), where you can print out electronic coupons for travel in the United States and Canada, including Hawaii.

Airlines of the Web (www.itn.net/airlines)—This new site might be the most comprehensive Internet airline information source to date. Among its many

Hawaiian Airlines Hawaiian offers a variety of discounts based on the number of flights you're taking and the number of passengers flying. The **Hawaiian Island Pass** gives you unlimited interisland flights for $299 per person for 5 consecutive days, $349 for 7 days, $369 for 10 days, and $409 for 2 weeks.

Because Hawaiian Airlines also flies to and from the mainland United States, you might also be able to apply your transpacific flight toward discounts on your interisland travel; be sure to inquire when booking.

CAR RENTALS

Maui has one of the lowest car-rental rates in the country. The average non-discounted, unlimited-mileage rate for a 1-day rental for an intermediate-sized car features are links to virtually every airline in the world, Internet-only airfare deals posted on one easy-to-scan page, and a terrific fare finder and online reservations service. A unique feature is ITN's Low Fare Ticker, which allows you to monitor fares around the clock—particularly useful during fare wars. Fare Mail will notify you via e-mail when a flight you're interested in dips below your personal price threshold.

Trip.Com (www.thetrip.com)   This site is really geared toward the business traveler, but vacationers-to-be can also use Trip.Com's valuable fare-finding engine, which will e-mail you every week with the best city-to-city airfare deals on your selected route or routes.

Discount Tickets (www.discount-tickets.com)   Operated by the ETN (European Travel Network), this site offers discounts on airfares, accommodations, car rentals, and tours. It deals in flights between the United States and other countries, not domestic U.S. flights, so it's most useful for travelers coming to Hawaii from abroad.

E-Savers Programs   Several major airlines, most of which service the Hawaiian Islands, offer a free e-mail service known as **E-Savers,** via which they'll send you their best bargain airfares on a weekly basis. Here's how it works: Once a week (usually Wednesday), subscribers receive a list of discounted flights to and from various destinations, both international and domestic. Now here's the catch: These fares are available only if you leave the very next Saturday (or sometimes Friday night) and return on the following Monday or Tuesday. It's really a service for the spontaneously inclined and for travelers looking for a quick getaway (for Hawaii, that usually means travelers from the West Coast). But the fares are cheap, so it's worth taking a look. If you have a preference for certain airlines (in other words, the ones you fly most frequently), sign up with them first.

Here's a list of airlines and their Web sites, where you can not only get on the e-mail lists, but also book flights directly:

- **American Airlines:** www.americanair.com
- **Continental Airlines:** www.flycontinental.com
- **Northwest Airlines:** www.nwa.com
- **TWA:** www.twa.com
- **US Airways:** www.usairways.com

Epicurious Travel (travel.epicurious.com), another good travel site, allows you to sign up for all of these airline e-mail lists at once.

was $39 in 1997. That's the fourth-lowest rate in the country, compared with the national average of $53.50 a day.

All major car-rental agencies are represented at Kahului Airport and most neighbor-island airports, including **Alamo** (☎ 800/327-9633; www.goalamo.com), **Avis** (☎ 800/321-3712; www.avis.com), **Budget** (☎ 800/935-6878; www.budgetrentacar.com), **Dollar** (☎ 800/800-4000; www.dollarcar.com), **Hertz** (☎ 800/654-3011; www.hertz.com), and **National** (☎ 800/227-7368; www.nationalcar.com). For discount car rentals and moped rentals, see chapter 5.

Rental cars are usually at a premium on Molokai and Lanai and might be sold out on the neighbor islands on holiday weekends, so be sure to book well ahead.

To rent a car in Hawaii, you must be at least 25 years of age and have a valid driver's license and a credit card. Your valid home-state license will be recognized here.

MULTI-ISLAND DEALS   If you're going to visit multiple islands, it's usually easiest—and cheapest—to book with one company and carry your contract through on each island for your entire stay; you just drop off your car on the island you're leaving, and there will be one waiting for you on the next island with the same company. By booking your cars this way, as one interisland rental, you can usually take advantage of weekly rates that you'd be excluded from if you treated each rental separately. Both **Avis** (☎ **800/321-3712;** www.avis.com) and **Hertz** (☎ **800/654-3011;** www.hertz.com) can do this for you; inquire about interisland rental arrangements when booking.

INSURANCE   Hawaii is a no-fault state, which means that if you don't have collision damage insurance, you are required to pay for all damages before you leave the state, whether the accident was your fault or not. Your personal car insurance might provide rental-car coverage; read your policy or call your insurer before you leave home. Bring your insurance identification card if you decline the optional insurance, which usually costs from $12 to $20 a day. Obtain the name of your company's local claim representative before you go. Some credit-card companies also provide collision damage insurance for their customers; check with yours before you rent.

DRIVING RULES   Hawaii has a mandatory seat-belt law; if you're caught without your seat belt buckled up, you'll get a $50 ticket. Infants must be strapped in car seats. Pedestrians always have the right of way, even if they're not in the crosswalk. You can turn right on red from the right lane after a full and complete stop, unless there is a sign forbidding you to do so.

ROAD MAPS   The foldout map at the back of this book should get you around all the islands well.

The best and most detailed road maps are published by *This Week Magazine,* a free visitor publication available on Maui. For island maps, check out those published by the University of Hawaii Press. Updated periodically, they include a detailed network of island roads, large-scale insets of towns, historical and contemporary points of interest, parks, beaches, and hiking trails. These maps cost about $3 each, or about $15 for a complete set. If you can't find them in a bookstore near you, write to **University of Hawaii Press,** 2840 Kolowalu St., Honolulu, HI 96822.

If you seek topographical maps of the Hawaiian Islands, write the **Hawaii Geographic Society,** P.O. Box 1698, Honolulu, HI 96806 (☎ **808/546-3952;** fax 808/536-5999).

9 Tips on Accommodations

Maui offers all kinds of accommodations, from simple rooms in restored plantation homes and quaint cottages on the beach to luxurious ocean-view condo units and opulent suites at palatial resorts. Each has its pluses and minuses—so before you book, make sure that you know what you're getting into. Below, we discuss the various accommodation options available in Hawaii, how to get the best possible rate, when you should consider using a booking agency, and what to do if your dream accommodation turns into a nightmare.

TYPES OF ACCOMMODATIONS

HOTELS   In Hawaii, "hotel" can indicate a wide range of options, from few or no on-site amenities to enough extras to qualify as a miniresort. Generally, a hotel offers daily maid service and has a restaurant, on-site laundry facilities, a swimming pool, and a sundries/convenience–type shop (as opposed to the shopping arcades that most resorts have these days). Top hotels also provide activities desks, concierge service, business centers, a bar and/or lounge, and perhaps a few more shops. The advantages of staying in a hotel are privacy and convenience; the disadvantage is generally noise: either thin walls between rooms, or loud music from a lobby lounge late into the night.

Compared with resorts, hotels offer similar accommodations but tend to be smaller, providing fewer facilities—you might get a swimming pool, but don't expect a golf course or tennis courts, more than one or two restaurants, and everything else that comes with a full-fledged resort.

RESORTS   In Hawaii, a resort offers everything a hotel offers and more. What you get varies from property to property, of course, but expect such facilities, services, and amenities as direct beach access, with beach cabanas and chairs; pools (often more than one) and a Jacuzzi; a spa and fitness center; multiple restaurants, bars, and lounges; a 24-hour front desk; concierge, valet, and bell services; room service (often around the clock); an activities desk; tennis and golf (some of the world's best courses are at Hawaii resorts); ocean activities; a business center; children's programs; and more.

The advantage of staying at a resort is that you have everything you could possibly want in the way of service and things to do; the disadvantage is that the price generally reflects this fact. Don't be misled by a name—just because a place is called "ABC Resort" doesn't mean it actually *is* a resort. Make sure that you're getting what you pay for.

CONDOS   The roominess and convenience of a condo—which is usually a fully equipped multiple-bedroom apartment—makes this a great choice for families. Condominium properties in Hawaii are generally several apartments set in either a single high-rise or a cluster of low-rise units. Condos generally have amenities such as some degree of maid service (ranging from daily to weekly; it might or might not be included in your rate, so be sure to ask), a swimming pool, laundry facilities (either in your unit or in a central location), and an on-site front desk or a live-in property manager. The advantages of a condo are privacy, space, and conveniences—which usually include full kitchen facilities, washer and dryer, private phone, and more. The downsides include the absence of an on-site restaurant and the density of the units (as opposed to the privacy you get with a single-unit vacation rental).

Condos vary in price according to size, location, and amenities. Many of them are located on or near the beach, and they tend to be clustered in resort areas. Although there are some very high-end condos, most tend to be quite affordable, especially if you're traveling in a group that's large enough to require more than one bedroom.

BED-AND-BREAKFASTS   Maui has a wide variety of places that fall under this category: everything from the traditional B&B—several bedrooms in a home (which might or might not share a bathroom), with breakfast served in the morning—to what is essentially a vacation rental on an owner's property that comes with fixings for you to make your own breakfast. Make sure that the B&B you're booking matches your own mental picture; would you prefer conversation around a big dining-room table as you eat a hearty breakfast, or just a muffin and juice to enjoy in your own private place? Laundry facilities and a private phone are not always available at B&Bs. We've reviewed lots of wonderful places in the island chapters that follow. If you have to share a bathroom, we've spelled it out in the listings; otherwise, you can assume that you will have a private bath.

The advantage to a traditional B&B is its individual style and congenial atmosphere. B&Bs are great places to meet other visitors to Maui, and the host is generally very happy to act as your own private concierge, offering tips on where to go and what to do. In addition, B&Bs are usually an affordable way to go (though fancier ones can run $150 or more a night). The disadvantages are lack of privacy, usually a set time for breakfast, few amenities, generally no maid service, and the fact that you'll have to share the quarters beyond your bedroom with others. In addition, B&B owners usually require a minimum stay of 2 or 3 nights, and it's often a drive to the beach.

VACATION RENTALS This is another great choice for families, as well as for long-term stays. "Vacation rental" usually means there will be no one on the property where you're staying. The actual accommodation can range from an apartment in a condominium building to a two-room cottage on the beach to an entire fully equipped house. Generally, vacation rentals are the kinds of places you can settle into for a while: they have kitchen facilities (which can be either a complete kitchen or just a kitchenette with microwave, refrigerator, burners, and coffeemaker), on-site laundry facilities, and phone; some also come outfitted with such extras as TV, VCR, and stereo. The advantages of a vacation rental are complete privacy, your own kitchen (which can save you money on meals), and lots of conveniences. The disadvantages are a lack of an on-site property manager, and generally no maid service; often, a minimum stay is required (sometimes as much as a week). If you book a vacation rental, be sure that you have a 24-hour contact so that when the toilet won't flush or you can't figure out how to turn on the air-conditioning, you'll have someone to call.

BARGAINING ON PRICES

Like the price of a car, accommodations rates can sometimes be bargained down, but it depends on the place. In general, each type of accommodation allows a different amount of latitude in bargaining on their rack (or published) rates.

The best bargaining can be had at **hotels** and **resorts.** Hotels and resorts regularly pay travel agents as much as 30% of the rate you're paying for sending clients their way; if business is slow, some hotels might give you the benefit of at least part of this commission if you book directly instead of going through an airline or travel agent. Most also have kamaaina, or "local," rates for islanders, which they might extend to visitors during slow periods. It never hurts to ask politely for a discounted or local rate; a host of special rates are also available for the military, seniors, members of the travel industry, families, corporate travelers, and long-term visitors. Ask about package deals, which might include a car rental or free breakfast for the same price as a room. Hotels and resorts offer packages for everyone: golfers, tennis players, families, honeymooners, and more. We've found that it's worth the extra few cents to call a hotel's local number; sometimes the local reservationist knows about package deals that the toll-free operators are unaware of. If all else fails, try to get the hotel or resort to upgrade you to a better room for the same price as a budget room, or to waive the parking fee or the extra fees for children. Persistence and polite inquiries can pay off.

Package-Buying Tip

For one-stop shopping on the Web, go to **www.vacationpackager.com**, a Web search engine that links you up with many different package-tour operators, who can then help you plan a custom-tailored trip to Hawaii. Be sure to look under both "Hawaii" and "Hawaiian Islands."

You'll find it more difficult to bargain a lower rate at **bed-and-breakfasts.** You might be able to bargain down the minimum stay, or negotiate a discount if you're staying a week or longer. But generally, a B&B owner has only a few rooms and has already priced the property at a competitive rate; expect to pay what's asked.

You have somewhat more leeway to negotiate with **vacation rentals** and **condos.** In addition to asking for a discount on multinight stays, also ask whether the condo or vacation rental can throw in a rental car to sweeten the deal; believe it or not, they often will.

GREAT DEALS AT HAWAII'S TOP HOTEL CHAINS

Hawaii's three major hotel chains—Outrigger, Aston, and Marc Resorts, which together represent 79 hotels, condominiums, resorts, a historic bed-and-breakfast, and even restored plantation homes—have a host of packages and ways to save money.

With some 28 properties in Hawaii, including four on Maui, **Outrigger** (☎ 800/OUTRIGGER; fax 800/622-4852; www.outrigger.com; e-mail reservations@outrigger.com) offers excellent affordable accommodations, all with consistently dependable, clean, and well-appointed rooms. The chain's price structure is based entirely on location, room size, and amenities. You'll be comfortable at any of the chain's outposts: the small rooms at the budget Outriggers are just as tastefully appointed as the larger, more expensive Outrigger rooms right on the beach. Package deals include discounted rates for spring and fall stays, a car package, deals on multinight stays, family plans, cut rates for seniors, and even packages for scuba divers (2 days of two-tank boat dives and a 3-night stay starts at $311 per person, double occupancy).

The **Aston** chain (☎ 800/92-ASTON; fax 808/922-8785; www.aston-hotels. com; e-mail reservations@aston-hotels.com), which celebrated 50 years in Hawaii in 1998, has some 29 hotels, condominiums, and resort properties scattered throughout the islands. They range dramatically in price and style, from the luxurious Aston Wailea to the comfortable Aston Maui Lu. Aston offers package deals galore, including family plans; discounted senior rates; car, golf, and shopping packages; and deals on multinight stays, including a wonderful "Island Hopper" deal that allows you to hop from island to island and get 25% off on 7 nights or more at Aston properties.

Marc Resorts Hawaii (☎ 800/535-0085; fax 800/633-5085; www. marcresorts.com; e-mail marc@aloha.net) has 22 properties on every island but Lanai, ranging from luxury resorts to an affordable condominium property on Molokai. The chain offers package deals for seniors, multinight stays, honeymooners, and golfers, as well as corporate discounts and car-rental deals.

USING A BOOKING AGENCY VS. DOING IT YOURSELF

Sometimes you can save money by making your travel arrangements yourself—not only can you bargain on the phone, but some accommodations also might be

What to Do If Your Dream Hotel Turns Out to Be a Nightmare

Don't panic! Even if you've booked into a small B&B and you absolutely hate both of the bedrooms once you show up, usually the host wants to make you happy, and might even get on the phone and book you at another place that will suit you better. Hotels, resorts, and condominiums are generally easier to deal with, since they have numerous units to offer and can probably satisfy your complaints by moving you to another room.

Here are some tips on how to complain if you're unhappy with your room:

• Find out beforehand exactly what the accommodation is offering you: the cost, the minimum stay, the included amenities. Ask whether there's any penalty fee for leaving early. Read the small print in the contract—especially that on cancellation fees.

• Discuss ahead of time with the B&B, vacation rental, condominium agent, or booking agency what their cancellation policy is if the accommodation doesn't meet your expectations. Get this policy in writing (so there are no misunderstandings later).

• When you arrive, if the room you're given doesn't meet your expectations, notify the front desk, rental agent, or booking agency immediately.

• Approach the management in a calm, reasonable manner. Voice your complaint clearly and suggest a solution. Be reasonable and be willing to compromise. Do not make threats or leave. If you leave, it might be harder to get your deposit returned.

• If all else fails, when you get home, write to your credit-card company or any association the accommodation might be a member of (such as the Hawaii Visitors and Convention Bureau, a resort association, or an island association). In the letter, state the name of the accommodation, the name you registered under, the date of the complaint, the exact nature of the complaint, and why the issue was not resolved to your satisfaction. And be sure to let us know if you have a problem with a place we recommend in this book!

willing to pass on a percentage of the commission they would normally have to pay a travel agent or a booking agency.

However, if you don't have the time or money to call several places to make sure that they offer the amenities you'd like and to bargain for a price you're comfortable with, then you might consider using a booking agency. The time the agency spends on your behalf might well be worth any fees you'll have to pay.

The top reservations service in the state is **Hawaii's Best Bed & Breakfasts,** P.O. Box 563, Kamuela, HI 96743 (☎ **800/262-9912** or 808/885-4550; fax 808/885-0559; www.bestbnb.com; e-mail bestbnb@aloha.net). This service charges $15 to book the first two locations and $5 for each additional location. Barbara and Susan Campbell will personally select from the traditional homestays, cottages, and inns they represent throughout the islands, based on each one's hospitality, distinctive charm, and attention to detail. Other great statewide booking agents are **Volcano Reservations,** P.O. Box 998, Volcano, HI 96785 (☎ **800/736-7140** or 808/967-7244; fax 800/577-1849; www.volcano-hawaii.com; e-mail reservations@volcano-hawaii.com), which doesn't charge a penny for booking your reservations and is always in the know about the best deals on every island; and **Ann and Bob Babson,** 3371 Keha Dr., Kihei, HI 96753 (☎ **800/824-6409** or

808/874-1166; fax 808/879-7906; www.maui.net/~babson; e-mail babson@
maui.net), who can steer you in the right direction for both accommodations and
car rentals. Not only do they personally inspect the units they recommend, but the
Babsons also are impeccably honest and dedicated to matching you up with
the place that's right for you.

For vacation rentals, contact **Hawaii Beachfront Vacation Homes**
(☎ **808/247-3637** or 808/235-2644; www.hotspots.hawaii.com/beachrent1.html;
e-mail hibeach@lava.net). **Hawaii Condo Exchange** (☎ **800/442-0404;**
http://wwte.com/condos) acts as a consolidator for condo and vacation-rental
properties.

10 Money-Saving Package Deals

Booking an all-inclusive travel package that includes some combination of airfare,
accommodations, rental car, meals, airport and baggage transfers, and sightseeing
can be the most cost-effective way to travel to Hawaii. You can sometimes save so
much money by buying all the pieces of your trip through a packager that your
transpacific airfare ends up, in effect, being free.

The best place to start looking for a package deal is in the travel section of your
local Sunday newspaper. Also check the ads in the back of such national travel
magazines as *Travel & Leisure, National Geographic Traveler,* and *Condé Nast
Traveler.* **Liberty Travel** (many locations; check your local directory, since there's
no central toll-free number), for instance, one of the biggest packagers in the
Northeast, usually boasts a full-page ad in Sunday papers. You won't find much
in the way of service, but you will get a good deal. **American Express Travel**
(☎ 800/AXP-6898; www.americanexpress.com/travel) can also book you a well-
priced Hawaiian vacation; it also advertises in many Sunday travel sections.

Hawaii is such an ideal destination for vacation packages that some packagers
book Hawaiian vacations as the majority of their business. **Pleasant Hawaiian
Holidays** (☎ 800/2-HAWAII or 800/242-9244; www.pleasantholidays.com
or www.2hawaii.com) is, by far, the biggest and most comprehensive packager
to Hawaii; it offers an extensive, high-quality collection of 50 condos and hotels
in every price range. **Sunscapes** (☎ 800/229-8376 or 425/643-1620;
www.sunscapes.com) sells only Hawaii vacations, concentrating on budget and
moderately priced hotels and condos.

Other reliable packagers include the airlines themselves, which often package
their flights together with accommodations. Among the airlines offering good-value
package deals to Hawaii are **American Airlines FlyAway Vacations** (☎ 800/
321-2121; www.2travel.com/americanair/hawaii.html), **Continental Airlines
Vacations** (☎ 800/634-5555 or 800/301-3800; www.coolvacations.com),
Delta Dream Vacations (☎ 800/872-7786; www.leisureweb.com/DELTA),
TWA Getaway Vacations (☎ 800/GETAWAY or 800/438-2929; www.twa
.com/html/vacation/tourvac.html), and **United Vacations** (☎ 800/328-6877;
www.unitedvacations.com). If you're traveling to the islands from Canada, ask
your travel agent about package deals through **Air Canada Vacations** (☎ 800/
776-3000; www.aircanada.ca).

4 For Foreign Visitors

by Jeanette Foster

The pervasiveness of American culture around the world might make the United States feel like familiar territory to foreign visitors, but leaving your own country for the States—especially the unique island state of Hawaii—still requires an additional degree of planning. This chapter will help prepare you for the more common problems—expected and unexpected—that visitors to the islands might encounter.

1 Preparing for Your Trip

ENTRY REQUIREMENTS

Immigration laws are a hot political issue in the United States these days, and the following requirements might have changed somewhat by the time you plan your trip. Check at any U.S. embassy or consulate for current information and requirements.

DOCUMENT REGULATIONS Canadian citizens may enter the United States without visas; they need only proof of residence.

The U.S. State Department has a **Visa Waiver Pilot Program** allowing citizens of certain countries to enter the United States without a visa for stays of up to 90 days. At press time, these included Andorra, Australia, Austria, Belgium, Brunei, Denmark, Finland, France, Germany, Iceland, Ireland, Italy, Japan, Liechtenstein, Luxembourg, Monaco, the Netherlands, New Zealand, Norway, San Marino, Spain, Sweden, Switzerland, and the United Kingdom. Citizens of these countries need only a valid passport and a round-trip air or cruise ticket in their possession upon arrival. If they first enter the United States, they may then visit Mexico, Canada, Bermuda, and/or the Caribbean islands and return to the United States without needing a visa. Further information is available from any U.S. embassy or consulate.

Citizens of all other countries must have (1) a valid **passport** with an expiration date at least 6 months later than the scheduled end of their visit to the United States, and (2) a **tourist visa,** which can be obtained without charge from the nearest U.S. consulate.

To obtain a visa, you must submit a completed application form (either in person or by mail) with a 1½-inch-square photo, and you must demonstrate binding ties to a residence abroad. Usually you

Travel Tip

Be sure to keep a copy of all your travel papers separate from your wallet or purse, and leave a copy with someone at home in case you need it faxed in an emergency.

can obtain a visa at once or within 24 hours, but it might take longer during the summer rush from June to August. If you cannot go in person, contact the nearest U.S. embassy or consulate for directions on applying by mail. Your travel agent or airline office might also be able to provide you with visa applications and instructions. The U.S. consulate or embassy that issues your visa will determine whether you will be issued a multiple- or single-entry visa and any restrictions regarding the length of your stay.

UK citizens can obtain up-to-date passport and visa information by calling the **U.S. Embassy Visa Information Line** at ☎ **0891/200-290** or the **London Passport Office** at ☎ **0990/210-410** (for recorded information).

Foreign driver's licenses are recognized in Hawaii, although you might want to get an international driver's license if your home license is not written in English.

MEDICAL REQUIREMENTS   Inoculations are not needed to enter the United States unless you are coming from, or have stopped over in, areas known to be suffering from epidemics, particularly cholera or yellow fever.

If you have a disease requiring treatment with medications containing narcotics or drugs requiring a syringe, carry a valid signed prescription from your physician to allay suspicions that you are smuggling drugs.

CUSTOMS REQUIREMENTS   Every adult visitor may bring in, free of duty, 1 liter of wine or hard liquor, 200 cigarettes or 100 cigars (but no cigars from Cuba) or 3 pounds of smoking tobacco, and $100 worth of gifts. These exemptions are offered to travelers who spend at least 72 hours in the United States and who have not claimed them within the preceding 6 months. It is altogether forbidden to bring into the country foodstuffs (particularly cheese, fruit, cooked meats, and canned goods) and plants (vegetables, seeds, tropical plants, and so on). Foreign tourists may bring in or take out up to $10,000 in U.S. or foreign currency with no formalities; larger sums must be declared to customs on entering or leaving.

In addition, you cannot bring fresh fruits and vegetables into Hawaii, even if you're coming from the U.S. mainland and have no need to clear customs. Every passenger is asked shortly before landing to sign a certificate declaring that he or she does not have fresh fruits or vegetables in his or her possession. The form also asks questions for the Hawaii Visitors and Convention Bureau about your visit, such as how long you plan to stay, which island or islands you will visit, and how many times you have been to Hawaii.

INSURANCE   There is no nationwide health system in the United States, and the cost of medical care in Hawaii is extremely high. Accordingly, we strongly advise every traveler to secure health insurance coverage before setting out.

You might want to take out a comprehensive travel policy that covers (for a relatively low premium) sickness or injury costs (medical, surgical, and hospital); loss or theft of your baggage; trip-cancellation costs; guarantee of bail in case you are arrested; and costs of accident, repatriation, or death. Such packages (for example, "Europ Assistance" in Europe) are sold by automobile clubs at attractive rates, as well as by insurance companies and travel agencies.

Insurance for British Travelers   Most big travel agents offer their own insurance, and they will probably try to sell you their package when you book a holiday. Think before you sign. Britain's Consumers' Association recommends that you insist on seeing the policy and reading the fine print before buying travel insurance. The **Association of British Insurers** (☎ **0171/600-3333**) gives advice by phone and publishes the free *Holiday Insurance,* a guide to policy provisions and prices. You might also shop around for better deals: try **Columbus Travel Insurance Ltd.** (☎ **0171/375-0011**) or, for students, **Campus Travel** (☎ **0171/730-2101**).

MONEY

CURRENCY   The American monetary system has a decimal base: one U.S. **dollar** ($1) = 100 **cents** (100¢). Dollar bills commonly come in $1 ("a buck"), $5, $10, $20, $50, and $100 denominations (the last two are not welcome when paying for small purchases and are not accepted in taxis or movie theaters).

There are six denominations of coins: 1¢ (1 cent or a "penny"), 5¢ (5 cents or a "nickel"), 10¢ (10 cents or a "dime"), 25¢ (25 cents or a "quarter"), 50¢ (50 cents or a "half-dollar"), and the rare $1 piece.

EXCHANGING CURRENCY   Exchanging foreign currency for U.S. dollars can be painless in Maui. Generally, the best rates are available through the bank; most major banks in Maui will exchange your foreign currency for U.S. dollars. Most of the major hotels also offer currency exchange services, but the rate of exchange is usually not as good as what you'll find at a bank. There are no currency exchange services on Maui, but there are currency services at the Honolulu International Airport.

TRAVELER'S CHECKS   It's actually cheaper and faster to get cash at an automatic teller machine (ATM) than to fuss with traveler's checks. As noted in the section "Visitor Information & Money" in chapter 3, Maui has ATMs almost everywhere. If you do bring traveler's checks, those denominated in U.S. dollars are readily accepted at most hotels, restaurants, and large stores. Do not bring traveler's checks denominated in any currency other than U.S. dollars.

CREDIT CARDS   The method of payment most widely used is the credit card: Visa (BarclayCard in Britain), MasterCard (EuroCard in Europe, Access in Britain, Chargex in Canada), American Express, Diners Club, Discover, and Carte Blanche. You can save yourself trouble by using "plastic money" rather than cash or traveler's checks in most hotels, restaurants, and retail stores (a growing number of food and liquor stores now accept credit cards). You must have a credit card to rent a car in Hawaii.

SAFETY

GENERAL   Although tourist areas are generally safe, crime is on the increase everywhere in the United States, and Maui is no exception. Visitors should always stay alert. It's wise to ask the island tourist office if you're in doubt about which neighborhoods are safe. Avoid deserted areas, especially at night. Generally speaking, you can feel safe in areas where there are many people and open establishments.

Avoid carrying valuables with you on the street, and don't display expensive cameras or electronic equipment. Hold onto your pocketbook, and place your billfold in an inside pocket. In theaters, restaurants, and other public places, keep your possessions in sight. When you go to the beach, do not leave valuables such as your wallet or passport on your beach towel when you go into the water.

Remember also that hotels are open to the public, and in a large hotel, security might not be able to screen everyone entering. Always lock your room door—don't assume that once inside your hotel you are automatically safe and no longer need to be aware of your surroundings.

DRIVING   Safety while driving is particularly important. Question your rental agency about personal safety, or ask for a brochure of traveler safety tips when you pick up your car. Ask the agency to provide written directions or a map with the route marked in red showing how to get to your destination.

Recently, more crime has involved burglary of tourist rental cars in hotel parking structures and at beach parking lots. Park in well-lighted and well-traveled areas if possible. Leaving your rental car unlocked and empty of your valuables is probably safer than locking your car with valuables in plain view. Never leave any packages or valuables in sight. If someone attempts to rob you or steal your car, do not try to resist the thief or carjacker—report the incident to the police department immediately.

For more information on driving rules and getting around by car in Maui, see "Getting There & Getting Around" in chapter 3.

2 Getting To & Around the United States

Airlines serving Hawaii from other than the U.S. mainland include **Air Canada** (☎ 800/776-3000; www.aircanada.ca); **Canada 3000** (☎ 888/CAN-3000; www.canada3000.com); **Canadian Airlines** (☎ 800/426-7000; www.cdnair.ca); **Air New Zealand** (☎ 0800/737-000 in Auckland, 64-3/379-5200 in Christchurch, 800/926-7255 in the U.S.), which runs 40 flights per week between Auckland and Hawaii; **Qantas** (☎ 008/177-767 in Australia, 800/227-4500 in the U.S.), which flies between Sydney and Honolulu daily (plus additional flights 4 days a week); **Japan Air Lines** (☎ 03/5489-1111 in Tokyo, 800/525-3663 in the U.S.); **All Nippon Airways** (ANA) (☎ 03/5489-1212 in Tokyo, 800/235-9262 in the U.S.); **China Airlines** (☎ 02/715-1212 in Taipei, 800/227-5118 in the U.S.); **Garuda Indonesian** (☎ 251-2235 in Jakarta, 800/342-7832 in the U.S.); **Korean Airlines** (☎ 02/656-2000 in Seoul, 800/223-1155 on the East Coast, 800/421-8200 on the West Coast, 800/438-5000 from Hawaii); and **Philippine Airlines** (☎ 631/816-6691 in Manila, 800/435-9725 in the U.S.).

Travelers coming from Europe can take advantage of the **APEX** (Advance Purchase Excursion) fares offered by all major U.S. and European carriers. Aside from these, attractive values are offered by **Icelandair** (☎ 354/5050-100 in Reykjavik, 0171/388-5599 in London, 800/223-5500 in the U.S.; www.icelandair.is) on flights from Luxembourg to New York, and by **Virgin Atlantic Airways** (☎ 0293/747-747 in Britain, 800/862-8621 in the U.S.; www.fly.virgin.com) from London to New York/Newark. You can then catch a connecting domestic flight to Honolulu.

Some large American airlines—such as **American Airlines, Delta, Northwest, TWA,** and **United**—offer travelers on transatlantic or transpacific flights special discount tickets under the name **Visit USA,** allowing travel between any U.S. destinations at reduced rates. These tickets are not on sale in the United States and must, therefore, be purchased before you leave your foreign point of departure. This system is the best, easiest, and fastest way to see the United States at low cost. You should obtain information well in advance from your travel agent or the office of the airline concerned, since the conditions attached to these discount tickets can be changed without advance notice.

The **ETN** (European Travel Network) operates a Web site offering discounts on international airfares to the United States, accommodations, car rentals, and tours; point your Internet browser to www.discount-tickets.com.

The visitor arriving by air should cultivate patience and resignation before setting foot on U.S. soil. Getting through immigration control can take as long as 2 hours on some days, especially during summer weekends. Add the time it takes to clear customs, and you'll see that you should make very generous allowance for delay in planning connections between international and domestic flights—an average of 2 to 3 hours at least.

For further information about travel to Maui, see "Arriving" and "Getting Around" in chapter 5.

FAST FACTS: For the Foreign Traveler

Automobile Rentals   See "Getting Around" in chapter 5.

Business Hours   See "Fast Facts: Maui" in chapter 5.

Climate   See "When to Go" in chapter 3.

Currency & Currency Exchange   See "Preparing for Your Trip" above.

Electricity   Maui, like the U.S. mainland and Canada, uses 110–120 volts, 60 cycles, compared to 220–240 volts, 50 cycles, as in most of Europe and in other areas of the world including Australia and New Zealand. In addition to a 100-volt transformer, small appliances of non-American manufacture, such as hair dryers or shavers, will require a plug adapter, with two flat, parallel pins.

Embassies & Consulates   All embassies are located in the national capital, Washington, D.C. Some consulates are located in major cities, and most nations have a mission to the United Nations in New York City. Listed here are the embassies and some consulates of the major English-speaking countries. Travelers from other countries can obtain telephone numbers for their embassies and consulates by calling directory information for Washington, D.C. (☎ 202/555-1212).

The embassy of **Australia** is at 1601 Massachusetts Ave. NW, Washington, DC 20036 (☎ 202/797-3000). There is also an Australian consulate in Hawaii, but it's on the island of Oahu (not on Maui) at 1000 Bishop St., Penthouse Suite, Honolulu, HI 96813 (☎ 808/524-5050).

The embassy of **Canada** is at 501 Pennsylvania Ave. NW, Washington, DC 20001 (☎ 202/682-1740). Canadian consulates are also at 1251 Avenue of the Americas, New York, NY 10020 (☎ 212/768-2400), and at 550 South Hope St., 9th floor, Los Angeles, CA 90071 (☎ 213/346-2700).

The embassy of the **Republic of Ireland** is at 2234 Massachusetts Ave. NW, Washington, DC 20008 (☎ 202/462-3939). There's a consulate office in San Francisco at 44 Montgomery St., Suite 3830, San Francisco, CA 94104 (☎ 415/392-4214).

The embassy of **New Zealand** is at 37 Observatory Circle NW, Washington, DC 20008 (☎ 202/328-4800). The only New Zealand consulate in the United States is at 12400 Wilshire Blvd., Los Angeles, CA 90025 (☎ 310/207-1605).

The embassy of the **United Kingdom** is at 3100 Massachusetts Ave. NW, Washington, DC 20008 (☎ 202/462-1340). British consulates are at 845 Third Ave., New York, NY 10022 (☎ 212/745-0200), and 11766 Wilshire Blvd., Suite 400, Los Angeles, CA 90025 (☎ 310/477-3322).

The embassy of **Japan** is at 2520 Massachusetts Ave. NW, Washington, DC 20008 (☎202/939-6700). The consulate general of Japan has an office on the island of Oahu (not on Maui), located at 1742 Nuuanu Ave., Honolulu, HI 96817 (☎808/536-2226). There are several other consulates, including one in New York at 299 Park Ave., New York, NY 10171 (☎212/371-8222).

Emergencies   Call ☎**911** to report a fire, call the police, or get an ambulance.

Gasoline (Petrol)   One U.S. gallon equals 3.8 liters, and 1.2 U.S. gallons equals 1 Imperial gallon. You'll notice that several grades (and price levels) of gasoline are available at most gas stations. And you'll also notice that their names change from company to company. The ones with the highest octane are the most expensive, but most rental cars take the least expensive "regular" gas with an octane rating of 87.

Holidays   See "When to Go," in chapter 3.

Languages   English is the official language. Major Maui hotels might have multilingual employees. Unless your language is very obscure, hotels can usually supply a translator on request. See "Life & Language," in chapter 2, for information about the Hawaiian language and the local version of pidgin.

Legal Aid   The ordinary tourist will probably never become involved with the American legal system. If you are pulled over for a minor infraction (for example, driving faster than the speed limit), never attempt to pay the fine directly to a police officer; you might wind up arrested on the much-more-serious charge of attempted bribery. Pay fines by mail, or directly into the hands of the clerk of the court. If you're accused of a more serious offense, it's wise to say and do nothing before consulting a lawyer (you have the rights both to remain silent and to consult an attorney under the U.S. Constitution). Under U.S. law, an arrested person is allowed one telephone call to a party of his or her choice; call your embassy or consulate.

Mail   If you want your mail to follow you on your vacation and you aren't sure of your address, your mail can be sent to you, in your name, c/o **General Delivery** at the main post office of the city or region where you expect to be. The addressee must pick up the mail in person and produce proof of identity (driver's license, passport, or the like).

Mailboxes, generally found at intersections, are blue with a blue-and-white eagle logo and carry the inscription U.S. POSTAL SERVICE. If your mail is addressed to a U.S. destination, don't forget to add the five-figure postal code, or **ZIP code,** after the two-letter abbreviation of the state to which the mail is addressed. The abbreviation for Hawaii is **HI.**

International air-mail rates are 60¢ for half-ounce letters (40¢ for letters going to Mexico and 46¢ for letters to Canada) and 50¢ for postcards (35¢ to Mexico and 40¢ to Canada). All domestic first-class mail goes from Hawaii to the U.S. mainland by air, so don't bother paying the extra amount to send a letter back to your grandmother in Michigan.

Newspapers/Magazines   National newspapers include the *New York Times* (often available at hotels in a condensed fax edition), *USA Today,* and the *Wall Street Journal.* These are available in major hotels, as are major West Coast newspapers like the *San Francisco Chronicle* and the *Los Angeles Times.* National news weeklies include *Newsweek, Time,* and *U.S. News and World Report.* The *Honolulu Advertiser* and the *Honolulu Star-Bulletin* are the major local newspapers on Oahu and throughout the islands; on Maui, the *Maui News* is the island's only daily newspaper.

Radio & TV The United States has numerous coast-to-coast television networks—ABC, CBS, NBC, Fox, the Public Broadcasting System (PBS), CNN, ESPN, MSNBC, MTV, and other cable networks play a major part in American life. On Maui, television viewers have a choice of about three dozen TV channels, most of which transmit all day long, plus the pay-TV channels showing recent movies or sports events. All options are usually indicated on your hotel TV set. You'll also find a wide choice of local radio stations, each broadcasting particular kinds of talk shows and/or music—classical, country, jazz, pop, gospel—punctuated by news broadcasts and frequent commercials. For more information, see "Fast Facts: Maui" in chapter 5.

Safety See "Safety" under "Preparing for Your Trip" above.

Taxes The United States has no VAT (Value-Added Tax) or other indirect taxes at a national level. Every state, and each city in it, has the right to levy its own local tax on all purchases, including hotel and restaurant checks, airline tickets, and so on. In Hawaii, sales tax is 4%; there's also a 6% hotel room tax, so the total tax on your hotel bill will be 10%.

Telephone & Fax The telephone system in the United States is run by private corporations, so rates, particularly for long-distance service and operator-assisted calls, can vary widely—especially on calls made from public telephones. Local calls—that is, calls to other locations on Maui—made from public phones cost 25¢.

Generally, hotel surcharges on long-distance and local calls are astronomical. You are usually better off using a **public pay telephone,** which you will find clearly marked in most public buildings and private establishments, as well as on the street.

Most **long-distance and international calls** can be dialed directly from any phone. For calls to Canada and to other parts of the United States, dial 1 followed by the area code and the seven-digit number. For international calls, dial 011 followed by the country code, the city code, and the telephone number of the person you want to call.

In Hawaii, interisland phone calls are considered long-distance and often are as costly as calling the U.S. mainland.

For **reversed-charge or collect calls,** and for **person-to-person calls,** dial 0 (zero, not the letter "O"), followed by the area code and number you want; an operator will then come on the line, and you should specify that you are calling collect, or person-to-person, or both. If your operator-assisted call is international, ask for the overseas operator.

Note that all phone numbers with the area code 800 or 888 are toll-free.

For **local directory assistance** ("information"), dial 411; for **long-distance information,** dial 1, then the appropriate area code and 555-1212.

Fax facilities are widely available and can be found in most hotels and many other establishments. Try **Mailboxes Etc., Kinko's,** or any photocopying shop.

Telephone Directory There are two kinds of telephone directories in the United States. The general directory is the so-called *White Pages,* in which private and business subscribers are listed in alphabetical order. The inside front cover lists the emergency number for police, fire, and ambulance, and other vital numbers (such as the Coast Guard, poison-control center, and crime-victims hot line). The first few pages are devoted to community-service numbers, including a guide to long-distance and international calling, complete with country codes and area codes.

The second directory, printed on yellow paper (hence its name, *Yellow Pages*), lists all local services, businesses, and industries by type of activity, with an index at the back. The listings cover not only such obvious items as automobile repairs by make of car, or drugstores (pharmacies), often by geographical location, but also restaurants by type of cuisine and geographical location, bookstores by special subject and/or language, places of worship by religious denomination, and other information that the tourist might otherwise not readily find. The *Yellow Pages* also includes city plans or detailed maps, often showing postal ZIP codes and public transportation routes.

Time   See "Fast Facts: Maui" in chapter 5.

Tipping   It's part of the American way of life to tip, on the principle that you must expect to pay for any service you get. Many personnel receive little direct salary and must depend on tips for their income. In fact, the U.S. federal government imposes income taxes on service personnel based on an estimate of how much they should have earned in tips relative to their employer's total receipts. In other words, they might have to pay taxes on a tip you didn't give them!

Here are some rules of thumb:

In **hotels,** tip bellhops at least $1 per piece of luggage ($2 to $3 if you have a lot of luggage), and tip the chamber staff $1 per person, per day. Tip the doorman or concierge only if he or she has provided you with some specific service (for example, calling a cab for you or obtaining difficult-to-get theater tickets). Tip the valet parking attendant $1 every time you get your car.

In **restaurants, bars, and nightclubs,** tip service staff 15% to 20% of the check, tip bartenders 10% to 15%, tip checkroom attendants $1 per garment, and tip valet-parking attendants $1 per vehicle. Tip the doorman only if he has provided you with some specific service (such as calling a cab for you). Tipping is not expected in cafeterias and fast-food restaurants.

Tip **cab drivers** 15% of the fare.

As for **other service personnel,** tip skycaps at airports at least $1 per piece ($2 to $3 if you have a lot of luggage), and tip hairdressers and barbers 15% to 20%.

Tipping gas-station attendants and ushers at movies and theaters is not expected.

Toilets   Foreign visitors often complain that public toilets are hard to find in most U.S. cities. True, there are none on the streets, but the visitor can usually find one in a bar, fast-food outlet, restaurant, hotel, museum, department store, or service station—and it will probably be clean (although those in service stations sometimes leaves much to be desired). Note, however, a growing practice in some restaurants and bars of displaying a notice that "toilets are for the use of patrons only." You can ignore this sign, or better yet, avoid arguments by paying for a cup of coffee or soft drink, which will qualify you as a patron. The cleanliness of toilets at parks and beaches is more open to question. Some public places are equipped with pay toilets, which require you to insert one or more coins into a slot on the door before it will open.

5 Getting to Know Maui

by Jeanette Foster

Each of us harbors different expectations of the perfect tropical paradise, but Maui just might fulfill all of them: cascading waterfalls set amidst lush rain forests; swaying palm trees bordering pristine white-sand beaches; a mysterious dormant volcano; Technicolor sunsets that will haunt your dreams forever; and starry nights so crystal clear that the profusion of constellations seems close enough to touch. Maui is the island that can satisfy all desires—it's the realization of the dream.

And everybody, it seems, knows it. Next to Waikiki, Maui is Hawaii's best-known destination, welcoming some 2½ million people each year to its sunny shores. As soon as you arrive at Kahului Airport, a huge banner greets you with the news that the readers of *Condé Nast Traveler* voted Maui the best island *in the world*—and they've done so 3 years running.

As the 20th century draws to a close, Maui has become *the* hip travel destination. Indeed, sometimes it feels a little too well-known—especially when you're stuck in bumper-to-bumper traffic around the airport or the wall-to-wall boat jam at Maui's popular snorkeling-diving atoll, Molokini crater. However, the congestion here pales in comparison to big-city Honolulu; Maui is really just a casual collection of small towns. Once you move beyond the resort areas, you'll find a slower, more peaceful way of life, where car horns are used only to greet friends, posted store hours mean nothing if the surf's up, and taking time to watch the sunset is part of the daily routine.

Visitors from other small towns in the United States and elsewhere find Maui just right: warm and friendly, with an easygoing lifestyle that's perfect for relaxing. But Maui also has an underlying energy that can nudge devout sunbathers right off the beach. The rest of the island soon beckons, and visitors find themselves inspired to do things they never dreamed of: rising before dawn to catch the sunrise over Haleakala Crater, then hopping on a bicycle to coast back down to sea level over 37 miles of switchbacks; heading out to sea on a lonely kayak to look for wintering humpback whales; or trekking through the lunar-like crater of a dormant volcano.

In this chapter, we have provided information to help you make your way from the airport and give you a feel for the lay of the land.

We've also offered logistical advice for getting around the island, as well as provided some handy facts and phone numbers to make your trip as hassle free as possible.

1 Arriving

If you think of the island of Maui as the shape of a head and shoulders of a person, you'll probably arrive on its neck, at **Kahului Airport.**

At press time, four airlines fly directly from the mainland to Maui: **United Airlines** (☎ 800/241-6522; www.ual.com), which offers one nonstop flight per day from San Francisco, and one from Los Angeles; **Hawaiian Airlines** (☎ 800/367-5320; www.hawaiianair.com), which has several daily flights from San Francisco and Los Angeles with a stopover in Honolulu but no plane change, plus direct flights from San Francisco and Seattle; **American Airlines** (☎ 800/433-7300; www.americanair.com), which flies direct from Los Angeles; and **Delta Airlines** (☎ 800/221-1212; www.delta-air.com), which offers direct flights from San Francisco and Los Angeles.

The other carriers fly to Honolulu, where you'll have to pick up an inter-island flight to Maui. **Aloha Airlines** (☎ 800/367-5250 or 808/484-1111; www.alohaair.com) and **Hawaiian Airlines** (☎ 800/367-5320 or 808/838-1555; www.hawaiianair.com; e-mail webmaster@hawaiianair.com) both offer jet service from Honolulu and other neighbor islands.

For additional advice on getting to and around Maui, see "Getting There & Getting Around" in chapter 3.

LANDING AT KAHULUI AIRPORT

If there's a long wait at baggage claim, step over to the state-operated **Visitor Information Center,** where you can pick up brochures and the latest issue of *This Week Maui,* which features great regional maps of the islands, and ask about island activities. After collecting your bags from the poky, automated carousels, step out, take a deep breath, proceed to the curbside rental-car pickup area, and wait for the appropriate rental-agency shuttle van to take you a half mile away to the rental-car checkout desk.

GETTING TO & FROM THE AIRPORT

Sadly, there is no public transportation on the island of Maui. To get around, you basically need to rent a car. You can get to your hotel via airline shuttle van or a very expensive taxi ride.

BY RENTAL CAR   All major rental companies have cars available at the Kahului Airport (see "Getting Around," below). Rental agency vans will pick you up outside and at the ocean end of the terminal (to your right as you stand with your back to the terminal) and take you to the agencies' off-site lots.

BY TAXI   You'll see taxis outside the airport terminal, but they are quite expensive—expect to spend around $60 to $75 for a ride from Kahului to Kaanapali and $50 from the airport to Wailea.

BY AIRPORT SHUTTLE   If you're not renting a car, the cheapest way to get to your hotel is **SpeediShuttle** (☎ 808/875-8070), which can take you from Kahului Airport to all the major resorts between 5am and 9pm daily. Rates vary, but figure on $20 for two passengers to Wailea (one-way) and $40 for two to Kapalua (one-way). Be sure to call before your flight to arrange pickup.

Maui

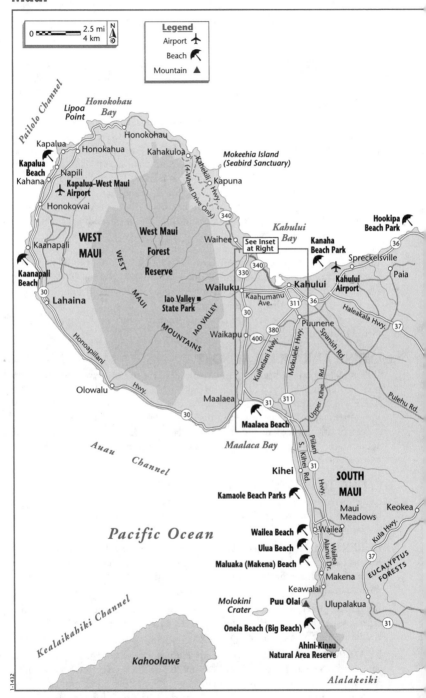

Legend
Airport ✈
Beach 🏖
Mountain ▲

0 ——— 2.5 mi
4 km

Pailolo Channel

Honokohau Bay

Lipoa Point

Honokohau

Kahakuloa

Mokeehia Island (Seabird Sanctuary)

Kapalua

Honokahua

Kapuna

Kapalua Beach

Napili

Kahana

Kapalua–West Maui Airport

Honokowai

Kaanapali

WEST MAUI

West Maui Forest Reserve

Kaahekili Hwy. (4-Wheel Drive Only)

Kahului Bay

Waihee

340

See Inset at Right

330

340

Hookipa Beach Park

Kanaha Beach Park

36

Spreckelsville

Paia

Kaanapali Beach

30

Lahaina

WEST MAUI MOUNTAINS

Iao Valley State Park

Wailuku

Kahului

Kahului Airport

Kaahumanu Ave.

311

36

Haleakala Hwy.

37

IAO VALLEY

Waikapu

400

380

Puunene

30

Honoapiilani Hwy.

Olowalu

Maalaea

Kuihelani Hwy.

Mokulele Hwy.

Spanish Rd.

Upper Kihei Rd.

Pulehu Rd.

31

311

Maalaea Beach

Auau Channel

Maalaea Bay

Kihei

S. Kihei Rd.

SOUTH MAUI

Maui Meadows

Keokea

Kamaole Beach Parks

Pacific Ocean

Wailea Beach

Wailea

Ulua Beach

Maluaka (Makena) Beach

Pilani Hwy.

Wailea Alanui Dr.

Kula Hwy.

31

37

EUCALYPTUS FORESTS

Makena

Keawalai

Molokini Crater

Puu Olai ▲

Ulupalakua

31

Kealaikahiki Channel

Onela Beach (Big Beach)

Ahini-Kinau Natural Area Reserve

Kahoolawe

Alalakeiki

1-1432

74

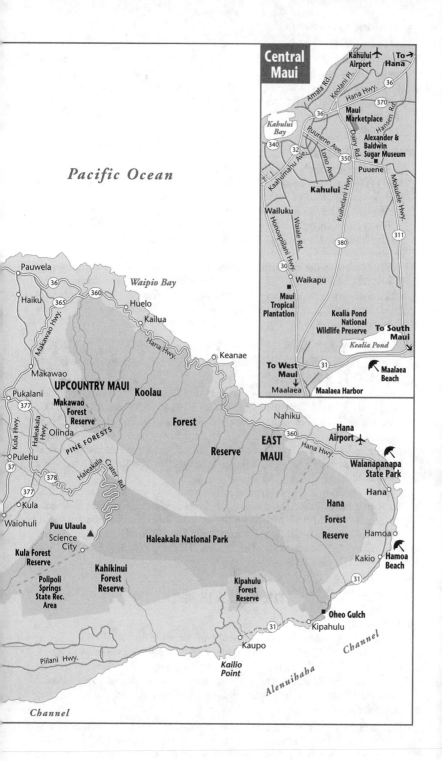

Pacific Ocean

Central Maui

Kahului Airport ✈ To → Hana

Amala Rd.
Keolani Pl.
Hana Hwy.
36
370

Kahului Bay

36

Maui Marketplace

Hansen Rd.

Puunene Ave.

340

32

Kaahumanu Ave.

Lono Ave.

Dairy Rd.

350

Alexander & Baldwin Sugar Museum

Puunene

Kahului

Kuihelani Hwy.

Mokulele Hwy.

Wailuku

Waiale Rd.

311

Honoapiilani Hwy.

380

30

Waikapu

Maui Tropical Plantation

Kealia Pond National Wildlife Preserve

To South Maui

Kealia Pond

To West Maui ↓ Maalaea

Maalaea Harbor

☂ Maalaea Beach

31

Pauwela

36

Waipio Bay

Haiku

365

360

Huelo

Makawao Hwy.

Kailua

Hana Hwy.

Keanae

Makawao

UPCOUNTRY MAUI

Pukalani

377

Koolau

Nahiku

Hana Airport ✈

Makawao Forest Reserve

Kula Hwy.

Haleakala Hwy.

Olinda

Forest

360

Hana Hwy.

☂ Waianapanapa State Park

PINE FORESTS

EAST MAUI

Hana

Pulehu

Haleakala

Reserve

37

378

Crater Rd.

Hamoa ☂

377

Kula

Hana

Waiohuli

Puu Ulaula ▲

Forest

Kakio

☂ Hamoa Beach

Science City

Haleakala National Park

Reserve

Kula Forest Reserve

Polipoli Springs State Rec. Area

Kahikinui Forest Reserve

Kipahulu Forest Reserve

31

■ Oheo Gulch

Kipahulu

31

Kaupo

Piilani Hwy.

Channel

Kailio Point

Alenuihaha

Channel

75

If you're staying in the Lahaina-Kaanapali area, transportation service is available through **Airporter Shuttle** (☎ **800/533-8765** or 808/661-6667), which runs every half hour from 9am to 4pm; the cost is $26 one-way, $56 round-trip.

If possible, avoid landing on Maui between 3 and 6pm, when the working stiffs on Maui are "pau work" (finished with work) and a major traffic jam occurs at the first intersection.

AVOIDING KAHULUI

You can avoid Kahului Airport altogether by taking an **Island Air** (☎ **800/ 323-3345**) flight to **Kapalua–West Maui Airport,** which is convenient if you're planning to stay at any of the hotels in Kapalua or at the Kaanapali resorts. If you're staying in Kapalua, it's only a 10- or 15-minute drive to your hotel; it takes 10 to 15 minutes to Kaanapali (as opposed to 35 or 40 minutes from Kahului). Island Air also flies into tiny **Hana Airport,** but you have to make a connection at Kahului to get there.

A newcomer on the interisland commuter scene is Kahului-based **Pacific Wings** (☎ **888/873-0877** or 808/575-4546; fax 808/873-7920; www.pacificwings.com), which flies eight-passenger, twin-engine Cessna 402C aircraft. They currently have flights from Kahului to Hana, Molokai, and Waimea (on the Big Island), with plans to expand to flights to Kapalua, Lanai, and Honolulu.

2 Orienting Yourself: The Lay of the Land

VISITOR INFORMATION

The **Maui Visitors Bureau** is located at 1727 Wili Pa Loop, Wailuku, Maui, HI 96793 (☎ **800/525-MAUI** or 808/244-3530; fax 808/244-1337; www.visitmaui.com). To get there from the airport, go right on Hi. 36 (the Hana Highway) to Kaahumanu Avenue (Hi. 32); follow it past Maui Community College and Wailuku War Memorial Park onto East Main Street in Wailuku; at North Market Street, turn right, and then right again on Mill Street; go left on Kala Street and left again onto Wili Pa Loop.

There are also a few regional tourist boards that can help you out. The **Kaanapali Beach Resort Association** is at 2530 Kekaa Dr., Suite 1-B, Kaanapali-Lahaina, HI 96761 (☎ **800/245-9229** or 808/661-3271; fax 808/661-9431; www.maui.net/~kbra; e-mail kbra@maui.net). The **Wailea Destination Association** is at 3750 Wailea Alanui Dr., Wailea, HI 96753 (☎ **800/78 ALOHA** or 808/879-4258; fax 808/874-5044).

THE ISLAND IN BRIEF

CENTRAL MAUI

This flat, often windy corridor between Maui's two volcanoes is where you'll most likely arrive—it's where the main airport is. It's also home to the majority of the island's population, the heart of the business community, and the local government (courts, cops, and county/state government agencies). You'll find good shopping and dining bargains on the windward side of the island, but very little in the way of accommodations.

KAHULUI   If you have a late arrival or an early departure, you can stay in "Dream City," home to thousands of former sugarcane workers who dreamed of owning their own homes away from the sugar plantations. Three small hotels located just 2 miles from the airport are convenient for 1-night stays if you have a late arrival or early departure, but we don't recommend them for your vacation headquarters on Maui.

WAILUKU   With its faded wooden storefronts, old plantation homes, shops straight out of the forties, and relaxed way of life, Wailuku is like a time capsule. Although most people race through the town on their way to see the natural beauty of **Iao Valley,** this quaint little town is worth a brief visit, if only to see a real place where real people actually appear to be working at something other than a suntan. This isn't a tourist town; it's the county seat, so you'll see men in neckties and women in dressy suits on important missions in the tropical heat. Centrally located, Wailuku is about 45 miles from the beaches, shops, and restaurants of Lahaina (in one direction) and Wailea (in the other direction). Beaches surrounding Wailuku are not great for swimming, but the old town does offer a spectacular view of Haleakala crater, a couple of hostels and one excellent historic B&B, great budget restaurants, a tofu factory, some interesting bungalow architecture, a Frank Lloyd Wright building on the outskirts of town, and the always-endearing Bailey House Museum.

WEST MAUI

This is the fabled Maui you see depicted on postcards. Jagged peaks, green velvet valleys, a wilderness full of native species—the majestic West Maui Mountains are the epitome of earthly paradise. The beaches here are some of the islands' best. And it's no secret: This stretch of coastline along Maui's "forehead," from Kapalua to the historic port of Lahaina, is the island's most bustling resort area (with South Maui close behind).

If you want to book into a resort or condo on this coast, first consider which community you'd like to base yourself in. Starting at the southern end of West Maui and moving northward, the coastal communities are as listed here:

LAHAINA   This old whaling seaport teems with restaurants, T-shirt shops, and a gallery on nearly every block, but there's still lots of real history to be found amid the gimcrack. This vintage village is a tame version of its former self, when whalers swaggered ashore in search of women and grog. The town serves as a great base for visitors: a few old hotels (like the newly restored 1901 Pioneer Inn on the harbor), quaint bed-and-breakfasts, and a handful of oceanfront condos offer a variety of accommodations to choose from. This is the place to stay if you want to be in the "center" of things: oodles of restaurants, shops, and nightlife.

KAANAPALI   Farther north along the West Maui coast is Hawaii's first master-planned family resort. Pricey mid-rise hotels line nearly 3 miles of gold-sand beach; they're linked by a landscaped parkway and separated by a jungle of plants. Golf greens wrap around the slope between beachfront and hillside properties. **Whalers Village**—a seaside mall with 48 shops and restaurants, including such fancy names as Tiffany and Louis Vuitton, plus the best little whale museum in Hawaii—and other restaurants are easy to reach on foot along the waterfront walkway or via resort shuttle, which also serves the small West Maui airport just to the north. Shuttles also go to Lahaina, 3 miles to the south, for shopping, dining, entertainment, and boat tours. Kaanapali is popular with meeting groups and families—especially those with teenagers, who will like all the action.

FROM HONOKOWAI TO NAPILI   In the building binge of the 1970s, condominiums sprouted along this gorgeous coastline like mushrooms after a rain. Today these older oceanside units offer excellent bargains for astute travelers.

The great location—along sandy beaches, within minutes of both the Kapalua and the Kaanapali resort areas, and close enough to the goings-on in the town of Lahaina—makes this area an accommodations heaven for the budget-minded.

In **Honokowai** and **Mahinahina,** you'll find mostly older units that tend to be cheaper; there's not much shopping here aside from convenience stores, but you'll have easy access to the shops and restaurants of Kaanapali (see above).

Kahana is a little more upscale than Honokowai and Mahinahina. Most of the condos here are big high-rise types, built more recently than those immediately to the south. You'll find a nice selection of shops and restaurants in the area, and Kapalua West Maui Airport is nearby.

Napili is a much-sought-after area for condo seekers: it is quiet; has great beaches, restaurants, and shops; and is close to Kapalua. Units are generally more expensive here (although we've found a few hidden gems at affordable prices; see the Napili Bay entry in chapter 6).

KAPALUA   North beyond Kaanapali and the shopping centers of Napili and Kahana, the road starts to climb and the vista opens up to fields of silver-green pineapple and manicured golf fairways. Turn down the country lane of Pacific pines toward the sea, and you could only be in Kapalua. It's the very exclusive domain of two gracious—and expensive—hotels, set on one of Hawaii's best gold-sand beaches, next to two bays that are marine-life preserves (with fabulous surfing in winter).

Even if you don't stay here, you're welcome to come and enjoy Kapalua. Both of the fancy hotels here provide public parking and beach access. The resort champions innovative environmental programs; it also has an art school (where you can learn local crafts), three golf courses, historic features, a collection of swanky condos and homes (many available for vacation rental at astronomical prices), and wide-open spaces that include a rain forest preserve—all open to the general public. Kapalua is a great place to stay put. However, if you plan to "tour" Maui, you will spend a lot of your vacation driving from this location and might want to consider a more central place to stay, because even Lahaina is a 15-minute drive away.

SOUTH MAUI

This is the hottest, sunniest, driest, most popular coastline on Maui for sun worshipers—Arizona by the sea. Rain rarely falls and temperatures stick around 85°F year-round. On former scrub land from Maalaea to Makena, where cacti once grew wild and cows grazed, are now four distinctive areas—Maalaea, Kihei, Wailea, and Makena—each appealing to a different crowd.

MAALAEA   If the western part of Maui is a head, Maalaea is just under the chin. Located directly across the isthmus from Wailuku-Kahului, this windy, oceanfront village centers around the small boat harbor (with a general store and a couple of restaurants) and the newly opened **Maui Ocean Center,** an aquarium/ocean complex. This quaint region offers several condominium units to choose from, but visitors staying here should be aware that it is often—as in 350 days a year—very windy (all the wind from the Pacific is funneled between the West Maui Mountains and Haleakala, coming out in Maalaea).

KIHEI   Kihei is less a proper town than a nearly continuous series of condos and minimalls lining South Kihei Road. This is Maui's best vacation bargain: budget travelers swarm like sun-seeking geckos over the eight sandy beaches along this scalloped, condo-packed, 7-mile stretch of coast. Kihei is neither charming nor quaint; what it lacks in aesthetics, though, it more than makes up for in sunshine, affordability, and convenience. If you want latte in the morning, beach in the afternoon, and Hawaii regional cuisine in the evening—all at budget prices—head to Kihei.

WAILEA   Only 2½ decades ago, this was wall-to-wall scrub kiawe trees; now Wailea is a manicured oasis of multimillion-dollar resort hotels situated along 2 miles of palm-fringed gold coast. It's like Beverly Hills–by-the-sea, except California never had it so good: warm, clear water full of tropical fish; year-round sunshine and clear blue skies; and hedonistic pleasure palaces on 1,500 acres of black lava shore. Amazing what a billion dollars can do.

This is the playground of the stretch-limo set. The planned resort development—practically a well-heeled town—has a shopping village, three prized golf courses of its own and three more in close range, and a tennis complex. A growing number of large homes sprawl over the upper hillside, some offering excellent bed-and-breakfast units at reasonable prices. The resorts along this fantasy coast are spectacular, to say the least. Next door to the Four Seasons, which is the most elegant, is the Grand Wailea Resort Hotel & Spa, a public display of ego by Tokyo mogul Takeshi Sekiguchi, who dropped $600 million in 1991 to create his own minicity. There's nothing like it in Hawaii, and maybe even on the planet. Stop in and take a look—it's so gauche you've gotta see it.

Appealing natural features include the coastal trail, a 3-mile round-trip path along the oceanfront with pleasing views everywhere you look—out to sea and to the neighboring islands, or inland to the broad lawns and gardens of the hotels. The trail's south end borders an extensive garden of native coastal plants, as well as ancient lava-rock house ruins juxtaposed with elegant oceanfront condos. But the chief attractions, of course, are those five outstanding beaches (the best is Wailea).

MAKENA   Suddenly, the road enters raw wilderness. After Wailea's overdone density, the thorny landscape provides welcome relief. Although beautiful, this is an end-of-the-road kind of place: it's a long drive from Makena to anywhere on Maui. If you're looking for an activity-filled vacation, you might want to book somewhere else, or spend a lot of time in your car. But if you crave a quiet, relaxing respite, where the biggest trip of the day is from your bed to the beach, Makena is your place.

Beyond Makena you'll discover Haleakala's last lava flow, which ran to the sea in 1790; the bay named for French explorer La Perouse; and a chunky lava trail known as the King's Highway, which leads around Maui's empty south shore past ruins and fish camps. Puu Olai stands like Maui's Diamond Head on the shore, where a sunken crater shelters tropical fish, and empty golden-sand beaches stand at the end of dirt roads.

UPCOUNTRY MAUI

After a few days at the beach, you'll probably take notice of the 10,000-foot mountain in the middle of Maui. The slopes of Haleakala ("House of the Sun") are home to cowboys, growers, and other country people who wave back as you drive by; they're all up here enjoying the crisp air, emerald pastures, eucalyptus, and flower farms of this tropical Olympus—there's even a misty California redwood grove. You can see a thousand tropical sunsets reflected in the windows of houses old and new, strung along a road that runs like a loose hound from Makawao, an old-paniolo-turned–New Age village, to Kula, where the road leads up to the crater and **Haleakala National Park.** The rumpled two-lane blacktop of Hi. 37 narrows on the other side of Tedeschi Winery, where wine grapes and wild elk flourish on the Ulupalakua Ranch, the biggest on Maui. A stay upcountry is usually affordable and is a nice contrast to the sizzling beaches and busy resorts below.

MAKAWAO   Until recently, this small, two-street upcountry town consisted of little more than a post office, gas station, feed store, bakery, and restaurant/bar serving the cowboys and farmers living in the surrounding community; the hitching posts outside storefronts were really used to tie up horses. As the population of Maui started expanding in the seventies, a health-food store sprung up, followed by boutiques, a chiropractic clinic, and a host of health-conscious restaurants. The result is an eclectic amalgam of old paniolo Hawaii and the baby-boomer trends of transplanted mainlanders. **Hui No'eau Visual Arts Center,** Hawaii's premier arts collective, is definitely worth a peek. The only accommodations here are reasonably priced bed-and-breakfasts, perfect for those who enjoy great views and don't mind slightly chilly nights.

KULA   A feeling of pastoral remoteness prevails in this upcountry community of old flower farms, humble cottages, and new suburban ranch houses with million-dollar views that take in ocean, isthmus, the West Maui Mountains, Lanai and Kahoolawe off in the distance, and, at night, the string of pearls that lights the gold coast from Maalaea to Puu Olai. Everything flourishes at a cool 3,000 feet (bring a jacket), just below the cloud line along a winding road on the way up to Haleakala National Park, and everyone here grows something—Maui onions, carnations, orchids, and proteas, that strange-looking blossom that looks like a *Star Trek* prop. The local B&Bs cater to guests seeking cool tropic nights, panoramic views, and a rural upland escape. Here you'll find the true peace and quiet that only rural farming country can offer—yet you're still just 30 to 40 minutes away from the beach and an hour's drive into the nightlife of Lahaina.

EAST MAUI

The Hawaii of your dreams: wild, lush jungles spilling out onto the road, thundering waterfalls, serene mountain pools, and the sweet smell of ginger wafting through the air.

ON THE ROAD TO HANA   When old sugar towns die, they usually fade away in rust and red dirt. Not Paia. A tangle of electrical, phone, and cable wires hanging overhead symbolizes the town's ability to adapt to the times—it might look messy, but it works. Here, trendy restaurants, eclectic boutiques, and high-tech windsurf shops stand next door to the ma-and-pa grocery, fish market, and storefronts that have been serving customers since the plantation days. Hippies took over in the seventies; although their macrobiotic restaurants and old-style artists' co-op have made way for Hawaii regional cuisine and galleries featuring the works of renowned international artists, Paia still manages to maintain a pleasant vibe of hippiedom. The town's main attraction, though, is Hookipa Beach Park, where the wind that roars through the isthmus of Maui brings windsurfers from around the world, who come to fly over the waves on gossamer wings linked to surfboards. A few bed-and-breakfasts are located just outside Paia in the tiny community of Kuau.

Ten minutes down the road from Paia and up the hill from the Hana Highway—the connector road to the entire east side of Maui—sits Haiku. Once a pineapple plantation village, complete with cannery (today a shopping complex), Haiku offers visitors a quiet, pastoral setting. Several vacation rentals and B&Bs tucked away in the bucolic hills overlooking the ocean make the perfect base for those who want to get off the beaten path and experience a quieter side of Maui, but don't want to feel too removed: the beach is only 10 minutes away.

About 15 to 20 minutes past Haiku is the largely unknown community of Huelo. Every day, thousands of cars whiz by on the road to Hana, but most passengers barely glance at the double row of mailboxes overseen by a fading Hawaii Visitors Bureau sign. But down the road lies a hidden Hawaii: a Hawaii of an earlier time, where Mother Nature is still sensual and wild, where ocean waves pummel soaring lava cliffs, and where an indescribable sense of serenity prevails. Huelo is not for everyone—but those who hunger for the magic of a place still largely untouched by "progress" should check into a B&B or vacation rental here.

HANA   Set between an emerald rain forest and a forever-blue Pacific is a village probably best defined by what it lacks: golf courses, shopping malls, McDonald's; except for two gas stations and a bank with an ATM, you'll find little of what passes for progress here. Instead, you'll discover the simple joys of fragrant tropical flowers, the sweet taste of backyard bananas and papayas, and the easy calm and unabashed small-town aloha spirit of Old Hawaii. What saved "Heavenly" Hana from the inevitable march of progress? The 52-mile road that winds around 600 curves and crosses more than 50 one-lane bridges that separates it from Kahului. You can go to Hana for the day—it's a 3-hour drive (and a half-century away)—but a 3-day trip is better. The tiny town has a surprising variety of accommodations, including a luxury first-class resort, a handful of great B&Bs, and some spectacular vacation rentals (where else can you stay in a tropical cabin in a rain forest?)—but be sure to read our warning on using booking agents before you plunk your money down (see page 61). Most vacation rentals and B&Bs have cooking facilities, because Hana offers limited restaurant choices.

3 Getting Around

The only way to see Maui is by rental car. There's no real island-wide public transit.

CAR RENTALS

All the major car-rental agencies are represented on Maui. Cars are usually plentiful, except on holiday weekends, which in Hawaii also means King Kamehameha Day, Prince Kuhio Day, and Admission Day (see "When to Go" in chapter 3).

The following national companies have offices on Maui, usually at both Kahului and West Maui Airports: **Alamo** (☎ 800/327-9633), **Avis** (☎ 800/321-3712), **Budget** (☎ 800/527-0700), **Dollar** (☎ 800/800-4000), **Hertz** (☎ 800/654-3011), and **National** (☎ 800/227-7368).

There also are a few frugal car-rental agencies offering used cars at discount prices. The only one that provides courtesy airport pickup is **Word of Mouth Rent-a-Used-Car** in Kahului (☎ **800/533-5929**). A four-door compact without air-conditioning costs $115 a week, plus tax; with air-conditioning, it's $130 a week, plus tax.

AA Rent-a-Dent, 1135 Makawao Ave., Makawao, HI 96768 (☎ **808/573-1722**; e-mail amariel@maui.net), has used cars from the 1980s in good condition (sorry—no air-conditioning); the weekly rate, with taxes and insurance, is $136 (drivers under 25 pay a $10 surcharge). AA Rent-a-Dent will pick you up at the airport for a $15 fee and drop you off there for $10. **LTAR,** 1992 S. Kihei Rd., Kihei, HI 96753 (☎ **808/874-4800**), rents used economy cars at a weekly rate (which allows you to keep the car for up to 11 days) of $160, plus tax, and a monthly rate of $295, plus tax. LTAR provides no airport pickup, however; you'll have to make your own way to Kihei (it's about $20 in the Speedy Shuttle van; see "Other Transportation Options," below, for details).

EASY RIDING AROUND MAUI

Don black denim and motorcycle boots and ride around Maui on a hog. Fatboys, DynaWide Glides, Softail Customs, and Road Kings—they're all for hire for $100 to $150 a day at **Island Riders** (☎ **800/529-2925**; www.islandriders.com). Forget the greasy Hell's Angels image; latter-day Wild Ones are button-down corporate types, or California Highway Patrol officers on holiday. Everybody's doing it—so get yourself a Harley for a day or more. Whether you blast up Haleakala's grand corniche or haul ass up to Hana, it's the most fun you can have on two wheels in the islands. This toy store for big boys and girls also rents exotic cars, from a Rolls Royce Corniche convertible to a red-hot Dodge Viper (exotic cars start at about $200 a day and top out around $350). Island Riders offers free pickup from most Maui hotels—convenient if you're throwing caution to the wind for just a day (half-day rentals are available, too).

MOPEDS

Mopeds are available for rent from **Rental Warehouse,** 578 Front St. (near Prison Street), Lahaina (☎ **808/661-1970**), and in Azeka Place II, on the mountain side of Kihei Road (near Lipoa Street), Kihei (☎ **808/875-4050**), starting at $19 a day. Mopeds are little more than motorized bicycles that get up to around 35mph (with a good wind at your back), so we suggest using them only locally (to get to the beach or to go shopping). Don't take them out on the highway, because they can't keep up with the traffic.

DRIVING AROUND MAUI

Maui has only a handful of major roads: one follows the coastline around the two volcanoes that form the island, Haleakala and Puu Kukui; one goes up to Haleakala's summit; one goes to Hana; one goes to Wailea; and one goes to Lahaina. It sounds simple, right? Well, it isn't, because the names of the few roads change en route. Study the island map on page 74 before you set out; you might also consult the foldout map in the back of this book.

TRAFFIC ADVISORY   The road from Central Maui to Kihei and Wailea, Mokulele Highway (Hi. 35), is a dangerous strip that's often the scene of head-on crashes involving intoxicated and speeding drivers; be careful. Also, be alert on the Honoapiilani Highway (Hi. 30) en route to Lahaina, since drivers who spot whales in the channel between Maui and Lanai often slam on the brakes and cause major tie-ups and accidents.

If you get in trouble on Maui's highways, look for the flashing blue strobe lights on 12-foot poles; at the base are emergency, solar-powered call boxes (programmed to dial 911 when you pick up the handset). There are 29 emergency call boxes on the island's busiest highways and remote areas, including along the Hana and Haleakala highways and on the north end of the island in the remote community of Kahakuloa.

Another Traffic Note: Buckle up your seat belt—Hawaii has stiff fines for noncompliance.

OTHER TRANSPORTATION OPTIONS

TAXIS   For island-wide 24-hour service, call **Alii Taxi** (☎ 808/661-3688 or 808/667-2605). You can also try **Kihei Taxi** (☎ 808/879-3000), **Wailea Taxi** (☎ 808/874-5000), or **Yellow Cab of Maui** (☎ 808/877-7000) if you need a ride.

SHUTTLES **SpeediShuttle** (☎ 808/875-8070) can take you between Kahului Airport and all the major resorts from 5am to 9pm daily (for details, see "Getting To & From the Aiport" under "Arriving," above).

Free shuttle vans operate within the resort areas of Kaanapali, Kapalua, and Wailea; if you're staying in those areas, your hotel can fill you in on exact routes and schedules.

Maui Trolley, a San Francisco–style trolley-on-wheels, offers shuttle-bus service from some 13 hotels in South Maui's Wailea-Kihei area to the West Maui commercial centers of Lahaina and Kaanapali, four times a day; the first hotel pickup is at the Maui Makena Prince Hotel at 9am. The cost is $15 from the South Maui hotels to West Maui ($10 for teenagers and $7.50 for children 12 and under) with unlimited reboarding; $5 for the return trip from West Maui to Kihei-Wailea ($3 for teenagers and $2 for children 12 and under); and $2 for rides from one hotel to another in the Kihei-Wailea area. For more information, call ☎ **800/824-8804.**

FAST FACTS: Maui

American Express For 24-hour traveler's check refunds and purchase information, call ☎ **800/221-7282.** Local offices are located in South Maui, at the **Grand Wailea Resort** (☎ 808/875-4526), and in West Maui, at the **Ritz-Carlton Kapalua** (☎ 808/669-6016) and the **Westin Maui** at Kaanapali Beach (☎ 808/661-7155).

Area Code All of the Hawaiian Islands are in the **808** area code. You must dial 1-808 if you're calling one island from another, and you will be billed at long-distance rates (which can be more expensive than calling the mainland).

Business Hours Most offices open at 8am and close by 5pm. The morning commute usually runs from 6 to 8am, and the evening rush is from 4 to 6pm. Many people work at two or three jobs and drive their children to and from private schools, which creates extra traffic. Bank hours are Monday through Thursday from 8:30am to 3pm, Fridays from 8:30am to 6pm. Some banks are open on Saturdays. Shopping centers are open Monday through Friday from 10am to 9pm, Saturdays from 10am to 5:30pm, and Sundays from noon to 5 or 6pm.

Dentists Emergency dental care is available at Maui Dental Center, 162 Alamaha St., Kahului (☎ **808/871-6283**).

Doctors No appointment is necessary at **West Maui Healthcare Center,** Whaler's Village, 2435 Kaanapali Pkwy., Suite H-7 (near Leilani's Restaurant), Kaanapali (☎ 808/667-9721; fax 808/661-1584), which is open 365 days a year, nightly until 10pm. In Kihei, call **Kihei Physicians,** 1325 S. Kihei Rd., Suite 103 (at Lipoa Street, across from Star Market), Kihei (☎ 808/879-7781), open daily from 8am to 7pm; doctors are on call 24 hours a day.

Driving Rules See "Getting There & Getting Around," in chapter 3.

Electricity Like the rest of the United States, Hawaii's electric power is 110 volts, 60 cycles.

Emergencies Dial ☎ **911** for police, fire, or ambulance. District stations are located in Lahaina (☎ **808/661-4441**) and in Hana (☎ **808/248-8311**).

Hospitals For medical attention, go to **Maui Memorial Hospital,** in Central Maui at 221 Mahalani, Wailuku (☎ 808/244-9056); East Maui's **Hana Medical Center,** on Hana Highway (☎ 808/248-8924); or **Kula Hospital,** in upcountry Maui at 204 Kula Hwy., Kula (☎ 808/878-1221).

Legal Aid Call the Legal Aid Society of Hawaii, 2287 Main St., Wailuku, HI 96793 (☎ **808/244-3731**).

Liquor Laws The legal drinking age in Hawaii is 21.

Newspapers The *Honolulu Advertiser* and the *Honolulu Star Bulletin* are circulated statewide. The *Maui News* is the island's daily paper.

Poison Control Center In an emergency, call ☎ **800/362-3585.**

Post Offices To find the nearest post-office branch, call ☎ **800/ASK-USPS.** In Lahaina, there are branches at the Lahaina Civic Center, 1760 Honoapiilani Hwy., and at the Lahaina Shopping Center, 132 Papalaua St.; in Kahului, there's a branch at 138 S. Puunene Ave.; and in Kihei, there's one at 1254 S. Kihei Rd.

Radio & TV Honolulu has a score of radio stations that broadcast in English, Hawaiian, Japanese, and Filipino throughout the islands. The most popular stations are KHPR (88.1 or 90.7 FM), the National Public Radio station; KGU (760 AM), for news and talk radio; KUMU (94.7 FM), for easy listening; and KSSK (590 AM), the pop-music station and the top morning-drive DJs.

All major Hawaiian islands are equipped with cable TV and receive major mainland network broadcast programs, which local stations delay by several hours so that they will appear during "prime time" in Hawaii's time zone. This delay includes sports events, so fans who want to follow their teams "live" should seek out establishments with satellite dishes. CNN is the prime source of 24-hour news.

Safety Although Hawaii is generally a safe tourist destination, visitors have been crime victims, so stay alert. The most common crime against tourists is rental car break-ins. Never leave any valuables in your car, not even in your trunk. Thieves can be in and out of your trunk faster than you can open it with your own keys. Especially be leery of high-risk areas such as beaches and resort areas. Also, never carry large amounts of cash with you. Stay in well-lighted areas after dark. Don't hike on deserted trails alone.

Smoking It's against the law to smoke in public buildings, including airports, grocery stores, retail shops, movie theaters, banks, and all government buildings and facilities. Hotels have nonsmoking rooms available, restaurants have nonsmoking sections, and car-rental agencies have nonsmoking cars. Most bed-and-breakfasts prohibit smoking inside their buildings.

Taxes Hawaii's sales tax is 4%. Hotel occupancy tax is 6%, and hoteliers are allowed by the state to tack on an additional .001666% excise tax. Thus, expect taxes of about 10.17% to be added to every hotel bill.

Telephone Hawaii's telephone system operates like any other state's. Long-distance calls can be directly dialed to the islands from the U.S. mainland and from most foreign countries. The international country code is 1, the same as for the rest of the United States and for Canada. Local calls costs 25¢ at a pay phone. Interisland calls are billed at the same rate as long distance. Hotels add a surcharge on local, interisland, mainland, and international calls.

Time   Hawaii Standard Time is in effect year-round. Hawaii is 2 hours behind Pacific standard time and 5 hours behind Eastern standard time. In other words, when it's noon in Hawaii, it's 2pm in California and 5pm in New York during standard time on the mainland. There's no daylight savings time here, so when daylight savings time is in effect on the mainland, Hawaii is 3 hours behind the West Coast and 6 hours behind the East Coast—so in summer, when it's noon in Hawaii, it's 3pm in California and 6pm in New York.

Hawaii is east of the international date line, putting it in the same day as the U.S. mainland and Canada, and a day behind Australia, New Zealand, and Asia.

Weather Reports   For the current weather, call ☎ **808/871-5054;** for Haleakala National Park weather, call ☎ **808/572-9306;** for marine weather and surf and wave conditions, call ☎ **808/877-3477.**

6

Accommodations

by Jeanette Foster

Maui has accommodations to fit every kind of dream vacation, from luxury oceanfront suites and historic B&Bs to reasonably priced condos that will sleep a family of four. Before you book, be sure to read "The Island in Brief" under the section "Orienting Yourself: The Lay of the Land" in chapter 5, which will help you decide on your ideal location; also check out "Tips on Accommodations" in chapter 3.

We've divided this section not only by geographic area, but also by the dent it will make in your pocketbook. For those dream vacations in which money is no object, look in the **Very Expensive** category, where rooms begin at more than $275 a night. For those in search of dream vacations within some spending limits, the **Expensive** category lists accommodations where rates start at $175 to $275 a night. For a vacation that won't mean taking out a second mortgage, look at the **Moderate** category, where rates start at $100 to $175 a night. For those on a frugal budget, check out the good buys in the **Inexpensive** category, with rates under $100 a night. Combined within these categories are a variety of accommodations: hotels, vacation rentals, bed-and-breakfast units, apartments, condominium units, and even hostels.

Remember to consider *when* you will be traveling to the islands. Hawaii has two seasons—high and low. The highest season, during which rooms are always booked and rates are at the top end, runs from mid-December to March. The second "high" season, when rates are high but bookings are somewhat easier, is summer, June to September. The low season, with fewer tourists and cheaper rates—and sometimes even "deals" on rooms—is April to June and September to mid-December.

Finally, remember to add Hawaii's 10.17% accommodations tax to your final bill. Parking is free unless otherwise noted.

1 Central Maui

KAHULUI

If you are arriving late at night or have an early morning flight out, the best of Kahului Airport's nearby hotels is the **Maui Seaside Hotel,** 100 Kaahumanu Ave. (near Lono Avenue), Kahului, HI 96732 (☎ **800/367-7000** or 808/877-3311). The rooms are small and somewhat dated, but they're clean and cheap ($80 to $140 double), and some come with kitchenettes. Otherwise, try the **Maui Beach Hotel,** 170 Kaahumanu Ave. (Hi. 32, at Hi. 340), Kahului, HI 96732 (☎ **800/367-5004** or 808/ 877-0051), which has nondescript, motel-like rooms ($90 to $110 double) and free airport shuttle service. These places are OK for a night, but don't bother spending more time in Kahului than you have to.

WAILUKU
MODERATE

✪ **Old Wailuku Inn at Ulupono.** 2199 Kahookele St. (at High St., across from the Wailuku School), Wailuku, HI 96732. ☎ **800/305-4899** or 808/244-5897. Fax 808/242-9600. E-mail: Mauibandb@aol.com. 11 units. A/C TV TEL. $120–$180 double. Rates include gourmet breakfast. Extra person $20. AE, MC, V.

This 1924 former plantation manager's home, lovingly restored by innkeepers Janice and Thomas Fairbanks, offers a genuine Old Hawaii experience. Inspired by Hawaii's poet laureate, Don Blanding, the theme is Hawaii of the 1920s and 1930s, with decor, design, and landscaping to match.

The guest rooms are wide and spacious—reminiscent of a day when land was cheap and building material affordable—with exotic ohia wood floors, high ceilings, and traditional Hawaiian quilts gracing the beds. The mammoth bathrooms (some with clawfoot tubs, some with Jacuzzis) have plush towels and "earth friendly" toiletries on hand. A full gourmet breakfast is served on the enclosed back lanai or delivered to your room if you prefer. You'll feel right at home lounging on the generously sized living-room sofa, or watching the world go by from an old wicker chair on the lanai.

Located in the old historic area of Wailuku, the inn is just a few minutes' walk from the Maui County seat, the state building, the courthouse, and a wonderful stretch of antiques shops. It's fully equipped to handle business travelers, with automated message service, modem jacks, and multiple phones in each room; fax and copy services and computers are available for guest use.

INEXPENSIVE

Backpackers might want to head for **Banana Bungalow Maui,** a funky Happy Valley hostel at 310 North Market St., Wailuku, HI 96793 (☎ **800/846-7835** or 808/244-5090; fax 808/244-3678; www.home1.gte.net/bungalow/bungalow.htm; e-mail bungalow@pac.get.net), with dorms ($14.50 per person) plus some private rooms ($36.50 double). Dorm-style accommodations ($15 dorm, $40 double) are also available at the **Northshore Inn,** in old Wailuku town, at 2080 Vineyard St., Wailuku, HI 96793 (☎ **808/242-8999;** fax 808/244-5004). Note, however, that women traveling alone might not feel safe in either of these areas after dark.

2 West Maui

LAHAINA
MODERATE

If you dream of an oceanfront condo but your budget is on the slim side, also consider **Lahaina Roads,** 1403 Front St. (reservations c/o Klahani Travel, 505 Front St., Lahaina, HI 96761; ☎ **800/669-MAUI** or 808/667-2712; fax 808/661-5875; e-mail robyn@maui.net), which offers small, reasonably priced units in an older building in the quiet part of town ($100 one-bedroom, $180 two-bedroom; 3-night minimum).

✪ **Aston Maui Islander.** 660 Wainee St. (between Dickenson and Prison sts.), Lahaina, HI 96761. ☎ **800/367-5226** or 808/667-9766. Fax 808/661-3733. 372 units. A/C TV TEL. High season $92 double, $105–$114 studio with kitchenette, $125 one-bedroom with kitchen, $182 two-bedroom with kitchen; low season $82 double, $95–$104 studio with kitchenette, $115 one-bedroom with kitchen, $172 two-bedroom with kitchen. Extra person $6; children 17 and under stay free using existing bedding. AE, CB, DC, DISC, JCB, MC, V.

These units are one of Lahaina's great buys—especially the kitchenette units; the larger ones are great for families on a budget. This wooden complex isn't on the beach, but it is on a quiet side street (a rarity in Lahaina) and within walking distance of restaurants, shops, attractions, and, yes, the beach (it's just 3 blocks away). All of the good-sized rooms, decorated in tropical-island style, are comfortable and quiet. The entire complex is spread across 10 landscaped acres and includes tennis courts (with lights for night play until 10pm), a pool, a sundeck, a barbecue, and a picnic area. The aloha-friendly staff will be happy to take the time to answer all of your questions.

Best Western Pioneer Inn. 658 Wharf St. (in front of Lahaina Pier), Lahaina, HI 96761. ☎ **800/457-5457** or 808/661-3636. Fax 808/667-5708. E-mail: pioneer@maui.net. 50 units. A/C TV TEL. $99–$159 double. Extra person $15. AE, CB, DC, DISC, MC, V. Parking $4 in lot 2 blocks away.

This historic hotel has come a long way from its origins as a turn-of-the-century whaler's saloon and inn. Until the 1970s, a room at the Pioneer Inn overlooking Lahaina Harbor went for $20 and included a can of Raid insect repellent; the honky-tonk bar downstairs went until the wee hours of the morning, so no one slept. But those days are long gone—and this old waterfront hotel has never looked better. At the end of 1997, it became a Best Western, and the finishing touches of its restoration were completed.

This once-rowdy home-away-from-home for sailors and whalers now seems almost respectable, like visiting your great-grandma's house—old but nice, even charming (a word never before associated with this relic). The hotel is a two-story plantation-style structure with big verandas that overlook the streets of Lahaina and the harbor. All the rooms are totally remodeled with vintage baths and new curtains and carpets; they even have TVs, VCRs, and direct-dial phones now. There are a new outdoor pool, three restaurants, the historic whalers' saloon (without the honky-tonk music), 20 shops, and the Lahaina Harbor just 50 feet away. The quietest rooms face either the garden courtyard—devoted to refined outdoor dining accompanied by live (but quiet) music—or the block-square banyan tree next door. We recommend room no. 47, over the banyan court, with a view of the ocean and the harbor. If you want a front-row seat for all the Front Street action, book no. 48.

House of Fountains Bed & Breakfast. 1579 Lokia St. (off Fleming Rd., north of Lahaina town), Lahaina, HI 96761. ☎ **800/789-6865** or 808/667-2121. Fax 808/667-2120. www.maui.net/~private/home. E-mail: private@maui.net. 6 units (private bathrooms with shower only). A/C TV. $85–$125 double. Rates include full breakfast. Extra person $15. AE, DISC, MC, V. From Hi. 30, take Fleming Rd. exit; turn left on Ainakea; in 2 blocks, turn right on Malanai St.; go 3 blocks, and turn left onto Lokia St.

Talk about escape: A young German couple ran away to Maui for their honeymoon, fell in love with the island, bought a big house above Lahaina, and turned it into one of the area's best B&Bs. Their 7,000-square-foot contemporary home, in a quiet residential subdivision at the north end of town, is very popular with visitors from around the world. This place is immaculate (hostess Daniela Clement provides daily maid service). The oversized rooms are fresh and quiet, with white ceramic tile

Lahaina & Kaanapali Accommodations

Aloha Lani Inn **17**
Aston Maui Islander **13**
Best Western Pioneer Inn **14**
Garden Gate B&B **9**
Guest House **9**
House of Fountains B&B **9**
Hyatt Regency Maui **8**
Kaanapali Beach Hotel **4**
Lahaina Inn **11**
Lahaina Roads **10**
Lahaina Shores Beach
  Resort **15**
Maui Eldorado Resort **2**
Maui Marriott Resort **7**
Old Lahaina House **16**
Plantation Inn **12**
Puamana **18**
Royal Lahaina Resort **1**
Sheraton Maui **3**
Wai Ola Vacation Paradise **9**
Westin Maui **6**
The Whaler on Kaanapali
  Beach **5**

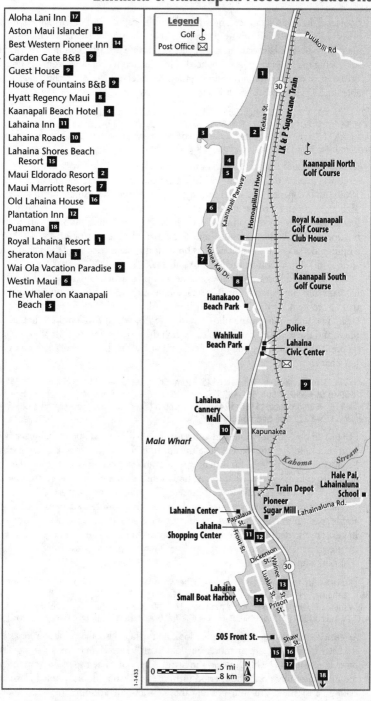

Legend
Golf
Post Office ⊠

Puukolii Rd

LK & P Sugarcane Train

Kaanapali North
Golf Course

Royal Kaanapali
Golf Course
Club House

Kaanapali South
Golf Course

Hanakaoo
Beach Park

Police

Wahikuli
Beach Park

Lahaina
Civic Center

Lahaina
Cannery
Mall

Kapunakea

Mala Wharf

Kahoma Stream

Hale Pai,
Lahainaluna
School

Train Depot

Pioneer
Sugar Mill

Lahaina Center

Lahainaluna Rd.

Lahaina
Shopping Center

Dickenson St.

Lahaina
Small Boat Harbor

505 Front St.

Shaw St.

Prison St.

Luakini St.

Wainee St.

Front St.

Papalaua St.

Honoapiilani Hwy.

Kekaa St.

Kaanapali Parkway

Nohea Kai Dr.

0   .5 mi
     .8 km

N

1-1433

floors, bright tropical fabrics, and wicker furnishings; the four downstairs rooms all open onto flower-filled private patios. Guests share a pool, Jacuzzi, well-equipped guest kitchen, and barbecue area, and you're welcome to curl up on the living-room sofa facing the fireplace (not really needed in Lahaina) with a book from the library. Breakfast is served in the sunny dining room. Self-service laundry facilities are available for $2. The nearest beach is about 10 minutes away.

✪ **Lahaina Inn.** 127 Lahainaluna Rd. (near Front St.), Lahaina, HI 96761. ☎ **800/ 669-3444** or 808/661-0577. Fax 808/667-9480. 12 units (most bathrooms have shower only). A/C TEL. $89–$149 double. Rates include continental breakfast. Children under 14 not accepted. AE, DISC, JCB, MC, V. Next-door parking $5.

If the romance of historic Lahaina catches your fancy, a stay here will really underscore the experience. Built in 1938 as a general store, swept by fire in the mid-1960s, and reopened as a hotel in the 1970s, this place deteriorated into a fleabag with an eyesore of a bar at street level. Then, in 1986, rescue came in a classy way: it was saved from extinction by Rick Ralston, the Waikiki airbrush artist who became the Crazy Shirts mogul—and a one-man historic restoration society. About a million dollars of T-shirt money has brought this place back to life as a charming, antique-filled inn right in the heart of Lahaina.

If you like old hotels that have genuine historic touches, you'll love this place. As in many old hotels, some of these Victorian antique–stuffed rooms are small; if that's a problem for you, ask for a larger unit. All come with a private bathroom and lanai. The best room in the house is no. 7 ($99), which overlooks the beach, the town, and the island of Lanai; you can watch the action below or close the door and ignore it. Downstairs is one of Hawaii's finest bistros, David Paul's Lahaina Grill (see chapter 7).

Lahaina Shores Beach Resort. 475 Front St. (near Shaw St.), Lahaina, HI 96761. ☎ **800/628-6699** or 808/661-4835. Fax 808/661-4696. 151 units. A/C TV TEL. High season $130–$165 studio double, $180–$245 one-bedroom (sleeps up to 4); low season $120–$145 studio, $155–$215 one-bedroom. AE, MC, V.

Lahaina Shores is affordable and convenient. What's special about this place is its location: right on the beach, just outside the rowdy, trafficky central core of Lahaina. It's a catbird seat for watching whales and ships coming and going, day and night, from Lahaina's busy harbor. Although the beach here isn't the greatest on the coast, it's just a short walk down the street to a good swimming beach.

The roomy, individually owned condo units come with full kitchens, VCRs, and ample space, plus daily maid service and a concierge; laundry facilities are available. In general, the bathrooms are small, but they do the job. There's a pool and spa off the newly renovated lobby. Shops and restaurants are right next door at the 505 Front St. complex.

✪ **Plantation Inn.** 174 Lahainaluna Rd. (between Wainee and Luakini sts., 1 block off Hi. 30), Lahaina, HI 96761. ☎ **800/433-6815** or 808/667-9225. Fax 808/667-9293. www.maui.net/~inn/. E-mail: inn@maui.net. 18 units (some bathrooms have shower only). A/C TV TEL. $135–$215 double. Rates include full breakfast. AE, CB, DC, DISC, JCB, MC, V.

Attention, romance-seeking couples: look no further. This charming inn looks like it's been here 100 years or more, but looks can be deceiving: the Victorian-style hotel is actually of 1990s vintage—an artful deception. The rooms are romantic to the max, tastefully done with period furniture, hardwood floors, stained glass, and ceiling fans; there are four-poster canopy beds and armoires in some rooms, brass beds and wicker in others. All come equipped with soundproofing (a plus in Lahaina), TV, VCR, fridge, private bathroom, and lanai; the suites have kitchenettes. The rooms wrap around the large pool and deck. Also on the property are a spa and an elegantly decorated pavilion lounge, as well as Gerard's, an excellent French restaurant (see chapter 7). It can be pricey, but hotel guests get a discount on dinner (you'll kick yourself if you don't eat here). Breakfast is served around the pool and in the pavilion lounge; ours featured fresh fruit, followed by a choice of Gerard's French toast or his homemade yogurt and granola.

Puamana. Front St. (at the extreme southern end of Lahaina, 1/2 mile from downtown), P.O. Box 11108, Lahaina, HI 96760. ☎ **800/669-6284** or 808/667-2712. Fax 808/661-5875. E-mail: robyn@maui.com. 40 units. TV TEL. $100–$175 one-bedroom double, $140–$250 two-bedroom, $300–$350 three-bedroom. 3-night minimum. AE, MC, V.

These 28 acres of town houses situated right on the water are the ideal choice for those who want the option of retreating from the crowds and cacophony of downtown Lahaina into the serene quiet of an elegant neighborhood. Private and peaceful are apt descriptions for this complex: each unit is an individual home, with no neighbors above or below. These town houses are all privately owned (most are exquisitely decorated), and they come with full kitchens, TVs, at least two bathrooms, lanais, and barbecues. There are three pools (one for adults only), a tennis court, table tennis, and on-site laundry facilities (some units have washers and dryers as well). Puamana was once a private estate in the 1920s, part of the sugar plantation that dominated Lahaina; the plantation manager's house has been converted into a clubhouse with oceanfront lanai, library, card room, sauna, and office.

Wai Ola Vacation Paradise on Maui. Kuuipo St. (P.O. Box 12580), Lahaina, HI 96761. ☎ **800/492-4652** or 808/661-7901. Fax 808/661-7901. www.maui.net/~tai/WaiOla.html. E-mail: tai@maui.net. 3 units. A/C TV TEL. $95 studio, $100 suite, $115 one-bedroom apt. Extra person $15. 5-night minimum high season, 3-night minimum low season. AE, DISC, MC, V.

Just 2 blocks from the beach, in a quiet, residential development behind a tall concrete wall, lies Hawaii's version of Shangri-la: shade trees, sitting areas, gardens, a pool, an ocean mural, and a range of accommodations—a suite inside the 5,000-square-foot home, a separate studio cottage, and a one-bedroom apartment. Hostess Julie Frank owned and operated Julie's Bed-and-Breakfast in Half Moon Bay, California, for years; as a veteran innkeeper, she knows how to provide comfortable accommodations and memorable vacations. The Kuuipo (Sweetheart) Suite comes complete with deck and sweeping views of the Lahaina coastline. Downstairs, just off the pool, hot tub, and deck, is the 1,000-square-foot one-bedroom apartment with full kitchen, queen bed, sofa bed, private phone, TV/VCR, and air-conditioning. The 500-square-foot studio cottage, located in the courtyard, has a full kitchen and tasteful white wicker furniture. Guests have full access to the pool, barbecue facilities, and outdoor wet bar.

INEXPENSIVE

Also consider value-priced **Old Lahaina House** (☎ **800/847-0761** or 808/667-4663; fax 808/667-5615; www.mauiweb.com/maui/olhouse/), which features comfy twin- and king-bedded doubles for $69 to $95.

Aloha Lani Inn—A Maui Guest House. 13 Kauaula Rd. (at Front St.), Lahaina, HI 96761. ☎ **800/57-ALOHA** or 808/661-8040. Fax 808/661-8045. www.maui.net/~tony/index.html. E-mail: tony@maui.net. 3 units (all with shared bathroom). $65–$69 double. Extra person $10. 2-night minimum. AE, MC, V.

ⓕ Family-Friendly Accommodations

If you're traveling with the kids, you'll be welcomed with open arms at many of Maui's accommodations. Our favorite family-friendly choices on the island are listed below. Note that by state law, hotels that offer supervised activity programs can accept only children ages 5 to 12.

Our Favorite: Four Seasons Resort Wailea *(see p. 113)* This is the most kid-friendly hotel on Maui. The complimentary "Kids for All Seasons" program (open year-round, daily from 9am to 5pm) features a range of activities, from sand sculpturing to kite flying. The resort goes out of its way to make the keikis feel welcome with such amenities as complimentary milk and cookies on the first day, children's menus in all restaurants (including room service), complimentary infant needs (crib, stroller, high chair, playpen, car seats, and more), and complimentary child-safety features (like toilet-seat locks, plug covers, and security gates). The resort can also prepurchase a range of necessities (such as diapers and baby food) for you before your arrival. Kids and teens have a huge list of recreational activities and equipment to choose from, including a game room (with Super Nintendo, Sony PlayStation, foosball, billiards, and more); a complimentary scuba clinic (for ages 12 and older); children's videos; and a host of sailing, snorkeling, and whale-watching activities.

WEST MAUI

Hale Kai *(see p. 100)* This small condo complex in Honokowai is ideally located for families: right on the beach, next door to a county park, and within a 10-minute drive of Lahaina's shops, restaurants, and attractions. Kids can hang out at the pool, swim in the ocean, or play in the park next door. There are a TV and a VCR in every unit, and the well-equipped kitchens (with dishwasher, disposal, microwave, even a blender) allow Mom and Dad to save money on eating out.

Hyatt Regency Maui *(see p. 96)* The Camp Hyatt program, for hotel guests only, operates daily from 9am to 3pm and offers a range of activities from "Olympic Games" to a scavenger hunt. The cost is $65, which includes lunch and snacks. The Camp also has nightly activities (from 6 to 10pm) such as table games, movies, and video games. The cost is $12 per hour, per child, and includes light snacks and refreshments.

Kaanapali Beach Hotel *(see p. 97)* The Kalo Patch Kids Program is offered to hotel guests only, Tuesday through Saturday from 8:30am to 1:30pm. The wide range of activities offered ranges from making Hawaiian crafts to riding on the Kaanapali Train. The cost is $15 per child.

If you're on a fixed budget and don't mind sharing a bathroom, this clean, casual B&B, just a block from the beach, is the place for you. Host Melinda Mower, who took over the operation formerly known as Aloha Tony's in June 1996, has livened up the place with tropical and floral interior decor. The entire house is guest-friendly: the living room is stuffed with books on the flora, fauna, history, and marine life of the islands, along with menus from dozens of nearby restaurants; all the drawers and cabinets in the communal kitchen are labeled with their contents; a map of Maui pinpoints great things to do; and loads of brochures are available to help you plan your stay. The guest rooms are small, but the location is dynamite: a stone's throw from the beach and within walking distance of downtown Lahaina

Maui Park *(see p. 101)* Located directly across the street from Honokowai Beach Park, the roomy apartments at this three-story complex are a good value for families. Extras include a large swimming pool, a jet spa, and barbecue and picnic areas.

Noelani Condominium Resort *(see p. 102)* If your kids love to swim, head to this Kahana condominium on the ocean. Right next door is great snorkeling at a sandy cove that's frequented by spinner dolphins and turtles in summer and humpback whales in winter. On-site are two freshwater swimming pools (one heated for night swimming). The units feature complete kitchens, entertainment centers, and spectacular views.

Ritz-Carlton Kapalua *(see p. 105)* The Ritz Kids is a year-round daytime activity center that features both educational activities (from exploring the ecosystems in streams to learning the hula) and sports (from golf to swimming). The cost for the program is $60 for a full day (non–Ritz-Carlton guests pay $75), which includes lunch and a T-shirt, and $40 for a half day (non–Ritz-Carlton guests pay $55).

SOUTH MAUI

Koa Resort *(see p. 109)* Right across the street from the ocean in Kihei, this deluxe condo complex is great for active families: on-site are two tennis courts, a swimming pool, a hot tub, and an 18-hole putting green. The spacious, privately owned one-, two-, and three-bedroom units are fully equipped and have plenty of room for even a large brood.

Mana Kai Maui Resort *(see p. 111)* This eight-story complex, an unusual combination of hotel and condominium, sits on a beautiful white-sand cove in Kihei that's one of the best snorkeling beaches on Maui's south coast. Families should consider the condo units, which feature full kitchens and open living rooms; sliding-glass doors lead to small lanais overlooking the sandy beach and ocean.

UPCOUNTRY MAUI

Nohona Laule'a *(see p. 121)* If you have children who need space to run and you don't want to worry about them bothering the neighbors, book this two-bedroom cottage on the slopes of Haleakala. The 700-square-foot cottage has open-beam ceilings, skylights, a complete kitchen, a huge deck with views, and 4 open acres—plenty of room for the kids to play and make as much noise as they want.

(no parking woes), yet in a quiet residential neighborhood. A continental breakfast is available for $3, or you're welcome to fix your own.

Garden Gate Bed & Breakfast. 67 Kaniau Rd. (across from Waihiku Park, north of Lahaina town), P.O. Box 12321, Lahaina, HI 96760. ☎ **808/661-8800.** Fax 808/667-7999. E-mail: ggbb@maui.net. 3 units. TV TEL. $60–$95 double. Rates include continental breakfast. Extra person $15. 3-night minimum. AE, MC, V. Take Fleming Rd. off Hi. 30, turn left on Ainakea, then right on Kaniau Rd.

This oasis of a B&B is located in a quiet residential area outside Lahaina. Hosts Wilmoet and Ron Glover, both working artists, have poured their talents into this place. Guests enter the main house and studio through an enchanting garden with a fountain. Our favorite room is the garden studio, a 500-square-foot room with private entrance and lanai, sitting area, full kitchen, and sleeper sofa—it's comfortable for as many as four to five people. Each of the two rooms in the house comes with private bathroom, small refrigerator, fan, and air-conditioning. At $55, the Molokai Room is a great deal for budget travelers. The Sea View Room offers a bit more luxury, with private entrance and queen-size platform bed.

Guests staying in the main house wake up to a continental breakfast, which is served in the dining room or outdoors on the deck overlooking the garden. Wilmoet fills the studio's kitchen with everything guests need to prepare their own morning repast, from eggs to Kona coffee, and delivers freshly baked bread each morning.

✪ **Guest House.** 1620 Ainakea Rd. (off Fleming Rd., north of Lahaina town), Lahaina, HI 96761. ☎ **800/621-8942** or 808/661-8085. Fax 808/661-1896. www.ourworld. compuserve.com/homepages/guesthouse. E-mail: guesthouse@compuserve. 5 units (1 unit shares a bathroom with hosts). A/C TV TEL. $59–$89 double. Rates include full breakfast. Extra person $15. AE, DISC, MC, V. Take Fleming Rd. off Hi. 30; turn left on Ainakea; house is 2 blocks down.

This is one of Lahaina's great bed-and-breakfast deals: a charming house with more amenities than the expensive Kaanapali hotels just down the road a piece. The roomy home features parquet floors, floor-to-ceiling windows, and a pool—surrounded by a deck and comfortable lounge chairs—that's larger than some at high-priced condos. Every guest room is air-conditioned and has a ceiling fan, small fridge, TV, and private phone; four of the rooms each have a quiet lanai and a romantic hot tub. The large kitchen (with every gadget imaginable) is available for guests' use. The Guest House also operates Trinity Tours and offers discounts on car rentals and just about every island activity.

KAANAPALI
VERY EXPENSIVE

In addition to those listed below, other options to consider include the **Royal Lahaina Resort,** 2780 Kekaa Dr., Lahaina, HI 96761 (☎ **800/44-ROYAL** or 808/661-3611; fax 800/432-9752 or 808/661-6150)—but skip the overpriced hotel rooms; stay here only if you can get one of the 122 cottages tucked among the well-manicured grounds ($295 to $385 double). If you aren't looking for something uniquely Hawaiian and you like the Marriott chain's style, consider the **Maui Marriott Resort,** 100 Nohea Kai Dr., Lahaina, HI 96761 (☎ **800/228-9290** or 808/667-1200; fax 808/667-8181; www.travelweb.com), where doubles run from $280 to $328.

✪ **Sheraton Maui.** 2605 Kaanapali Pkwy., Lahaina, HI 96761. ☎ **800/STAY-ITT** or 808/ 661-0031. Fax 808/661-9991. www.sheraton-maui.com. 510 units. A/C TV TEL. $290–$465 double, from $575 suite. Extra person $40; children 17 and under stay free using existing bedding. AE, CB, DC, DISC, MC, V. Valet parking $8, self-parking $5.

Terrific facilities for families and fitness buffs and a premier beach location make this beautiful resort an all-around great place to stay. The first to set up camp in Kaanapali (in 1963), the hoteliers took the best location on the beach: the curving white-sand cove next to Black Rock (a lava formation that rises 80 feet above the beach), where they built into the side of the cliff. The grand dame of Kaanapali Beach reopened in April 1997 after a $160 million, 2-year renovation; the resort is virtually new, with six buildings of six stories or less set in well-established tropical gardens. The lobby has been elevated to take advantage of panoramic views, and a new lagoon-like pool features lava-rock waterways, wooden bridges, and an open-air spa.

The new emphasis is on family appeal, with a class of rooms dedicated to those traveling with children (665-square-foot units with two double beds and a pull-down wall bed) and other kid-friendly amenities. Every room is outfitted with all the comforts that make for easy travel—from minifridges and free Kona coffee for the coffeemakers to irons, hair dryers, and even toothbrushes and toothpaste. Other pluses include a "no hassle" check-in policy, in which the valet takes you and your luggage straight to your room—no time wasted standing in line at registration.

But not everything has changed, thankfully. Cliff divers still swan-dive off the torch-lit lava-rock headland in a traditional sunset ceremony—a sight to see. And the views of Kaanapali Beach, with Lanai and Molokai in the distance, are some of the best in Kaanapali.

Dining/Diversions: Three restaurants, with cuisine ranging from teppanyaki to steaks and seafood, plus a snack bar and three bars and cocktail lounges to choose from.

Amenities: Nightly cliff-diving show, free summer children's program, in-room dining from 6:30am to 10:30pm (delivery guaranteed in 30 minutes or less), valet laundry, baby-sitting, express checkout, in-house doctors' office. Two pools, three tennis courts, conference facilities, activities desk. A fitness center, game center, full beach services, 24-hour coin-op laundry, and hospitality suite for early arrivals or late departures extend the usual list of Kaanapali features: golf, tennis, ocean sports, shopping, and the beach.

Westin Maui. 2365 Kaanapali Pkwy., Lahaina, HI 96761. ☎ **800/228-3000** or 808/667-2525. Fax 808/661-5831. 793 units. A/C MINIBAR TV TEL. $265–$495 double, from $800 suite. Special wedding/honeymoon and other packages available. Extra person $30 ($50 in Royal Beach Club rooms). AE, DC, DISC, ER, JCB, MC, V. "Resort fee" of $6 for such amenities as free local phone calls, use of fitness center, complimentary coffee and tea, free parking, and free local paper.

The "Aquatic Playground"—an 87,000-square-foot pool area with five free-form heated pools joined by swim-through grottoes, waterfalls, and a 128-foot-long water slide—sets this resort apart from its peers along Kaanapali Beach. Thanks to megahotelier Christopher Hemmeter, who waved his magic wand over the property in the late 1980s, this is the Disney World of water-park resorts—and your kids will be in water-hog heaven.

The fantasy theme extends from the estate-like grounds into the interior's public spaces, which are filled with the shrieks of tropical birds and the splash of waterfalls; the oversized architecture, requisite colonnade, and $2 million art collection make a pleasing backdrop for all of the action. Guests seem to love it: the resort has taken top honors in various readers' surveys, from *Condé Nast Traveler* to *Travel & Leisure*. With lots of indoor and outdoor meeting spaces, it's also a big hit with wedding parties and groups.

The majority of the rooms (refurbished in 1995) in the two 11-story towers overlook the aquatic playground, the ocean, and the island of Lanai in the distance. In addition to the standard features, each comes with a safe, an ironing board and iron, a coffeemaker, and its own lanai. The top-floor Royal Beach Club rooms feature a hospitality lounge and special amenities.

Dining/Diversions: Several outdoor restaurants and lounges, ranging from a sushi bar to a seafood buffet, take advantage of the casual mood and balmy weather. The Sound of the Falls features an elegant Sunday brunch amid flamingos and the sound of waterfalls.

Amenities: Twice-daily maid service; nightly turndown; multilingual staff; American Express and Hertz desks; secretarial services. Guest Services will help you plan sightseeing and activities. Extensive health club and spa facilities. Extensive supervised kids' program weekdays. Five pools, Jacuzzi, aquacise classes, scuba lessons for beginners and refresher courses; guided outdoor adventure hikes. Coin-op laundry, ATM, and hospitality suite for early check-ins and late departures. Beauty salon, retail shops, business center, conference facilities. Golf, tennis, and shopping are all at hand. A wedding coordinator, known as the Director of Romance, can help you throw an unforgettable wedding.

EXPENSIVE

Hyatt Regency Maui. 200 Nohea Kai Dr., Lahaina, HI 96761. ☎ **800/233-1234** or 808/661-1234. Fax 808/667-4714. 815 units. A/C MINIBAR TV TEL. $260–$495 double, from $600 suite. Packages available. Extra person $25 ($45 in Regency Club rooms); children 18 and under stay free using existing bedding. AE, DC, DISC, JCB, MC, V. Valet parking $8, free self-parking.

People either absolutely love this fantasy resort or hate it. One of several built by Christopher Hemmeter for Hyatt in the 1980s, this hotel—the southernmost of the Kaanapali properties—has lots of imaginative touches: a collection of exotic species (flaming pink flamingos, unhappy-looking penguins, and an assortment of loud parrots and macaws in the lobby), nine waterfalls, and an eclectic Asian and Pacific art collection. This huge place covers some 40 acres; even if you don't stay here, you might want to walk through the expansive tree-filled atrium and the park-like grounds, with their dense riot of plants and fantasy pools with grottoes, slides, and a suspended walking bridge. There's even a man-made beach in case the adjacent public beach is just too crowded.

All the rooms are pleasantly decorated in rich colors, floral prints, and Asian lamps—a welcome change from the typical beiges—and feature separate sitting areas and private lanais. In-room extras include safes, hair dryers, coffeemakers, and irons and ironing boards.

Dining/Diversions: Swan Court is a romantic setting for dinner; its rollaway walls open wide to let in the moonlight, and diners sit beside a waterfall pool where black and white swans cruise for handouts. Steaks and seafood are served in the open-air Lahaina Provisions Company, whereas Spats serves Italian fare; the Pavilion is a casual poolside choice. The "Drums of the Pacific" dinner show keeps things rolling at night. In addition to numerous lounges, the cool pool has a swim-up bar for cocktails.

Amenities: Twice-daily maid service; concierge; room service; activity desk; baby-sitting on request. Two Regency Club floors have private concierge, complimentary breakfast, sunset cocktails, and snacks. Camp Hyatt kids' program offers daytime and evening supervised activities for 3- to 12-year-olds. Special programs include a rooftop astronomy program. In addition to the Great Pool, there's a health club with weight and exercise rooms, Jacuzzi, sauna, and massage studio; six hard-surface tennis courts; three nearby golf courses; game room; and a small lending library. Snorkeling gear, bicycles, kayaks, boogie boards, and video and underwater cameras are available for rent. *Kiele V,* the Hyatt's 55-foot catamaran, sponsors snorkel trips, whale-watching excursions, and evening cruises.

✪ **Maui Eldorado Resort.** 2661 Kekaa Dr., Lahaina, HI 96761. ☎ **800/688-7444** or 808/661-0021. Fax 808/667-7039. www.outrigger.com. E-mail: reservations@outrigger.com. 98 units. AC TV TEL. High season $175–$200 studio double, $220–$250 one-bedroom (sleeps up to 4), $285–$325 three-bedroom (sleeps up to 6); low season $160–$185 studio, $200–$255 one-bedroom, $285–$325 three-bedroom; spring/fall, $150–$175 studio, $185–$210 one-bedroom, $260–$290 three-bedroom. Numerous packages available, including 1 night free with 7-night stay, car packages, senior rates, and more. AE, CB, DC, DISC, JCB, MC, V.

These spacious condominium units—all with full kitchens, washer/dryers, and daily maid service—were built at a time when land in Kaanapali was cheap, contractors took pride in their work, and visitors expected large, spacious units with views from every window. You'll find it hard to believe that this was one of Kaanapali's first properties in the late 1960s—this first-class choice looks like new. The Outrigger chain has managed to keep prices down to reasonable levels, especially if you come in spring or fall. This is a great place for families, with its big units, grassy areas that are perfect for running off excess energy, and beachfront that's usually safe for swimming.

Amenities: Daily maid service, travel desk, fax services, personal safe. Three pools, beach cabana, barbecue areas, shops, laundry facilities.

✪ **The Whaler on Kaanapali Beach.** 2481 Kaanapali Pkwy. (next to Whalers Village), Lahaina, HI 96761. ☎ **800/367-7052** or 808/661-4861. Fax 510/939-6644. www.ten-io.com/vri. 360 units; 150 in rental pool. A/C TV TEL. High season $195–$205 studio double, $250–$380 one-bedroom (sleeps up to 4), $415–$495 two-bedroom (sleeps up to 6); low season $195–$205 studio double, $230–$350 one-bedroom, $360–$470 two-bedroom. Extra person $15; crib $10. 2-night minimum. Packages available. AE, MC, V.

Location, location, location—in the heart of Kaanapali, right on the world-famous beach, lies this oasis of elegance, privacy, and luxury. The relaxing atmosphere strikes you as soon as you enter the open-air lobby, where light reflects off the dazzling koi in the meditative lily pond. No expense has been spared on these gorgeous accommodations; all have full kitchens, washer/dryers, marble bathrooms, 10-foot beamed ceilings, and blue-tiled lanais. Add to that daily maid service, in-room safes, pool and spa, exercise room, tennis, and a rarity in Kaanapali these days: free parking. Every unit boasts spectacular views, which include vistas of both Kaanapali's gentle waves and the humpback peaks of the West Maui Mountains.

Dining/Diversions: Next door is Whalers Village, where you'll find Peter Merriman's terrific Hula Grill (see chapter 7) and a handful of other restaurant and bar choices.

Amenities: Daily maid service, pool and spa, exercise room, five tennis courts. The Kaanapali Golf Club's 36 holes are across the street, and all the ocean activities Maui has to offer are just out back.

MODERATE

Kaanapali Beach Hotel. 2525 Kaanapali Pkwy., Lahaina, HI 96761. ☎ **800/262-8450** or 808/661-0011. Fax 808/661-5978. www.kaanapalibeachhotel.com. 433 units. A/C TV TEL. $150–$235 double, from $210 suite. Extra person $25. Free car, bed-and-breakfast, golf, and romance packages available, as well as discount rates for seniors. AE, CB, DC, DISC, JCB, MC, V.

This old beach hotel, set in a garden by the sea, is Maui's most genuinely Hawaiian place to stay—you live aloha here.

This isn't a luxury property, but it's not bad, either. Three low-rise wings are set around a wide, grassy lawn with coco palms and a whale-shaped swimming pool, bordering a fabulous stretch of beach. The spacious, spotless motel-like rooms are done in wicker and rattan, with Hawaiian-style bedspreads and a lanai that looks toward the courtyard and the beach. The beachfront rooms are separated from the water only by Kaanapali's landscaped walking trail.

The Kaanapali is older and less high-tech than its upscale neighbors, but it has an irresistible local style and a real Hawaiian warmth that are absent in many other Maui hotels. Old Hawaii values and customs are always close at hand, and in true aloha style, the service is some of the friendliest around. Tiki torches, hula, and

Hawaiian music create a festive atmosphere in the expansive open courtyard every night. As part of the hotel's extensive Hawaiiana program, you can learn to cut pineapple, weave *lauhala,* and even dance the *real* hula; there are also an arts-and-crafts fair 3 days a week, a morning welcome reception weekdays, and a Hawaiian library.

The hotel's three restaurants feature native Hawaiian dishes as well as modern Hawaiian cuisine; there's also a poolside bar that fixes a mean piña colada. Amenities include concierge, coin-op laundry, in-room movies, and ice, drink, and snack machines, as well as baby-sitting, a United Airlines desk, free scuba and snorkeling lessons, convenience shops and salon, conference rooms, beach-equipment rentals, and access to tennis and Kaanapali golf.

FROM HONOKOWAI TO NAPILI
VERY EXPENSIVE

Embassy Suites. 104 Kaanapali Shores Pl. (in Honokowai), Lahaina, HI 96761. ☎ **800/ 669-3155** or 808/661-2000. Fax 808/661-1353. www.maui.net/~embassy. E-mail: embassy@maui.net. 413 units. A/C TV TEL. $260–$400 one-bedroom suite (sleeps up to 4), $550 two-bedroom suite (sleeps up to 4). Rates include full breakfast and 2-hour cocktail party daily. Extra person $20; children 18 and under stay free using existing bedding. AE, CB, DC, DISC, MC, V. Parking $5. Take the first turn off Hwy. 30 after Kaanapali on Lower Honoapiilani Rd.; turn left at Kaanapali Shores Pl.

Welcome to kid-heaven. The all-suite property features a mammoth 1-acre pool with a 24-foot water slide, a great beach for swimming and snorkeling, and complete entertainment centers in every unit that will satisfy even the surliest teenager: 35-inch TV (with HBO), VCR (there's a vast video library on-site), and stereo system. With roomy condo-like suites (ranging from 820 to 1,100 square feet) that feature hotel-style amenities, all-you-can-eat breakfasts, and free daily cocktail parties included in the price, Mom and Dad will be happy, too.

You can't miss this place: the shockingly pink pyramid-shaped building is visible from the highway. It's composed of three towers, each set around a central atrium amidst tropical gardens with interlocking waterfalls and waterways; a huge wooden deck overlooks the koi-filled ponds and streams.

Every unit has a full-sized sofa bed, a good-sized lanai, a minikitchen (microwave, small fridge with ice maker, wet bar, and coffeemaker with free Kona coffee), two phones, a soaking tub big enough for two in the bathroom, and a second TV in the bedroom.

Dining/Diversions: There are three on-site dining choices: the oceanfront North Beach Grille, the poolside Ohana Bar and Grill, and a sandwich/snack bar, The Deli Planet.

Amenities: Concierge, laundry facilities, dry cleaning, tour desk, children's program (during holidays and in summer). Pool, health club, Jacuzzi, sauna, sundeck, 18-hole minigolf. Kaanapali's shops, golf, tennis, and restaurants are just minutes away.

EXPENSIVE

Families might want to consider the **Sands of Kahana,** 4299 Lower Honoapiilani Rd., in Kahana (☎ **888/669-0400** or 808/669-1199; fax 808/669-8409; www.sands-of-kahana.com; e-mail vacation@maui.net). Despite the austere appearance of the high-rise buildings, these condo units offer many amenities for those traveling with children, including pools and a playground ($165 to $225 one-bedroom, $220 to $280 two-bedroom, $275 to $335 three-bedroom; 5-night minimum).

Accommodations from Honokowai to Kapalua

Embassy Suites **21**
Hale Kai **17**
Hale Maui Apt. Hotel **16**
Honokeana Cove **9**
Hoyochi Nikko **15**
Kahana Sunset **10**
Kaleialoha **14**
Kapalua Bay Hotel **3**
Kapalua Villas **2**
Mauian on Napili Bay **5**
Maui Park **18**
Maui Sands **19**
Napili Bay **7**
Napili Kai Beach Club **4**
Napili Sunset **6**
Napili Surf Beach
    Resort **8**
Noelani Condominium
    Resort **12**
Papakea **20**
Polynesian Shores **13**
Ritz-Carlton Kapalua **1**
Sands of Kahana **11**

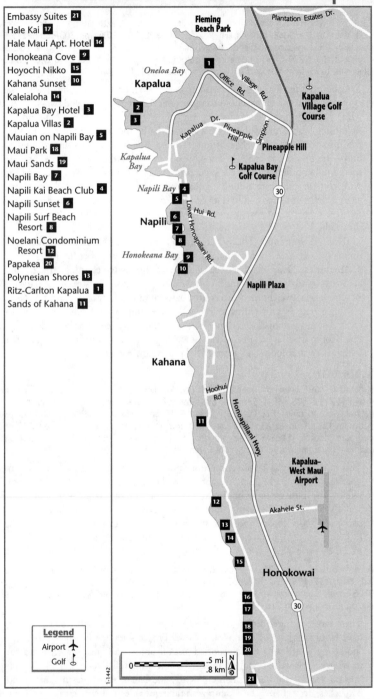

○ **Napili Kai Beach Club.** 5900 Honoapiilani Rd. (at the extreme north end of Napili, next door to Kapalua), Lahaina, HI 96761. ☎ **800/367-5030** or 808/669-6271. Fax 808/669-0085. www.napilikai.com. E-mail: nkbc@maui.net. 162 units. TV TEL. $170–$265 double studio, $270–$550 one-bedroom suite (sleeps up to 4), $270–$550 two-bedroom (sleeps up to 6). Extra person $10. Packages available. AE, MC, V.

Just south of the Bay Club restaurant in Kapalua, nestled in a small white-sand cove, lies this comfortable oceanfront complex. Clusters of one- and two-story units with double-hipped Hawaii-style roofs face their very own gold-sand safe-swimming beach; many units have a view of the Pacific, with Molokai and Lanai in the distance. The older beachfront Lahaina Building units—with ceiling fans only—are a good buy at $215. Those who prefer air-conditioning should book into the Honolua Building—for the same price, you'll get a fully air-conditioned room set back from the shore around a grassy park-like lawn and pool. All units (except eight hotel rooms) have fully stocked kitchenettes with full-sized refrigerator (with ice maker), cooktop stove, microwave, toaster oven, and coffeemaker; some have dishwashers.

Dining/Diversions: The Sea House Restaurant serves breakfast, lunch, and dinner (see chapter 7); the Whale Watcher's Bar takes care of cocktails.

Amenities: Daily maid service, laundry facilities, dry cleaning, free children's activities (available Easter, June 15 to August 31, and Christmas), activity desk. Beach pagoda, two shuffleboard courts, barbecue areas, four pools, and two 18-hole putting greens. Nearby tennis courts; golf just minutes away. Complimentary beach chairs, mats, swim masks, and snorkels; complimentary tennis rackets and golf putters. Complimentary coffee at the beach pagoda every morning, free tea in the lobby every afternoon, and a free Mai Tai party once a week.

MODERATE

Hale Kai. 3691 Lower Honoapiilani Rd. (in Honokowai), Lahaina, HI 96761. ☎ **800/446-7307** or 808/669-6333. Fax 808/669-7474. www.halekai.com. E-mail: halekai@halekai.com. 40 units. TV TEL. High season $110 one-bedroom double, $140–$145 two-bedroom (sleeps up to 4), $180 three-bedroom (sleeps up to 6); low season $95 one-bedroom double, $125–$130 two-bedroom, $180 three-bedroom. Extra person $10; children 3 and under stay free. 3-night minimum. MC, V.

This small, two-story condo complex is ideally located, right on the beach and next door to a county park; shops, restaurants, and ocean activities are all within a 6-mile radius. The units are older but in excellent shape, and they come with a full kitchen and TV/VCR. Many guests clamor for the oceanfront pool units; but we find the park-view units cooler, and they still have ocean views (upstairs units also have cathedral ceilings). Book early, because units fill up fast; repeat guests make up most of the clientele.

Honokeana Cove. 5255 Lower Honoapiilani Rd. (in Napili), Lahaina, HI 96761. ☎ **800/237-4948** or 808/669-6441. Fax 808/669-8777. 33 units. A/C TV TEL. $105 one-bedroom double, $147 two-bedroom (sleeps up to 4), $175 three-bedroom (sleeps up to 6). Extra person $10–$15. 3-night minimum. MC, V.

These large, secluded units—cozily set around a pool in a lush tropical setting—have fabulous views of Honokeana Cove. The cobblestone beach is excellent for snorkeling—turtles have been spotted just offshore—and great for whale watching in winter. The well-appointed units all come with full kitchens, TVs (including Spectra Vision at no extra charge), VCRs, and lanais. Amenities include laundry, barbecues, deck chairs, and a ramp with railing that leads down to that great beach. All in all, a well-priced option in an expensive neighborhood.

⊙ **Kahana Sunset.** 4909 Lower Honoapiilani Rd. (at the northern end of Kahana, almost in Napili), c/o P.O. Box 10219, Lahaina, HI 96761. ☎ **800/669-1488** or 808/669-8011. Fax 808/669-9170. E-mail: sun2set@maui.net. 49 units; 29 in rental pool. A/C TV TEL. High season $160–$180 one-bedroom (sleeps up to 6), $165–$265 two-bedroom (sleeps up to 6); low season $120–$160 one-bedroom, $140–$200 two-bedroom. 3-night minimum. AE, MC, V. From Hwy. 30, turn makai (toward the ocean) at the Napili Plaza (Napilihau St.), then left on Lower Honoapiilani Rd.

Lying in the crook of a sharp horseshoe curve on Lower Honoapiilani Road is this series of wooden condo units, stair-stepping down the slide of a hill to a postcard-perfect white-sand beach. The unique location, nestled between the coastline and the road above, makes Kahana Sunset a very private place to stay. A small pool and Jacuzzi sit in the midst of a grassy lawn; down by the sandy beach are gazebos and picnic areas. The units feature full kitchens, washer/dryers, large lanais with terrific views, and sleeper sofas. This is a great complex for families: the beach out front is safe for swimming, the grassy area is away from traffic, and the units are roomy enough for all. The two-bedroom units have parking just outside, making carrying luggage and groceries that much easier.

Maui Park. 3626 Lower Honoapiilani Rd. (in Honokowai), Lahaina, HI 96761. ☎ **800/367-5004** or 808/669-6622. Fax 800/477-2329 or 808/669-9647. 288 units. A/C TV TEL. High season $109 double room, $129–$135 double studio, $145–$155 one-bedroom (sleeps up to 4), $189 two-bedroom (sleeps up to 6); low season $99 double room, $109–$115 double studio, $125–$135 one-bedroom, $169 two-bedroom. Extra person $17. AE, DC, DISC, MC, V.

Directly across the street from Honokowai Beach Park, this three-story, six-building complex offers a haven for families. The property features a large pool, a jet spa, and barbecue and picnic areas; a convenience store is just next door, and coin-op laundry facilities are on-site. The large, roomy units all come with balconies and kitchens. There are no elevators, but wheelchair-accessible rooms are available on the ground level.

Maui Sands. Maui Resort Management, 3600 Lower Honoapiilani Rd. (in Honokowai), Lahaina, HI 96761. ☎ **800/367-5037** or 808/669-1902. Fax 808/669-8790. www.mauigetaway.com. E-mail: getaway@maui.net. 76 units. A/C TV TEL. $85–$130 one-bedroom (sleeps up to 3), $115–$160 two-bedroom (sleeps up to 5). Extra person $9. 7-night minimum. MC, V.

The Maui Sands was built back when property wasn't as expensive and developers took the extra time and money to surround all their condo units with lush landscaping. It's hard to get a unit with a bad view: all face either the ocean (with views of Lanai and Molokai) or tropical gardens blooming with brilliant heliconia and sweet-smelling ginger. Each roomy unit has a big lanai and full kitchen. With two big bedrooms plus space in the living room for a fifth person (or even a sixth), the larger units are good deals for families. There are a narrow beach out front and a pool and laundry facilities on-site. In case you have any problems or questions, the management agency is just across the street.

Mauian on Napili Bay. 5441 Lower Honoapiilani Rd. (in Napili), Lahaina, HI 96761. ☎ **800/367-5034** or 808/669-6205. Fax 808/669-0129. E-mail: Mauian@maui.net. 44 units. High season $145–$175 double, low season $125–$155 double. Extra third or fourth person $10 each. AE, DISC, MC, V.

The Hawaiian family who built this low-rise hotel in 1961 now own it once again, and they've restored the studio units to their original Old Hawaiian style. This is a good choice to get away from it all: the Mauian is perched above a beautiful half-mile-long white-sand beach with great swimming and snorkeling in the turquoise waters just offshore; there's a pool with chaise lounges, umbrellas, and tables on the sundeck; and the verdant grounds are bursting with tropical color. The renovated rooms feature hardwood floors, Indonesian-style furniture, and big lanais with great views. Return guests have been drawn back for more than 3 decades by the small touches, such as the fresh flowers welcoming visitors upon arrival (plus chilled champagne for those celebrating a special occasion) and the "Breakfast with the Manager" every Thursday. There are no phones or TVs in the rooms (this place truly is about getting away from it all), but the large Ohana (family) room does have a TV, a VCR, and an extensive library for those who can't bear the solitude, plus complimentary coffee; phones and fax service are available in the business center. Great restaurants are just a 5-minute walk away, Kapalua Resort is right up the street, and the nightly sunsets off the beach are spectacular.

Napili Surf Beach Resort. 50 Napili Pl. (off Lower Honoapiilani Rd. in Napili), Lahaina, HI 96761. ☎ **800/541-0638** or 808/669-8002. Fax 808/669-8004. www.napilisurf.com. 53 units (some with shower only). TV TEL. $95–$152 studio double, $152–$199 one-bedroom double. Extra person $20; children 6 and under stay free. 5-night minimum. No credit cards.

This well-maintained, superbly landscaped complex has a great location on Napili Beach. Facilities include two pools, three shuffleboard courts, and three gas barbecue grills. The well-furnished units were renovated in 1997, and free daily maid service—a rarity in condo properties—keeps the units clean. Management encourages socializing: in addition to weekly Mai Tai parties and coffee socials, the resort hosts annual shuffleboard and golf tournaments, as well as get-togethers on July 4th, Thanksgiving, Christmas, and New Year's. Many guests arrange their travel plans around these events at the Napili Surf.

✪ **Noelani Condominium Resort.** 4095 Lower Honoapiilani Rd. (in Kahana), Lahaina, HI 96761. ☎ **800/367-6030** or 808/669-8374. Fax 808/669-7904. www. noelani-condo-resort.com. E-mail: noelani@maui.net. 50 units. TV TEL. $97–$107 studio double, $120 one-bedroom (sleeps up to 3), $167 two-bedroom (sleeps up to 4), $197 three-bedroom (sleeps up to 6). Rates include continental breakfast on first morning. Extra person $10; children under 12 stay free. Packages for honeymooners, seniors, and AAA members available. 3-night minimum. AE, MC, V.

This oceanfront condo is a great value, whether you stay in a studio or a three-bedroom unit (ideal for large families). The top-notch property is AAA-approved and, after extensive exterior and interior renovations, has just been awarded a three-diamond designation. Everything is first class, from the furnishings to the oceanfront location, with a sandy cove next door at the new county park. There's good snorkeling off the cove, which is frequented by spinner dolphins and turtles in the summer and humpback whales in the winter. All units feature full kitchens, entertainment centers, and spectacular views. Our favorites are in the Antherium building, where the one-, two-, and three-bedrooms have oceanfront lanais just 20 feet from the water. There are two freshwater swimming pools (one heated for night swimming) and an oceanfront Jacuzzi. Guests are invited to a continental breakfast orientation on their first day, and Mai Tai parties at night.

Polynesian Shores. 3975 Lower Honoapiilani Rd. (in Mahina Beach, near Kahana), Lahaina, HI 96761. ☎ **800/433-6284** or 808/669-6065. Fax 808/669-0909. 32 units. TV TEL. $100–$110 one-bedroom double, $115–$125 two-bedroom double, $165 two-bedroom (sleeps up to 4), $185 three-bedroom (sleeps up to 4). Extra person $10; children under 4 stay free using existing bedding. 3-night minimum. DISC, MC, V.

Every unit in this complex—from the cheapest to the most expensive—has a private lanai with ocean view. Floor-to-ceiling sliding-glass doors provide an open, airy feel. The units we inspected had new rattan furnishings and fully equipped kitchens (even down to a blender). In the midst of the 2-acre, well-maintained grounds sits a large heated pool; a redwood deck with barbecue facilities is situated at water's edge. Ocean-oriented guests can snorkel right offshore or walk down to a nearby sandy beach for great swimming. If you're coming to Maui from Honolulu, you're best off flying into Kapalua West Maui Airport; it's just 2 minutes from the complex. If forced to choose, we'd probably call the Noelani Condominium Resort (see above) first, but we'd gladly stay here too.

INEXPENSIVE

In addition to the choices listed below, also consider **Hoyochi Nikko,** 3901 Lower Honoapiilani Rd. (in Honokowai), Lahaina, HI 96761 (☎ **800/487-6002** or 808/669-8343; fax 808/669-3937), which features just 17 one- and two-bedroom units sharing 180 feet of oceanfront; the units are older, but well maintained and outfitted with everything you could want ($85 to $105 double, 1-week minimum). If you seek privacy but still want to get the inside scoop on surrounding activities, try the **Hale Maui Apartment Hotel,** 3711 Lower Honoapiilani Hwy., in Honokowai (☎ **808/669-6312;** fax 808/669-1302), where one-bedroom apartments go for $65 to $95 double. Frugal travelers should also consider the **Kaleialoha,** 3785 Lower Honoapiilani Rd. (in Honokowai), Lahaina, HI 96761 (☎ **800/ 222-8688** or 808/669-8197; fax 808/669-2502; e-mail dwhipple@maui.net), offering recently upgraded condo units; studios with mountain views are cheapest ($75 studio double, $90 to $100 one-bedroom double, 3-night minimum).

❍ Napili Bay. 33 Hui Dr. (off Lower Honoapiilani Hwy.), in Napili). Reservations c/o Maui Beachfront Rentals, 256 Papalaua St., Lahaina, HI 96767. ☎ **888/661-7200** or 808/ 661-3500. Fax 808/661-5210. www.involved.com/baldys/napili.htm. E-mail: maui-pru@ maui.net. 33 units. TV TEL. $58–$75 double. 5-night minimum. MC, V.

One of Maui's best secret bargains is this small, two-story complex, located right on Napili's half-mile white-sand beach. Couples in search of a romantic getaway, look no further. The atmosphere here is comfortable and relaxing; the ocean lulls you to sleep at night; and birdsong wakes you in the morning. The beach here is one of the best on the coast, with great swimming and snorkeling—in fact, it's so beautiful that people staying at much more expensive resorts down the road frequently haul all their beach paraphernalia here for the day. The compact studio apartments have everything you need to feel at home, from full kitchens (including microwave, coffeemaker, toaster, blender, and more) to big TVs, comfortable queen beds, and roomy lanais that are great for watching the sun set over the Pacific. Louvered windows and ceiling fans keep the units cool during the day. Our favorite is no. 201, a corner unit with fabulous views and a king bed.

Within walking distance of restaurants and a convenience store, the complex is just a mile from a shopping center, 10 minutes from world-class golf and tennis, and 15 minutes from Lahaina town. A resident on-site manager is a walking encyclopedia of information on where to go and what to do while you're on Maui. All this for as little as $58 a night—unbelievable! Book early, and tell 'em Frommer's sent you.

Napili Sunset. 46 Hui Rd. (in Napili), Lahaina, HI 96761. ☎ **800/447-9229** or 808/ 669-8083. Fax 808/669-2730. www.napilisunset.com. E-mail: info@napilisunset.com. 42 units. TV TEL. High season $95 studio double, $185 one-bedroom double, $265 two-bedroom (sleeps up to 4); low season $75 studio, $159 one-bedroom , $219 two-bedroom. Extra person $12; children under 3 stay free. 3-night minimum. MC, V.

Housed in three buildings (two on the ocean and one across the street) and located just down the street from Napili Bay (see above), these clean, older but well-maintained units offer good value. At first glance, the plain two-story structures don't look like much, but the location, the bargain prices, and the friendly spirit of the staff are the real hidden treasures here. In addition to daily maid service, the units all have free in-room safes, full kitchens (with dishwasher), ceiling fans, sofa beds in the living room, small dining rooms, and small bedrooms. Laundry facilities are on-site (you provide the quarters, they provide the free laundry soap). The beach—one of Maui's best—can get a little crowded, because the public beach access is through this property (and everyone on Maui seems to want to come here). The studio units are all located in the building off the beach and a few steps up a slight hill; they're good-sized, with complete kitchens and either a sofa bed or a queen Murphy bed, and they overlook the small swimming pool and garden. The one- and two-bedroom units are all on the beach (the downstairs units have lanais that lead right to the sand). The staff makes sure each unit has the basics—paper towels, dishwasher soap, coffee filters, condiments—to get your stay off to a good start.

Papakea. Maui Resort Management, 3600 Lower Honoapiilani Rd. (in Honokowai), Lahaina, HI 96761. ☎ **800/367-5037** or 808/669-1902. Fax 808/669-8790. www. mauigetaway.com. E-mail: getaway@maui.net. 28 units. TV TEL. $80–$100 studio double, $100–$150 one-bedroom (sleeps up to 4), $120–$189 two-bedroom (sleeps up to 6). Extra person $9. 7-night minimum. MC, V.

Just a mile down the beach from Kaanapali lie these low-rise buildings, surrounded by manicured, landscaped grounds and ocean views galore. Palm trees and tropical plants dot the property, a putting green wraps around two kidney-shaped pools, and a foot bridge arches over a lily pond brimming with carp. Each pool has its own private cabana with sauna, Jacuzzi, and barbecue grills; a poolside shop rents snorkel gear for exploring the offshore reefs. As if that weren't enough, there are three private tennis courts on the grounds for guests' use. All units have big lanais, dishwashers, and washer/dryers. The studios have pull-down beds to save space during the day. Definitely a value property.

KAPALUA
VERY EXPENSIVE

Kapalua Bay Hotel. 1 Bay Dr., Kapalua, HI 96761. ☎ **800/367-8000** or 808/669-5656. Fax 808/669-4694. www.kapaluabayhotel.com. 209 units. A/C MINIBAR TV TEL. $275–$525 double, $400–$550 villa suite, from $800 one- and two-bedroom suite. Extra person $50; children 17 and under stay free using existing bedding. AE, CB, DC, JCB, MC, V.

When we visited this hotel in fall 1997, it had just reopened after a year of complete restoration and was still in the "shakedown" phase of operations. We expect to see great things here, because the management consultant is no other than the Halekulani Corporation, of Waikiki's Halekulani, one of Hawaii's finest luxury hotels.

Few Hawaiian resorts have the luxury of open space like this one. It sits seaward of 23,000 acres of green fields lined by spiky Norfolk pine windbreaks. The 1970s-style rectilinear building sits down by the often windy shore, full of angles that frame stunning views of ocean, mountains, and blue sky. The tastefully designed maze of oversized rooms fronts a palm-fringed gold-sand beach that's one of the best in Hawaii, as well as an excellent Ben Crenshaw golf course. Each guest room has a sitting area with a sofa, a king or two double beds, and an entertainment center; plantation-style shutter doors open onto private lanais with a view of Molokai across the channel. The renovated bathrooms feature two granite vanities, a large soaking tub, and a glass-enclosed shower.

The one- and two-bedroom villas are situated on the ocean at the very private Oneloa Bay. Each one has several lanais, a full kitchen, a washer/dryer, ceiling fans, an oversized tub, and access to three swimming pools with cabanas and barbecue facilities.

Dining: The most appealing dining spot is The Bay Club (see chapter 7), in its own plantation-style building overlooking the sea, specializing in seafood for lunch and dinner. The casual Gardenia Court serves breakfast, lunch, and dinner.

Amenities: 24-hour room service; twice-daily maid service; ice service every afternoon and on request; resort shuttle; complimentary transfer to Kapalua–West Maui Airport; secretarial services; baby-sitting services. Two pools, exercise facility, a famous trio of golf courses (each with its own pro shop). Ten Plexi-pave tennis courts for day and night play (villa guests have access to two additional tennis courts). Kamp Kapalua, for kids ages 5 to 12, offers activities ranging from snorkeling and surfing to lei making and cookie baking. Adults can plan similar activities through the hotel's Beach Activity Center. The Kapalua Shops are within easy walking distance.

✪ **Ritz-Carlton Kapalua.** 1 Ritz-Carlton Dr., Kapalua, HI 96761. ☎ **800/262-8440** or 808/669-6200. Fax 808/665-0026. www.kapaluamaui.com. 598 units. A/C MINIBAR TV TEL. $260–$595 double, from $495 suite. Extra person $40 ($80 in Club Floor rooms). Wedding/honeymoon and other packages available. AE, DC, DISC, MC, V. Valet parking $10, free self-parking.

Of all the Ritz-Carltons in the world, this is probably the best. It's in the best place (Hawaii) near the best beach (Kapalua), and it's got a friendly staff who go above and beyond the call of duty to make sure that your vacation is a dream come true.

The Ritz is a complete universe, one of those resorts where you can sit by the pool with a book for 2 whole weeks. It rises proudly on a knoll, in a singularly spectacular setting between the rain forest and the sea. During construction, the remains of hundreds of early Hawaiians were discovered buried in the sand, so the hotel was moved inland to avoid disrupting the graves. The setback improved the hotel's outlook, which now has a commanding view of Molokai.

The style is fancy plantation, elegant but not imposing. The public spaces are open, airy, and graceful, with plenty of tropical foliage and landscapes by artist Sarah Supplee that recall the not-so-long-ago agrarian past. Rooms are up to the usual Ritz standard, outfitted with marble baths, private lanais, in-room fax capability, and voice mail. Hospitality is the keynote here; you'll find the exemplary service you expect from Ritz-Carlton seasoned with good old-fashioned Hawaiian aloha.

Dining/Diversions: Dining is excellent at the Anuenue Room (also great for elegant Sunday brunch), the outdoor Terrace (for breakfast and dinner), and poolside (for lunch). Whether you prefer your gourmet fare regular or macrobiotic, it'll be memorable, thanks to executive chef Patrick Callarec and crew. It's a small hike to the beach, so fortunately the Beach House serves daytime drinks and light fare. Cocktails are served in the Lobby Lounge, which doubles as an espresso bar in the morning. A new pool bar serves drinks by the three pools.

Amenities: 24-hour room service, twice-daily towels, nightly turndowns; private club floors with concierge, continental breakfast, afternoon drinks, private lounge, and other extras. Airport and golf shuttle, secretarial services, daily kids' programs, lei greetings, multilingual employees. Three top-rated golf courses, tennis complex, three pools, nine-hole putting green, croquet lawn, beach volleyball, fitness center and salon, guests-only full-day guided backcountry hikes, and a historic plantation-style wedding chapel. Meeting facilities and ballrooms accommodate incentives winners and groups.

EXPENSIVE

Golfers and families will like the upscale **Kapalua Villas,** 500 Office Rd., Kapalua, HI 96761 (☎ **800/545-0018** or 808/669-8088; fax 808/669-5234; www.kapaluavillas.com), which come fully equipped and can accommodate groups (high season, $185 to $245 one-bedroom condo, $255 to $375 two-bedroom condo, $800 to $995 three-bedroom home, $3,000 five-bedroom home). Guests have access to all of the resort's amenities and enjoy special golf rates.

3 South Maui

MAALAEA

Contact **Maalaea Bay Rentals,** 280 Hauoli St., Wailuku, HI 96793 (☎ **800/ 367-6084** or 808/244-7012; Fax 808/242-7476; e-mail maalaea@sprynet.com), which has a variety of units in nearly every condominium in Maalaea, ranging from a low of $60 for a one-bedroom garden unit in an older building to $175 for a two-bedroom oceanfront unit. If your stay is shorter than 5 nights, an extra charge will be added for cleaning. Laundry facilities are on-site, and all units have full kitchens and complete furnishings down to the TV, phones, linens, and beach towels.

KIHEI
EXPENSIVE

Maalaea Surf Resort. 12 S. Kihei Rd. (at S. Kihei Rd. and Hi. 350), Kihei, HI 96743. ☎ **800/423-7953** or 808/879-1267. Fax 808/874-2884. 34 units in rental pool. A/C TV TEL. High season $186 one-bedroom double, $252 two-bedroom (sleeps up to 4); low season $165 one-bedroom, $217 two-bedroom. Extra person $15. MC, V.

Located at the quiet end of Kihei Road, this two-story condominium complex sprawls over 5 acres of lush tropical gardens. This is the place for people who want a quiet, relaxing vacation on a well-landscaped property, with a beautiful white-sand beach right outside. The large, luxury town-house units all have ocean views, big kitchens, air-conditioning, cable TV, VCRs, and phones. Maid service (Monday through Saturday) is included in the price.

✪ **Maui Hill.** 2881 S. Kihei Rd. (across from Kamaole Park III, between Keonekai St. and Kilohana Dr.), Kihei, HI 96753. ☎ **800/922-7866** or 808/879-6321. Fax 808/879-8945. 140 units. A/C TV TEL. High season $205 one-bedroom, $235 two-bedroom, $315 three-bedroom; low season $170 one-bedroom, $200 two-bedroom, $280 three-bedroom. AE, CB, DC, DISC, JCB, MC, V.

If you can't decide between the privacy of a condominium unit and the conveniences a hotel offers, this place will solve your dilemma. Managed by the respected Aston chain, Maui Hill gives you the best of both options. Located on a hill above the heat of Kihei town, this large, Spanish-style resort (with white stucco buildings, red-tile roof, and arched entries) combines all the amenities and activities of a hotel—large pool, hot tub, tennis courts, Hawaiiana classes, and more—with large luxury condominium units that have full kitchens, lots of space, and plenty of privacy. Nearly all units have ocean views, dishwashers, washer/dryers, queen sofa beds, big lanais, and daily maid service. Beaches are within easy walking distance. The management here goes out of their way to make sure that your stay is as perfect as you planned it.

Amenities: Daily maid service, concierge service, weekly complimentary continental breakfast, weekly manager's party. Large pool, hot tub, putting green,

South Maui Coast Accommodations

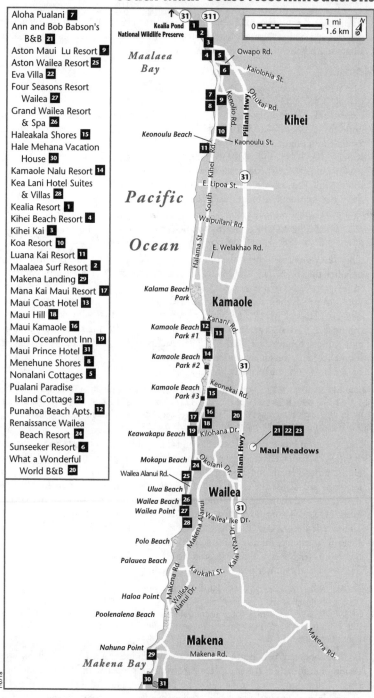

Aloha Pualani 7
Ann and Bob Babson's B&B 21
Aston Maui Lu Resort 9
Aston Wailea Resort 25
Eva Villa 22
Four Seasons Resort Wailea 27
Grand Wailea Resort & Spa 26
Haleakala Shores 15
Hale Mehana Vacation House 30
Kamaole Nalu Resort 14
Kea Lani Hotel Suites & Villas 28
Kealia Resort 1
Kihei Beach Resort 4
Kihei Kai 3
Koa Resort 10
Luana Kai Resort 11
Maalaea Surf Resort 2
Makena Landing 29
Mana Kai Maui Resort 17
Maui Coast Hotel 13
Maui Hill 18
Maui Kamaole 16
Maui Oceanfront Inn 19
Maui Prince Hotel 31
Menehune Shores 8
Nonalani Cottages 5
Pualani Paradise Island Cottage 23
Punahoa Beach Apts. 12
Renaissance Wailea Beach Resort 24
Sunseeker Resort 6
What a Wonderful World B&B 20

Maalaea Bay

Kealia Pond National Wildlife Preserve

Owapo Rd.
Kaiolohia St.
Kenolio Rd.
Ohukai Rd.

Kihei

Keonoulu Beach
Kaonoulu St.

Piilani Hwy.
South Kihei Rd.

E. Lipoa St.

Pacific Ocean

Waipuilani Rd.

Halama St.

E. Welakhao Rd.

Kalama Beach Park

Kamaole

Kanani Rd.

Kamaole Beach Park #1

Kamaole Beach Park #2

Kamaole Beach Park #3

Keonekai Rd.

Keawakapu Beach
Kilohana Dr.

Maui Meadows

Mokapu Beach
Wailea Alanui Rd.
Ulua Beach

Okolani Dr.
Piilani Hwy.

Wailea Beach
Wailea Point

Wailea

Wailea 'Ike Dr.
Wailea Alanui
Kalai Waa Dr.

Polo Beach

Palauea Beach

Kaukahi St.

Haloa Point

Poolenalena Beach

Makena Rd.
Wailea Alanui Dr.
Makena Rd.

Nahuna Point

Makena
Makena Rd.

Makena Bay

0   1 mi
1.6 km

1-0718

tennis courts, shuffleboard, 14 barbecue areas, and classes in Hawaiiana such as lei making and crafts. A variety of restaurants and shops are just a short walk away along South Kihei Road.

MODERATE

Also consider the **Kihei Beach Resort,** 36 S. Kihei Rd., Kihei, HI 96753 (☎ **800/367-6034** or 808/879-2744; fax 808/875-0306), which has spacious, comfortable condo units right on the beach—the downside is the constant traffic noise from Kihei Road ($110 to $125 one-bedroom, $140 to 160 two-bedroom; 3-night minimum). Another good deal is the **Maui Kamaole,** 2777 S. Kihei Rd., Kihei, HI 96753 (☎ **800/367-5242** or 808/874-5151; fax 808/879-6900; www.maui.net/~crh/), right across from beautiful Kamaole Beach Park III. The roomy, fully furnished units (high season, $135 to $150 one-bedroom, $170 to $190 two-bedroom; 4-night minimum) are great for families.

✪ **Aston Maui Lu Resort.** 575 S. Kihei Rd. (between Kaonoulu and Ohukai sts.), Kihei, HI 96753. ☎ **800/92-ASTON** or 808/879-5881. Fax 808/879-4627. 120 units. A/C TV TEL. High season $120–$185; low season $99–$165. Packages available. AE, DC, DISC, JCB, MC, V.

They just don't make them like this anymore. Located at the quieter northern end of Kihei, the Polynesian-style Maui Lu offers a nostalgic Old Hawaii atmosphere on its 28 green acres by the sea. Ask for a beach unit if you'd like to be right on the sand; the rest of the resort is across the road and up on a rise, around a pool shaped like the island of Maui. The big, airy rooms are outfitted with rattan furniture, ceiling fans, Hawaiian art, two double beds, coffeemakers, and small fridges. Tennis and laundry facilities are available. The restaurant, Ukulele Grill, has an inspired local chef and a reasonably priced continental/Hawaiian gourmet menu; it serves breakfast, dinner, and Sunday brunch.

Haleakala Shores. 2619 S. Kihei Rd. (across from Kamaole Park III, at Keonekai St.), Kihei, HI 96753. ☎ **800/869-1097** or 808/879-1218. Fax 808/879-2219. 144 units; 76 in rental pool. TV TEL. High season $120 two-bedroom (sleeps up to 4), 7-night minimum; low season $90 two-bedroom, 5-night minimum. Extra person $10. MC, V.

This is a great buy for frugal travelers and for families on a budget. Each large unit (some 1,200 square feet) sleeps up to six people and comes with two bedrooms, two baths, private lanai, full kitchen with dishwasher, and washer/dryer. The great location, just across the street from Kamaole Park III, makes it an easy walk to restaurants and shopping. Even the parking situation is ideal: there's a free covered garage. OK, now for the bad news: the units were built in 1974, and most still sport 1970s-style decor. Also, the units can be noisy—due not only to traffic on Kihei Road (you can ask for a unit inside the complex), but also to thin walls (you can hear your neighbors' TV and conversations quite clearly). If you manage to get a quiet unit and can overlook the nostalgic decor, these units are winners.

Kamaole Nalu Resort. 2450 S. Kihei Rd. (between Kanani and Keonekai rds., next to Kamaole Beach Park II), Kihei, HI 96753. ☎ **800/767-1497** or 808/879-1006. Fax 808/879-8693. www.mauigateway.com/~kamaole. E-mail: abeach@maui.net. 36 units. TV TEL. High season $145–$165 double, low season $90–$110 double. Extra person $10–$15. 3-night minimum. MC, V.

Located between two beach parks, Kamaole I and Kamaole II, this six-story condominium boasts fabulous ocean views. The property, right across the street from a shopping complex housing the popular restaurant Radio Cairo, has an oceanside pool and barbecue facilities that are great for a sunset cookout. The units have large living rooms and private lanais; the kitchens are a bit small but come fully equipped. We recommend no. 306 for its wonderful bird's-eye ocean view. Be warned: Since the building is located on Kihei Road, the units can be noisy.

✪ **Koa Resort.** 811 S. Kihei Rd. (between Kulanihakoi St. and Namauu Pl.), c/o Bello Realty, P.O. Box 1776, Kihei, HI 96753. ☎ **800/541-3060** or 808/879-3328. Fax 808/875-1483. www.bellowmaui.com. E-mail: bello@maui.net. 54 units. TV TEL. High season $105–$180 double, low season $85–$160 double. No credit cards.

Located just across the street from the ocean, Koa Resort consists of five two-story wooden buildings on more than 5½ acres of landscaped grounds. The spacious, privately owned one-, two-, and three-bedroom units are decorated with care and come fully equipped. Each kitchen comes complete with fridge (with ice maker), dishwasher, disposal, microwave, blender, and coffeemaker. The larger units have both showers and tubs, whereas the smaller units have showers only. All feature large lanais, ceiling fans, and washer/dryers. The property has two tennis courts, a pool, a hot tub, and an 18-hole putting green. For maximum peace and quiet, ask for a unit far from Kihei Road.

Maui Coast Hotel. 2259 S. Kihei Rd. (1 block from Kamaole Beach Park I), Kihei, HI 96753. ☎ **800/895-6284** or 808/874-6284. Fax 808/875-4731. 370 units. A/C TV TEL. $129–$139 double, $149–$159 suite, $169–$179 one-bedroom double, $240 two-bedroom (sleeps up to 4). Extra person $10. Rental-car packages available. AE, DC, DISC, JCB, MC, V.

For the price of a room (or a one- or two-bedroom apartment), the Maui Coast's "Extra Value" package gives you a rental car free. Built in 1993, this off-beach mid-rise stands out as one of the only moderately priced new hotels in Hawaii. That's big news—especially on Maui, where luxury abounds. The chief advantage of this hotel is not only its price, but also its location—about a block from Kamaole Beach Park I, with plenty of diversions within walking distance, including bars, restaurants, and shopping. Rooms are clean and simple; they remind us of college dorms, only with lots of extras: sitting areas, coffeemakers and free coffee, hair dryers, whirlpool tubs, minifridges, safes, ceiling fans, furnished private lanais. There's a casual restaurant, a sushi bar, and a poolside bar with nightly entertainment. Additional amenities include room service, an activities desk, laundry, two pools (one for the kids), two Jacuzzis, tennis, and a gift shop. This ain't the Ritz, but you'll be very comfortable here—and your wallet will thank you.

INEXPENSIVE

In addition to the choices listed below, you might want to consider **Aloha Pualani,** 15 Wailana Pl., Kihei, HI 96753 (☎ **800/PUALANI** or 808/874-9265; fax 808/874-9127; www.mauigateway.com/~pualani), which offers five suites surrounding a heated pool ($89 to $109 double, 3-night minimum). Also noteworthy is **Luana Kai Resort,** 940 S. Kihei Rd., Kihei, HI 96753 (☎ **800/ 669-1127** or 808/879-1268; fax 808/879-1455; e-mail luanakai@mauigateway.net), an older condo complex with 113 one- and two-bedroom units ($80 to $130 one-bedroom, $100 to $160 two-bedroom; 4-night minimum), pool, tennis, and other facilities; children are welcome. **Kihei Kai,** 61 N. Kihei Rd., Kihei, HI 96753 (☎ **800/735-2357** or 808/879-2357; fax 808/874-4960; www. maui.net/~kiheikai/; e-mail kiheikai@maui.net), has one-bedroom apartments ($80 to $105) that are ideal for families. Finally, **Sunseeker Resort,** 551 S. Kihei Rd., P.O. Box 276, Kihei, HI 96753 (☎ **800/532-MAUI** or 808/879-1261; fax 808/874-3877; www.maui.net/~sunseekr), offers older, sometimes noisy budget units with great ocean views—somewhat of a rarity on Maui ($55 to $60 studio, $65 to $70 one-bedroom; 3-night minimum).

✪ Ann and Bob Babson's Bed & Breakfast and Vacation Rentals. 3371 Keha Dr. (in Maui Meadows), Kihei, HI 96753. ☎ **800/824-6409** or 808/874-1166. Fax 808/879-7906. www.mauibnb.com. E-mail: babson@mauibnb.com. 4 units. TV TEL. $80–$95 double room (rates include breakfast Mon–Sat), $95 apt double, $115 cottage double. Extra person $15. 3-night minimum. MC, V.

In addition to the wonderful accommodations on their property, Ann and Bob Babson also operate a B&B booking service, in which they go above and beyond the call of duty to find the ideal place for you. We highly recommend just staying right here on the landscaped half-acre property, which boasts 180-degree views of the islands of Lanai, Kahoolawe, and Molokini (and on a clear day, part of Molokai), and sunsets not to be missed. Accommodations include two rooms in the house (one with panoramic ocean views, skylights, and a whirlpool tub), a one-bedroom apartment, and a two-bedroom cottage.

Eva Villa. Kumulani Dr. (in Maui Meadows), Kihei. Reservations c/o Hawaii's Best Bed & Breakfast, P.O. Box 563, Kamuela, HI 96743. ☎ **800/262-9912** or 808/885-4550. Fax 808/885-0559. E-mail: bestbnb@aloha.net. 3 units. TV TEL. $95 studio double, $100 cottage double, $95 two-bedroom apt double. Extra person $15. 3-night minimum. DISC.

Eva's location is great: at the top of Maui Meadows, overlooking Wailea, and just minutes from the white-sand beaches, six championship golf courses, and restaurants and shopping in Kihei and Wailea. There are three different units to choose from: a separate cottage, a small two-bedroom apartment, and a one-room studio. The 500-square-foot cottage is a separate house with complete kitchen (with dishwasher), washer/dryer, smallish living/dining room (with sofa bed), and one bedroom with queen bed and wraparound lanai (complete with Weber barbecue). If the cottage's offbeat 1960s decor (blue toilet and blue basin in the bathroom, with checked linoleum flooring) doesn't bother you in the least, you'll be happy here. Two units inside the main house each have private entry and use of laundry facilities. The 600-square-foot studio, which is essentially one large room with a full kitchen, looks out to the pool and Jacuzzi. We thought the $95 rate, considering the mishmash of furniture and the presence of numerous fans (indicating the room temperature during the day), placed this a little on the high side compared with other B&B studios in the same area. Also in the main house is a two-bedroom apartment, perfect for families with children. (The trundle bed in the second bedroom makes this a little on the uncomfortable side for two couples.) The apartment doesn't have a full kitchen (there's no oven), but a large refrigerator, microwave, and two-burner hot plate should suffice.

Kealia Resort. 191 N. Kihei Rd. (north of Hi. 31, at the Maalaea end of Kihei), Kihei, HI 96753. ☎ **800/265-0686** or 808/879-0952. Fax 808/875-1540. E-mail: kealia@juno.com. 51 units. TV TEL. $55–$70 studio double, $75–$110 one-bedroom double, $135–$155 two-bedroom (sleeps up to 4). Extra person $10. 4-night minimum. MC, V.

This oceanfront property at the northern end of Kihei is well maintained and nicely furnished—and the price is excellent. As tempting as the $55 studio units might sound, don't give in: they face noisy Kihei Road and are near a major junction, so big trucks downshifting can be especially noisy at night. Instead, go for one of the ocean-view units; they all have full kitchens, washer/dryers, and private lanais. The grounds, which abut a 5-mile stretch of beach, feature a recently retiled pool with sundeck. The management goes out of its way to provide opportunities for guests to meet; social gatherings include free coffee-and-donut get-togethers every Friday morning and pupu parties on Wednesdays.

Mana Kai Maui Resort. 2960 S. Kihei Rd. (between Kilohana and Keonekai rds., at the Wailea end of Kihei), Kihei, HI 96753. ☎ **800/367-5242** or 808/879-1561. Fax 808/876-5042. www.maui.net/~crh. E-mail: crh@maui.net. 132 units. A/C TV TEL. $80–$100 double hotel rm, $150–$180 one-bedroom (sleeps up to 4), $180–$220 two-bedroom (sleeps up to 6). AE, DC, MC, V.

This eight-story complex, situated on a beautiful white-sand cove, is an unusual combination of hotel and condominium. The hotel rooms, which constitute half of the total number of units, are small but nicely furnished. The condo units feature full kitchens and open living rooms with sliding-glass doors that lead to small lanais overlooking the sandy beach and ocean. Some units are beginning to show their age in this 20-something-year-old building, but they're all clean and comfortable. There are laundry facilities on each floor, an open-air restaurant in the building, a swimming pool on the property, and one of the best snorkeling beaches on the coast just steps away.

Maui Oceanfront Inn. 2980 S. Kihei Rd. (near Kilohana Rd., at the Wailea end of Kihei), Kihei, HI 96753. ☎ **800/367-5004** or 808/879-7744. Fax 800/447-2729 or 808/874-0145. 85 units (with showers only). A/C TV TEL. $80–$105 double rm, $150–$160 one-bedroom (sleeps up to 4). Extra person $17. AE, DC, MC, V.

If you don't mind noise and uninspired decor, this fabulously located budget choice—formerly the Wailea Oceanfront Hotel—might be right for you. Stretched out between Kihei Road and the ocean, the box-shaped Maui Oceanfront offers tiny rooms with the basics: bed, desk, nightstand, TV, and dresser. The units are noisy—you can hear not only guests in adjoining rooms and down the hall, but also people in the parking lot, cars on the road, and noise from the restaurant next door, Carelli's On the Beach. Thankfully, there's air-conditioning—the rooms can get stiflingly hot. But the location is great: the hotel is right on Keawakapu Beach, which is good for swimming, and close to Wailea Resort's shops, tennis, golf, restaurants, and ocean activities. The staff is friendly and helpful, the rooms are kept immaculately clean, and free coffee and donuts are available at the front desk every day.

Menehune Shores. 760 S. Kihei Rd. (between Kaonoulu and Hoonani sts.), P.O. Box 1327, Kihei, HI 96753. ☎ **800/558-9117** or 808/879-3428. Fax 808/879-5218. 70 units. TV TEL. $75–$100 one-bedroom double, $88.50–$120 two-bedroom double, $100–$140 two-bedroom (sleeps up to 4), $140–$160 three-bedroom (sleeps up to 6). Weekly car/condo package $789 one-bedroom double, $889 two-bedroom double, $989 two-bedroom (sleeps up to 4), $1,189 three-bedroom (sleeps up to 6). Extra person $7.50. 5-night minimum. No credit cards.

If you plan to stay on Maui for a week, you might want to look into the car/condo packages here; they're a real deal, especially for families on a budget. The six-story Menehune Shores is more than 2 decades old and is showing its age in some places, but all units are well maintained and have ocean views. The design is straight out of the 1970s, but the view from the private lanais is timeless. The kitchens are fully equipped, all units have washer/dryers, and the oceanfront location guarantees a steady breeze that keeps the rooms cool. The U-shaped building sits in front of the ancient Hawaiian fish ponds of Kalepolepo; some Hawaiians still fish them using traditional throw nets, but generally the pond serves as protection from the ocean waves, making it safe for children (and those unsure of their ability) to swim in the relatively calm waters. There are also a heated pool, shuffleboard courts, and a whale-watching platform on the roof garden.

Nonalani Cottages. 455 S. Kihei Rd. (just south of Hi. 31 Junction), P.O. Box 655, Kihei, HI 96753. ☎ **800/733-2688** or 808/879-2491. Fax 808/891-0273. 11 units. TV. $60 double rm, $60–$80 cottage. Extra person $7–$15. 4-night minimum. No credit cards.

Picture this: right across the street from a white-sand beach, a grassy expanse dotted with eight small cottages tucked among palm and fruit trees. Built in 1975, the 400-square-foot cottages are tiny, but they contain everything you'll need: a small but complete kitchen, two twin beds that double as couches in the living room, a separate bedroom with queen bed, and a lanai with table and chairs, ideal for watching the ocean waves as you eat your breakfast. The cottages are slightly worn, but the setting and the privacy of your own bungalow make up for this drawback. There are no phones in the cabins (a blessing if you're trying to escape civilization), but there's a public phone near the coin-op laundry facilities.

If the cabins are booked, or you want a bit more luxury in your accommodations, you might opt for one of the private guest rooms in host David Kong's main house. Each beautiful room features cathedral-like open-beam ceilings, plush carpet, koa bed frames, air-conditioning, and private entrance.

✪ **Pualani Paradise Island Cottage.** 3134 Hoomua Dr. (in Maui Meadows), Kihei, HI 96753. ☎ **808/875-8522.** Fax 808/874-9129. www.maui.net/~mcwebb. E-mail: mcwebb@maui.net. 1 cottage. A/C TV TEL. $95 double. Rates includes stocked refrigerator with breakfast fixings. Extra person $10. 3-night minimum. No credit cards.

Tucked away on a quiet street in the residential area above Wailea known as Maui Meadows, you'll find this quaint cottage, surrounded by lush landscaped grounds and a large swimming pool. The cozy cottage, with fully equipped kitchen, is decorated with Balinese works of art. In addition to the queen bed in the separate bedroom, there's also a queen sofa bed in the living room that's great for kids. The immaculate grounds, the charming cottage, and the cool pool regularly draw guests back. If you love animals, the Webbs' two friendly golden retrievers (who regularly show off by diving into the pool) will entertain you for hours.

✪ **Punahoa Beach Apts.** 2142 Iliili Rd. (off S. Kihei Rd., 100 yards from Kamaole Beach I), Kihei, HI 96753. ☎ **800/564-4380** or 808/879-2720. Fax 808/875-3147. E-mail: pb6110@aol.com. 12 units. TV TEL. High season $93 studio double, $127 one-bedroom double, $130 two-bedroom double, low season $66 studio double, $85 one-bedroom, $94 two-bedroom. Extra person $12. 5-night minimum. AE, MC, V.

Book this place—we can't put it any more simply than that. The location— off noisy, traffic-ridden Kihei Road, on a quiet side street with ocean frontage—is fabulous; a grassy lawn rolls about 50 feet down to the beach; there are great snorkeling just offshore and a popular surfing spot next door; and shopping and restaurants are all within walking distance. All of the beautifully decorated units in this small, four-story building have lanais with great ocean views and fully equipped kitchens. Rooms go quickly during the winter months, so book early.

✪ **What a Wonderful World B&B.** 2828 Umalu Pl. (off Keonakai St., near Hi. 31), Kihei, HI 96753. ☎ **808/879-9103.** Fax 808/874-9352. E-mail: amauibnb@maui.net. 4 units. A/C TV TEL. $65 rm double, $75 studio double, $85–$95 one-bedroom apt. All rates include full gourmet breakfast. Children 11 and under stay free. AE, DC, DISC, MC, V.

We couldn't believe what we'd discovered here: an impeccably done B&B with thought and care put into every room, a great location, and excellent rates. Then we met hostess Eva Tantillo, who has not only a full-service travel agency, but also a master's degree in hotel management, along with several years of experience in managing all aspects of the hotel business. The result? One of Maui's finest bed-and-breakfasts, centrally located in Kihei (a half mile to Kamaole II Beach Park,

5 minutes from Wailea Golf Courses, and convenient to shopping and restaurants). Choose from one of four units: the master suite (which has a small fridge, a coffeemaker, and a barbecue grill on the lanai), the studio apartment (with fully equipped kitchen), or two one-bedroom apartments (also with fully equipped kitchens). All come with private bathrooms, phones, and entrances. Guests are welcome to use the barbecue, laundry facilities, and hot tub. Eva serves a gourmet family-style breakfast (eggs Benedict, Alaskan waffles, skillet eggs with mushroom sauce, fruit blintzes, and more) on her lanai, which has views of white-sand beaches, the West Maui Mountains, and Haleakala.

WAILEA

For a complete selection of condominium units throughout Wailea and Makena, contact **Destination Resorts Hawaii,** 2750 Wailea Alanui Dr., Wailea, HI 96753 (☎ **800/367-5246** or 808/879-1595; fax 808/874-3554; http://maui.net/~drh). The luxury units represented include one-bedroom doubles, from $140 to $435; two-bedroom units that sleep up to 4, from $170 to $510; and three-bedroom units that sleep up to 6, from $450 to $600 (extra person $20). Minimum stays vary by property.

VERY EXPENSIVE

In addition to the choices listed below, you might want to consider the Arabian Nights–style fantasy resort, **Kea Lani Hotel Suites & Villas,** 4100 Wailea Alanui Dr., Wailea, HI 96753 (☎ 800/882-4100 or 808/875-4100; fax 808/875-1200). Its fabulous villas are a good choice for families, but we were slightly disappointed with the obstructed view and the slow service ($295 to $525 suite, $900 to $1,000 one-bedroom villa, $1,100 to $1,200 two-bedroom villa, $1,300 to $1,400 three-bedroom villa; all villa rates include car rental).

✪ **Four Seasons Resort Wailea.** 3900 Wailea Alanui Dr., Wailea, HI 96753. ☎ **800/ 334-MAUI** or 808/874-8000. Fax 808/874-6449. 463 units. A/C MINIBAR TV TEL. $295–$690 double, from $545 suite. Packages available. Extra person $80 ($140 in Club Floor rms); children under 18 stay free using existing bedding. AE, DC, JCB, MC, V.

All of the luxury hotels in Wailea are fabulous, boasting terrific views and luxurious accommodations. What sets the Four Seasons apart is its relaxing, casual atmosphere, combined with service so great you hardly notice it. If money's not a factor, this is the place to spend it. And bring the kids too: There's a complete activity program designed just for them.

It's hard to beat this modern version of a Hawaiian palace by the sea, complete with columns, fountains, reflecting pools, waterfalls, and views of the Pacific and Haleakala. Although it sits on the beach between two other hotels, the Four Seasons inhabits its own separate world, thanks to the open courtyard of pools and gardens—so you won't feel like you're on chockablock resort row.

The spacious (about 600 sq. ft.) rooms feature furnished private lanais (nearly all with ocean views) and TV/VCRs hidden away in teak armoires. The grand bathrooms have deep marble bathtubs, showers for two, and lighted French makeup mirrors. Other amenities include safes, irons and ironing boards, hair dryers, and plush terry robes.

Service is attentive but not cloying. At the pool, guests lounge in Casbah-like tents, pampered with special touches like iced Evian and chilled towels. And you'll never see a housekeeping cart in the hall: the cleaning staff work in teams, so they're as unobtrusive as possible and in and out of your room in minutes.

This ritzy neighborhood is home to great restaurants, Wailea Shopping Village, the Wailea Tennis Center (known as Wimbledon West), and six nearby golf courses—not to mention that great beach, with gentle waves and islands framing the view on either side. From your lanai, you can watch whales spouting and leaping in winter, and sunsets year-round.

Dining: Chef George Mavrothalassitis was lured from Honolulu's famed Halekulani to the resort's signature restaurant, Seasons (see chapter 7), where he dazzles guests with his Hawaii Regional Cuisine. The combination of open-air dining, great views, and Chef Mavro's masterpieces guarantees a memorable experience. During the day, the Seaside Restaurant offers a casual atmosphere overlooking the Pacific; by night, it's transformed into Ferraro's at Seaside, serving authentic Italian creations. The Pacific Grill, overlooking the ocean and pool, offers lavish breakfast buffets and dinners featuring Pacific Edge cuisine and Chef Mavro's specials.

Amenities: Twice-daily maid service, 24-hour room service, same-day dry cleaning and laundry, 1-hour and overnight pressing, free overnight shoe shine or sandal repair, complimentary valet and shuttle around resort, airport limousine service, rental cars at concierge desk, 24-hour medical service. Lei greeting and oshibori towel on arrival, early arrival/late departure facility. Voice mail, safes, hair dryers, irons and ironing boards, terry robes. Special amenities on Club Floors, including breakfast, afternoon tea and snacks, cocktails, pupus, and open bar. Two pools (one for adults only), 41 pool and beach cabanas, two whirlpools (one for adults only), fitness center with weight room and steam room, tennis (two lighted Plexi-pave courts with rackets and tennis balls provided), putting green and nearby golf. Beach pavilion with snorkels, boogie boards, kayaks, and other water sports gear; 1 hour free use of snorkel equipment; complimentary use of bicycles; complimentary exercise and tennis attire on loan. Game room, video library, salon, shops, conference facilities. Year-round kids' program with loads of activities and a complete children's facility, plus a teen recreation center; children's video library and toys.

Grand Wailea Resort Hotel & Spa. 3850 Wailea Alanui Dr., Wailea, HI 96753. ☎ **800/888-6100** or 808/875-1234. Fax 808/879-4077. 814 units. A/C MINIBAR TV TEL. $380–$580 double, from $1,100 suite. Packages available. Extra person $30 ($50 in Napua Club rooms and suites). AE, DC, DISC, JCB, MC, V.

Here's where grand becomes grandiose. When it opened in 1991, this was the world's most expensive hotel project ($600 million), the pinnacle of Hawaii's brief fling with fantasy megaresorts. This monument to excess is extremely popular with families, incentive groups, and conventions; it's the grand prize in Hawaii vacation contests and the dream of many honeymooners.

This hotel really is too much. It has a Japanese restaurant decorated with real rocks hewn from the slopes of Mount Fuji; 10,000 tropical plants in the lobby; an intricate pool system with slides, waterfalls, rapids, and a water-powered elevator to take you up to the top; Hawaii's most elaborate spa (not even the Romans had it this good); Hawaii's most expensive hotel suite, a 5,500-square-foot pad with a 180-degree view of paradise; a restaurant in a man-made tide pool; a floating New England–style wedding chapel; and nothing but ocean-view rooms, outfitted with every amenity you could ask for. And it's all crowned with a $30 million collection of original art, much of it created expressly for the hotel by Hawaii artists and sculptors. There's also a fantastic beach out front.

Dining/Diversions: Six restaurants and 12 bars range from fine dining to casual poolside snacks, serving everything from Japanese and Italian specialties to local seafood and spa cuisine. A nightclub features laser light shows, a hydraulic dance floor, and 20 video monitors. There are also luau grounds for 300.

Amenities: Lei greeting; complimentary valet parking; 24-hour room service; twice-daily towel service; same-day laundry and dry cleaning; multilingual concierge; infant care center; art and hotel tours; Budget Rent-A-Car and American Express tour desks; 100 Napua Club rooms with attendants, complimentary continental breakfast, cocktails, and tea service. Hawaii's largest spa, the 50,000-square-foot Spa Grande, with a blend of European-, Japanese-, and American-style techniques; 2,000-foot-long Action Pool, featuring a 10-minute swim/ride through mountains and grottoes; complimentary dive and windsurf lessons; seaside wedding chapel; conference facilities. Kids enjoy a computer center, video game room, arts and crafts, 60-seat children's theater, and outdoor playground. Five golf courses, including two 18-hole championship courses, nearby.

✪ **Renaissance Wailea Beach Resort.** 3550 Wailea Alanui Dr., Wailea, HI 96753. ☎ **800/9-WAILEA** or 808/879-4900. Fax 808/879-6128. 345 units. A/C TV TEL. $290–$515 double, from $820 suite. Extra person $40; children 18 and under stay free using existing bedding. AE, CB, DC, DISC, MC, V. Parking $3.

This is the place for visitors in search of the luxury of a Wailea hotel, but in a smaller, more intimate setting. Located on 15 acres of rolling lawn and tropical gardens, Renaissance Wailea has the feeling of a small boutique hotel. Perhaps it's the resort's U-shaped design, the series of small coves and beaches, or the spaciousness of the rooms—whatever the reason, you just don't feel crowded here.

Each room has a sitting area, a large lanai, a TV and VCR hidden away in the armoire, three phones (with computer data ports), a fridge, and a safe. The bathrooms include such extras as double vanities (one with lighted makeup mirror) and *hapi* coats (japanese-style cotton robes). Bedspreads, drapes, and towels in all rooms have recently been upgraded.

The resort also offers rooms in the Mokapu Beach Club, an exclusive two-story building just steps from a crescent-shaped beach, featuring such extras as private check-in, in-room continental breakfast, and access to a private pool and beach cabanas.

Dining/Diversions: Palm Court, a casual, open-air restaurant surrounded by tropical gardens, serves a breakfast buffet and, at dinner, a choice of a buffet or an oven-baked pizza. Hana Gion, a small Japanese restaurant, features a sushi bar and teppanyaki grill. Maui Onion, a casual poolside restaurant surrounded by lush gardens and a cascading waterfall, serves breakfast and lunch (see chapter 7). Every Monday, a traditional luau is offered at sunset.

Amenities: Room service (from 6am to 11pm); lei greeting; concierge; complimentary in-room coffee and daily newspaper; complimentary video library; traditional Hawaiian craft classes; massage therapy; baby-sitting; Camp Wailea children's program. Complete fitness center, two freshwater swimming pools, two whirlpools, golf at nearby Wailea Golf Club, tennis at nearby Wailea Tennis Club, shopping arcade, hair salon, basketball court, ping-pong, and shuffle board.

EXPENSIVE

✪ **Aston Wailea Resort.** 3700 Wailea Alanui Dr., Wailea, HI 96753. ☎ **800/92-ASTON** or 808/879-1922. Fax 808/875-4878. 566 units. A/C TV TEL. $219–$309 double, from $499 suite. AE, DC, DISC, JCB, MC, V.

Aston Wailea gives you a sense of what Maui was like before the big resort boom: this classic 1970s-style hotel is like a tropical garden by the sea. Airy and comfortable, with touches of Hawaiian art (and a terrific aquarium that stretches forever behind the front desk), it just feels right. The open-air hotel is filled with tapa (Hawaiian cloth made from tree bark), weavings, and authentic carvings; it was the first resort built in Wailea (in 1976), yet it remains the most Hawaiian of them all.

What's truly special about this hotel is how it fits into its environment without overwhelming it. Eight buildings, all low-rise except for an eight-story tower, are spread along 22 gracious acres of lawns and gardens spiked by coco palms, with lots of open space and a half mile of oceanfront on a point between Wailea and Ulua beaches. The vast, parklike expanses are a luxury on this now-crowded coast.

All of the rooms have private lanais and separate dressing and bathroom areas with marble-topped basins. When Aston took over management in 1996, it did a million dollars' worth of renovations to restore this once grande dame to her former glory.

Dining/Diversions: Hula Moons, a casual outdoor restaurant, serves pizza, burgers, and cool drinks at lunch, and fresh Hawaii seafood specialties at dinner; there's a free hula show nightly. The open-air, ocean-view Lanai Terrace serves breakfast daily and dinner Tuesday through Saturday. Kai Puka Lounge offers full cocktail service with dramatic ocean views, Hawaiian music, and seasonal pupus. A luau takes place on Tuesday, Thursday, and Friday, featuring two-time world-champion fire/knife dancer Efi.

Amenities: Same-day laundry and valet, multilingual concierge. A comprehensive Hawaiian Culture Program offers free activities like lei making and hula lessons; there's also an activities and culture program for the kids. Three pools, gift shop, newsstand, beauty salon, barber shop. Three championship golf courses nearby.

MAKENA
EXPENSIVE

✪ **Hale Mehana Vacation House.** 176 Makena Rd. (by the Keawalai Church in S. Makena), Kihei, HI 96753. ☎ 808/875-8231. Fax 808/877-2046. E-mail: dugal@maui.net. TV TEL. 3-bedroom/2-bathroom home. $200 double. Extra person $25, maximum 6 people. 5-night minimum. No credit cards.

Located right on the ocean at Makena (with the waves lapping just a few feet from the magnificent deck), Hale Mehana ("warm-hearted house") consists of the entire upstairs floor of a luxury home. Not a penny has been spared to make this property a dream oceanfront accommodation. A huge deck wraps around the house, offering breathtaking views of Molokini and Kahoolawe in the distance and easy access to swimming, snorkeling, and kayaking. The living area has big picture windows, polished wooden floors, a huge sofa, and a complete entertainment center. The kitchen opens onto the living/dining area, taking advantage of those incredible views; it contains every possible appliance a cook could want. The master bedroom is simply fabulous: a huge bay window looks out on the ocean, and the large master bathroom has a Jacuzzi big enough for two. Two smallish bedrooms share a full bathroom. Makena golf and tennis courts are just 2 minutes away, and restaurants and shopping at the hotels in Wailea are a 5-minute drive.

Maui Prince Hotel. 5400 Makena Alanui, Makena, HI 96753. ☎ **800/321-MAUI** or 808/874-1111. Fax 808/879-8763. 304 units. A/C MINIBAR TV TEL. $230–$395 double, $440–$840 suite. Packages available. AE, DC, JCB, MC, V.

The Maui Prince is located in a beautiful, tranquil spot next to a golden-sand beach. But it's also at the end of the road—far, far away from anything else on the island. If you're looking for a vacation setting of serene gardens and secluded beaches, here's your place. But if you plan to tour Maui, this is definitely far out of your way.

When you first see the stark white hotel, it looks like a high-rise motel stuck in the woods—from the outside. Inside, you'll discover an atrium garden with a koi-filled waterfall stream, an ocean view from every room, and a simplicity to the furnishings that makes some people feel uncomfortable and others blissfully clutter free. Rooms are small but come with private lanais with great views.

Dining/Diversions: Japanese cuisine tops the menu at the Hakone (see chapter 7), an elegant restaurant that serves lunch and dinner and also has a sushi bar. For dinner, the Prince Court specializes in Hawaii Regional cuisine (see chapter 7), and the casual Cafe Kiowai offers seasonal and international specialties. The Makena Clubhouse Restaurant serves lunch and snacks. The Molokini Lounge has local Hawaiian music nightly.

Amenities: Lei greeting, complimentary early-morning coffee and tea, complimentary valet parking, multilingual concierge, same-day dry cleaning and laundry, daily kids' program, early arrival and late departure services. Tennis (six Plexi-pave courts, two lit for night play), 36 holes of Robert Trent Jones–designed golf at North and South Courses, separate pools for adults and children, fitness center, six-station fitness trail, conference facilities, library.

INEXPENSIVE

✪ **Makena Landing.** 5100 Makena Rd. (next to the county beach park), Makena, HI 96753. ☎ **808/879-6286.** 2 units. TV TEL. $95 double. Extra person $10. 3-night minimum. No cards.

This has to be the most fabulous location for a bed-and-breakfast: right on the ocean at Makena Landing. Once you settle in, you might not want to leave. The view is incredible; the sunsets are to die for; some of the best swimming, snorkeling, diving, and shoreline fishing are within walking distance; and the hosts are the nicest people you'll ever meet. The property has been in the Lu'uwai family for seven generations; hosts Boogie and Vi are both Native Hawaiians, and they're brimming with generosity.

To ensure privacy, the two units are at opposite ends of the two-story cedar house. Both have private entrances, full baths, kitchens, and private balconies that overlook the ocean, with Molokini and Kahoolawe off in the distance. The kitchens have everything you can think of, and Vi makes sure that you have all the fixings for breakfast. Outside are a barbecue area and a sundeck; here you'll have the ocean splashing at your feet, and a ringside seat to watch the humpback whales from December to April.

4 Upcountry Maui

MAKAWAO, OLINDA & HALIIMAILE
MODERATE

In addition to Olinda Country Cottage, also consider **Angel's Nest of Mother Maui,** 576-T Olinda Rd., 3.6 miles above Makawao town (☎ **808/572-6773;** fax 808/573-2013; www.angelsnest.com), a New Age-y B&B set in an architect's dream of a home on 3½ heavenly acres. The five rooms (which share two luxurious baths with Jacuzzi and steam room) run $105 to $125 double, and the two cottages are $150 to $190 each.

☼ Olinda Country Cottage & Inn. 536 Olinda Rd. (near the top of Olinda Rd., a 15-minute drive from Makawao), Makawao, HI 96768. ☎ **800/932-3435** or 808/572-1453. Fax 808/572-1453. www.maui.net/~bbinn. E-mail: bbinn@maui.net. 5 units. TV TEL. $95–$110 double rm (rate includes continental breakfast), $110–$120 suite double (rate includes first morning's breakfast in fridge), $125–$140 cottage double (sleeps up to 5; rate includes first morning's breakfast in fridge). Extra person $15. 2-night minimum for rooms and suite, 3- to 5-night minimum for cottages. No credit cards.

When Ellen Unterman and Rupa McLaughlin bought this old Tudor mansion, formerly known as McKay Country Cottage, they saw distinct possibilities. The couple lovingly refurbished it; then Ellen, owner of a trendy antique store in Santa Monica, California, shipped almost a warehouse-full of antiques and collectibles to furnish it—and the result is one of the best-decorated country inns in Hawaii.

Set on the slopes of Haleakala in the crisp, clean air of Olinda, this charming B&B is located on an 8½-acre protea farm, surrounded by 35,000 acres of ranch lands (with miles of great hiking trails). The 5,000-square-foot country home, outfitted with a professional eye to detail, has large windows with incredible panoramic views of all of Maui. Upstairs are two guest rooms with antique beds, private full baths, and a separate entryway. Connected to the main house but with its own private entrance, the Pineapple Sweet has a full kitchen, an antique-filled living room, a marble-tiled full bathroom, and a separate bedroom. Located about 100 yards from the main house, the cottage is 1,000 square feet of cozy country luxury, with a fireplace, a bedroom with queen bed, cushioned window seats (with great sunset views), wall-to-wall carpet, and open-beam cathedral ceilings. Just added in 1997, the 950-square-foot Hidden Cottage (located in a truly hidden, secluded spot surrounded by protea flowers) features three decks, 8-foot French glass doors, a full kitchen, a washer/dryer, and a private bathtub for two on the deck.

Restaurants are a 15-minute drive away in Makawao, and beaches are another 15 minutes beyond that. Once ensconced, however, you might never want to leave this enchanting inn.

INEXPENSIVE

If you'd like your own private cottage, consider **Peace of Maui,** 1290 Haliimaile Rd. (just outside of Haliimaile town), Haliimaile, HI 96768 (☎ **808/572-5045;** e-mail pom@maui.net), with full kitchen, a bedroom, a day bed, and a large deck; the cottage goes for $50 to $65. Children are welcome.

☼ Banyan Tree House. 3265 Baldwin Ave. (next to Veteran's Cemetery, just .8 mile below Makawao), Makawao, HI 96768. ☎ **808/572-9021.** Fax 808/579-8180. www.maui.net/~banyantree.html. E-mail: holter@maui.net. 1 house, 2 cottages. $185 three-bedroom/3-bathroom house (sleeps up to 6), $45–$65 cottage double. 2- to 3-night minimum for house only. MC, V.

Huge monkeypod trees (complete with swing and hammock) extend their branches over this 2½-acre property like a giant green canopy. The restored 1920s plantation manager's house is decorated with Hawaiian furniture from the 1930s; the large guest rooms have big, comfortable beds and private marble-tiled bathrooms. A fireplace stands at one end of the huge living room, a large lanai runs the entire length of the house, and the hardwood floors shine throughout. The guest cottages have been totally renovated and also feature hardwood floors and marble bathrooms. The small cottage has a queen bed, private bathroom, microwave, coffeepot, and access to the fridge in the laundry room. The larger cottage has a queen bed and a twin bed, private bathroom, small fridge, microwave, coffeemaker, toaster, and TV. Guests have use of laundry facilities. The quiet neighborhood and nostalgic Old

Hawaii ambiance give this place a comfortable, easygoing atmosphere. Restaurants and shops are just minutes away in Makawao; the beach is a 15-minute drive—but this place is so relaxing that guests often find themselves wanting to do nothing more than lie in the hammock and watch the clouds float by.

Hale Ho'okipa Inn Makawao. 32 Pakani Pl., Makawao, HI 96768. ☎ **808/572-6698.** E-mail: cherie@mauigateway.com. 3 units (2 with shower only). $60—$70 double. Rates include continental breakfast. Extra person $8. No credit cards. From Haleakala Hwy., turn left on Makawao Ave., then turn right on the fifth street on the right off Makawao Ave. (Pakani Pl.); go to the last house on the right.

Step back in time at this 1924 plantation-style home, rescued by owner Cherie Attix in 1996 and restored to its original charm. Cherie, who owns an interior-design store, lovingly refurbished the old wooden floors, filled the rooms with antique furniture from the 1920s, and hung works by local artists on the walls. The result is a charming, serene place to stay, just a 5-minute walk from the shops and restaurants of Makawao town, 15 minutes from beaches, and a 1½-hour drive from the top of Haleakala. The guest rooms have separate outside entrances and private baths. The house's front and back porches are both wonderful for sipping tea and watching the sunset. The living room, decorated in period pieces, has a TV and a private phone line for guest use. Continental breakfast is served in the dining room, but most guests prefer to take their coffee out onto the porch to contemplate that majestic, century-old tree.

KULA
MODERATE

If you'd like to stay in a former sea captain's cottage, also consider **Country Garden Cottage** (☎ **888/878-2858** or 808/878-2858; fax 808/876-1458). This meticulously restored 1940s home on the slopes of Haleakala has a comfy living/dining room with a floor-to-ceiling stone fireplace, spacious bathroom, kitchenette, and small wooden deck that extends into flowering jungle. This sweet cottage is $100 double with a 2-night minimum; children are welcome.

✪ **Silver Cloud Ranch.** Old Thompson Rd. (1.2 miles past Hi. 37). RR 2, Box 201, Kula, HI 96790. ☎ **800/532-1111** or 808/878-6101. Fax 808/878-2132. www.maui.net/~slvrcld. E-mail: slvrcld@maui.net. 6 units in main house, 5 studios in bunkhouse, 1 cottage. $85–$125 double rm, $105–$145 double studio, $150 double cottage. Rates include full breakfast. Extra person $15. AE, DISC, MC, V.

Old Hawaii lives on at Silver Cloud Ranch, founded in 1902 by a sailor who jumped ship when he got to Maui. The former working cattle spread has a commanding view of four islands, the West Maui Mountains, and the valley and beaches below. The Lanai Cottage, a favorite among honeymooners, is nestled in a flower garden and has an ocean-view lanai, clawfoot bathtub, full kitchen, and wood-burning stove to warm chilly nights; a futon is available if you're traveling with a third person. The best rooms in the main house are on the second floor: the King Kamehameha Suite (with king bed) and the Queen Emma Suite (with queen bed). Each has a royal view, though some prefer Emma's. The Paniolo Bunkhouse, once used by real cowboys, is now fully restored and houses five studios, each with private bathroom, kitchenette, and views of the Pacific or Haleakala (go for the ocean view). All guests are free to use the main house and kitchen.

You'll find it cool and peaceful up here at 2,800 feet (bring a sweater). One-lane Thompson Road makes an ideal morning walk (about 3 miles round-trip), and you can go horseback riding next door at Thompson Ranch. There's a TV available if you feel visually deprived, but after a few Maui sunsets, you won't even remember why you bothered to ask.

INEXPENSIVE

In addition to the choices below, also consider **Elaine's Upcountry Guest Rooms,** 2112 Naalae Rd. (1½ miles from Kula Hwy.), Kula, HI 96790 (☎ **808/878-6623;** fax 808/878-2619); the warm and welcoming hosts let three rooms in their spacious pole house ($65 double), plus a wonderful cottage ($100 for four) with a separate bedroom plus a twin-bedded loft, full kitchen, and bathroom with sunken tub and a floor-to-ceiling window (Elaine's has a 3-night minimum).

Halemanu. 221 Kawehi Pl. (off Hi. 377), Kula, HI 96790. ☎ **808/878-2729.** Fax 808/878-2729. 1 unit. $85 double. Rate includes continental breakfast. 2-night minimum. No credit cards.

Carol Austin (owner, hostess, cook, and general renaissance woman) named her B&B Halemanu, which loosely translates as perch, because it's literally perched on the side of Haleakala at 3,600 feet. Way, way off the usual tourist path, Halemanu, built in 1990, is surrounded by farms and eucalyptus groves; it boasts 180-degree views of Maui from the ocean to the mountains. Staying here is like visiting an old, dear friend. There's only one guest room, with a queen bed with lace bedspread, a private full bathroom, and a private deck; its large picture windows look out over the island. There is a loft with a TV/VCR and a fabulous collection of movies that Blockbuster would be proud to call its own. Breakfast consists of fresh island fruit, homemade muffins, and cereals. Carol provides an extra fridge for her guests, as well as everything you could possibly need for the beach: cooler, beach mats, towels, and lots of advice on where to go. Beaches are about 30 minutes away, and Haleakala is about 45 minutes away.

✪ **Kula Cottage.** 206 Puakea Pl. (off Lower Kula Rd.), Kula, HI 96790. ☎ **808/878-2043** or 808/871-6230. Fax 808/871-9187. E-mail: gilassoc@maui.net. 1 cottage. $85 double. Rate includes continental breakfast. 2-night minimum. No credit cards.

We can't imagine having a less-than-fantastic vacation here. Tucked away on a quiet street amidst a half-acre of blooming papaya and banana trees, Cecilia and Larry Gilbert's romantic honeymoon cottage is very private—it even has its own driveway and carport. The 700-square-foot cottage has a full kitchen (complete with dishwasher), a washer/dryer, and three huge closets that offer enough storage space for you to move in permanently. An outside lanai has a big gas barbecue and an umbrella table and chairs. Cecilia delivers a continental breakfast daily (visitors rave about her homemade bread in the guest book). If you're an animal lover, Hana, the dog, will be more than happy to be a surrogate pet to you during your vacation; otherwise, Cecilia makes sure that Hana stays out of your way. Groceries and a small take-out lunch counter are within walking distance; it's a 30-minute drive to the beach.

Kula View. 140 Holopuni Rd. (off Kula Hwy.), P.O. Box 322, Kula, HI 96790. ☎ **808/878-6736.** 1 suite (with shower only). $85 double. Rate includes continental breakfast. Additional person $15. 2-night minimum. No credit cards.

On the slopes of Haleakala, at 2,000 feet, former flight attendant Susan Kauai maintains a quaint studio suite on the upper level of her home. A private entrance takes you up the stairs to a wide deck with views, views, views: in one direction Haleakala rises majestically; in another, all of Maui is spread out before you. Because the studio is located up a flight of stairs, it's not really an appropriate place for children under 5 years old. Surrounding the B&B are 2 lush acres blooming with fruits, flowers, and banana and coffee trees. The studio, tastefully decorated in Laura Ashley fabrics, is outfitted with a queen bed, a reading area, a wicker breakfast nook with small kitchenette, and a private shower.

✪ **Nohona Laule'a.** 763-2 Kamehameiki Rd. (off Kula Hwy.), Kula, HI 96790. ☎ **808/ 878-6646.** Fax 808/878-6646. 1 two-bedroom cottage. TV TEL. $85 double. Extra person $10. 3-night minimum. No credit cards.

What a deal—an impeccable two-bedroom cottage for $85 for two! Located on a windy road at about 2,500 feet, Nohona Laule'a (which means "peaceful dwelling") is 4 acres of tropical paradise with the cottage smack-dab in the middle. The 700-square-foot cottage, decorated in Asian style, features open-beam ceilings, skylights, a complete gourmet kitchen, a full bathroom, a living room, a huge deck, and a washer/dryer. The whole cottage has great island views: one bedroom, with Japanese shoji doors and two twin beds, looks out onto Haleakala; the other, with a double bed, has a big picture window overlooking the garden and the north shore beyond. The living room has a comfortable couch, a wooden rocker, and another huge picture window. Owners Brian and Sue Kanegai are congenial hosts; Sue greets guests with her delicious mango or banana bread. True to its name, this place is indeed peaceful. Kick back in a comfortable chair on the big deck and survey the blooming landscape at your feet, and you'll know what it must have been like to experience Eden.

5 East Maui: On the Road to Hana

KUAU
INEXPENSIVE

✪ **Kuau Cove Plantation.** 2 Wa'a Pl. (on the ocean side off Hana Hwy., 1 mile from stoplight in Paia), Paia, HI 96779. ☎ **808/579-8988.** Fax 808/579-8710. 2 units, 2 studio apts. TV TEL. $85 double rm, $95 studio apt. Rates include continental breakfast. Extra person $10 (a rollaway bed is available). 2-night minimum. MC, V.

This 1930s plantation doctor's home has been restored and decorated with antiques, wicker, and rattan furniture. An old-fashioned porch greets you upon arrival, and Douglas fir floors run throughout the house. The dining room overlooks a large lawn with two ancient monkeypod trees and lots of exotic blooming plants. Two large bedrooms in the main house each have a queen bed, private bathroom, TV, and phone. Each of the two studios (separate from the main house) has a small kitchenette, bedroom, sitting area, and full bathroom. Our favorite is the upstairs studio, which has its own small lanai with an ocean view. A continental breakfast is served buffet style in the dining room from 7:30 to 9am every day; breakfast is delivered to the two studio apartments.

Quiet accommodations, gorgeous surroundings, and excellent location. But the coup de grâce is the private path leading to a secluded ocean cove lined with coconut palms (access is tricky, so you generally have this beach all to yourself). There are world-class windsurfing just a short walk away at Hookipa Beach, restaurants within a 5-minute drive, and great boutiquing a mile away in Paia; it's just 10 minutes to Kahului Airport.

✪ **Mama's Beachfront Cottages.** 799 Poho Pl. (off the Hana Hwy. in Kuau), Paia, HI 96779. ☎ **800/860-HULA** or 808/579-9764. Fax 808/579-8594. www.maui.net/~mamas. E-mail: mamas@maui.net. 6 units. TV TEL. $90 one-bedroom apt (sleeps up to 4), $175 two-bedroom apt (sleeps up to 6). 3-night minimum. AE, DC, DISC, MC, V.

The fabulous location (nestled in a coconut grove on the secluded Kuau beach), beautifully decorated interior (with island-style rattan furniture and works by Hawaiian artists), and plenty of extras (Weber gas barbecue, 27-inch TVs, and all the beach toys you can think of) make this place a must-stay for people looking for a centrally located vacation rental. It has everything, even Mama's Fish House next door (where guests get a 20% discount). The one-bedrooms are nestled in a tropical jungle, whereas the two-bedrooms face the beach. Both have terra-cotta tiled floors, complete kitchens, sofa beds, and laundry facilities. We loved Mama's sense of humor: we opened the closet in one unit and found a grass hula skirt complete with a coconut-shell top tacked to the back wall.

HAIKU
MODERATE

Also consider **Haikuleana Bed & Breakfast,** 555 Haiku Rd., Haiku, HI 96708 (☎ **808/575-2890;** fax 808/575-9177; e-mail blumblum@maui.net), an 1850s former plantation doctor's house furnished with turn-of-the-century period pieces ($95 to $125 double, 2-night minimum).

✪ **Pilialoha B&B Cottage.** 2512 Kaupakalua Rd. (.7 mile from Kokomo intersection), Haiku, HI 96708. ☎ **808/572-1440.** Fax 808/572-4612. www.mauigateway.com/~heyde. E-mail: Heyde@mauigateway.com. 1 cottage. TV TEL. $100–$110 double. Rate includes continental breakfast. 3-night minimum. No credit cards.

The minute you arrive at this split-level country cottage, located on 2 acres of eucalyptus, you'll see owner Machiko Heyde's artistry at work. Just in front is a garden blooming with some 200 varieties of roses; you'll find more of her handiwork inside the quaint cottage. The cottage is great for couples but can sleep up to five: there are a queen bed in the master bedroom, a twin bed in a small adjoining room, and a queen sleeper sofa in the living room. A large lanai extends from the master bedroom. You'll find a great movie collection for rainy days or cool country nights, a washer/dryer, beach paraphernalia (including snorkel equipment), and a garage. Machiko delivers breakfast daily; if you plan on an early-morning ride to the top of Haleakala, she'll make sure that you go with a thermos of coffee and her homemade bread. *Pilialoha* translates as "friendship," which is how you will feel about your hostess by the time you leave.

INEXPENSIVE

Those in search of a peaceful retreat should try the **Bamboo Mountain Sanctuary,** 1111 Kaupakalua Rd., Haiku, HI 96708 (☎ **808/572-5106**), a 1940s plantation house that has served as a Zen monastery for 17 years; it offers five rooms (all with shared bathroom) on the edge of the Koolau Forest Reserve ($50 double).

Conveniently located near Twin Falls and Baldwin Beach is the **Golden Bamboo Ranch,** Kaupakalua Road (at Holokai Road), Haiku (☎ **800/262-9912** or 808/885-4550; fax 808/885-0559; e-mail bestbnb@aloha.net), situated on 7 fruit tree–covered acres with wonderful views ($80 suite double, $85 apt double, $90 cottage double).

Maui Dream Cottages. 265 W. Kuiaha Rd. (1 block from Pauwela Cafe), Haiku, HI 96708. ☎ **808/575-9079.** Fax 808/575-9477. E-mail: gblue@aloha.net. 2 cottages (with showers only). TV. $70 for 4. 7-night minimum. MC, V.

Essentially a vacation rental, this 2-acre country estate is located atop a hill overlooking the ocean. The grounds are dotted with fruit trees (bananas, papayas, and avocados, all free for the picking), and the front lawn is comfortably equipped with a double hammock, chaise lounges, and table and chairs. One cottage has two bedrooms, one bathroom, full kitchen (with microwave and coffeemaker), washer/dryer, and entertainment center. The other is basically the same, but with only one bedroom (plus a sofa bed in the living room). They're both very well maintained, comfortably outfitted with furniture that's not only attractive but also casual enough for families with kids.

The Haiku location is quiet and restful, and it offers the opportunity to see how real islanders live. However, be aware that you'll have to drive a good 20 to 25 minutes to restaurants in Makawao or Paia for dinner. The famous windsurfing mecca, Hookipa Beach, is about a 20-minute drive, and Baldwin Beach (good swimming) is about 25 minutes away.

TWIN FALLS
INEXPENSIVE

Also consider the private studio at **Halfway to Hana House,** off Hana Highway past Twin Falls Bridge, P.O. Box 675, Haiku, HI 96708 (☎ **808/572-1176;** fax 808/572-3609; www.maui.net\~gailp; e-mail gailp@maui.net), a cozy room with Polynesian-style decor ($70 double, 3-night minimum).

✪ **Maluhia Hale.** P.O. Box 687 (off Hana Hwy., nearly 1 mile past Twin Falls bridge), Haiku, HI 96708. ☎ **808/572-2959.** Fax 808/572-2959. E-mail: djg@maui.net. 3 units. TV. $85 cottage double, $105 suite double. Rates include continental breakfast on the first morning. Extra person $15. 2-night minimum. No credit cards.

Diane and Robert Garrett design and build homes that are works of art. Here, they've created a private country cottage by the sea that has the feeling of a gracious old Hawaiian plantation home. An open, airy screened veranda leads to a glassed-in sitting room and kitchenette; antiques fill the cottage, and Diane's exquisite flower arrangements add splashes of color. A traditional Hawaiian bathhouse is adjacent, with an old clawfoot tub and a separate shower. In the main house are two suites: one with a solarium, complete with small kitchenette and screened porch; and a more romantic suite with cherry-wood floors, a lacy bedspread, and a view of the lily pond outside. Diane does light housekeeping daily. When your stay is over, you'll no doubt depart with the warm feeling of having been pampered in paradise.

HUELO
MODERATE

✪ **Huelo Point Flower Farm.** Off Hana Hwy., between mile markers 3 and 4 (P.O. Box 1195), Paia, HI 96779. ☎ **808/572-1850.** www.maui.net/~huelopt. E-mail: huelopt@maui.net. 3 cottages, 1 main house. $110–$200 cottage double (rates include continental breakfast); $2,300 per week for main house for 6. Extra person $15. No credit cards.

Here's where the celebs escape to a little Eden by the sea: a 2-acre estate on a remote 300-foot sea cliff overlooking Waipio Bay, with guest cottages and a main house all available for rental. Despite its seclusion, it's just a half hour to Kahului Airport (so is just about everything else on Maui), or about 20 minutes to Paia's shops and restaurants. The studio-sized Gazebo Cottage has a glass-walled oceanfront, koa-wood captain's bed, TV, stereo, kitchenette, private oceanside patio, private hot tub, and half-bathroom with outdoor shower. The new 900-square-foot Carriage House apartment sleeps four and has glass walls facing mountain and sea, plus kitchen, den, decks, and loft bedroom. The two-bedroom main house has an exercise room, a fireplace, a sunken bathtub, and cathedral ceilings. There's a natural pool with waterfall and an oceanfront hot tub. You're welcome to pick fruit, vegetables, and flowers from the extensive garden. Homemade scones, tree-ripened papayas, and fresh-roasted coffee are available to start your day.

❖ **Huelo Point Lookout B&B.** Off Hana Hwy., between mile markers 3 and 4. Reservations c/o Hawaii's Best Bed & Breakfasts, P.O. Box 563, Kamuela, HI 96743. ☎ **800/262-9912** or 808/885-4550. Fax 808/885-0559. E-mail: bestbnb@aloha.net. 3 cottages. TV TEL. $95–$275 cottage double. Rates include a welcome breakfast on arrival. Extra person $20. 3-night minimum. DISC.

About a quarter-mile from the 300-foot cliffs of Waipio Bay is this lovely B&B, situated on 2 acres of tropical jungle with a hot tub, 40-foot freeform swimming pool, and view all the way down the coastline to Hana. The main house has pentagonal glass walls that offer sweeping views, two private entrances, a large bedroom with king bed, a kitchenette, a big bathroom with a tub for two, and a lotus pond and waterfall outside on the private deck. The Honeymoon cottage is a totally renovated old fisherman's residence, with an upstairs bedroom; a full kitchen; a sitting room; and a solarium with lots of windows, skylights, and a deck. The bathroom has a Victorian tub and glass all around, with views of Haleakala on one side and the ocean on the other. The Halekala cottage is smaller but full of amenities, including a full kitchen, king bed, and tiled bathroom that extends outside into the garden so that you can actually take a hot shower under the stars, surrounded by white lattice and tropical flowers. The newest cottage, Rainbow, located next to the swimming pool, features 25-foot-high glass walls with nothing but views. Other unique amenities include a private indoor hot tub, glass-ceilinged bathroom, and work-of-art wooden staircase. The owners, Jeff and Sharyn, also own a video store in Paia, so they can get you the movies of your choice.

Pali Uli. Off Hana Hwy., between mile markers 3 and 4 (P.O. Box 1059), Haiku, HI 96708. ☎ and fax **808/573-0693.** www.maui.net/~paliuli/. E-mail: paliuli@maui.net. 1 house. TV TEL. $200 double. Extra person $25. 3-night minimum. No credit cards.

This cliff house sits on a 22-acre estate overlooking a 150-foot waterfall on the cliff below. Glass, teak, and marble dominate the unusual architect-designed 900-square-foot house. The complete kitchen features teak cabinets and marble floors and countertops; the living room has a built-in king sofa bed, a 10-foot marble fireplace, and a huge skylight. Outside, a hot tub on the deck overlooks the ocean, waterfall, and majestic cliffs below. You can sleep either on the built-in sofa bed in front of the fireplace or in the detached Asian-style sleeping quarters, next to the large swimming pool. The prices aren't cheap, but then this is a luxury accommodation well worth the price.

INEXPENSIVE

Hale Akua Shangri-la Resort. Star Rte. 1, Box 161 (off Hana Hwy. between mile markers 3 and 4), Haiku, HI 96708. ☎ **888/368-5305** or 808/572-9300. Fax 808/572-6666. www.maui.net/~shangrla.html. E-mail: shangrla@maui.net. 11 units (some with shared bathrooms), 2 cottages. $50–$140 double rm, $100–$125 cottage double. Rates include breakfast. Extra person $20. AE, DISC, MC, V.

This place isn't for everyone; the hang-loose atmosphere might or might not be your style. Way off the beaten path, Hale Akua is a collection of eclectic buildings on 2 tropical acres where, at certain times of the year, guests can choose to go "clothing optional" (translation: naked). The main house on the property has breathtaking ocean views and private lanais off most rooms; guests share the living room, bathroom, and kitchen. The Cabana building, next to the 60-foot pool, is a two-story house with five separate rooms, two kitchens, and a dining area. Also on the property is a cottage with two rooms, one pyramid-shaped. Other features on the property include a hot tub, fountain, lily pond, hammock in the trees, trampoline, and maze formed by panex trees. Yoga classes are available.

6 At the End of the Road in East Maui: Hana

In past editions, we've recommended a couple of booking agencies located in Hana; however, on our most recent site inspection of their properties, we found that several listings needed repairs, were way overpriced, or were downright dirty. At this time we cannot recommend these booking agencies, but we'll continue to inspect their properties and, in the next edition, let you know if they have made the necessary repairs and maintained standards of cleanliness.

VERY EXPENSIVE

✪ **Hotel Hana-Maui.** P.O. Box 8, Hana, HI 96713. ☎ **800/321-HANA** or 808/248-8211. Fax 808/248-7202. 143 units. TEL. $395 garden rm double, $450–$495 suite double, $525–$795 cottage double. Packages available. Extra person $50. AE, DC, JCB, MC, V.

Picture Shangri-la, Hawaiian-style: 66 acres rolling down to the sea in a remote Hawaiian village, with a wellness center, two pools, and access to one of the best beaches in Hana. It all adds up to make this one of the best locations in the state. Since it was built in 1946, Hotel Hana-Maui has been the luxury getaway for celebrities around the globe. As we went to press, there were rumors in the wind that a new management team (of impeccable international stature) was poised to take over. We hope so, because the property is in need of massive overall renovation.

This bastion of tranquillity has large suitelike rooms in single-story buildings set on shady lawns; all come with private patios, bleached wood floors, Hawaiian quilts on the beds, wonderful bathrooms (with large soaking tubs overlooking private gardens), fridges, and coffeemakers. Terry robes and fresh coffee beans assure a pleasant start to the day. Our favorites are the Sea Ranch cottages, small but exquisite plantation-style units at water's edge, with hot tubs on the lanais.

There's no swimming here, but much-celebrated Hamoa Beach, with pavilion and beach amenities for guests, is about 3 miles away via free shuttle or down a pleasant country lane. We love the multitude of trails, the quiet starry nights, and the genuine Hawaiian atmosphere here.

Dining: The dining room was once home to two of the finest chefs in Hawaii (Jean-Marie Josselin and Amy Ferguson-Ota), but it has since suffered a decline in quality and service, coupled with escalating prices. Hopefully the rumored new management will institute significant changes: a revamped menu, new training, and a reinvigorated spirit for a flagging operation that has failed to maintain the high standards of its heyday.

Amenities: Free airport pickup from Hana Airport; lei greetings; nightly turndowns on request; free beach shuttle. Library, riding stables, hiking trails, tennis, pool, three-hole practice golf course, bicycles, beach equipment, rental cars. Salon, wellness/health center with spa treatments and activities, shops.

MODERATE

If you'd like an unusual place to stay, consider the series of huts at **Ho'onanea Farm,** Star Route 165A (10 miles from Hana, next to Oheo Gulch and Haleakala National Park in Kipahulu Valley), Hana, HI 96713 (☎ **808/248-7816;** fax 808/248-8648). Two huts serve as sleeping "hales," or houses; one is the common area; and another houses bathroom facilities. It's not for everyone, but it's certainly unique and beautiful ($105 double, 2-night minimum or $15 cleaning fee added).

✪ **Ekena.** Off Hana Hwy., above Hana Airport (P.O. Box 728), Hana, HI 96713. ☎ **808/248-7047.** Fax 808/248-7047. www.maui.net/~ekena. E-mail: ekena@maui.net. 2 deluxe two-bedroom apts. TV TEL. $150 double, $190–$275 for 4. Extra person $15. 3-night minimum. No credit cards.

Only one floor (and one two-bedroom unit) in this elegant two-story pole house is rented at any one time to ensure privacy. Just one glance at the 360-degree view and you can see why hosts Robin and Gaylord gave up their careers on the mainland and moved here. This 8½-acre piece of paradise in rural Hana boasts views of the coastline, the ocean, and the verdant rain forest; the floor-to-ceiling sliding-glass doors in the spacious Hawaiian-style home bring the outside in. The house is exquisitely furnished, from the comfortable U-shaped couch that invites you to relax and take in the view to the top-of-the-line mattress on the king bed. The kitchen is fully equipped (guests have made complete Thanksgiving and holiday meals here), and it contains every high-tech convenience you can imagine. The grounds are impeccably groomed with tropical plants and fruit trees. Hiking trails into the rain forest start right on the property, and the beaches, waterfalls, and pools are just minutes away. Robin places fresh flowers in every room and makes sure that guests are comfortable. She's available to answer questions about what Hana has to offer, but she also respects her guests' privacy and lets them enjoy their vacation in peace.

✪ **Hamoa Bay Bungalow.** P.O. Box 773, Hana, HI 96713. ☎ **808/248-7884.** Fax 808/248-8642. E-mail: jody@maui.net. 1 cottage. TV TEL. $145 double. Rate includes continental breakfast. 2-night minimum. No credit cards.

Down a country lane guarded by two Balinese statues stands a little bit of Indonesia in Hawaii, a carefully crafted bungalow overlooking Hamoa Bay. Only 2 miles beyond Hasegawa's General Store on the way to Kipahulu, this enchanting retreat sits on 4 verdant acres within walking distance of black-sand Hamoa Beach (which James Michener considered one of the most beautiful in the Pacific). The romantic, 600-square-foot Balinese-style cottage is distinctly tropical, with giant Elephant bamboo furniture from Indonesia, batik prints, a king bed, a full kitchen, and a screened porch with hot tub and shower. Host Jody Baldwin, a lifelong Mauian who lives on the estate, serves a tropical breakfast of fruit, yogurt, and muffins; she'll be happy to share the secrets of the Hana Coast, including the great mountain hiking trail nearby.

Hana Hale Malamalama. Hana (across from the Mormon Church). Reservations c/o Hawaii's Best Bed & Breakfast, P.O. Box 563, Kamuela, HI 96743. ☎ **800/262-9912** or 808/885-4550. Fax 808/885-0559. E-mail: bestbnb@aloha.net. TV TEL. 3 units. $110–$175 suite double, $150 cottage double. Extra person $15. 2-night minimum. DISC.

Located on a historic site with ancient fish ponds and a cave mentioned in ancient chants, Hana Hale Malamalama definitely exudes the spirit of Old Hawaii. Host John takes excellent care of the ponds (he feeds the fish at 5pm every day, to the delight of his guests) and is fiercely protective of the hidden cave on-site ("it's not a tourist attraction, but a sacred spot"). The property has access to a nearby rocky beach, which is not good for swimming but is a wonderful place to watch the sun set and the moon rise. All the accommodations include fully equipped kitchens, baths, bedrooms, living/dining areas, and private lanais. The main house, with the two duplex suites, is an architectural masterpiece, built entirely of Philippine mahogany with 4-foot-wide skylights the entire length of the house. Entry to the house is down stone steps, so this is not a place for small children or anyone who has trouble climbing steep steps. Downstairs is the garden suite, with a separate bedroom, kitchen, and bathroom shower overlooking a private garden. Upstairs, the royal suite offers more than 1,800 square feet of open living area, with a deck around the entire house. The master bedroom contains a king bed; a queen bed is in the open loft. The skylights are wonderful at night, but I found that they made the entire house too hot in the summer. In a separate building is the tree-house cottage, nestled between a kamani tree and a coconut palm. Downstairs is the bathroom with a Jacuzzi tub for two; upstairs is a Balinese bamboo bed, a small kitchen/living area, and a small deck outside. Although the view is wonderful, we weren't too fond of walking up and down the steep steps at night to go to the bathroom.

Papalani. Star Route 27 (3 miles past Hasagawa's General Store, before the bridge at mile marker 48), Hana, HI 96713. ☎ **808/248-7204.** Fax 808/248-7285. 1 apt, 1 cottage. TEL. $150 double. Extra person $25. 3-night minimum. No credit cards.

These luxurious, romantic accommodations are hidden from the road, offering privacy and quiet in a first-class setting. There is only one tiny drawback: mosquitoes—swarms of them, in fact. A stream runs through the property, and although hostess Cybil has done everything possible to eliminate this nuisance (like providing screened-in lanais so that you can enjoy the outdoors without experiencing these biting pests), bring your insect repellent.

Otherwise, Papalani lives up to its name, which means "heaven and all the spiritual powers." The apartment and the cottage, both decorated by a professional designer, have white leather couches, wood floors, and expensive artwork. Everything is first-class, from the kitchen appliances to the bathroom faucets. The apartment has a kitchenette with minifridge, blender, and coffeemaker, whereas the cottage has a full kitchen. Both units have their own laundry facilities and private hot tubs. In addition, this is a TV-free environment, so you can really get in touch with nature. The great location means you're just a 5-minute walk to Waioka Stream (where there's good swimming in the pools), a mile from beautiful Hamoa Beach, and 5 minutes from Hana. Cybil asks that guests not smoke on the property and that meat be cooked on a barbecue outside; no children under 8 are permitted.

INEXPENSIVE

If you'd like your own cottage, consider the simple but adequately furnished **Aloha Cottages,** 83 Keawa Pl., P.O. Box 205, Hana, HI 96713 (☎ **808/248-8420**), which go for $60 to $95 double. For million-dollar views at budget rates, consider **Koholaimi,** HCR Box 34 (3 miles past Hasagawa's General Store, just past mile marker 48), Hana, HI 96713 (☎ **808/248-8366**); the warm hosts and the mesmerizing vistas will make you forget the slightly funky decor ($75 rm double, $135 cottage double, 3-night minimum).

✪ **Tradewinds Cottage.** 135 Alalele Pl. (P.O. Box 385), Hana, HI 96713. ☎ **800/327-8097** or 808/248-8980. Fax 808/248-7735. www.maui.net/~twt/cottage.html. E-mail: twt@maui.net. 2 cottages. TV TEL. $95 studio cottage double, $115 two-bedroom cottage double. Extra person $10. 2-night minimum. MC, V.

Nestled amongst the ginger and heliconias on a 5-acre flower farm are these two separate cottages, each with complete kitchen, carport, barbecue, private hot tub, TV, ceiling fan, and sleeper sofa. The cabana is a studio cottage that sleeps up to four; a bamboo shoji blind separates the sleeping area (with queen bed) from the sofa bed in the living room. The Tradewinds cottage has two bedrooms (with queen bed in one room and two twins in the other), one bathroom (with shower only), sleeper sofa, and huge front porch. The atmosphere is quiet and relaxing, and hosts

Mike and Rebecca Buckley, who have been in business for a decade, welcome families (they have two children, a cat, and a very sweet golden retriever). You can use their laundry facilities at no extra charge.

Waianapanapa State Park Cabins. Off Hana Hwy. c/o State Parks Division, 54 S. High St., Rm. 101, Wailuku, HI 96793. ☎ **808/984-8109.** 12 cabins. $45 for 4 (sleeps up to 6). Extra person $5. 5-night maximum. No credit cards.

These 12 rustic cabins are the best lodging deal on Maui. Everyone knows it, too—so make your reservations early (up to 6 months in advance). The cabins are warm and dry and come complete with kitchen, living room, bedroom, and bathroom with hot shower; furnishings include bedding, linen, towels, dishes, and very basic cooking and eating utensils. Don't expect luxury—this is a step above camping, albeit in a beautiful tropical jungle setting unlike any other in the islands. The key attraction at this 120-acre state beach park is the unusual horseshoe-shaped black-sand beach on Pailoa Bay, popular for shore fishing, snorkeling, and swimming. There's a caretaker on-site, along with rest rooms, showers, picnic tables, shoreline hiking trails, and historic sites. But bring mosquito protection—this *is* the jungle.

Dining 7

by Jocelyn Fujii

If there are any doubts in your mind that Maui is a dining mecca, consider the latest in the restaurant scene. Superchef Sam Choy of the hugely successful Sam Choy's restaurant chain has opened a large new eatery in a prime spot at the Kaahumanu Center, with plans to convert the former site of Shark's Tooth Brewery and Grill (in the same shopping center) into a contemporary Chinese restaurant. Peter Merriman, chef extraordinaire and a pioneer of Hawaii Regional Cuisine, plans to open his new restaurant in late 1998, in the new Maui Ocean Center in Maalaea. The emphasis will be on seasonal produce and fresh local ingredients, an imaginative menu, and "shared dining"—a perfect concept in a region where combination platters and "family style" ethnic dining are commonplace. Merriman also oversees Hula Grill in Kaanapali.

New dining adventures beckon elsewhere on Maui. This is the island of cuisine as luscious as the West Maui Mountains, the place where Hawaii's chefs first became as celebrated as their glamorous clients from the mainland. In the past decade, with the ascension of Hawaii Regional Cuisine into national prominence, and with Maui as Hawaii's visitor-industry success story, the state's best chefs have opened their Maui doors and turned this island into a culinary nexus.

Good food on this island means chefs like David Paul, Beverly Gannon, Eric Leterc (the newly arrived wunderkind at Maui Prince's Prince Court), Steve Amaral at his new Cucina Pacifica, and arrivals from outer islands: Peter Merriman (Big Island), Jean-Marie Josselin (Kauai), Roy Yamaguchi (Oahu), and George Mavrothalassitis, the former Halekulani chef who moved to Maui to become the best thing about the Four Seasons Resort at Wailea.

You can also dine well at Lahaina's open-air oceanfront watering holes. You'll find budget eateries there, but not many; Maui's old-fashioned, multigeneration mom-and-pop diners are disappearing by attrition, eclipsed by the flashy newcomers or clinging to the edge of existence in the older neighborhoods of central Maui. Although you'll have to work harder to find them, you won't have to go far to find creative cuisine, pleasing style, and stellar views in upcountry, south, and west Maui.

In the listings below, reservations are not necessary unless otherwise noted.

1 Central Maui

Maui is in the midst of a Sam Choy's invasion. The irrepressible chef has opened his fourth Hawaii restaurant in Kahului, where the **Kaahumanu Center,** as much a dining as a shopping attraction, is located (5 minutes from Kahului Airport on Hi. 32, at 275 Kaahumanu Ave.). The second floor of Kaahumanu Center, the structure that looks like a white *Star Wars* umbrella in the center of town, has its own very popular food court with concessions and small take-out counters that serve, for the most part, excellent food. The **Juiceland** kiosk near the top of the elevator offers vitamin-rich (and delicious!), freshly squeezed vegetable and fruit juices, as well as smoothies made from the legendary fresh fruits of Maui. Busy shoppers seem more than willing to dispense with fine china and other formalities to enjoy a no-nonsense meal that efficiently refreshes them between spurts of shopping. Among the standouts: **Maui Tacos,** one of Mark Avalon's string of palate-pleasing Mexican diners sprinkled throughout Maui (see page 141). (Watch for them on the mainland; founder/chef Mark Ellman has formed a partnership with Blimpie International to open Maui Tacos outlets nationwide.) The green burritos, painted naturally with spinach, are the best this side of the Rio Grande. **Edo Japan** teppanyaki is a real find, its flat Benihana-like grill dispensing marvelous flavorful mounds of grilled fresh vegetables and chicken teriyaki for $4.15. **Yummy Korean B-B-Q,** part of a chain well-known on Oahu, proffers soups, sesame bean sprouts, potato salad, and many combinations of vegetables, meats, fish, and ribs infused with the assertive flavors of Korea. One spot that's always abuzz is the Kaahumanu Center's **The Coffee Store** (see page 145), a no-nonsense java stop that serves sandwiches, salads, pasta, and nearly two dozen different coffee drinks for shopping-mall regenerates.

When you leave Kaahumanu Center, take a moment to gaze at the West Maui Mountains to your left from the parking lot. You'll see one of Maui's wonders, a kaleidoscopic show of clouds, sunlight, textured canyons, and deep greens that reflect the mystical qualities of the old mountain.

EXPENSIVE

Sam Choy's Kahului. Kaahumanu Center, 275 Kaahumanu Ave. ☎ **808/893-0366.** Reservations recommended. Breakfast $4.25–$9.50, lunch $4.95–$9.95, dinner main courses $22.95–$29.95. AE, DC, JCB, MC, V. Sun–Thurs 7am–3pm and 5:30–9pm, Fri–Sat 7am–3pm and 5–9:30pm. LOCAL/HAWAII REGIONAL CUISINE.

Despite his widespread appeal as a chef, Sam Choy's new Maui eatery has received mixed reviews since its opening in Kahului. The Maui-style favorites on the menu sound good, but have disappointed many diners. Let's hope that changes and this new and busy dining room can reach the culinary heights of its Oahu and Big Island sister restaurants. Local items abound at breakfast and lunch; at dinner, the menu shifts gears to more ambitious fare. This means gargantuan servings and such local ravishments as baked stuffed shiitake mushrooms; a seafood sampler of mahimahi, lau lau, macadamia nut–crusted ono, and salmon Wellington; vegetarian tofu lasagna; Oriental lamb chops; Brie wonton (a favorite); and Sam's signature garlic mashed potatoes, a hit.

MODERATE

Marco's Grill & Deli. 444 Hana Hwy., Kahului. ☎ **808/877-4446.** Main courses $12.95–$19.95. AE, CB, DC, DISC, JCB, MC, V. Daily 7:30am–10pm. ITALIAN.

Located in the elbow of central Maui, where the roads to upcountry, west, and south Maui converge, Marco's is popular among area residents who like its homemade Italian fare and friendly informality. This is one of those comfortable neighborhood fixtures favored by all generations. The antipasto salad, vegetarian lasagna, and roasted peppers with garlic, provolone cheese, and anchovies are tasty treats, but don't ignore the meatballs and Italian sausage: homemade and robust, they're served on French bread with all the trimmings. Hot entrees start streaming out of the kitchen at 10am.

INEXPENSIVE

✪ **A Saigon Cafe.** 1792 Main St., Wailuku. ☎ **808/243-9560.** Main courses $6.50–$16.95. DC, MC, V. Mon–Sat 10am–9:30pm, Sun 10am–8:30pm. VIETNAMESE.

Saigon's feisty flavors find expression in Jennifer Nguyen's authentic Vietnamese cuisine, which enjoys a sterling reputation even among picky Maui residents. There's no sign, but the cafe is always busy with regulars (the Maui grapevine is hyperactive). The menu runs the gamut, from a dozen different soups to cold and hot noodles (including the popular beef noodle soup called *pho*) and chicken and shrimp cooked in a clay pot. Wok-cooked Vietnamese specialties—sautéed with spicy lemongrass and sweet-and-sour sauces—highlight the produce of the season, and the fresh catch (ono, opakapaka) comes whole and crisp or steamed with ginger and garlic. You can create your own Vietnamese "burritos" from a platter of tofu, noodles, and vegetables that you wrap in rice paper and dip in garlic sauce. Our favorites include the piquant and refreshing shrimp lemongrass ($8.50) and the tofu curry ($6.75), swimming in herbs and vegetables straight from the garden. The Nhung Dam, the Vietnamese version of fondue—a hearty spread of basil, cucumber, mint, romaine, bean sprouts, pickled carrots, turnips, and vermicelli, wrapped in rice paper and dipped in a legendary sauce—is cooked at your table.

Class Act. At Maui Community College, 310 Kaahumanu Ave., Wailuku. ☎ **808/984-3480.** Reservations required. Four-course lunch $13. No credit cards. Wed and Fri 11am–12:15pm, last seating. Cuisine changes weekly.

This restaurant is part of a program run by the Food Service Department of Maui Community College; it has quite a following on the island. Student chefs show their stuff in their "classroom," where they pull out all the stops as if it were their own place. Linen, china, servers in ties and white shirts, and a four-course lunch make this a four-star value. The appetizer, soup, salad, and dessert are set, but you can choose between the regular entree and a heart-healthy option prepared in the culinary tradition of the week. The filet mignon offered during French week is popular, as are the other international menus (including Japanese, Austrian, and Moroccan cuisine) served throughout the months. There's no air-conditioning, but there are fans and balcony seating. With soup, salad, and grilled lamb or eggplant Napoleon, capped with a gourmet dessert for $11, it's no wonder they're always busy. Tea and soft drinks are offered—and they can get pretty fancy, with fresh fruit and spritzers—but otherwise it's BYOB.

Hamburger Mary's. 2010 Main St., Wailuku. ☎ **808/244-7776.** Reservations suggested for dinner and Sun brunch. Most items under $8; Sun brunch $20. DISC, MC, V. Mon 10am–4pm, Tues–Sat 10am–9pm and bar until 2am, Sun brunch 10am–2pm. AMERICAN.

Hamburger Mary's is famous for its one-third–pound hamburgers; it's also popular as a gay hangout and as Wailuku's version of Cheers, a place where gays and straights are equally at home, enjoying wholesome food in an upbeat atmosphere. Among the specialties: excellent homemade soups (fish chowder, spicy black bean, lentil) and burgers on three different types of bread, heaped high with vegetables and smothered in homemade dressings. Fans rave about the veggie burgers, crowned with grilled onions and homemade Thousand Island dressing. They're made with larger, meatier garden *steaks* (as opposed to garden *burgers*), and you can pile them high with sautéed mushrooms and other toppings for a small extra charge. Only fresh seafood is used, so pay attention to the specials—like the Sunday brunch, they're also très populaire.

Ichiban. 47 Kaahumanu Ave., Kahului Shopping Center. ☎ **808/871-6977.** MC, V. Mon–Fri 6:30am–2pm and 5–9pm, Sat 10:30am–2pm and 5–9pm. JAPANESE/SUSHI.

What a find: an informal neighborhood restaurant that serves inexpensive, home-cooked Japanese food *and* good sushi, at realistic prices. Local residents consider Ichiban a staple for breakfast, lunch, or dinner. Offerings include egg-white omelets for $4.75, great saimin for $4.25, shrimp omelets for $5.25, combination plates (teriyaki chicken, teriyaki meat, *tonkatsu* [pork cutlet], rice, and pickled cabbage) for $8.50, chicken yakitori for $5.50, plus sushi—everything from unagi and scallop to California roll. The sushi items might not be inexpensive, but, like the specials (such as steamed opakapaka for $18.75), they're a good value. *Tip:* We love the tempura, miso soup, and spicy ahi hand roll.

Maui Bake Shop. 2092 Vineyard St., Wailuku. ☎ **808/242-0064.** Most items under $5. AE, DC, DISC, MC, V. Mon–Fri 6am–5pm, Sat 7am–3pm. BAKERY/DELI.

Sleepy Vineyard Street has seen many a mom-and-pop business come and go, but Maui Bake Shop is here to stay. Maui native Claire Fujii-Krall and her husband, baker José Krall (who was trained in the south of France and throughout Europe), are turning out buttery brioches, healthy nine-grain and two-tone rye breads, focaccia, strudels, sumptuous fresh fruit gâteaux, puff pastry, and dozens of baked goods and confections. The breads are baked in one of Maui's oldest brick ovens, installed in 1935; a high-tech European diesel oven handles the rest. The front window displays the more than 100 bakery and deli items, which include salads, a popular eggplant marinara focaccia, and a moist $3 calzone with a chicken/pesto/mushroom/cheese filling. Homemade soups team up nicely with sandwiches made with freshly baked bread, and they're light enough (well, almost) to justify the Ultimate Dessert: white-chocolate macadamia-nut cheesecake.

Norm's Café. 740 Lower Main St., Wailuku. ☎ **808/242-1667.** Main courses $5.35–$6.95. MC, V. Mon–Sat 5am–2pm, Wed–Thurs 5–8pm, Fri–Sat 5–9pm, Sun 6am–2pm. AMERICAN/LOCAL.

The newest rage for the diner crowd, Norm's welcomes you with a plaid yellow concrete-block entrance lined with lava rock—an apt foreshadowing of the old-fashioned, Formica-table celebration that awaits you inside. Hot-pink paper menus issue the call for Norm's signature Paukukalo Burger, an 8-ounce hamburger with bleu cheese dressing and all the trimmings; Fran's Club, a turkey-bacon-avocado fantasy on grilled sourdough; and the universal fave, bamboo-steamed ono—at $6.45, a catch. There's always a gaggle of habitués somewhere in the far corner, trying to decide between saimin, dry mein, BLT, and the humongous hamburger, and then winding up with the steamed ono, the dish that put Norm's on the map.

Restaurant Matsu. In the Maui Mall, 70 E. Kaahumanu Ave., Kahului. ☎ **808/871-0822.** Most items under $6. No credit cards. Mon–Thurs 9am–6pm, Fri 9am–9pm, Sat 9am–5:30pm, Sun 10am–4pm. JAPANESE/LOCAL.

Customers have come from Hana (more than 50 miles away) just for Matsu's California rolls; regulars line up for the cold saimin, made with julienned cucumber, egg, *char siu* (Chinese-style sweet pork), and red ginger on noodles. The bento plates—various assemblages of chicken, teriyaki beef, fish, and rice—make great take-out lunches for working folks and picnickers. The new nigiri sushi items are popular, especially for the don't-dally lunch crowd. The katsu pork and chicken, breaded and deep-fried, are another specialty of this casual Formica-style diner. We love the tempura udon and the saimin, steaming mounds of wide and fine noodles swimming in homemade broths and topped with condiments. The daily specials are a changing lineup of home-cooked classics: ox-tail soup, roast pork with gravy, teriyaki ahi, miso butterfish, and breaded mahimahi.

Siam Thai. 123 N. Market St., Wailuku. ☎ **808/244-3817.** Reservations recommended for parties of 4 or more. Main courses $5.95–$8.50. AE, CB, DC, DISC, JCB, MC, V. Mon–Fri 11am–2:30pm and 5–9pm, Sat–Sun 5–9pm. THAI.

This local favorite specializes in Evil Prince chicken and other coconut- and spice-infused Thai specialties that are much favored by Westerners. Expect lots of fresh basil, lemongrass, ginger, cabbage, spices, and tofu, as well as a feisty Siam Chicken—a whole Cornish game hen deep-fried with garlic and soy sauce. The Thai snapper (*pla rad prik*) is deep-fried crisp and whole in a sweet-and-sour sauce and heaped with onions, red peppers, and condiments—tasty, but not for the faint-hearted.

Stanton's of Maui. In the Maui Mall, 70 E. Kaahumanu Ave., Kahului. ☎ **808/877-3711.** Most items under $6.95. AE, DC, DISC, MC, V. Mon–Sat 9am–6pm, Fri 9am–9pm. COFFEE SHOP/DELI.

Local Kaanapali coffee from Maui, Kona coffee from the Big Island, Ethiopian mocha, Haitian Blue French Roast, and many other versions of the bean are sold here, in light, dark, decaf, and rotating flavors of the day. Accompanying the high-octane libations is a small, attractive menu of soups, sandwiches, and salads. This being Maui, a growing list of vegetarian items is de rigueur, and much appreciated. The lean machines love the tofu burger, piled high with sprouts, tomatoes, cucumbers, and a special dressing. There's live music from 6 to 9pm on Fridays and from noon to 2pm on Mondays, Wednesdays, and Fridays. If coffee isn't your cup of tea, there's a full bar.

Wei Wei BBQ and Noodle House. In Millyard Plaza, 210 Imi Kala St., Wailuku. ☎ **808/242-7928.** Combination plates $4.95–$6.95; main dishes $3–$8.50. No credit cards. Daily 10am–9pm. CHINESE/NOODLE HOUSE.

Noodles are rapidly gaining on Big Macs as the fast-food choice of Hawaii these days, and Wei Wei is a good example. Open less than a year, it's the new darling of the on-the-go, no-nonsense, noodle-loving Maui crowd. You order at the counter, fast-food style, from a menu that includes Chinese classics: saimin with roast duck, shrimp-vegetable chow mein, dim sum, and the extremely popular house fried noodles. American favorites—hamburger, teriyaki chicken burger, turkey sandwich, and the popular chicken katsu burger—are winning fans, too. The hot-and-sour soup is a Szechuan touch, and the combination and mini plates (steak, chicken, katsu, ahi, sweet-and-sour spareribs) are gaining the attention of budget-conscious diners.

2 West Maui

LAHAINA
EXPENSIVE

Avalon. 844 Front St. ☎ **808/667-5559.** Reservations recommended. Lunch $5.95–$15.95, dinner main courses $14.95–$26.95. AE, CB, DC, DISC, JCB, MC, V. Daily 11am–11pm. HAWAII REGIONAL.

Ten-year-old Avalon is now one among Mark and Judy Ellman's many other Maui enterprises, including six Maui Tacos "healthy Maui Mex" take-out stands throughout the island. Avalon's signature dishes still tower (as in the salmon-tiki salad) and titillate (as in its signature Caramel Miranda dessert). Order and share the appetizers, which range from summer rolls to potstickers to luau-roasted garlic seafood. The column called chili-seared salmon-tiki is an edible high-rise of mashed potatoes, eggplant, greens, tomato salsa, and salmon with a plum vinaigrette; it's one of the more flamboyant of Ellman's signature dishes. The only dessert, Caramel Miranda, is a heroic mound of macadamia-nut–brittle ice cream, caramel sauce, and exotic local fruit (the best of what's in season).

Chart House. 1450 Front St., at Honoapiilani Hwy. (Hi. 30). ☎ **808/661-0937.** Main courses $16.95–$44.95. AE, CB, DC, DISC, MC, V. Daily 5–10pm, lounge until 1am. AMERICAN.

Chart House restaurants have a knack for finding terrific locations with ocean views, and Lahaina's has one of the best. (The other Maui locations are at 100 Wailea Ike Dr. in Wailea, and at 500 N. Puunene in Kahului.) The location is Chart House's strongest suit: perched at the north end of Front Street, removed from congested Lahaina proper, and elevated for optimum view, the restaurant offers a singular look at Lanai, Molokai, the ocean, and the sunset. Otherwise, expect the predictable fare that marks all other Chart Houses: prime rib, East-West prawns, garlic steak, and an assortment of fresh fish in teriyaki, garlic herb, and mayonnaise sauces. Especially indulgent is the signature mud pie, a weighty dessert of Kona coffee ice cream, Oreo cookie crust, fudge, almonds, and whipped cream.

✪ **David Paul's Lahaina Grill.** 127 Lahainaluna Rd. ☎ **808/667-5117.** Reservations required. Main courses $19–$38. AE, CB, DC, DISC, MC, V. Daily 5:30–10pm. Bar, daily until midnight. NEW AMERICAN.

Nationally applauded and a recipient of numerous culinary awards, David Paul's is most people's favorite restaurant on Maui. On an island where excellent dining is as ubiquitous as Haleakala, that's saying a lot. With two restaurants—including his new David Paul's Diamond Head Grill on Oahu—he's been dividing his attentions between two islands, yet the creativity of his cuisine shows no signs of neglect. His chic Lahaina oasis is located in a historic building next to the faithfully restored Lahaina Hotel. Special custom-designed degustation dinners can be arranged with 48 hours' notice for parties of five to eight, but the daily menu is completely satisfying. The Kula salad is a masterpiece (olives, beet tops, feta cheese, Maui onions, and a superb vinaigrette), the kalua duck is fork-tender, and a roster of other classics keeps diners returning: spicy crab cake in a sesame-Dijon sauce, Kona coffee–roasted rack of lamb, eggplant napoleon, and many other seductions. The bar is the busiest spot in Lahaina, and the ambiance—black-and-white tile floors, pressed tin ceilings, eclectic 1890s decor—is a good match for the cuisine.

Gerard's. Plantation Inn, 174 Lahainaluna Rd. ☎ **808/661-8939.** Reservations recommended. Main courses $26.50–$32.50. AE, DC, DISC, JCB, MC, V. Daily 6–10pm. FRENCH.

Winner of the *Wine Spectator* Award of Excellence for 1994, 1995, and 1997, Gerard's Gallic offerings still score high in this competitive culinary atmosphere. A worthy starter is the shiitake and oyster mushroom appetizer, savory and steaming in puff pastry, or the ahi tartar with taro chips, followed by the roasted Hawaiian snapper in a spicy orange and ginger butter sauce. Gerard Reversade specializes in fresh seafood, which he buys daily from the fishermen at the harbor, then transforms into haute cuisine. Game lovers also have some sophisticated choices: venison with peppered sauce and poha berry compote, Ulupalakua lamb

Lahaina & Kaanapali Dining

Aloha Mixed Plate **6**
Avalon **8**
Beachside Grill and Leilani's on the Beach **1**
Chart House **4**
Cheeseburger in Paradise **9**
Compadres Bar & Grill **5**
David Paul's Lahaina Grill **10**
Gerard's **11**
Groovy Smoothies **13**
Hard Rock Cafe **7**
Hula Grill **1**
Kimo's **8**
Lahaina Coolers **14**
Lahaina Fish Company **9**
Pacific'o Restaurant **16**
Pizza Paradiso **1**
Planet Hollywood **12**
Spats **3**
Swan Court **3**
Swiss Café **15**
The Villa **2**
Village Pizzeria **16**

Legend
Post Office ✉

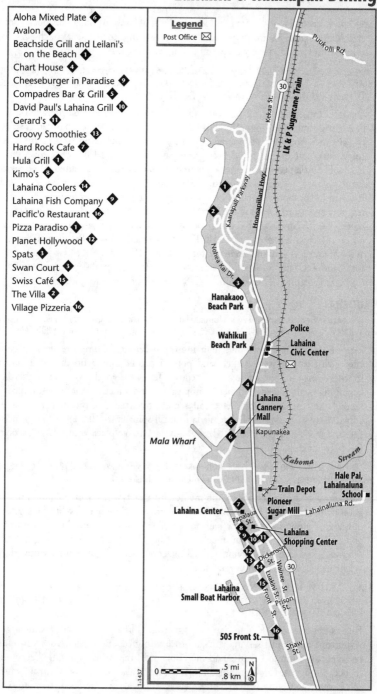

Puukolii Rd.
LK & P Sugarcane Train
Kekaa St.
Kaanapali Parkway
Honoapiilani Hwy.
Nohea Kai Dr.
1
2
3
Hanakaoo Beach Park
Wahikuli Beach Park
Police
Lahaina Civic Center
4
Lahaina Cannery Mall
Kapunakea
5
6
Mala Wharf
Kahoma Stream
Hale Pai, Lahainaluna School
Train Depot
Pioneer Sugar Mill
Lahainaluna Rd.
Lahaina Center
Papalaua St.
7
8
9
10 **11**
Lahaina Shopping Center
12
13 Dickenson St.
14
30
Wainee St.
Luakini St.
15
Front St.
Prison St.
Lahaina Small Boat Harbor
16
505 Front St.
Shaw St.

0 .5 mi
  .8 km
N

1-1437

135

and pork cassoulet, and a popular rosemary rack of lamb. Although his duck confit and filet mignon in mustard sauce are noteworthy, there are also choices for vegetarians: Gerard's is very accommodating with vegetarian requests.

Pacific'o Restaurant. 505 Front St. ☎ **808/667-4341.** Reservations recommended. Lunch $9–$14, dinner main courses $19–$26. AE, DC, MC, V. Daily 11am–4pm and 5:30–10pm. PACIFIC RIM/CONTEMPORARY PACIFIC.

You couldn't get closer to the ocean than the tables here, located literally on the beach; the award-winning seafood dishes are served with a backdrop of Lanai across the channel. You can't go wrong with the shrimp wonton appetizer or the shiso spicy tuna, seared and served over green papaya tomato salad with a miso sauce ($12). The Asian Gravlox is another winner, a marriage of house-cured salmon with sweet-potato applejack, wasabi sour cream, and caviar ($8). Fresh fish comes grilled, steamed in bamboo, bathed in Indonesian spices and Mandarin fennel sauce, fried tempura style, and coated in crisp coconut-macadamia with a Thai peanut coconut sauce. Vegetarians love this place for the marvelous quinoa-lentil-shiitake-Maui onion entree with roasted tofu steak. The many awards won by Pacific'o include the *Wine Spectator* Award of Excellence for 1996 and 1997 and three first-place awards for seafood in the Taste of Lahaina culinary festival in the past several years. Live jazz is featured Thursday through Saturday from 9pm to midnight.

MODERATE

Compadres Bar & Grill. 1221 Honoapiilani Hwy., Lahaina Cannery Mall. ☎ **808/ 661-7189.** Main courses $12–$18.50. DC, JCB, MC, V. Daily 8am–11:30pm. MEXICAN.

Despite its concrete floor and high industrial ceilings, Compadres exudes good cheer with its oversized baskets and pots of plants, dining on the lanai, and a split-level area indoors. The food is classic Tex-Mex, good any time of the day, beginning with huevos rancheros, hot cakes, and omelets (the $8 Acapulco is heroic), and progressing to enchiladas and appetizers for the margarita-happy crowd. Stay spare (vegetable enchilada in fresh spinach tortilla, $9.50) or go hefty (Texas T-bone and enchiladas, $18.50)—it's a carefree place with a large capacity for merrymaking.

Hard Rock Cafe. 900 Front St. ☎ **808/667-7400.** Main courses $7–$17. AE, DC, MC, V. Daily 11:30am–10pm. Bar, daily 11:30am–midnight. AMERICAN.

You know the formula: rock 'n' roll memorabilia everywhere you look; loud music; good chili; fresh grilled fish with baked potato; and sky-high, jaw-breaking grilled burgers weighing in at a hefty half pound. The famous country burger with fries and unlimited soda is still an unbelievable value, but our favorite is the grilled ahi sandwich, smoky and satisfying with all the condiments. Vegetarians say the grilled veggie burger puts garden burgers to shame.

Kimo's. 845 Front St. ☎ **808/661-4811.** Reservations recommended for dinner. Lunch $5.95–$10.95; dinner main courses $12.95–$23.95. AE, MC, V. Daily 11am–3pm and 5–10:30pm. STEAK/SEAFOOD.

Kimo's has a loyal following that keeps it from falling into the faceless morass of waterfront restaurants serving surf-and-turf with great sunset views. It's a formula restaurant (sibling to Leilani's and the Hula Grill) that works not only because of its oceanfront patio and upstairs dining room, but also because of its menu, which offers some satisfying (for the price) choices. It's always crowded, buzzing with people having fun on a deck that takes in Molokai, Lanai, and Kahoolawe. Burgers and sandwiches are affordable and reliable, and the fresh catch in garlic-lemon and a sweet-basil glaze is a top seller, rivaling the hefty prime rib; it comes complete with salad, carrot muffins, herb rolls, and herb rice. Keep in mind that the waistline-defying Hula Pie—macadamia-nut ice cream in a chocolate-wafer crust with fudge and whipped cream—originated here.

Lahaina Fish Company. 831 Front St. ☎ **808/661-3472.** Main courses $7.95–$22.95. AE, JCB, MC, V. Daily 11am–midnight. SEAFOOD.

This open-air dining room, which is literally right above the water, has flickering torches after sunset and an affordable menu that covers the seafood and pasta basics. If you have to wait for a table—and many people do—the beach end of Hammerheads Fish Bar, with the draft from the huge fridge, is not where you want to be. Between noon and 3pm, head to an oceanside table and order a hamburger, cheeseburger, chickenburger, fishburger, generous basket of peel-and-eat shrimp, or sashimi; lingering is highly recommended. From noon to 5pm, the Mai Tai and the Tropical Itch cost just $2.50, a big attraction to accompany the appetizer-happy menu. Nightly specials range from island fish-and-chips to several pasta dishes; standard steak-and-seafood combinations; and four types of fresh island fish prepared in Asian, American, and European styles.

INEXPENSIVE

Aloha Mixed Plate. 1285 Front St. ☎ **808/661-3322.** Main courses $2.95–$9.95. MC, V. Sun–Wed 10am–10:30pm, Thurs–Sat 10:30am–1am. PLATE LUNCH/NOODLE HOUSE.

The operators of the Old Lahaina Luau have moved north in a big way. Recently, they opened Aloha Mixed Plate in a charming, freestanding, plantation-style building directly across from the Lahaina Cannery, to be followed later in 1998 with a move of the luau from its 505 Front St. location to a spot next door, adjacent to its new plate-lunch restaurant. At Aloha Mixed Plate, you can sit on an open deck under umbrellas and tuck into inexpensive mahimahi, kalua pig and cabbage, shoyu chicken, and other local plate-lunch specials, all for less than $5. Garden burgers and hamburgers cost even less. Five ethnic noodle dishes, including Thai noodles, udon, and saimin, round out what is a great concept in informal—and mostly pricey—Lahaina.

Cheeseburger in Paradise. 811 Front St. ☎ **808/661-4855.** Main courses $5.95–$9.95. AE, MC, V. Daily 8am–10:15pm. AMERICAN.

Wildly successful, always crowded, highly visible, and very noisy with its live music in the evenings, Cheeseburger is a shrine to the American classic. This is burger country, tropical style, with everything from tofu and garden burgers to the biggest, juiciest beef and chicken burgers, served on whole-wheat and sesame buns baked fresh daily. The two-story green-and-white building next to the seawall is always packed, but for good reasons: good value, good grinds, and a great ocean view. The Cheeseburger in Paradise—a hefty hunk with jack and cheddar cheeses, sautéed onions, lettuce, fresh tomatoes, and Thousand Island dressing—is a paean to the basics. Or you can build your own burger, by adding sautéed mushrooms, bacon, grilled ortega chiles, and other condiments for an extra charge. Onion rings, chili cheese fries, and a cold beer complete the carefree fantasy.

Groovy Smoothies. 708 Front St. ☎ **808/661-8219.** Smoothies under $4.50. No credit cards. Daily 9am–9:30pm. SMOOTHIES.

This closet-size take-out stand makes the best smoothies in Lahaina. But if these treats are too pure for you, there are always muffins, espresso, and Danishes. We love the mango and banana smoothie, but others might pine for the piña colada or the Elvis Peachly, or any of the berry delights. Protein powders, bee pollen, and other nutritious ingredients are blended into these tasty, healthy treats.

Lahaina Coolers. 180 Dickenson St. ☎ **808/661-7082.** Most items under $14. AE, MC, V. Daily 7am–midnight, bar until 2am. AMERICAN.

A huge marlin hangs above the bar, and epic wave shots and wall sconces made of surfboard fins line the walls at this indoor/outdoor restaurant. Open windows on three sides take advantage of the shade trees to create a cordial, cheerful atmosphere. The bar is open until 2am, so you can go from the Surfer Special (a gourmet bean burrito) or fruit pancakes to the famous mango daiquiri at the end of the day. The pasta machine is a special touch for a place that's more Beach Boys than Puccini. Great bites: smoked salmon fettuccine in dill-caper cream sauce, and nightly steak and fish specials at $16 to $18.50, two of Lahaina's terrific deals. The Evil Jungle Pizza, grilled chicken in a spicy Thai peanut sauce, is a novelty and one of several successful "tropic pizzas." A big plus: everything can be prepared vegetarian upon request.

Planet Hollywood. 744 Front St. ☎ **808/667-7877.** Main courses $8.50–$19.95. AE, DC, JCB, MC, V. Daily 11am–midnight. AMERICAN/CALIFORNIA.

You have to say this about Planet Hollywood: its hyped-up souvenir menus cost $3, but you can order a great meal for $8.50. This is the Hard Rock Cafe with a *Blade Runner* twist, with vinyl accents, zebra-printed booths and carpets, and a bloody Arnold Schwarzenegger statue in your face. Chrome, suspended acrylic cages, neon galore, and blaring rock music greet you as you step in off Front Street. For $6.50 you can order a basket of Cap'n Crunch–covered chicken with a Creole-mustard sauce, and for a few cents more, Texas nachos. Prices have gone up recently but remain within reason: the world-famous cheeseburgers and french fries are $8.95; the Thai shrimp pasta, $13.95; and the Caesar salad, $8.95.

Swiss Café. 640 Front St. ☎ **808/661-6776.** Seven-inch pizza $6.95–$7.95, sandwiches $5.95–$6.95. No credit cards. Mon–Sat 8am–7pm, Sun 10am–7pm. SANDWICHES/PIZZA.

This tiny cafe, a take-out stand with a few outdoor tables just off Lahaina's main drag, serves a Swiss breakfast, but it's mainly a sandwich and pizza shop. Despite its no-frills menu, there's always a line out front. Cold sandwiches, hot sandwiches (such as Italian boboli or turkey-broccoli melt), small pizzas, salads, and garden burgers are cheap and fast, and on a hot day, the ice cream and the mocha coffee shakes move swiftly. The coffee shakes, smoothies, milk shakes, and other high-octane espresso drinks are Swiss Café specialties.

Village Pizzeria. 505 Front St. ☎ **808/661-8112.** Salad and pizza $3.95; main courses $6.95–$24.50 for special pizzas. AE, DC, DISC, MC, V. Daily 11am–9:30pm. PIZZA.

With thin or thick crust, more than a dozen toppings, and the signature clam-and-garlic pizza that you can smell from around the corner, the pizzeria draws a steady stream of diners to its location at the popular shopping complex called 505 Front St. Appetizers, sandwiches (made with homemade bread), pasta, and famous tiramisu make this more than just a pizza joint.

KAANAPALI
EXPENSIVE

Spats. 200 Nohea Kai Dr., Hyatt Regency Maui. ☎ **808/661-1234.** Reservations recommended. Main courses $20–$30. AE, DISC, MC, V. Daily 6–10pm. ITALIAN.

Descend the stairs into the lavishly Italianate entrance and behold the host of sensory stimuli, including the aromas of garlic and tomato and the sounds of an Italian aria. Spats is all seduction. The "Spats salad" is a notable celebration of simplicity and freshness. The puttanesca and assorted pastas get appreciative nods, and the service is excellent. For dessert, the tiramisu is lighter and more cakey than most, delicious without being frothy.

Swan Court. 200 Nohea Kai Dr., Hyatt Regency Maui. ☎ **808/661-1234.** Reservations recommended for dinner. Main courses $28–$36. AE, DC, DISC, JCB, MC, V. Daily 6:30–11:30am and 6–10pm. CONTINENTAL.

Even as a resort restaurant (one of four at the Hyatt Regency Maui), Swan Court is hard to resist. Come here as a splurge, or on a bottomless expense account, and enjoy its continental menu in incomparable surroundings. The combination of waterfalls, ocean view, Japanese gardens, and swans and flamingos serenely gliding by is irresistibly romantic, especially with alfresco dining and appropriately extravagant fare. The menu changes nightly in this tiered dining room. Hunan marinated lamb chops and the island-style bouillabaisse are perennial favorites, but many other seafood and game specials will also compete for your attention.

The Villa. 2365 Kaanapali Pkwy., Westin Maui. ☎ **808/667-2525.** Reservations recommended. Main courses $18–$32; prix fixe menu $28. AE, DC, DISC, JCB, MC, V. Daily 6–10pm. HAWAII REGIONAL.

The Westin's signature restaurant offers a romantic ambiance with tables encircling a man-made lagoon near waterfalls and a large banyan tree. The dining room is surrounded by water, and even with its soaring ceilings and enormous visual scale, it's an informal and comfortable place, with dishes that range from good to excellent. The prix fixe menu might offer black turtle bean soup or smoked ahi risotto; grilled marinated chicken with radicchio; wild mushroom-and-sage pasta; and many other pleasures. Order what you will, but do not miss the ahi poke martini. Served in a martini glass, the fresh, finely cubed ahi comes topped with seaweed, *chiso* (a savory flat leaf used as an accompaniment in sushi), *tobiko* (flying-fish roe), finely cubed cucumber, green onions, and a daringly spicy garlic sauce. Vegetarian specials, such as eggplant terrine, are gourmet fare. Bravo.

MODERATE

Beachside Grill and Leilani's on the Beach. In Whalers Village, 2435 Kaanapali Pkwy. ☎ **808/661-4495.** Reservations suggested for dinner. Lunch (Beachside Grill) $5.95–$9.95; dinner (Leilani's) $14.95 and up. AE, DC, DISC, MC, V. Beachside Grill, daily 11am–11pm (bar, daily until 12:30am); Leilani's, daily 5–10pm. STEAK/SEAFOOD.

The Beachside Grill is the informal, less expensive room downstairs, where folks wander in off the beach for a frothy beer and a burger. It's open for lunch and dinner (the top price is $9.95, except for fresh fish at market price). Leilani's is the dinner-only room with more expensive, but still not outrageously priced, steak and seafood offerings. At Leilani's, spinach, cheese, and mushroom raviolis cost $10.95; the lobster and steak are at higher market prices. Still, children can order a quarter-pound hamburger for just $4.95 or broiled chicken breast for $2 more—a value for sure. Pasta, rack of lamb, a $25.95 filet mignon, and Alaskan king crab at market price are among the temptations in the upstairs room. We love the informality of both rooms, but the downstairs Beachside Grill is geared toward the budget-conscious. This is a lively spot, a Kaanapali oasis, with live Hawaiian music every afternoon except Fridays, when the Rock 'n' Roll Aloha Friday set gets those decibels climbing. Free concerts are offered on a stage outside the restaurant, usually on the last Sunday of the month. The popular program, Music on the Beach, is always a big draw—another big reason to love Leilani's. Any way you cut it, the view, food, prices, and location make this a hard-to-beat Kaanapali staple.

✪ **Hula Grill.** In Whalers Village, 2435 Kaanapali Pkwy. ☎ **808/667-6636.** Reservations recommended for dinner. Lunch and Barefoot Bar menus $5.95–$11.95; dinner main courses $14.95–$35. AE, MC, V. Barefoot Bar, daily 11am–midnight; dining room, daily 5–9:30pm. HAWAII REGIONAL/SEAFOOD.

Who wouldn't want to be tucking into *poisson cru* (Tahitian-style raw fish, cubed and marinated in lime juice with onions), crab and corn cakes, or ahi poke rolls under a thatched umbrella, with a sand floor and palm trees at arm's length, and a view of Lanai across the channel? What a cheerful place this Kaanapali magnet is, *the* place to dine while watching swimmers and catamarans bobbing in the sea. Peter Merriman, a culinary guru and one of the originators of Hawaii Regional Cuisine, has literally redefined chain-restaurant cuisine. You'll dine in a charming setting of vintage Hawaiiana accented with kitschy hula dolls, koa walls, and authentic Hawaiian canoes. The superb menu includes his signature wok-charred ahi, firecracker mahimahi (baked in tomato, chili, and cumin aioli), scallop and lobster potstickers, and six different fresh fish preparations, including his famous ahi poke rolls, lightly sautéed rare ahi wrapped in rice paper with Maui onions. Lunchtime burgers are de rigueur, or order gourmet appetizers from the Barefoot Bar menu (macadamia-nut/ crab wonton, fresh ono fish and chips, pizza, smoked-turkey sandwiches). There's happy hour entertainment from 3 to 5pm daily and Hawaiian music with a hula dancer from 6:30 to 9pm. Hula Grill is one of those dining rooms with a wide range in prices and choices; although it can be expensive, it doesn't have to be.

INEXPENSIVE

Pizza Paradiso. In Whaler's Village. ☎ **808/667-0333.** Breakfast pizza $3.35–$3.85 (by the slice); 12-inch pizzas $13–$18. No credit cards. Daily 7:30am–9:30pm. PIZZA.

From the Nutty Vegan to the Maui Wowie (with ham and pineapple), the Godfather (roasted chicken, artichoke hearts, sun-dried tomatoes), and the Clam Slam (with juicy clams and tons of garlic), these pizzas are always described in superlatives, even by jaded New Yorkers. It's not Little Italy (see: Thai chicken pizza with spicy peanut sauce), but it earns high ratings in both flavor and quality. Create your own pizza with a long menu of possibilities (roasted eggplant, artichoke hearts, MacNut pesto, and more); then enjoy it in this mall-like fast-food atmosphere or take it to Kaanapali beach, just a few steps away.

FROM HONOKOWAI TO NAPILI
MODERATE

Fish & Games Sports Grill. 4405 Honoapiilani Hwy., Kahana Gateway Shopping Center. ☎ **808/669-3474.** Reservations recommended for dinner. Lunch main courses $6.95–$10.95, dinner main courses $13.95–$25.95. AE, CB, DC, DISC, JCB, MC, V. Daily 11am–1am. SEAFOOD.

One of the owners is a major fresh-seafood distributor for Maui, so guess what the specialties are. A recent expansion has added space, a microbrewery, and a new rotisserie oven to the seafood delights in this formerly unremarkable corner of a mall in Kahana. A constant stream of fresh clams, oysters, fish, and mussels flows out of the kitchen, and a small retail section sells fresh seafood. The menu for sit-down meals covers basic tastes but covers them well: an oyster bar, soups, salads, and sandwiches for lunch, and seafood pastas and entrees for dinner, with a flame-broiled New York steak (with homemade Cognac–green peppercorn sauce), rack of lamb, and steak/seafood combinations for heftier tastes.

✪ **Roy's Kahana Bar & Grill/Roy's Nicolina Restaurant.** Kahana Gateway, 4405 Honoapiilani Hwy. ☎ **808/669-6999.** Reservations strongly suggested. Main courses $13–$26. AE, CB, DC, DISC, JCB, MC, V. Roy's Kahana, daily 5:30–10pm; Roy's Nicolina, daily 5:30–9:30pm. EURO-ASIAN.

These two sibling restaurants are next door to each other, have the same menu, and are busy, busy, busy. Both are bustling with young, hip servers impeccably trained to deliver the blackened ahi or perfectly seared lemongrass shutome (broadbill swordfish) hot to your table, in rooms that sizzle with cross-cultural tastings. Roy's Nicolina now features dining on the lanai. Both restaurants are known for their rack of lamb and fresh seafood (usually eight or nine choices) and for the large, open kitchens that turn out everything from pizza to sake-grilled New York steak and roasted half chickens in garlic and orange, glistening in cardamom-and-cabernet sauce. If potstickers are on the menu, don't resist. Large picture windows open up Roy's Kahana Bar & Grill but don't quell the noise, another tireless trait long ago established by Roy's Restaurant in Honolulu, the flagship of the burgeoning empire of Roy Yamaguchi.

Sea House Restaurant. At the Napili Kai Beach Club, 5900 Honoapiilani Hwy. ☎ 808/669-1500. Reservations required for dinner. Main courses $14–$25. AE, MC, V. Daily 8–11am and noon–2pm; Sat–Thurs 6–9pm, pupus available Sat–Thurs 2–9pm, Fri 2–5:30pm. Friday-night show 6–8:30pm; bar open Fri 10am–9:30pm, Sat–Thurs 10am–10pm. PACIFIC RIM.

The Sea House is not glamorous, famous, or hip, but it's worth mentioning for its view of Napili Bay, one of the two most gorgeous in West Maui. The Napili Kai Beach Club, where Sea House is located, is a charming throwback to the days when hotels blended in with their surroundings, had lush tropical foliage, and were sprawling rather than vertical. The dining room is comfortable and informal; Friday nights, a Polynesian dinner show features the children of the Napili Kai Foundation, an organization devoted to supporting Hawaiian culture. Dinner entrees come complete with soup or salad, vegetables, and rice or potato. The lighter appetizer menu is a delight—more than a dozen choices range from sautéed or blackened crab cake to crisp Pacific Rim sushi and scallops grilled with portobello mushrooms. The biggest plus, however, is the million-dollar view.

INEXPENSIVE

Maui Tacos. In Napili Plaza, 5095 Napili Hau St. ☎ 808/665-0222. Most items under $6.95. No credit cards. Mon–Sat 11am–9pm, Sun 11am–8pm. MEXICAN.

Mark Ellman of Lahaina's Avalon fame put gourmet Mexican on paper plates and on the island's culinary map. Barely more than a take-out counter with a few tables, this and the other three Maui Tacos on the island (in the Kaahumanu Center in Kahului, in Lahaina Square in Lahaina, and in the Kamaole Beach Center in Kihei) are the rage of hungry surfers, discerning diners, burrito buffs, and Hollywood glitterati like Sharon Stone, whose picture adorns a wall or two. Regardless, the food is worth seeking out: excellent fresh fish tacos, chimichangas, searing salsas, and mouth-breaking compositions such as the Hookipa, a "surf burrito" of fresh fish, black beans, and salsa. The green spinach burrito contains four kinds of beans, rice, and potatoes—a knockout.

KAPALUA
EXPENSIVE

The Bay Club. Kapalua Bay Hotel & Villas, 1 Bay Dr. ☎ 808/669-5656. Reservations recommended for dinner. Dress code at dinner: collared shirts with long slacks for men; no jeans, shorts, or T-shirts for women. Main courses $24–$38. AE, CB, JCB, MC, V. Daily 11:30am–2pm and 6–9:30pm. SEAFOOD.

The classic enjoyments—a stellar view, beatific sunsets, attentive service from bow-tied servers—are matched by a seafood menu that has lost none of its luster over the years. The Caesar salad is still tossed tableside, the seafood is fresh, the peppered steak is just so, and the vegetarian dishes are quite elegant. Duck, rack of lamb, excellent salads, fresh catch, sandwiches and pasta for lunch, and a host of simple delights can be enjoyed in this open-air dining room with the view of Molokai and Lanai, one that changes as the sun moves south to eventually set behind Lanai in the winter months. Tried and true, the Bay Club is one of Maui's lasting pleasures.

Plantation House. 200 Plantation Club Dr. (at Kapalua Plantation Golf Course), Kapalua Resort. ☎ **808/669-6299.** Reservations recommended. Main courses $18–$24. AE, MC, V. Daily 8am–3pm and 5:30–10pm. SEAFOOD/ISLAND REGIONAL.

With its teak tables, fireplace, and open sides, Plantation House gets high marks for ambiance: the 360-degree view from high among the resort's pine-studded hills takes in Molokai and Lanai, the ocean, the rolling fairways and greens, the northwestern flanks of the West Maui Mountains, and the daily sunset spectacular. Readers of the *Maui News* have deemed this the island's "Best Ambiance," a big honor on this island of ubiquitous views. Choices include fresh fish prepared seven ways, among them Mediterranean (seared), Upcountry (sautéed with Maui onion and vegetable stew), Island (pan-seared in sweet sake and chili-sesame sauce), and Rich Forest (with roasted wild mushrooms), the top seller. Salads utilizing fresh Maui produce are also strong. The menu is bolstered by other seafood, pasta, and meat entrees, such as the rosemary-infused double-cut lamb chops at dinner, also a hit.

MODERATE

Jameson's Grill & Bar at Kapalua. 200 Kapalua Dr. (at the 18th hole of the Kapalua Golf Course). ☎ **808/669-5653.** Reservations recommended for dinner. Lunch $5.95–$11.95; main courses $6.95–$12.95 on the cafe menu, $15.95–$39.95 at dinner. AE, DC, DISC, JCB, MC, V. Daily 8am–10pm, cafe menu 3–10:30pm. AMERICAN.

Jameson's is now an all-day eatery where diners can enjoy breakfast, lunch, and dinner on the 18th hole of the Kapalua Bay Golf Course. It's the quintessential country-club restaurant, open-air with mountain views—and the familiar Jameson's mix of fresh fish (sautéed, wok-seared, or grilled), rack of lamb, ahi steak, and other basic surf-and-turf selections for dinner. For duffers dashing to make tee time, grab a "Golf Sandwich" for $5.95. All the favorites are here: fish and chips, patty melt, crab cakes, and an affordable cafe menu with gourmet appetizers (Thai summer rolls, seared sashimi, baked artichoke). At dinner, herb-roasted chicken is a favorite.

☼ **Sansei Seafood Restaurant and Sushi Bar.** 115 Bay Dr., Kapalua Shops, Kapalua Resort. ☎ **808/669-6286.** Reservations recommended. Main courses $15–$19.75. AE, DC, DISC, MC, V. Sat–Wed 5:30–10pm; sushi bar open until 11pm; Thurs–Fri 5:30pm–1am. SEAFOOD/SUSHI.

Sansei opened its doors on the site of the old Garden Café and quickly put a stop to the Kapalua dining doldrums. People drive from central Maui to dine here—and that's a long drive. Why do they come? Part Japanese fusion, part Hawaii Regional Cuisine, and all parts sushi, Sansei is tirelessly creative, with a menu that manages to please both the purists and the adventurous: nori ravioli of shrimp, opah, and Chinese sausage with shiitake mushroom sauce; roasted Japanese eggplant with a sweet miso sauce; ahi carpaccio; udon and ramen; traditional tempura. The Asian rock shrimp cake in ginger-lime chili butter and cilantro pesto is a first-place "Taste of Lahaina" winner, but there is simpler fare as well, such as pastas and wok-tossed upcountry vegetables. And don't forget the desserts: tempura fried ice cream with chocolate sauce, crème brûlée, and, an autumn phenomenon, persimmon crème brûlée made with Kula persimmons.

3 South Maui

MAALAEA & KIHEI
EXPENSIVE

✪ **A Pacific Cafe Maui.** Azeka's Place II, 1279 S. Kihei Rd. ☎ **808/879-0069.** Reservations recommended. Main courses $24.75–$32. AE, CB, DC, MC, V. Daily 5:30–10pm. HAWAII REGIONAL.

This is a busy restaurant every night of the week—so make your reservations as early as possible. You'll dine on rattan chairs at hammered copper tables, under very high ceilings in a room bordered with windows (but you'll be so busy enjoying the food that you won't notice the parking lot). The menu changes daily and offers an abundance of marvels: the delectable signature tiger-eye ahi sushi tempura; the garlic-sesame pan-seared mahimahi, a Pacific Cafe staple; salmon firecracker roll; and many others. Jean-Marie Josselin, chef extraordinaire, recently introduced hormone-free Hawaii-grown specialty meats, such as lamb, elk, veal, and Kobe beef.

Carelli's on the Beach. 2980 S. Kihei Rd. ☎ **808/875-0001.** Reservations recommended. Main courses $22–$38. AE, MC, V. Daily 6–10pm, bar until 11pm. ITALIAN/SEAFOOD.

Kihei's well-tanned, chic set come here for pasta, seafood, and the view. Carelli's is stupendous: with its prime on-the-sand location at Keawakapu Beach, you can enjoy the sunset in ravishing surroundings over top-drawer entrees such as cioppino (the most popular item, at $36), fresh fish, ravioli, carpaccio, and other Italian favorites. The wood-burning brick oven turns out great pizzas. To sit at a table on the dining floor, though, there's a $25 minimum order.

Steve Amaral's Cucina Pacifica. Upstairs in the Rainbow Mall, 2439 S. Kihei Rd., #201A. ☎ **808/875-7831.** Reservations recommended. Main courses $15–$28. DC, DISC, MC, V. Daily 5:30pm–closing. MEDITERRANEAN/SEAFOOD.

Kihei, for all its disappointments, is shaping up to be quite a dining destination. Amaral's new restaurant is stirring up excitement with a menu that features the best of Mediterranean culinary traditions *and* a striking way with fresh Maui ingredients. Maui/Mediterranean, we like to call it. The menu changes seasonally to honor and utilize fresh seasonal produce. In the winter: Italian winter truffle and potato soup, spicy elk sausage with slow-cooked fagioli in garlic sage, wild mushroom risotto, spanakopita of pan-seared diver scallops (with spinach, feta, pine nuts, and nine-olive tapenade!), and something as simple as four-cheese manicotti. The remarkable menu and Amaral's irrepressible imagination cater to vegetarians, seafood lovers, and beef lovers—in short, anyone who loves good food. The vegetarian sampler, a medley of grilled zucchini, wild mushrooms, polenta, couscous, garlic mashed potatoes, and pan-seared tofu, is a triumph.

The Waterfront at Maalaea. 50 Hauoli St., Maalaea Harbor. ☎ **808/244-9028.** Reservations recommended. Main courses $18–$38. AE, DC, DISC, JCB, MC, V. Daily 11:30am–1:30pm and 5:30–8:30pm (last seating). SEAFOOD.

The Waterfront has won awards for wine excellence, service, and seafood, but its biggest boost is word of mouth. Loyal diners rave about the friendly staff and seafood, served in unfancy surroundings with a bay and harbor view. You have nine choices of preparations for the five to eight varieties of fresh Hawaiian fish, ranging from *en papillote* (baked in buttered parchment) to light cuisine (broiled or poached, then topped with steamed and fresh vegetables). The baked triple-cream Danish appetizer is an excellent starter, but so are the Kula onion soup and the excellent Caesar salad. Vegetarians favor the grilled eggplant layered with Maui onions, tomatoes, and spinach, served with red pepper coulis and Big Island goat cheese.

MODERATE

Buzz's Wharf. Maalaea Harbor. ☎ **808/244-5426.** Reservations suggested. Main courses $10.95–$24.95. AE, CB, DC, DISC, JCB, MC, V. Daily 11am–10pm. AMERICAN.

Another formula restaurant with a superb view and surf-and-turf fare that's satisfying, but not sensational. Still, it's a fine way station for whale watching over a cold beer and a fresh mahimahi sandwich with fries or, if you're feeling extravagant, the house specialty, Prawns Tahitian ($18.95 at lunch, $24.95 at dinner). Many diners opt for several appetizers (stuffed mushrooms, bucket of steamer clams, artichoke, onion soup) and a salad, but it's hard to keep the resolve at dessert time. Buzz's prize-winning dessert—Tahitian Baked Papaya, a warm, fragrant melding of fresh papaya with vanilla and coconut—is the pride of the house.

The Greek Bistro. 2511 S. Kihei Rd. ☎ **808/879-9330.** Reservations recommended. Combination and family-style dinners $14.95–$21.95 per person; family-style platter $35 for 2. AE, DC, CB, JCB, MC, V. Daily 5–10pm. GREEK.

The banana trees, yellow ginger, and hibiscus that surround the tile-floored terrace add immeasurably to the dining experience at this indoor/outdoor bistro, especially in chaotic Kihei. Homemade pita bread, quality feta and spices, classic spanakopita (spinach pie in microthin layers of phyllo dough), and chicken and lamb souvlaki (the Greek version of shish kebab) are some of the authentic and well-received Mediterranean offerings. Popular items include the family-style combination platters and the fresh fish of the day. Also popular is the Greek lasagna and the Mediterranean chicken breast, an elaborate platter of mushroom-and-wine–infused organic skinless chicken, served with linguine and vegetables. Children's portions are also available for considerably less.

Hapa's Brew Haus & Restaurant. In the Lipoa Shopping Center, 41 E. Lipoa St. ☎ **808/879-9001.** Reservations recommended. Main courses $8–$18.95. AE, DISC, JCB, MC, V. Daily 11am–2am. BREW HOUSE/INTERNATIONAL.

Food, beer, and music are the primary offerings here. In addition to being a full-service restaurant and a nightclub, Hapa's is a microbrewery with four lagers to accompany the seafood, prime rib, sandwiches, gourmet pizza, and pasta on the menu. The appetizers—blackened ahi, potstickers, steamer clams, and baked artichoke—reflect the gregarious, happy-hour nature of the place. A top happy-hour special: from 5 to 6pm daily, drafts are $2 and free pizza is served— a happy marriage indeed. Gourmet pizzas come heaped with grilled chicken, pesto shrimp, garlic sauce, and any number of other combinations, on thin or thick crust. On Sundays from 2 to 6pm, members of the Maui Symphony Swing Band take over the stage. It's worth searching out this bistro from among the faceless strip malls of Kihei, because it works hard to keep up the value. (See also chapter 11, "Maui After Dark.")

Stella Blues Cafe & Deli. In Long's Center, 1215 S. Kihei Rd. ☎ **808/874-3779.** Main courses $9.95–$16.95. DISC, MC, V. Daily 8am–9pm. AMERICAN.

Stella Blues gets going at breakfast and continues through dinner with something for everyone—vegetarians, children, pasta and sandwich lovers, hefty steak eaters, and sensible diners alike. Grateful Dead posters line the walls of this corner cafe, and a covey of gleaming motorcycles is invariably parked outside. It's loud and lively, casual and unpretentious. Sandwiches are the highlight, with two dozen selections ranging from Tofu Extraordinaire to Mom's egg salad on a croissant to garden burgers and grilled chicken. Tofu wraps and a mountain-size Cobb salad are popular, and, for the carefree, so are large coffee shakes with mounds of whipped cream. The Stella Special is a hit: spiced grilled eggplant with roasted garlic and sweet red peppers, feta cheese, and greens with pesto mayonnaise on homemade herb bread. At dinner, selections are geared toward good-value family dining, from affordable full dinners (Thai sweet-chili chicken for $14.95, including rice pilaf or potato, vegetable of the day, fresh Kula greens, and French bread) to pastas and burgers.

INXPENSIVE

✪ **Alexander's Fish & Chicken & Chips.** 1913 S. Kihei Rd. ☎ **808/874-0788.** Fish and chips $6.75–$9.50. MC, V. Daily 11am–9pm. FISH & CHIPS/SEAFOOD.

Look for the ocean mural in front, Kalama Park across the street, and a marketplace next door to this friendly neighborhood take-out stand with patio seating outside. Fresh ono, mahimahi, and ahi, broiled or fried, fly out of the kitchen with baskets of french fries or rice. Equally popular are the 13-piece shrimp, chicken, oyster, calamari, rib, or fish baskets ($16.50 to $19.95). Fresh fish, teriyaki chicken, barbecued beef, and shrimp sandwiches, along with onion rings, cornbread, and other side orders, make this a budget-friendly family favorite.

The Coffee Store. In Azeka's Place II, 1279 Kihei Rd. ☎ **808/875-4244.** All items under $8.50. AE, CB, DC, DISC, MC, V. Sun–Thurs 6am–10pm, Fri–Sat 6am–11pm. COFFEEHOUSE.

This simple, classic coffeehouse serves two dozen types of coffee drinks, from mochas, lattes, and frappes to cappuccino, espresso, and toddies. Breakfast items include smoothies, lox and bagels, quiches, granola, and pastries. Pizza, salads, vegetarian lasagna, veggie-and-shrimp quesadillas, and sandwiches also move briskly from the take-out counter. The recently introduced turkey and veggie tortilla-wrapped sandwiches have proven to be a hit. There are only a few small tables and they fill up fast, often with musicians and artists who spent the previous evening entertaining at the Wailea and Kihei resorts.

Hawaiian Moons Pizza & Deli. 2411 Kihei Rd. ☎ **808/875-4356.** Pizzas $15.50–$20.95; sandwiches $5.50–$7.50. Sun–Thurs 11am–7pm, Fri–Sat 11am–9pm. (Pizzas on Fri–Sat nights only.) PIZZA/DELI.

Our favorite Kihei health-food store also runs this deli/pizzeria, which always uses wholesome ingredients in its healthy gourmet salads, sandwiches, and smoothies. Among the special touches: it uses unbleached, organically grown wheat for the pizza flour; organically grown herbs and tomatoes; and free-range, antibiotic- and chemical-free turkey and chicken. Although pizzas are baked only on weekends, they are sensational: healthy, Maui style, with loads of flavor, gourmet toppings, and fresh local produce. We love the deli sandwiches (tempeh burger, roasted vegetarian, smoked turkey, and more), and the lasagna and a salad are hard to beat.

Peggy Sue's. In Azeka Place II, 1279 S. Kihei Rd. ☎ **808/875-8944.** Burgers $6–$11, plate lunches $5–$10. DC, MC, V. Sun–Thurs 11am–9pm, Fri–Sat 11am–10pm. AMERICAN.

Just for a moment, forget that diet and take a leap. Peggy Sue's, a 1950s-style diner with oodles of charm, is a swell place to spring for a malt and fries. You'll find the best chocolate malt on the island here, as well as sodas, shakes, floats, and egg creams. Old-fashioned diner stools, an Elvis Presley Boulevard sign, and jukeboxes serve as backdrop for the famous burgers, served with all the goodies, as well as garden burgers and plate lunches—chicken, steak, and mahimahi. We think the Maui-made Roselani ice cream used here is the secret to the oh-so-creamy malts.

Señor Taco. In the Dolphin Shopping Plaza, 2395 S. Kihei Rd. ☎ **808/875-2910.** Most items $1.90–$6.25. No credit cards. Mon–Sat 10am–9pm. TACOS/MEXICAN.

The smells and menu—beef-tongue tacos, smoked meat with chile sauce, chimichangas, steak burritos, fresh fish tacos, and many other savory concoctions— exude authenticity. Beef, chicken, steak, and the popular pork burrito (top of the line at $6.25); beef, chicken, and potato chimichangas ($6.50,including rice and beans); and a $5.75 combination plate are tasty and affordable, and nothing less than the real thing. On these as well as the daily specials, Oscar Del Campo, whose mother's secret recipes are featured, makes a promise not to disappoint.

Shaka Sandwich & Pizza. 1295 S. Kihei Rd. ☎ **808/874-0331.** Sandwiches $3.75–$8; pizzas $12.95–$25.95. Daily 10:30am–9pm (deliveries, daily 10:30am–9pm). PIZZA.

Award-winning pizzas share the limelight with New York–style hoagies and Philly cheese steaks, and they're all top-drawer. Shaka uses fresh Maui produce and home-made Italian bread. Choose thin or Sicilian thick crust, with gourmet toppings: Maui onions, spinach, jalapeño peppers, and a spate of other vegetables. Clam-and-garlic pizza, spinach pizza (with olive oil, spinach, garlic, and mozzarella), and the Shaka Supreme (with at least 11 toppings!) will satisfy even the insatiable.

WAILEA
EXPENSIVE

Joe's Bar & Grill. At the Wailea Tennis Club, 131 Wailea Ike Place. ☎ **808/875-7767.** Reservations recommended. Main items $17–$30. AE, DC, MC, V. Daily 5:30–10:30pm. AMERICAN GRILL.

Beverly Gannon's style of American home-cooking with a regional twist is inspiring and inimitable, with hearty staples you're not likely to forget: mashed Molokai potatoes, perhaps the best you'll have on Maui; the smoky and sublime grilled applewood salmon, the signature item; mixed grill of mushrooms with spinach, tomatoes, toasted walnuts, and crumbled Roquefort; grilled lamb chops; and chocolate cake, layered with bittersweet chocolate with a hint of orange. The 360-degree view spans the golf course, tennis courts, ocean, and Haleakala. At night, the theater lighting, 43-foot copper bar, high ceilings, and plank floors add to the enormously pleasing dining experience.

Kea Lani Restaurant. Kea Lani Hotel, 4100 Wailea Alanui Dr. ☎ **808/875-4100.** Reservations recommended for dinner. Main courses $26–$38. AE, DC, JCB, MC, V. Daily 6:30–11am and 5:30–10pm. EURO-PACIFIC.

The organic herb garden still fuels the kitchens of Kea Lani, where the Grand Chefs on Tour series presents culinary explorations on a regular basis. The year-round programs unite renowned chefs from Hawaii and the mainland for tastings, demonstrations, and bountiful dinners. Breakfast in this open-air dining room is a generous buffet with cornucopian carts that spill over with lilikoi, figs, starfruit, mangoes and litchis in season, edible flowers, and countless other colorful things from the garden and throughout Maui. From its Hollandaise to its home-cured Canadian bacon, the eggs Benedict ($11.50) is perfect. The dining room reopens at dinner, when it's transformed into a Mediterranean fantasy: ocean view, candlelight flickering over tile floors, and a menu of Pacific Rim specialties. Diners report favorably on the ginger hoisin hibachi rack of lamb with plum wine sauce and the nori-wrapped ono, prepared à la California, with crab, avocado, and wasabi beurre blanc.

Pacific Grill. 3900 Wailea Alanui, at the Four Seasons Resort Wailea. ☎ **808/874-8000.** Breakfast $9.25–$24.50, dinner main courses $23–$28.50. AE, CB, DC, DISC, JCB, MC, V. Daily 6–11:30am and 6–9:30pm. PACIFIC EDGE.

This is a good alternative for those wanting something between very casual and super-luxe. Open for lunch only occasionally, Pacific Grill features gourmet breakfasts and smashing dinners, ranging from Oriental-style steamed snapper to lemongrass mahimahi baked in parchment paper with shiitake mushrooms and spinach. One could dine happily on the starters alone, from the *limu kohu ahi poke* (cubed ahi with seasonings that include a pungent variety of seaweed) with watercress and fried taro (a favorite) to the scallop and goat cheese wonton (another favorite). You don't have to be vegan to love the vegan miso risotto with spinach, mushrooms, and tomatoes, or the Kula tomato salad, a paean to the rich volcanic soil of Maui.

✪ **Seasons.** 3900 Wailea Alanui, at the Four Seasons Resort Wailea. ☎ **808/874-8000.** Reservations recommended. Main courses $36–$46; prix fixe $75–$95. AE, CB, DC, DISC, JCB, MC, V. Tues–Sat 6–9pm. HAWAII REGIONAL/PROVENÇAL.

"Sometimes I get fish in the morning, and it's still alive!" exclaims chef George Mavrothalassitis, who has found his match in Maui's abundance of fresh produce and seafood. The menu for this tony, open-air seaside room is a showcase for his mastery of Provençal and Hawaii Regional cuisines, featuring inventions such as onaga baked in a Hawaiian salt crust, with an *ogo* (seaweed) sauce; and a whole *kumu* (goatfish) filled with watercress, garnished with Swiss chard and wild mushrooms. The seared *hamachi* (yellowfin tuna) is marinated for 48 hours in garlic, basil, Hawaiian chiles, and olive oil, and served on organic tomato coulis. In the winter, try truffle rotisserie chicken (slivers of fresh truffles are nestled between the meat and skin), served with fresh creamed corn and fresh mashed Molokai sweet potatoes and a hint of French vanilla. With his perfectly balanced flavors and his masterful use of spices, Mavrothalassitis has won a loyal following among foodies here and beyond. The walnut bread and French cheeses are still the best dessert in the Islands, and the room—elegant, understated, and open to the Wailea sea—is a temple of fine dining.

MODERATE

SeaWatch. 100 Wailea Golf Club Dr. ☎ **808/875-8080.** Reservations required for dinner. Lunch $4.50–$12; dinner main courses $18–$30. AE, DC, MC, V. Daily 8am–10pm. ISLAND CUISINE.

SeaWatch's use of fresh Maui produce, Big Island goat cheese, and island fish in ethnic preparations sets it apart from most other upscale clubhouse restaurants, and in fact, it is one of the more affordable stops in tony Wailea. Lunchtime sandwiches, pastas, salads, crab cakes, and soups are moderately priced, and you get the 360-degree view to go with them. You'll dine on the terrace or under high ceilings in a room with pretty views, on a menu that carries the tee-off-to-19th-hole crowd with ease. Pacific crab cakes, Chinese chicken salad, and fresh fish tacos are some of the lunchtime stars. At dinner, the nightly fresh catch, which can be ordered in one of three preparations, is a SeaWatch staple. Favorites include the Island Breeze, fresh fish seared in a black-bean crab broth; the Makai, bamboo-steamed fresh catch; and the Upcountry, kiawe-grilled fish on garlic mashed potatoes, served with oyster mushrooms from Haiku and an herb-tomato-butter sauce.

INEXPENSIVE

Maui Onion. At the Stouffer Renaissance Wailea Beach Resort, 3550 Wailea Alanui Dr. ☎ **808/879-4900.** Most items under $13.50. AE, DISC, JCB, MC, V. Daily 11am–5:30pm. AMERICAN.

Poolside dining on patio furniture, under a canopy of white alamandra blossoms dripping from vines in the trellises, with an ocean view—that's Maui Onion. We recommend it for the bold souls who love onion rings, french fries, hamburgers, and smoothies. The Maui onion rings are the best in the world: thick, juicy, and crisp, cooked in a miracle batter that seals in moisture and flavor. The fries, Cajun style and thin, are equally commendable. After these successes, a so-so sandwich would be acceptable. Thankfully, they also come heartily recommended— particularly the mahimahi with honey-mustard and the tuna melt on sourdough; for the more discreet, there's Cobb salad with shrimp.

MAKENA
EXPENSIVE

✪ **Hakone.** Maui Prince Hotel, 5400 Makena Alanui. ☎ **808/874-1111.** Reservations recommended. Complete dinners $22–$42; Mon night buffet $38, Sun sushi buffet $45; Kaiseki (multi-course Kyoto-style dinners, requiring 24-hour advance notice) $85. AE, JCB, MC, V. Mon–Sat 6–9:30pm, Sun 6–9pm. JAPANESE.

The Prince Hotels know Japanese cuisine and spared no effort to create a slice of Kyoto here, complete with sandalwood walls and pillars that were imported and assembled by Japanese craftsmen. Hakone offers super-luxe Japanese fare— gorgeously presented, and pricey. But the difficulty of choosing has been tempered by the popular Sunday night sushi buffet and Monday night Japanese dinner buffet. The latter includes sushi, broiled miso butterfish, shrimp tempura, and several appealing salads, as well as pupus, miso soup, and rice. Sashimi, tempura, broiled fish, California roll, and other traditional Japanese delicacies are offered on the regular Hakone menu.

✪ **Prince Court.** Maui Prince Hotel, 5400 Makena Alanui. ☎ **808/874-1111.** Reservations recommended. Main courses $27–29; Sun brunch $34. AE, JCB, MC, V. Thurs–Mon 6–9:30pm, Sun 9:30am–1pm. HAWAII REGIONAL.

Half of the Sunday brunch experience is the fabulous view of Makena Beach, the crescent-shaped islet called Molokini, and Kahoolawe island. The other half is the lavish buffet, spread over several tables: omelets, cheeses, pastries, sashimi, smoked salmon, fresh Maui produce, and an eye-popping array of ethnic and continental foods. As for dinner at the Prince Court, it's truly something to write home about. Chef Eric Leterc's guava-glazed shredded baby back ribs with ginger and hoisin are brilliant, and his seafood risotto, with Kona lobster, chiso butter sauce, and poi (the master touch), is a great idea that is perfectly executed. The chef's special changes weekly, but if the grilled ono with warm herb salad and *musubi* fried rice (a triangular Japanese rice ball) is offered, don't miss it.

4 Upcountry Maui

MAKAWAO
MODERATE

Casanova Italian Restaurant. 1188 Makawao Ave. ☎ **808/572-0220.** Reservations recommended for dinner. Main courses $8–$23. CB, DC, DISC, MC, V. Mon–Sat 11:30am–2pm and 5:30–9pm, Sun 5:30–9pm. Lounge, daily until 12:30am or 1am; deli, Mon–Sat 8am–6:30pm, Sun 8:30am–6:30pm. ITALIAN.

Look for the tiny veranda with a few stools, always occupied, in front of a deli at Makawao's busiest intersection—that's the most visible part of Casanova's restaurant and lounge. The center of Makawao's nightlife consists of a stage and dance floor adjoining a cozy cafe and bar in the wing next to the deli. Pizza, rosemary lamb chops, and pasta in a dozen shapes, colors, and flavors appear on a menu that has made this Maui's long-lasting Italian star. You can dine simply or lavishly, from a tomato, garlic, and four-cheese pizza to penne with lobster tail and scallops in a tomato-garlic-sherry sauce. The 12-inch, thin-crust, wood-fired Neapolitan pizzas are all fabulous, with 10 varieties and dozens of additional toppings to choose from (from $10).

Makawao Steak House. 3612 Baldwin Ave. ☎ **808/572-8711.** Reservations recommended. Main courses $13.95–$24.95. DC, DISC, MC, V. Mon–Thurs 5–9:30pm, Fri–Sat 5–10pm. STEAK/SEAFOOD.

The new owners (who also owned it in the mid-1970s) installed a new carpet, redid the kitchen, revised the menu, and put some spit and polish into an old Makawao fixture. Only 2 weeks old at this writing, the new Makawao Steak House has brought back its popular salad bar and a menu of chicken, fish, shrimp, crab, pork, steaks, and prime rib—plain old basics with friendly service. The king crab legs are a big seller in this paniolo town, and so is the prime rib.

Polli's Mexican Restaurant. 1202 Makawao Ave. ☎ **808/572-7808.** Main courses $6–$15. AE, DC, DISC, MC, V. Daily from about 9am (call to see if they're open) to 10pm. MEXICAN.

The extensive menu here is equally considerate to health foodies, vegetarians, and carnivores. There's something for everyone, from baby back ribs and steak dinners to substitutions of tofu or vegetarian taco mix, happily accommodated on all menu items. Sizzling fajitas ($12.95 to $13.95) are the house special, featuring fish, shrimp, chicken, tofu, or steak on a crackling hot platter with vegetables and spices, flour tortillas, sour cream, and guacamole—a good group endeavor. Expect the full roster of south-of-the-border favorites, from the usual tamales, tacos, and burritos to cheese-, mushroom-, and Mexi-burgers, laced with jalapeños and pepper jack cheese. Best of all, the menu is lard free.

INEXPENSIVE

✪ **Café 'O Lei.** 3673 Baldwin Ave. ☎ **808/573-9065.** Sandwiches and salads $4.50–$5.95. No credit cards. Mon–Sat 11am–4pm. AMERICAN/ISLAND.

Dana Pastula managed restaurants at Lanai's Manele Bay Hotel and the Four Seasons Resort Wailea before opening her tiny, charming outdoor cafe in this sunlit sliver of Makawao. Everything on the menu, from the sandwiches (roast chicken breast, turkey breast, prosciutto) and salads to the soup of the day, is homemade and excellent. The chic Makawao shopkeepers lunch here daily and never tire of the quinoa salad, the ginger chicken soup, the roasted-beet-and-potato soup, and the talk of the town—a towering Asian salad of Oriental vegetables, tofu, and baby greens, tossed in a sesame vinaigrette with fresh mint, ginger, and lemongrass, and served over Chinese noodles.

Kitada's Kau Kau Corner. 3617 Baldwin Ave. ☎ **808/572-7241.** Most items under $6.75. No credit cards. Mon–Sat 6am–1:30pm. AMERICAN/JAPANESE.

This is saimin central, a cross between grandma's kitchen and a cowboy diner known for its paniolo-size servings and the tastiest saimin in Upcountry Maui. Kitada's plate lunches are legendary (the hamburger plate is adored by the reckless), and the dry mein, a heap of noodles, is a cross between saimin and Chinese fried noodles. You'll see everyone from upcountry ranch hands to expensively dressed Makawao ladies digging in. Lots of local color and cheap eats.

HALIIMAILE & PUKALANI
MODERATE

✪ **Haliimaile General Store.** Haliimaile Rd., Haliimaile. ☎ **808/572-2666.** Reservations recommended. Lunch $6–$14; dinner $14–$28. AE, DC, MC, V. Mon–Fri 11am–2pm and 5:30–9:30pm, Sat 5:30–9pm, Sun 10am–2:30pm (brunch) and 5:30–9:30pm. AMERICAN.

You'll dine in a peach-colored room with old wood floors, high ceilings (sound ricochets fiercely here), and works by local artists. The food, a blend of eclectic American with ethnic touches, manages to avoid the usual pitfalls of Hawaii Regional Cuisine: the same-old, same-old, I'm-bored-with-seared-ahi syndrome. Even the fresh-catch sandwich on the lunch menu is anything but prosaic. The chicken tortilla soup and salade niçoise disappear quickly at lunch, when soups, salads, fresh fish, and salads dominate. Dinner splurges include the spicy rack of lamb, Hunan style, and paniolo ribs in tangy barbecue sauce. One of the 12 original Hawaii Regional Cuisine chefs, Bev Gannon has proven her staying power.

INEXPENSIVE

Upcountry Cafe. In the Andrade Building, 7-2 Aewa Place (just off the Haleakala Hwy.), Pukalani. ☎ **808/572-2395.** Lunch $5.95–$8.95; most dinner items under $14.95. MC, V. Mon 6:30am–3pm, Wed–Thurs 6:30am–3pm and 5:30–8:30pm, Fri–Sat 6:30am–3pm and 5:30–9pm, Sun 6:30am–1pm. AMERICAN/LOCAL.

Pukalani's inexpensive, casual, and very popular cafe features cows everywhere: on the walls, chairs, menus, aprons, even the exterior. But the food is the draw: simple home-cooked comfort food like meat loaf, roast pork, and humongous hamburgers, plus home-baked bread, oven-fresh muffins, and local faves such as saimin and Chinese chicken salad. Soups and salads and shrimp scampi with bow-tie pasta are among the cafe's other pleasures. The signature dessert is the cow pie, a naughty pile of chocolate cream cheese with macadamia nuts in a cookie crust, shaped like you-know-what.

KULA
EXPENSIVE

Kula Lodge. Haleakala Hwy. (Hi. 377). ☎ **808/878-2517.** Reservations recommended for dinner. Lunch $7.25–$14; dinner main courses $18–$26. MC, V. Daily 6:30am–9pm. HAWAII REGIONAL/AMERICAN.

Don't let the dinner prices scare you, because the Kula Lodge is equally enjoyable—if not more so—for breakfast and lunch, when the prices are lower and the views through the large picture windows have an eye-popping intensity. A new feature is the outdoor dining area with its wood-burning oven, open from 11am daily for as long as the weather permits. The million-dollar view spans the flanks of Haleakala, rolling 3,200 feet down to central Maui, the ocean, and the West Maui Mountains; if possible, go for sunset cocktails. When darkness descends, a roaring fire and lodge atmosphere heighten the coziness of the room. For breakfast, the Kula Lodge serves eggs Benedict and is famous for its banana–macadamia nut pancakes. At lunch, choices include smoked-turkey sandwiches, garden burgers, soups, salads, seared ahi, mahimahi burgers, and pizza.

INEXPENSIVE

Grandma's Coffee House. At the end of Hi. 37, Keokea. ☎ **808/878-2140.** Most items under $8.95. MC, V. Daily 7am–7pm. COFFEEHOUSE/AMERICAN.

Alfred Franco's grandmother started what is now a five-generation coffee business back in 1918, when she was 16 years old. Today the tiny wooden coffeehouse, named after her and still fueled by home-grown Haleakala coffee beans, is the quintessential roadside oasis. About 6 miles before the Tedeschi Vineyard in Ulupalakua, Grandma's is a gathering place for espresso drinks, fresh juices, home-baked pastries, inexpensive pasta, sandwiches (including sensational avocado and garden burgers), homemade soups, and plate-lunch specials that change daily. The rotating specials include Hawaiian beef stew, ginger chicken, saimin, lentil soup, and sandwiches piled high with Kula vegetables.

Kula Sandalwoods Restaurant. Haleakala Hwy. (Hi. 377). ☎ **808/878-3523.** Most items under $8.75. DISC, MC, V. Mon–Sat 6:30am–2pm, Sun 6:30am–noon (brunch). AMERICAN.

Chef Eleanor Loui, a graduate of the Culinary Institute of America, makes hollandaise sauce every morning from fresh upcountry egg yolks, sweet butter, and Myers lemons, which her family grows in the yard above the restaurant. This is Kula cuisine, with produce from the backyard and everything made from scratch: French toast with home-baked Portuguese sweet bread, hamburgers in a special sauce made with grated sharp cheddar, grilled teriyaki chicken breast, and an outstanding garden veggie burger. The Kula Sandalwoods omelet is an open-faced marvel with cheddar and jack cheeses, tomatoes, and green onions, served with cottage potatoes—a gourmet treat. The Kula Sandalwoods salad features grilled chicken breast with crimson Kula tomatoes and onions, and, when the garden allows, just-picked red oak, curly green, and red leaf lettuces. You'll dine in the gazebo or on the terrace, with dazzling views in all directions—including, in the spring, a yard dusted with lavender jacaranda flowers and a hillside ablaze with fields of orange akulikuli blossoms.

5 East Maui: On the Road to Hana

PAIA

MODERATE

Impromptu Café. 71 Baldwin Ave. ☎ **808/579-8477.** Main courses $9.95–$18.95. AE, DISC, MC, V. Daily 7:30am–11pm. NEW AMERICAN.

The next time you have a yen for grilled vegetable pasta, Caribbean jerk pork tenderloin, coconut and ginger lamb kebab with spicy peanut sauce, scallops on weed (nori), white clam and garlic pizza, and fantastic salads with ingredients like feta, shiitake, pine nuts, gorgonzola, and organic greens, try Impromptu. It's a hit in Paia, with a menu sufficiently sophisticated but not terribly pricey, offered in a chic environment with windows looking out to Baldwin Avenue and original works by local artists.

Jacques Bistro. 89 Hana Hwy. ☎ **808/579-6255.** Reservations accepted. Brunch main courses $5–$18, dinner main courses $8–$19. MC, V. Daily 10:30am–10:30pm. FRENCH/AMERICAN/ISLAND.

Fresh local seafood with a French touch, served in a room with a 42-foot monkeypod bar and arches, columns, and garden lanai—that's Paia's newest bistro.

New owners with fresh ideas and a likable chef proffer a menu of affordable delights: catch of the day (from Paia fishermen), ahi poke, bouillabaisse, sashimi, and special touches such as seasoned purple potatoes and lightly steamed Kula vegetables. Pasta dishes (from $7.50) are a good deal after a day of windsurfing (or even shopping); meat lovers can choose ribeye steak, baby back ribs, or rack of lamb. The garden area is lush with palms and bromeliads and towering banyan trees—a world of serenity in quirky Paia.

INEXPENSIVE

Milagros Food Company. Hana Hwy. and Baldwin Ave. ☎ **808/579-8755.** Breakfast about $7; lunch $3–$8; dinner $7–$16. DC, DISC, MC, V. Daily 8am–9:30pm. SOUTHWESTERN/SEAFOOD.

Milagros quickly gained a following with its great food, upbeat atmosphere, and highly touted margaritas. Although the fish tacos are fabulous ($7.25 for a plate of two with beans and rice), this is much more than Mexican food. Regulars anticipate the fresh ahi creation of the evening, a combination of Southwestern and Pacific Rim flavors accompanied by fresh veggies and Kula greens. The $15.95 chile rellenos plate comes with grilled ahi, beans, rice, and Kula greens—a sensation, and very generous. The daily happy hour features $2.50 margaritas ($12 for a pitcher) from 3 to 6pm.

Paia Fish Market. 110 Hana Hwy. ☎ **808/579-8030.** Lunch and dinner plates $6.95–$14.95. AE, DC, MC, V. Daily 11am–9:30pm. SEAFOOD.

It really is a fish market, with fresh fish to take home—and cooked seafood, salads, pastas, fajitas, and quesadillas to take out or enjoy at the few picnic tables inside the restaurant. Peppering the walls are photos of the number-one regional sport here, windsurfing. It's an appealing and budget-friendly selection: Cajun-style fresh catch, fresh fish tacos and quesadillas, and seafood and chicken pastas. You can also order hamburgers, cheeseburgers, and fish and chips (shrimp and chips, too), and wonderful lunch and dinner plates, both cheap and tasty.

Pic-nics. 30 Baldwin Ave. ☎ **808/579-8021.** Most items under $6.95. JCB, MC, V. Daily 7am–7pm. SANDWICHES/PICNIC LUNCHES.

Breakfast is terrific here—omelets, eggs to order, Maui Portuguese sausage, Hawaiian pancakes—and so is lunch. Pic-nics is famous for many things, among them the spinach nut burger, an ingenious vegetarian blend topped with vegetables and cheddar cheese (a cold version is topped with vegetables and Pic-nics's own homemade nonfat yogurt dressing). Stop here to fill your picnic basket for the drive to Hana or Upcountry Maui. These are gourmet sandwiches (Kula vegetables, home-baked breast of turkey, Cajun fish) worthy of the most idyllic picnic spot. The rosemary herb-roasted chicken can be ordered as a plate lunch for $7.95, or as part of the Hana Bay picnic ($22.95 for two), which includes sandwiches, meats, Maui-style potato chips, and home-baked cookies and muffins. You can order old-fashioned fish and chips too, or shrimp and chips, as well as pastries baked fresh daily. Fresh breads from the Maui Bake Shop add to the appeal. Several coffee drinks made with Maui blend coffee can give you the jolt you need for the drive ahead.

The Vegan. 115 Baldwin Ave. ☎ **808/579-9144.** Main courses $4.95–$8.95. MC, V. Daily 11:30am–9pm. GOURMET VEGETARIAN/VEGAN.

The Vegan proves that "vegan" doesn't have to mean boring. Wholesome foods with ingenious soy substitutes and satisfying flavors appear on a menu that defies deprivation. Garlic noodles are the best-selling item, cooked in a creamy coconut sauce and generously seasoned with garlic and spices. Curries, grilled polenta, pepper steak made of seitan (a meat substitute), and organic hummus are among the items that draw vegetarians from around the island. Proving that desserts are justly deserved, the Vegan offers a coconut milk–flavored tapioca pudding that hints of Thailand and doesn't contain dairy milk.

HAIKU
INEXPENSIVE

✪ **Pauwela Cafe.** 375 W. Kuiaha Rd. ☎ **808/575-9242.** Most items under $6. No credit cards. Mon–Sat 7am–3pm, Sun 8am–2pm. INTERNATIONAL.

It's a long drive from anywhere, but the kalua turkey sandwich is reason enough for the journey. Because it's located in an industrial center of sailboard and surfboard manufacturers, you might find a surf legend dining at the next table. The tiny cafe with concrete floors and six tables has a strong local following for many reasons. Becky Speere, a gifted chef, and her husband, Chris, a food-service instructor at Maui Community College and a former sous chef at the Maui Prince Hotel, infuse every sandwich, salad, and muffin with a high degree of culinary finesse. We never dreamed we could dine so well with such pleasing informality. The scene-stealing kalua turkey is one success layered on the other: warm, smoky, moist shredded turkey, served with cheese on home-baked French bread and covered with a green-chili and cilantro sauce. It gets our vote as the best sandwich on the island. The black-bean chili bursts with flavor and is served over brown rice with sour cream, cheese, and onions—a hearty, healthy choice. The salads, too, are fresh and uncomplicated, served with homemade dressings. For breakfast, eggs chilaquile are a good starter, with layers of corn tortillas, pinto beans, chiles, cheese, and herbs, topped with egg custard and served hot with salsa and sour cream—the works, for an unbelievable $5.

6 At the End of the Road in East Maui: Hana

We haven't included the main dining room at the Hotel Hana-Maui in the reviews below because the hotel was undergoing much managerial distress at press time. A new management team is rumored to take over, hopefully reinvigorating the spirit of a flagging operation that has suffered a decline in quality and service since its heyday.

EXPENSIVE

Hana Ranch Restaurant. Hana Hwy. ☎ **808/248-8255.** Reservations recommended for dinner. Main courses $16.95–$34.95. DC, DISC, MC, V. Sun–Thurs 11am–2:30pm, Fri–Sat 11am–2:30pm and 6–8:30pm. Buffet, daily 11am–2:30pm. Takeout, daily 6:30am–6:30pm. AMERICAN.

Part of the Hotel Hana-Maui operation, the Hana Ranch Restaurant is an informal alternative to the hotel's dining room. Dinner choices include New York steak; prawns and pasta; and a few Pacific Rim options, such as spicy shrimp wontons and the predictable fresh fish poke. Aside from the weekly, warmly received Wednesday "Pizza Night," the lunch buffet is a more affordable prospect: barbecued ribs, chicken, baked potatoes, beans, and salads for $10.95. There are indoor tables as well as two outdoor pavilions that offer stunning ocean views. At the take-out stand adjoining the restaurant, saimin, a $6.25 teriyaki plate lunch, a $5.95 chicken Caesar salad, and a mahi sandwich for $4.25 are reasonable alternatives for the dine-and-dash set.

INEXPENSIVE

The Cafe at Hana Gardenland. Hana Hwy. at Kalo Rd. ☎ **808/248-8975.** Most items under $8.95. MC, V. Daily 8:30am–5pm. HEALTHY/AMERICAN.

Hot sellers at this roadside cafe are the Hana Wraps, rice and vegetables wrapped in the tortilla of your choice. The light, healthy fare and foliage both indoors and out are pure, garden-style Hana. The koi pond, art gallery, and gift shop complement a menu that has won the hearts of diners with its honest simplicity: ahi salad in Hana papaya halves, garlic potato salad, and generously towering sandwiches on whole-wheat Maui Crunch bread. When Hillary Rodham Clinton and her daughter, Chelsea, came to Hana, they dined on steamed eggs with salsa on Maui Crunch bread, and waffles topped with fresh mangos. Most of the produce is grown on the Gardenland property, and the espresso bar serves teas; Hana-blend coffee; fresh orange, carrot, and lemon juices; and smoothies made with freshly picked bananas and papayas.

Fun in the Surf & Sun 8

by Jeanette Foster

This is why you have come to Maui—the sun, the sand, the surf. In this chapter, we'll tell you about the best beaches, from where to go to soak up the rays to the best place to plunge beneath the waves for a fish's-eye view of the underwater world. We've covered a range of ocean activities on Maui, as well as the best places and operators for these marine adventures. Also in this chapter are things to do on dry land: the best spots for hiking and camping, the greatest golf courses, and the lowdown on other outdoor activities.

1 Beaches

Maui has more than 80 accessible beaches of every conceivable description, from rocky black-sand beaches to powdery golden sands; there's even a rare red-sand beach. What follows is a selection of the finest of Maui's beaches, carefully chosen to suit a variety of needs, tastes, and interests.

For beach toys and equipment, contact **Rental Warehouse,** in Lahaina at 578 Front St., near Prison Street (☎ **808/661-1970**), or in Kihei at Azeka Place II, on the mountain side of Kihei Road near Lipoa Street (☎ **808/875-4050**). Beach chairs rent for $2 a day, coolers (with ice!) for $2 a day, and a host of toys (Frisbees, volleyballs, and more) for $1 a day.

WEST MAUI
✪ D. T. FLEMING BEACH PARK

This quiet, out-of-the-way beach cove, named after the man who started the commercial growing of pineapple on the Valley Isle, is a great place to take the family. The crescent-shaped beach, located north of the Ritz-Carlton Hotel, starts at the 16th hole of the Kapalua golf course (Makaluapuna Point) and rolls around to the sea cliffs at the other side. Ironwood trees provide shade on the land side. Offshore, a shallow sandbar extends to the edge of the surf. The waters are generally good for swimming and snorkeling; sometimes, off on the right side near the sea cliffs, the waves build enough for bodyboarders and surfers to get a few good rides in. This park has lots of facilities: rest rooms, showers, picnic tables, barbecue grills, and a paved parking lot.

Beaches & Outdoor Activities on Maui

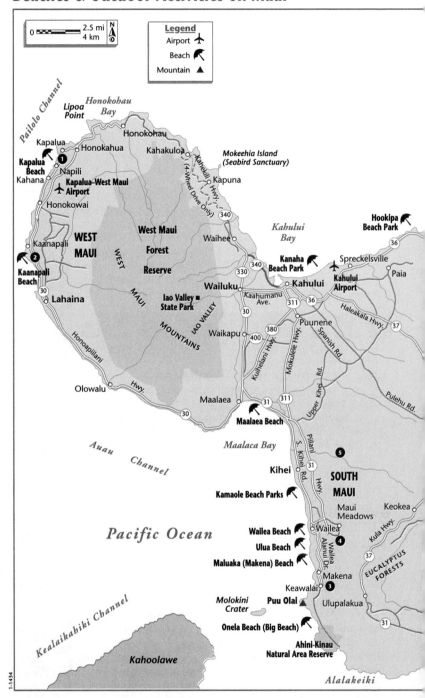

Legend
✈ Airport
🏖 Beach
▲ Mountain

0 — 2.5 mi / 4 km N

Pailolo Channel

Honokohau Bay

Lipoa Point

Kapalua
Kapalua Beach ①
Napili
Kahana
Kapalua–West Maui Airport
Honokowai

Honokohau
Honokahua
Kahakuloa
Mokeehia Island (Seabird Sanctuary)
Kapuna
Kahekili Hwy. (4-Wheel Drive Only)
340

WEST MAUI

WEST MAUI FOREST RESERVE

Kaanapali
Kaanapali Beach ②
30
Lahaina

WEST MAUI MOUNTAINS

Waihee
330
340

Kahului Bay

Kanaha Beach Park
Spreckelsville
Kahului Airport
Paia
36

Hookipa Beach Park

Wailuku
Iao Valley State Park ■
Iao Valley
Kaahumanu Ave.
311
36

Waikapu
380
400
30

Puunene
Haleakala Hwy.
37
Kuihelani Hwy.
Mokulele Hwy.
Spanish Rd.

Honoapiilani Hwy.

Olowalu

Maalaea
31
311

Pulehu Rd.

Auau Channel

Maalaea Beach

Maalaca Bay

Pacific Ocean

Kihei
31
S. Kihei Rd.
Piilani Hwy.
Upper Kihei Rd.

⑤

SOUTH MAUI

Maui Meadows
Keokea

Kamaole Beach Parks
Wailea Beach
Ulua Beach
Maluaka (Makena) Beach
Wailea ④
Makena ③
Wailea Alanui Dr.
Kula Hwy.
37

EUCALYPTUS FORESTS

Keawalai
Molokini Crater
Puu Olai ▲
Ulupalakua
31

Onela Beach (Big Beach)
Ahini-Kinau Natural Area Reserve

Kealaikahiki Channel

Kahoolawe

Alalakeiki

1-1434

156

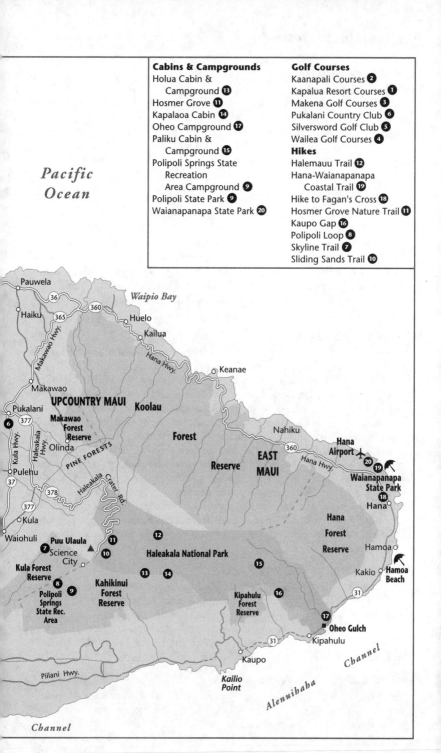

Cabins & Campgrounds

Holua Cabin & Campground **13**
Hosmer Grove **11**
Kapalaoa Cabin **14**
Oheo Campground **17**
Paliku Cabin & Campground **15**
Polipoli Springs State Recreation Area Campground **9**
Polipoli State Park **9**
Waianapanapa State Park **20**

Golf Courses

Kaanapali Courses **2**
Kapalua Resort Courses **1**
Makena Golf Courses **3**
Pukalani Country Club **6**
Silversword Golf Club **5**
Wailea Golf Courses **4**

Hikes

Halemauu Trail **12**
Hana-Waianapanapa Coastal Trail **19**
Hike to Fagan's Cross **18**
Hosmer Grove Nature Trail **11**
Kaupo Gap **16**
Polipoli Loop **8**
Skyline Trail **7**
Sliding Sands Trail **10**

Pacific Ocean

Pauwela

36

Waipio Bay

Haiku

365

360

Huelo

Kailua

Hana Hwy.

Keanae

Makawao Hwy.

Makawao

UPCOUNTRY MAUI

Koolau

Pukalani

377

6

Makawao Forest Reserve

Olinda

Kula Hwy.

Haleakala Hwy.

PINE FORESTS

Forest

Nahiku

360

Hana Airport

Hana Hwy.

20 **19**

Waianapanapa State Park

Pulehu

37

Reserve

EAST MAUI

18

Hana

Kula

377

378

Haleakala

Crater Rd

Waiohuli

Puu Ulaula

11

12

Hana Forest Reserve

Hamoa

7 Science City

10

Haleakala National Park

15

Kula Forest Reserve

8

13

14

Kakio

Hamoa Beach

Polipoli Springs State Rec. Area

9

Kahikinui Forest Reserve

Kipahulu Forest Reserve

16

31

17

Oheo Gulch

Kipahulu

Piilani Hwy.

31

Kaupo

Kailio Point

Alenuihaha

Channel

Channel

✪ KAPALUA BEACH

The beach cove that fronts the Kapalua Bay Hotel is the stuff of dreams: a golden crescent bordered by two palm-studded points. The sandy bottom slopes gently to deep water at the bay mouth; the water's so clear that you can see where the gold sands turn to green, and then deep blue. Protected from strong winds and currents by the lava-rock promontories, Kapalua's calm waters are great for snorkelers and swimmers of all ages and abilities, and the bay is big enough to paddle a kayak around without getting into the more challenging channel that separates Maui from Molokai. Waves come in just right for riding. Fish hang out by the rocks, making it great for snorkeling. The beach is accessible from the hotel on one end, which provides sun chairs with shades and a beach activities center for its guests, and a public access way on the other. It isn't so wide that you'll burn your feet getting in or out of the water, and the inland side is edged by a shady path and cool lawns. Outdoor showers are stationed at both ends. Parking is limited to about 30 spaces in a small lot off Lower Honoapiilani Road, by Napili Kai Beach Club, so arrive early; next door is a nice but somewhat pricey oceanfront restaurant, Kapalua's Bay Club. Facilities include showers, rest rooms, lifeguard, rental shack, and plenty of shade.

✪ KAANAPALI BEACH

Four-mile-long Kaanapali is one of Maui's best beaches, with grainy gold sand as far as the eye can see. The beach parallels the sea channel through most of its length, and a paved beach walk links hotels and condos, open-air restaurants, and Whalers Village shopping center. Because Kaanapali is so long and most hotels have adjacent swimming pools, the beach is crowded only in pockets—there's plenty of room to find seclusion. Summertime swimming is excellent. The best snorkeling is around Black Rock, in front of the Sheraton; the water is clear, calm, and populated with clouds of tropical fish. Facilities include outdoor showers; you can use the rest rooms at the hotel pools. Various beach activity vendors line up in front of the hotels, offering nearly every type of water activity and equipment. Parking is a problem, though. There are two public entrances: at the south end, turn off Honoapiilani Highway into the Kaanapali Resort, and pay for parking there; or continue on Honoapiilani Highway, turn off at the last Kaanapali exit at the stoplight near the Maui Kaanapali Villas, and park next to the beach signs indicating public access.

WAHIKULI COUNTY WAYSIDE PARK

This small stretch of beach, adjacent to Honoapiilani Highway between Lahaina and Kaanapali, is one of Lahaina's most popular beach parks. It's packed on weekends, but during the week it's a great place for swimming, snorkeling, sunbathing, and picnics. Offshore, the bottom is composed of rocks and sand, gradually sloping down to deeper water. Facilities include paved parking, rest rooms, showers, and small covered pavilions with picnic tables and barbecue grills.

LAUNIUPOKO COUNTY WAYSIDE PARK

Families with children will love this small park off Honoapiilani Highway, just south of Lahaina. A large man-made wading pool for kids fronts the shady park, with giant boulders protecting the wading area from the surf outside. Just to the left is a small sandy beach with good swimming when conditions are right. Offshore, the waves are occasionally big enough for surfing. The view from the park is one of the best: you can see the islands of Kahoolawe, Lanai, and Molokai in the distance. Facilities include paved parking lot, rest rooms, showers, picnic tables, and barbecue grills. It's crowded on weekends.

SOUTH MAUI
KAMAOLE III BEACH PARK

Three beach parks—Kamaole I, II, and III—stand like golden jewels in the front yard of the funky seaside town of Kihei, which all of a sudden is sprawling like suburban blight. The beaches are the best thing about Kihei (if you don't count Pacific Cafe). All three are popular with local residents and visitors because they're easily accessible. On weekends they're jam-packed with fishermen, picnickers, swimmers, and snorkelers. The most popular is Kamaole III, or Kam-3, as locals say. The biggest of the three beaches, with wide pockets of golden sand, it's the only one with a playground for children and a grassy lawn that meets the sand. Swimming is safe here, but scattered lava rocks are toe stubbers at the water line, and parents should watch to make sure that their kids don't venture too far out, because the bottom slopes off quickly. Both the north and south shores are rocky fingers with a surge big enough to attract fish and snorkelers, and the winter waves attract bodysurfers. Kam-3 is also a wonderful place to watch the sunset. Facilities include rest rooms, showers, picnic tables, barbecue grills, and lifeguard. There's also plenty of parking on South Kihei Road, across from the Maui Parkshore condos.

✪ WAILEA BEACH

Wailea, which means "water of Lea," the Hawaiian goddess of canoe makers, is the best golden-sand crescent on Maui's sunbaked southwestern coast. One of five beaches within Wailea Resort, Wailea is big, wide, and protected on both sides by black lava points. It's the front yard of the Four Seasons Wailea and the Grand Wailea Resort Hotel and Spa, respectively Maui's most elegant and outrageous beach hotels. From the beach, the view out to sea is magnificent, framed by neighboring Kahoolawe and Lanai and the tiny crescent of Molokini, probably the most popular snorkel spot in these parts. The clear waters tumble to shore in waves just the right size for gentle riding, with or without a board. From shore, you can see Pacific humpback whales in season (December through April), and unreal sunsets nightly. Facilities include rest rooms, outdoor showers, and limited free parking at the blue SHORELINE ACCESS sign, on Wailea Alanui Drive, the main drag of this resort. Wailea Resort's beaches might seem off-limits, hidden from plain view by an intimidating wall of luxury resorts, but they're all open to the public.

ULUA BEACH

One of the most popular beaches in Wailea, Ulua is a long, wide, crescent-shaped gold-sand beach between two rocky points. When the ocean is calm, Ulua offers Wailea's best snorkeling; when it's rough, the waves are excellent for bodysurfers. The ocean bottom is shallow and gently slopes down to deeper waters, making swimming generally safe. The beach is usually occupied by guests of nearby resorts; during the high season (from Christmas to March and June to August), it's carpeted with beach towels and packed with sunbathers like sardines in cocoa butter. Facilities include showers and rest rooms. A variety of equipment is available for rent at the nearby Wailea Ocean Activity Center. To find Ulua, look for the new blue SHORELINE ACCESS sign on South Kihei Road, near Stouffer Wailea Beach Resort. A tiny parking lot is nearby.

✪ MALUAKA (MAKENA) BEACH

On the southern end of Maui's resort coast, development falls off dramatically, leaving a wild, dry countryside of green kiawe trees. The Maui Prince sits in isolated splendor, sharing Makena Resort's 1,800 acres with only a couple of first-rate golf courses and a necklace of perfect beaches. The strand nearest the hotel is Maluaka Beach, often called Makena, notable for its beauty and its views of Molokini Crater, the offshore islet, and Kahoolawe, the so-called "target" island. It's a short, wide, palm-fringed crescent of golden, grainy sand set between two black lava points and bounded by big sand dunes topped by a grassy knoll. Swimming in this mostly calm bay is considered the best on Makena Bay, which is bordered on the south by Puu Olai cinder cone and historic Keawala'i Congregational Church. Facilities include rest rooms, showers, a landscaped park, a lifeguard, and roadside parking. Along Makena Alanui, look for the SHORELINE ACCESS sign near the hotel, turn right, and head down to the shore.

ONELOA BEACH (BIG BEACH)

Oneloa, which means "long sand" in Hawaiian, is one of the most popular beaches on Maui. Locals call it "Big Beach"—it's 3,300 feet long and more than 100 feet wide. Mauians come here to swim, fish, sunbathe, surf, and enjoy the view of Kahoolawe and Lanai. Snorkeling is good around the north end at the foot of Puu Olai, a 360-foot cinder cone. During storms, however, big waves lash the shore and a strong rip current sweeps the sharp drop-off, posing a danger for inexperienced open-ocean swimmers. No facilities are available except for portable toilets, but there is plenty of parking. To get there, drive past the Maui Prince Hotel to the second dirt road, which leads through a kiawe thicket to the beach.

On the other side of Puu Olai is Little Beach, a small pocket beach where assorted nudists work on their all-over tans, to the chagrin of uptight authorities who take a dim view of public nudity. You can get a real nasty sunburn and a lewd-conduct ticket too.

EAST MAUI
BALDWIN PARK

Located off the Hana Highway between Sprecklesville and Paia, this popular beach park is well used by Maui residents, especially bodyboard enthusiasts. Named after Harry Baldwin, who was a delegate to Congress, the park was originally developed for the employees of Hawaiian Commercial and Sugar Co., who lived in the nearby area. In 1963, the company turned the park over to the county. It's easy to see why this place is so popular: the surf breaks along the entire length of the white-sand beach, creating perfect conditions for bodyboarding. On occasion, the waves get big enough for surfing. A couple of swimming areas are safe enough for children: one in the lee of the beach rocks near the large pavilion, and another at the opposite end of the beach, where beach rocks protect a small swimming area. Facilities include a large pavilion with picnic tables and kitchen facilities, barbecue grills, additional picnic tables on the grassy area, rest rooms, showers, and a semi-paved parking area. The park also contains a baseball diamond and a soccer field. The park is well used on weekends; weekdays are much quieter.

HOOKIPA BEACH PARK, PAIA

Two miles past Paia, on the Hana Highway, you'll find one of the most famous windsurfing sites in the world. Due to constant wind and endless waves, Hookipa attracts top windsurfers and wave jumpers from around the globe. Surfers and fishermen also enjoy this small, gold-sand beach at the foot of a grassy cliff, which provides a natural amphitheater for spectators. Except when international competitions are being held, weekdays are the best time to watch the daredevils fly over the waves. When the water is flat, snorkelers and divers explore the reef. Facilities include rest rooms, showers, pavilions, picnic tables, barbecue grills, and a parking lot.

✪ HAMOA BEACH, HANA

This half moon–shaped, gray-sand beach (a mix of coral and lava) in a truly tropical setting is a favorite among sunbathers seeking rest and refuge at Hotel Hana-Maui (which maintains the beach and acts as though it's private—which it isn't, so just march down those lava-rock steps and grab a spot on the sand). James Michener said of Hamoa: "Paradoxically, the only beach I have ever seen that looks like the South Pacific was in the North Pacific—Hamoa Beach . . . a beach so perfectly formed that I wonder at its comparative obscurity." The 100-foot-wide beach is three football fields long and sits below 30-foot black-lava sea cliffs. An unprotected beach open to the ocean, Hamoa is often swept by power rip currents. Surf breaks offshore and rolls ashore, making this a popular surfing and bodysurfing area. The calm left side is best for snorkeling in the summer. The hotel has numerous facilities for guests; there are an outdoor shower and rest rooms for nonguests. Parking is limited. Look for the Hamoa Beach turnoff from Hana Highway.

✪ WAIANAPANAPA STATE PARK

This beach park is located 4 miles before Hana, off the Hana Highway. It takes its name from the legend of the Waianapanapa Cave, where Chief Kaakea, a jealous and cruel man, suspected his wife, Popoalaea, of having an affair. Popoalaea left her husband and hid herself in a chamber of the Waianapanapa Cave. She and her attendant ventured out only at night, for food. Nevertheless, a few days later, Kaakea was passing by the area and saw the shadow of the servant. Knowing he had found his wife's hiding place, Kaakea entered the cave and killed her. During certain times of the year, the water in the tide pool turns red as a tribute to Popoalaea, commemorating her death. Scientists claim, however, that the change in color is due to the presence of small red shrimp.

Waianapanapa State Park's 120 acres have 12 cabins, a caretaker's residence, a beach park, picnic tables, barbecue grills, rest rooms, showers, a parking lot, a shoreline hiking trail, and a black-sand beach (it's actually small black pebbles). This is a wonderful area for both shoreline hikes (bring insect repellent, because the mosquitoes are plentiful) and picnicking. Swimming is generally unsafe, though, due to powerful rip currents and strong waves breaking offshore, which roll into the beach unchecked. Because Waianapanapa is crowded on weekends with local residents and their families, as well as tourists, weekdays are generally a better bet.

2 Hitting the Water

Maui is a haven for every type of water activity for enthusiasts of all kinds, from windsurfers twirling in the ocean breezes to beginners donning a mask and snorkel for the first time to view the dazzling array of underwater life. You can skim across the water on a fast-moving sailing boat, plunge beneath the waves in a high-tech submarine, and soar above the water in a parasail. Whatever your interest, you can find it on Maui.

BODYBOARDING (BOOGIE BOARDING) & BODYSURFING

Bodysurfing—riding the waves without a board, becoming one with the rolling water—is a way of life in Hawaii. Some bodysurfers just rely on their outstretched hands (or hands at their sides) to ride the waves; others use handboards (flat, paddle-like gloves).

For additional maneuverability, try a boogie or bodyboard (also known as belly boards or *paipo* boards). These 3-foot-long vehicles, which support the upper part of your body, are easy to carry and very maneuverable in the water. Both body-surfing and bodyboarding require a pair of open-heeled swim fins to help propel you through the water. Both kinds of wave riding are very popular in the islands because the equipment is inexpensive and easy to carry, and both sports can be prac-ticed in the small, gentle waves.

You can rent boogie boards and fins for $6.50 a day or $26 a week from **Snorkel Bob's,** open from 8am to 5pm daily at two locations: Napili Village Hotel, 5425 Lower Honoapiilani Rd., Napili (☎ 808/669-9603); and 161 Lahainaluna Rd., Lahaina (☎ 808/661-4421). They're also available for rent from **West Hawaii Surfing Academy,** 658 Front St. (in front of the Wharf Cinema Center and across the street from the Banyan Tree), Lahaina (☎ 808/667-5399), for $5 for 2 hours. The cheapest place to rent boogie boards is **Rental Warehouse,** 578 Front St. (near Prison Street), in Lahaina (☎ 808/661-1970), or in Kihei at Azeka Place II, on the mountain side of Kihei Road, near Lipoa Street (☎ 808/875-4050), where they go for as little as $2 a day.

Baldwin Beach, just outside of Paia, has great bodysurfing waves nearly year-round. In winter, Maui's best bodysurfing spot is Mokuleia Beach, known locally as Slaughterhouse because of the cattle slaughterhouse that once stood here, not because of the waves—although they are definitely for expert bodysurfers only. To get to Mokuleia, take Honoapiilani Highway just past Kapalua Bay Resort; various hiking trails will take you down to the pocket beach.

Storms from the south bring fair bodysurfing conditions and great boogie boarding to the lee side of Maui. Good choices include Oneloa (or Big Beach) in Makena, Ulua and Kamaole III in Kihei, and Kapalua beaches.

OCEAN KAYAKING

Gliding silently over the water, propelled by a paddle, seeing Maui from the sea the way the early Hawaiians did—that's what ocean kayaking is all about. One of Maui's best kayak routes is along the Kihei Coast, where there's easy access to calm water. Mornings are always best, because the wind comes up around 11am, making seas choppy and paddling difficult.

Kayak rentals are available for $15 per hour from **West Hawaii Surfing Academy,** 658 Front St. (in front of the Wharf Cinema Center and across the street from the Banyan Tree), Lahaina (☎ 808/667-5399). The island's cheapest kayak rentals are at **Rental Warehouse,** 578 Front St. (near Prison Street), in Lahaina (☎ 808/661-1970), or in Kihei at Azeka Place II, on the mountain side of Kihei Road, near Lipoa Street (☎ 808/875-4050), where one-person kayaks are $20 a day and two-person kayaks are $40 a day.

For the uninitiated, our favorite kayak tour is **Makena Kayak Tours** (☎ 808/879-8426). Dino, the professional guide, leads the 2½-hour tour from Makena Landing and loves taking first-time kayakers over the secluded coral reefs and into remote coves. Dino has been swimming, snorkeling, and diving in these waters most of his life; his wonderful tour will be the highlight of your trip.

The cost for the tour, which includes refreshment, snorkeling equipment, and kayak equipment, is only $55.

Gordon Godfrey, Suzanne Simmons, and the expert guides of **South Pacific Kayaks**, 2439 S. Kihei Rd., Kihei, HI 96753 (☎ **800/776-2326** or 808/875-4848; fax 808/875-4691; www.maui.net/~kayak; e-mail seakayak@maui.net), are Maui's oldest kayak tour company. They offer ocean kayak tours (with snorkeling) that include lessons and a guided tour. Tours run from 2½ to 5 hours and range in price from $59 to $89. Kayak rentals start at $20 a day.

In Hana, **Hana Kayak and Snorkel Tours** (☎ **808/248-7711**) runs 4½-hour tours of Hana's coastline on wide, stable "no roll" kayaks for $59 per person. You can also spend a day learning how to kayak-surf with an instructor—it costs $59 for 7 hours—or rent your own kayak for $27.50 per hour.

OCEAN RAFTING

If you're semi-adventurous and looking for a more intimate experience with the sea, try ocean rafting. The inflatable rafts hold 6 to 24 passengers, and tours usually include snorkeling and coastal cruising. One of the best (and most reasonable) outfitters is **Hawaiian Ocean Raft**, P.O. Box 381, Lahaina, HI 96761 (☎ **888/677-RAFT** or 808/667-2191; fax 808/878-3574), which operates out of the Lahaina Harbor. The best deal here is the 5-hour morning tour, which heads over to Lanai, goes searching for dolphins, and includes two snorkeling stops; it costs $69 for adults, $49 for children ages 5 to 12 (children under 5 ride free). The all-day (8am to 4pm) tour with eight snorkel stops and lunch costs $109 for adults and $79 for children ages 5 to 12.

PARASAILING

Soar high above the crowds (at around 400 ft.) for a bird's-eye view of Maui. This ocean adventure sport, which is something of a cross between skydiving and waterskiing, involves sailing through the air, suspended under a large parachute attached by a tow line to a speedboat. Keep in mind, though, that parasailing tours don't run during whale season, which is roughly December through May.

We recommend **UFO Parasail** (☎ **800/FLY-4UFO** or 808/661-7UFO), which picks you up at Kaanapali Beach. The Early Bird Special (arrive by 7am) costs $37 (as opposed to $42) for a 7-minute ride. During whale season, the company converts its 37-foot speedboat into a whale-watching machine, and offers 1½-hour whale-watching trips for $25 per person.

SAILING & BOATING

To really appreciate Hawaii, you need to get off the land and get on the sea. Almost every type of nautical experience is available in the islands. You can go to sea on old-fashioned Polynesian outrigger canoes, high-tech kayaks, fast-moving catamarans, inflatable rubber Zodiacs, smooth-moving SWATH (Small Waterplane Area Twin Hull) vessels that promise not to make you seasick, gaff-rigged schooners, America's Cup racing sloops, charter fishing boats, ferries, booze cruise barges, snorkel and dive boats, submarines, or even an interisland cruise ship.

Trade winds off the Lahaina Coast and the strong wind that rips through Maui's isthmus make sailing around the island exciting. Many different boats, from a three-masted schooner to spacious trimarans, offer day cruises from Maui.

You can experience the thrill of competition sailing with **World Class Yacht Charters**, 107 Kahului Heliport, Kahului, HI 96732 (☎ **800/600-0959** or 808/667-7733). There's nothing like it, especially when all you have to do is hold on and cheer. *World Class,* a 65-foot custom yacht designed for Maui waters, takes 24 passengers for a variety of sailing adventures: 2-hour whale-watching tours for $25; 4-hour morning snorkel sails for $59; high-performance sails for $35; and a 2-hour trade-winds sunset sail for $45. The 2pm high-performance sailing tour is the most exciting. Be prepared to get wet: the captain and crews of this cutter-rigged, high-tech yacht are serious about sailing. All trips leave from Kaanapali Beach.

You can also take a ride on *America II,* slip #5, Lahaina Harbor (☎ **888/ 667-2133** or 808/667-2195; www.galaxymall.com/stores/americaii), a U.S. contender in the America's Cup. It's a true racing boat, offering a morning whale-watching sail, an afternoon sail, and a sunset sail. Each trip lasts 2 hours and costs $29.95 for adults, $14.95 for children ages 6 to 12; free for children 5 and under.

DAY CRUISES TO LANAI

Hop aboard ✪ **Trilogy Excursions'**s 50-foot catamaran for a 90-mile sail to Lanai and a fun-filled day of sailing, snorkeling, swimming, and whale watching. This is the only cruise that offers a personalized ground tour of the island. Breakfast (homemade cinnamon buns and freshly brewed Kona coffee) and lunch (a Hawaiian barbecue) are included. The trip is $159 for adults, $79.50 for children ages 3 to 12, and free for children under 3—we think it's worth every penny. Call ☎ **800/ 874-2666** or 808/661-4743.

The ✪ **Expedition's Lahaina/Lanai Passenger Ferry** (☎ **808/661-3756**) will take you from Maui to Lanai and back for $50 round-trip. The ferry services run daily, five times a day. Before you catch the first ferry, which leaves Lahaina at 6:45am, call **Red Rover** (☎ **808/565-7722**), which rents four-wheel Land Rovers on Lanai; staffers will meet you upon arrival in Lanai with a Land Rover, snorkeling equipment, boogie board, fishing tackle, and beach toys for a day of four-wheel exploring and beach activities (prices for the Land Rover range from $119 to $159). For an extra $25, they will provide a gourmet picnic lunch for two, complete with basket, blanket, and more. The last ferry leaves Lanai at 6:45pm, and you can return the Land Rover at the ferry departure area at Manele Bay for no extra charge.

A day with **Club Lanai** (☎ **808/871-1144**) consists of a trimaran trip departing from Lahaina Harbor, slip 4, at 7:30am to Lanai's eastern shore, where you can spend the day snorkeling, kayaking, bicycling, and relaxing in a hammock at an 8-acre beachfront estate. An all-you-can-eat buffet lunch and an open bar are included in the cost: $89 for adults, $69 for children ages 13 to 20, $29 for children ages 4 to 12, and free for children 3 and under.

Scotch Mist (☎ **808/661-0386**), a 50-foot Santa Cruz sailboat anchored in Lahaina Harbor, slip 9, offers half-day sail and snorkeling cruises to Lanai; you won't actually set foot on Lanai, but you'll swim with the fish in its sparkling off-shore waters. The price—$55 for adults, $45 for kids ages 10 to 16, $35 for kids ages 4 to 10, and free for kids under 4—includes snorkeling gear, plus fruit juice, fresh pineapple spears, Maui chips, beer, wine, and soda. All you have to bring is a swimsuit and towel.

Navatek II (☎ **800/852-4183** or 808/661-8787) is a new and unusual 82-foot SWATH vessel, designed to operate in heavy seas without spilling your Mai Tai. The ship's superstructure (the part you ride on) rests on twin torpedo-like hulls that slash the water, creating a remarkably smooth ride. For all of you who approach the sea with patches stuck behind your ears, this boat's for you; you couldn't get sick if you tried. A trip on the *Navatek II,* which glides across the 9-mile Auau Channel from Maalaea, Maui, to Lanai, includes a 90-minute snorkel off Lanai's rugged west coast, breakfast, lunch, a sail along Lanai's remote coastline, and whale watching in season. Cruises depart from Maalaea Harbor and cost $125 for adults, $95 for juniors (ages 12 to 17), and $75 for children (ages 5 to 11).

For an amazingly smooth, stable, and swift ride, call *Maui Nui Explorer* (☎ **808/661-3776**). This 48-foot, 49-passenger adventure craft leaves Lahaina Harbor for a 4-hour journey along the coast of Lanai, where you'll be able to swim and snorkel in remote coves and bays. Coffee, juice, and a deli-style lunch (sandwiches, Maui potato chips, fresh fruit, and cookies) are included, along with snacks, snorkel gear, and whale watching (in season). There's always a Hawaiian cultural specialist/marine-life expert on board to answer questions about the Hawaiian Islands and their surrounding waters. The cost is $65 for adults and $45.50 for children ages 5 to 11.

DINNER CRUISES

Navatek II, 162 Lahainaluna Rd., Lahaina (☎ **800/852-4183** or 808/661-8787), offers one of Hawaii's best sunset dinner cruises. The boat is souped up using revolutionary technology that makes the ride incredibly smooth—out on the water, you'll forget that you're even on a boat. It's perfect for those prone to seasickness. On board, you can watch porpoises play as the sun sets, then watch the stars come out. The 2-hour dinner cruise, accompanied by Hawaiian entertainment, operates Saturday through Thursday. It departs from Maalaea Harbor and costs $87 for adults and $55 for children ages 2 to 11 (free for children under 2).

SCUBA DIVING

Some people come to the islands for the sole purpose of plunging into the tropical Pacific and exploring the underwater world. You can see the great variety of tropical marine life (more than 100 endemic species found nowhere else on the planet), explore sea caves, and swim with sea turtles and monk seals in the clear tropical waters off Hawaii, one of the world's top-10 dive destinations.

If you dive, go early in the morning. Trade winds often rough up the seas in the afternoon, so most dive operators schedule early-morning dives that end at noon and then take the rest of the day off.

If you're not certified, take classes before you come to Hawaii so that you can dive right in. Unsure about scuba diving? Take an introductory dive; most operators offer no-experience-necessary dives, ranging from $70 to $95. You can learn from this glimpse into the sea world whether diving is for you.

Everyone dives Molokini, a marine-life park and one of Hawaii's top dive spots. This crescent-shaped crater has three tiers of diving: a 35-foot plateau inside the crater basin (used by beginning divers and snorkelers), a wall sloping to 70 feet just beyond the inside plateau, and a sheer wall on the outside and backside of the crater that plunges 350 feet. This underwater park is very popular thanks to calm, clear, protected waters and an abundance of marine life, from manta rays to clouds of yellow butterfly fish.

For personalized diving, **Ed Robinson's Diving Adventures** (☎ **800/635-1273** or 808/879-3584; fax 808/874-1939; www.mauiscuba.com; e-mail robinson@ maui.net) is one of the best on Maui. This widely published underwater photographer offers specialized charters for small groups. Most of his business comes from repeat customers. Ed offers two-tank dives for $104 ($10 extra for equipment); his dive boats depart from Kihei boat ramp.

If Ed is booked, call **Mike Severns Diving,** P.O. Box 627, Kihei (☎ **808/ 879-6596;** www.severns.maui.hi.us; e-mail severns@mauigateway.com), for small (12-person maximum, divided into two groups of six people each) personal diving tours on his 38-foot Munson/Hammerhead boat with freshwater shower. Mike and

An Expert Shares His Secrets: Maui's Best Dives

Ed Robinson, of Ed Robinson's Diving Adventures (see above), knows what makes a great dive. Here are five of his favorites on Maui—and he'll be happy to take you to any or all of them:

Hawaiian Reef   This area off the Kihei-Wailea coast is so named because it hosts a good cross-section of topography and marine life typical of Hawaiian waters. Diving to depths of 85 feet, you'll see everything from lava formations and coral reef to sand and rubble, plus a diverse range of both shallow and deep-water creatures. You'll see for yourself why this area was so popular with ancient Hawaiian fishermen: large helmet shells, a healthy garden of large antler coral heads, and large schools of snapper are common.

Third Tank   Located off Makena Beach at 80 feet, this World War II tank is one of the most picturesque artificial reefs you're likely to see around Maui. It acts like a fish magnet: because it's the only large solid object in the area, any fish or invertebrate looking for a safe home comes here. Surrounding the tank is a cloak of schooling snapper and goat fish just waiting for a photographer with a wide-angle lens. For its small size, the Third Tank is loaded with more marine life per square inch than any other site off Maui.

Molokini Crater   The backside is always done as a live boat drift dive. The vertical wall plummets from over 150 feet above sea level to around 250 feet below. Looking down to unseen depths gives you some idea of the vastness of the open ocean. Pelagic fish and sharks are often sighted, and living coral perches on the wall, which is home to lobster, crabs, and a number of photogenic black coral trees at 50 feet.

There are actually two great dive sites around Molokini crater. Named after common chub or rudder fish, **Enenue Side** gently slopes from the surface to about 60 feet, then drops rapidly to deeper waters. The shallower area is an easy

his wife, Pauline Fiene-Severns, are both biologists who make diving in Hawaii not only fun, but also educational (they also have a spectacular underwater photography book called *Molokini Island*). In their 18 years of operation, they have been accident free. Two-tank dives are $100 without equipment ($109 with equipment).

Maui's largest diving retailer, with everything from rentals to scuba-diving instruction to dive-boat charters, is **Maui Dive Shop,** which can be found all over the island: in Kihei at Azeka Place II Shopping Center (☎ **808/879-3388**), Kamaole Shopping Center (☎ **808/879-1533**), and Kihei Town Center (☎ **808/879-1919**); and in Lahaina at Lahaina Cannery Mall (☎ **808/661-5388**) and 626 Front St. (☎ **808/667-0722**). Other locations include Wailea Shopping Village (☎ **808/879-3166**); Whalers Shopping Village, Kaanapali (☎ **808/661-5117**); Kahana Gateway, Kahana (☎ **808/669-3800**); and 444 Hana Hwy., Kahului (☎ **808/871-2111**).

If you dive on your own, order the *Dive Hawaii Guide,* which describes 44 locations on a chart created by Dive Hawaii and the University of Hawaii Sea Grant. Send $2 to **UH/SGES,** attention: Dive Guide, 1000 Pope Rd., MSB 226, Honolulu, HI 96822.

SNORKELING

Snorkeling is the main attraction in Maui—and almost anyone can do it. To enjoy the underwater world, all you need are a mask, a snorkel, fins, and some basic dive, with lots of tame butterfly fish. It's also the home of Morgan Bentjaw, one of our friendliest moray eels. Enenue Side is often done as a live boat drift dive to extend the range of the tour. Diving depths vary. Divers usually do a 50-foot dive, but on occasion advanced divers drop to the 130-foot level to visit the rare boar fish and the shark condos.

Almost every kind of fish found in Hawaii can be seen in the crystalline waters of **Reef's End.** Reef's End is an extension of the rim of Molokini crater, which runs for about 200 yards underwater, barely breaking the surface. Reef's End is shallow enough for novice snorkelers and exciting enough for experienced divers. The end and outside of this shoal drop off in dramatic terraces to beyond diving range. In deeper waters, there are shark ledges at varying depths, and dozens of eels, some of which are tame, including moray, dragon, snowflake, and garden eels. The shallower inner side is home to Garbanzo, one of the largest and first eels to be tamed. The reef is covered with cauliflower coral; in bright sunlight, it's one of the most dramatic underwater scenes in Hawaii.

La Perouse Pinnacle   In the middle of scenic La Perouse Bay, site of Haleakala's most recent lava flow, is a pinnacle rising from the 60-foot bottom to about 10 feet below the surface. Getting to the dive site is half the fun: the scenery above water is as exciting as that below the surface. Underwater, you'll enjoy a very diversified dive. Clouds of damsel and trigger fish will greet you on the surface. Divers can approach even the timid bird wrasse. We find more porcupine puffers here than anywhere else, as well as schools of goat fish and fields of healthy finger coral. La Perouse is good for snorkeling and those long, shallow second dives.

—Rick Carroll

swimming skills. Floating over underwater worlds through colorful clouds of tropical fish is like a dream. In many places, all you have to do is wade into the water and look down.

If you've never snorkeled before, you can take advantage of the snorkeling equipment and lessons offered by most resorts and excursion boats. However, you won't really need lessons; it's plenty easy to figure out for yourself, especially once you're at the beach—everybody around you will be doing it.

Always snorkel with a buddy. Look up every once in a while to see where you are, how far offshore you are, and whether there's any boat traffic. Don't touch anything; not only can you damage coral, but camouflaged fish and shells with poisonous spines might surprise you. Always check with a dive shop, lifeguards, and others on the beach about the area in which you plan to snorkel: Are there any dangerous conditions you should know about? What are the current surf, tide, and weather conditions?

Snorkel Bob's can rent everything you need at their two Maui locations: Napili Village Hotel, 5425 Lower Honoapiilani Rd., Napili (☎ **808/669-9603**); and 161 Lahainaluna Rd., Lahaina (☎ **808/661-4421**). Snorkeling gear (fins, mask, and snorkel) rents for $2.50 to $6.50 a day, or $9 to $39 a week.

Rental Warehouse, in Lahaina at 578 Front St., near Prison Street (☎ **808/ 661-1970**), and in Kihei at Azeka Place II, on the mountain side of Kihei Road, near Lipoa Street (☎ **808/875-4050**), also has everything you need to experience the underwater world. The snorkel sets include mask, fins, snorkel, gear bag, map of great snorkeling areas, no-fog lotion (for your mask), and fish identification chart—just add water and you're ready to go.

Maui's best snorkeling beaches include Kapalua; Black Rock, at Kaanapali; along the Kihei coastline, especially at Kamaole III; and along the Wailea coastline, particularly at Ulua Beach. Mornings are best, because local winds don't kick in until around noon.

Two truly terrific places are worth the effort to get to, because they're home to Hawaii's tropical marine life at its best: Molokini and Ahihi-Kinau Natural Preserve.

Molokini   Like a crescent moon fallen from the sky, this sunken crater sits almost midway between Maui and the uninhabited island of Kahoolawe. Tilted so that only the thin rim of its southern side shows above water in a perfect semicircle, Molokini stands like a scoop against the tide, and it serves, on its concave side, as a natural sanctuary for tropical fish and snorkelers, who commute daily in a fleet of dive boats to this marine-life preserve. See "Taking a Snorkel Cruise," below, for details on getting there.

Ahihi-Kinau Natural Preserve   You can't miss in Ahihi Bay, a 2,000-acre State Natural Area Reserve in the lee of Cape Kinau, on Maui's rugged south coast, where Haleakala spilled red-hot lava that ran to the sea in 1790. Fishing is strictly kapu here, and the fish know it; they're everywhere in this series of rocky coves and black-lava tide pools. The black, barren, lunar-like land stands in stark contrast to the green-blue water, which covers a sparkling mosaic of tropical fish that thrive in this marine preserve, making for excellent snorkeling. Après-snorkel, check out La Perouse Bay on the south side of Cape Kinau, where the French admiral La Perouse became the first European to set foot on Maui. A lava rock pyramid known as Perouse Monument marks the spot. To get there, drive south of Makena past Puu Olai to Ahihi Bay, where the road turns to gravel and sometimes seems like it'll disappear under the waves. At Cape Kinau, there are three four-wheel-drive trails that lead across the lava flow; take the shortest one, nearest La Perouse Bay.

TAKING A SNORKEL CRUISE

If you'd like take a snorkel boat to Molokini (see the box above), check with the **Ocean Activities Center,** 1847 S. Kihei Rd., Kihei (☎ **800/798-0652** or 808/879-4485), which also operates out of a number of hotels and condos. The best deal is the Maka Kai cruise, which includes a continental breakfast, deli lunch, snorkel gear, and instruction; it's $55 for adults, $35 for children ages 3 to 12. The 5-hour cruise departs from Maalaea Harbor, slip 62, at 7am. Or you can call **Maui Classic Charters** (☎ **800/736-5740** or 808/879-8188; www.maui.net/~charters/MCC.html). Its snorkeling-sailing cruises on the 63-foot *Lavengro* leave Maalaea, slip 80, at 7am for a 6-hour journey that includes a continental breakfast and a deli lunch; the cruise costs $59 for adults and $40 for children under 12. This outfit also has a new boat, *Four Winds II,* a 53-foot glass-bottom catamaran, which offers both 5-hour snorkel trips ($69 for adults, $45 for children ages 3 to 12) and 3½-hour trips ($39.95 for adults, $29.95 for children). For an action-packed snorkel-sail experience, check out *Pride of Maui,* which operates out of Maalaea Harbor (☎ **808/875-0955**). The 5½-hour cruises not only go to Molokini, but also stop at Turtle Bay, off the cost of the Maui Prince Hotel, and in Makena, for more snorkeling. Continental breakfast, barbecue lunch, gear, and instruction are included in the price ($76 for adults, $69 for kids 13 to 17, $49 for kids 3 to 12, and free for kids under 3).

For trips that combine snorkeling with whale watching, see "Whale-Watching Cruises," below. If you'd like to head over to Lanai for a pristine day of snorkeling, see "Day Cruises to Lanai" under "Sailing & Boating," above.

SPORTFISHING

The largest blue marlin taken on a rod and reel in the waters around Maui tipped the scale at more than 1,200 pounds. Marlin, tuna, ono, and mahimahi await the baited hook in Maui's coastal and channel waters. No license is required; just book a sportfishing vessel out of Lahaina or Maalaea harbors. Most charter boats that troll for big game fish carry a maximum of six passengers. You can walk the docks, inspecting boats and talking to captains and crews, or book through an activities desk or one of the outfits recommended below.

If you want to fish out of Maalaea, you can spend the day with **Capt. Joe Yurkanin** and **Capt. Ermin Fergerstrom** on their 37-foot Tollycraft, the *No Ka Oi III* (☎ **800/798-0652** or 808/879-4485). For other ideas, try the **Maalaea Activities** desk at the harbor (☎ **808/242-6982**).

At Lahaina Harbor, go for one of the following charter companies: **Hinatea Sportfishing,** slip 27 (☎ 808/667-7548); **Lucky Strike Charters,** slips 50 and 51 (☎ 808/661-4606); or **Aerial Sportfishing Charters,** slip 2 (☎ 808/667-9089). Or check with **West Maui Charter** (☎ 808/669-6193), which offers everything from light- to heavy-tackle fishing.

Shop around. Prices vary widely according to the boat, the crowd, and the captain. A shared boat for a half-day of fishing starts at $100; a shared full day of fishing starts at around $140. A half-day exclusive (you get the entire boat) is around $300 to $535; a full-day exclusive boat can range from $450 to $900. Also, many boat captains tag and release marlin or keep the fish for themselves (sorry, that's Hawaii style). If you want to eat your mahimahi for dinner or have your marlin mounted, tell the captain before you go.

SURFING

The ancient Hawaiian sport of *hee nalu* (which translates as "wave sliding") is probably the sport most people picture when they think of Hawaii. Believe it or not, you too can be doing some wave sliding—just sign up at any one of the numerous surfing schools listed below.

Always wanted to learn to surf, but didn't know who to ask? Contact the **Nancy Emerson School of Surfing,** P.O. Box 463, Lahaina, HI 96767 (☎ **808/244-SURF;** fax 808/874-2581; www.maui.net/~ncesurf/ncesurf.html; e-mail ncesurf@maui.net). Nancy has been surfing since 1961—she was a stunt performer for various movies, including *Waterworld*. She's pioneered a new instructional technique called "Learn to Surf in One Lesson." It's $50 per person for 1 hour, $65 per person for 2 hours with a group; private classes run $110 per person for 2 hours.

Even if you've never seen a surfboard before, Andrea Thomas claims she can teach you the art of riding the waves. She's instructed thousands at **Maui Surfing School,** P.O. Box 424, Puunene, HI 96784 (☎ **808/875-0625;** www.mauisurf.com). She has taken students as young as 3 and as "chronologically gifted" as 70; she backs her classes with a guarantee that she'll get you surfing, or you'll get 110% of your money back. Two-hour lessons are $60, available by appointment only.

Steve and Ava McNanie, owners of the **West Maui Surfing Academy,** 658 Front St. (in front of the Wharf Cinema Center, across the street from the Banyan Tree), Lahaina (☎ **808/667-5399**), teach surfing the Hawaiian way; 2½-hour lessons run

$65, and surfboards rent for $10 for 2 hours. Surfboards are also available for rent from **Hunt Hawaii Surf and Sail** in Paia (☎ 808/575-2300), starting at $20 a day.

Surfers on a budget will find the least expensive rates on rental boards at **Rental Warehouse,** in Lahaina at 578 Front St., near Prison Street (☎ 808/661-1970), and in Kihei at Azeka Place II, on the mountain side of Kihei Road, near Lipoa Street (☎ 808/875-4050). "Goober's" boards rent for $10 a day and "shredder's" boards go for $19 a day. Cool, dude.

Expert surfers visit Maui in winter when the surf's really up. The best surfing beaches include Honolua Bay, Lahaina Harbor (in the summer, there'll be waves just off the channel entrance with a south swell), Maalaea (a clean, world-class left), and Hookipa (surfers get the waves until noon; after that—in a carefully worked-out compromise to share this prized surf spot—the windsurfers take over).

WHALE WATCHING

Every winter, pods of Pacific humpback whales make the 3,000-mile swim from the chilly waters of Alaska to bask in Maui's summery shallows, fluking, spy hopping, spouting, and having an all-around swell time.

The humpback whale is a cottage industry here. No creature on earth is celebrated in so many ways: you'll see whale posters, whale T-shirts, whale jewelry, and whale art, some of it quite awful. Don't waste your money on whale stuff; go for the real thing. The humpback is the star of the annual whale-watch season, which usually begins in December and lasts, sometimes, until May. If you're here in season and haven't seen a whale, you haven't seen Maui.

Humpbacks are one of the world's oldest, most impressive inhabitants. Adults grow to be about 45 feet long and weigh a hefty 40 tons; when they splash, it looks as though a 747 has hit the drink. Humpbacks are officially an endangered species; in 1997, some of the waters around the state were designated the Hawaiian Islands Humpback Whale National Marine Sanctuary, the country's only federal single-species sanctuary. About 1,500 to 3,000 humpback whales appear in Hawaii waters each year.

WHALE WATCHING FROM SHORE

The best time to whale-watch is between mid-December and April. Just look out to sea. There's no best time of day for whale watching, but the whales seem to appear when the sea is glassy and the wind calm. Once you see one, keep watching in the same vicinity; they might stay down for 20 minutes. Bring a book—and binoculars, if you can. You can rent them for $2 a day at **Rental Warehouse,** in Lahaina at 578 Front St., near Prison Street (☎ 808/661-1970), and in Kihei at Azeka Place II, on the mountain side of Kihei Road, near Lipoa Street (☎ 808/875-4050).

Some good whale-watching points on Maui are:

McGregor Point   On the way to Lahaina, there's a Scenic Lookout at mile marker 9 (just before you get to the Lahaina Tunnel); it's a good viewpoint to scan for whales.

Aston Wailea Resort   On the Wailea coastal walk, stop at this resort (formerly the Maui Inter-Continental) to look for whales through the telescope installed by the Hawaiian Island Humpback Whale National Marine Sanctuary as a public service.

Olowalu Reef   Along the straight part of Honoapiilani Highway, between McGregor Point and Olowalu, you'll see whales leap out of the water. Sometimes, their appearance brings traffic to a screeching halt: people abandon their cars and run down to the sea to watch, causing a major traffic jam. If you stop, pull off the road so that others can pass.

Puu Olai It's a tough climb up this coastal landmark near the Maui Prince Hotel, but you're likely to be well rewarded: this is the island's best spot for offshore whale watching. On the 360-foot cinder cone overlooking Makena Beach, you'll be at the right elevation to see Pacific Humpbacks as they dodge Molokini and cruise up Alalakeiki Channel between Maui and Kahoolawe. If you don't see one, you'll at least have a whale of a view.

WHALE-WATCHING CRUISES

For a closer look, take a whale-watching cruise. The **Pacific Whale Foundation,** 101 N. Kihei Rd., Kihei, HI 96753 (☎ **800/942-5311** or 808/879-8811; www.pacificwhale.org), is a nonprofit foundation in Kihei that supports its whale research by offering cruises and snorkel tours, some to Molokini and Lanai. The organization operates a 53-foot motor vessel called *Whale I,* a 50-foot sailing ketch called *Whale II,* a 65-foot power catamaran called *Ocean Spirit,* and a sea kayak. The rates for a 2-hour whale-watch cruise would make Moby Dick smile: $19 for adults, $17 for kids; there are 15 daily trips to choose from. Cruises are offered December through May, out of both Lahaina and Maalaea Harbors.

The **Ocean Activities Center** (☎ **800/798-0652** or 808/879-4485) runs three 2-hour whale-watching cruises on its spacious 65-foot catamaran, which leaves out of Maalaea Harbor; trips are $30 for adults and $18 for children 3 to 12. Bring a towel and your swimsuit; everything else—fins, mask, snorkel, and usually whales—is provided.

To see the whales in comfort in the patented SWATH (which means the boat doesn't rock and you won't get seasick), take a cruise on the *Navatek II* (☎ **800/852-4183** or 808/661-8787). The comfortable, air-conditioned boat (with spacious outside decks and hot and cold showers) offers a 6-hour morning whale-watch snorkel cruise with full breakfast (waffle and pancake bar) plus lunch (barbecue buffet); the cost is $125 for adults, $95 for children ages 12 to 17, $75 for children ages 5 to 11, and free for children under 5. Navatek II also offers a 2-hour afternoon whale watch, $39 for adults and $26.50 for children ages 2 to 11.

If you want to combine ocean activities, then a snorkel or dive cruise to Molokini, the sunken crater off Maui's south coast, might be just the ticket. You can see whales on the way there, at no extra charge. See "Scuba Diving" and "Taking a Snorkel Cruise," above.

WHALE WATCHING BY KAYAK & RAFT

Seeing a humpback whale from an ocean kayak or raft is awesome. The best budget deal for rafting is **Capt. Steve's Rafting Excursions,** P.O. Box 12492, Lahaina, HI 96761 (☎ **808/667-5565**), which offers 2-hour whale-watching excursions out of Lahaina Harbor. Take the early-bird trip at 7:30am and spot some whales for only $35 per person. Kayakers should call **South Pacific Kayaks,** 2439 S. Kihei Rd., Kihei (☎ **800/776-2326** or 808/875-4848; www.maui.net/~kayak; e-mail seakayak@maui.net), which leads small groups on 3-hour trips in the calm waters off Maui for $59 per person.

WINDSURFING

Maui has Hawaii's best windsurfing beaches. **Hookipa,** known all over the globe for its brisk winds and excellent waves, is the site of several world championship contests. **Kanaha** also has dependable winds; when conditions are right, it's packed with colorful butterfly-like sails. When the winds turn northerly, **Kihei** is the spot to be; some days you can spot whales in the distance behind the windsurfers. During the winter, windsurfers from around the world flock to the town of **Paia** to ride the waves.

Complete equipment rental (board, sail, rig harness, and roof rack) is available from $45 a day and $295 a week. Lessons, from beginner to advanced, range in price from $50 to $75 for 2 hours. **Hawaiian Island Surf and Sport,** 415 Dairy Rd., Kahului (☎ **800/231-6958** or 808/871-4981; fax 808/871-4624; www.hawaiianisland.com; e-mail hisurf@maui.net), offers lessons, rentals, and repairs. Other shops offering rentals and lessons are **Hawaiian Sailboarding Techniques,** 444 Hana Hwy., Kahului (☎ **808/871-5423**); and **Maui Windsurf Co.,** 520 Keolani Place, Kahului (☎ **800/872-0999** or 808/877-4816).

For daily reports on wind and surf conditions, call the **Wind and Surf Report** at ☎ **808/877-3611.**

3 Hiking & Camping

In the past 2 decades, Maui has grown from a rural island to a fast-paced resort destination, but its natural beauty remains largely inviolate; there are still many places that can be explored only on foot. Those interested in seeing the backcountry—complete with virgin waterfalls, remote wilderness trails, and quiet meditative settings—should head for Haleakala's upcountry or the tropical Hana coast.

Camping on Maui can be extreme (inside a volcano) or benign (by the sea in Hana). It can be wet, cold, and rainy, or hot, dry, and windy—often all on the same day. If you're heading for Haleakala, remember that U.S. astronauts trained for the moon inside the volcano; bring survival gear. Don't forget both your swimsuit and rain gear if you're bound for Waianapanapa, and bring your own equipment, because there's no place to rent gear on Maui yet. If you need to buy equipment, check out **Gaspro,** 365 Hanakai, Kahului (☎ 808/877-0056); **Maui Expedition,** Kihei Commercial Center, (☎ 808/875-7470); or **Maui Sporting Goods,** 92 N. Market, Wailuku (☎ 808/244-0011).

For more information on Maui camping and hiking trails and to obtain free maps, contact **Haleakala National Park,** P.O. Box 369, Makawao, HI 96768 (☎ 808/572-9306; www.nps.gov/hale), and the **State Division of Forestry and Wildlife,** 54 S. High St., Wailuku, HI 96793 (☎ 808/984-8100; www.hawaii. gov). For information on trails, hikes, camping, and permits for state parks, contact the **Hawaii State Department of Land and Natural Resources,** State Parks Division, 54 S. High St., Rm. 101, Wailuku, HI 96793 (☎ 808/984-8109; www.hawaii.gov). For information on Maui County Parks, contact **Maui County Parks and Recreation,** 1580-C Kaahumanu Ave., Wailuku, HI 96793 (☎ 808/ 243-7380; www.mauimapp.com).

TIPS ON SAFE HIKING & CAMPING   Water might be everywhere in Hawaii, but it more than likely isn't safe to drink. Most stream water must be treated because cattle, pigs, and goats have probably contaminated the water upstream. The Department of Health continually warns campers of bacterium leptospirosis, which is found in freshwater streams throughout the state and enters the body through breaks in the skin or through the mucous membranes. It produces flulike symptoms and can be fatal. Make sure that your drinking water is safe to drink by vigorously boiling it, or if boiling is not an option, use tablets with hydroperiodide; portable water filters will not screen out the bacterium leptospirosis.

Since firewood isn't always available, it's a good idea to carry a small, light backpacking stove, which you can use both to boil water and to cook meals for your hiking and camping adventures.

Remember, there is crime in paradise: never leave your valuables (wallet, airline ticket, and so on) unprotected. Carry a day pack if you have a campsite, and never camp alone.

Some more do's and don'ts: Do bury personal waste away from streams, don't eat unknown fruit, do carry your trash out, and don't forget there is very little twilight in Hawaii when the sun sets—it gets dark quickly.

HIKING WITH A GUIDE   If you would like a knowledgeable guide to accompany you on a hike, contact **Maui Hiking Safaris,** P.O. Box 11198, Lahaina, HI 96761 (☎ **888/445-3963** or 808/573-0168; fax 808/572-3037; www.maui.net/~mhs; e-mail mhs@maui.net). Owner Randy Warner takes visitors on half-day (4 to 5 hours) and full-day (8 to 10 hours) hikes into valleys, rain forests, and coastal areas. Randy has been hiking around Maui for more than 10 years and is wise in the ways of Hawaiian history, native flora and fauna, and volcanology. His rates are $49 for a half day, $89 for a full day (children 13 and under get 10% off on all hikes), and include day packs, rain parkas, snacks, water, and, on full-day hikes, sandwiches.

Maui's oldest hiking-guide company is **Hike Maui,** P.O. Box 330969, Kahului, HI 96733 (☎ **808/879-5270;** www.hikemaui.com; e-mail hikemaui@ hikemaui.com), headed by Ken Schmitt, who pioneered guided hikes on the Valley Isle. Hike Maui offers five different hikes a day, ranging from an easy 3½-mile stroll through the rain forest to a waterfall ($70 for adults, $50 for children 15 and under) to a strenuous, full-day hike in the rain forest and along a mountain ridge ($110 for adults, $85 for children 15 and under). Rates include equipment and transportation.

An all-day hike to the lush rain forests and waterfall pools of the West Maui Mountains is offered exclusively by **Kapalua Nature Society** (☎ **800/KAPALUA** or 808/669-0244). Groups of up to nine hikers can go on guided hiking tours, which include a picnic lunch and transportation to and from the trails. Two exclusive hikes are offered: the easy, 1¾-mile Maunalei Arboretum/Puu Kaeo Nature Walk, which starts at 1,200 feet above sea level and goes to the 1,635-foot summit of Puu Kaeo; and the breathtaking, 4-mile Manienie Ridge Hike, a more strenuous hike with moderate slope, some uneven footing, and close vegetation. Kapalua Nature Society is a not-for-profit organization dedicated to preserving the island's natural and cultural heritage. Proceeds go toward the education and preservation of Puu Kukui rain forest. Each hike goes from 8am to noon on Saturday. The cost is $59; children must be 12 or older to participate.

HALEAKALA NATIONAL PARK

For complete coverage of the national park, see "House of the Sun: Haleakala National Park," in chapter 9.

INTO THE WILDERNESS: SLIDING SANDS & HALEMAUU TRAILS

Hiking into Maui's dormant volcano is the best way to see it. The terrain inside the wilderness area of the volcano ranges from burnt-red cinder cones to ebony-black lava flows; it's simply spectacular. Inside the volcano's crater, there are some 27 miles of hiking trails, two camping sites, and three cabins.

Of the National Park's 34 miles of trails, the best route takes in two of them: into the crater along **Sliding Sands Trail,** which begins on the rim at 9,800 feet and descends into the belly of the beast, to the valley floor at 6,600 feet, and back out along **Halemauu Trail.** The hardiest hikers can consider making the 11.3-mile one-way descent, which takes 9 hours, and the equally long return ascent in 1 day. The rest of us will need to extend this steep but wonderful hike to 2 days. The descending and ascending trails aren't loops; the trailheads are miles (and several thousand feet in elevation) apart, so you'll need to make transportation arrangements in advance. Arrange to stay at least 1 night in the park; 2 or 3 nights will allow you more time to actually explore the fascinating interior of the volcano. See below for details on the cabins and campgrounds in the wilderness area in the valley.

Before you set out, stop at park headquarters to get camping and hiking updates. There is no registration for day hikers.

A word of warning about the weather: The weather at nearly 10,000 feet can change suddenly and without warning. Come prepared for cold, high winds, rain, and even snow in the winter. Temperatures can range from 77°F down to 26°F (they feel even lower with the wind-chill factor), and high winds are frequent. Rainfall varies from 40 inches a year on the west end of the crater to more than 200 inches on the eastern side. Bring boots, waterproof wear, warm clothes, extra layers, and lots of sunscreen—the sun shines very brightly up here.

The trailhead for Sliding Sands is well marked and the trail easy to follow over lava flows and cinders. As you descend, look around: the view is breathtaking. In the afternoon, waves of clouds flow into the Kaupo and Koolau gaps. Vegetation is sparse to nonexistent at the top, but the closer you get to the valley floor, the more vegetation you'll see: bracken ferns, pili grass, shrubs, even flowers. On the floor, the trail travels across rough lava flows of basalt and cinder-covered cones, passing by rare silversword plants, volcanic vents, and multicolored cinder cones.

The Halemauu Trail goes over red and black lava and past vegetation like evening primrose as it begins its ascent up the valley wall. Occasionally, riders on horseback use this trail as an entry and exit from the park. The proper etiquette is to step aside and stand quietly next to the trail as the horses pass.

SOME SHORTER & EASIER OPTIONS Hiking into it is the best way to experience this curious crater. Take a half-mile walk down the **Hosmer Grove Nature Trail**, or start down **Sliding Sands Trail** for a mile or two to get a hint of what lies ahead. Even this short hike can be exhausting at the high altitude. A good day hike is **Halemauu Trail** to Holua Cabin and back, an 8-mile, half-day trip.

GUIDED HIKES A 20-minute orientation presentation is given daily in the Summit Building at 9:30, 10:30, and 11:30am. The park rangers offer two guided hikes. The 2-hour, 2-mile Cinder Desert Hike takes place Tuesday and Friday at 10am and starts from the Sliding Sands Trailhead at the end of the Haleakala Visitor Center Parking Lot. The guided 3-hour, 3-mile Waikamoi Cloud Forest Hike leaves every Monday and Thursday at 9am; it starts at the Hosmer Grove, just inside the Park entrance, and traverses through the Nature Conservancy's Waikamoi Preserve.

STAYING IN THE WILDERNESS AREA

Most people stay at one of two tent campgrounds, unless they get lucky and win the lottery—the lottery, that is, for one of the three wilderness cabins. For more information, contact **Haleakala National Park,** P.O. Box 369, Makawao, HI 96768 (☎ **808/572-9306;** www.nps.gov/hale).

THE CABINS It can get really cold and windy down in the valley (see above), so try for a cabin. They're warm, protected from the elements, and reasonably priced. Each has 12 padded bunks (but no bedding; bring your own), table, chairs, cooking utensils, a two-burner propane stove, and a wood-burning stove with firewood (you might also have a few cockroaches). The cabins are spaced so that each one is an easy walk from the other: Holua cabin is on the Halemauu Trail, Kapalaoa cabin on Sliding Sands Trail, and Paliku cabin on the eastern end by the Kaupo Gap. The rates are $40 a night for groups of one to six and $80 a night for groups of 7 to 12.

The cabins are so popular that the National Park Service has a lottery system for reservations. Requests for cabins must be made 3 months in advance (be sure to request alternate dates). You can request all three cabins at once; you're limited to no more than 2 nights in one cabin and no more than 3 nights within the wilderness per month.

THE CAMPGROUNDS   If you don't win the cabin lottery, all isn't lost, because there are three tent camping sites that can accommodate you: two in the wilderness, and one just outside at Hosmer Grove. There is no charge for tent camping.

Hosmer Grove, located at 6,800 feet, is a small, open grassy area surrounded by a forest. Trees protect campers from the winds, but nights still get quite cold. Hard to believe, but sometimes there's ice on the ground up here. This is the best place to spend the night in a tent if you want to see the Haleakala sunrise. Come up the day before, enjoy the park, take a day hike, and then turn in early. The enclosed, glass summit building opens at sunrise for those who come to greet the dawn—a welcome windbreak. Facilities include a covered pavilion with picnic tables and grills, chemical toilets, and drinking water. Food is 17 miles away and gas is 27 miles away. No permits are needed at Hosmer Grove, and there's no charge; but you can stay for only 3 nights in a 30-day period.

The two tent camping areas inside the volcano are **Holua,** just off Halemauu at 6,920 feet; and **Paliku,** just before the Kaupo Gap at the eastern end of the valley, at 6,380 feet. Facilities at both campgrounds are limited to pit toilets and nonpotable catchment water. Water at Holua is limited, especially in summer. No open fires are allowed inside the volcano, so bring a stove if you plan to cook. Tent camping is restricted to the signed area. No camping is allowed in the horse pasture. The inviting grassy lawn in front of the cabin is kapu. Camping is free, but limited to 2 consecutive nights, and no more than 3 nights a month inside the volcano. Permits are issued daily at Park Headquarters on a first-come, first-served basis. Occupancy is limited to 25 people in each campground.

HIKING & CAMPING AT KIPAHULU

You can set up at **Oheo Campground,** a first-come, first-served drive-in campground with tent sites for 100 near the ocean, with a few tables, barbecue grills, and chemical toilets. No permit is required, but there's a 3-night limit. No food or drinking water is available, so bring your own. Bring a tent, because it rains 75 inches a year here. Contact **Kipahulu Ranger Station,** Haleakala National Park, HI 96713 (☎ **808/248-7375;** www.nps.gov/hale).

HIKING FROM THE SUMMIT   If you hike from the crater rim down **Kaupo Gap** to the ocean, more than 20 miles away, you'll pass through climate zones ranging from arctic to tropical. On a clear day, you can see every island except Kauai on the trip down.

HIKING KIPAHULU   If you drive to Kipahulu, you'll have to approach it from the Hana Highway, because it's not accessible from the summit. Always check in at the ranger station before you begin your hike; not only can they inform you of current conditions (trail conditions, flash-flood warnings, and more), but they also can share their wonderful stories about the history, culture, flora, and fauna of the area.

There are two hikes you can take here. The first is a short, easy half-mile loop along the Kaloa Point Trail (Kaloa Point is a windy bluff overlooking Oheo Gulch), which leads toward the ocean along pools and waterfalls and back to the ranger station. The clearly marked path leaves the parking area and rambles along the flat, grassy peninsula. Crashing surf and views of the Island of Hawaii are a 5-minute walk from the Ranger Station. Along the way you'll see the remnants of an ancient fishing shrine, a house site, and a lauhala-thatched building depicting an earlier time. The loop stops at the bridge you drove over when you entered the park; this is the best place for a photo opportunity. The pools are above and below the bridge; the best for swimming are usually above the bridge.

The second hike is for the more hardy. Although just a 4-mile round-trip, the trail is steep and you'll want to stop and swim in the pools, so allow 3 hours. You'll be climbing over rocks and up steep trails, so wear hiking boots. Take water, snacks, swim gear, and insect repellent (to ward off the swarms of mosquitoes). Always be on the lookout for flash-flood conditions. This walk will pass two magnificent waterfalls, the 181-foot Makahiku Falls and the even bigger 400-foot Waimoku Falls. The trail starts at the ranger station, where you'll walk uphill for a half mile to a fence overlook at the thundering Makahiku Falls. The tired can turn around here, but the true adventurers will press on.

Behind the lookout, the well-worn trail picks up again and goes directly to a pool on the top of the Makahiku Falls. The pool is safe to swim in as long as the waters aren't rising; if they are, get out and head back to the ranger's station. Back on the trail, you'll cross a meadow and then a creek, where you'll scramble up the rocky bank and head into a bamboo forest jungle. At the edge of the jungle is another creek, but the trail doesn't cross this one. A few minutes more, and the vertical Waimoku Falls will be in sight.

GUIDED HIKES   The rangers at Kipahulu conduct a 1-mile hike to the Bamboo Forest at 9am daily; half-mile hikes or orientation talks are given at 12, 1:30, 2:30, and 3:30pm daily; and a 4-mile round-trip hike to Waimoku Falls takes place Saturdays at 9:30am. All programs and hikes begin at the Ranger Station.

SKYLINE TRAIL, POLIPOLI SPRINGS STATE RECREATION AREA

This is some hike—strenuous but worth every step if you like to see the big picture. It's 8 miles, all downhill, with a dazzling 100-mile view of the islands dotting the blue Pacific, plus the West Maui Mountains, which seem like a separate island.

The trail is located just outside Haleakala National Park at Polipoli Springs National Recreation Area; however, you access the trail by going through the national park to the summit. The Skyline Trail starts just beyond the Puu Ulaula summit building on the south side of Science City and follows the southwest rift zone of Haleakala from its lunar-like cinder cones to a cool redwood grove. The trail drops 3,800 feet on a 4-hour hike to the recreation area, in the 12,000-acre Kahikinui Forest Reserve. If you aren't on foot, you need a four-wheel-drive vehicle to access the trail.

There is a **campground** at the recreation area, at 6,300 feet. No fee or reservations are required, but your stay must be limited to 5 nights. Tent camping is free, but you'll need a permit. One 10-bunk cabin is available for $45 a night for one to four guests ($5 for each additional guest); it has a cold shower, a gas stove, and no electricity. There is no drinking water available, so bring in your own. To reserve, contact the **State Parks Division,** 54 High St., Rm. 101, Wailuku, HI 96793 (☎ **808/984-8109** between 8am and 4pm weekdays; www.hawaii.gov).

POLIPOLI STATE PARK

One of the most unusual hiking experiences in the state can be found at Polipoli State Park, part of the 21,000-acre Kula and Kahikinui Forest Reserve on the slope of Haleakala. At Polipoli, it's hard to believe that you're in Hawaii. First of all, it's cold, even in the summer, since the loop is up at 5,300 to 6,200 feet. Second, this former forest of native koa, ohia, and mamane trees, which was overlogged in the 1800s, was reforested in the 1930s with introduced species: pine, Monterey cypress, ash, sugi, red adler, redwood, and several varieties of eucalyptus. The result is a cool area, with muted sunlight filtered by towering trees.

The **Polipoli Loop** is an easy, 5-mile hike that takes about 3 hours; dress warmly for it. To get there, take the Haleakala Highway (Highway 37) to Keokea and turn right onto Highway 337; after less than a half-mile, turn on Waipoli Road, which climbs swiftly. After 10 miles, Waipoli Road ends at the Polipoli State Park campgrounds. The well-marked trailhead is next to the parking lot, near a stand of Monterey cypress; the tree-lined trail offers the best view of the island.

Polipoli Loop is really a network of three trails: Haleakala Ridge, Plum Trail, and Redwood Trail. After a half-mile of meandering through groves of eucalyptus, blackwood, swamp mahogany, and hybrid cypress, you'll join the Haleakala Ridge Trail, which, about a mile into the trail, joins with the Plum Trail (named for the plums that ripen in June and July). It passes through massive redwoods and by an old Conservation Corps bunkhouse and a rundown cabin before joining up with the Redwood Trail, which climbs through Mexican pine, tropical ash, Port Orford cedar, and—of course—redwood.

Camping is allowed in the park with a permit from the **Division of State Parks,** 54 S. High St., Rm. 101, Wailuku, HI 96793 (☎ **808/984-8109**). There's one cabin, available by reservation.

KANAHA BEACH PARK CAMPING

The only Maui County camping facility on the island is Kanaha Beach Park, located next to the Kahului Airport. The county has two separate areas for camping: seven tent sites on the beach and an additional 10 tent sites inland. This well-used park is a favorite of windsurfers, who take advantage of the strong winds that roar across this end of the island. Facilities here include a paved parking lot, portable toilets, outdoor showers, barbecue grills, and picnic tables. Camping is limited to no more than 3 consecutive days; the permit fee is $3 per person, per night, and can be obtained from the **Maui County Parks and Recreation Department,** 1580-C Kaahumanu Ave., Wailuku, HI 96793 (☎ **808/243-7380;** www.mauimapp.com). Since this is Maui's only county camping facility, the 17 sites book up quickly; reserve your dates far in advance (the County will accept reservations a year in advance).

WAIANAPANAPA STATE PARK
HANA-WAIANAPANAPA COAST TRAIL

This is an easy, 6-mile hike that takes you back in time. Allow 4 hours to walk along this relatively flat trail, which parallels the sea, along lava cliffs and a forest of lauhala trees. The best time to take the hike is in either the early morning or the late evening, when the light on the lava and surf makes for great photos. Midday is the worst time; not only is it hot (lava intensifies the heat), but there's no shade or potable water available.

There's no formal trailhead; join the route at any point along the Waianapanapa Campground and go in either direction. Along the trail, you'll see remains of an ancient heiau; stands of lauhala trees; caves; a blowhole; and a remarkable plant, *naupaka,* that flourishes along the beach. Upon close inspection, you'll see that the naupaka has only half-blossoms; according to Hawaiian legend, a similar plant living in the mountains has the other half of the blossoms. One ancient explanation is that the two plants represent never-to-be-reunited lovers: as the story goes, the two lovers bickered so much that the gods, fed up with their incessant quarreling, banished one lover to the mountain and the other to the sea.

CAMPING AT WAIANAPANAPA

Tucked in a tropical jungle, on the outskirts of the little coastal town of Hana, is Waianapanapa State Park, a black-sand beach set in an emerald forest. Waianapanapa has 12 cabins and a tent campground. Go for the cabins, because it rains torrentially here, sometimes turning the campground into a mud-wrestling arena. If you opt to tent-camp, it's free, but limited to 5 nights in a 30-day period. Permits are available from the **State Parks Division,** 54 S. High St., Rm. 101, Wailuku, HI 96793 (☎ **808/984-8109**). Facilities include rest rooms, outdoor showers, drinking water, and picnic tables.

HANA: THE HIKE TO FAGAN'S CROSS

This 3-mile hike to the cross erected in the memory of Hana Ranch and Hotel Hana-Maui founder Paul Fagan offers spectacular views of the Hana coast, particularly at sunset. The uphill trail starts across Hana Highway from the Hotel Hana-Maui. Enter the pastures at your own risk; they're often occupied by glaring bulls with sharp horns and cows with new calves, so beware the bulls, avoid the nursing cows, and don't wear red. Watch your step as you ascend this steep hill on a jeep trail across open pastures; you'll be rewarded at the cross with the breathtaking view.

KEANAE ARBORETUM

About 47 miles from Kahului, along the Hana Highway and just after the Keanae YMCA Camp (and just before the turnoff to the Keanae Peninsula), is an easy family walk through the Keanae Arboretum, which is maintained by the State Department of Land and Natural Resources, Division of Forestry and Wildlife. The walk, which is just over 2 miles, passes through a forest with both native and introduced plants. Allow 1 to 2 hours; swimming is available, so you might want to stay longer. Take rain gear and mosquito repellent.

Park at the Keanae Arboretum and pass through the turnstile. Walk along the fairly flat jeep road to the entrance. For a half mile, you will pass by plants introduced to Hawaii (ornamental timber, pummelo, banana, papaya, hibiscus, and more), all with identifying tags. At the end of this section is a taro patch showing the different varieties the Hawaiians used as their staple crop. After the taro, a 1-mile trail leads through a Hawaiian rain forest. The trail crisscrosses a stream as it meanders through the rain forest. Our favorite swimming hole is just to the left of the first stream crossing, at about 100 yards.

WAIHEE RIDGE

This 3- to 4-mile strenuous hike, with a 1,500-foot climb, offers spectacular views of the valleys of the West Maui Mountains. Allow 3 to 4 hours for the round-trip hike. Pack a lunch, carry water, and pick a dry day, because this area is very wet. There's a picnic table at the summit with great views.

   To get there from Wailuku, turn north on Market Street, which becomes the Kahekilii Highway (Highway 340) and passes through Waihee. Go just over 2½ miles from the Waihee Elementary School and look for the turnoff to the Boy Scouts' Camp Maluhia on the left. Turn into the camp and drive nearly a mile to the trailhead on the left side of the road. Park at the trailhead.

   Pass through the turnstile and walk on the jeep road. About a third of a mile in, there will be another gate, marking the entrance to the West Maui Forest Reserve. A foot trail, kept in good shape by the State Department of Land and Natural Resources, begins here. The trail climbs to the top of the ridge, offering great views of the various valleys. The trail is marked by a number of switchbacks and can be extremely muddy and wet. In some areas, it's so steep that you have to grab on to the trees and bushes for support. There's temporary relief to this climb after about 1½ miles, when the trail crosses a flat area (which can be so wet that it's impassable). After the swampy area, the trail ascends again for about a mile to Lanilili Peak, where a picnic table and magnificent views await.

4 Great Golf

In some circles, Maui is synonymous with golf. The island's world-famous golf courses start at the very northern tip of the island and roll right around to Kaanapali, jumping down to Kihei and Wailea in the south. There are also some lesser-known municipal courses that offer challenging play for less than $100. Golfers new to Hawaii should know that it's windy here, especially between 10am and 2pm, when winds of 10 to 15mph are the norm. Play two to three clubs up or down to compensate for the wind factor. Also, we recommend that you bring extra balls—the rough is thicker here and the wind will pick your ball up and drop it in very unappealing places (like water hazards). If your heart is set on playing on a resort course, book at least a week in advance. For the ardent golfer on a tight budget: play in the afternoon, when discounted twilight rates are in effect. There's no guarantee you'll get 18 holes in, especially during the winter when it's dark by 6pm, but you'll have an opportunity to experience these world-famous courses at half the usual fee.

   If you don't bring your own, rent clubs from **Rental Warehouse,** in Lahaina at 578 Front St., near Prison Street (☎ **808/661-1970**), or in Kihei at Azeka Place II, on the mountain side of Kihei Road, near Lipoa Street (☎ **808/875-4050**), where "not-so-top quality" clubs go for $10 a day and "top quality" clubs run $15 a day. **Golf Club Rentals** (☎ **808/665-0800**) offers custom-built clubs for men, women, and juniors in both right- and left-handed versions. Their rates are just $15 a day and they offer delivery island-wide.

   For last-minute and discount tee times, contact **Stand-by Golf** (☎ **888/ 645-BOOK** in Hawaii, 808/322-BOOK from the mainland), which offers discounted and guaranteed tee times for same-day or next-day golfing. Call between 7am and 9pm, Hawaii Standard Time, to get a guaranteed tee time at a 10% to 40% discount.

✪ KAPALUA RESORT COURSES

The views from these championship courses at Kapalua Resort are worth the greens fees alone. Choose from three courses: the Bay, the Village, or the Plantation. The first to open was the **Bay Course** (☎ **808/669-8820**), a par-72, 6,761-yard course inaugurated in 1975. Designed by Arnold Palmer and Ed Seay, this course is a bit forgiving with its wide fairways; the greens, however, are difficult to read.

The well-photographed 5th overlooks a small ocean cove; even the pros have trouble with this rocky par-3, 205-yard hole.

The **Village Course** (☎ 808/669-8830), another Palmer/Seay design, is a par-71, 6,632-yard course. It's the most scenic of the three courses; the hole with the best vista is definitely the 6th, which overlooks a lake with the ocean in the distance. But don't get distracted by the view—the tee is between two rows of Cook pines.

The **Plantation Course** (☎ 808/669-8877), scene of the Lincoln/Mercury Kapalua International and the Kirin Cup World Championship of Golf, was designed by Ben Crenshaw and Bill Coore. A 6,547-yard, par-73 course on a rolling hillside of the West Maui Mountains, this one is excellent for developing your low shots and precise chipping.

Facilities for the three courses include locker rooms, a driving range, and an excellent restaurant. Regular greens fees at the Village Course and the Bay Course are $140, and fees at the Plantation are $150. Play twilight rates after 2pm for $65 at the Village and Bay courses, $70 at the Plantation Course; you'll get a world-class golfing experience at half the price. Fifty-four holes gives you a better chance at getting a tee time; weekdays are best.

✪ KAANAPALI COURSES

Both courses at the **Kaanapali Resort** (☎ 808/661-3691) offer a challenge to all golfers, from high handicappers to near-pros. The North Course (originally called the Royal Lahaina Golf Course) is a true Robert Trent Jones design: an abundance of wide bunkers; several long, stretched-out tees; and the largest, most contoured greens on Maui. The par-72, 6,305-yard course has a tricky 18th hole (par 4,435 yd.) with a water hazard on the approach to the green.

The South Course, a par-72, 6,250-yard course, is an Arthur Jack Snyder design; although shorter than the North Course, it does require more accuracy on the narrow, hilly fairways. Just like its sister course, it has a water hazard on its final hole, so don't tally up your score card until the final putt is sunk.

Facilities include driving range, putting course, and clubhouse with dining. Regular greens fees are $120 ($100 for guests staying in Kaanapali); weekday tee times are best. For frugal golfers, the twilight rates (after 2pm) are $62 for non-Kaanapali guests ($60 for Kaanapali guests) for 18.

SILVERSWORD GOLF CLUB

This is a course for golfers who love the views as much as the fairways and greens. Located on the foothills of Haleakala, **Silversword,** at 1345 Piilani Hwy. (near the Lipoa Street turnoff) in Kihei (☎ 808/874-0777), sits just high enough to afford spectacular ocean views from every hole. This course is very forgiving, especially for duffers and high handicappers. Just one caveat: go in the morning. Not only is it less sunny and hot, but, more important, it's also less windy. In the afternoon, the winds really pick up, blustering down Haleakala with great gusto. Silversword is a fun course to play, with some challenging holes (the par-5 no. 2 is a virtual minefield of bunkers, and the par-5 no.8 shoots over a swale and then up a hill). Greens fees vary with the season: from April 1 to October 31, they're $59, with twilight rates of $42 for 18. The rest of the year, greens fees are $70, with twilight rates of $44. You can play nine holes after 3:30pm, year-round, for $23.

✪ WAILEA COURSES

There are three courses to choose from at Wailea. The Blue Course, a par-72, 6,700-yard flat, open course designed by Arthur Jack Snyder and dotted with bunkers and water hazards, is a golf course for duffers and pros alike. The wide fairways appeal to beginners, and the undulating terrain makes it a course everyone can enjoy. A little more difficult is the par-72, 7,073-yard championship Gold Course, with narrow fairways, several tricky dogleg holes, and the classic Robert Trent Jones, Jr., challenges: natural hazards, like lava-rock walls, and native Hawaiian grasses. The Orange Course, originally an Arthur Jack Snyder design, was renovated by Robert Trent Jones, Jr., into a more challenging course.

With 54 holes to play, getting a tee time is slightly easier here on weekends than at other resorts, but weekdays are best (the Gold Course is usually the toughest to book). Facilities include a pro shop, a restaurant, locker rooms, and a complete golf training facility. Greens fees are $130. Call ☎ **808/879-2966** or 808/875-5111.

✪ MAKENA COURSES

Here you'll find 36 holes of "Mr. Hawaii Golf"—Robert Trent Jones, Jr.—at its best. Add to that spectacular views: Molokini islet looms in the background, humpback whales gambol offshore in the winter, and the tropical sunsets are spectacular. This is golf not to be missed; the par-72, 6,876-yard **South Course** has a couple of holes you'll never forget. The view from the par-4 15th hole, which shoots from an elevated tee 183 yards downhill to the Pacific, is magnificent. The 16th hole has a two-tiered green that's blind from the tee 383 yards away (that is, if you make it past the gully off the fairway). The par-72, 6,823-yard **North Course** is more difficult and more spectacular. The 13th hole, located partway up the mountain, has a view that makes most golfers stop and stare. The next hole is even more memorable: a 200-foot drop between tee and green. Facilities include clubhouse, driving range, two putting greens, pro shop, lockers, and lessons. Beware of crowded conditions on weekends. Greens fees are $100 for Makena Resort guests and $120 for nonguests. Call ☎ **808/879-3344.**

PUKALANI COUNTRY CLUB

This cool course at 1,100 feet offers a break from the resort's high greens fees, and it's really fun to play. The par-72, 6,962-yard course has 19 greens. There's an extra green because the third hole offers golfers two different options: a tough iron shot from the tee (especially into the wind), across a gully (yuck!) to the green, or a shot down the side of the gully across a second green into sand traps below. (Most people choose to shoot down the side of the gully; it's actually easier than shooting across a ravine.) High handicappers will love this course; more experienced players can make it more challenging by playing from the back tees. Greens fees, which include the cart fee, are only $35 for 18; the early twilight rate (after 12pm) is $30, and the later one (after 2:30pm) is just $15. Facilities include club and shoe rentals, practice areas, lockers, a pro shop, and a restaurant. For tee times and other information, contact the **Pukalani Country Club,** 360 Pukalani St., Pukalani, HI 96768 (☎ **808/572-1314**). To reach this upcountry course, take Haleakala Highway (Hi. 37) off the Hana Highway (Highway 36) up to the Pukalani exit; turn right on Pukalani Street, and go 2 blocks to the country club.

WAIEHU MUNICIPAL GOLF COURSE

This public oceanside golf course is like playing two different courses: the first nine holes, built in 1930, are set along the dramatic coastline, whereas the back nine holes, added in 1966, head toward the mountains. This par-72 course is a fun playing course that probably won't challenge your handicap. The only hazard here is the wind, which can rip off the ocean and play havoc with your ball.

Basically, this is a flat and straight course. The only hole that can raise your blood pressure is the 511-yard, par 5, 4th hole, which is very narrow and very long. To par here, you have to hit a long accurate drive, then another long and accurate fairway drive, and finally a perfect pitch over the hazards to the greens (yeah, right). Since this is a public course, the greens fees are low—$25 on weekdays and $30 on weekends—but getting a tee time is tough. Facilities include snack bar, driving range, practice greens, golf club rental, and clubhouse. For tee times and information, contact **Waiehu Municipal Golf Course,** P.O. Box 507, Wailuku, HI 96793 (☎ **808/244-5934**). To get there from the Kahului Airport, turn right on the Hana Highway (Highway 36), which becomes Kaahumanu Avenue (Highway 32). Turn right at the stoplight at the junction of Waiehu Beach Road (Highway 340). Go another 1½ miles down the road, and you'll see the entrance on your right.

5 Bicycling, Horseback Riding & Other Outdoor Activities

BICYCLING

It's not even close to dawn, but here you are, rubbing your eyes awake, riding in a van up the long, dark road to the top of Maui's sleeping volcano. It's colder than you ever thought possible for a tropical island. The air is thin. You stomp your chilly feet while you wait, sipping hot coffee. Then comes the sun, exploding over the yawning Haleakala Crater, which is big enough to swallow Manhattan whole—a mystic moment you won't soon forget, imprinted on a palette of dawn colors. Now you know why Hawaiians named it the House of the Sun. But there's no time to linger: decked out in your screaming yellow parka, you mount your special steed and test its most important feature, the brakes—because you're about to coast 37 miles down a 10,000-foot volcano.

Cruising down Haleakala, from the lunar-like landscape at the top, past flower farms, pineapple fields, and eucalyptus groves, is quite an experience—and just about anybody can do it. This is a safe, comfortable, no-strain bicycle trip for everyone, from the kids to the grandparents. The trip usually costs between $100 and $120, which includes hotel pickup, transport to the top, bicycle and safety equipment, and meals. Wear layers of warm clothing, because there might be a 30-degree change in temperature from the top of the mountain to the ocean. You don't have to be an expert cyclist; you just have to be able to ride a bike. Generally, the tour groups will not take riders under 12, but the younger children can ride along in the van that accompanies the groups. Pregnant women should also ride in the van.

Maui's oldest downhill company is **Maui Downhill,** 199 Dairy Rd., Kahului, HI 96732 (☎ **800/535-BIKE** or 808/871-2155; e-mail mauidown@gte.net), which has a sunrise-safari bike tour, including continental breakfast and brunch, starting at $100. Haleakala rides for $120 are offered by both **Maui Mountain Chasers** in Makawao (☎ **808/871-6014** or 800/232-6284) and **Mountain Riders Bike Tours** in Kahului (☎ **808/242-9739**).

For bike excursions on other parts of Maui, contact **Chris' Adventures,** P.O. Box 869, Kula, HI 96790 (☎ **800/224-5344** or 808/871-2453). Chris offers various bike tours, with costs ranging from $49 to $110. We recommend the Waihee-Kahakuloa Coastal Adventure ($59): you'll hike the Waihee Valley or Ridge and then bike along the spectacular northwestern coast, which feels like Old Hawaii.

If you want to venture out on your own and cruise around the Valley Isle on a bike, cheap rentals—$10 a day for cruisers and $20 a day for mountain bikes—are available from **Rental Warehouse,** in Lahaina at 578 Front St., near Prison Street (☎ **808/661-1970**), and in Kihei at Azeka Place II, on the mountain side of Kihei Road, near Lipoa Street (☎ **808/875-4050**).

For maps and information on bikeways, contact Walter Enomoto, chair of the **Mayor's Advisory Committee on Bicycling** (☎ **808/871-6886**). The local bike club is **Maui Mountain Bike Club,** P.O. Box 689, Makawao, HI 96768. A great book for mountain bikers who want to venture out on their own is ***Mountain Biking the Hawaiian Islands*** by John Alford, published by Ohana Publishing, P.O. Box 240170, Honolulu, HI 96824-0170 (www.bikehawaii.com; e-mail mtnbike@aloha.net).

HORSEBACK RIDING

Maui offers spectacular adventure rides through rugged ranch lands, into tropical forests, and to remote swimming holes. For a 5½-hour tour on horseback—complete with swimming and lunch—call **Adventure on Horseback,** P.O. Box 1419, Makawao, HI 96768 (☎ **808/242-7445** or 808/572-6211); the cost is $175 per person. According to owner Frank Levinson, the philosophy behind the 5½-hour tours is "to provide a trip that's really special for the people who go on it—something that will move them. I can't do that in an hour. I need the whole day." The day begins over coffee and pastries, when Frank matches the horses to the riders, in terms of not only skill, but also personality. Frank leads small groups across pastures, through thick rain forests, along side streams, and up to waterfalls and pools. After a hearty lunch, the group retraces the route back.

Out in Hana, **Oheo Stables,** Kipahulu Ranch, Start Route 1, Box 151 A., on Highway 31 (1 mile past Oheo Gulch), Kipahulu (☎ **808/667-2222;** e-mail ray@maui.net), offers two daily rides through the mountains above Oheo Gulch (Seven Pools). The best deal is the 10:30am ride ($119), which includes brunch and snacks during the 4-hour adventure (2½ hours in the saddle). The ride ventures into the Haleakala National Park, stopping at scenic spots like the Pipuwai lookout, where you can glimpse the 400-foot Waimoku Falls. If you enjoy your ride, kiss your horse and tip your guide.

HALEAKALA ON HORSEBACK

If you'd like to ride down into Haleakala's crater, contact **Pony Express Tours,** P.O. Box 535, Kula, HI 96790 (☎ **808/667-2200** or 808/878-6698; fax 808/878-3581); they offer half-day rides down to the crater floor and back up, lunch included, for $130 per person. A full-day ride, at $160 per person, explores the crater floor extensively. The Deluxe Picnic Ride, a 3-hour ride with lunch, costs $85. Gentler 1- and 2-hour rides are also offered at Haleakala Ranch, located on the beautiful lower slopes of the volcano, for $40 and $65. Pony Express provides well-trained horses and experienced guides, and accommodates all riding levels. In order to ride, you must be at least 10 years old, weigh no more than 230 pounds, and wear long pants and closed-toe shoes.

WAY OUT WEST ON MAUI: RANCH RIDES

We recommend riding with **Mendes Ranch & Trail Rides,** on Kahekili Highway, 4 miles past Wailuku (☎ **808/871-5222**). The morning (8:15am) ride, which lasts 3 hours and includes lunch, costs $130; the afternoon (12:15pm) ride, a 2½-hour ride with snacks, costs $85. Rides are offered Monday through Saturday.

The 300-acre Mendes Ranch is a real-life working cowboy ranch that has all the essential elements of an earthly paradise—rainbows, waterfalls, palm trees, coral-sand beaches, lagoons, tide pools, a rain forest, and its volcanic peak. Allan Mendes, a third-generation wrangler, raises 300 head of beef cattle, Brahmas, Texas Longhorns, and painted ponies.

Allan will take you from the edge of the rain forest and out to the sea. On the way, you'll cross tree-studded meadows where Texas longhorns sit in the shade like surreal lawn statues, and past a dusty corral where Allan's father, Ernest, a champion roper, is at work on the day's task—breaking in a wild horse. All the while, Allan keeps close watch, turning often in his saddle on his pinto, Pride, to make sure that everyone is happy. He points out flora and fauna, and fields questions, but generally just lets you soak up Maui's natural splendor in golden silence. The morning ride ends with a high-noon barbecue back at the corral, complete with ribs, baked beans, and potato salad—the perfect ranch-style lunch after a full morning in the saddle.

SPELUNKING

Most people come to Maui to get outdoors and soak up some Hawaiian sunshine, not to go underground and traipse through cold, dark caves. But if you're into cave exploration or you're looking for an offbeat adventure, you might want to contact Chuck Thorne of **Island Spelunkers,** P.O. Box 40, Hana, HI 96713 (☎ **808/ 248-7308;** www.maui.net/~hanacave; e-mail hanacave@maui.net). After leading scuba tours through underwater caves for more than 10 years around Hawaii, Chuck discovered some caves on land that he wanted to show visitors. When the land surrounding the largest cave on Maui went on the market in 1996, Chuck snapped it up and started his own tour company. He'll take you hiking into subterranean passages of a huge, extinct lava tube that has 40-foot ceilings. This geology lesson you won't soon forget—Chuck is a long-time student of the science of volcano-speleology and can discuss every little formation in the cave, how it came to be, and what its purpose is. All the equipment you'll need (lights, hard hats, gloves, water bottles) is supplied on the 2-hour tours, which cost $50 for adults and $25 for children ages 7 to 17 (when accompanied by an adult). Wear long pants and closed shoes, and bring your imagination.

TENNIS

Maui County has excellent tennis courts located all over the island. All are free and available from daylight to sunset; a few even have night lights, allowing play to continue until 10pm. The courts are available on a first-come, first-served basis. When someone's waiting for a court, please limit your play to no more than 45 minutes. For a complete list of all public tennis courts, contact **Maui County of Parks and Recreation,** 1580-C Kaahumanu Ave., Wailuku, HI 96793 (☎ **808/243-7389**).

Private tennis courts are available at most resorts and hotels on the island. The **Kapalua Tennis Garden and Village Tennis Center,** Kapalua Resort (☎ **808/669-5677**), is home to the Kapalua Open, featuring the largest purse in the state, on Labor Day weekend, and the Kapalua Betsy Nagelsen Tennis Invitational Pro-Am in November. Court rentals are $10 an hour for resort guests and $15 an hour for nonguests. In Wailea, the **Wailea Tennis Club,** 131 Wailea Iki Place, Wailea (☎ **808/879-1958**), has Plexi-pave courts. Per-day court rentals are $25 for Wailea resort guests and $30 an hour for players not staying in Wailea.

Seeing the Sights

by Jeanette Foster

After a few days of just relaxing on the beach, the itch to explore the rest of Maui sets in: What's on top of Haleakala, looming in the distance? Is the road to Hana really the tropical jungle everyone raves about? What does the inside of a 19th-century whaling boat look like?

There is far more to the Valley Isle than just sun, sand, and surf. Get out and see for yourself the other-worldly interior of a 10,000-foot volcanic crater; watch endangered sea turtles make their way to nesting sites in a wildlife sanctuary; wander back in time to the days when whalers and missionaries fought for the soul of Lahaina; and feel the energy of a thundering waterfall cascade into a serene mountain pool.

1 By Air, Land & Sea: Guided Island Adventures

Admittedly, the adventures below aren't cheap. However, each one offers such a wonderful opportunity to see Maui from a unique perspective that, depending on your interests, you might make one of them the highlight of your trip—it'll be worth every penny.

FLYING HIGH: HELICOPTER RIDES

Pablo Picasso once said that the three greatest inventions of the 20th century were the blues, cubism, and Polish vodka. Had he ever visited Hawaii, he might have added the helicopter.

Only a helicopter can bring you face-to-face with remote sites like Maui's little-known Wall of Tears, up near the summit of Puu Kukui in the West Maui Mountains. A helicopter ride on Maui isn't a wild ride; it's more like a gentle gee-whiz zip into a seldom-seen Eden. You'll glide through canyons etched with 1,000-foot waterfalls, and over dense rain forests; you'll climb to 10,000 feet, high enough to glimpse the summit of Haleakala, and fly by the dramatic vistas at Molokai.

The first chopper pilots in Hawaii were good ol' boys on their way back from Vietnam—hard-flying, hard-drinking cowboys who cared more about the ride than the scenery. But not anymore. Today, pilots, like the ones at Blue Hawaiian (see below), are an interesting hybrid: part Hawaiian historian, part DJ, part tour

Especially for Kids

A Submarine Ride   Atlantis Submarines (☎ **800/548-6262**) takes you and the kids down into the shallow coastal waters off Lahaina in a real sub. They'll love seeing all the fish—maybe even a shark!—and you'll stay dry the entire time. See below for details.

The Sugarcane Train   This ride will appeal to small kids as well as train buffs of all ages. A steam engine pulls open passenger cars of the Lahaina/Kaanapali and Pacific Railroad on a 30-minute, 12-mile round-trip through sugarcane fields between Lahaina and Kaanapali. The conductor sings and calls out the landmarks, and along the way, you can see Molokai, Lanai, and the backside of Kaanapali. Tickets are $13 for grown-ups, $6.50 for kids; call ☎ **808/661-0089.**

Star Searches   After sunset, the stars over Kaanapali shine big and bright because the tropical sky is almost entirely free of both pollutants and the interference of big-city lights. Amateur astronomers can probe the Milky Way, see the rings of Saturn's and Jupiter's moons, and scan the Sea of Tranquillity in a 60-minute star search on the world's first recreational computer-driven telescope. Not just for kids, this cosmic adventure on the rooftop takes place every night at 8, 9, and 10pm for $12 adults and $6 children. Anyone who's starry-eyed should contact the Hyatt Regency Maui (200 Nohea Kai Dr., Kaanapali Beach; ☎ **808/661-1234**).

In-Line Skating   Bring your own skates and roll, glide and skid around the free, newly constructed rink in Kihei's Kalama Park. It's open daylight hours, with the occasional Maui In-Line Hockey Association game scheduled. For information, call ☎ **808/874-4860**.

Sharks, Stingrays, and Starfish   Hawaii's largest aquarium, **Maui Ocean Center** (☎ **808/875-1962**), has a range of sea critters—from tiger sharks to tiny starfish—that are sure to fascinate kids of all ages. At this 5-acre facility in Maalaea, visitors can take a virtual walk from the beach down to the ocean depths via the three dozen tanks, countless exhibits, and 100-foot-long, 600,000-gallon main oceanarium.

A Dragonfly's View   Kids will think this is too much fun to be educational. Don a face mask and get the dizzying perspective of what a dragonfly sees as it flies over a mountain stream, or watch the tiny *oopu* fish climb up a stream at the Hawaii Nature Center (☎ **808/244-6500**) in beautiful Iao Valley, where you'll find some 30 hands-on, interactive exhibits and displays of Hawaii's natural history.

guide, and part amusement-ride operator. As you soar through the clouds, absorbing Maui's scenic terrain, you'll learn about Hawaii's flora and fauna, history, and culture.

Among the many helicopter-tour operators on Maui, the best is **Blue Hawaiian,** at Kahului Airport (☎ **800/745-BLUE** or 808/871-8844; www.maui.net/~blue), which not only takes you on the ride of your life, but also entertains, educates, and leaves you with an experience you'll never forget. Flights vary from 45 minutes to a half-day affair and range from $130 to $220. A keepsake videotape of your flight is available for $19.95 (so your friends at home can ooh and aah).

If Blue Hawaiian is booked, try **Sunshine Helicopters** (☎ **800/544-2520** or 808/ 871-0722; www.sunshinehelicopters.com; e-mail sales@sunshinehelicopters.com), which offers a variety of flights from short hops around the West Maui Mountains to island tours. Prices range from $99 to $179.

GOING UNDER: SUBMARINE RIDES

This is the stuff dreams are made of: plunge 100 feet under the sea in a state-of-the-art, high-tech submarine and experience swarms of vibrant tropical fish up close and personal as they flutter through the deep blue waters off Lahaina. **Atlantis Submarines,** 665 Front St., Lahaina, HI 96761 (☎ **800/548-6262** or 808/667-7816), offers trips out of Lahaina Harbor; they leave every hour on the hour from 8am to 3pm. Tickets are $79 each. Budget tip: The 8am, 1pm, 2pm, and 3pm tours are $10 cheaper than the other tours. Allow 2 hours for your underwater adventure.

ECO-TOURING

Venture into the lush West Maui Mountains with an experienced guide on one of the **Ritz-Carlton Kapalua's Eco-Tours** (☎ **808/669-6200**). After a continental breakfast, you'll hike by streams and waterfalls, through native trees and plants, and on to breathtaking vistas. The tour takes breaks for a picnic lunch, swimming in secluded pools, and memorable photo opportunities. The 6-hour excursion (offered Tuesday through Friday at 8am) costs $110 for adults, $90 for children 13 to 18; the 4-hour excursion (offered Saturday through Monday at 8am) is $65. The 2- to 3-mile, 4-hour hike is classified as "easy"; the 4- to 5-mile, 6-hour hike is classified as "easy-moderate." Ritz-Carlton Kapalua suggests that you wear comfortable walking or hiking shoes and bring a swimsuit, sunscreen, and a camera. The tour company supplies the meals, a fanny pack with bottled water, and rain gear if necessary. No children under 13 are allowed.

About 1,500 years ago, the verdant Kahakuloa Valley was a thriving Hawaiian village. Today, only a few hundred people live in this secluded hamlet, but Old Hawaii still lives on here. Explore the valley with **Ekahi Tours** (☎ **808/877-9775**). Your guide, a Kahakuloa resident and a Hawaiiana expert, walks you through a taro farm, explains the mystical legends of the valley, and provides you with a peek into ancient Hawaii. The Kahakuloa Valley Tour is $60 for adults, $50 for children under 12. It starts at 7am daily and lasts 7½ hours (until 2:30pm). Snack, beverages, and hotel pickup are included in the price.

2 Central Maui

Central Maui isn't exactly tourist central; this is where real people live. You'll most likely land here and head directly to the beach. However, there are a few sights worth checking out if you need a respite from the sun 'n' surf.

KAHULUI

Under the airport flight path, next to Maui's busiest intersection and across from Costco and K-Mart in Kahului's new business park, is the most unlikely place: **Kanaha Wildlife Sanctuary,** Haleakala Highway Extension and Hana Highway (☎ **808/984-8100**). Look for a parking area off Haleakala Highway Extension (behind the mall, across the Hana Hwy. from Cutter Automotive), and you'll find a 50-yard trail that meanders along the shore to a shade shelter and lookout. Look for the sign proclaiming this the permanent home of the endangered black-neck Hawaiian stilt, whose population is now down to between 1,000 and 1,500. Naturalists say this is a good place to see endangered Hawaiian Koloa ducks, stilts, coots, and other migrating shorebirds. At one time this area was a bit more remote and a lot more rural, until Maui County built a sewer treatment plant near the Sanctuary (after a protracted court battle with environmentalists and bird lovers); after that, the commercial area of Kahului continued to grow closer and closer to the Sanctuary. For a quieter, more natural-looking wildlife preserve, try the Kealia Pond National Wildlife Preserve in Kihei (see "Kihei" under "The South Maui Resorts," below).

PUUNENE

This town, located in the middle of the Central Maui plains, is nearly gone. Once a thriving sugar plantation town with hundreds of homes, a school, a shopping area, and a community center, today Puunene is little more than the sugar mill, a post office, and a museum. The Hawaiian Commercial & Sugar Company, owners of the land and the mill, has slowly phased out the rental plantation housing to open up more land to plant sugar.

The **Alexander & Baldwin Sugar Museum,** at the intersection of Puunene Avenue (Hwy. 350) and Hansen Road (☎ **808/871-8058**), is a former sugar mill superintendent's home converted into a museum that tells the story of sugar in Hawaii. Exhibits explain how sugar is grown, harvested, and milled. An eye-opening display shows how Samuel Alexander and Henry Baldwin managed to acquire huge chunks of land from the Kingdom of Hawaii and how they ruthlessly fought to gain access to water on the other side of the island, making sugarcane an economically viable crop. The museum is open Monday through Saturday from 9:30am to 4:30pm; admission is $3 for adults and $1.50 for children 6 to 17.

WAIKAPU

Across the sugarcane fields from Puunene, and about 3 miles south of Wailuku on the Honoapiilani Highway, lies the tiny, one-street village of Waikapu, which has two attractions that are worth a peek, especially if you're trying to kill time before your flight out.

Relive Maui's past by taking a 40-minute narrated tram ride around fields of pineapple, sugarcane, and papaya trees at **Maui Tropical Plantation,** 1670 Honoapiilani Hwy., Waikapu (☎ **800/451-6805** or 808/244-7643). A shop sells fresh and dried fruit. The working plantation is open daily from 9am to 5pm. Admission is free; the tour is $8.50 for adults and $3.50 for kids 5 to 12.

Marilyn Monroe and Frank Lloyd Wright meet for dinner every night at **Waikapu Golf and Country Club,** 2500 Honoapiilani Hwy. (☎ **808/244-2011;** fax 808/242-8089), one of Maui's most unusual buildings. Neither actually visited Maui in real life, but these icons of architecture and glamour who traded on the curvilinear live on in this paradise setting. Wright designed the place for a Pennsylvania family in 1949, but it was never actually constructed. In 1957, Marilyn and husband Arthur Miller wanted it built for them in Connecticut, but they separated the following year. When Tokyo billionaire Takeshi Sekiguchi went shopping at Taliesen West for a signature building to adorn his 18-hole golf course, he found the blueprints, and he had Marilyn's Wright House cleverly redesigned as a clubhouse. A horizontal in a vertical landscape, it doesn't quite fit the setting, but it's still the best-looking building on Maui today. You can walk in and look around at Wright's architecture and the portraits of Marilyn in Monroe's, the restaurant.

WAILUKU

This historic gateway to Iao Valley (see below) is worth a visit, if only for a brief stop at **Bailey House Museum,** 2375-A Main St. (☎ **808/244-3326;**

fax 808/244-3920). Missionary and sugar planter Edward Bailey's 1833 home is a treasure trove of Hawaiiana. The house is an architectural hybrid of stones laid by Hawaiian craftsmen and timbers joined in a display of Yankee ingenuity. Inside, you'll discover an eclectic collection, from precontact artifacts like scary temple images, dog-tooth necklaces, and a rare lei made of tree snail shells, to latter-day relics like Duke Kahanamoku's 1919 redwood surfboard and a koa wood table given to President Ulysses S. Grant, who had to refuse it because he couldn't accept gifts from foreign countries. There's also a gallery devoted to a few of Bailey's landscapes, painted from 1866 to 1896, which capture on canvas a Maui we can only imagine today.

The museum is open daily from 10am to 4pm. Admission is $4 for adults, $3.50 for seniors, and $1 for children 6 to 12.

WALKING TOUR
Historic Wailuku

The historic town of Wailuku, which most visitors merely glance at through their car windows as they whiz by on the way to Iao Valley, has played a significant role in Maui's history over the past 200 years. One of Hawaii's bloodiest battles took place here in 1790, when Kamehameha I fought the Maui chiefs in his bid to unite the Hawaiian Islands. The town of Wailuku (which means "bloody waters") took its name from that battle, in which the carnage was so intense that the 4-mile Iao Stream actually turned red from the slaughter.

Wailuku was also where the missionaries landed in the mid-1800s to "save" the natives and convert them to Christianity. You can still see the New England architectural influences they brought with them in this quaint community today.

Sugar, which was to dominate Maui for the next century, came to Wailuku in 1860, when the Wailuku Sugar Company housed its operations, mill, and plantation in the old town. The industry drew immigrant groups from China, Japan, Okinawa, Korea, the Philippines, and Europe, each contributing aspects of its culture to the local way of life.

In 1905, Wailuku became the county seat of Maui's government; soon the small town became the center not only of government, but also of finance, commerce, and entertainment. Vaudeville thrived, movie houses were packed, and Wailuku was in its heyday.

At the beginning of the 1970s, however, sugar lost its sweetness, and sugar planters began to cut back operations due to economic conditions. Wailuku began to shrink. As modern subdivisions popped up in nearby Kahului and retail shops moved to shopping centers there, Wailuku became frozen in history.

Today, visitors can experience the past 200 years of Maui's history by spending an hour wandering through Wailuku.

Getting There: From Lahaina and Kihei, take Honoapiilani Highway (Hi. 30) north across the central plains of the island. The Honoapiilani Highway becomes High Street in Wailuku. Park on High Street by the Wailuku Elementary School.

Start: Wailuku Elementary School, High Street.

Finish: Same location.

Time: About an hour, depending on how much time you spend in the shops.

Best Times: When the shops are open, Monday through Saturday from 9am to 4pm.

Begin your walk at the:

1. Wailuku Elementary School. This old stone building has housed Maui school-children since 1904. It was designed by C. W. Dickey, one of Wailuku's most prolific architects in his day, known for developing a Hawaiian style of architecture characterized by a distinctive double-hipped roof.

Right next door is:

2. Wailuku Union Church, a brick structure built in 1911 that still holds church services every Sunday at 10am.

Continue down High Street to Apuni Street; on the corner is:

3. Wailuku Public Library. When the white-columned library (also designed by C. W. Dickey) was built in 1928, no one ever imagined that computers would be used to locate the books within the arched doorways and that children would line up to communicate over the Internet.

Now cross Apuni Street to the:

4. Territorial Building, yet another C. W. Dickey design. Built in 1930, it was once home to the business of the Territory of Hawaii, but now the thick white concrete walls house the State District Court and traffic court.

Next door is:

5. Kaahumanu Church. On the spreading lawns beneath a huge monkeypod tree is one of the most important churches on the island. Named after Queen Kaahumanu, the monarch whose conversion to Christianity prompted thousands of her subjects to follow her lead, this was one of Maui's first stone churches. It was originally a grass-hut chapel where the queen often attended services, until 1832, when missionaries built an adobe-type church that the frequent rains of Wailuku eventually washed away. In 1837, the adobe structure was replaced by a stone church, designed by Edward Bailey (see below). In 1876, the stone church we see today replaced the existing stone structure. When the steeple needed repairing in 1984, the company hired was Skyline Engineers, from Massachusetts, the same place the missionaries came from some 150 years earlier. A small cemetery on the far side of the church property contains graves of the first missionaries and their families. Services at this grande dame church are held at 9:30am on Sundays; the congregation sings hymns in Hawaiian.

Now turn left on Main Street and head up the hill toward the West Maui Mountains; on the left is:

6. Bailey House Museum, first built in 1833, with various rooms added on until 1850. During the 1840s, the building was used as Hawaii's first boarding school for girls, the Wailuku Female Seminary, with Edward Bailey serving as principal. Bailey, who went on to manage the Wailuku Sugar Company, is also widely known as a prolific landscape painter. His works, which depict Maui from 1866 to 1886, are on display at the Bailey House today, along with ancient Hawaiian artifacts, furniture, clothing, and tools from the missionaries. The Maui Historical Society has its offices here. See the Bailey House Museum listed above.

Continue up Main Street and turn right at Ilima Street, where at the bend in the road you'll see the:

7. Cemetery. At the elbow in the road where Ilima and Vineyard streets meet is a cemetery that reflects Wailuku's history. The various ethnic groups who flocked to Maui during the sugar boom years buried their dead in this quiet area with breathtaking views of Iao Valley and the West Maui Mountains.

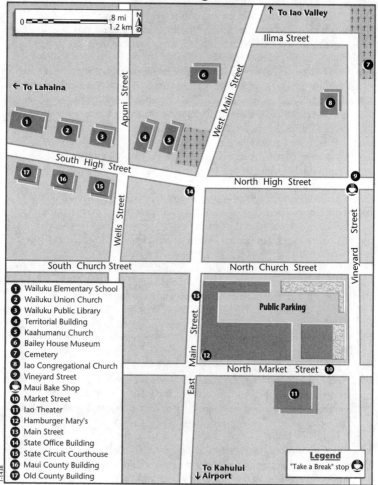

1 Wailuku Elementary School
2 Wailuku Union Church
3 Wailuku Public Library
4 Territorial Building
5 Kaahumanu Church
6 Bailey House Museum
7 Cemetery
8 Iao Congregational Church
9 Vineyard Street
☺ Maui Bake Shop
10 Market Street
11 Iao Theater
12 Hamburger Mary's
13 Main Street
14 State Office Building
15 State Circuit Courthouse
16 Maui County Building
17 Old County Building

Legend
"Take a Break" stop ☺

Continue down Vineyard; on your right is:

8. Iao Congregational Church, built in 1895 and still an active member of the surrounding community, offering day-care facilities and Sunday services at 9:30am. Various community groups use the church for meetings.

Turn left upon leaving the church and continue down:

9. Vineyard Street, an eclectic combination of old plantation houses, now-defunct stores, and a modern high-rise condominium plopped down in the middle. The next 2 blocks consist of boarded-up stores beside thriving businesses, and renovated old buildings alongside dilapidated shacks.

☺ **TAKE A BREAK** On the corner of Vineyard and High streets is **Maui Bake Shop** (☎ 808/242-0064), a world-class European bakery offering more than 100 bakery and deli items and breads baked in one of Maui's oldest brick ovens. You won't be able to resist the white-chocolate macadamia-nut cheesecake here. (See chapter 7 for a complete review.)

Walk further down Vineyard and turn right onto:

10. **Market Street.** Local residents call this street Antique Row for the curios, collectibles, memorabilia, and antiques shops that line the street.

In the middle of the block is:

11. **Iao Theater.** This restored art-deco building, constructed in 1928, has had numerous lives. It first housed vaudeville, then became a movie theater, and finally fell into disrepair. In the 1970s, it reopened as a movie theater, showing art house flicks, and was eventually fully restored to its former glory. It now hosts plays performed by the Maui Community Theater.

Walk to the corner of Main Street to:

12. **Hamburger Mary's.** A legend in Wailuku for its good grinds (see chapter 7 for review), this is where gays and straights dine together, enjoying both the food and the eclectic decor.

Turn right at the corner of Market and Main streets and continue up:

13. **Main Street,** where the collection of small shops offers everything from knick-knacks to antiques from the Orient.

Continue up Main Street and turn left on High Street, where on the corner is the:

14. **State Office Building.** One of the few modern buildings in old Wailuku town, it houses most of the state agencies, including Land and Natural Resources, which offers information on state parks and camping permits.

Continue down High Street and cross Wells Street, and on the corner you'll see the:

15. **State Circuit Courthouse.** Built in 1907, trials are still being heard in this stately old building today.

Next door on High Street is the:

16. **Maui County Building.** The modern, nine-story structure stands out among the historic buildings surrounding it. When it was being built in the early 1970s, the mayor at the time said he wanted it to be the biggest building in Wailuku. He got his wish.

Next door is the:

17. **Old County Building.** When it was built in 1925, this old stone edifice was large enough to serve all the needs of Maui County. Fifty years later, a nine-story building was needed to serve the same purpose. When the county government moved into its current building, the police department operated out of this structure for a couple of decades, until it got its own brand-new building on Kaahumanu Avenue (by the Maui Memorial Hospital). This historic site is now home to the County Department of Planning's Land Use and Codes.

If you continue down High Street, you'll be back at your car in front of the Wailuku Elementary School.

IAO VALLEY

A couple of miles north of the historic town of Wailuku, past the Bailey House museum where the little plantation houses stop and the road climbs ever higher, Maui's true nature begins to reveal itself. The transition between suburban sprawl and raw nature is so abrupt that most people who drive up into the valley don't realize they're suddenly in a rain forest. The walls of the canyon begin to close around them, and a 2,250-foot needle pricks gray clouds scudding across the blue sky. After the hot tropic sun, the air is moist and cool, and the shade is a welcome comfort. This is Iao Valley, a 6.2-acre state park of great nature, history, and beauty, enjoyed by millions of people from around the world for more than a century.

Iao (literally "Supreme Light") Valley, 10 miles long and encompassing 4,000 acres, is the eroded volcanic caldera of the West Maui Mountains. The head of the Iao Valley is a broad circular amphitheater where four major streams—the Nakalaloa, the Poohoahoa, the Kinihipai, and the Ae—converge into Iao Stream. At the back of the amphitheater is rain-drenched Puu Kukui, the West Maui Mountains' highest point. No other Hawaiian valley lets you go from seacoast to rain forest so easily. This peaceful valley, full of tropical plants, rainbows and waterfalls, swimming holes, and hiking trails, is a place of solitude, reflection, and escape for residents and visitors alike.

JUST THE FACTS

WHEN TO GO   The park is open daily from 7am to 7pm year-round. Go early in the morning or late in the afternoon, when the sun's rays slant into the valley and create a mystical atmosphere. You can bring a picnic and spend the day, but be prepared at any time for a tropical cloudburst, which often soaks the valley and swells both waterfalls and streams.

ACCESS POINTS   There's only one way in and one way out. From Wailuku, take Main Street, then turn right on Iao Valley Road to the entrance to the state park.

INFORMATION & VISITOR CENTERS   For information, contact **Iao Valley State Park,** State Parks and Recreation, 54 High St., Rm 101, Wailuku (☎ **808/984-8109;** fax 808/984-8111). The ✪ **Hawaii Nature Center,** 875 Iao Valley Rd. (☎ **808/244-6500**), home of the Iao Valley Nature Center, features hands-on, interactive exhibits and displays relating the story of Hawaiian natural history; it is an important stopping point for all who want to explore Iao Valley on their own or on guided trips. It's open daily from 10am to 4pm; admission is $5 for adults and $3 for children under 12.

SEEING THE HIGHLIGHTS

You're invited to follow two paved walkways that loop into the massive green amphitheater, across the bridge of Iao Valley Stream, and along the stream itself. The one-third–mile loop on a paved trail is Maui's easiest hike—you can even take your grandmother on this one. The leisurely walk will allow you to enjoy the lush vegetation and the lovely views of the Iao Needle. Others often proceed beyond the state park border, taking two trails deeper into the valley, but the trails enter private land, and NO TRESPASSING signs are posted.

The feature known as **Iao Needle** is an erosional remnant composed of basalt dikes. The phallic rock juts an impressive 2,250 feet above sea level. Youngsters play in **Iao Stream,** a peaceful brook that belies its bloody history. In 1790, King Kamehameha the Great and his men engaged in the bloody battle of Iao Valley to gain control of Maui. When the battle ended, so many bodies blocked Iao Stream that the battle site was named Kepaniwai, or "damning of the waters." An architectural heritage park of Hawaiian, Japanese, Chinese, Filipino, and New England–style houses stands in harmony by Iao Stream at **Kepaniwai Heritage Garden.** This is a good picnic spot, because there are plenty of picnic tables and benches. You can see ferns, banana trees, and other native and exotic plants in the **Iao Valley Botanic Garden** along the stream. The park was designed by architect Richard C. Tongg, who wanted to create an area showing the various cultures that make up Maui. There's a thatched-roof Hawaiian grass shack, a New England "salt box" constructed house, a Portuguese villa with outdoor oven, a Japanese teahouse with garden, and a Chinese pagoda.

3 Lahaina & West Maui

THE SCENIC ROUTE TO WEST MAUI: KAHEKILI HIGHWAY

The usual road to West Maui from Wailuku is the Honoapiilani Highway, which takes you across the isthmus to Maalaea and around to Lahaina, Kaapanali, and Kapalua. But for an off-the-beaten-path, back-to-nature driving experience, take the Kahekili Highway instead. ("Highway" is a bit of a euphemism for this paved but somewhat precarious narrow road; check your rental-car agreement before you head out.) It was named after the great chief Kahekili, who built houses from the skulls of his enemies.

On the way, stop at the **Halekii and Pihanakalani Heiau,** which most visitors rarely see. To get there from Wailuku, turn north from Main Street onto Market Street. Make a right on Mill Street and follow it until it ends; then make a left on Lower Main Street. Follow Lower Main until it ends at Waiehu Beach Road (Hwy. 340), and turn left. Turn left on Kahio Street and again at the first left onto Hea Place, and drive through the gates.

These heiau, built in 1240, were among Maui's first. Kahekili, the last chief of Maui, lived here; Keopuolani, the wife of Kamehameha I and the mother of both Kamehameha II and Kamehameha III, was born here. And after the bloody battle at Iao Stream, Kamehameha I reportedly came to the temple here to pay homage to the war god, Ku, with a human sacrifice.

The two heiau, made with stones carried up from the Iao Stream below, sit on a hill with a commanding view of central Maui and Haleakala. Halekii ("House of the Idol") is made of stone walls with a flat grassy top, whereas Pihanakalani ("gathering place of supernatural beings") is a pyramid-shaped mount of stones. Although both sites are state monuments, they are somewhat in disrepair, surrounded by overgrown weeds. If you sit quietly nearby (never walk on any heiau, because that's considered disrespectful), the view alone explains why this spot was chosen.

Go back to Waiehu Beach Road (Hwy. 340), which passes through the tiny town of Waiehu, and then on to the true wild nature of Maui: a narrow and winding road that weaves for 20 miles along an ancient Hawaiian coastal footpath.

If you want views, these are photo opportunities from heaven: steep ravines, rolling pastoral hills, tumbling waterfalls, exploding blowholes, crashing surf, jagged lava coastlines, and a tiny Hawaiian village straight off a postcard.

Along the route, nestled in a crevice between two steep hills, is the picturesque village of **Kahakuloa** ("the tall hau tree"), with a red-tiled-roof church, a dozen weather-worn houses, and vivid green taro patches. From the northern side of the village, you can look back at the great view of Kahakuloa, the dark boulder beach, and the 636-foot Kahakuloa Head rising in the background.

A couple of miles down the road, just past the 16-mile marker, look for the **POHAKU KANI** sign, marking the huge, 6-foot-by-6-foot, bell-shaped stone. To "ring" the bell, look on the side facing Kahakuloa for the deep indentations, and strike the stone with another rock.

A little farther down the road (less than a half mile), you'll come to a wide turnoff providing a great photo op: a view of the jagged coastline down to the crashing surf.

Just past the 20-mile mark, after a sharp turn in the road, look for a small turnoff on the mauka side of the road (just after the guardrail ends). Park here and walk across the road, and on your left you'll see a spouting **blow hole.** During the winter months, this is an excellent spot to look for whales.

As the road rounds the point, the island of Molokai comes into view. At Honokohau, the road becomes Honoapiilani Highway (Hwy. 30). At the next valley, you'll come to the twin bays, **Honolua** and **Mokuleia,** which have been designated as Marine Life Conservation Areas (the taking of fish, shells, or anything else is prohibited). In the 1970s, Colin Cameron, head of Maui Land and Pineapple (and owner of the not-yet-developed Kapalua Resort area), was a pioneer in the preservation of Maui's resources; he personally fought to protect these two incredibly fragile marine systems in perpetuity.

KAPALUA

If you're taking the Kahekili Highway (Hi. 340), Kapalua is the first resort area you'll see in West Hawaii.

For generations, West Maui meant one thing: pineapple. Hawaii's only pineapple cannery today, **Maui Pineapple Co.,** offers tours of its pineapple plantation through the Kapalua Resort Activity Center (☎ **808/669-8088**). Real plantation workers lead the 2½-hour tours, which feature the history of West Maui, facts about growing and harvesting pineapple, and lots of trivia about plantation life. Participants are even allowed to pick and harvest their own pineapple. The tours, which depart from the Kapalua Shops (next door to the Kapalua Bay Hotel), are given twice daily from Monday to Friday; fees are $19 per person, and children must be at least 12 years old. Before or after the tour, you might want to take some time to wander through the Kapalua resort (see chapters 6 and 8).

A WHALE OF A PLACE IN KAANAPALI

Heading south from Kapalua, the next resort area you'll come to is Kaanapali. If you haven't seen a real whale yet, go to **Whalers Village,** 2435 Kaanapali Pkwy., a shopping center that has adopted the whale as its mascot. You can't miss it: a huge, almost life-size metal sculpture of a mother whale and two nursing calves greets you. A few more steps, and you're met by the looming, bleached-white bony skeleton of a 40-foot sperm whale; it's pretty impressive.

On the second floor of the mall is the **Whale Center of the Pacific** (☎ **808/661-5992**), a museum celebrating the "Golden Era of Whaling" (1825 to 1860) from the whaler's point of view: harpoons and scrimshaw are on display, and the museum has even re-created the cramped quarters of a whaler's seagoing vessel.

Across the way, you'll find the **House of the Whale,** or "Hale Kohola" (☎ **808/661-6752**), which tells the story from the whale's point of view, as it were. Here's where you can learn about the evolution of the whale: the museum houses exhibits on 70 species of whales and more whale lore than you could hope to absorb during your entire 2-week vacation in Hawaii. Venture into the Bone Room, where volunteers scrape and identify the bones of marine mammals that wash ashore in Hawaiian waters to use in future exhibits. You can also watch movies about whales, buy any number of whale souvenirs, and get a free *Whale Watch Guide* that points you out the door and toward the ocean, now that you more or less know what whales look like.

Both museums are open during mall hours, daily from 9:30am to 10pm. Admission is free.

SIGHTSEEING IN HISTORIC LAHAINA

Back when "there was no God west of the Horn," Lahaina was the capital of Hawaii and the Pacific's wildest port. Today, it's a mild, mollified version of its old self—mostly a hustle-bustle of whale art, timeshares, and "Just Got Lei'd" T-shirts. I'm not sure the rowdy whalers would have been pleased. But, if you look hard, you'll still find the historic port town they loved, filled with the kind of history that inspired James Michener to write his best-selling epic novel, *Hawaii.*

At the headquarters of the **Lahaina Restoration Foundation,** at the Masters' Reading Room, Front & Dickenson streets (☎ **808/661-3262**), you can pick up a self-guided walking tour map. This map will take you to Lahaina's historic sites—from the Royal Taro Patch and the ruins of King Kamehameha's Brick Palace to the Seamen's Cemetery and old jail yard, where the most drunk and disorderly sailors were thrown for a day of drying out. Here, you'll learn the stories of those who lived Lahaina's colorful past, from the missionary doctor who single-handedly kept a cholera epidemic from wiping out Maui's people to the boy king who lived on his very own island.

Below are our favorite places to rediscover historic Lahaina.

Baldwin Home Museum. 696 Front St. (at Dickenson St.). ☎ **808/661-3262.** Admission $3 adults, $2 seniors, $1 children, $5 family. Daily 10am–4:30pm.

The oldest house in Lahaina, this coral-and-rock structure was built in 1834 by Rev. Dwight Baldwin, a doctor with the fourth company of American missionaries to sail around the Horn to Hawaii. Like many missionaries, he came to Hawaii to do good—and did very well. After 17 years of service, Baldwin was granted 2,600 acres for farming and grazing in Kapalua. His ranch manager experimented with what Hawaiians called *hala-kahiki,* or pineapple, on a 4-acre plot; the rest is history. Open for guided tours, the house looks as though Baldwin had just stepped out for a minute to tend a sick neighbor down the street.

Next door is the **Masters' Reading Room,** Maui's oldest building. This became visiting sea captains' favorite hangout once the missionaries closed down all of Lahaina's grog shops and banned prostitution; but by 1844, once hotels and bars started reopening, it lost its appeal. It's now the headquarters of the plucky band of historians who try to keep this town alive and antique at the same time.

Banyan Tree. At the Courthouse Building, 649 Wharf St.

Of all the banyan trees in Hawaii, this is the biggest, most sheltering of all—it's so big that you can't get it in your camera's viewfinder. It was only 8 feet tall when it was planted in 1873 by Maui Sheriff William O. Smith to mark the 50th anniversary of Lahaina's first Christian mission; the big old banyan from India is now more than 50 feet tall, has 12 major trunks, and shades two-thirds of an acre in Lahaina's courthouse square.

The Brig *Carthaginian II.* Lahaina Harbor. ☎ **808/661-8527.** Admission $3 adults, $2 seniors, $5 family. Daily 10am–4:30pm.

This authentically restored square-rigged brigantine is an authentic replica of a 19th-century whaling ship, the kind that brought the first missionaries to Hawaii. This floating museum features exhibits on whales and 19th-century whaling life. You won't believe how cramped the living quarters were—they make today's cruise ship cabins look downright roomy.

Hale Pai. Lahainaluna High School Campus, 980 Lahainaluna Rd. (at the top of the mountain). ☎ **808/661-3262.** Free admission. Mon–Sat 10am–3pm.

Where to Park Free—or Next to Free—in Lahaina

Lahaina is the worst place on Maui for parking. The historic town was created and filled with shops, restaurants, and historic sites before the throngs of tourists (and their cars) invaded. Street parking is hit-or-miss (actually more miss—there are Lahaina residents who haven't seemed to move their cars since the Bush administration). You can either drive around the block for hours looking for a free place to park on the street or park in one of the nearly 20 parking lots. We've divided the lots into four classes: free; free for customers; discount with validation; and pay.

Free: Of the free lots, the best is the public lot on the south side of Prison Street, between Front and Luakini Streets (the lot across the street is pay), which offers 3 hours of free parking. Another free lot is on the corner of Front and Shaw Streets, for the users of Maluuluolele Park.

Free for Customers: The three lots on Papalaua Street are all free for customers. The largest is the Lahaina Shopping Center lot, with 2 free hours. Next in size is the Lahaina Center, across the street (which allows 4 hours free, but you must get a validation from a store in the Lahaina Center); the smallest is the Lahaina Square lot on Papalaua and Wainee streets, which offers 2 free hours for customers.

Discount with Validation: Customers of the Wharf Cinema Center, located on Front Street, can get a discount by parking at either of the theater's two lots: one on Wainee Street, between Dickenson and Prison streets; and the other on Luakini Street, between Dickenson and Prison streets.

Pay: Lahaina is filled with pay lots ranging from 50¢ for a half hour to all-day parking for $8 to $10. Pay lots on Front Street are located between Papalaua and Lahainaluna streets, on the corner of Dickenson Street, and underground at the 505 Front Street shopping center. Pay lots on Luakini Street are located near the Prison Street intersection and near the Lahainaluna Street intersection. Lahainaluna Street has several pay lots between Wainee and Front streets. Dickenson Street has three pay lots between Wainee and Luakini streets.

When the missionaries arrived in Hawaii wanting to spread the word of God, they found the Hawaiians had no written language. They quickly rectified the situation by converting the Hawaiian sounds into a written language. They then built the first printing press in order to print educational materials that would assist them on their mission. Hale Pai was the printing house for the Lahainaluna Seminary, the oldest school west of the Rockies. Today Lahainaluna is the public high school for the children of West Maui.

Lahaina Jodo Mission. 12 Ala Moana St. (off Front St., near the Mala Wharf). ☎ **808/ 661-4304.** Free admission. Daily, during daylight hours.

This site has long been held sacred. The Hawaiians called it Puunoa Point, which means "the hill freed from taboo." Once a small village named "Mala" (which translates as "garden"), the Japanese immigrants, who came to Hawaii in 1868 as laborers for the sugarcane plantations, loved to spend time in this peaceful place and eventually built a small wooden temple to worship here. In 1968, on the 100th anniversary of the Japanese in Hawaii, a Great Buddha statue, the largest outside of Japan (some 12 feet high and weighting 3.5 tons) was brought here from

Lahaina

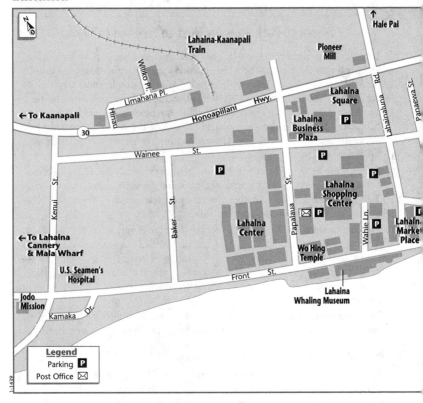

Japan. The immaculate grounds also contain a replica of the original wooden temple and 90-foot-tall pagoda.

Lahaina Whaling Museum. Front Street Crazy Shirt Shop, 865 Front St. (ocean side of the street by Papalaua St.). ☎ **808/661-4775.** Free admission. Daily 9:30am–9pm.

Yankee whalers came to Lahaina to reprovision ships' stores, get drunk, and raise hell with "the girls of old Mowee." Everything was fine and dandy until the Congregational missionaries arrived and declared the port town "one of the breathing holes of hell." They tried to curb drinking and prostitution, but failed; Lahaina grew ever more lawless until the whaling era came to an end with the discovery of oil in Pennsylvania and the birth of the petroleum industry. That rambunctious era is recalled in this small museum full of art and relics from Lahaina's glory days.

Maluuluolele Park. Front and Shaw streets.

At first glance, this Front Street park appears to be only a hot, dry, dusty softball field. But under home plate is the edge of Mokuula, where a royal compound once stood more than 100 years ago, now buried under tons of red dirt and sand. Here, Prince Kauikeaolui, who ascended the throne as King Kamehameha III when he was only 10, lived with the love of his life, his sister Princess Nahienaena. Missionaries took a dim view of incest, which was acceptable to Hawaiian nobles in order to preserve the royal bloodlines. Torn between love for her brother and the new Christian morality, Nahienaena grew despondent and died at the age of 21.

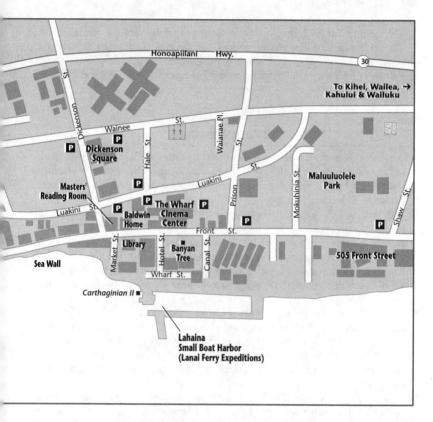

King Kamehameha III, who reigned for 29 years—longer than any other Hawaiian monarch—presided over Hawaii as it went from kingdom to constitutional monarchy, and absolute power over the islands began to transfer from island nobles to missionaries, merchants, and sugar planters. Kamehameha died in 1854 at the age of 39. In 1918, his royal compound, containing a mausoleum and artifacts of the kingdom, was demolished and covered with dirt to create a public park. The baseball team from Lahainaluna School, the first American school founded by missionaries west of the Rockies, now plays games on the site of this royal place, still considered sacred to many Hawaiians.

U.S. Seaman's Hospital. Front St. near Kenui St. ☎ 808/661-3262.

During the whaling days, from 1820 to 1860, some sea captains considered sick sailors a liability to get rid of at the next port. Records from the 1850s refer to "2,000 to 3,000 destitute sailors on Hawaiian beaches during the month of October." The United States finally leased this former residence of King Kamehameha III (built in 1833), which you can view from the outside, to serve as a hospital for seamen in 1844.

Wo Hing Temple. Front St. (between Wahie Lane and Papalaua St.). ☎ 808/661-3262.
Admission $3 adults, $2 seniors, $1 children, $5 family. Daily 10am–4pm.

The Chinese were among the various immigrants brought to Hawaii to work in the sugarcane fields. In 1909, several of the Chinese workers formed the Wo Hing society, a chapter of Chee Kun Tong, a Chinese society that dates back to the

17th century. In 1912, they built this social hall in downtown Lahaina for the Chinese community. Completely restored, the Wo Hing Temple has displays and artifacts on the history of the Chinese in Lahaina; next door in the old cookhouse is a theater with movies of Hawaii taken by Thomas Edison in 1898 and 1903.

WALKING TOUR
Historic Lahaina

Located between the waving green sugarcane blanketing the West Maui Mountains and the deep azure ocean offshore, Lahaina stands out as one of the few places in Hawaii that has managed to preserve its 19th-century heritage while still accommodating 20th-century guests.

In the past 200 years, Lahaina has gone from capital of the united kingdom of Hawaii to whaler's playground to missionaries' holy ground to fertile sugarcane ground and finally to tourist mecca. In ancient times, powerful chiefs and kings ruled this hot, dry oceanside village. At the turn of the 19th century, after King Kamehameha united the Hawaiian Islands, he made Lahaina the royal capital—which it remained until 1845, when Kamehameha III moved the capital to the larger port of Honolulu.

In the 1840s, the whaling industry was at its peak: hundreds of ships called into Lahaina every year. The streets were filled with sailors 24 hours a day. Even Herman Melville, who later wrote *Moby Dick,* was among the throngs of whalers in Lahaina.

Just 20 years later, the whaling industry was waning, and sugar had taken over the town. The Pioneer Sugar Mill Company, which still exists today, reigned over Lahaina for the next 100 years.

Today, the drunken and derelict whalers who wandered through Lahaina's streets in search of bars, dance halls, and brothels have been replaced by hordes of tourists crowding into the small mile-long main section of town in search of boutiques, art galleries, and chic gourmet eateries.

Lahaina's colorful past continues to have a profound influence today. This is no quiet seaside village, but a vibrant, cutting-edge kind of place, filled with a sense of history, but definitely with its mind on the future.

Members of the Lahaina Restoration Foundation have worked for 3 decades to preserve Lahaina's past. They have marked a number of historical sites with brown and white markers; below, we've provided explanations of the significance of each site as you walk through Lahaina's historic past.

Getting There: From the Kahului Airport, take the Kuihelani Highway (Highway 38) to the intersection of Honoapiilani Highway (Highway 30), where you turn left. Follow Honoapiilani Highway to Lahaina and turn left on Lahainaluna Street. When Lahainaluna Street ends, make a left on Front Street. A block down, the walk begins on Front and Dickenson streets (see the box on parking below).

Start: Front and Dickenson streets.

Finish: Same location.

Time: Approximately 1 hour.

Best Time: Daylight hours.

1. Masters' Reading Room. This coral-and-stone building looks just as it did in 1834, when Rev. William Richards and Rev. E. Spaulding convinced the whaling ship captains that they needed a place for the ships' masters and captains, many of whom traveled with their families, to stay while they were ashore. The bottom floor was used as a storage area for the mission; the top floor, from

Walking Tour–Historic Lahaina

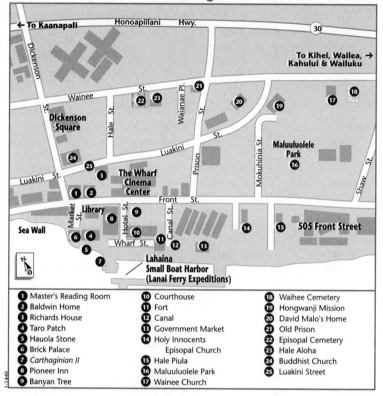

| To Kaanapali ← | Honoapiilani Hwy. | 30 |

To Kihei, Wailea, → Kahului & Wailuku

Dickenson St.

Wainee St.

Dickenson Square

Hale St.

Waianae Pl.

Luakini St.

Prison St.

Mokuhinia St.

Maluuluolele Park ⑯

Shaw St.

Luakini St.

The Wharf Cinema Center

Front St.

Library

Sea Wall

Market St.

Hotel St.

Canal St.

Wharf St.

Lahaina Small Boat Harbor (Lanai Ferry Expeditions)

❶ Master's Reading Room
❷ Baldwin Home
❸ Richards House
❹ Taro Patch
❺ Hauola Stone
❻ Brick Palace
❼ *Carthaginian II*
❽ Pioneer Inn
❾ Banyan Tree

❿ Courthouse
⓫ Fort
⓬ Canal
⓭ Government Market
⓮ Holy Innocents
   Episopal Church
⓯ Hale Piula
⓰ Maluuluolele Park
⓱ Wainee Church

⓲ Waihee Cemetery
⓳ Hongwanji Mission
⓴ David Malo's Home
㉑ Old Prison
㉒ Episopal Cemetery
㉓ Hale Aloha
㉔ Buddhist Church
㉕ Luakini Street

which you could see the ships at anchor in the harbor, was for the visiting ships' officers.

Next door is the:

2. Baldwin Home. Harvard-educated physician Rev. Dwight Baldwin, with his wife of just a few weeks, sailed to Hawaii from New England in 1830. Baldwin was first assigned to a church in Waimea, on the Big Island, and then to Lahaina's Wainee Church in 1838. He and his family lived in this house until 1871. The Baldwin Home (built in 1834) and the Masters' Reading Room are the oldest standing buildings in Lahaina, made from thick walls of coral and hand-milled timber. Baldwin also ran his medical office and his missionary activities out of this house. See the Baldwin Home Museum, above, for information on hours and admission.

On the other side of the Baldwin Home is the former site of the:

3. Richards House. The open field is empty today, but it represents the former home of Lahaina's first Protestant missionary, Rev. William Richards, who had quite an influence on the Kingdom of Hawaii. Richards went on to become the chaplain, teacher, and translator to Kamehameha III. He also was instrumental in drafting Hawaii's constitution and acted as the king's envoy to the United States and England, seeking recognition of Hawaii as an independent nation. After his death in 1847, he was buried in the Wainee Churchyard.

From here, cross Front Street and walk toward the ocean, with the Lahaina Public Library on your right and the green Pioneer Inn on your left, until you see the:

4. Taro Patch. The lawn in front of the Lahaina Library was once a taro patch stretching back to the Baldwin Home. The taro plant was a staple of the Hawaiian diet: the root was used to make poi, and the leaves were used in cooking. At one time, Lahaina looked like Venice of the tropics, with streams, ponds, and waterways flooding the taro fields. As the population of the town grew, the water was siphoned off for drinking water.

To get to the next marker, walk away from the Lahaina Harbor toward the edge of the lawn, where you'll see the:

5. Hauola Stone. Hawaiians believed that certain stones placed in sacred places had the power to heal. Kahunas of medicine used stones like this to help cure illnesses.

For the next historic marker, turn around and walk back toward the Pioneer Inn; look for the concrete depression in the ground, which is all that's left of the:

6. Brick Palace, the first Western-style building in Hawaii. King Kamehameha I had this 20-by-40-foot, two-story brick building constructed for his wife, Queen Kaahumanu (who is said to have preferred a grass thatched house nearby). The building was begun in 1798 by two ex-convicts from the British penal colony in Botany Bay, Australia, who fired the brick from the soft red mud they found in Lahaina. Inside, the walls were constructed of wood and the windows were glazed glass. King Kamehameha I lived here from 1801 to 1802, when he was building his war canoe, Peleleu, and preparing to invade Kauai. A handmade stone seawall surrounded the palace to protect it from the surf. Amazingly, the building stood for 70 years; in addition to being a royal compound, it was also used as a meeting house, storeroom, and warehouse.

Behind you, dockside of the loading pier of the Lahaina Harbor, is the:

7. *Carthaginian,* a replica of a 19th-century brig, which carried commerce back and forth to Hawaii. It also serves as a museum and exhibit of 19th-century boating and whaling. For details on hours and fees, see the entry for The Brig *Carthaginian II,* above.

Directly opposite the Carthaginian is the:

8. Pioneer Inn. The scene of some wild parties just after the turn of the century, the Pioneer Inn, Lahaina's first hotel, got its start from a criminal investi-gation. George Freeland, of the Royal Canadian Mounted Police, tracked a criminal to Lahaina and then fell in love with the town. He built the hotel in 1901 but soon discovered that it wasn't the tourist mecca it is today. To make ends meet, Freeland built a movie theater, which was wildly successful. The Pioneer Inn remained the only hotel in all of West Hawaii until the 1950s. As visitors slowly started to trickle in after Hawaii became a state in 1959, Freeland's family expanded the hotel rooms and shops. You can stay at this restored building today (see chapter 6).

From the Pioneer Inn, cross Hotel Street and walk along Wharf Street, which borders the harbor. On your left is:

9. Banyan Tree. Hard to believe that this huge tree (a *Ficus benghalensis*) was only 8 feet tall when it was planted in 1873 by Maui Sheriff William O. Smith in celebration of the 50th anniversary of the missionaries in Lahaina. The tree has witnessed decades of luaus, dances, concerts, private chats, public rallies, and resting sojourners under its mighty boughs.

Continue along Wharf Street; near the edge of the park is the:

10. Courthouse. In 1858, a violent windstorm destroyed about 20 buildings in Lahaina, including Hale Piula, which served as the courthouse and palace of King Kamehameha III. It was rebuilt immediately, using the stones from the previous building; it served not only as courthouse, but also as custom house, post office, tax collector's office, and government offices.

Continue down Wharf Street to Canal Street. On the corner is the:

11. Fort. The remains of a 1-acre fort with 20-foot-high walls can be seen here. In 1830, some whalers fired a few cannonballs into Lahaina in protest of Rev. William Richards's meddling in their affairs. (Richards had convinced Governor Hoapili to create a law forbidding the women of Lahaina from swimming out to greet the whaling ships.) The fort was constructed from 1831 to 1832 with coral blocks taken from the ocean where the Lahaina Harbor sits today. As a further show of strength, cannons were placed along the waterfront, where they remain today. Historical accounts seem to scoff at the "fort," saying it appeared to be more for show than for force. It was later used as a prison, until it was finally torn down in the 1850s; its stones were used for construction of the new prison, Hale Paahao (see no. 21, below).

Cross Canal Street to the:

12. Canal. Unlike Honolulu with its natural deep water harbor, Lahaina was merely a roadstead with no easy access to the shore. Whalers would anchor in deep water offshore, then board smaller boats (which they used to chase down and harpoon whales) to make the passage over the reef to shore. If the surf was up, coming ashore could be dangerous. In the 1840s, the U.S. consular representative recommended digging a canal from one of the freshwater streams that ran through Lahaina and charging a fee to the whalers who wanted to obtain fresh water. In 1913, the canal was filled in to construct Canal Street.

Next door is:

13. Government Market. A few years after the Canal was built (see above), the government built a thatched marketplace with stalls for Hawaiians to sell goods to the sailors. Merchants quickly took advantage of this marketplace and erected drinking establishments, grog shops, and other pastimes of interest nearby. Within a few years, this entire area became known as "Rotten Row."

Make a right onto Front Street and continue down the street, past Kamehameha III Elementary School. On the ocean side of the street across from the park is:

14. Holy Innocents Episcopal Church. When the Episcopal missionaries first came to Lahaina in 1862, they built a church across the street from the current structure. In 1909, the church moved to its present site, which was once a thatched house built for the daughter of King Kamehameha I. The present structure, built in 1927, features unique paintings of a Hawaiian Madonna and endemic birds and plants to Hawaii, executed by DeLos Blackmar in 1940.

Continue down Front Street, and at the next open field look for the white stones by the ocean, marking the former site of:

15. Hale Piula, the "iron-roofed house." In the 1830s, the two-story stone building with a large surrounding courtyard was built for King Kamehameha III. However, the king preferred sleeping in a small thatched hut nearby, so the structure was never really completed. In the 1840s, Kamehameha moved his capital to Honolulu and wasn't using Hale Piula, so it became the local courthouse. The wind storm of 1858, which destroyed the Courthouse on Wharf Street (see no. 10, above), also destroyed the iron-roofed house. The stones from Hale Piula were used to rebuild the Courthouse on Wharf Street.

Continue down Front Street; across from the 505 Front St. complex is:

16. Maluuluolele Park, a sacred spot to Hawaiians and now site of a park and ball field. This used to be a village, Mokuhinia, with a sacred pond that was the home of a *moo* (a spirit in the form of a lizard), which the royal family honored as their personal guardian spirit. In the middle of the pond was a small island, Mokuula, home to Maui's top chiefs. After conquering Maui, Kamehameha I claimed this sacred spot as his own; he and his two sons, Kamehameha II and III, lived here when they were in Lahaina. In 1918, in the spirit of progress, the pond was drained and the ground leveled for a park.

Make a left onto Shaw Street and then another left onto Wainee Street; on the left side, just past the cemetery, is:

17. Wainee Church, the first stone church built in Hawaii (between 1828 and 1832). At one time the church could sit some 3,000 people, albeit tightly packed together, complete with "calabash spittoons" for the tobacco-chewing Hawaiian chiefs and the whale ship captains. That structure didn't last long—the 1858 wind storm that destroyed several buildings in Lahaina also blew the roof off the original church, knocked over the belfry, and picked up the church's bell and deposited it 100 feet away. The structure was rebuilt, but that too was destroyed—this time by Hawaiians protesting the 1894 overthrow of the monarchy. Again the church was rebuilt, and again it was destroyed—by fire, in 1947. The next incarnation of the church was destroyed by yet another wind-storm, in 1951. The current church has been standing since 1953, and so far, so good. Be sure to walk around to the back of the church: the row of palm trees on the ocean side are among the oldest in Lahaina.

Wander next door to the:

18. Waihee Cemetery. Established in 1823, this was the first Christian cemetery in Hawaii. The graves tell a fascinating story of old Hawaii, with graves of Hawaiian chiefs, commoners, missionaries and their families (infant mortality was high then), and sailors. Enter this ground with respect, because Hawaiians consider it sacred—many members of the royal family were buried here, including Queen Keopuolani, who was wife of King Kamehameha I, mother of Kings Kamehameha II and III, and the first Hawaiian baptized as a Protestant. Among the other graves are Rev. William Richards (the first missionary in Lahaina), Princess Nahienaena (sister of Kings Kamehameha II and III), King Kaumualii (last king of Kauai), and Queen Kekauonohi (wife of Kamehameha II).

Continue down Waihee Street to the corner of Luakini Street and the:

19. Hongwanji Mission. The temple was originally built in 1910 by members of Lahaina's Buddhist sect. The current building was constructed in 1927, housing a temple and language school. The public is welcome to attend the New Year's Eve celebration, Buddha's birthday (in April; see the calendar in chapter 3), and O Bon Memorial Services in August.

Continue down Wainee Street; just before the intersection with Prison Street, look for the historical marker for:

20. David Malo's Home. Although no longer standing, the house that once stood here was the home of David Malo, Hawaii's first scholar, philosopher, and well-known author. Educated at Lahainaluna School, his book on ancient Hawaiian culture, *Hawaiian Antiquities,* is considered *the* source on Hawaiiana today. His alma mater celebrates David Malo Day every year in recognition of his contributions to Hawaii.

Cross Prison Street; on the corner of Prison and Waihee is the:

21. Old Prison. The Hawaiians called this Hale Paahao ("stuck in irons house"), due to the shackles that attached prisoners to either a wall or a ball and chain. The need for a prison became apparent when sailors would refuse to return to their boats at sunset. Hawaiian guards would arrest them and take them to the old Fort (see no. 11, above). In 1851, however, the fort physician told the government that sleeping on the ground at night made the prisoners ill, costing the government quite a bit of money to treat them—so the Kingdom of Hawaii used the prisoners to build a prison from the coral block of the old fort. Most prisoners here had terms of a year or less (those with longer terms were shipped off to Honolulu) and were convicted of crimes like deserting ship, drunkenness, working on Sunday, or reckless horseback riding. Today the grounds of the Prison have a much more congenial atmosphere, because they are rented out to community groups for parties.

Continue down Waihee Street, just past Waianae Place, to the:

22. Episcopal Cemetery. This small cemetery tells another story in Hawaii's history. During the reign of King Kamehameha IV, his wife, Queen Emma, formed close ties with the British Royalty. She encouraged Hawaiians to join the Anglican Church after asking the Archbishop of Canterbury to form a church in Hawaii. This cemetery contains the burial sites of many of those early Anglicans.

Next door is:

23. Hale Aloha. This "house of love" was built in 1858 by Hawaiians in "commemoration of God's causing Lahaina to escape the small pox, while it desolated Oahu in 1853, carrying off 5,000 to 6,000 of its population." The building served as a church and school until the turn of the century, when it fell into disrepair.

Turn left on Hale Street and then right on Luakini Street to the:

24. Buddhist Church. This green, wooden Shingon Buddhist temple is very typical of the myriad of Buddhist churches that sprang up all over the island when the Japanese laborers were brought to work in the sugarcane fields. Some of the churches were little more than elaborate false "temple" fronts on existing buildings.

On the side of Village Galleries, on the corner of Luakini and Dickenson streets, is the final historical marker, for:

25. Luakini Street. "Luakini" translates as a heiau or temple where the ruling chiefs prayed and where human sacrifices were held. This street received its unforgettable name after serving as the route for the funeral procession of Princess Harriet Naiehaena, sister of King Kamehameha III. The princess was a victim of the rapid changes in Hawaiian culture. A convert to Protestantism, she had fallen in love with her brother at an early age. Just 20 years earlier, their relationship would have been nurtured in order to preserve the purity of the royal bloodlines. The missionaries, however, frowned on brother and sister marrying. In August 1836, the couple had a son, who only lived a few short hours. Nahienaena never recovered and died in December of that same year (the King was said to mourn her death for years, frequently visiting her grave at the Waihee Cemetery; see no. 18, above). The route of her funeral procession through the breadfruit and koa trees to the cemetery became known as "Luakini," in reference to the gods "sacrificing" the beloved princess.

Turn left on Dickenson and walk down to Front Street, where you'll be back at the starting point.

OLOWALU

Most people drive right by Olowalu, 5 miles down Honoapiilani Highway from Lahaina; there's little to mark the spot but a small general store and Chez Paul, an expensive—but not very good—French restaurant. Olowalu (which translates as "many hills") was the scene of a bloody massacre in 1790. The Hawaiians, fascinated with iron nails and fittings, stole a skiff from the U.S. ship *Eleanora,* took it back to shore here, and burnt it for the iron parts. The captain of the ship, Simon Metcalf, was furious and tricked the Hawaiians into sailing out in their canoes to trade with the ship. As the canoes approached, he mowed them down with his cannons, killing a hundred people and wounding many others.

Olowalu has great snorkeling around the 14-mile marker, where there is a turtle cleaning station about 50 to 75 yards out from shore. Turtles line up here to have cleaner wrasses pick small parasites off.

MAALAEA

At the bend in the Honopiilani Highway (Highway 30), Maalaea Bay runs along the south side of the isthmus between the West Maui Mountains and Haleakala. This is the windiest area on Maui: trade winds blowing between the two mountains are funneled across the isthmus, and by the time they reach Maalaea, gusts of 25 to 30 m.p.h. are not uncommon.

This creates ideal conditions for windsurfers out in Maalaea Bay. Surfers also are seen just outside the small boat harbor in Maalaea, which has one of the fastest breaks in the state.

At the entry to Maalaea, in the 18-acre Maalaea Harbor Village shopping center, is the recently opened ✪ **Maui Ocean Center,** at the triangle between Honoapiilani Highway and Maalaea Road (☎ **808/875-1962;** www.coralworld.com/moc). The 5-acre facility, which opened in early 1998, houses the largest aquarium in the state and features one of Hawaii's largest predators—the tiger shark. As visitors enter the site and walk through some three dozen tanks and countless exhibits, they slowly descend from the "beach" to the deepest part of the ocean, without ever getting wet. The focus of the Maui Ocean Center is regional, meaning that all exhibits are geared toward the residents of Hawaii's ocean waters. Starting at the surge pool, where visitors walk past shallow-water marine life like spiny urchins and cauliflower coral, visitors proceed past the reef tanks, a turtle pool, a "touch" pool (with starfish and sea urchins), and an eagle ray pool, before seeing the main 100-foot-long, 600,000-gallon main tank, featuring tiger, gray, and white tip sharks, as well as tuna, surgeon fish, trigger fish, and numerous other tropical fish. Also on the property are two restaurants, an ocean shop, and a logo store. The center is open daily from 9am to 5pm; admission is $17 for adults, $12 for children ages 3 to 12, and free to children under age 3.

4 The South Maui Resorts

The South Maui resorts aren't about sightseeing; this hot, dry, sunny coast is where you come for fun in the sun. Still, there's a little worthwhile exploring to do.

KIHEI

Kihei, which translates to "shoulder cloak," was renowned for its ocean facilities before the tourists began arriving. In ancient times, the calm waters off this coast were frequented by Hawaiians in fishing canoes or by warriors about to embark on territorial skirmishes. Capt. George Vancouver "discovered" Kihei in 1778, when it was only a collection of fisherman's grass shacks on the hot, dry, dusty coast (hard to believe, eh?). A **totem pole** stands today where he's believed to have landed, across from Aston Maui Lu Resort (575 S. Kihei Rd.). Vancouver sailed on to discover British Columbia, where a great international city and harbor now bear his name.

During World War II, the Territorial Government of Hawaii feared that Kihei, with its sparse population, would be the perfect place for an invasion by the Japanese. You can still see remnants today of eroding pillboxes and rusting tank traps along the beach: a reminder that Hawaii is the United States's westernmost front.

West of the junction of Piilani Highway (Highway 31) and Mokulele Highway (Highway 350) is **Kealia Pond National Wildlife Preserve** (☎ 808/875-1582), a 700-acre U.S. Fish and Wildlife wetland preserve where endangered Hawaiian stilts, coots, and ducks hang out and splash. These ponds work two ways: as bird preserves and as sedimentation basins that keep the coral reefs from silting from runoff. You can take a self-guided tour along a boardwalk dotted with interpretive signs and shade shelters, through sand dunes, and around ponds to Maalaea Harbor. The boardwalk starts at the outlet of Kealia Pond on the ocean side of North Kihei Road (near the 2-mile marker on Piilani Highway). Among the Hawaiian water birds seen here are the black-crowned high heron (*aukuu*), Hawaiian coot (*alae keokeo*), Hawaiian duck (*Koloa maoli*), and Hawaiian stilt (*aeo*). There are also shore birds like sanderling (*hunakai*), Pacific golden plover (*kolea*), ruddy turnstone (*akekeke*), and wandering tattler (*ulili*). From July to December, the hawksbill turtle (*honuea*) comes ashore here to lay her eggs.

If you're interested in going to one of the many beaches along Kihei's 6-mile coast, eating in one of the dozens of restaurants, or taking in some shopping, the South Kihei Road borders the ocean and goes through the heart of town. If you're bypassing Kihei, take the Piilani Highway (Highway 31), which parallels the South Kihei Road, and avoid the hassle of stoplights and traffic.

WAILEA

The dividing line between arid Kihei and artificially green Wailea is distinct. Wailea (which can translate to "the waters of Lea," the goddess of canoe makers, or "joyful waters") once had the same kiawe-strewn, dusty landscape as Kihei until Alexander and Baldwin Inc. (of sugarcane fame) began developing a resort here in the 1970s (after piping water from the other side of the island to the desert terrain of Wailea). Today, the manicured 1,450 acres of this affluent resort stand out like an oasis along the normally dry leeward coast.

The best way to explore this golden resort coast is to rise with the sun and head for Wailea's 1½-mile **coastal nature trail,** stretching between the Kea Lani Hotel and the kiawe thicket just beyond the Renaissance Wailea. It's a great morning walk on Maui, a serpentine path that meanders uphill and down past native plants, old Hawaiian habitats, and a billion dollars worth of luxury hotels. You can pick up the trail at any of the resorts or from clearly marked Shoreline Access points along the coast. The best time to go is when you first wake up; by midmorning, the coastal trail is too often clogged with pushy joggers (somebody should tell them that this is a scenic nature walk, not a fitness loop), and it grows crowded with beachgoers as the day wears on. As the path crosses several bold black lava points, it affords new vistas of islands and ocean; benches allow you to pause and contemplate the view across Alalakeiki Channel, which jumps with whales in season. Sunset is another good time to hit the trail; many come down here to watch the glorious end of yet another perfect day in paradise.

MAKENA

A few miles south of Wailea, the manicured coast turns to wilderness; now you're in Makena (Hawaiian for "abundance").

In the 1800s, **Makena Landing** was the scene of cattle shipping. Cattle were driven down the slope from upland ranches, lashed to rafts, and sent into the water to swim to boats that waited to take them to market. By 1900, interisland shipping had moved to Kahului Harbor—and Makena Landing was left behind. It's now a beach park with boat-launching facilities, showers, toilets, and picnic tables. It's great for snorkeling and for launching kayaks bound for Perouse Bay and Ahihi-Kinau preserve.

From the landing, go south on Makena Road; near the end of the road on the right side, you'll see **Keawali Congregational Church** (☎ **808/879-5557**). Surrounded by ti leaf, which by Hawaiian custom provides protection, and built of 3-foot-thick coral block cut from the reef in 1831, this Protestant church sits on its own cove with a gold-sand beach and always attracts a Sunday crowd for its part-Hawaiian/part-English service at 9:30am. Take some time to wander through the cemetery; you'll see some great examples of the old custom of having a ceramic picture of the deceased on the tombstone.

The road reaches a cul-de-sac at the Maui Prince Hotel; to continue down the coast, backtrack to Alanui Road. The Maui Prince Hotel is the last place to get food or water on this coastline.

Alanui Road ends as Makena Road begins again, on the other side of the Maui Prince Hotel. The first beach you will come to is **Makena Beach,** which in the 1960s and 1970s was an enclave of hippies who had an encampment on the beach. The days of love and peace came to an end in 1972, when the police broke up the squatters and Maui entered a period of unprecedented growth, meaning that future visitors would have to pay for their accommodations and not stay on the beach free. There are actually two beaches here: the Big Beach and, over a barrier of rocks, the Little Beach. For years, Little Beach was known as a clothing-optional, or nude, beach. Be warned: Maui County still has strict laws about "indecent exposure," and periodically the police will arrest nude sunbathers.

After Big Beach, Makena Road is paved for another 2½ miles into the **Ahihi-Kinau Natural Area Reserve,** before ending at **La Perouse Bay.** From Ahihi Bay to Cape Kinau, some 2,045 acres make up the unique marine-life habitat of the Ahiki-Kinau National Area Reserve. This is the site of Maui's most recent lava flow in 1790, which contributed to this distinctive area with features such as anchialine ponds (brackish water ponds) and *kipukas* (areas of land that the lava flowed around, trapping an oasis in the midst of the lava). Since this is an underwater park, the marine life here is spectacular, but remember: do not take anything from the ocean or land. On land, look between the lava at Ahihi Bay for the remains of an ancient Hawaiian village.

Continuing down Makena Road, the paved portion ends just before **La Perouse Bay.** Park here and walk about 10 minutes along the trail, which passes over the lava and alongside the ocean to La Perouse Bay, where French explorer Adm. Jean Francois de Galaup La Perouse set foot on Maui in 1786. At the time, this area had a series of thriving Hawaiian villages. The first Westerner to "discover" the island, he described the "burning climate" of the leeward coast, and noted: "During our excursion we observed four small villages of about ten or twelve houses each, built and covered with straw." From Hawaii, La Perouse sailed on into oblivion, never to be seen again; some believe he might have been eaten by cannibals in what is now New Hebrides. A monument to this explorer—actually, a pyramid of lava rocks that marks the spot where La Perouse came ashore—sits amid a clearing in black lava at the end of the dirt trail.

The rocky coastline and sometimes rough seas contribute to the lack of appeal for water activities here; hiking opportunities, however, are excellent. Prepare in advance, bring plenty of water and sun protection, and wear hiking boots that can withstand walking on lava. From La Perouse Bay, you can pick up the old King's Highway trail, which at one time circled the island. Walk along the sandy beach at La Perouse and look for the trail indentation in the lava, which leads down to the lighthouse at the tip of Cape Hanamanioa, about a three-quarter–mile round-trip. Or you can continue on the trail as it climbs up the hill for 2 miles, then ventures back toward the ocean, where there are quite a few old Hawaiian home foundations and rocky/coral beaches.

5 House of the Sun: Haleakala National Park

At once forbidding and compelling, Haleakala National Park (the "House of the Sun") is Maui's main natural attraction. More than 1.3 million people a year go up the 10,023-foot-high mountain to peer down into the crater of the world's largest dormant volcano. (Haleakala is officially considered to be "active, but not currently erupting," even though it has not rumbled or spewed lava since 1790.) That hole would hold Manhattan: 3,000 feet deep, 7½ miles long by 2½ miles wide, and encompassing 19 square miles, with its own mini-mountain range of nine cinder cones ranging from 600 to 1,000 feet high.

But there's far more to do than simply stare in a big black hole: just going up the mountain is an experience in itself. Where else on the planet can you climb from sea level to 10,000 feet in just 37 miles, or a 2-hour drive, without ever leaving the ground? The snaky road passes through big puffy cumulus clouds to offer magnificent views of the isthmus of Maui, the West Maui Mountains, and the calm blue Pacific Ocean.

The Hawaiians recognized the mountain as a sacred site. Ancient chants tell of Pele, the volcano goddess, and one of her siblings, doing battle on the crater floor where Kawilinau ("Bottomless Pit") now stands. Commoners in ancient Hawaii didn't spend much time here, though. Evidence shows that they might have made forages into the crater to quarry tools from the stone, but they didn't stay long. The only people "allowed" into this sacred area were the kahunas, who took their apprentices into the crater to live for periods of time in this intensely spiritual place. In fact, there are stories about power struggles taking place on Haleakala between the *kahuna lapaau* (medical doctors who practice healing) and their rivals, *kahuna anaana* (sorcerers who practice black magic by praying people to death). Today, New Agers also revere Haleakala as one of the earth's powerful energy points, and even the Air Force has a not-very-well-explained presence here.

Impressions

There are few enough places in the world that belong entirely to themselves. The human passion to carry all things everywhere, so that every place is home, seems well on its way to homogenizing our planet, save for the odd unreachable corner. Haleakala crater is one of those corners.

—Barbara Kingsolver, the *New York Times*

Many drive up to the summit in predawn darkness to watch the sunrise over Haleakala; writer Mark Twain called it "the sublimest spectacle" of his life. Others take a trail ride inside the bleak lunar landscape of the wilderness inside the crater (see "Horseback Riding," page 183), or coast down the 37-mile road from the summit on a bicycle with special brakes (see "Bicycling," page 182). Hardy adventurers hike and camp inside the crater's wilderness (see "Hiking & Camping," page 172). Those bound for the interior bring their survival gear, because the terrain is raw, rugged, and punishing—not unlike the moon. However you choose to experience Haleakala National Park, it will prove memorable—guaranteed.

JUST THE FACTS

Haleakala National Park is composed of some 27,468 acres and extends from the Hosmer Grove, just below the summit of Mount Haleakala, across the summit, into the crater, down the volcano's southeast flank to Maui's eastern coast, beyond Hana, and ends at the ocean. Within the park's boundaries, there's an unimaginably dramatic range of geological terrain: both rain and dry forests, desert and subtropical beaches. There are actually two separate and distinct destinations within the park: **Haleakala Summit** and the **Kipahulu** coast (See "Just Beyond Hana," page 229). The Summit gets all the publicity, but Kipahulu draws crowds, too—it's lush, green, and tropical, and home to Oheo Gulch, which was misnamed Seven Sacred Pools in the 1940s and hasn't been able to lose the misnomer ever since. No road links the summit and the coast; you must approach each separately, and you need at least a day to see each place.

WHEN TO GO   At the 10,023-foot summit, weather changes fast. Temperatures with wind chill can be below freezing any time of year. Summer can be dry and warm, winters wet, windy, and cold. Before you go, call the park for current weather conditions (☎ 808/572-9306), or the **National Weather Service** (☎ **808/ 871-5054**) for a recorded forecast.

From sunrise to noon the light is weak, but the view is usually free of clouds. The best time for photos is in the afternoon, when the sun lights the crater and clouds are few. Go on full-moon nights for spectacular viewing.

ACCESS POINTS   **Haleakala Summit** is 37 miles, or about a 2-hour drive, from Kahului. To get there, take Highway 37 to Highway 377 to Highway 378. For details on the drive, see "The Drive to the Summit," below. Pukalani is the last town for water, food, and gas.

Kipahulu, on Maui's east end near Hana, is 60 miles from Kahului on Highway 36 (the Hana Highway). Due to traffic and rough road conditions, plan on 4 hours for the drive, one-way. (see "Driving the Road to Hana," below). Hana (see below) is the only nearby town for services, water, gas, food, and overnight lodging; some facilities might not be open after dark.

INFORMATION, VISITOR CENTERS & RANGER PROGRAMS   For information before you go, contact Haleakala National Park, Box 369, Makawao, HI 96768 (☎ 808/572-9306).

Haleakala National Park Headquarters (☎ 808/572-9306) is located 1 mile from the park entrance, at 7,000 feet; it's open daily from 7am to 4pm. Here you can pick up information on park programs and activities, get camping permits, and, occasionally, see a Hawaiian nene—one or more are often here to greet visitors. Rest rooms, a pay phone, and drinking water are available.

Rangers also offer excellent, informative, and free **naturalist talks** at 9:30, 10:30, and 11:30am daily in the Summit Building.

Haleakala National Park

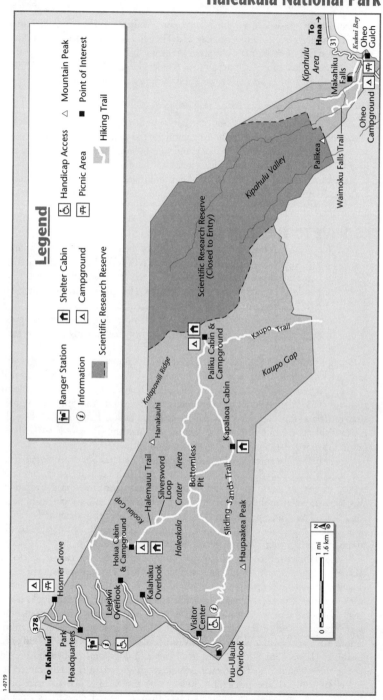

Free 3-hour guided hikes are offered into **Waikamoi Preserve.** The hikes leave from Hosmer Grove on Monday and Thursday at 9am and take you into a cloud forest full of native plants, birds, and insects that live nowhere else on earth. Park rangers also offer 2-hour guided Cinder Desert Hikes on the Sliding Sands Trail on Tuesday and Friday at 10am. Wear sturdy shoes and carry rain gear and water.

Haleakala Visitor Center, open daily from sunrise to 3pm, is near the summit of Mount Haleakala, 11 miles from the park entrance. It offers a panoramic view of the volcanic landscape, with photos identifying the various features, and exhibits that explain its history, ecology, geology, and volcanology. Park staff are often handy to answer questions. The only facilities are rest rooms and water.

Haleakala National Park offers a number of **hiking and camping** possibilities in both the Summit and Kipahulu districts, including cabins and campgrounds in the wilderness itself. See "Hiking & Camping," in chapter 8, for details.

THE DRIVE TO THE SUMMIT

If you look on a Maui map almost in the middle of the part that resembles a torso, there's a black wiggly line that looks like this: WWWWW. That's **Highway 378,** also known as **Haleakala Crater Road**—one of the few roads in the world that climb from sea level to 10,000 feet in just 37 miles. This grand corniche, which has at least 33 switchbacks, passes through numerous climate zones; goes under, in, and out of clouds; takes you past rare silversword plants and endangered Hawaiian geese sailing through the clear, thin air; and offers a view that extends for more than 100 miles.

Going to the summit takes about 2 hours from Kahului. No matter where you start out, you'll follow Highway 37 (Haleakala Highway) to Pukalani, where you'll pick up Highway 377 (which is also Haleakala Highway), which you'll take to Highway 378. Along the way, expect fog, rain, and wind. You might encounter stray cattle and downhill bicyclists. Fill up your gas tank before you go—the only gas available is 27 miles below the summit at Pukalani. There are no facilities beyond the ranger stations. Bring your own food and water.

Remember, you're entering a high-altitude wilderness area. Some people get dizzy due to the lack of oxygen; you might also suffer lightheadedness, shortness of breath, nausea, or worse: severe headaches, increased flatulence, and dehydration. People with asthma, pregnant women, heavy smokers, and people with heart conditions should be especially careful in the rarefied air. Bring water and a jacket or a blanket, especially if you go up for sunrise. You might want to go up to the summit for sunset, but it's less spectacular and sometimes cloudy.

At the **park entrance,** you'll pay an entrance fee of $4 per car (or $2 for a bicycle). About a mile from the entrance is **Park Headquarters,** where an endangered **nene,** or Hawaiian goose, might greet you with its unique call. With a black face, buff cheeks, and partially webbed feet, the gray-brown bird looks like a small Canada goose with zebra stripes; it brays out "nay-nay" (thus its name), doesn't migrate, and prefers lava beds to lakes. The unusual goose clings to a pre-carious existence on these alpine slopes. Vast populations of more than 25,000 once inhabited Hawaii, but hunters, pigs, feral cats and dogs, and mongooses preyed on the nene; coupled with habitat destruction, these predators nearly caused its extinction. By 1951, there were only 30 left. Now protected as Hawaii's state bird, the wild nene on Haleakala numbers fewer than 250—and the species remains endangered.

The Legend of the House of the Sun

According to ancient legend, Haleakala got its name from a very clever trick that the demigod Maui pulled on the sun. Maui's mother, the goddess Hina, complained one day that the sun sped across the sky so quickly that her tapa cloth couldn't dry.

Maui, known as a trickster, devised a plan. The next morning, he went to the top of the great mountain and waited for the sun to poke its head above the horizon. Quickly, Maui lassoed the sun, bringing its path across the sky to an abrupt halt.

The sun begged Maui to let go, and Maui said he would on one condition: that the sun slow its trip across the sky to give the island more sunlight. The sun assented. In honor of this agreement, the Hawaiians call the mountain Haleakala, or "House of the Sun."

To this day, the top of Haleakala has about 15 minutes more sunlight than the communities on the coastline below.

Beyond headquarters, two scenic overlooks on the way to the summit are worth a stop, if only to get out, stretch, and get accustomed to the heights. Stop at Leleiwi on the way up, and Kalahaku on the way back down. Take a deep breath, look around, and pop your ears. If you feel dizzy or drowsy, or get a sudden headache, consider turning around and going back down.

Leleiwi Overlook is just beyond mile marker 17. From the parking area, a short trail leads you to a panoramic view of the lunar-like crater. When the clouds are low and the sun is in the right place, usually around sunset, you can experience a phenomenon known as the "Specter of the Brocken"—you can see a reflection of your shadow, ringed by a rainbow, in the clouds below. It's an optical illusion caused by a rare combination of sun, shadow, and fog that occurs in only three places on the planet: Haleakala, Scotland, and Germany.

Two miles farther along is **Kalahaku Overlook,** the best place to see a rare **silversword.** You can turn into this overlook only when you are descending from the top. The silversword is the punker of the plant world, its silvery bayonets displaying tiny purple bouquets—like a spacey artichoke with an attitude. This botanical wonder proved irresistible to humans, who gathered them in gunnysacks for Chinese potions, for British specimen collections, and just for the sheer thrill of having something so rare. Silverswords grow only in Hawaii, take from 4 to 50 years to bloom, and then, usually between May and October, send up a 1- to 6-foot stalk with a purple bouquet of sunflower-like blooms. They're now very rare, so don't even think about taking one home.

Continue on, and you'll quickly reach **Haleakala Visitor Center,** which offers spectacular views. You'll feel as if you're at the edge of the earth. But don't turn around here; the actual summit's a little farther on, at **Puu Ulaula Overlook** (also known as Red Hill), the volcano's highest point, where you'll find a mysterious cluster of buildings officially known as Haleakala Observatories, but unofficially called **Science City.** If you do go up for sunrise, the building at **Puu Ulaula Overlook,** a triangle of glass that serves as a wind break, is the best viewing spot. After the daily miracle of sunrise—the sun seems to rise out of the vast crater (hence the nickname, "the House of the Sun")—you can see all the way across Alenuihaha Channel to the often snowcapped summit of Mauna Kea on the Big Island.

MAKING YOUR DESCENT   Put your car in low gear; that way, you won't suddenly see smoke coming from your brakes, and you won't destroy your brakes by riding them the whole way down.

6 More in Upcountry Maui

Come upcountry and discover a different side of Maui: on the slopes of Haleakala, cowboys, planters, and other country people make their homes in serene, neighborly communities like Makawao and Kula, a world away from the bustling beach resorts. Even if you can't spare a day or two in the cool upcountry air, there are some sights that are worth a look on your way to or from the crater. Shoppers and gallery hoppers might really want to make the effort; see chapter 10 for details.

On the slopes of Haleakala, Maui's breadbasket has been producing vegetables since the 1800s. In fact, during the gold rush in California, the Hawaiian farmers in Kula shipped so many potatoes that it was nicked named Nu Kaleponi, a sort of pidgin Hawaiian pronunciation of "New California." At the end of the 1800s, Portuguese and Chinese immigrants, who had fulfilled their labor contracts with the sugarcane companies, moved to this area, drawn ·by the rural agricultural lifestyle. That lifestyle continues today, among the fancy gentlemen's farms that have sprung up in the past two decades. Kula continues to be a breadbasket, growing the well-known onions, lettuce, tomatoes, carrots, cauliflower, and cabbage. It is also a major source of cut flowers for the state: most of Hawaii's proteas come from Kula, and nearly all the carnations used in leis are from here.

To experience a bit of the history of Kula, turn off the Kula Highway (Highway 37) onto Lower Kula Road. Well before the turnoff, you'll see a white octagonal building with a silver roof, the **Holy Ghost Catholic Church.** Hawaii's only eight-sided church, it was built between 1884 and 1897 by Portuguese immigrants, who began arriving in Hawaii in the 1870s. The church resembles something out of Portugal; it's worth a stop to see the hand-carved altar and works of art for the stations of the cross, with inscriptions in Portuguese. For information on mass, call ☎ **808/878-1091.**

To experience some of the floral beauty in this area, continue down the Kula Highway (Highway 37) about seven-tenths of a mile, to the intersection of Highway 377 and the **Kula Botanical Garden** (☎ **808/878-1715**). Here you can take a self-guided, informative, leisurely stroll through more than 700 native and exotic plants. The 5-acre garden offers a good overview of Hawaii's exotic flora in one small, cool place with three unique collections of orchids, proteas, and bromeliads. It's open daily from 9am to 4pm; admission is $4 for adults, $1 for children ages 6 to 12.

Continuing on the Kula Highway (Highway 37), on the southern shoulder of Haleakala, you'll enter cattle country. The road narrows after the tiny village of Keokea, and you'll see some of the 6,000 cattle, 600 merino sheep, and 150 Rocky Mountain elk on the **Ulupalakua Ranch,** a 25,000-acre spread once owned by legendary sea captain James Makee, celebrated in the Hawaiian song and dance *Hula O Makee.* Wounded in a Honolulu waterfront brawl in 1843, Captain Makee moved to Maui and bought Ulupalakua. He renamed it Rose Ranch and planted sugar as a cash crop. He grew rich and toasted life until his death in 1879. Still in operation, the ranch (now owned by Pardee Erdman) is home to **Tedeschi Vineyards and Winery,** P.O. Box 953, Ulupalakua, HI 96790 (☎ **808/ 878-6058**). It was established in 1974 by Napa vintner Emil Tedeschi, who began growing California and European grapes here and producing serious still and sparkling wines, plus a silly wine made of pineapple juice. The rustic grounds of Maui's only winery are the perfect place for a picnic. Pack a basket before you go, but don't BYOB: there's plenty of great wine to enjoy at Tedeschi's free wine tasting. Spread your picnic lunch under the sprawling camphor tree, pop the cork on a Blanc du Blanc, and toast your good fortune in being here. Winery tours are offered daily from 9am to 5pm.

Across from the winery are the remains of the three smokestacks of the **Makee Sugar Mill,** built in 1878. This is home to Maui artist Reems Mitchell, who carved the mannequins on the front porch of the Ulupakalua Ranch Store: a Filipino with his fighting cock, a cowboy, a farmhand, and a sea captain, all representing the people of Maui's history.

7 Driving the Road to Hana

Top down, sunscreen on, radio tuned to a little Hawaiian music on a Maui morning: it's time to head out to Hana along the Hana Highway (Highway 36), a wiggle of a road that runs along Maui's northeastern shore. The drive takes at least 3 hours—but take all day. Going to Hana is about the journey, not the destination. If you race along the scenic road to get to the village of Hana or to the Oheo Gulch (Seven Pools) beyond Hana, you'll be disappointed. You'll wonder what all the fuss is about. The "fuss" is the adventure into a wild place, where Mother Nature still reigns and man is but a speck in the continuous march of time.

There are wilder roads and steeper roads and even more dangerous roads, but in all of Hawaii no road is more celebrated than this one. It winds for 50 miles past taro patches, magnificent seascapes, waterfall pools, botanical gardens, and verdant rain forests, and it ends at one of Hawaii's most beautiful tropical places.

The outside world discovered the little village of Hana in 1926 and 1927, when the narrow coastal road, carved by pick-ax–wielding convicts, opened with 56 bridges and 600 hairpin switchbacks. The mud and gravel road, often subject to landslides and washouts, was paved in 1962, when tourist traffic began to increase; it now exceeds 1,000 cars and dozens of vans a day, according to storekeeper Harry Hasegawa. That equals about 500,000 people a year on this road, which is way too many. Go at the wrong time, and you'll be stuck in a bumper-to-bumper rental-car parade—peak traffic hours are midmorning and midafternoon year-round, especially on weekends.

In the rush to "do" Hana in a day, most visitors spin around town in 10 minutes flat and shake their heads at the seemingly innocuous village. It takes time to take in Hana (like a week or two), play in the waterfalls, sniff the tropical flowers, hike to bamboo forests, and take in the spectacular scenery (see "The End of the Road: Heavenly Hana," below).

However, if you really must "do" the Hana Highway in a day, go just before sunrise and return after sunset: on a full-moon night, you'll believe in magic when you see the sea and the waterfalls glowing in soft white light, with mysterious shadows appearing in the jungle. And you'll have the road almost to yourself on the way back. Better yet, spend the night in a B&B, or pitch a tent at Oheo Gulch in Kipahulu (see chapter 6 for B&B listings, or "Hiking & Camping," in chapter 8), and come home, with a smile, in a day or two.

AKAMAI TIPS   Forget your mainland road manners. Practice aloha, give way at the one-lane bridges, wave at oncoming motorists, let the big guys in four-by-fours with pig-hunting dogs in the back have the right-of-way—it's just common sense,

Hana Highway

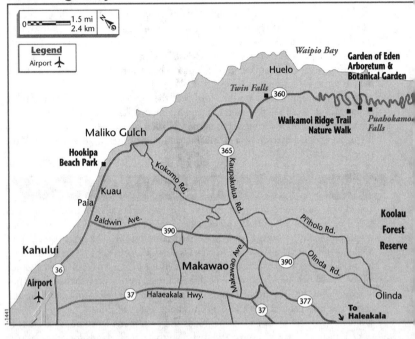

brah. If the guy behind you blinks his lights, let him pass. Oh, yeah, and don't honk your horn—in Hawaii, it's considered rude.

THE JOURNEY BEGINS IN PAIA   Before you even start out, fill up your gas tank. Gas in Paia is mucho expensive ($2-plus a gallon), and it's the last place for gas until you get to Hana, some 42 miles, 54 bridges, and 600 hairpin turns down the road.

The former plantation village of Paia was once a thriving sugar mill town; in the 1930s, its population of 10,000 people lived in the six subdivisions (called "camps") around the town. The mill is still there, but the population shifted to Kahului in the 1950s when subdivisions opened there, leaving Paia to shrivel up and die. But the town refused to give up, and it has proven its ability to adapt to the times. Now chic eateries and trendy shops stand next door to the ma-and-pa establishments that have been serving generations of Paia customers.

Plan to be in Paia early, around 7am, when **Charley's,** 142 Hana Hwy. (☎ **808/579-9453**), opens. Enjoy a big, hearty breakfast for a reasonable price. After your meal, head up Baldwin Avenue; about a half a block from the intersection of the Hana Highway and Baldwin Avenue, go to **Pic-nics,** 30 Baldwin Ave. (☎ **808/579-8021**), to stock up for a picnic lunch for the road (see chapter 7).

As you leave Paia, on your right you'll see acres of sugarcane fields, the crop that kept Maui alive for more than a century. Just before the bend in the road, you'll pass the Kuau Mart on your left; a small general store, it's the only reminder of the once-thriving community of **Kuau.** The road then bends into an S-turn; in the middle of the S is the entrance to **Mama's Fish House,** depicted by a restored 1935 panel truck with Mama's logo on the side. Just past the truck on the ocean side is the entrance to Mama's parking lot and adjacent small sandy cove in front of

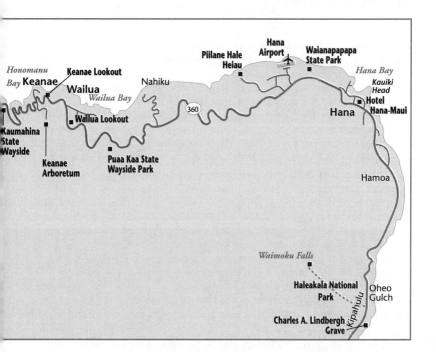

the restaurant. Mainly surfers use this treacherous ocean access over very slippery rocks into strong surf, but the beach is a great place to sit and soak up some sun.

WINDSURFING MECCA A mile from Mama's, just before mile marker 9, is a place known around the world as one of the greatest windsurfing spots on the planet, **Hookipa Beach Park.** Hoopika lives up to its Hawaiian name, which translates to "hospitality," as the site where the world's top-ranked windsurfers come to test themselves against the forces of nature: thunderous surf and forceful wind. World championship contests are held here (see "Maui Calendar of Events" in chapter 3), but on nearly every windy day after noon (the board surfers have the waves in the morning), you can watch dozens of windsurfers twirling and dancing in the wind like colored butterflies. To watch the windsurfers, do not stop on the highway, but go past the park and turn left at the entrance on the far side of the beach. You can either park on the high grassy bluff or drive down to the sandy beach and park alongside the pavilion. The park also has rest rooms, a shower, picnic tables, and a barbecue area.

INTO THE COUNTRY Past Hookipa Beach, the road winds down into a **Maliko** ("Budding") **Gulch** at mile marker 10. At the bottom of the gulch, look for the road on your right, which will take you out to **Maliko Bay.** Take the first right turn, which will take you under the bridge and past a rodeo arena (scene of competitions by the Maliko Roping Club in the summer) and on to the rocky beach. There are no facilities here except a boat-launch ramp. In the 1940s, Maliko had a thriving community at the mouth of the bay, but its residents rebuilt farther inland after a strong tidal wave wiped it out.

Back on the Hana Highway, as you leave Maliko Gulch, you'll see acres of pineapple fields on your right around mile marker 11. Don't be tempted to stop and pick pineapples, because they're the private property of Maui Land and Pineapple Co.; picking is considered stealing. For the next few miles, you'll pass through the rural area of Haiku, with banana patches; glimpses of farms; cane grass blowing in the wind; and forests of guava trees, avocados, kukui trees, palms, and Christmas berry. Just before mile marker 15 is the **Maui Grown Market and Deli** (☎ **808/572-1693**), a good stop for drinks or snacks for the ride.

At mile marker 16, the curves begin, one right after another. Slow down and enjoy the view of bucolic rolling hills, fruiting mango trees, and vibrant ferns. After the 16-mile marker, the road is still called the Hana Highway; but the number changes from Highway 36 to Highway 360, and the mile markers go back to 0.

A GREAT PLUNGE ALONG THE WAY   A dip in a waterfall pool is everybody's tropical island fantasy. The first great place to stop is **Twin Falls,** at mile marker 2. Just before the wide, concrete bridge, pull over on the mountain side and park (but not in front of the sign that says DO NOT BLOCK DRIVEWAY). Keep in mind that there have been thefts in this area, and remember that a good thief can get into your locked trunk faster than you can with your key.

Hop over the ladder on the right side of the red gate and walk about 3 to 5 minutes to the waterfall and pool off to your left, or continue on another 10 to 15 minutes to the second, larger waterfall and pool (do not go in if it has been raining recently). What a way to start the trip to Hana.

HIDDEN HEULO   Just before mile marker 4 on a blind curve, look for a double row of mailboxes overseen by a fading HAWAII VISITORS BUREAU sign. Down the road lies a hidden Hawaii: a Hawaii of an earlier time, where ocean waves pummel soaring lava cliffs and where an indescribable sense of serenity prevails.

Protruding out of Maui's tumultuous northern coastline, hemmed in by Waipo and Hoalua Bays, is the remote, rural community of **Huelo.** Once, this fertile area supported a population of 75,000; today, only a few hundred live among the scattered homes on this windswept land, where a handful of bed-and-breakfast oases and exquisite vacation rentals are known only to a select few travelers (see chapter 6).

The only reason Huelo even has a Hawaii Visitors Bureau marker (albeit one faded to a dull pink) is the historic 1853 **Kaulanapueo Church,** which sits in the center of a putting-green–perfect lawn, bordered with hog wire fence and accessible through a squeaky, metal turnstile. Reminiscent of New England architecture, this coral-and-cement church, topped with a plantation-green steeple and a cloudy gray tin roof, is still in use, although services are held just once or twice a month. It still has the same austere, stark interior of 1853: straight-backed benches, a no-nonsense platform for the minister, and no distractions on the walls to tempt you from paying attention to the sermon.

Next to the church is a small graveyard, a personal history of this village in concrete and stone. The graves, facing the setting sun and bleached white over the decades, are the community's garden of memories, each well-tended and oft-visited.

KOOLAU FOREST RESERVE   After Huelo, the vegetation seems lusher, as though Mother Nature had poured Miracle Grow on everything. This is the edge of the **Koolau Forest Reserve.** Koolau means "windward," and this certainly is one of the greatest examples of a lush windward area: the coastline here gets about 60 to 80 inches of rain a year, and farther up the mountain, the rainfall is from 200 to 300 inches a year.

Here you will see 20- to 30-foot-tall guava trees, their branches laden with green (not ripe) and yellow (ripe) fruit. The skin is peeled and the fruit inside of the guava eaten raw, squeezed for juice, or cooked for jams or jellies. Also in this prolific area are mangos, java plums, and avocados the size of softballs. The spiny, long-leafed plants you see are hala trees, which the Hawaiians used for roofing material and for weaving baskets, mats, and even canoe sails.

The very tall trees, up to 200 feet tall, are eucalyptus, brought to Hawaii from Australia to supply the sugarcane mills with power for the wood-burning engines. Unfortunately, in the nearly 100 years since the fast-growing tree was first introduced, it has quickly taken over Hawaiian forests, forcing out native plants and trees.

The 200 to 300 inches of rainfall up the mountain means a waterfall (and one-lane bridge) around nearly every turn in the road from here on out, so drive slowly and be prepared to stop and yield to oncoming cars.

WAILUA   Between mile markers 5 and 6, the tiny village of **Wailua** appears on your left. This is company headquarters for EMI, **East Maui Irrigation Company,** which supplies water from the rain forests of East Maui to the dry sugarcane fields in the central plains. Most of the people who live here work for EMI, maintaining the 75 miles of ditches and tunnels that carry the water from one side of the island to the other. The system, which was built 100 years ago, is still in operation, carrying some 450 million gallons of water a day.

DANGEROUS CURVES   About half a mile after mile marker 6, there's a sharp U-curve in the road, going uphill. The road is practically one-lane here, with a brick wall on one side and virtually no maneuvering room. Sound your horn at the start of the U-curve to let approaching cars know you are coming. Take this curve, as well as the few more coming up in the next several miles, very slowly.

Just before mile marker 7 is a forest of waving bamboo. The sight is so spectacular that drivers are often tempted to take their eyes off the road. Be very cautious. Wait until just after mile marker 7, at the **Kaaiea** ("breathtaking") **Bridge** and stream below, to pull over and take a closer look at the hand-hewn stone walls. Then turn around to see the vista of bamboo, a photo opportunity that will certainly "take your breath away."

A GREAT FAMILY HIKE   At mile marker 9, there is a small state wayside area with rest rooms, a pavilion, picnic tables, and a barbecue area. The sign says **Koolau State Forest Reserve,** but the real attraction here is the **Waikamoi Ridge Trail,** an easy three-quarter–mile loop that the entire family can do. The start of the trail is just behind the QUIET TREES AT WORK sign. The well-marked trail meanders through eucalyptus (including the unusual paper bark eucalyptus), ferns, and hala trees.

THE GARDEN OF EDEN   Just past mile marker 10 is the **Garden of Eden Arboretum and Botanical Garden** (☎ 808/572-6453), some 26 acres of nature trails, picnic areas, and more than 500 exotic plants and trees from around the Pacific (wild ginger, an assortment of ti plants, and an impressive palm collection). The Garden of Eden is the dream of arborist/landscape designer Alan Bradbury, who wanted to help restore a natural ecosystem and promote Hawaii's native and indigenous species. He and his staff have been nurturing plants since 1991. This place might look familiar—it's in the opening sequence of the film *Jurassic Park.* It's open daily from 9am to 2pm; admission is $3 per person.

MORE GREAT PLUNGES   Another great waterfall is **Puohokamoa Falls,** a 30-foot falls that spills into an idyllic pool in a fern-filled amphitheater. Naturalist Ken Schmidt says that its name, loosely translated, means "valley of the chickens bursting into flight"—which is what hot, sweaty hikers look like as they take the plunge.

Park at the bridge at mile marker 11 and take the short walk up the trail, which is lined with stone walls. The spectacular waterfall and deep swimming pool are surrounded by banana trees, colorful heliconias, and sweet-smelling ginger. Bring mosquito repellent. There's a picnic table at the pool.

Back at your car, be sure to check out the view toward the ocean from the bridge: dozens of kinds of heliconias blanket the valley below.

CAN'T-MISS PHOTO OPPORTUNITIES   Just past mile marker 12 is the **Kaumahina** ("moonrise") **State Wayside Park.** Not only is this a good pit stop (rest rooms are available here) and a wonderful place for a picnic under the tall eucalyptus trees (with tables and barbecue area), but it's also a great vista point. The view of the rugged coastline makes an excellent photo—you can see all the way down to the jutting Keanae Peninsula. Just past the park on the ocean side, there's another scenic turnoff (be careful crossing the oncoming traffic) and great photo opportunity.

Another mile and a couple of bends in the road and you'll enter the Honomanu Valley ("valley of the bird"), with its beautiful bay. To get down to the **Honomanu Bay County Beach Park,** look for the turnoff on your left, just after mile marker 14, as you begin your ascent up the other side of the valley. The rutted dirt and cinder road takes you down to the rocky black-sand beach. There are no facilities here, except for a stone fire pit someone has made in the sand. This is a popular site among surfers and net fishermen. There are strong rip currents offshore, so swimming is best in the stream inland from the ocean. You'll consider the drive down worthwhile as you stand on the beach, well away from the ocean, and turn to look back on the steep cliffs covered with vegetation.

THE ROAD DILEMMA   Back on the Hana Highway, you'll notice that the already narrow road grows even more narrow. Years of erosion on the 1927 highway are finally taking their toll: the ocean side of this carved road is literally falling into the ocean. The community now faces a daunting question: how to fix it? Close the Hana Highway for the several months it would take to shore up the road for the necessary repairs, or keep the road open and work on it during off-peak hours (with long, long delays to traffic), or work at night (which would be a very pricey solution for the state of Hawaii and its taxpayers)? The debate continues.

HAWAII'S BOTANICAL WORLD   Farther along the winding road, between mile markers 16 and 17, is a cluster of bunkhouses composing the YMCA Camp Keanae. A quarter-mile down lies the **Keanae Arboretum,** where the region's botany is divided into three parts: native forest; introduced forest; and traditional Hawaiian plants, food, and medicine. You can swim in the pools of Piinaau Stream, or press on along a mile-long trail into Keanae Valley, where a lovely tropical rain forest waits at the end (see "Hiking & Camping," in chapter 8).

KEANAE PENINSULA   The old Hawaiian village of **Keanae** stands out against the Pacific like a place time forgot. Here, on an old lava flow graced by an 1860 stone church and swaying palms, is one of the last coastal enclaves of native Hawaiians. They still grow taro in patches and pound it into poi, the staple of the old Hawaiian diet; they still pluck *opihi* (shellfish) from tide pools along the jagged coast and cast throw-nets at schools of fish.

The turnoff to the Keanae Peninsula is on the left, just after the Arboretum. The road passes by farms, taro patches, and banana bunches as it hugs the peninsula.

Where the road bends, there's a small beach where fishermen gather to catch dinner. A quarter-mile farther is the **Kaenae Congregational Church** (☎ **808/ 248-8040**), built in 1860 of lava rocks and coral mortar, standing out in stark contrast to the green fields surrounding it. Beside the church is a small beach-front park, with false kamani trees against a backdrop of black lava and a roiling turquoise sea.

For an experience in an untouched Hawaii, follow the road until it ends. Park by the white fence and take the short, 5-minute walk along the shoreline over the black lava. Continue along the footpath through the tall California grass to the black rocky beach, separating the freshwater stream, **Pinaau,** which winds back into the Keanae Peninsula, nearly cutting it off from the rest of Maui. This is an excellent place for a picnic and a swim in the cool waters of the stream. There are no facilities here, so be sure you leave no evidence that you were here (carry every-thing out with you and use rest room facilities before you arrive). As you make your way back, notice the white PVC pipes sticking out of the rocks—they're fishing-pole holders for fishermen, usually hoping to catch ulua.

ANOTHER PHOTO OP: KEANAE LOOKOUT   Just past mile marker 17 is a wide spot on the ocean side of the road, where you can see the entire Keanae Penin-sula's checkerboard pattern of green taro fields and its ocean boundary etched in black lava. Keanae was the result of a postscript eruption of Haleakala, which flowed through the Koolau Gap and down Keanae Valley and added this geological punctuation to the rugged coastline.

FRUIT & FLOWER STANDS   Around mile marker 18, the road widens; you'll start to see numerous small stands advertising fruit or flowers for sale. Many of these stands work on the honor system: you leave your money in the basket and select your purchase. We recommend you stop at **Uncle Harry's,** which you'll find just after the Keanae School around mile marker 18. Harry Kunihi Mitchell was a legend in his time. The native Hawaiian, who was an expert in Hawaiian native plants and herbs, devoted his life to the Hawaiian-rights and nuclear-free move-ments. Mitchell's family sells a variety of fruit and juices at this small stand, open Monday through Saturday from 9am to 4pm (see chapter 10).

WAILUA   Just after Uncle Harry's, look for the Wailua Road off on the left. This will take you through the hamlet of homes and churches of Wailua, which also contains a shrine depicting what the community calls a "miracle." Behind the pink **St. Gabriel's Church** is the smaller blue-and-white **Coral Miracle Church,** home of the **Our Lady of Fatima Shrine.** According to the story, in 1860, the men of this village were building a church by diving for coral to make the stone. But the coral offshore was in deep water and the men could only come up with a few pieces at a time, making the construction of the church an arduous project. A freak storm hit the area and deposited the coral from the deep on a nearby beach. The Hawaiians gathered what they needed and completed the church. This would make a nice enough miracle story, but there's more—after the church was completed, another freak storm hit the area and swept all the remaining coral on the beach back out to sea.

If you look back at Haleakala from here, on your left you can see the spectacular, near-vertical **Waikani Falls.** On the remainder of the dead-end road is an eclectic collection of old and modern homes. Turning around at the road's end is very difficult, so we suggest you just turn around at the church and head back for the Hana Highway.

Back on the Hana Highway, just before mile marker 19, is the **Wailua Valley State Wayside Park** on the right side of the road. For a photo opportunity, climb up the stairs for a view of the Keanae Valley, waterfalls, and Wailua Peninsula. On a really clear day, you can see up the mountain to the Koolau Gap.

For a better view of the Wailua Peninsula, continue down the road about a quarter-mile; on the ocean side, there will be a pull-off area with parking.

PUAA KAA STATE WAYSIDE PARK   You'll hear this park long before you see it, about halfway between mile markers 22 and 23. The sound of waterfalls provides the background music for this small park area with rest rooms, a phone, and a picnic area. There's a well-marked path to the falls and to a swimming hole. Ginger plants are everywhere: pick some flowers and put them in your car so that you can travel with that sweet smell.

OLD NAHIKU   Just after mile marker 25 is a narrow 3-mile road leading from the highway, at about 1,000 feet elevation, down to sea level—and to the remains of the old Hawaiian community of **Nahiku** (which means "seven," referring to the constellation of the Big Dipper). At one time, this was a thriving Hawaiian community of thousands; today, the population has dwindled to fewer than a hundred—including a few Hawaiian families, but mostly extremely wealthy mainland residents who jet in for a few weeks at a time to their luxurious vacation homes. (The most prominent part-time resident is former Beatle George Harrison.) At the turn of the century, this site saw brief commercial activity as home of the Nahiku Rubber Company, the only commercial rubber plantation in the United States. You can still see rubber trees along the Nahiku Road. However, growing a few rubber trees as ornamentals and growing them as a commercial endeavor turned out to be two different things. The amount of rainfall, coupled with the damp conditions, could not support the commercial crop; the plantation closed in 1912, and Nahiku was forgotten until the 1980s, when multimillionaires "discovered" the remote and stunningly beautiful area.

At the end of the road, you can see the remains of the old wharf from the rubber plantation days. Local residents come down here to shoreline fish; there's a small picnic area off to the side. Dolphins are frequently seen in the bay here.

STRETCH YOUR LEGS   Just before mile marker 31, on the right side of the road, is **The Café at Hana Gardenland** (☎ **808/248-8975**), a great place to stop for a bite to eat (see chapter 7) and to stretch your legs while you take a look at the plants, flowers, and local artwork for sale.

HANA AIRPORT   After mile marker 31, a small sign points to the **Hana Airport,** down Alalele Road on the left. **Island Air** (☎ **800/323-3345** from the mainland, **800/652-6541** from Hawaii) has two flights a day to Kahului with connections to other islands. Newly formed commuter airline **Pacific Wings** (☎ **888/575-4546**), flying 8-passenger, twin-engine Cessna planes, offers three flights daily to and from Hana, with connecting flights from Kahului as well. There is no public transportation in Hana. Car rentals are available through **Dollar Rent A Car** (☎ **800/800-4000** or 808/248-8237).

WAIANAPANAPA STATE PARK   A half-mile down the Hana Highway from the turnoff to the airport, at mile marker 32, is the turnoff to this 122-acre park. Shiny black-sand Waianapanapa Beach appears like a vivid dream, with bright-green jungle foliage on three sides and cobalt blue water lapping at its feet. Waiana-panapa is Hawaiian for "glistening water," which you can see for yourself on a day trip to this great beach on the outskirts of Hana. The oceanside park on an ancient aa lava flow includes sea cliffs, lava tubes, arches, and the black-sand beach, plus 12 cabins, tent camping, picnic pavilions, rest rooms, showers, drinking water, and hiking trails. For information, contact the **Department of Land and Natural Resources,** 54 S. High St., Rm. #101, Wailuku, HI 96793 (☎ **808/984-8109;** fax 808/989-8111). Also see "Beaches" and "Hiking & Camping," in chapter 8.

8 The End of the Road: Heavenly Hana

Hana is Paradise on Earth—or just about as close as you can get to it, anyway. In and around Hana, you'll find a lush tropical rain forest dotted with cascading waterfalls and sparkling blue pools, skirted by red- and black-sand beaches. This is probably what you came to Maui looking for.

But Hana is even more than a destination—it's a memory, a state of mind, one of those magical escapes from the humdrum world that occupy your daydreams.

Beautiful Hana enjoys more than 90 inches of rain a year—more than enough to keep the scenery lush. Banyans, bamboo, breadfruit trees—everything seems larger than life in this small town, especially the flowers, such as wild ginger and plumeria. Several roadside stands offer exotic blooms for $1 a bunch. Just "put money in box." It's the Hana honor system.

HANA'S HISTORY

The Hana coast is rich in Hawaiian history and the scene of many turning points in Hawaiian culture. The ancient chants tell of a ruler's pride and arrogance destroying a community—a pointed reference to Hana's King Hua, who, in the 12th century, killed a priest and caused a 3-year drought in Hana and on the Big Island. The chants also discuss good rulers like the 15th-century Piilani, who united the island of Maui and built fish ponds, irrigation fields, paved roads (4 to 6 feet wide), and the massive Piilanihale Heiau, which still stands today. It was Piilani's sons and grandson who finished the Heiau and also built the first road to Hana from West Maui, not only along the coast, but also up the Kaupo Gap and through the Haleakala Crater.

In more modern history, Hana played a role in the turbulent 1700s, when Kamehameha united the Hawaiian Islands. In 1759, the Big Island chief Kalaniopuu captured Hana and held control for 20 years, primarily because he had such a strong fortress in the Kauiki, the cinder cone on Hana Bay. During this time, the ruler of Molokai was overthrown by a powerful Maui chief, Kahikili. The Molokai chief and his wife escaped to Hana, where Kalaniopuu welcomed him. The Molokai chief and his wife had a baby girl in 1768, named Kaahumanu, who later married Kamehameha, and in her lifetime changed many tabus in the Hawaiian culture, such as the tabu against women eating with men. Her conversion to Christianity led the way for numerous Hawaiians to adopt the religion of their queen.

The 1800s saw commerce coming to this isolated village. In 1849, the cantankerous sea captain George Wilfong started the first sugar plantation in Hana on some 60 acres, where he built a mill near the historic Kauiki fortress. Because his harsh personality and set demands for plantation work did not sit well with the Hawaiians, Wilfong brought in the first Chinese immigrants to work his fields.

In 1864, two Danish brothers, August and Oscar Unna, contributed to the growth of the local sugar industry when they established the Hana Plantation. Four years later, they brought in Japanese immigrants to work the fields. The big boost to sugar—not only in Hana, but also across the entire state—came in 1876, when King Kalakaua negotiated the Sugar Reciprocity Treaty with the United States, giving Hawaiian sugar a "sweet" deal on price and tariff.

By the turn of the century, sugar wasn't the only crop booming in Hana (there were some six plantations in and around the town); rubber was being commercially grown in Nahiku, wheat in Kaupo, pineapple in Kipahulu, and tobacco in Ulupalakua.

In the 1920s and 1930s, several self-sufficient towns lined the Hana coast (Keanae, Nahiku, Kipuhulu, Kaupo, and, in the area where the current Hana Airport stands, the town of Kaeleku), each with its own general store, school, and churches; some had movie theaters as well. Hana has all of the above plus some 15 stores, three barber shops, a pool hall, and several restaurants.

We can only guess what those towns would be like today, if tragedy hadn't struck. On April 1, 1946, a huge tidal wave hit the state. The damage along the Hana coast was catastrophic: the Keanae Peninsula was swept clear (only the stone church remained), Hamoa was totally wiped out, and entire villages completely disappeared.

After World War II, the labor movement became a powerful force in Hawaii. C. Brewer, owner of the largest sugar plantation in Hana, decided that it would shut down its operation there instead of fighting the labor union. The closure of the plantation meant not only the loss of thousands of jobs, but also the loss of plantation-supplied homes and the entire plantation lifestyle. Thankfully, Paul I. Fagan, an entrepreneur from San Francisco who had purchased the Hana Sugar Co. from the Unna Brothers in the 1930s, became the town's guardian angel.

Fagan wanted to retire to Hana, so he focused his business acumen on the tiny town with big problems. Recognizing that sugar in isolated Hana was no longer economically feasible, he looked at the community and saw other opportunities. He bought 14,000 acres of land in Hana, stripped it of sugarcane, planted grass, and shipped in cattle from his ranch on Molokai.

Next, he did something that was years ahead of his time: he thought tourism might have a future in Hana, so he built a small six-room inn, called Kauiki Inn, which later became the **Hotel Hana-Maui.** When he opened it in October 1946, he said it was for first-class wealthy travelers (like his friends). Not only did his friends come, but he also pulled off a public-relations coup, which is still talked about today. Fagan owned a baseball team, the San Francisco Seals, and figured they needed a spring training area—so why not Hana? He brought out the entire team to train, and, more important, he brought out the sportswriters as well. The writers loved Hana and wrote glowing reports about the town; one even gave the town a nickname that stuck: "Heavenly Hana."

When the state paved the Hana Highway in 1962, it was still barely a one-lane road, but at least it was a paved one-lane road—giving Hana yet another break. In the 1970s, tourists not only "discovered" Maui, but they also were willing to make the long trek out to Hana.

The biggest change to the Hana lifestyle came on December 5, 1977, when television finally arrived. The isolated community was unable to get TV reception until a local cable operator spent 6 months laying cable over cinder cones, mountain streams, and cavernous gulches from one side of the island to the other. Some 125 homes tuned in to the tube—and the rural Hawaiian community was never the same.

The small coastal village is now inhabited by 2,500 people, many part Hawaiian.

SEEING THE SIGHTS

Most visitors will zip through Hana, perhaps taking a quick look out their car windows at a few sights before buzzing on down the road. They might think they

Hana

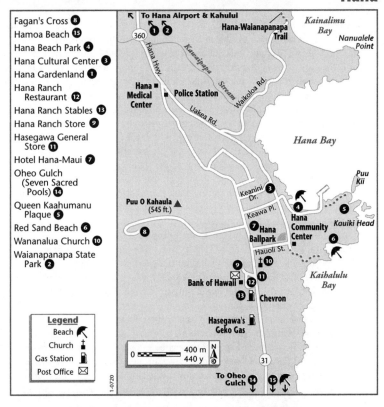

Fagan's Cross **8**
Hamoa Beach **15**
Hana Beach Park **4**
Hana Cultural Center **3**
Hana Gardenland **1**
Hana Ranch Restaurant **12**
Hana Ranch Stables **13**
Hana Ranch Store **9**
Hasegawa General Store **11**
Hotel Hana-Maui **7**
Oheo Gulch (Seven Sacred Pools) **14**
Queen Kaahumanu Plaque **5**
Red Sand Beach **6**
Wananalua Church **10**
Waianapanapa State Park **2**

Legend
Beach
Church
Gas Station
Post Office

"saw" Hana, but they definitely didn't "experience" Hana. Allow at least 2 or 3 days to really let this land of legends show you its breathtaking beauty and quiet serenity.

As you enter Hana, the road splits about a half-mile past mile marker 33, at the police station. Both roads will take you to Hana, but the lower road, Uakea Road, is more scenic. Just before you get to Hana Bay on the right side, you'll see the old wood-frame **Hana District Police Station and Courthouse.** Next door is the **Hana Museum Cultural Center** on Uakea Road (☎ **808/248-8622;** fax 808/248-8620; www.planet/hawaii.com/hana; e-mail hccm@aloha.net), open daily from 10am to 4pm (most of the time). This small building has an excellent collection of Hawaiian quilts, some 560 artifacts, 600 books, and 5,000 photos. Also on the grounds are Kauhala O Hana, composed of four hale (houses) for living, meeting, cooking, and canoe building or canoe storage. A $2 donation is suggested for admission to the Hana Cultural Center, which also allows you to look at the police station, courthouse, and jail next door. The three-bench courthouse is a no-nonsense affair; restored in 1989, it's still used today when a judge comes out to Hana from Wailuku every other month. The adjacent jail, no longer in use, was in service from 1871 to 1979. Hana residents love to tell the story about how they could always tell when a prisoner was in jail: the lawn outside would be mowed (one of the jobs the prisoner had to perform as part of his punishment).

Catercorner from the Hana Cultural Center is the entrance to **Hana Bay.** You can drive right down to the pier and park. There are rest rooms, showers, picnic tables, barbecue areas, and even a snack bar here. The 386-foot, red-faced cinder cone beside the bay is **Kauiki Hill,** the scene of numerous fierce battles in ancient Hawaii and the birthplace of Queen Kaahumanu in 1768. A short, 5-minute walk will take you to the spot. Look for the trail along the hill on the wharf side, and follow the path through the ironwood trees; the lighthouse on the point will come into view, and you'll see pocket beaches of red cinder below. Grab onto the ironwood trees for support, because the trail has eroded in some areas. A copper plaque on a rock marks the site of the queen's birthplace. This is a perfect place for a secluded picnic, or you can continue on the path out to the lighthouse. To get to the lighthouse, which sits on a small island, watch the waves for about 10 minutes to get a sense of how often and from which direction the waves are coming. Between wave sets, either swim or wade in the shallow, sandy bottom channel or hop across the rocks to the island.

To get to the center of town, leave Hana Bay, cross Uakea Road, and drive up Keawa Place; turn left on Hana Highway, and on the corner will be the **Hotel Hana-Maui,** the luxurious hotel established by Paul Fagan in 1946 (see above; for a review, see chapter 6). On the green hills above Hotel Hana-Maui stands a 30-foot-high white cross made of lava rock. Citizens erected the cross in memory of Paul Fagan, who founded the Hana Ranch as well as the hotel, and helped keep the town alive. The hike up to **Fagan's Cross** provides a gorgeous view of the Hana coast, especially at sunset, when Fagan himself liked to climb this hill. See "Hiking & Camping," in chapter 8, for details.

Back on the Hana Highway, just past Hauoli Road, the historic **Wananalua Congregation Church** stands majestically. It's on the National Historic Register not only because of its age (it was built from 1838 to 1842 from coral stones), but also because of its location, atop an old Hawaiian heiau. *Wananalua* means "double prophecy," appropriate for this location. This is also the site of the battle between Maui warriors and Kamehameha, part of his efforts to unite the islands.

Just past the church on the right side of the Hana Highway is the turnoff to the **Hana Ranch Center,** the commercial center for Hana, with a post office, a bank, a general store, the Hana Ranch Stables, and a restaurant and snack bar (see chapter 7). But the real shopping experience is across the Hana Highway at the **Hasegawa General Store,** a Maui institution (see chapter 10), which carries oodles of merchandise from soda and fine French wines to fishing line to name-brand clothing, plus everything you need for a picnic or a gourmet meal. This is also the place to find out what's going on in Hana: the bulletin board at the entrance has fliers and hand-written notes advertising everything from fund-raising activities to classes to community-wide activities. You cannot make a trip to Hana without a stop at this unique store.

If you need gas before heading back, note that the two service stations, **Chevron** and **Hasegawa's Hana Geko Gas,** sit nearly side by side on the right side of the Hana Highway as you leave town.

OUTDOOR ACTIVITIES

Most day-trippers to Hana can't imagine what there is to do in this tiny community. The answer is: everything. One of the best areas on Maui for ocean activities, it also boasts a wealth of incredible nature hikes, remote places to explore on horseback, waterfalls to discover, and even lava tube caves to investigate.

For more information on the lava tubes, see **Island Spelunkers** (☎ 808/ 248-7308) on page 184. For details on horseback riding, see **Oheo Stables** (☎ 808/ 667-2222) on page 183. If you're a tennis player, you can take advantage of the free public courts located next to the Hotel Hana-Maui, available on a first-come, first-served basis.

BEACHES & OCEAN ACTIVITIES

Hana's beaches come in numerous varieties: white, black, gray or red sand; perfectly shaped coves, crescents, or long stretches; and excellent for just about every kind of ocean activity you can think of. Call ☎ **808/248-7711** if you'd like to snorkel or kayak with **Hana Kayak and Snorkel Tours** (see "Ocean Kayaking" under "Hitting the Water," in chapter 8), or venture out on your own at our favorite beaches:

HANA   The waters in the Hana Bay are calm most of the time and great for swimming. Excellent snorkeling and diving can be found by the lighthouse. Strong currents can run through here, so don't venture farther than the lighthouse. See Hana Bay, above, for more details on the facilities and hikes here.

RED SAND BEACH   The Hawaiian name for this beach is Kaihalulu Beach, which means "roaring sea," and it's easy to understand why: the beach is as red as a Ferrari at a five-alarm fire. It's truly a sight to see. The beach is on the ocean side of Kauiki Hill, just south of Hana Bay, in a wild, natural setting on a pocket cove, where the volcanic cinder cone lost its seaward wall to erosion and spilled red cinders everywhere to create the red sands. Before you put on your bathing suit, there are two things to know about this beach: you have to trespass to get here (trespassing is against the law and you could face charges), and nudity (also illegal in Hawaii—arrests have been made) is common here.

To reach the beach, put on solid walking shoes (no flip-flops), and walk south on Uakea Road, past Haoli Street and the Hotel Hana-Maui, to the parking lot for the hotel's Sea Ranch Cottages. Turn left and cross the open field next to the Hana Community Center. Look for the dirt trail and follow it to the huge ironwood tree, where you turn right (do not go ahead to the old Japanese cemetery). If it's wet, do not attempt to go down the treacherous trail. Use the ironwood trees to maintain your balance as you follow the ever-eroding cinder footpath a short distance along the shoreline, down the narrow cliff trail. The trail suddenly turns the corner, and into view comes the burnt-red beach, set off by the turquoise waters, black lava, and vivid green ironwood trees—a vision that will haunt you forever.

The lava outcropping protects the bay and makes it safe for swimming. Snorkeling is excellent and there's a natural whirlpool area on the Hana Bay side of the cove. Stay away from the surge area where the ocean enters the cove.

KOKI BEACH   One of the best surfing and boogie-boarding beaches on the Hana Coast lies just a couple of miles from the Hasegawa General Store in the Oheo Gulch direction. There is a very strong rip current here, so unless it is dead calm and you are a strong swimmer, do not attempt swimming here. In fact, a sign on the emergency call box—installed after a drowning in 1996—warns of the strong currents. It's a great place, though, to sit on the white sand and watch the surfers. The only facility is a big parking area. To get here, drive toward Oheo Gulch from Hana, where Highway 36 changes to Highway 31. About 1½ miles outside of Hana, turn left at Haneoo Road.

HAMOA BEACH   For one of Hana's best beaches—great for swimming, boogie boarding, and lying out—continue another half mile down the Haneoo Road loop to Hamoa Beach. There is easy access from the road down to the sandy beach, and facilities include a small public rest room and an outdoor shower. The large pavilion and beach accessories are for the guests of the Hotel Hana-Maui.

WAIOKA POND Locally, this swimming hole in a series of waterfalls and pools is called Venus Pool, and the rumor is that in ancient Hawaii, only the royalty were allowed to use this exquisite swimming site. The freshwater swimming area is a great place to spend a secluded day. Only two warnings here: don't go to the pond if it has been raining (flash floods), and don't go near the surf at the ocean end of the stream (strong undertow). To get here, park your car well off the Hana Highway at mile marker 48, before the bridge. Hop over the fence on the ocean side of the bridge, and follow the well-worn footpath that parallels the stream. At the stream, turn to your right to take the path down to the smooth rocks above the stream. There's a huge pond just off the white-rock waterfall with a little island you can swim to in the middle.

HIKING

Hana is woven with hiking trails along the shoreline, through the rain forest, and up in the mountains. See "Hiking & Camping," in chapter 8, for a discussion of hiking in Waianapanapa and up to Fagan's Cross.

Another excellent hike leads you to **Blue Pool and Hawaii's largest heiau.** This easy 3-mile round-trip hike takes you to a freshwater, oceanside waterfall and swimming pool at the halfway point. On the way back, you can tour a tropical botanical garden and see the largest heiau in the state. The hike is on a jeep trail with some climbing over boulders, so wear good hiking boots or tennis shoes (no slippers or flip-flops) and bring your swimsuit and mosquito repellent. Go in the morning, when the sun lights up the oceanside pool, and you'll have plenty of time for a picnic lunch before touring the garden and heiau in the afternoon.

Turn toward the ocean on Ulaino Road, by mile marker 31. Drive down the paved road (which turns into a dirt road but is still drivable) to the first stream (about 1½ miles). If the stream is flooded, turn around and go back. If you can forge the stream, cross it and park on the right side of the road by the huge bread-fruit trees. The trees are part of the 122-acre **Kahanu Garden** (☎ **808/248-8912**), owned and operated by the National Tropical Botanical Garden (www.ntbg.org), which also has two gardens on Kauai. Call before you go to reserve a spot on the guided tours of the garden and **Piilanihale Heiau.** Tours (limited to 15) are given Monday through Friday from 1 to 3pm; they cost $10 for adults and are free for children 12 and under.

After you park your car, walk down the jeep road that parallels the Kahanu Gardens. You'll have to forge two more streams before the road ends at the beach. Cross the rocky and gravel beach. If it has been dry, you can just walk along the shoreline. If there has been rain, you will need to cross over the big boulders in the stream. Continue walking down the beach to the 100-foot waterfall on your left with its deep freshwater pool, known locally as **Blue Pool.**

If you've brought a picnic lunch, you can eat on the large boulders as you sun yourself after swimming in the bracing spring water.

If you have made reservations for the tour of Kahanu Garden, be back at your car before the 1pm tour begins. The tour offers a history of Hawaii through its discussion of Hawaii's native plants, plus the history of the Piilanihale Heiau and a chance to see the rugged coastline of this remote area. The 122 acres encompass plant collections from the Pacific Islands, concentrating on plants of value to the people of Polynesia, Micronesia, and Melanesia. Fringed by a vast native pandanus forest, Kahanu Garden contains the largest known collection of breadfruit cultivars. This collection serves as a germplasm repository for this important South Pacific food crop, housing cultivars from more than 17 Pacific Island groups and Indonesia, the Philippines, and the Seychelles.

The heiau is the real draw here. Believed to be the largest in the state, the **Piilanihale Heiau** ("House of Piilani," one of Maui's greatest chiefs—see "Hana's History," above) measures 340 feet by 415 feet, and it was built in a unique terrace design not seen anywhere else in Hawaii. The walls are some 50 feet tall and 8 to 10 feet thick. Historians now believe that Piilani's two sons and his grandson built the mammoth temple, which was dedicated to war, sometime in the 1500s.

JUST BEYOND HANA
TROPICAL HALEAKALA: OHEO GULCH AT KIPAHULU

If you're thinking about heading out to the so-called Seven Sacred Pools, out past Hana at the Kipahulu end of Haleakala National Park, let's clear this up right now: there are more than seven pools—about 24, actually—and *all* water in Hawaii is considered sacred. It's all a public-relations scam that has spun out of control into contemporary myth. Folks here call the attraction by its rightful name, Oheo Gulch, although visitors sometimes refer to it as Kipahulu, which is actually the name of the area where Oheo Gulch is located. The dazzling series of waterfall pools and cataracts cascading into the sea is a beautiful sight—and so popular that it now has its own roadside parking lot.

GETTING THERE   Even though Oheo is part of Haleakala National Park, you cannot drive from Haleakala to Oheo. Even hiking from Halekala to Oheo is tricky: the access trail out of Haleakala is down Kaupo Gap, which ends at the ocean, a good 6 miles down the coast from Oheo. To drive to Oheo, head for Hana, some 60 miles from Kahului on the Hana Highway (Highway 36). Oheo is about 30 to 50 minutes beyond Hana, along Highway 31. The Highway 31 bridge passes over pools near the ocean; the other pools, plus magnificent 400-foot Waimoku falls, are reachable via an often-muddy but rewarding, hour-long uphill hike (see "Hiking & Camping," in chapter 8). Expect showers on the Kipahulu coast.

KIPAHULU RANGER STATION   The ranger station, at the Oheo Gulch part of the Haleakala National Park (☎ **808/248-7375**), is staffed from 9am to 5pm daily. Rest room facilities, but no drinking water, are available. Kipahulu rangers offer park safety information, exhibits, and books, plus a variety of walks and hikes year-round; check at the station for current activities.

HIKING & CAMPING IN THE PARK   There are a number of hikes in the park, and tent camping is allowed. See "Hiking & Camping," in chapter 8, for details. Check with the Haleakala Park rangers before hiking up to or swimming in the pools, and always keep one eye on the water in the streams; the sky can be sunny near the coast, but flood waters travel 6 miles down from 8,000 acres of Kipahulu Valley and can rise 4 feet in less than 10 minutes.

LINDBERGH'S GRAVE

A mile past Oheo Gulch on the ocean side of the road is **Lindbergh's Grave.** First to fly across the Atlantic Ocean, Charles A. Lindbergh (1902 to 1974) found peace in the Pacific; he settled in Hana, where he died of cancer in 1974. The famous aviator is buried under river stones in a seaside graveyard behind the 1857 **Palapala Hoomau Congregational Church,** where his tombstone is engraved with his own words: "If I take the wings of the morning and dwell in the uttermost parts of the sea. . . ."

FARTHER AROUND THE BEND

Those of you who are continuing on around Maui to the fishing village of **Kaupo** and beyond should be warned that Kaupo Road, or Old Piilani Highway (Highway 31), is rough and unpaved in parts, often full of potholes and ruts. About 2½ miles past Oheo Gulch, the pavement ends for about 5 miles—5 very rough miles as the narrow road becomes one lane around blind bends hugging the ocean cliffs, wandering in and out of valleys with sharp rock walls lining the single-car road. You might encounter wild pigs and stray cows. There are no phones or services until you reach **Ulupalakua Ranch** (see "More in Upcountry Maui," above), where there are a winery, a general store, and a gas station, which is likely to be closed. Ask around about road conditions, or call the **Maui Public Works Department** (☎ 808/ 248-8254) or the **Police Department** (☎ 808/248-8311). This road frequently washes out in the rain. You'd really be better off retracing your route through Hana.

About 6 miles and about 60 minutes from Oheo Gulch, you'll see the restored **Huialoha Congregationalist "Circuit" Church,** originally constructed in 1859. Across from the church and down the road a bit is the **Kaupo Store** (☎ 808/ 248-8054), which marks the center of the ranching community of Kaupo. Store hours are supposedly Monday through Friday from 7:30am to 4:30pm, but in this arid cattle country, posted store hours often prove meaningless. The Kaupo Store is the last of the Soon family stores, which at one time stretched from Kaupo to Keanae.

From the Kaupo Store, the landscape turns into barren, dry desert. In the lee of Haleakala, this area gets little rain. Between mile markers 29 and 30, look for the ancient lava flow that created an arch as it rolled down Haleakala. Keep an eye peeled for cattle, because this is open range country. Eventually the road will wind uphill, and suddenly the forest and greenery of Ulupalakula come into sight. The upcountry town is about 45 minutes from Kahului.

by Jocelyn Fujii

Like dining, shopping is a major Maui activity. And why not? You can leapfrog from one shopping mall to the next simply by following the main road—and rationalize that walking from store to store is a form of aerobic exercise. But Maui is also the arts center of the Islands, with a large number of resident artists who show their works in more than four dozen galleries and countless gift shops scattered throughout the island. Concerts at the Maui Arts and Cultural Center, Lahaina gallery openings on Friday nights, Hui No'eau activities in Makawao, the Art School at Kapalua, and year-round fund-raisers for worthy causes are motivating factors in the arts. Maui also possesses an active social environment in which people dress up and are seen, whether in a chic restaurant, a culinary festival, or a sold-out concert at the Maui Arts and Cultural Center.

From Kula to Hana, Maui is also the queen of specialty products, an agricultural cornucopia that includes Kula onions, upcountry protea, Kaanapali coffee, world-renowned potato chips, and many other tasty treats that are shipped worldwide.

As with any popular visitor destination, you'll have to wade through bad art (in this case, oceans of trite marine art) and mountains of trinkets, particularly in Lahaina and Kihei, where touristy boutiques line the streets between rare pockets of treasures. If you shop in south or west Maui, expect to pay inflated resort prices, clear down to a bottle of Evian or sunscreen. But Maui's gorgeous finds are particularly rewarding. Residents work, live, and shop for everyday needs in central Maui, which is home to first-rate boutiques for specialized tastes as well: Wailuku has its own antiques alleys (North Market and Main streets), and the Kaahumanu Center in neighboring Kahului is becoming more fashionable by the month. Also in Kahului is the $28 million Maui Arts and Cultural Center, a dream venue for the performing and visual arts, with two theaters and a 3,500-square-foot gallery. Upcountry, Makawao's boutiques are worth seeking out, despite some attitude and high prices.

1 Central Maui

KAHULUI

Kahului's best shopping is concentrated in two places. Almost all of the shops listed below are at one of these centers:

Kaahumanu Center, Kaahumanu Avenue (☎ 808/877-3369), is a commercial hub only 5 minutes from the Kahului Airport, offering more than 100 shops, restaurants, and theaters. More manageable than Honolulu's Ala Moana, with a thoughtful selection of food and retail shops, Kaahumanu covers all the bases. It offers everything from the finest arts and crafts to a Foodland Supermarket, plus everything in between: a thriving food court; the island's best beauty-supply store; mall standards like Sunglass Hut, The Gap, Radio Shack, Local Motion (surf and beach wear, including the current fad, women's board shorts—a combination of hot pants and men's surf trunks), department stores like JC Penney, Liberty House, and Shirokiya; and attractive boutique/galleries such as Ki'i and Maui Hands. From 11:30am to 1:30pm on the last Friday of every month, there are food demonstrations and samplings, fashion shows, and live entertainment in the center's Queen's Market Food court. The center is open Monday through Friday from 9:30am to 9pm, Saturday from 9:30am to 9pm, and Sunday from 11am to 6pm.

Rough around the edges and dramatically eclipsed by the Kaahumanu Center down the street, **Maui Mall,** 70 E. Kaahumanu Ave. (☎ 808/877-7559), is still a place of everyday good things, from Longs Drugs, which anchors the modest mall, to 60-minute photo processing and a Star Market.

Caswell-Massey. Kaahumanu Center. ☎ 808/877-7761.

What makes this Caswell-Massey special is the presence of Maui-made soaps and bath products that utilize tropical fragrances and botanicals. Although part of a worldwide chain, this is a Maui store of distinction. As America's oldest perfume company, established in 1752, Caswell-Massey triple-mills all its soaps (so that they last three times longer), scents them with natural oils, and uses old-fashioned, tried-and-true methods and ingredients. Most notable for visitors is the line of made-on-Maui perfumes, eight scents made of botanical (not synthetic) ingredients, ranging from Ginger and Plumeria to Victorian Vanilla. They prepare handsome, custom-designed baskets at no extra charge. You can hand-pick your selection from hundreds of specialty products, from decadent bath salts with 23k gold flakes to Damask rose shampoo and bath gels, eye creams, body lotions, old Swedish soaps, freesia bath gel, sachets, candles, perfume bottles, potpourris, room mists, oil lamps, and an array of pamperings.

Cost Less Imports. Maui Mall. ☎ 808/877-0300.

Natural fibers are everywhere in this tiny corner of the mall: lauhala, sea-grass mats, bamboo blinds, grassy floor and window coverings, shoji-style lamps, burlap yardage, baskets, tactile Balinese cushions. Plus Asian, Indonesian, and Polynesian imports, as well as top-of-the-line, made-on-Maui soaps and handicrafts. This is the only direct importer in Hawaii of Chinese seagrass-rush mats.

Hoaloha Heirlooms. Kaahumanu Center. ☎ 808/877-4325.

Lavish ukuleles by Maui Ukulele and leis made of kukui nuts, wiliwili seeds, and Job's tears are part of the Hawaiian offerings at this new Maui gift shop. Paintings, place mats, koa tables, small Hawaiian quilts, children's clothes, muumuus and dresses, hair ornaments, handmade paper, fiber baskets, and hundreds of gift items from Hawaii, Indonesia, and the South Pacific are available here.

Ki'i Gallery. Kaahumanu Center. ☎ 808/871-4557.

The eclectic collection includes glass art and black pearls, as well as a wide assortment of made-on-Maui crafts. Chinese porcelains, clay teapots, jewelry, hand-painted maple wood bowls, perfume bottles, and an occasional esoteric item (such as the Yiking clay forms from Shanghai) keep regulars coming back. But it's the glass vases that dominate the room with their brilliance and luminosity. All handcrafted, of the highest quality, the glass reflects excellent craftsmanship and design, from Venetian and Czech glass to Pizzo from Maui and Vandemark Merritt from New Jersey.

Lightning Bolt Maui Inc. 55 Kaahumanu Ave. ☎ **808/877-3484.**

There's an excellent selection of women's board shorts, aloha shirts, swimwear, sandals and shoes, beach towels, and everything else needed for fun in the sun. Quality labels such as Patagonia and high-tech, state-of-the-art outdoor gear like Polartec sweaters and moccasins attract adventurers heading for the chilly hinterlands as well as the sun-drenched shores.

Lisa's Beauty Supply & Salon. Kaahumanu Center. ☎ **808/877-6463.**

The shop is a sensory overload, with every imaginable item for a well-groomed life—every product you've seen or heard advertised, and many you've never heard of. These are professional products of high quality, at often lower-than-drugstore prices. If you've lost your emery boards or hair dryer, or have broken a nail or forgotten your favorite shampoo, Lisa's is a must. Browse among the shelves of Matrix, Paul Mitchell, Aveda, Joico, $2 eye crayons that are as good or better than name brands, hairbrushes and accessories, Sorme lipsticks, Cici lip colors, aromatherapy oils, soaps, cosmetics cases, and numerous other items for pampering yourself in the days ahead.

Maui Farmers Market. Kahului Shopping Center (next to Ah Fook's Super Market). ☎ **808/573-1934.**

Maui's produce has long been a source of pride for islanders, and this is where you'll find a fresh, inexpensive selection of Maui-grown fruit, vegetables, flowers, and plants in season. Local color too. Crafts and gourmet foods add to the event, and the large monkeypod trees provide welcome shade.

Maui Hands. Kaahumanu Center. ☎ **808/877-0368.**

Maui hands have made most of the items in this tiny store. The assortment of arts and crafts includes paintings, prints, and things whimsical and serious, from jewelry to glass marbles (a tchotchke handsomer than it sounds) and the works of the 200 artists represented, 90% of them from Maui. This is an ideal stop for made-on-Maui products of good quality. There are paintings and prints aplenty, in all price ranges.

The original Maui Hands remains in Makawao at The Courtyard, 3620 Baldwin Ave. (☎ **808/572-5194**).

Maui Swap Meet. S. Puunene Ave. (next to the Kahului Post Office). ☎ **808/242-0240.**

Throughout the year there are more than 100 vendors, making Maui Swap Meet, the pioneer of neighbor island markets, a large and popular event. After Thanksgiving and throughout the month of December, the number of booths nearly doubles and the activity reaches fever pitch. The colorful assortments of Maui specialties include Kula vegetables, vegetables from Keanae, fresh taro, plants, protea, crafts, household items, homemade ethnic foods, and baked goods. Every Saturday from early morning to noon, vendors spread out their wares in booths, under tarps, in a festival-like atmosphere that is pure Maui with a touch of kitsch. Admission is 50¢, and if you go before 7am while the vendors are setting up, no one will turn you away.

Summerhouse. In the Dairy Center, 385 Dairy Rd. ☎ **808/871-1320.**

Sleek and chic, tiny Summerhouse is big on style. Linens by Russ Berens, FLAX, Kiko, and Christy Allen; hats by Mui Milner and Emi Azeka Preston; unique jewelry; up-to-the-minute evening dresses; and high-quality T-shirts take women from day to evening.

WAILUKU

Just as they love to dine out, Mauians love to shop, and Wailuku, the old part of town, makes it easy for everyone to indulge this passion. Wailuku is the center of antiquing on Maui, and very likely all of Hawaii. There is some junk, but a stroll along Main and Market streets usually turns up a treasure or two. Maui residents *love* to decorate their homes, and when they're buying or getting rid of things, they're likely to end up in Wailuku.

Enter a varied world of nostalgia, kitsch, posh antiquities, humor, and collectible fervor. Some of the shops in Wailuku have classic antiques sharing space with lighthearted, borderline ephemera, or whimsical 1950s ashtrays in the shadow of priceless, centuries-old armoires. A mixed bag, for sure, but thoroughly enjoyable.

✪ **Bailey House Gift Shop.** At the Bailey House Museum, 2375-A Main St. ☎ **808/244-3920.**

If you're shopping for made-in-Hawaii items and have to pick just one shop in Wailuku, make it Bailey House. The small space, discriminating taste, and high level of integrity have honed a selection of remarkable gift items, from Hawaiian music albums to exquisite woods, traditional Hawaiian games (konane, checkers, and ticktacktoe), pareus, and an impressive selection of books. Koa-framed prints by Madge Tennent, a legendary Hawaii artist; lauhala hats hanging in mid-air; hand-sewn pheasant hat bands (with Ulupalakua fathers, by Diane Masumura); Tutuvi T-shirts; jams and jellies; Maui cookbooks; children's clothes; and an occasional Hawaiian quilt are some of the treasures to be found here. Hawaiian music often wafts in from a neighboring room, where a class in slack-key guitar playing might be in session. This is a thoroughly enjoyable browse through authoritative Hawaiiana, in a museum that is one of the finest examples of missionary architecture, dating back to 1833.

✪ **Bird of Paradise Unique Antiques.** 56 N. Market St. ☎ **808/242-7699.**

The owner, Joe Myhand, loves furniture, old Matson liner menus, blue willow china, kimonos for children, and anything nostalgic that happens to be Hawaiian. The furniture in the strongly Hawaiian collection ranges from 1940s rattan to wicker and old koa—those items tailor-made for informal island living and leisurely moments on the lanai. Myhand also collects bottles and mails his license plates all over the world. The collection ebbs and flows with his finds, keeping buyers waiting in the wings for his Depression glass, California pottery from the 1930s and 1940s (Bauer, Metlox, Vernon, Friscan ware, the occasional precious Roseville), old dinnerware, perfume bottles, vintage aloha shirts, and vintage Hawaiian music on cassettes. Items from the South Pacific are showing a stronger presence in the shop.

✪ **Brown-Kobayashi.** 160-A N. Market St. ☎ **808/242-0804.**

From self-adornment to interior design, graceful living is the theme here. Prices range from $2 to $7,000 in this 750-square-foot treasure trove. Asian antiques mingle quietly with old and new French, European, and Hawaiian objects, expressing an eclectic yet cohesive esthetic. Japanese kimono and obi, Bakelite and

Peking glass beads, breathtaking Japanese lacquerware, woven cricket carriers ($38 for the woven to $1,400 for the one of antique carved ivory), cloisonné, and a lotus-leaf basket carved of bamboo are among the many treasures here. Exotic and precious Chinese woods (purple sandalwood and huanghauali) glow discreetly from quiet corners, and an occasional monarchy-style lidded milo bowl comes in and flies out. Marc Kobayashi and Ronald Brown opened the shop in 1995, and word spread swiftly about their treasures: carved bamboo teapots, made by an aging master; the 1890s red lacquer Chinese bridal cabinet with large brass medallions and calligraphy pole; Chinese lacquer, antique crystal, Peking glass, or rock coral jewelry; Matson liner menus; armoires, tables, desks, and one-of-a-kind furnishings for indoor-outdoor beachfront living or upcountry chalets.

Gima Designs. 2058 Main St. ☎ **808/242-1839.**

Elaine Gima creates art to wear with her original silk designs, a blend of traditional forms with a modern eye and a timeless sense of style. Her clothing, accessories, and silk forms, and her collaborations with husband Thomas Calhoun, a fine wood-worker, have won top honors at the "Woods of Hawaii" show. Call ahead to make sure that she's there; she doesn't keep regular hours.

Memory Lane. 130 N. Market St. ☎ **808/244-4196.**

The 1,500-square-foot showroom is filled with fine art, Hawaiian collectibles, Oriental antiques, kitsch, vintage textiles and aloha shirts, English crystal from the 1700s, Depression glass, antique silver, and furniture "from the very old to the 1950s and Federal," says the owner. Like all shop owners in Wailuku, Joe Ransberger, a painter, finds that old koa furniture is a rarity that flies out of the store to collectors, who must lie in wait. Some things he can't part with, such as the curly koa chest made in the 1800s, and some of the one-of-a-kind wood-pulp rayon textiles. Prices range from $1 to $30,000, with many pieces over $1,000. It's a treasure hunt from the moment you enter: one elderly man, searching for a needle for his antiquated 78 r.p.m. phonograph, miraculously found one here.

Traders of the Lost Art. 62 N. Market St. ☎ **808/242-7753.**

It's a mixed bag and you might have to wade through a dense landscape with musty recesses, but you never know what the store promises: collectibles, kitsch, tribal art, African trade-bead bracelets, carpets from Katmandu, Hawaiian carvings, nautical Oceanic art, vintage koa furniture.

CENTRAL MAUI EDIBLES

The **Star Market** in the Maui Mall, **Foodland** in the Kaahumanu Center, and **Safeway** at 170 E. Kamehameha Ave. will satisfy your ordinary grocery needs. On Saturday you might want to check out the **Maui Swap Meet** (see above). A few sources of local specialties, flowers, health foods, and other mighty morsels are worth checking out:

The good news is that **Down to Earth Natural Foods** has expanded with its move from Wailuku to 305 Dairy Rd. in Kahului (☎ **808/877-2661**), and its service, like its selection, has improved. Fresh organic Maui produce, a bountiful salad bar, sandwiches and smoothies, vitamins and supplements, freshly baked goods, chips and snacks, whole grains, and several packed aisles of vegetarian and health foods have made Down to Earth a health-food staple for many years.

Established in 1941, the **Ooka Super Market,** 1870 Main St., Wailuku (☎ **808/244-3931**), Maui's ultimate home-grown supermarket, is a mom-and-pop business that has grown by leaps and bounds but still manages to keep its neighborhood flavor. Ooka sells inexpensive produce (fresh Maui mushrooms for a song), fresh island seafood, certified Angus beef, Maui specialties such as manju and mochi, and a rainbow of potted and freshly cut flowers at the best prices in town. Protea cut the same day, freesias in season, hydrangeas, fresh lei, torch gingers from Hana, upcountry calla lilies in season, and multicolored anthuriums compose what is one of Maui's finest and most affordable retail flower selections. Prepared foods are also a hit: bentos and plate lunches, roast chicken and laulau, and specialties from all the islands abound. The fresh fish is always fresh, and the seaweed, poi, Kula persimmons in the fall, fresh Haiku mushrooms, and dried marlin from Kona are among the local delicacies that make Ooka a Maui favorite.

Most of the space at **Shirokiya,** in the Kaahumanu Center, Kaahumanu Avenue (☎ 808/877-5551), is devoted to food, with a well-stocked prepared-foods section, but check out the fresh produce (bananas, papayas), juices, health-food supplements, and home appliances and audio-video equipment as well. The Dee Lite Bakery has a small corner, with its famous haupia cakes and other white-and-bright pastries, but most of the other foods are local or Japanese plate-lunch fare, offered in neatly packaged bento boxes or hot from the counter. Specialties such as Maui manju and Maui mochi are also available.

Located in the northern section of Wailuku, **Takamiya Market,** 359 N. Market St., Wailuku (☎ 808/244-3404), is much loved by local folks and visitors, who often drive all the way from Kihei to stock up on picnic fare and mouth-watering ethnic foods for sunset gatherings and beach parties. This is a highly recommended stop for all those with adventurous palates. Unpretentious home-cooked foods from East and West are prepared daily and served on Styrofoam plates from an ethnic smorgasbord. From the chilled-fish counter come fresh sashimi and poke, and in the renowned assortment of prepared foods are mounds of shoyu chicken, tender fried squid, roast pork, kalua pork, laulau, Chinese noodles, fiddlehead ferns, and Western comfort foods such as corn bread and potato salad. Fresh produce and paper products are also available, but it's the prepared foods that have made Takamiya's a household name in central Maui.

2 West Maui

LAHAINA

Lahaina's merchants and art galleries go all-out from 6:30 to 9pm on Friday night, when **Art Night** evokes an extra measure of hospitality and community spirit. The Art Night openings are usually marked with live entertainment and refreshments and a livelier-than-usual street scene.

If you're in Lahaina on the second or last Thursday of each month, stroll by the front lawn of the **Baldwin Home,** 696 Front St. (at Dickenson Street), for a splendid look at lei making and an opportunity to meet the gregarious senior citizens of Lahaina. In a program sponsored by the American Association of Retired Persons, they gather from 10am to 4pm to demonstrate lei making, to sell their floral creations, and, equally important, to socialize.

SHOPPING CENTERS Any day of the week, the waterfront shopping/dining complex at the southern end of Lahaina simply known as **505 Front St.** (☎ 808/667-0727) is a place to tuck into pizza (**Village Pizzeria**), shop (**Foreign Intrigue Imports and Maui To Go**), attend Maui's best luau (the **Old Lahaina Luau;** see chapter 11), have a sunset drink (**Pacific'o Restaurant**), buy art-deco posters or rock-star paintings (**New York–Paris**), and ease into Avanti's popular retro silk aloha shirts. It's not a large complex, and it gets mixed reviews; but there are some surprises there.

What was formerly a big belching pineapple cannery is now a maze of shops and restaurants at the northern end of Lahaina town known as the **Lahaina Cannery Mall,** 1221 Honoapiilani Hwy. (☎ **808/661-5304**). Find your way through the T-shirt and sportswear shops (**Reyn's** has fabulous aloha shirts) to **Lahaina Printsellers,** home of rare maps, antique originals, prints, paintings, and wonderful 18th- to 20th-century cartography representing the largest collection of engravings and antique maps in Hawaii. You can buy a book at **Waldenbooks** and follow the scent of coffee to **Sir Wilfred's Coffee House** a few doors away, where you can unwind with espresso and croissants, or you can head for **Compadres Bar and Grill,** where the margaritas flow freely and the Mexican food is tasty. The artist **Guy Buffet** has his gallery here. For film, water, notebooks, aspirin, groceries, sunscreen, and other things you can't live without, nothing beats **Longs Drugs** and **Safeway,** two old standbys that anchor the Cannery.

The **Lahaina Center,** 900 Front St. (☎ **808/667-9216**), is north of Lahaina's most congested strip, where Front Street begins. Across the street from the center, the seawall is a much-sought-after front-row seat to the sunset. There's plenty of free validated parking with easy access to more than 30 shops, a hair salon, restaurants, a nightclub, and a four-plex movie theater complex. Among the shopping stops: **Banana Republic,** the **Hilo Hattie Fashion Center** (a dizzying emporium of aloha wear), **McInerny** (wonderfully discounted designer clothes), **Local Motion,** an **ABC Discount Store,** and a dozen other recreational, entertainment, dining, and shopping prospects.

The recent conversion of 10,000 square feet of parking space into the re-creation of a traditional Hawaiian village is a welcome touch of Hawaiiana. With the commercialization of modern Lahaina, it's easy to forget that it was once the capital of the Hawaiian kingdom and a significant historic site. The village, called **Hale Kahiko,** features three main houses, called hale: a sleeping house, the men's dining house, and the craft house, where women pounded lauhala for mats and baskets. Construction of the houses consumed 10,000 feet of ohia wood from the island, 20 tons of pili grass, and more than 4 miles of hand-woven coconut sennit for the lashings. Artifacts, weapons, a canoe, and indigenous trees are among the authentic touches in this village, which can be toured privately or with a guide.

David Lee Galleries. 712 Front St. ☎ **808/667-7740.**

The gallery is devoted to the works of David Lee, who uses natural powder colors to paint on silk, creating a luminous, ethereal quality. He has also opened a new gallery at the Kahala Mandarin on Oahu.

Foreign Intrigue Imports. 505 Front St. ☎ **808/667-4004.**

The large selection of interior accents puts a new spin on the often-tired world of Indian and Balinese imports. Gorgeous hand-painted wooden trays, gilded Buddhas, cat benches, chests and armoires of all sizes, and sturdy hemp pouches and accessories make the collection an intriguing one. Furniture, textiles, wood carvings, wall hangings, masks, and hundreds of functional and nonfunctional accessories line the shop and reflect the mastery of detail that Balinese villagers possess. Although hand-painted cabinets, trunks, and household accessories from India are a new hit in the store, there are items in all price ranges—and intrepid shoppers might find some wonderful deals among the vast and colorful selection, including one-of-a-kind, made-on-Maui necklaces of antique beads and jades.

Bath & Beauty, Maui Style

It was only a matter of time before Maui botanicals and tropical fragrances gained a noticeable presence in the retail world. Like jams, jellies, vinegars, chutneys, and sauces that celebrate the produce of the Islands, bath products—soaps, aromatherapy oils, potpourris, lotions, and perfumes—are quite the new medium of expression in the Islands, especially on ethereal Maui. Plumeria, pikake, macadamia nut oil, kukui, Hawaiian seaweed, mango, ginger, and gardenia are some of the tropical infusions appearing more prominently in locally made bath and beauty products.

Maui Tropical Soaps are top-quality, made on Maui, and terrific, with names like Hawaiian Sunset, Seafoam Mint, Jacaranda Morning, and Jungle Java. Look for these soaps at Maui gift shops and galleries, where they are becoming more widely available. Great gifts to go, they are nonperishable, are easily packed, and can serve as delightful sachets in your luggage. Hawaiian Botanical's Pikake Shower Gel is another top-quality Maui product.

The specialty shops that carry notable selections of Maui soaps, oils, and bath products include **Lahaina Body & Bath,** 713 Front St. (☎ 808/661-1076); **Lei Spa Maui,** in Lahaina at 505 Front St. (☎ 808/661-1178), and at the Westin Maui, 2365 Kaanapali Pkwy. (☎ 808/667-9579); and **Caswell-Massey,** in Kaahumanu Center, Kahului (☎ 808/877-7761). In all of these shops, you can discover new frontiers in body pampering while enjoying the fruits and flowers of Maui.

✪ **Gallery Ltd.** 716 Front St. ☎ **808/661-0696.**

One of the beauties of Lahaina, the Gallery is easy to miss among the bright windows of Front Street. You'll need a good chunk of browsing time here; the jade and pearls alone could account for the better part of an afternoon. The Gallery is awash in gorgeous antiquities, from snuff bottles and netsuke to lacquerware, jade carvings, Buddhas, scrolls, screens, and precious jewelry, most of it Chinese and Japanese. Although antiques make up half of the impressive selection, there are also some remarkable contemporary works of Asian art. The Japanese screens and larger porcelains are upstairs. Here since 1959, the Gallery has recently been renovated. Children whose parents were customers are now looking for their own wedding strands among the Biwa, South Seas black pearls, and stunning Japanese strands, which can be lengthened and clasped according to the customer's design.

Martin Lawrence Galleries. In the Lahaina Market Place, 126 Lahainaluna Rd. ☎ **808/661-1788.**

The front is garish, with pop art, kinetic sculpture, and bright, carnivalesque glass objects. Toward the back of the gallery, however, there's a sizable inventory of two-dimensional art and some plausible choices for collectors of Keith Haring, Andy Warhol, and other controversial artists. The focus is on pop art and national and international artists; only one artist represented here is from Maui.

Maui to Go. 505 Front St. ☎ **808/667-2292.**

Shop here for high-quality, made-on-Maui products: plump sun-dried macadamia nuts (with no cholesterol), upcountry jams in several flavors, Maui coffee, Maui teas and potpourris, Maui onion mustards and condiments, cookies, chocolates, and many other island delectables. Throw in a nostalgic aloha shirt while you're at it, in retro prints that were worn by Elvis, Tony Curtis, and President Eisenhower. The owners, Colleen Noah-Marti and her husband, Gerard, make sure that their shop is stocked with Maui's finest specialty products. Other items from far-flung islands include fiber handbags, place mats, books, ceramics, lauhala mats from the South Pacific, and other accessories for the home.

Miki's. 762 Front St. ☎ **808/661-8991.**

Walk in off the sidewalk onto the bleached wood floors and see why aloha shirts are so fab. Tiny, busy, and bursting with color, Miki's has a tasteful assortment of aloha wear, from Tommy Bahama shirts and coordinates to Honu Bay T-shirts, Jams, surf shorts, and beach slippers.

South Seas Trading Post. 780 Front St. ☎ **808/661-3168.**

Treasures from the South Pacific, from masks to jewelry to wall hangings and puppets, acknowledge the tribal arts of Borneo, Papua New Guinea, Thailand, Kashmir, and the Himalayas. Take a journey to these exotic destinations through the carvings, drums, implements, and arts of their cultures.

Totally Hawaiian. 1221 Honoapiilani Hi. ☎ **808/667-2558.**

A good browse for its selection of Niihau shell jewelry, excellent Hawaiian CDs, Norfolk pine bowls, and Hawaiian quilt kits. Hawaiian quilt patterns sewn in Thailand (at least they're honest about it) are labor-intensive, less expensive, and attractive, although not totally Hawaiian.

✪ **Village Galleries in Lahaina.** 120 and 180 Dickenson St. ☎ **808/661-4402** and 808/661-5559.

The 27-year-old Village Galleries is the oldest continuously running gallery on Maui, and it's highly esteemed as one of the few with consistently high standards. The recent addition of a contemporary gallery (with colorful gift items and jewelry!) has upped the enjoyment and value of dropping by. The selection of mostly original two- and three-dimensional art offers a good look at the quality of work emanating from the island. Art collectors know the Village Galleries as a respectable showcase for regional artists.

There's another location in the Ritz-Carlton Kapalua, 1 Ritz-Carlton Dr. (☎ **808/669-1800**).

LAHAINA EDIBLES

Westside Natural Foods. 193 Lahainaluna Rd. ☎ **808/667-2855.**

A longtime Lahaina staple, Westside is serious about providing tasty food that's healthy and affordable. Its excellent food bar attracts a healthy clientele with its vegetarian lasagna, marinated tofu strips, vegetarian pot pie, crisp salads, grains, curries, and gorgeous organic produce.

KAANAPALI

Rhonda's Quilts. In the Hyatt Regency Maui, 210 Nohea Kai Dr., Kaanapali Beach. ☎ **808/667-7660.**

Rhonda's has increased its made-in-Hawaii selection. Some T-shirts, tote bags, mouse pads, and Hawaiian quilt designs are designed in-house, but there are also dolls, children's clothing, locally made tiles in Hawaiian quilt patterns, books, stuffed animals, and other eclectic goods in this cheerful store. The assortment includes a small selection of women's clothing among the antique quilts and Americana. The Hawaiian quilts are made both here and, much less expensively, in the Philippines, and all are of high quality. Quilt pillows, supplies, patterns, and kits are sold here, and quilting classes are offered on Friday.

✪ **Sandal Tree.** In the Westin Maui, at Kaanapali Beach. ☎ **808/667-5330.**

It's unusual for a resort shop to draw local customers on a regular basis (add time and parking costs to that pair of sandals), but the Sandal Tree has a flock of footwear fanatics who come here from throughout the islands for their chic kicks. The shop sells rubber thongs and topsiders, sandals and dressy heels, athletic shoes and hats, Yves St. Laurent pumps, Arche comfort footwear, and much more. Accessories range from fashionable knapsacks to indulgences such as avant-garde geometrical handbags. Prices are realistic, too.

Three of the six Sandal Tree resort shops throughout Hawaii are on Maui. There's another at the Hyatt Regency Maui, 200 Nohea Kai Dr., Kaanapali Beach (☎ 808/661-3495), and the third is at the Grand Wailea Resort.

Whalers Village. 2435 Kaanapali Pkwy. ☎ **808/661-4567.**

Whalers Village has gone shockingly upscale. No one would have dreamed that Prada would come to Whaler's Village, but it has. Once you've stood under the authentic whale skeleton or squeezed the plastic whale blubber at the **Whale Center of the Pacific** (see chapter 9), you can blow a bundle at **Tiffany, Prada, Chanel, Ferragamo, Dolce & Gabbana,** and **Sharper Image,** or any of the other 70 shops and restaurants that have sprouted up in this beachfront shopping center. The posh Euro trend doesn't bode well; there's next to nothing here that's Hawaiian. Some of the village's mainstream possibilities: the **Body Shop** for the best and most globally conscious products for bath and home; **Hobie Hawaii** for swim and surf things; **Paradise Clothing** for Speedos and bathing suits; and **Canoe** for crisp, tasteful aloha shirts. **The Eyecatcher** has one of the most extensive selections of sunglasses on the island, located just across from the busiest **ABC** store in the state. The most comforting stop of all is the **Maui Yogurt Company,** where Maui-made Roselani ice cream is sold in mouth-watering flavors, including a bracing mint chocolate chip. The Whalers Village is open daily from 9:30am to 10pm.

FROM HONOKOWAI TO NAPILI

Kahana Gateway is an unimpressive mall built to serve the condominium community that has sprawled along the coastline north of Kaanapali, before Kapalua. If you need a woman's bathing suit, however, **Rainbow Beach Swimwear** is a find, boldly situated near the waistline-challenging dining mecca, Roy's Kahana Bar and Grill, and a stone's throw from Fish & Games Sports Grill. At Rainbow, you'll find a wide selection of suits for all shapes, at lower-than-resort prices, slashed even further during the frequent (and welcome) sales.

Also in Kahana Gateway, **Hutton's Fine Jewelry** is a breath of fresh air for lovers of fine adornments. High-end jewelry from designers around the country (a lot of platinum and diamonds) reflects discerning tastes for those who can afford it. Tahitian black pearls and jade (some hundreds of years old, all certified) are among the Hutton's specialties, but we love the Carleton Kinkade oil paintings hanging on the walls.

KAPALUA

Honolua Store. 502 Office Rd. (next door to the Ritz-Carlton Kapalua). ☎ **808/669-6128.**

Walk on the old wood floors peppered with holes from golf shoes and find your everyday essentials: bottled water, stationery, mailing tape, jackets, chips, wine, soft

A Creative Way to Spend the Day: The Art School at Kapalua

Make a bowl from clay or paint a premade one, then fire it and take it home. Or paint a picture, learn ballet, or learn to sketch like the masters. West Maui's only art school, featuring local and visiting instructors, is open daily for people of all ages and skill levels. (A group of students, ages 8 to 10, recently beautified a construction site by painting an oceanic mural at Lahaina Cannery Mall.) Projects, programs, classes, and workshops at this nonprofit organization highlight creativity in all forms. Classes in photography, sketching, painting on silk, throwing at the potter's wheel, and the performing arts (ballet, creative dramatics, yoga, and the Pilates stretch for muscular development) are offered in a charming 1920s plantation building that was part of an old cannery operation in the heart of the Kapalua Resort. Costs range from $7 for nonmembers for a children's creative-movement class to $360 for nonmembers for a twice-weekly, 4-week class in potting on the wheel and hand-building ceramics. Contact the **Art School at Kapalua,** Kapalua Resort (☎ **808/665-0007**).

drinks, paper products, fresh fruit and produce, and aisles of notions and necessities. One corner of the store is dedicated to the Kapalua Nature Society, which leads hikes into the West Maui Mountains. With its take-out counter offering deli items—13 types of sandwiches; salads; and a $3.50 breakfast of eggs, biscuits and gravy—and its picnic tables on the veranda, there are always long lines of customers. Golfers and surfers love to come here for the morning paper and coffee.

Kapalua Shops. At the Kapalua Bay Hotel and Villas, in the Kapalua Resort. ☎ **808/ 669-1029.**

Shops have come and gone in this small, exclusive, and once-chic shopping center, now much quieter than in days past. Tiny **Mandalay** still sells East-West luxe with its silk clothing and handful of interior accents. Kapalua old-timer **South Seas Trading Post** brims with exotic artifacts such as Balinese beads, tribal masks, jewelry, and stunning coconut-shell bowls with mother-of-pearl inlay. Around the corner is **San Luigi,** an Italian shoetique with a small and not overwhelmingly expensive selection of footwear in all grades of leather, fiber, and even futuristic plastic. In one of its many Maui locations, the sleek **Lahaina Galleries** occupies a corner of the mall with artwork by Guy Buffet, Macedo, Andrea Smith, and others. **Reyn's** and **McInerny's** purvey clothing for resort life, and **Kapalua Kids** weighs in with equal time (and toys) for kids.

Village Galleries. In the Ritz-Carlton Kapalua, 1 Ritz-Carlton Dr. ☎ **808/669-1800.**

Maui's finest exhibit their works here and in the other two Village Galleries in Lahaina. Take heart, art lovers: there's no clichéd marine art here. Translucent, delicately turned bowls of Norfolk pine gleam in the light, and George Allan, Betty Hay Freeland, Joyce Clark, Diana Lehr, and Pamela Andelin are included in the pantheon of respected artists represented in the tiny gallery. Watercolors, oils, sculpture, hand-blown glass, Niihau shell lei, jewelry, and all media are represented. The Ritz-Carlton's monthly Artist-in-Residence program features Village Gallery artists in demonstrations and special hands-on workshops, free including materials.

3 South Maui

KIHEI

Kihei is one long strip of strip malls. Most of the shopping here is concentrated in the **Azeka Place Shopping Center** on South Kihei Road. Fast foods abound at Azeka's—Taco Bell, Pizza Hut, Baskin-Robbins—as do tourist-oriented clothing shops like Crazy Shirts and the overly tropical Tropical Tantrum. The shopping center also houses several prominent attractions, including the popular restaurant called A Pacific Café, General Nutrition Center, and a cluster of specialty shops with everything from children's clothes to shoes, sunglasses, beauty services, a nail salon, and swimwear. Also on South Kihei Road is the **Kukui Mall** with its movie theaters, Waldenbooks, Subway, Whaler's General Store, and I Can't Believe It's Not Yogurt.

Here are some of the worthy shopping stops in Kihei:

Aloha Books. In the Kamaole Beach Center, 2411 S. Kihei Rd. ☎ **808/874-8070.**

The owner, Tom Holland, has been a collector and dealer in Hawaiian antiques, collectibles, and art, and his new bookstore reflects his passion. The shelves are stocked with books on and about Hawaii, particularly vintage Hawaiiana, and the walls are draped with vintage Hawaiian and Polynesian art. There are new, used, and rare books, and, although this isn't a big bookstore, the titles cover a range of tastes, from popular fiction to historic novels and Dick Francis whodunits. If there's an out-of-print Don Blanding or 1940s music sheet to be found in the neighborhood, it's likely to be here.

✪ **Hawaiian Moons Natural Foods.** 2411 S. Kihei Rd. ☎ **808/875-4356.**

Hawaiian Moons is a health-food store, and a great one, but it's also a mini-supermarket with one of the best selections of made-on-Maui products we've encountered on the island. Those who love wholesome, unadulterated food that is not boring love Hawaiian Moons. The Mexican tortillas are made on Maui (and are good!), and much of the produce here, such as organic vine-ripened tomatoes and organic onions, is grown in the fertile upcountry soil of Kula. There's Ono Farms Organic Coffee grown in Hana, and there's also a spate of Maui teas by the Hawaiian Tea Company in Wailuku. Chocolate-covered macadamia nuts from Captain Cook are aptly named Tropical Temptations, and there are Tropical Gourmet Salsas to follow the Dave's 100% Natural muffins and cakes. Big Island tempeh (a sensible soybean meat substitute), eggs from upcountry, Watler's Tofu and Volcano Spices (spicy garlic-lemon powdered seasonings) made on Maui, Maui bagels, Maui shiitake mushrooms, organic lemongrass and okra, Maui Crunch bread, free-range Big Island turkeys and chickens (no antibiotics or artificial nasties), and fresh Maui juices are some of the reasons for coming here. The juice bar/deli puts out pizzas and gourmet sandwiches. Cosmetics are also top of the line: sunblocks, fragrant floral oils, healthy kukui-nut oil from Waialua on Oahu, and the Island Essence made-on-Maui mango-coconut and vanilla-papaya skin lotions, the ultimate in body pampering.

Maui Sports & Cycle. In Dolphin Plaza, 2395 S. Kihei Rd. ☎ **808/875-2882.**

South Maui's upbeat water-sports retail and rental shop is a hit among beachgoers and water-sports enthusiasts. A friendly, knowledgeable staff helps you choose from among the mind-boggling selection of snorkel gear, boogie boards, kayaks, beach umbrellas, coolers, and view boards for "snorkeling lying down." Swimwear and mountain bikes too, and gear for riding on land or sea. There is good-quality snorkel gear, with a selection so extensive you can tailor your choice to your budget as well as your fit. Prescription masks are available, as are underwater cameras, sunscreens and lotions, jewelry, T-shirts, postcards, and hats and visors by the bushel.

There's a second Maui Sports & Cycle in Longs Center, 1215 S. Kihei Rd. (☎ **808/875-8448**).

Old Daze. In Azeka I, 1280 S. Kihei Rd. ☎ **808/875-7566.**

Nineteenth-century Americana and Hawaiian collectibles are nicely married in this charming shop. Some recent finds: an 1850s German sideboard, a Don Blanding teapot, 1940s head vases, a turn-of-the-century pie safe, an antique kimono, framed vintage music sheets, and Hawaiian silver collectible spoons. The collection features a modest furniture selection, Hawaiian pictures, 1960s ashtrays, Depression glass, old washboards, souvenir plates from county fairs, and an eclectic assortment of items for table and home. Choices range from hokey to rustic to pleasantly nostalgic, with many items for the kitchen.

Tuna Luna. 1941 S. Kihei Rd., Kihei Kalama Village. ☎ **808/874-9482.**

There are treasures to be found in this small cluster of tables and booths, where Maui artists display their work. Ceramics, exotic wood photo albums, jewelry, candles and soaps, handmade paper, and fiber accessories are functional and not, and make great gifts to go.

WAILEA

Wailea consists largely of upscale resort shops that sell expensive souvenirs, gift items, clothing, and accessories for both active lives and lives of leisure. **Sandal Tree** (see "Kaanapali," above), with its affordable-and-up designer wear, raises the footwear banner at the Grand Wailea Resort, and stores like **Mandalay,** in the Grand Wailea Shops and the Four Seasons Resort Maui, specialize in sumptuous Thai silks and Asian imports, from resort wear to the very dressy. More Wailea highlights for your day of splurge shopping:

Coast Gallery Wailea. 3750 Wailea Alanui Dr., in the Wailea Shopping Village. ☎ **808/879-2301.**

This venerable Maui gallery recently moved from the Aston Wailea to an attractive space in the Shopping Village, where the same level of service and selection prevails. From its inception in the mid-1980s, the Coast Gallery has maintained a high profile and level of esteem for its well-balanced mix of local, national, and international artists. Wood carvings, feather art, oil paintings, jewelry, bronze sculpture, prints, ceramics, and tasteful marinescapes reflect the discriminating tastes of the gallery owners, who include old masters and new talent in the selected works. This is a powerful and attractive venue for island artists, who are well represented in the collection.

Grand Wailea Shops. At the Grand Wailea Resort, 3850 Wailea Alanui Dr. ☎ **808/875-1234.**

The gargantuan Grand Wailea Resort has always been known for its long arcade of shops and galleries tailored to hefty pocketbooks. However, gift items in all price ranges can be found at **Lahaina Printsellers** (the premier store for old maps and prints), **Dolphin Galleries, H. F. Wichman, Sandal Tree,** the blindingly white resort shop called **Cruise,** and the **Napua Gallery,** which houses the private collection of the resort owner. And these are only some of the shops that line the arcade.

Ki'i Gallery. 3850 Wailea Alanui, Grand Wailea Resort. ☎ **808/871-4557.**

Its new location is slightly larger than a corner, but what a corner it is. Sleek and taut, the gallery is luminous with studio glass and the warm glow of exquisitely turned woods. Dale Zarella's naio wood sculpture on a koa and marble base is breathtaking, as is the Romeo glass vase from Amsterdam. The first Ki'i Gallery remains in Kaahumanu Center in Kahului.

⭐ **Mango Club.** In the Kea Lani Hotel, 4100 Wailea Alanui Dr. ☎ **808/874-1885.**

Shop here if you like the hip retro look, or if you just need a spiffy swimsuit. Treasures await on those racks of aloha shirts, vintage muumuus, 1940s tea-timer tops, and contemporary silk aloha shirts in authentic fabric prints from the 1920s to 1940s. Draped on the walls are collectible treasures with collectible prices, such as aloha shirts and Chinese-collared muumuus from the 1940s in vintage rayon. A dress or an aloha shirt in good shape could carry a price tag in the hundreds of dollars, but the modern retros by Avanti, Kamehameha, and Reyn Spooner offer the same look at a fraction of the price. Nicole Miller dresses, La Perla and Diva swimwear, Private Eyes sunglasses—we love Mango Club for its spirited tropical chic.

Wailea Shopping Village. 3750 Wailea Alanui Dr.

Wailea's only shopping complex is a mediocre assemblage of usually empty boutiques, a couple of galleries and gift shops, and the ubiquitous **Whalers General Store,** where people shop for macadamia nuts, newspapers, postcards, ice, sunscreen, Hawaiian teas, and wines at inflated prices. Otherwise, you'll find great shades at **For Your Eyes Only,** and rare, luminous pearls at the **Black Pearl Gallery.** Two bright spots in this complex are **The Elephant Walk** gift shop, where you can find quilted palaka house slippers, Lilikoi Gold Passion Fruit Butter, and coconut lidded bowls; and the tiny **Wailea Espresso,** a kiosk near the parking lot where cappuccino and cinnamon rolls move briskly.

4 Upcountry Maui

MAKAWAO

Besides being a shopper's paradise, Makawao is the home of the island's most prominent arts organization, the **Hui No'eau Visual Arts Center,** 2841 Baldwin Ave. (☎ **808/572-6560**). Designed in 1917 by C. W. Dickey, one of Hawaii's most prominent architects, the two-story, Mediterranean-style stucco home that houses the center is located on a sprawling, manicured, 9-acre estate called Kaluanui. A tree-lined driveway leading here features two of Maui's largest hybrid Cook and Norfolk Island pines. Also part of the estate is a former sugar mill that was once run by mule power. A legacy of Maui's prominent kamaaina, Harry and Ethel Baldwin, the estate became an art center in 1976 and remains a complete esthetic experience. Visiting artists offer lectures, classes, and demonstrations, all at reasonable prices, in basketry, jewelry making, ceramics, printmaking, painting, and all conceivable media. Half-day classes on Hawaiian art, culture, and history are available to visitors and residents. The Hui is also one of the few facilities available on Maui for independent art study and studios. Call ahead for schedules and details. A unique gift shop is worth a special stop, featuring many one-of-a-kind works by local artists and artisans. The exhibits at Hui No'eau are drawn from a wide range of disciplines and include both contemporary and traditional art from established and emerging artists. Maui artists long to exhibit here, because they consider it the most prestigious of venues. Gift shop and gallery hours are Monday through Saturday from 10am to 4pm.

✪ **Collections.** 3677 Baldwin Ave. ☎ **808/572-0781.**

Collections is a longtime Makawao attraction that shows renewed vigor after more than 2 decades on Baldwin Avenue. Its selection of sportswear, soaps, jewelry, candles, and tasteful, marvelous miscellany reflects the buyer's good sense and good style. Dresses, separates, home and bath accessories, sweaters, and a shop full of good things make this a Makawao must.

Holiday & Co. 3681 Baldwin Ave. ☎ **808/572-1470.**

Attractive women's clothing in natural fibers hang from racks, and jewelry to go with it beckons from the counter. Recent finds include lotus-fiber bags from Bali, unlike any you've seen before, and Ambre bubble bath, expensive and French and worth it. The latest in comfortable clothing and interchangeable styles in easy-care fabrics are the Holiday signature. Classic linen dresses, cotton and chenille sweaters, tasteful T-shirts, and silks in all weaves fill this understated store.

Hurricane. 3639 Baldwin Ave. ☎ **808/572-5076.**

Sigrid Olsen's clothing line for women claims a larger part of the floor space, but who cares? It's expensive but wonderful—knitted shells, Tencel jeans and skirts, cardigans, extraordinary silk tank dresses. The split-level boutique with gleaming knotty-pine floors and a cache of finds carries clothing two steps ahead of the competition. Tommy Bahama silk pique aloha print dresses and jeans, Sigrid Olsen dresses and T-shirts, and hard-to-find, eccentric books and home accessories are part of the Hurricane appeal. Next door is the men's version of Hurricane, **Tropo,** where stylish, sensitive men can shop for the latest in shirts, and the literary tomes to go with them.

Maui Girl. 3663 Baldwin Ave. ☎ **808/572-9576.**

Makawao's ever-changing commercial landscape has sprouted a chic new boutique with—surprise!—some things you're not likely to find anywhere else. Splashing the shop with color are gorgeous linen separates by Kleen, City Lights sportswear, loungewear too good for lounging, and clothing and accessories that will take you from a hot Lahaina lunch to a cool Makawao evening. A favorite: those bright, kicky retro aloha-printed pajama sets by Nick & Nora Sleepwear, party wear for the bold. There are a small selection of jewelry and a bigger selection of leather bags.

A branch in Paia, 12 Baldwin Ave. (☎ **808/579-9266**), carries mucho swimwear for the windsurfing culture.

The Mercantile. 3673 Baldwin Ave. ☎ **808/572-1407.**

The jewelry, home accessories (especially the Tiffany-style glass-and-shell lamps), dinnerware, Provençal soaps, pocket knives, and clothing are tastefully selected—a salute to the good life. Soothing eye pillows filled with flax seeds, scented neck pillows, and a riveting section of Bopla dinnerware, decorated by different designers and made of durable hotel porcelain, make it hard to stick to the clothing. Italian linen clothing for men and women, and designer jewelry by Dana Kellin and Beth Orduna, are fun to look at, but expensive.

⭕ **Ola's.** In the Paniolo Building, 1156 Makawao Ave. ☎ **808/573-1334.**

Doug Britt's scintillating paintings and photographs by his wife, Sharon, line the walls of Makawao's top gift gallery. The Britts own Ola's Hanalei on Kauai and helped set up Makawao's version, under different ownership (sisters Cindy Heacock and Shari O'Brien) but designed around the same concept of handmade American-made art by more than 100 artists, including Hawaii's best. Ola's is a bright, crisp, uncluttered, and thoughtfully designed space with a beach-glass counter, concrete floors, and objects that look great, feel good, and have varying degrees of utility. There's the koa-maple checkerboard, a masterpiece of detail; melodious thumb pianos, called kalimbas; elegant Lundberg studio glass, including a celestial lamp; cards; jewelry; and exquisite porcelain vases, with Picassoesque anatomical features, by Donna Polseno. Enjoy the chopsticks, silks, glass, wood, ceramics, bath products, and art, but don't forget Bella's at Ola's, a line of fourth-generation, handmade chocolates from Brooklyn, offered in 12 pricey but irresistible varieties.

Viewpoints Gallery. 3620 Baldwin Ave. ☎ **808/572-5979.**

Maui's only fine-arts cooperative showcases the work of dozens of Maui artists in an airy, attractive gallery located in a restored theater with a courtyard, a glass-blowing studio, and restaurants. This is a delightful odyssey through the creative atmosphere of Maui, where painters, sculptors, printmakers, and jewelers are fortunate to have a space like Viewpoints. The gallery features two-dimensional art, jewelry, fiber art, stained glass, papermaking, sculpture, and other media. A high degree of professionalism is maintained because the artists involved have passed a rigorous screening, and all are full-time professionals. Viewpoints is a fine example of what can happen in a collectively supportive artistic environment.

UPCOUNTRY EDIBLES

Working folks in Makawao who long to eat in arrive at the **Rodeo General Store,** 3661 Baldwin Ave. (☎ **808/572-7841**), to pick up their spaghetti and lasagna, sandwiches, salads, and changing specials from the deli. Even in their plastic-wrapped paper trays, the pastas are tasty, as if they came from a neighborhood trattoria in Little Italy. You can pick up all the necessary accompaniments here, from fresh produce, wine, and soft drinks to paper products and baked goods.

Down to Earth Natural Foods, 1169 Makawao Ave. (☎ **808/572-1488**), always has fresh salads and sandwiches at the salad bar, a full section of organic produce (Kula onions, strawberry papayas, mangos and litchis in season), bulk grains, vitamins and supplements, beauty aids, herbs, juices, snacks, condiments, tofu, seaweed, soy products, and aisles of vegetarian and health foods—canned, packaged, prepared, and fresh. Whether it's a smoothie, Ginger Blast, or burrito, it's Down to Earth territory.

Untold numbers have creaked over the wooden floors to pick up Komoda's famous cream puffs in the more than 6 decades that the **T. Komoda Store and Bakery,** 3674 Baldwin Ave. (☎ **808/572-7261**), has spent in this spot. Old-timers know to come early or the cream puffs will be sold out. Then the cinnamon rolls, doughnuts, pies, chocolate cake, and assorted edibles take over, keeping the aromas of fresh baking wafting through the old store. Pastries are just the beginning; poi, macadamia nut candies and cookies, and small bunches of local fruit in season keep the customers coming.

FRESH FLOWERS IN KULA

Like anthuriums on the Big Island, proteas are a Maui trademark and an abundant crop on Haleakala's rich volcanic slopes. They also travel well, dry beautifully, and can be shipped worldwide with ease. Among Maui's most prominent sources are **Sunrise Protea** (☎ 808/876-0200) in Kula. It has a walk-through garden and gift shops and provides friendly service and a larger-than-usual selection. The freshly cut flowers arrive from the fields on Tuesday and Friday afternoons. You can order individual blooms, baskets, arrangements, or wreaths for shipping all over the world. (Next door, the Sunrise Country Market proffers fresh local fruits, snacks, and sandwiches, with picnic tables for lingering.) **Proteas of Hawaii** (☎ 808/878-2533), another reliable source, offers regular walking tours of the University of Hawaii Extension Service gardens across the street in Kula. **Clouds Rest Protea** (☎ 808/878-2544) has a garden and an extensive selection, and will ship anywhere in the United States.

For flower shopping in other parts of Maui, **Ooka Super Market** (see "Central Maui Edibles," above) and the Saturday-morning **Maui Swap Meet** (see "Kahului," above) are among the best and least expensive places for tropical flowers of every stripe.

5 East Maui: On the Road to Hana

PAIA

Katie's Place Gifts & Collectibles. At Baldwin Ave. and Hana Hwy. ☎ 808/579-8660.

More hula dolls! Find the wiggling collectibles here in all price ranges, a good match for the Don Blanding dinnerware (popular and hard to find), Depression glass, salt and pepper shakers, Matson liner menus, music sheets, vintage 1940s bark-cloth curtains, tablecloths and linens, and countless other snippets of the past, ephemera and textiles galore, with prices ranging from $10 to $60. As with all collectibles shops, there are things for both serious and whimsical collectors, and the selection changes constantly.

Maui Crafts Guild. 43 Hana Hwy. ☎ 808/579-9697.

The old wooden storefront at the gateway to Paia houses local crafts of high quality and in all price ranges, from pit-fired Raku to bowls of Norfolk pine and other Maui woods fashioned by Maui hands. Basketry, scarves, jewelry, bamboo flutes, koa accessories, prints, pressed flowers, and hundreds of items are displayed in the rustic two-story gift gallery. The shop ships anywhere, and all artists are selectively screened.

EDIBLES ON THE ROAD TO HANA

A golden retriever named Mahi holds court with his growing public at the **Maui Grown Market,** 914 Hana Hwy., Paia (☎ 808/572-1693). As much of an attraction as the Maui produce sold here, Mahi has a gregarious nature that prompts some dog-sick visitors to take her to Hana for the day. But the friendly country store holds its own, with avocado trees, a white picket fence, and picnic tables on a deck. Maui produce abounds: fresh bananas, papayas, starfruit, chirimoyas, pineapples, tomatoes, onions, mangoes in season, lettuces, and whatever can be harvested from all corners of the island. Jams made in Makawao and Maui onion mustards are big sellers, as are the sandwiches drenched in homemade dressings. There are many options for the 54-mile Hana drive, among them the Hana box lunches in coolers loaned for the day for a returnable $5 deposit.

Home-grown aloha is what you'll find at the roadside oasis known as **Uncle Harry's Hawaiian Crafts and Fresh Fruits,** on the Hana Highway, Keanae (☎ **808/248-7019**), about halfway to Hana. Local papayas, bananas, lilikoi, coconuts, and other produce from the region are sold at this Keanae landmark, a legacy of the late Uncle Harry Mitchell, a local legend and respected Hawaiian elder who devoted his life to the Hawaiian-rights and nuclear-free movements. You can browse among the wood carvings and Hawaiian crafts and stock up on smoothies, chips, and snacks for the road.

6 At the End of the Road in East Maui: Hana

Hasegawa General Store. Hana Hwy. ☎ **808/248-8231.**

Established in 1910, immortalized in song since 1961, burned to the ground in 1990, and back in business in 1991, this legendary store is indefatigable and more colorful than ever in its third generation in business. The aisles are choked with merchandise: Hana-blend coffee specially roasted and blended for the store, Ono Farms organic dried fruit, fishing equipment, every tape and CD that mentions Hana, the best books on Hana to be found, T-shirts, beach and garden essentials, mugs, baseball caps, film, baby food, napkins, and other necessities for the Hana life.

11

Maui After Dark

by Jocelyn Fujii

The island's most prestigious entertainment venue is the $28 million **Maui Arts and Cultural Center** in Kahului (☎ **808/242-7469**), a long-awaited, first-class center for the visual and performing arts. It has proved to be an astonishing success, a Maui star. Bonnie Raitt has performed here, as have Pearl Jam, Ziggy Marley, and Tony Bennett, not to mention the finest in local and Hawaii talent. It has booked world-class cultural exhibits, rock and reggae, the Lakota Sioux Indian Dance Theatre, Santana, the Maui Symphony Orchestra, the stars of the Moscow Ballet, magic shows, the Hawaii International Film Festival, and many other notable acts. The center is as precious to Maui as the Met is to New York, with a visual-arts gallery, an outdoor amphitheater, offices, rehearsal space, a 300-seat theater for experimental performances, and a 1,200-seat main theater. Since its 1994 opening, the state-of-the-art facilities have attracted first-rate performers and sold-out shows. Whether it's Willie Nelson or Hawaiian music icon Keali'i Reichel, only the best will appear at the Maui Arts and Cultural Center. The center's activities are well publicized locally, so check the *Maui News* or ask your hotel concierge what's going on at the center during or before your visit.

HAWAIIAN MUSIC

Except for Casanova in Makawao, Hapa's in Kihei, and Tsunami in Wailea, nightlife options on this island are limited. The major hotels generally have lobby lounges offering regular Hawaiian music, soft jazz, or hula shows beginning at sunset. If the duo called **Hapa, Willie K and Amy Gilliom** or the soloist called **Keali'i Reichel** are playing anywhere on their native island, don't miss them; they're a Hawaiian music bonanza, among the finest Hawaiian musicians around today.

JAZZ & BLUES

To find out what's happening in jazz or blues, look in at **Hapa's Brew Haus** (☎ **808/879-9001**) in Kihei (see "South Maui," below). It seems to be the nightlife nexus for this genre, with quality music and overflow crowds that linger into the wee hours. The thriving blues scene throughout Hawaii can be credited to the efforts of Louie Wolfenson, his partner Kurt Kangas, and the **Maui Blues Association** (☎ **808/879-6123**), which books sold-out

It Begins with Sunset . . .

Nightlife in Maui begins at sunset, when all eyes turn westward to see how the day will end. Like spotting the same whale or school of spinner dolphins, sunset viewers seem to bond in the mutual enjoyment of a natural spectacle. And what better way to take it all in than over cocktails? Maui is a haven for lovers of both. With its view of Molokai to the northwest and Lanai to the west, Kaanapali and the west Maui destinations are graced with panoramic vistas unique to this island. In south Maui's Wailea and Makena, tiny Kahoolawe and the crescent-shaped Molokini islet are visible as familiar forms on the horizon, and the West Maui Mountains look like an entirely separate island. No matter what your vantage point, you are likely to be treated to an astonishing view.

Sunset viewers along south and west Maui shorelines need only head for the ocean and find a seat. Our favorite sunset watering holes begin with **the Bay Club at Kapalua** (☎ 808/669-5656), where the northwesterly view of Molokai and Lanai is enhanced by the elegant surroundings. It's quiet here, removed from the hubbub that prevails in the more populated Kaanapali Beach Resort to the south.

In Kaanapali, park in Whaler's Village and head for **Leilani's** (☎ 808/661-4495) or **Hula Grill** (☎ 808/667-6636), next to each other on the beach. Both have busy, upbeat bars and tables bordering the sand. These are happy places for great people-watching, gazing at the lump of Lanai that looks to be a stone's throw away, and enjoying end-of-day rituals like Mai Tais and margaritas. Hula Grill's Barefoot Bar appetizer menu is a cut above, offering such treats as macadamia-nut/crab wontons, fresh fish and chips, and pizza.

And Lahaina: It's a sunset-lover's nirvana, lined with restaurants that hang over the ocean and offer fresh fish in a multitude of forms—and Mai Tais elevated to an art form. If you love loud rock, head for **Cheeseburger in Paradise** (☎ 808/661-4855). A few doors away, **Lahaina Fish Company** (☎ 808/661-3472) and **Kimo's** (☎ 808/661-4811) are magnets all day long and

events at clubs throughout the state. Check the papers to see what's on while you're on Maui. The annual Islands Blues Mele, a festival around Memorial Day, grows by the year and has assumed a life of its own.

MOVIES

Film buffs can check the local newspapers to see what's playing at the few theaters around town: the **Kaahumanu Theatres** in the Kaahumanu Center in Kahului (☎ 808/873-3133); the **Maui Theatre** in the Kahului Shopping Center (☎ 808/877-3560); the **Kukui Mall Theater** at 1819 S. Kihei Rd. in Kihei (☎ 808/875-4533); and the **Wallace Theatres** in Lahaina (☎ 808/661-3347), at the Wharf Cinema Center, 658 Front St., and the Front Street Theatres at the Lahaina Center, 900 Front St.

1 West Maui

LAHAINA

At **Longhi's** (☎ 808/667-2288), live music spills out into the streets from 9:30pm to midnight on Fridays and Saturdays. Usually it's salsa or jazz, but call ahead to confirm. Other special gigs can be expected if rock 'n' rollers or jazz musicians who especially at sunset, when their open decks fill up with happy revelers. These three restaurants occupy the section of Front Street between Lahainaluna Road and Papalaua Street. At the southern end of Lahaina town, in the 505 Front St. complex, **Pacific'o** (☎ 808/667-4341) is a solid hit, with a raised bar, seating on the ocean, and a backdrop of Lanai across the channel. Besides the view and the friendly service, the food is notable, having won many awards for seafood in its brief history.

Moving south toward Wailea, the harbor stop called Maalaea is famous for its whale sightings during the winter months. Year-round, **Buzz's Wharf** (☎ 808/244-5426) is a formula restaurant with a superb ocean view and continuous service between lunch and dinner. Those are the basic makings of a sunset-viewing way station. Add an ice-cold beer or Mai Tai and a steaming order of fish and chips, and the sunset package is complete.

In Wailea, our favorite stop is the **Hula Moons** outdoor terrace at Aston Wailea Resort (☎ 808/879-1922)—for the ambience if not the food. It's more open than its fancier neighbors, and, in a corny but romantic touch, live Hawaiian music with a hula dancer is offered daily from 5:30 to 9:30pm. In Makena resort further south, you can't beat the Maui Prince's **Molokini Lounge** (☎ 808/874-1111), with its casual elegance and unequalled view of Molokini islet on the ocean side and, on the mountain side, a graceful, serene courtyard with ponds, rock gardens, and lush foliage. Adding to the setting is the appetizer menu, which comes from the esteemed Prince Court kitchen. From 5 to 9:30pm nightly, the pupu menu features a $15 Molokini sampler platter (Thai-style spring rolls, shrimp summer rolls, ahi sashimi), a $10 seared ahi seaweed salad on a tortilla shell, and pan-fried tiger shrimp ($12). Live Hawaiian music is offered from 6:30 to 10:30pm nightly, with a mini hula show (a duo plus two dancers) from 6 to 6:45pm.

are friends of the owner happen to be passing through. It wouldn't hurt to ask what's happening here.

You won't have to ask what's going on at **Cheeseburger in Paradise** (☎ 808/661-4855), the two-story green-and-white building at the corner of Front and Lahainaluna streets. Just go outside and you'll hear it: loud, live, and lively tropical rock blasting into the streets and out to sea daily from 4:30 to 11pm.

AN INTIMATE AFFAIR: LUAU, MAUI STYLE

Most of the larger hotels in Maui's major resorts offer luaus and Polynesian entertainment on a regular basis. You'll pay about $60 or more to attend one, and to protect yourself from disappointment, don't expect it to be a home-grown affair prepared in the traditional Hawaiian way. The labor-intensive nature of this traditional Hawaiian feast makes it an impossible endeavor for large-scale commercial operations offered on a regular basis. There are, however, commercial luaus that capture the romance and spirit of the affair with quality food and entertainment in outdoor settings.

Maui's best luau is indisputably the nightly **Old Lahaina Luau,** on the beach side of 505 Front St. in Lahaina (☎ 808/667-1998). At this writing, there are plans to move the luau a few blocks north in Lahaina, to a presently vacant 2-acre site just oceanside of the Lahaina Cannery. In the works are thatched buildings, an amphitheater seating, and a price increase of less than 10%, but the phone number will remain the same. This is the consummate luau, with a healthy balance of entertainment, showmanship, good food, educational value, and sheer romantic beauty. It begins at sunset and features Tahitian and Hawaiian entertainment, including ancient hula and an intelligent narrative on its rocky course of survival into modern times. The entertainment is riveting, even for jaded locals, and the food is entirely authentic: imu-roasted kalua pig, lomi salmon, poi, dried fish, poke, breadfruit, sweet potato, and, for the more cautious, teriyaki steak, barbecued chicken, and mahimahi. The cost is $62 plus tax for adults, $30 for children. The event is often booked a week in advance, so call ahead.

The **Maui Marriott Luau** (☎ **808/667-1200**) is, of course, beachside in Kaanapali, and it costs $60 for adults and $27 for children, free for those under 5. An open bar, a Hawaiian menu, and an after-dinner show add up to a pleasing experience, with fire dancers and traditional hula. The luau is offered from 5 to 8pm nightly.

If you'd like to be prepared for your luau, head over to **Wailea Shopping Village,** 3750 Wailea Alanui Dr., where free hula lessons are offered every Wednesday; there's also Polynesian entertainment every Tuesday.

2 South Maui

KIHEI

Hapa's Brew Haus (☎ **808/879-9001**) is the only game in town. And with its fairly recent renovations, tiered seating, state-of-the-art sound and lighting, and 40-seat oval bar, it's quite popular. Happy hours here are generous, with free pizza and $2 drafts from 5 to 6pm daily. Every Tuesday is comedy night, followed by DJ spins. When visiting bands are featured, improvisation and jamming bring a pulsing spontaneity to the scene. Call the hotline, ☎ **808/875-1990,** to find out whether jazz, blues, rock, reggae, funk, Hawaiian, or the duo Hapa's slack key will be filling the house. (See also page 144 in chapter 7.)

WAILEA

The Grand Wailea Resort's **Tsunami** (☎ **808/875-1234**), Maui's most high-tech club, happens to be South Maui's only nightspot for dancing. But what a club: 10,000 square feet, with marble, laser lights, huge video screens, futuristic decor, and well-dressed revelers. It's all disco, no live music, and is open Thursday, Friday, and Saturday from 9pm to 2am. The DJ plays everything from 1980s hits to Top 40. Thursday is ladies' night: no cover charge for women, drink specials, and a flower or other memento for the wily females who turn out to "dress and impress." On Fridays, "Flashback Fever" (music from the '70s and '80s) takes over. Cover charge is $5 on Thursday and Friday and $10 on Saturday.

3 Upcountry Maui

Upcountry in Makawao, the partying never ends at **Casanova** (☎ **808/572-0220**), the popular Italian ristorante where the good times roll with the pasta (see the full review in chapter 7). If a big-name mainland band is resting up on Maui following a sold-out concert on Oahu, you might find its members setting up for an impromptu night here. On Maui, word spreads quickly. DJs take over on

Wednesday (ladies' night) and Thursday nights. Every other Thursday is a fund-raiser for the Maui AIDS Society, and on Friday and Saturday, live entertainment draws fun-lovers from even the most remote reaches of the island. Entertainment starts at 9:45pm and continues to 1:30am. Expect good blues, rock 'n' roll, reggae, jazz, Hawaiian, and the top names in local and visiting entertainment. Elvin Bishop, the local duo Hapa, Los Lobos, and many others have filled Casanova's stage and limelight. The cover charge is usually $5.

12

Molokai, the Most Hawaiian Isle

Born of volcanic eruptions 1½ million years ago, Molokai remains a time capsule on the eve of the 21st century. It has no deluxe resorts, no fancy restaurants, no stoplights, and no buildings taller than a coconut tree. Less is definitely more on this languid island—and, fortunately for adventure travelers, Molokai is the least developed, most "Hawaiian" of all the islands.

The cradle of Hawaiian dance (the hula was born here), the ancient science of aquaculture, and sacred rites, Molokai lives up to its reputation as the most Hawaiian place chiefly through its lineage; there are, in fact, more people here of Hawaiian blood than anywhere else. An aura of ancient mysticism clings to the slipper-shaped island, and the old ways still govern life here. The residents survive by taking fish from the sea and hunting wild pigs and Axis deer on the range. Some folks still catch reef fish in throw nets and troll the reef for squid, a traditional Hawaiian delicacy. Families are important, friendship ties are cherished, and the Hawaiian concept of taking care of the land remains a priority. Modern Hawaii's high-rise hotels, shopping centers, and other trappings of tourism haven't been able to gain a foothold here—one lone low-rise resort, Kaluakoi, built more than 20 years ago, is Molokai's token attempt at contemporary tourism.

The only "new" development since Kaluakoi is the Molokai Ranch's eco-tourism project of upscale "camping," in semi-permanent "tentalows" (a combination of a bungalow and a tent) on the 53,000-acre ranch. The focus here is on outdoor recreation and adventure with a comfortable place to sleep in the wilderness.

The slow-paced, simple life of the people and the absence of contemporary landmarks are what attracts those in search of the "real" Hawaii. But what makes them stand in awe is this little island's diverse natural wonders: Hawaii's highest waterfall and greatest collection of fishponds, the world's tallest sea cliffs, sand dunes, coral reefs, rain forests, hidden coves—and empty, gloriously empty, beaches.

Exploring the "Most Hawaiian" Isle   Only 38 miles from end to end and just 10 miles wide, Molokai stands like a big green wedge in the blue Pacific. It has an east side, a west side, a back side, and a top side. Formed by three volcanic eruptions, the long, narrow island is like yin and yang: one side is a flat, austere, arid desert; the other is a lush, green, steepled tropical Eden. But the volcanic gods weren't done

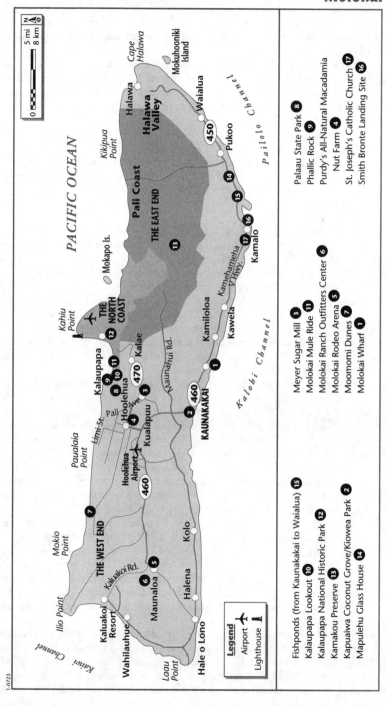

Molokai

Legend
✈ Airport
🗼 Lighthouse

Meyer Sugar Mill ③
Molokai Mule Ride ⑪
Molokai Ranch Outfitters Center ⑥
Molokai Rodeo Arena ⑤
Moomomi Dunes ⑦
Molokai Wharf ①

Fishponds (from Kaunakakai to Waialua) ⑮
Kalaupapa Lookout ⑩
Kalaupapa National Historic Park ⑫
Kamakou Preserve ⑬
Kapuaiwa Coconut Grove/Kiowea Park ②
Mapulehu Glass House ⑭

Palaau State Park ⑧
Phallic Rock ⑨
Purdy's All-Natural Macadamia
Nut Farm ④
St. Joseph's Catholic Church ⑰
Smith Bronte Landing Site ⑯

255

with Molokai until a third eruption produced the island's "thumb"—a peninsula jutting out of the steep cliffs of the north shore, like a punctuation mark on the island's geological story.

The few tourists who come here are separated from the adventurers at Hoolehua, home to Molokai's tin-roofed, lava-rock airport. Those who deplane in boots—hiking or cowboy—are going one place, and those in tasseled loafers or white tennies are heading for quite another. Most everyone ends up barefoot on the beach, but the transition is toughest on city slickers.

On the red-dirt southern plain, where most of the island's 6,000 residents live, the rustic village of Kaunakakai looks like the set of an old Hollywood western, with sun-faded clapboard houses and horses tethered in tall grass on the side of the road. At mile marker 0, in the center of town, the island is divided into East and West so dramatically that an arid cactus desert lies on one side, and a lush coco-palm jungle on the other.

Eastbound, along the coastal highway named for King Kamehameha V, are Gauguin-like, palm-shaded cottages, set on small coves or near fishponds; spectacular vistas that take in Maui, Lanai, and Kahoolawe; and a fringing coral reef visible through the crystal-clear waves.

Out on the sun-scorched west end is the island's lone destination resort, Kaluakoi, overlooking a gold-sand beach too big to fit on a postcard with water usually too rough to swim. A few old-timers inhabit the old hilltop plantation town of Maunaloa, now being remade into an upscale version of itself. Cowboys ride the range on Molokai Ranch, a 53,000-acre spread. Adventure travelers and outdoor recreation buffs stay at the tentalows on the ranch property and spend their days mountain biking, kayaking, horseback riding, sailing, hiking, snorkeling, and just vegetating on the endless white-sand beaches.

Elsewhere around the island, in hamlets like Kualapuu, old farmhouses with pickup trucks in the yards and sleepy dogs under the shade trees stand amid row crops of papaya, coffee, and corn—just like farm towns in Anywhere, USA.

But that's not all there is. The "back side" of Molokai is a rugged wilderness of spectacular beauty. On the outskirts of Kaunakakai, the land rises gradually from sea-level fishponds to cool uplands and the Molokai Forest, long ago stripped of sandalwood for the China trade. All that remains is an indentation in the earth that natives shaped like a ship's hull, a crude matrix that gave them a rough idea of when they'd cut enough sandalwood to fill a ship (it's identified on good maps as Luanamokuiliahi, or Sandalwood Boat).

The land inclines sharply to the lofty mountains and the nearly mile-high summit of Mount Kamakou, then ends abruptly with emerald-green cliffs, which plunge into a lurid aquamarine sea dotted with tiny deserted islets. These breathtaking 3,250-foot sea cliffs, the highest in the world, stretch 14 majestic miles along Molokai's north shore, laced by waterfalls and creased by five Eden-like valleys—Halawa, Papalaua, Wailau, Pelekunu, and Waikolu—once occupied by early Hawaiians who built stone terraces and used waterfalls to irrigate taro patches.

Long after the sea cliffs were formed, a tiny volcano erupted out of the sea at their feet and spread lava into a flat, leaflike peninsula called Kalaupapa—the infamous 1860s leper exile where Father Damien de Veuster of Belgium devoted his life, caring for the afflicted. A few people remain in the remote colony by choice, keeping it tidy for the daily company that arrives on mules and small planes.

What a Visit to Molokai Is *Really* Like   There's plenty of aloha on Molokai, but the so-called "friendly island" remains ambivalent about vacationers. One of the least-visited Hawaiian islands, Molokai welcomes visitors on its own take-it-or-leave-it terms and makes few concessions beyond that of gracious host; it never wants to attract too big of a crowd, anyway. A sign at the airport offers the first clue: SLOW DOWN, YOU ON MOLOKAI NOW—a caveat to heed on this island, where life proceeds at its own pace.

Rugged, red-dirt Molokai isn't for everyone, but those who like to explore remote places and seek their own adventures should love it. The best of the island can be seen only on foot, mule, or horse, or via kayak or sailboat. The sea cliffs are accessible only by sea in the summer, when the Pacific is calm, or via a 10-mile trek through the Wailau Valley—an adventure only a handful of hardy hikers attempt each year. The great Kamakou Preserve is open just once a month, by special arrangement with the Nature Conservancy. Even Moomomi, which holds bony relics of prehistoric flightless birds and other Lost World creatures, requires a guide to divulge the secrets of the dunes.

Those in search of nightlife have come to the wrong place; Molokai shuts down after sunset. The only public diversions are softball games under the lights of Mitchell Pauole Field, movies at Maunaloa, and the few restaurants that stay open after dark, serving everything from local brew to pizza.

The "friendly" island might captivate you—on the other hand, you might leave with your head shaking, never to return. It all depends on how you approach Molokai. Boots or loafers. Either way, take it slow.

—Jeanette Foster

1 Orientation

by Jeanette Foster

ARRIVING

BY PLANE   Molokai has two airports, but you'll most likely fly into **Hoolehua Airport,** on a dusty plain about 6 miles from Kaunakakai town, which everyone calls "the Molokai Airport." From Maui, **Island Air** (☎ 800/323-3345 from the mainland, 800/652-6541 from Maui) offers four direct flights a day. A new Maui-based carrier, **Pacific Wings** (☎ 888/575-4546 from the mainland, 808/873-0877 from Maui; www.pacificwings.com), has just recently begun offering flights from Kahului to both Molokai airports, in eight-passenger, twin-engine Cessna 402-C aircraft.

Molokai Air Shuttle (☎ 808/545-4988) and **Hawaiian Airlines** (☎ 800/367-5320 or 808/553-3644) both have direct daily flights from Honolulu to Molokai.

VISITOR INFORMATION

Look for a sun-faded yellow building on the main drag, Kamehameha V Highway (Highway 460), on the right just past the town's first stop sign, at mile marker 0; it's the **Molokai Visitors Association,** P.O. Box 960, Kaunakakai, HI 96748 (☎ **800/800-6367,** 808/553-3876 from the U.S. mainland and Canada, 800/553-0404 or 808/553-3876 interisland; www.molokai.com). The staff can give you all the information you need on what to see and do while you're on the friendly isle.

THE ISLAND IN BRIEF
KAUNAKAKAI

Dusty cars are parked diagonally along Ala Malama Street. The family car is a pickup truck. It could be any small town, except it's Kaunakakai, Molokai, 96748, where Friendly Isle Realty and Friendly Isle Travel offer islanders dream homes and impossible vacations; Rabang's Filipino Food posts bad checks in the window; antlered deer-head trophies guard the grocery aisles at Misaki's Market; and Kanemitsu's, the town's legendary bakery, churns out fresh loaves of onion-cheese bread daily.

Once an ancient canoe landing, Kaunakakai was the royal summer place of King Kamehameha V. The port town bustled when pineapple and sugar were king, but those days, too, are gone. With Old West–style storefronts laid out in a 3-block grid on a flat, dusty plain, Kaunakakai is a town from the past. Molokai's main settlement might appear rustic, but the spirit of aloha—the generous giving of one's self—still reigns. At the end of Wharf Road is **Molokai Wharf,** a rather picturesque place to fish, photograph, and just hang out.

THE NORTH COAST

Upland from Kaunakakai, the land tilts skyward and turns green with scented plumeria in yards and glossy coffee trees all in a row until it blooms into a true forest—then abruptly ends at a great precipice, falling 3,250 feet to the sea. The green cliffs are creased with five V-shaped cliffs so deep that light in the crevices is seldom seen (to paraphrase a Hawaii poet).

The north coast is the wild coast, a remote, forbidding place with a solitary peninsula—**Kalaupapa**—once the home for exiled lepers (it's now a national historical park). Easy on the eyes, difficult to visit.

THE WEST END

This end of the island, home to **Molokai Ranch,** is miles of stark, minimal desert terrain, bordered by the most beautiful white-sand beaches in Hawaii. The rugged rolling terrain slopes down to Molokai's only destination resort, **Kaluakoi,** a cul-de-sac of condos clustered around a 20-year-old seafront hotel near 3-mile-long Papohaku, the island's biggest beach. On the way to Kaluakoi—where everyone shows up at least once, if only to wait in line to eat dinner at Ohia Lodge—you'll find **Maunaloa,** a 1920s-era pineapple plantation town that, in Molokai's first and only urban renewal project, is in the midst of being transformed into a master-planned community, Maunaloa Village.

THE EAST END

The area east of Kaunakakai becomes lush, green, and tropical, with golden pocket beaches and a handful of cottages and condos that are popular with thrifty travelers. Beyond Kaunakakai, the two-lane road curves along the coast past piggeries, palm groves, and a 20-mile string of fishponds, as well as an ancient heiau, Damien-built churches, and a few contemporary condos by the sea. It ends in the earthly paradise of **Halawa Valley,** one of Hawaii's most beautiful valleys.

2 Getting Around

by Jeanette Foster

Getting around Molokai isn't easy if you don't have a rental car, and rental cars are often hard to find on Molokai. On holiday weekends—and remember, Hawaii celebrates different holidays than the rest of the United States (see "When to Go" in chapter 3)—car-rental agencies simply run out of cars. Book before you go. There's no municipal transit or shuttle service, but a 24-hour taxi service is available.

CAR-RENTAL AGENCIES   Rental cars are available from **Budget** (☎ 808/ 567-6877) and **Dollar** (☎ 808/567-6156); both agencies are located at the Molokai Airport.

TAXI & TOUR SERVICES   Regular taxi service and island tours are offered by **Molokai Off-Road Tours & Taxi** (☎ 808/553-3369). **Kukui Tours & Limousines** (☎ 808/553-5133) has air-conditioned limos available for tours, airport shuttle, and 24-hour taxi service.

FAST FACTS: Molokai

Molokai, like Lanai, is part of Maui County. For **local emergencies,** call **911.** For non-emergencies, call ☎ 808/553-5355 for police, ☎ 808/553-5601 for fire, and ☎ 808/553-5331 for **Molokai General Hospital,** in Kaunakakai. Downtown Kaunakakai also has a **post office** (☎ 808/553-5845) and several banks, including the **Bank of Hawaii** (☎ 808/553-3273), which has a 24-hour ATM.

Rawlins Chevron Service (mile marker 0, Kaunakakai; ☎ 808/553-3214) is the "last stop to the airport from Kaunakakai"—where you'll rush to fill up your rental car with 87-octane at the self-serve pump. Or wish you had. It's open Monday through Thursday from 6:30am to 8:30pm, Friday and Saturday until 9pm, and Sunday from 7am to 6pm.

3 Accommodations

by Jeanette Foster

Molokai is Hawaii's most affordable island; in fact, hotel prices here are lower than those on any other island. Plus, because the island's restaurants are few, most hotel rooms and condos come with kitchens, which can save you a bundle on dining costs.

There aren't a ton of accommodations options on Molokai—mostly B&Bs, condos, and a handful of funky hotels that are really more like motels. Camping on Molokai involves two options: the upscale tentalows offered by Molokai Ranch, along with a host of activities; or, for hardy souls, camping with your own tent at the beach or in the cool upland forest (see "Hiking & Camping," below). We've listed our top picks below; you might want to contact **Destination Molokai Association** (☎ 800/800-6367; fax 808/553-5288) for additional options.

Note: Taxes of 10.17% will be added to your hotel bill.

KAUNAKAKAI
MODERATE

Molokai Shores Suites. Kamehameha V Hwy. (P.O. Box 1037), Kaunakakai, HI 96748. ☎ **800/535-0085** or 808/553-5954. Fax 808/553-5954. E-mail: marc@marcresorts.com. 100 oceanfront apts. TV. $129 one-bedroom apt (sleeps up to 4); $159 two-bedroom apt (sleeps up to 6). AE, DC, JCB, MC, V.

Bright, clean, basic units with kitchens and large lanais face a small gold-sand beach and the ocean beyond in this quiet complex of three-story Polynesian-style buildings, less than a mile from Kaunakakai. Alas, the beach is mostly for show (offshore, it's shallow mud flats underfoot), fishing, or launching kayaks, but the swimming pool comes with an ocean view. Well-tended gardens, spreading lawns, and palms frame a restful view of fishponds, offshore reefs, and neighbor islands. The central location can be a plus, minimizing driving time from the airport or town, and it's convenient to the mule ride, as well as the lush East End countryside. Discounted rates for weekly and extended stays; corporate, military, and seniors as well.

INEXPENSIVE

In addition to the choices listed below, you might check with **Hotel Molokai,** Kamehameha V Highway (P.O. Box 546), Kaunakakai, HI 96748 (☎ **800/ 423-6656** or 808/553-5347; fax 808/553-5047), once one of the island's prized oceanfront hotels, but now looking rather sad and neglected. In late 1997, the property was sold at auction; hopefully the new owners will give the place a much-needed facelift.

Kahale Mala Bed and Breakfast. 7 Kamakana Pl. (P.O. Box 1582), Kaunakakai, HI 96748. ☎/fax **808/553-9001.** www.Molokai.com/kahalemala. E-mail: cpgroup@aloha.net. 1 studio. TV. $60 double. Breakfast for an extra $10 for 2; extra person $15. No credit cards.

In a subdivision just outside of town (off Kamehameha V Highway, before the 5-mile marker), you'll find the home of Jack Pugh and Cheryl Corbeil. When they moved here from Western Canada, Jack and Cheryl loved the property but thought it was too big for two. So in 1995, they bought the house and started a one-room B&B. The large unit has a private entrance through the garden, with a Jacuzzi just outside. Inside, the decor consists of white rattan furnishings, including two twin beds, and a full kitchen—Cheryl will happily share her home-grown, organic produce. Although you'll pay less if you make your own breakfast, we recommend Cheryl's: taro pancakes, sourdough waffles, or a vegetable-egg pie, along with fresh fruit, homemade bread, muffins, and cinnamon buns.

Pau Hana Inn. 40 Oki Pl., off Kamehameha V Hwy. (P.O. Box 860), Kaunakakai, HI 96748. ☎ **800/433-6656** or 808/553-5342. Fax 808/553-3928. 40 units. $45 Long House double, $55 double in main hotel, $55–$69 cottage double (sleeps up to 4), $90 oceanfront double (sleeps up to 4). Extra person $10. AE, MC, V.

If you want to experience true Molokai living, we recommend this funky seaside hotel. It's not the plushest place on the island—just a quaint collection of cottages, studios, and hotel rooms that's been around for years—but it might be the friendliest. The Inn languished a bit when it was up for sale. At the end of 1997, the property was sold at a public auction, so the new owners might breathe life into this historic hotel. The grounds here remain tropically lush, and the pool is always crystal clear. There's a restaurant (yes, they still serve mahi-burgers), and the open-air bar attracts quite a crowd, especially on Friday nights, when you might encounter live music, dancing, and plenty of storytelling.

WEST END
MODERATE

Also consider **Kaluakoi Villas,** Kaluakoi Resort, 1131 Kaluakoi Rd., Maunaloa, HI 96770 (☎ **800/367-5004** or 808/552-2721; fax 800/477-2329 or 808/552-2201). The aging, Polynesian-style units are comfortable but could definitely use some work ($125 to $150 studio; $150 to $180 one-bedroom apt; $200 cottage). Another option is the **Kaluakoi Hotel & Golf Club,** Kaluakoi Resort (P.O. Box 1977), Kepuhi Beach, HI 96770 (☎ **888/552-2550** or 808/552-2555; fax 808/ 552-2821), the only resort hotel on the island, with a faultless location—but we still consider it way overpriced and in need of dire renovations. If you choose to stay here, book a condo with a kitchen ($105 to $130 double room; $205 to $275 suite; $155 to $170 studio; $185 to $195 one-bedroom condo; $220 one-bedroom cottage).

① Family-Friendly Accommodations

✪ **Great Molokai Ranch Trail** *(see p. 275)* The upscale, luxurious "camping" at the Panaolo Camp (on Molokai Ranch property, just outside of Maunalao) features comfortable bungalow-tents (called "tentalows") and lots of outdoor activities, including special activities for children. Prices ($185 each for adults and $75 each for children) include three all-you-can-eat meals and snacks every day, two activities, transportation (including airport pickup), and daily maid services.

Ke Nani Kai Resort *(see p. 261)*   Located in Kaluakoi Resort, these one- and two-bedroom condo units offer families lots of space with complete kitchens, washer/dryers, VCRs, attractive furnishings, and breezy lanais. For the active families, there's a huge pool, a volleyball court, tennis courts, and golf at neighboring Kaluakoi.

Molokai Shores Suites *(see p. 259)* At this great central location, just outside of Kaunakakai, families can choose from large one- and two-bedroom units in a tropical garden complex with great views of the fishponds, offshore reefs, and neighbor islands. Amenities include a swimming pool and laundry facilities; shopping is nearby.

✪ **Puunana/Pauwalu Beachfront Cottages** *(see p. 263)*   Private two-bedroom cottages, located on the beach in the lush East End—the perfect spot for a family getaway vacation. Each cottage sits on its own secluded beach and features complete kitchens, washer/dryers, VCRs, large decks, and breathtaking views (great for watching whales in the winter).

Ke Nani Kai Resort. Kaluakoi Resort, Kaluakoi Rd., off Hwy. 460 (P.O. Box 289), Maunaloa, HI 96770. ☎ **800/888-2791** or 808/552-2761. Fax 808/552-0045. E-mail: marc@marcresorts.com. 100 apts. TV TEL. $139–$159 one-bedroom apt (sleeps up to 4), $169–$199 two-bedroom apt (sleeps up to 4). 2-night minimum; 4-night minimum Dec 15–Jan 4. AE, CB, DC, DISC, JCB, MC, V.

A home away from home, especially for families who'll like the space and quiet. These large apartments are set up for full-time living with real kitchens, washer/dryers, VCRs, attractive furnishings, and breezy lanais. There are a huge pool, a volleyball court, tennis courts, and golf on the neighboring Kaluakoi course. These condos are the farthest from the sea of those at Kaluakoi Resort, but it's just a brief walk down to the hotel facilities and the beach beyond. The two-story buildings are surrounded by parking and garden areas.

✪ **Paniolo Hale.** Next door to Kaluakoi Resort, Lio Place (P.O. Box 190), Maunaloa, HI 96770. ☎ **800/367-2984** or 808/552-2731. Fax 808/552-2288. www.lava.net/paniolo. E-mail: paniolo@lava.net. 77 units. TV. $95–$155 double studio; $115–$180 one-bedroom apt (sleeps up to 4); $145–$215 two-bedroom apt (sleeps up to 6). Extra person $10. 2-night minimum; 1-week minimum Dec 20–Jan 5. AE, MC, V.

This is far and away Molokai's most charming lodging, and probably its best value—be sure to ask about discounted weekly rates and special condo/car packages when booking your reservations here. Paniolo Hale's two-story Old Hawaii ranch-house design is airy and homey, with oak floors and walls of folding glass doors that open to huge screened verandas, doubling your living space. The one- and two-bedrooms come with two baths, so they accommodate three or four easily. Some have hot tubs on the lanai. Units are spacious and well equipped, with full kitchens and washer/dryers. They're comfortably furnished by the owners, who run their own rental operation.

The whole place overlooks the Kaluakoi Golf Course, a green barrier that separates these condos from the rest of Kaluakoi Resort. Hotel shops, a restaurant, and a lounge are just across the fairway, as is Kepuhi Beach (these are the closest units to the beach); it's a scenic place to walk and beachcomb, but the seas are too hazardous for most swimmers. There are a pool, paddle tennis, and barbecue facilities on the property, which adjoins open grassland countryside.

EAST END
MODERATE

Wavecrest Resort. Kamehameha V Hwy. (P.O. Box 1037), Kaunakakai, HI 96748. ☎ **800/535-0085** or 808/558-8103. Fax 808/558-8206 or 800-633-5085. E-mail: marc@ marcresorts.com. 126 units. TV. $109–$139 one-bedroom apt (sleeps up to 4); $169 two-bedroom apt (sleeps up to 6). AE, MC, V.

When you want to get away and pull up the drawbridge, this is a good place to go. The condos—some of them newly remodeled, some in need of remodeling—are in three-story tropical structures surrounded by lawns, palms, mountainous inland slopes, and the solitude of the island's lush East End. The units, individually decorated by the owners, come with full kitchens, large lanais, and either garden or ocean views. If the complex is full, it can be noisy. Wavecrest is more remote than Molokai Shores—it's about 12 miles of leisurely driving to Kaunakakai (translation: 30-plus minutes), 7 more to the airport, and a substantial drive to West End activities—but more appropriately tropical than West End properties. Fortunately, there's a small store on the property for snacks, drinks, and video rentals, as well as two lighted tennis courts and a pool. The haunting views of the three neighboring islands provide a truly unique sense of place, but the shoreline here isn't Molokai's best for swimming.

INEXPENSIVE

Country Cottage at Puu O Hoku Ranch. Kamehameha V Hwy., at mile marker 25 (HC-01, Box 900), Kaunakakai, HI 96748. ☎ **808/558-8109.** Fax 808/558-8100. 1 two-bedroom cottage (sleeps up to 6). $85 double. Extra person $10. 2-night minimum. No credit cards.

Escape to a working cattle ranch! Ranch manager Jack Spruance welcomes visitors to *Puu o Hoku* (Star Hill) Ranch, which spreads across the East End of Molokai. The ranch, on 14,000 acres of pasture and forests, is the last place to stay before Halawa Valley—it's at least an hour's drive from Kaunakai along the shoreline. Two acres of tropically landscaped property circle the ranch's rustic cottage, which has breathtaking views of rolling hills and the Pacific ocean. The wooden cottage features comfortable country furniture, a fully equipped kitchen, two bedrooms (one with double bed, one with two twins), two baths, a big living area, and a separate dining room on the enclosed lanai. TVs and VCRs are available on request. We recommend stargazing at night, watching the sunrise in the morning, and playing in the afternoon: croquet, hiking, swimming, or just roaming the grounds.

Honomuni House. Kamehameha V Hwy., just after mile marker 17 (HC-01, Box 700), Kaunakakai, HI 96748. ☎ **808/558-8383.** 1 one-bedroom cottage. TV. $80 double. Extra person $10 adult, $5 child. No credit cards.

Old stonework taro terraces and house foundations testify that Honomuni Valley was popular with early Hawaiians, whose groves of breadfruit, coconut, fruit, ginger, and coffee still flourish in the wilderness. Modern folks can sample this mini-Eden at a remote cottage—17½ miles from Kaunakakai, a mile or more from the nearest public beach area—set in the forest along the foot of the East End up slope. Freshwater prawns and native fish hide out in the stream that carved the valley. Experienced hikers will enjoy exploring upstream, where they'll find pools for swimming and watching (or catching) prawns and, farther up, a waterfall of their very own. The small cottage has a complete kitchen, a separate bedroom, a full bathroom, and an outside shower for rinsing off the sand from the beach. You're welcome to enjoy the tropical fruits growing right on the premises, which are dominated by a huge monkeypod tree. The cottage does sit right on the road, but there's generally little traffic after dark.

✪ **Kamalo Plantation Bed & Breakfast.** Kamehameha V Hwy., just past mile marker 10 (HC-01, Box 300), Kaunakakai, HI 96748. ☎/fax **808/558-8236.** 1 cottage, with shower only (sleeps up to 4); 1 unit in main house. TV. $75 cottage double, $65 rm double. Rates include continental breakfast. Extra person $10. 2-night minimum in cottage. No credit cards.

Glenn and Akiko Foster's 5-acre spread includes an ancient heiau ruin in the front yard, plus leafy tropical gardens and a working fruit orchard. The genial Fosters have lived and sailed in the islands for many years, and they are full of island lore. The Eden-like property, which they bought in 1992, is easy to find: it's right across the East End road from Father Damien's historic St. Joseph church. The plantation-style cottage is tucked under flower trees and surrounded by swaying palms and tropical foliage; it has its own lanai, a big living room with a queen-size pull-out couch, and a separate bedroom with king bed, so it can sleep four comfortably. The kitchen is fully equipped (including spices), and there's a barbecue outside. The room in the home has a separate entrance, private lanai, bathroom, coffeemaker, microwave, and fridge. Guests are provided with beach mats and towels. A breakfast of fruit and freshly baked bread is served every morning.

✪ **Puunana/Pauwalu Beachfront Cottages.** Kamehameha V Hwy., past mile marker 18. Reservations c/o Sunscapes, 3538 207th SE, Issaquah, WA 98029. ☎ **800/637-0861** or 206/391-8932. Fax 206/391-9121. 2 two-bedroom cottages (each sleeps up to 4). TV. $100 cottage; $600 per week. 3-night minimum. No credit cards.

As clichéd as it sounds, these two five-star cottages by the sea really are the stuff that dreams are made of. Some 18 miles from Kaunakakai, this is one of the most peaceful, comfortable, and elegant properties on Molokai's East End, and the setting is simply stunning. Built in 1996, each of these green-and-white plantation-style cottages sits on its own secluded beach—you'll feel like you're on your own private island. The Puunana Cottage has a king bed and two twins, and Pauwalu has a queen, a double, and a sofa bed. Both have full kitchens, VCRs, washer/dryers, ceiling fans, comfortable tropical furniture, large furnished decks, and views of Maui, Lanai, and Kahoolawe across the channel; in the winter, the deck is a perfect place for whale watching. Your hosts, whose family has held this property for generations, live nearby.

4 Dining

by Jocelyn Fujii

Despite the lamentable disappearance of JoJo's Café in Maunaloa, a few new eateries have opened up recently on this traditionally slow-moving island. Most of them are fast-food or take-out places, but a few of them have a home-cooked touch.

Even with these new developments, one of the best things about Molokai is its glacial pace of change. Lovers of the fast lane might consider this aspect of the island's personality a "con" rather than a "pro," but they wouldn't choose to come here anyway. Molokai is for those who want to get away from it all, who consider the lack of high-rises and traffic lights a welcome change from the urban chaos that keeps nibbling at the edges of the more popular and populated islands. Sybarites, foodies, and pampered oenophiles had best lower their expectations upon arrival, or turn around and leave the island's natural beauty to nature lovers.

Personally, we like the unpretentiousness of the island; it's an oasis in a state where plastic aloha abounds. Most Molokai residents fish, collect seaweed, grow potatoes and tomatoes, and prepare for backyard luaus; if you happen to be walking past on the beach (as we were on a first trip to the island many years ago), they might invite you in with a broad, generous wave of the arm, hollering, "Come eat, come eat! Got plenty food."

Unlike Lanai (see chapter 13), which is small and rural but offers some of the finest dining in the islands, Molokai—although more than double Lanai's population—provides no such mix of innocence and sophistication. You must meet this island on its own terms: it doesn't pretend to be anything more than a combination of old ways and an informal lifestyle, a lifestyle closer to the land than to a chef's toque.

You'll even find a certain defiant stance against the trappings of modernity. Although some of the best produce in Hawaii is grown on this island, you're not likely to find much of it served in its restaurants, other than in the take-out items at Outpost Natural Foods, at the Molokai Pizza Cafe (which we found to be one of the most pleasing eateries on the island), and at the newly opened Village Grill.

The rest of the time, content yourself with ethnic or diner fare or the fresh fish from the Molokai Ice House—or by cooking for yourself. The many visitors who stay in condos find that it doesn't take long to sniff out the best sources of produce, groceries, and fresh fish to fire up at home when the island's other dining options are exhausted. The "Edibles" sections in "Shops & Galleries," later in this chapter, will point you to the shops and markets where you can pick up foodstuffs for your own island-style feast.

All of Molokai's restaurants are inexpensive or moderately priced, and many of them don't accept credit cards. The Ohia Lodge in the Kaluakoi Hotel and Golf Club, as well as the newly opened Village Grill, will be more expensive than diner fare—but you certainly won't have to dress up on Molokai. In most cases, we've listed just the town rather than the street address, because, as you'll see, street addresses are as meaningless on this island as fancy cars and sequins.

Reservations are not accepted unless otherwise noted.

KAUNAKAKAI

Codi's Lunch Wagon. 90 Makaena Place, Kaunakakai. ☎ **808/553-3443.** $4.25–$5. No credit cards. Mon–Fri 10:30am–1:30pm. LOCAL.

Only days after opening in March 1998, residents were touting the spare ribs, oxtail soup, and pork adobo served up at this tiny lunch wagon. "A welcome addition to Kaunakakai" is how Codi's is commonly described. The four different plate lunches a day are served with rice, macaroni salad, and kimchee—a good value. The rotating menu includes chicken broccoli, chicken papaya, roast pork, meat loaf, shrimp curry, and other ethnic fare, served with a smile.

Kamoi Snack-N-Go. Kamoi Professional Center. ☎ **808/553-3742.** Ice cream $1.65 to $3.40. No credit cards. Mon–Sat 9am–9pm, Sun 12–9pm. ICE CREAM/SNACK SHOP.

Sweets and icy treats are the Kamoi specialty. Ice cream made by Dave's on Oahu comes in flavors like green tea, lychee sherbet, and many other tropical and traditional flavors. Schoolchildren and their parents line up for the ice cream cones, shakes, floats, sundaes, and popular Icee floats (in four flavors instead of the usual two) served at this tiny snack shop. No tables, but there are aisles of candies.

Kanemitsu's Bakery & Restaurant. 79 Ala Malama St., Kaunakakai. ☎ **808/553-5855.** Most items under $5.50. No credit cards. Restaurant, Wed–Sat 5:30am–1pm, Sun 5:30–11am; bakery, Wed–Mon 5:30am–6:30pm. BAKERY/DELI.

Morning, noon, and night, this local legend fills the Kaunakakai air with the sweet smells of baking. *Taro lavosh* is the hot new seller, joining Molokai bread, developed in 1935 in a cast-iron, kiawe-fired oven as a Kanemitsu signature. Flavors range from apricot-pineapple to mango (in season), but the classics remain the regular white and wheat, cheese, and onion-cheese breads. For those who like their bread warm, the bread mixes (regular, sweet, and macadamia-nut) offer a way to take Molokai home.

In the adjoining coffee shop/deli, all sandwiches come on their own freshly baked buns and breads. The hamburgers, egg-salad sandwiches, mahi burgers, and honey-dipped fried chicken are all popular.

Not many people know about Kanemitsu's other life as a late-night institution for die-hard bread lovers. Those in the know line up at the bakery's back door beginning at 10:30pm, when the bread is whisked hot out of the oven and into waiting hands. You can order your fresh bread with butter, jelly, cinnamon, cream cheese, "whatever," say the bakers, and they'll cut the hot loaves down the middle and slather on the works so that it melts in the bread.

Molokai Drive-Inn. Kaunakakai. ☎ **808/553-5655.** Most items under $6. No credit cards. Mon–Fri 5:30am–10pm, Sat–Sun 6am–10:30pm. AMERICAN/TAKE-OUT.

The $6 plate-lunch prices are a bit steep at this greasy spoon, but it's one of the rare drive-up places with fresh *akule* (big-eyed scad) and ahi (when available), and fried saimin for $2.75. The honey-dipped fried chicken is a favorite among residents, who also come here for the floats, shakes, potstickers, and other artery-clogging choices. But don't expect much in terms of ambiance: this is a fast-food take-out counter with the smells of frying in the surrounding air—and no pretensions otherwise.

Molokai Mango. 93-D Ala Malama St. ☎ **808/553-3981.** MC, V. Mon–Sat 9am–8:30pm, Sun noon–8:30pm. DELI/AMERICAN.

The former owner of JoJo's restaurant in Maunaloa opened this video store and popular sandwich shop in downtown Kaunakakai, where he sells sandwiches and nachos from the take-out counter. Turkey, ham, and roast beef (Angus beef) are served on five different breads, and all are popular. The $2.90 nachos are a big hit too, for those evenings at home with a rented old movie. Molokai Mango also rents and sells videos, games, and equipment, including TV sets.

✪ **Outpost Natural Foods.** 70 Makaena, Kaunakakai. ☎ **808/553-3377.** Most items under $5. No credit cards. Sun–Fri 10am–3pm. VEGETARIAN.

The healthiest and freshest food on the island is served at the lunch counter of this health-food store, around the corner from the main drag on the makai side of Kaunakakai town. The tiny store abounds in dewy-fresh Molokai papayas, bananas, herbs, potatoes, watermelon, and other produce, complementing its selection of vitamins, cosmetics, and health aids. But the real star is the closet-size lunch counter. The salads, burritos, tempeh sandwich, tofu-spinach lasagna special, and mock chicken, turkey, lamb, and meat loaf (made from oats, sprouts, seeds, and seasonings) will likely dispel the notion most folks have about vegetarian food being boring. Not so! Outpost serves hearty, creative lunches using no animal or un-wholesome products. The Eastern taco salad, for example, contains brown rice topped with lentil stew and a cashew-pimento cheese poured over the works.

Greens, sprouts, and a soy sour cream crown this marvel—invented, like all items on the menu, by the loving hands that prepare it.

Rabang's. Kaunakakai. ☎ **808/553-5841.** Most items under $4.50; combination plate $6. No credit cards. Daily 7am–9pm. FILIPINO.

Specialties here include sweet-and-sour turkey tail prepared Ilocano style (as opposed to Tagalog) and a Filipino dish called *pinat bet*—a mixture of eggplant, string beans, pumpkin, lima beans, and other vegetables, with a smidgen of pork and some assertive seasonings. The diner is a bit more in the thick of things and more inviting than Oviedo's down the street, but it's still extremely casual, with only a few tables that are always full at lunchtime. The Friday Hawaiian plate ($6.50), barbecued chicken plate, and sweet-and-sour pork are among the Molokai favorites.

✪ **Molokai Pizza Cafe.** At Kahua Center, on the old Wharf Rd. ☎ **808/553-3288.** Large pizzas $12.70–$22.15. No credit cards. PIZZA.

This place was the talk of the town when it opened—"Molokai has pizza now," locals announced proudly—and its excellent pizzas and sandwiches have made it a Kaunakakai staple as well as our favorite eatery on the island. There are seven different pizzas, each named after a Hawaiian island. (Niihau has yet to arrive in the Kaunakakai pizza pantheon.) The best-selling pizzas: the Molokai (pepperoni and cheese), the Big Island (pepperoni, ham, mushroom, Italian sausage, bacon, and vegetables), and the Molokini (simple individual cheese slices). Coin-operated cars and a toy airplane follow the children's theme, but adults should feel equally at home with the very popular barbecued baby back rib plate or the oven-roasted chicken dinner. Children's art and letters in the tiled dining room add an entertaining and charming touch. "Dear Uncle Sean," reads one of them, "thank you from the bottom of our tummies."

Sundown Deli. 145 Puali St. ☎ **808/553-3713.** Sandwiches and salads $3–$5.95. No credit cards. Mon–Fri 10:30am–6pm, Sat 10:30am–2pm. DELI.

Across the street from the Veteran's Memorial Park, Sundown is another Molokai newcomer serving sandwiches and food-to-go with a home-cooked flavor. Eight types of sandwiches (like smoked turkey and chicken salad) and several salads (Caesar, Oriental, stuffed tomato) are served daily, with a soup that changes by the day (it might be clam chowder, Portuguese bean, or cream of broccoli); saimin is $3.50. There are a couple of tables for those who want to eat in.

EN ROUTE TO THE NORTH COAST

Kualapuu Cook House. Kualapuu. ☎ **808/567-6185.** Main courses $7.50–$17.95. No credit cards. Mon–Sat 7am–9pm. AMERICAN.

The rusting wagon frame in front of the old plantation house marks this popular diner and breakfast spot where local farmers and cowboys gather to chitchat over coffee and one of the renowned omelets (humongous), steak and eggs (more humongous!), or other American dishes with a local twist. At lunch and dinner, burgers, chili, fresh fish, and surf-and-turf items are the norm. Thursday is prime rib night, when you can order a sizable dinner for $14.25. You can dine indoors or out. Unsolicited advice: Save room for the chocolate–macadamia-nut pie.

THE WEST END

The Village Grill. Maunaloa Hi. ☎ **808/552-0012.** Reservations recommended for lunch and dinner. Lunch $5.25–$8.50; dinner main courses $8–$22.50. AE, MC, V. Daily 11am–1:30pm and 6–9pm; bar with pupu menu opens from 5pm daily. AMERICAN.

Recent renovations to the former JoJo's location have been unobtrusive. The plantation architecture remains, with a wraparound veranda and indoor dining room around an antique bar from the 1800s. (Owners say the bar sailed here on a ship from the East Coast.) On a clear day, you can see Oahu from the deck—the back side of Diamond Head is a surprising sight from Molokai.

The menu is basically American steakhouse, featuring Molokai vegetables (but not beef), affordable fresh fish, and catchy names around the paniolo theme that prevails throughout this island. Thus you have Cactus Charley's Big Catch of the Day, usually pink snapper, mahimahi, or ono ($14.95). Heavier tastes may go for Pistol Pete's Prime Rib (24 ounces for $22.50); the 10-ounce New York steak, called the Mare Cut ($18); and the Stallion T-bone steak ($22.50). Also popular are the jumbo prawns, shrimp-and-scallop stir-fry, and vegetable tempura, featuring Molokai sweet potatoes.

The Grill is busy at sunset, when diners gather on the cool veranda over appetizer platters of seafood ($10); ethnic specialties ($9.50 for spiced beef and chicken, egg rolls, wonton, barbecued ribs); and El Cheapo, a nacho platter for $5. After a day of horseback riding, mountain biking, or hiking, the Grill is a popular place to quench your thirst and nurse those kiawe thorn scratches.

Ohia Lodge. Kaluakoi Hotel and Golf Club, Maunaloa. ☎ **808/552-2555.** Reservations recommended at dinner. Main courses $12–$22. AE, DC, DISC, MC, V. CONTINENTAL/ HAWAII REGIONAL.

The view of Kepuhi Beach has always been the best thing about this room, well positioned for spectacular sunsets and close enough to hear the waves. On a clear day, diners can even see the Makapuu Lighthouse on Oahu, and whales are in full view during the height of the winter whale season. This is the only full-service restaurant serving the West End.

The food: well, they try. The Friday night prime rib buffet is a popular choice on this paniolo island. Some of the options on the current menu: Molokai baby back ribs (we've heard good reports on this one); seafood linguine in a creamy basil alfredo; and fresh fish served broiled (with papaya pineapple salsa), sautéed (with lemon, butter, capers, and macadamia nuts), and wok-seared (with Asian black bean beurre blanc). The fresh catch is served with aromatic basmati rice, a plus.

THE EAST END

Neighborhood Store 'N Counter. Pukoo. ☎ **808/558-8498.** Most items under $6. No credit cards. Thurs–Tues 8am–6pm. AMERICAN.

The store/lunch counter appears like a mirage near mile marker 16 in the Pukoo area en route to the East End. The food stop serves omelets, Portuguese sausage, and other breakfast specials, then segues into sandwiches, salads, chicken katsu, mahimahi plates, and varied over-the-counter lunch offerings. There are daily specials, ethnic dishes, and some vegetarian dishes, such as the new vegetable pita at $4.95. The Neighborhood Store is nothing fancy, but most welcome on the long drive to east Molokai. (Also see "Shops & Galleries," later in this chapter.)

5 Beaches

by Jeanette Foster

With imposing sea cliffs on one side and lazy fishponds on the other, Molokai has little room for beaches along its 106-mile coast. Still, a big gold-sand beach flourishes on the West End, and you'll find tiny pocket beaches on the East End.

The emptiness of Molokai's beaches is both a blessing and a curse: the welcome seclusion means no lifeguards, and nobody to rely on except yourself.

KAUNAKAKAI'S BEACH
ONE ALI'I BEACH PARK

This thin strip of sand, once reserved for the ali'i (chiefs), is the oldest public beach park on Molokai. You'll find One Ali'i Beach Park (pronounced *onay*, not *won*) by a coconut grove on the outskirts of Kaunakakai. Safe for swimmers of all ages and abilities, it's often crowded with splashy families on weekends, but it can be all yours on weekdays. Facilities include outdoor showers, rest rooms, and free parking.

WEST END BEACHES
PAPOHAKU BEACH

Nearly 3 miles long and 100 yards wide, gold-sand Papohaku Beach is one of the biggest in Hawaii (17-mile-long Polihale Beach on Kauai is the biggest). The big surf and riptides make swimming risky except in summer, when the calm waters make it hospitable. Papohaku is great for walking, beachcombing, picnicking, and sunset watching year-round. Go early in the day when the tropic sun is less fierce and the wind calm. The beach is so big that you might never see another soul except at sunset, when a few people gather on the shore to watch the sun sink into the Pacific in hopes of spotting the elusive green flash, a daily natural wonder when the horizon is cloud free. Facilities include outdoor showers, rest rooms, picnic grounds, and free parking.

KEPUHI BEACH

Duffers see this picturesque golden strand in front of the Kaluakoi Resort and Golf Course as just another sand trap, but sunbathers like the semiprivate grassy dunes; they're seldom, if ever, crowded. Beachcombers often find what they're looking for here, but swimmers won't: they'll have to dodge lava rocks and risk riptides to survive. Oh, yes—look out for errant golf balls. There are no facilities or lifeguard, but cold drinks and rest rooms are handy at the resort.

EAST END BEACHES
SANDY BEACH

Molokai's most popular swimming beach—ideal for families with small kids—is a roadside pocket of gold sand protected by a reef with a great view of Maui and Lanai. You'll find it off the King Kamehameha V Highway (Highway 450) at mile marker 20. There are no facilities—just you, the sun, the sand, and the surf.

MURPHY BEACH PARK (KUMIMI BEACH PARK)

In 1970, the Molokai Jaycees wanted to create a sandy beach park with a good swimming area for the children of the East End. They chose a section known as Kumimi Beach, which was owned by the Puu o Hoku Ranch. The beach was a dump, literally. The ranch owner, George Murphy, immediately gave his permission to use the site as a park; the Jaycees cleaned it up and built three small pavilions, plus picnic tables and barbecue grills. Officially, the park is called the George Murphy Beach Park (shortened to Murphy Beach Park over the years)—but some old-timers still call it Kumimi Beach, and, just to make things real confusing, some people call it Jaycees Park.

No matter what you call it, this small park is shaded by ironwood trees that line a white-sand beach. Generally, it's a very safe swimming area. On calm days,

Molokai Beaches & Outdoor Activities

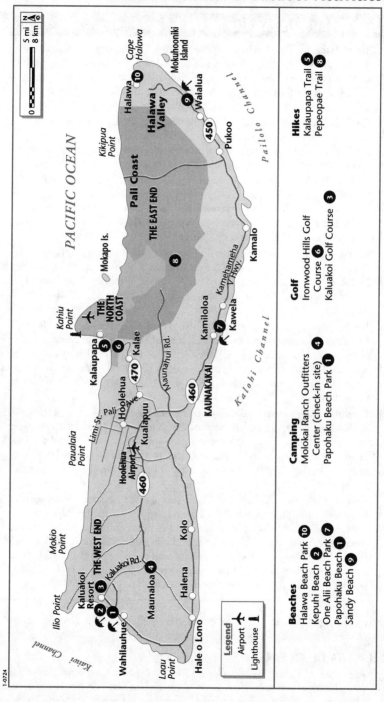

Beaches
- Halawa Beach Park ⑩
- Kepuhi Beach ②
- One Alii Beach Park ⑦
- Papohaku Beach ①
- Sandy Beach ⑨

Camping
- Molokai Ranch Outfitters Center (check-in site) ④
- Papohaku Beach Park ①

Golf
- Ironwood Hills Golf Course ⑥
- Kaluakoi Golf Course ③

Hikes
- Kalaupapa Trail ⑤
- Pepeopae Trail ⑧

Legend
- ✈ Airport
- 🗼 Lighthouse

✪ Frommer's Favorite Molokai Experiences

Travel Back in Time on the Pepeopae Trail. This awesome hike takes you through the Molokai Forest Reserve and back a few million years to a time before any human or creature set foot on the island. Along the misty trail (actually a boardwalk across the bog), expect close encounters of the botanical kind: mosses, sedges, violets, lichens, and knee-high ancient ohias.

Stroll the Sands at Papohaku. Go early, when the tropic sun isn't so fierce, and stroll this 3-mile stretch of unspoiled golden sand—it's one of the longest in Hawaii. The big surf and riptides make swimming somewhat risky, but Papohaku is perfect for walking, beachcombing, and, in the evening, sunset watching.

Soak in the Warm Waters off Sandy Beach. On Molokai's East End, about 20 miles outside of Kaunakakai—just before the road starts to climb to Halawa Valley—lies a small pocket of white sand known as Sandy Beach. Submerging yourself in the warm, calm waters (an outer reef protects the cove) is a sensual experience par excellence—and it's absolutely free.

Snorkel Among Clouds of Butterfly Fish. You don't have to pay for a boat ride or an expensive guide to explore the calm waters at Kumimi Beach on the East End. Just don a snorkel, a mask, and fins, and head to the reef, where you'll find lots of exotic tropical fish, including long-nosed butterfly fish (*lau wiliwili nukunuku oioi*), saddle wrasses (*hinalea lau wili*), and convict tang (*manini*).

Venture into the Garden of Eden. Drive the 30 miles of road along Molokai's East End. Take your time. Stop to smell the flowers and pick guavas by the side of the road. Pull over for a swim. Wave at every car you pass and every person you see. At the end of the road, stand on the beach at Halawa Valley and see Hawaii as it must've looked in A.D. 650, when the first people arrived in the islands.

Celebrate the Ancient Hula. Hula is the heartbeat of Hawaiian culture, and Molokai is the birthplace of the hula. Although most visitors to Hawaii never get to see the real thing, it's possible to see it here—once a year, on the third Saturday in May, when Molokai celebrates the birth of the hula at its Ka Hula Pikoi Festival. The daylong affair at Papohaku Beach Park includes dance, music, food, and crafts.

Ride a Mule into Kalaupapa. Don't pass up the opportunity to see this hauntingly beautiful peninsula. It's a once-in-a-lifetime ride for most, and the cliffs are taller than a 300-story skyscraper; but Buzzy Sproats's mules go up and down the 2.9-mile trail (with 26 switchbacks, it can be a bit tricky) to Molokai's famous leper colony. The views are breathtaking: you'll see the world's highest sea cliffs and waterfalls plunging thousands of feet into the ocean. If you're afraid of heights, catch the views from the Kalaupapa Lookout.

snorkeling and diving are great outside the reef. Fishermen are also frequently spotted here looking for papio and other island fish.

HALAWA BEACH PARK

At the foot of scenic Halawa Valley is this beautiful black-sand beach with a palm-fringed lagoon, a wave-lashed island offshore, and a distant view of the West Maui Mountains across the Pailolo Channel. The swimming is safe in the shallows close to shore, but where the waterfall stream meets the sea, the ocean is often murky and unnerving. A winter swell creases the mouth of Halawa Valley on the north side of the

Kayak Along the North Shore. This is the Hawaii of your dreams: waterfalls thundering down sheer cliffs, remote sand beaches, miles of tropical vegetation, tropical sea birds soaring overhead, and the sounds of the sea splashing on your kayak and the wind whispering in your ear. Best times to go are the brief window in early spring, around March to April, or during the summer months, especially August to September, when the normally galloping ocean lies down flat.

Sample the Local Brew. Saunter up to the Espresso Bar at the Coffees of Hawaii Plantation Store in Kualapuu for a fresh cup of java made from beans that were grown, processed, and packed on this 450-acre plantation. Afterward (or while you sip), survey the vast collection of native crafts.

Taste Aloha at a Macadamia Nut Farm. It could be the owner, Tuddie Purdy, and his friendly disposition that make the macadamia nuts here taste so good. Or it could be his years of practice in growing, harvesting, and shelling them on his 1½-acre farm. Either way, Purdy produces a perfect crop. You can see how he does it on a short, free tour of Purdy's All Natural Macadamia Nut Farm in Hoolehua, just a nut's throw from the airport.

Talk Story with the Locals. The number-one favorite pastime of most islanders is "talking story," or exchanging experiences and knowledge. It's an old Hawaiian custom that brings people, and generations, closer together. You can probably find residents more than willing to share their wisdom with you while fishing from the wharf at Kaunakakai, hanging out at Molokai Fish & Dive, or having coffee at any of the island's restaurants.

Post a Nut. Why send a picturesque postcard to your friends and family back home when you can send a fresh coconut? The Hoolelua Post Office will supply the free coconuts, if you'll supply the $3 postage fee.

Watch the Sunset from a Coconut Grove. Kapuaiwa Coconut Beach Park, off Maunaloa Highway (Hi. 460), is a perfect place to watch the sunset: the sky behind the coconut trees fills with a kaleidoscope of colors as the sun sinks into the Pacific. Molokai's tropical sunsets—often red, sometimes orange, always different—are an everyday miracle that stops people in their tracks. Be careful where you sit, though: falling coconuts could have you seeing stars well before dusk.

Stay at the Beach for Just $3. You can sleep under the stars at the West End's Papohaku Beach Park, the island's largest beach. All the facilities you need are here: rest rooms, drinking water, showers, barbecue grills. Just bring your own tent or sleeping bag and $3—and you'll have the best oceanfront accommodations on the island.

bay and attracts a crowd of local surfers. Facilities are minimal; bring your own water. To get there, take the King Kamehameha V Highway (Hi. 450) east to the end.

6 Hitting the Water

by Jeanette Foster

For details on the activities listed below, see "The Active Vacation Planner" in chapter 3.

BODYBOARDING (BOOGIE BOARDING) & BODYSURFING

Molokai only has three beaches that offer ridable waves for bodyboarding and bodysurfing: Papohaku, Kepuhi, and Halawa. Even these beaches are only for experienced bodysurfers, due to the strength of the rip currents and undertows. Bring your own boogie boards, because no one rents them on Molokai. However, **Molokai Ranch & Fun Hogs** (☎ 808/552-2791) offers surfing or bodyboarding excursions on Monday, Wednesday, Friday, and Sunday afternoons for $60 for 3 hours, including lesson, equipment, and transportation.

OCEAN KAYAKING

During the summer months, when the waters on the north shore are calm, Molokai offers some of the most spectacular kayaking in Hawaii. You can paddle from remote valley to remote valley, spending a week or more exploring the exotic terrain. However, Molokai is for experienced kayakers only, especially those adept in open ocean swells and through rough waves. Kayak tours are available through **Molokai Ranch & Fun Hogs** (☎ 808/552-2791); during the winter, this is a great way to whale-watch. The escorted tours cost $60 per person (minimum age, 10) and are available on Saturday only from 1 to 4pm.

SAILING

Molokai Charters (☎ 808/553-5852) offers a variety of sailing trips on *Satan's Doll*, a 42-foot sloop: 2-hour sunset sails for $40 per person; half day of sailing and whale watching for $50; full-day sail to Lanai with swimming and snorkeling for $90 (which includes lunch, cold drinks, snacks, and all equipment). Owners Richard and Doris Reed have been sailing visitors around Molokai's waters since 1975.

    Molokai Ranch & Fun Hogs (☎ 808/552-2791) offers catamaran sailing by expert sailor/diver/kayaker Mike Holmes in his 28-foot boat, *Nanea*, every Tuesday, Thursday, and Saturday afternoon, at a cost of $60 per person.

SCUBA DIVING

Want to see turtles or manta rays up close? How about sharks? Molokai resident Bill Kapuni has been diving the waters around Molokai his entire life; he'll be happy to show you whatever you're brave enough to encounter. **Bill Kapuni's Snorkel & Dive,** Kaunakakai (☎ 808/553-9867), can provide everything you need: gear, boat, even instruction. Two tank dives are $85 in his 22-foot Boston Whaler, and they include Bill's voluminous knowledge of the legends and lore of Hawaii.

SNORKELING

When the waters are calm, Molokai offers excellent snorkeling; you'll see a wide range of butterfly fish, tangs, and angelfish. Good snorkeling can be found—when conditions are right—at many of Molokai's beaches (see box). Snorkeling gear can be rented for $8.95 a day from **Molokai Fish & Dive** in Kaunakakai (☎ 808/553-5926); staffers will also point out that day's best snorkeling spots. Snorkeling tours are available for $45 from **Bill Kapuni's Snorkel & Dive** (☎ 808/553-9867), which also rents snorkeling gear for $25 a day (see "Scuba Diving," above).

    Walter Naki of **Molokai Action Adventures** (☎ 808/558-8184) offers snorkeling, diving, and swimming trips in his 21-foot Boston Whaler for $75 per person for a 4- to 6-hour custom tour.

    Molokai Ranch & Fun Hogs (☎ 808/552-2791) offers snorkeling excursions in a 25-foot hard-bottom inflatable boat (certified for 18 passengers) daily from

Molokai's Best Snorkeling Spots

Most Molokai beaches are too dangerous to snorkel in winter, when big waves and strong currents are generated by storms that sweep down from Alaska. Stick to the Kumimi or Murphy's Beach on the East End in winter. In summer, roughly May to mid-September, when the Pacific Ocean takes a holiday and turns into a flat lake, the whole west coast of Molokai opens up for snorkeling. "Fun Hog" Mike Holmes's favorite snorkel spots are:

- **Kawakiu Nui, Ilio Point, and Pohaku Moiliili,** on the West End: These are all special places seldom seen by even those who live on Molokai. You can reach Kawakiu Nui and Pohaku Moiliili on foot after a long, hot, dusty ride in a four-wheel-drive vehicle, but it's much easier and quicker to go by sea.
- **Kapukahehu or Dixie Maru,** on the West End: This is a good, gold-sand family beach, because the cove is well protected and the reef is close and shallow. The name Dixie Maru comes from a 1920s Japanese fishing boat, stranded off the rocky shore. One of the Molokai Ranch cowboys hung the wrecked boat's nameplate on a gate by Kapukahehu beach, and the name Dixie Maru stuck. To get there, take Kaluakoi Road to the end of the pavement, and then take the footpath 100 yards to the beach.
- **Murphy Beach Park or Kumimi Beach,** on the East End. Located at mile marker 20–21, off Kamehameha V Highway, the reef here is easily reachable, and the waters are calm year-round.

9am to noon, for $60 per person, which includes lunch and all snorkeling equipment.

SPORTFISHING

Molokai's waters can provide prime sporting opportunities, whether you're looking for big-game sportfishing or bottom fishing. When customers are scarce, Captain Joe Reich, who has been fishing the waters around Molokai for 2 decades, goes commercial fishing, so he always knows where the fish are biting. He runs *Alyce C* **Sportfishing** out of Kaunakakai Harbor (☎ **808/558-8377**). A full day of fishing for up to six people is $400, three-quarters of a day is $350, and a half day is $300. You can persuade him to do a whale-watching cruise during the winter months.

For fly-fishing or for light-tackle reef fish trolling, contact Walter Naki at **Molokai Action Adventures** (☎ **808/558-8184**). Walter's been fishing his entire life and loves to share his "secret spots" with visiting fishermen—he knows *the* place for bone fishing on the flats. A half-day trip in his 21-foot Boston Whaler is $50 per person (minimum two people), $100 per person for a full day.

For light-tackle/deep-sea fishing, **Molokai Ranch & Fun Hogs** (☎ **808/ 552-2791**) has afternoon (from 1 to 4pm) fishing excursions on Tuesday, Thursday, and Saturday on a 25-foot hard-bottom inflatable boat, for $250 for one to four passengers.

WHALE WATCHING

The humpback whales that frequent the waters around Molokai from mid-December to mid-March can be seen up-close-and-personal with **Molokai Charters,** Kaunakakai (☎ **808/553-5852**), which has a 42-foot sloop, *Satan's Doll* (see "Sailing," above).

Also contact **Molokai Ranch & Fun Hogs** (☎ 808/552-2791), which offers a variety of whale-watching charters during the winter months.

7 Hiking & Camping

by Jeanette Foster

HIKING MOLOKAI'S PEPEOPAE TRAIL

Molokai's most awesome hike is the **Pepeopae Trail;** it takes you back a few million years to a time before any human or creature set foot on the island. On the cloud-draped trail (actually a boardwalk across the bog), you'll see mosses, sedges, native violets, knee-high ancient ohias, and lichens that evolved in total isolation over eons. Eerie intermittent mists blowing in and out will give you an idea of this island at its creation.

The narrow boardwalk, built by volunteers, protects the bog and keeps you out of the primal ooze. Don't venture off of it; you could damage this fragile environment or get lost. The 3-mile round-trip takes about 90 minutes to hike—after you drive about 20 miles from Kaunakakai, deep into the Molokai Forest Preserve on a four-wheel-drive road. Plan a full day for this outing. Better yet, go on a guided nature hike with **The Nature Conservancy of Hawaii,** which guards this unusual ecosystem. For information, write The Nature Conservancy of Hawaii, 1116 Smith St., Suite 201, Honolulu, HI 96817. No permit is required for this easy hike. You should call ahead (☎ **808/537-4508,** or 808/553-5236 on Molokai), to check on the condition of the ungraded four-wheel-drive red-dirt road that leads to the trailhead and to let people know that you are up there.

To get there, take Highway 460 west from Kaunakakai for 3½ miles, and turn right before the Maunawainui Bridge onto the unmarked Molokai Forest Reserve Road (sorry, there aren't any road signs). The pavement ends at the cemetery; continue on the dirt road. After about 2 to 2½ miles, you'll see a sign telling you that you are now in the Molokai Forest Reserve. At the Waikolu Lookout and picnic area, which is just over 9 miles on the Molokai Forest Reserve Road, sign in at the box near the entrance. Continue on the road for another 5 miles to a fork in the road with a sign PUU KOLEKOLE pointing to the right side of the fork. Do not turn right; instead, continue straight at the fork, which will lead to the clearly marked trailhead.

HIKING TO KALAUPAPA

This hike is like going down a switchback staircase with what seems like a million steps. You don't always see the breathtaking view because you're too busy watching your step. It's easier going down—you go from 2,000 feet to sea level in 2½ miles—which takes about an hour; it sometimes takes twice as long on the way up. The trailhead starts on the mauka side of Highway 470, just past the Mule Barn (you can't miss it). Check in there at 7:30am, get a permit, and go before the mule train departs. You must be 16 or older (it's an old state law that kept kids out of the leper colony) and should be in good shape. Wear good hiking boots or sneakers; you won't make it past the first turn in zoris.

CAMPING

AT THE BEACH

One of the best year-round places to camp on Molokai is **Papohaku Beach Park** on the island's West End, a drive-up seaside site that's a great getaway. The island's largest beach is ideal for rest and relaxation. Facilities include rest rooms, drinking water, outdoor showers, barbecue grills, and picnic tables. Groceries and gas are available in Maunaloa, 6 miles away. Kaluakoi Resort is a mile away. Obtain camping permits by contacting **Maui County Parks Department,** P.O. Box 526, Kaunakakai, HI 96748 (☎ **808/553-3204**). Camping is limited to 3 days, but if nobody has applied, the time limit is waived. Cost is $3 a person per night.

IN AN IRONWOOD FOREST

At the end of Hi. 470 is the 234-acre piney woods known as **Palaau State Park,** home to the Kalaupapa Lookout (the best vantage point for seeing the historic leper colony if you're not hiking or mule riding in). It's airy and cool in the park's ironwood forest, where many love to camp at the designated state campground. Camping is free here, but you need a permit from the **State Division of Parks** (☎ **808/567-6618**). For more on the park, see "Seeing the Sights," below.

ON MOLOKAI RANCH

For a unique experience, the ✪ **Molokai Ranch Outfitters Center,** P.O. Box 259, Maunaloa, HI 96770 (☎ **800/254-8871** or 808/552-2791; www.molokai-ranch. com), offers an eco-adventure called the Great Molokai Ranch Trail. It features upscale, "comfortable" camping in a bungalow/tent called a tentalow, plus lots of outdoor activities. Paniolo Camp, the first camp to open in 1997, is located just south of Molokai Ranch headquarters in Maunaloa. The camp is a collection of 40 comfortable tents mounted on wooden platforms. All tents have queen-size beds, ceiling fans, private bathrooms with self-composting toilets, hot-water showers, and solar-powered lights. Each campsite is located on a footpath that meanders through ironwood trees.

Within the Paniolo Camp is an open-air dining pavilion, a swimming pool, a fire pit, nature trails, mountain-bike paths, and volleyball and horseshoe areas. Rates are $185 per person (double occupancy) and include meals, snacks, transportation (including airport pickup), daily maid service, and two major adventures per day (mountain biking, hiking, snorkeling, kayaking, beach and ocean sports, cultural experiences, and children's program). Equestrian and aquatic adventures are available for an additional charge.

The Paniolo Camp is set up for families with children. The newer Kalo Camp, which features 20 "yurts" (circular canvas shelters on platforms) down by the beach, is for adults only. Rates are $215 per person, double occupancy. In either camp, don't miss the mountain-biking adventures, conducted by Bob Ward of Hairbrain Adventures; he offers the best tours on the best mountain-bike trails in the state.

Even if you aren't a "camping" fan, don't miss this fabulous opportunity to experience a comfortable yet adventuresome side of Molokai.

8 Other Outdoor Activities: Golf & Tennis

by Jeanette Foster

GOLF

Golf is one of Molokai's best-kept secrets; it's challenging and fun, tee times are open, and the rates are lower than your score will be. Most popular is the par-72, 6,564-yard **Kaluakoi Golf Course,** which designer Ted Robinson calls "the most spectacular and unusual course in the islands." The course is cut along the ocean (six holes are along the shoreline) and through the woods (pheasants, Axis deer, and wild turkeys freely roam the fairways); it offers hilly, wooded fairways bisected by ravines, and a grand finish, beginning at the par-3, 16th hole. Called "The Gorge," the 16th plays 190 yards over a deep ravine to a two-tiered green. When you finish that, both the 17th and the 18th holes are very long par-4s, with greens blind from the tee. Facilities include driving range, putting green, pro shop, and restaurant. It's rarely crowded; greens fees are $40 for Kaluakoi Resort guests and $60 for nonguests, and twilight rates are $40 for nonguests and $32 for guests. Call ☎ **808/552-2739.**

The real find in golf courses is the **Ironwood Hills Golf Course,** off Kalae Highway (☎ **808/567-6000**). It's located just before the Molokai Mule Ride mule barn, on the road to the Lookout. One of the oldest golf courses in the state, Ironwood Hills (named after the two predominant features of the course, ironwood trees and hills) was built in 1929 by Del Monte Plantation for its executives. This unusual course, which sits in the cool air at 1,200 feet, delights with its rich foliage, open fairways, and spectacular views of the rest of the island. Surrounded by bushes, the third hole—a par-3, 158-yard shot from the tee over a gully—could qualify as the signature hole. If you play here, use a trick developed by the local residents: after teeing off on the 6th hole, just take whatever clubs you need to finish playing the hole, and a driver for the seventh hole, and park your bag under a tree. The climb to the 7th hole is steep—you'll be glad that you're carrying only a few clubs. Greens fees are $10 for 9 holes, $14 for 18 holes. Cart fees are $7 for 9 holes, $14 for 18. You can also rent a hand cart for just $2.50, and club rentals are $7 for 9 holes and $12 for 18.

TENNIS

Maui County has only two tennis courts on Molokai. Both are located at the **Mitchell Pauole Center** in Kaunakakai (☎ **808/553-5141**). Both courts have night lights and are available on a first-come, first-served basis.

9　Outfitters & Adventure Tour Operators

by Jeanette Foster

OUTFITTERS & TOUR GUIDES

Molokai Fish & Dive (☎ **808/553-5926**) in Kaunakakai is a mind-boggling store filled with outdoor gear. You can rent snorkeling gear, fishing gear, and even ice chests here. This is also the hot spot for fishing news and tips on what's running where.

If it's action you're looking for, call **Molokai Action Adventures** (☎ **808/ 558-8184**). Island guide Walter Naki will take you skin diving, reef trolling, kayaking, hunting, or hiking into Molokai's remote hidden valleys. Hiking tours are $50 per person for 4 hours, and he limits the number of participants to no more than four. Not only does Walter know Molokai like the back of his hand, but he also loves being outdoors and talking story with visitors; he tells them about the island, the people, the politics, the myths, and anything else his guests want to know.

AN ADVENTURE FOR EVERYONE: A WAGON RIDE TO ILI'ILI'OPAE HEIAU

In a wagon drawn by two horses, you bump along a dirt trail through an incredible mango grove, bound for an ancient temple of human sacrifice. The temple of doom—right out of *Indiana Jones*—is Ili'ili'opae, a huge rectangle of stone made of

90 million rocks, overlooking the once-important village of Mapulehu and four ancient fishponds. The wagon glides under the perfumed mangoes, then heads uphill through a kiawe forest filled with Java plums to the heiau, which stands across a dry stream bed under cloud-spiked Kaunolu, the 4,970-foot island summit.

Hawaii's most powerful heiau attracted kahunas from all over the islands, who came to learn the rules of human sacrifice at this university of sacred rites. Contrary to Hollywood's version, historians say the victims here were always men, not young virgins, and they were strangled, not thrown into a volcano, while priests sat on lauhala mats watching silently. Spooky, eh?

This is the biggest, oldest, and most famous heiau on Molokai. It's a massive 22-foot-high stone altar, dedicated to Lono, the Hawaiian god of fertility. The heiau resonates with mana (power) strong enough to lean on. Legend says Ili'ili'opae was built in a single night by a thousand men, who passed rocks hand over hand through the Wailau Valley from the other side of the island; each received a shrimp ('opae) in exchange for the rock (ili'ili). Others say it was built by *menehunes*, the mythic elves who accomplished Herculean feats.

After the visit to the awesome temple, the horse-drawn wagon takes you back to the mango grove for a beachside lunch and an old-fashioned backyard ukulele songfest. Popular with families, this little adventure might sound too down-home for some, but the search for the "real" Molokai begins here.

Contact **Molokai Wagon Rides**, P.O. Box 1528, King Kamehameha V Highway (Highway 450), at the 15-mile marker, Kaunakakai, HI 96748 (☎ **808/ 558-8132**). The adventure via the wagon ride is $35 per person and includes lunch; it begins daily at 10am and lasts at least a couple of hours, sometimes longer. The company also offers a tour to the heiau on horseback for $40 per person (no lunch). The hour-long ride goes up to the heiau, then beyond it to the top of the mountain for those breathtaking views, and finally back down to the beach.

✪ MULE RIDES TO KALAUPAPA

The first turn's a gasp, and it's all downhill from there. You can close your eyes and hold on for dear life, or slip the reins over the pommel and sit back, letting the mule do the walking down the precipitous path to Kalaupapa National Historic Park, Molokai's famous leper colony.

Even if you have only 1 day to spend on Molokai, spend it on a mule. It's a once-in-a-lifetime ride for most—the cliffs are taller than a 300-story skyscraper— but Buzzy Sproat's mules go up and down the narrow 2.9-mile trail daily, rain or shine, without ever losing a rider or mount on 26 switchbacks. From 1,600 feet on the nearly perpendicular ridge, the sure-footed mules step down the muddy trail, pausing often on switchbacks to calculate their next move—and always, it seems to me, veering a little too close to the edge. Each switchback is numbered; by the time you get to number 4, you'll catch your breath, put the mule on cruise control, and begin to enjoy Hawaii's most awesome trail ride.

The mule tours are offered once daily starting at 8am, and they last until about 3:30pm. They're $135 per person for the all-day adventure, which includes the round-trip mule ride, a guided tour of the settlement, a visit to Father Damien's church and grave, lunch at Kalawao, and souvenirs. To go, you must be at least 16 years old and physically fit. Contact **Molokai Mule Ride,** 100 Kalae Hwy., Suite 104, on Highway 470, 6 miles north of Highway 460 (☎ **800/567-7550** or 808/567-6088, or 808/567-6400 between 8 and 10pm; fax 808/567-6244; www.muleride.com; e-mail muleman@aloha.net). Advance reservations are required.

10 Seeing the Sights

by Jeanette Foster

IN & AROUND KAUNAKAKAI

Kapuaiwa Coconut Grove/Kiowea Park. Along Maunaloa Hwy. (Hi. 460), 2 miles west of Kaunakakai.

This royal grove—a thousand coconut trees on 10 acres planted in 1863 by the island's high chief Kapua'iwa (later King Kamehameha V)—is a major roadside attraction in Molokai. The shoreline park, 2 miles west of Kaunakakai, is a favorite subject of sunset photographers and visitors who delight in a hand-lettered sign that warns, DANGER: FALLING COCONUTS. In its backyard, across the highway, stands "Church Row": seven churches, each a different denomination, stark evidence of the missionary impact on Hawaii.

Post-A-Nut. Hoolehua Post Office, Puu Peelua Ave., near Maunaloa Hwy. (Hi. 460). ☎ **808/567-6144.** Mon–Fri 7:30–11:30am and 12:30–4:30pm.

Postmaster Margaret Keahi-Leary will help you say "Aloha" with a dried Molokai coconut: write a message on the coconut with a felt-tip pen, and she'll send it via U.S. mail over the sea. Coconuts are free, but postage is $3 for a mainland-bound 2-pound coconut.

Purdy's All-Natural Macadamia Nut Farm. Lihipali St., Hoolehua. ☎ **808/567-6601.** Mon–Fri 9:30am–3:30pm, Sat 10am–2pm, Sun by appointment only.

The Purdys have made macadamia nut–buying an entertainment event, offering tours of the 1½-acre homestead and lively demonstrations of nutshell-cracking in the shade of their towering trees. The tour of the 70-year-old nut farm explains the growth, bearing, harvesting, and shelling processes so that by the time you crunch into the luxurious macadamia nut, you'll have more than a passing knowledge of its entire life cycle.

Tuddie Purdy has invented a rubber holding device that has conquered the otherwise slippery (and hazardous) shelling process. The nuts sold here are grown on Molokai and the Big Island and packaged on the farm—they make a great, affordable souvenir.

THE NORTH COAST

Most people never get a chance to see Hawaii's most dramatic coast in its entirety, but nobody should miss the opportunity to glimpse it from the Kalaupapa Lookout at Palaau State Park. On the way, there are a few diversions (arranged here in geographical order).

EN ROUTE TO THE NORTH COAST

Coffees of Hawaii. The Plantation Store, Hi. 480 (near the junction of Hi. 470). ☎ **800/709-BEAN** or 808/567-9023. Fax 808/567-9270.

The defunct Del Monte pineapple town of Kualapuu is rising again—only this time coffee is the catch, not pineapple. Located in the cool foothills, Coffees of Hawaii has planted coffee beans on 600 acres of former pineapple land. The plantation is irrigating the plants with a high-tech, continuous water and fertilizer drip system (using the world's largest rubber-lined reservoir, which holds 1.4 billion gallons of water). Stop by the Espresso Bar for a "Mocha Mama" (Molokai coffee, ice, chocolate, chocolate ice cream, chocolate syrup, whipped cream, and chocolate shavings on top). It'll keep you going all day, maybe even all night.

Especially for Kids

Flying a Kite *(see p. 287)*   Not only can you get a guaranteed-to-fly kite at the **Big Wind Kite Factory** (☎ 808/552-2634) in Maunaloa, but kite designer Jonathan Socher also offers free kite-flying classes to kids, who'll learn how to make their kites soar, swoop, and, most important, stay in the air for more than 5 minutes.

Spending the Day at Kumimi Beach Park *(see p. 268)*   Just beyond Wailua on the East End, Kumimi Beach Park (also known as Murphy Beach Park) is a small wayside park that's perfect for kids. There are safe swimming conditions for children, plenty of shade from the ironwood trees, and useful facilities like small pavilions with picnic tables and barbecue grills.

Riding a Wagon *(see p. 276)*   Kids will love being in a wagon drawn by two horses as it traverses a dirt trail through a mango grove bound for an ancient temple of sacrifice. After the ride, the whole family is treated to a beachside lunch and an old-fashioned ukulele songfest.

Watching Whales *(see p. 273)*   From mid-December to mid-March, whale watching for kids of all ages on Molokai Charters's 42-foot sloop, *Satan's Doll,* offers a variety of ways to spot these leviathans that visit Hawaiian waters in the winter.

Visiting the Past *(see p. 279)*   The Molokai Museum and Cultural Center lets kids step into the past and see how sugar was made (with a restored 1878 sugar mill, complete with old steam engine, mule-driven cane crusher, and redwood evaporating pans).

Molokai Museum and Cultural Center. Meyer Sugar Mill, Hi. 470 (just after the turnoff for the Ironwood Hills Golf Course, and 2 miles below Kalaupapa Overlook), Kaunakakai. ☎ **808/567-6436.** Admission $2.50 adults, $1 students. Mon–Sat 10am–2pm.

En route to the California Gold Rush in 1849, Rudolph W. Meyer, a German professor, came to Molokai, married the high chiefess Kalama, and, after planting corn, wheat, and potatoes, began to operate a small sugar plantation near his home. Now on the National Register of Historic Places, the restored 1878 sugar mill, with its century-old steam engine, mule-driven cane crusher, copper clarifiers, and redwood evaporating pans—all in working order—is the last of its kind in Hawaii. The mill also houses a museum that traces the history of sugar growing on Molokai and features special events such as wine tastings every 2 months, taro festivals, an annual music festival, and occasional classes in ukulele making, loom weaving, and sewing; call for schedule.

Palaau State Park. At the end of Hi. 470.

This 234-acre piney woods park 8 miles out of Kaunakakai is a sleeper. It doesn't look like much until you get out of the car and take a hike, which literally puts you between a rock and a hard place: go right, and you end up on the edge of Molokai's magnificent sea cliffs, with its panoramic view of the infamous Kalaupapa leper colony; go left, and you come face-to-face with a stone phallus.

If you have no plans to scale the cliffs on mule or foot (see "Outfitters & Tour Guides" and "Hiking & Camping," above), the ✪ **Kalaupapa Lookout** is the only place from which to see the former place of exile. The trail is marked and there are historic photos and interpretive signs to explain what you're seeing.

It's airy and cool in the ironwood forest, where camping is free at the designated state campground. You'll need a permit from the **State Division of Parks** (☎ **808/ 567-6618**). Not many people seem to camp here, probably because of the legend associated with the **Phallic Rock.** Six feet high, pointed at an angle that means business, Molokai's famous Phallic Rock is a legendary fertility tool that appears to be working today. According to Hawaiian legend, a woman who wishes to become pregnant need only spend the night near the rock and . . . voilà! It's probably just a coincidence, of course, but Molokai does have a growing population of young, pregnant women. If you want to avoid an unwanted pregnancy, it might be wise to avoid camping in the rock's vicinity.

Phallic Rock is at the end of a well-worn uphill path, through an ironwood grove past other rocks that vaguely resemble sexual body parts. No mistaking the big guy, though—it's definitely a giant erect male penis. Supposedly, it belonged to Nanahoa, a demigod who quarreled with his wife, Kawahuna, over a pretty girl. In the tussle, Kawahuna was thrown over the cliff, and both husband and wife were turned to stone.

Of all the phallic rocks in Hawaii and the Pacific, this is the one to see. It's so famous, it's featured on a postcard with a tiny, awe-struck Japanese woman standing next to it.

THE LEGACY OF FATHER DAMIEN: KALAUPAPA NATIONAL HISTORIC PARK

An old tongue of lava that sticks out to form a peninsula, Kalaupapa became infamous because of man's inhumanity to victims of a formerly incurable contagious disease.

King Kamehameha V sent the first lepers—nine men and three women—into exile on this lonely shore, at the base of ramparts that rise like temples against the unbroken Pacific, on January 6, 1866. More than 11,000 lepers arrived between 1865 and 1874, dispatched to disfigure and die in one of the world's most beautiful— and lonely—places. They called Kalaupapa "The Place of the Living Dead."

One of the world's least contagious diseases, leprosy is caused by a germ, *Mycobacterium leprae,* that attacks the nerves, skin, and eyes. It's transmitted by direct, repetitive, person-to-person contact over a long period of time. American scientists found a cure for the disease, sulfone, in the 1940s.

Before science intervened, there was Father Damien. Born to wealth in Belgium, Joseph de Veuster traded a life of excess for exile among lepers; he devoted himself to caring for the afflicted at Kalaupapa. Father Damien, as he became known, volunteered to go out to the Pacific in place of his ailing brother when he was 33. Horrified at the conditions in the leper colony, Father Damien worked at Kalaupapa for 16 years, building houses, schools, and churches, and giving patients hope of redemption. He died on April 15, 1889, in Kalaupapa, of leprosy. He was 49.

A hero nominated for Catholic sainthood, Father Damien is buried not in his tomb next to St. Philomena Church, but in his native Belgium. His hand was recently returned to Molokai, however, and was re-interred at Kalaupapa as a relic of his martyrdom.

This small peninsula is probably the final resting place of more than 11,000 souls. The sand dunes are littered with grave markers, sorted by the religious affiliation—Catholic, Protestant, Lutheran, Buddhist—of those who died here. But so many are buried in unmarked graves that no census of the dead is believed to be either accurate or complete.

In the chronicle of man there is perhaps no more melancholy landing than this. . . .

—Robert Louis Stevenson, on Kalaupapa

Smile. It No Broke Your Face.

—sign at Kalaupapa

Kalaupapa is now a National Historic Park and one of Hawaii's richest archaeo-logical preserves, with sites that date to A.D. 1000. About 60 former patients chose to remain in the tidy village of whitewashed houses with tombstones on the coast and statues of angels in their yards. The original name for their former affliction, "leprosy," was officially banned in Hawaii by the State Legislature in 1981. The politically correct name now is "Hansen's Disease," for Dr. Gerhard Hansen of Norway, who discovered the germ in 1873. The few residents of Kalaupapa still call their disease leprosy, although they aren't too keen on being called lepers.

Kalaupapa welcomes visitors who arrive on foot, by mule (see "Mule Rides to Kalaupapa," page 277), or by small plane. You can visit Father Damien's St. Philomena church, built in 1872. Once off-limits, the quiet village is now open to visitors, who can see it from a yellow school bus driven by resident tour guide Richard Marks, an ex-seaman and sheriff who survived the disease. You won't be able to roam freely, and you'll be allowed to enter only the museum, the craft shop, and the church.

Father Damien Tours, P.O. Box 1, Kalaupapa, HI 96742 (☎/fax **808/ 567-6171**), picks you up at the Kalaupapa Airport and takes you to some of the area's most scenic spots, including Kalawao, where Father Damien's church still stands; the Kauhako Crater; and the town of Kalaupapa. The $30 fee includes the tour and the permit to enter this secluded area. Bring your own lunch and drinks, and arrange for air transportation to Kalaupapa Airport (contact **Molokai-Lanai Air Shuttle,** ☎ 808/567-6847; **Island Air,** ☎ 800/652-6541; or **Paragon Air,** ☎ 808/244-3356). You must be at least 16 years old.

THE WEST END
MAUNALOA

"Eleven hundred feet above the ocean in the rolling hills of west Molokai, some-thing wonderful is happening," the real estate prospectus says. "A classic island town is becoming new again."

In the first and only urban renewal on Molokai, the 1920s-era pineapple plantation town of Maunaloa is coming down. The termite-filled houses built by Libby, McNeil, and Libby are being scrapped by bulldozers; in their place is rising a new tract of $125,000 houses. Streets are being widened and paved, curbs and sidewalks are going in. Historic Maunaloa is being transformed into Maunaloa Village, and already there's a movie theater and a Kentucky Fried Chicken outlet.

All this gentrification is unsettling to longtime residents, who resisted the change—and the end of an era of cheap rents. Only Jonathan Socher's Big Wind Kite Factory (see "Shops & Galleries," below), the town's main attraction, remains in place for now, his kites and books wrapped in cellophane against constant clouds of red dust raised by construction crews. Even the Cooke Island pines of Maunaloa need a bath.

The only master-planned village on Molokai will have a museum, a bed-and-breakfast lodge, a town park with playing field, new restaurants, artisan's studios, and tidy new plantation-style houses with steel rafters, solar water heaters, and low-flow fixtures and toilets—uptown stuff for Molokai. And with the newly opened Molokai Ranch Outfitters Center, the old plantation town is moving up in the world as a destination for both cowboys and those who dream of being cowboys.

The very popular Molokai Ranch Wildlife Conservation Park, which offered entertaining tours of the collection of exotic African and Indian animals in the wild, has closed. Tours are no longer available.

KALUAKOI

At the end of the stark desert of the West End lies an oasis: spectacular beaches; a cluster of seacoast condos that hug an 18-hole, par-72 golf course; and the island's only resort hotel, Kaluakoi Hotel and Golf Club.

"Kaluakoi" is Hawaiian for "adz quarry"; many have been found on the rocky West End. This area is riddled with historical sites: heiau (temples), ancient Hawaiian house sites, calendar rock fields (similar to Stonehenge), huge stone boulders marking district boundaries, and even an enchanted forest. At the 110-foot Puu o Kaiaka, a crumbly cinder cone that separates Kepuhi and Papohaku beaches, San Francisco hotelier Ben Swig once planned to build a Fairmount Hotel, but his plans were defeated by islanders; so the coast is clear, just as it was more than 200 years ago.

ON THE NORTHWEST SHORE: MOOMOMI DUNES

Undisturbed for centuries, the Moomomi Dunes, on Molokai's northwest shore, are a unique treasure chest of great scientific value. They might look like just a pile of sand to you as you fly over on final approach to Hoolehua Airport, but Moomomi Dunes are much more than that. Archaeologists have found adz quarries, burial sites, and shelter caves; botanists have identified five endangered plant species; and marine biologists are finding evidence that endangered green sea turtles are hauling out from the waters once again to lay eggs here. The greatest discovery, however, belongs to Smithsonian Institute ornithologists, who have found bones of prehistoric birds—some of them flightless—that existed nowhere else on earth. The shifting dunes were also burial sites for ancient Hawaiians.

Accessible by jeep trails that thread downhill to the shore, this wild coast is buffeted by strong afternoon breezes. It's hot, dry, and windy, so take water, sunscreen, and a windbreaker. At Kawaaloa Bay, a 20-minute walk to the west, there's a broad golden beach that you can have all to yourself. Stay on the trails, out of the water, and along the beach.

This 920-acre preserve is open to guided nature tours once a month, led by **The Nature Conservancy of Hawaii;** call ☎ **808/553-5236** or 808/524-0779 for exact schedule and details.

To get to Moomomi Dunes, take Hi. 460 (Maunaloa Highway) from Kaunakakai; turn right onto Hi. 470, and follow it to Kualapuu. At Kualapuu, turn left on Hi. 480 and go through Hoolehua Village; it's 3 miles to the bay.

THE EAST END

The East End is a cool and inviting green place that's worth a drive to the end of King Kamehameha V Highway (Hi. 450), even if one of the island's greatest natural attractions, Halawa Valley, is now essentially off-limits.

KAMAKOU PRESERVE

It's hard to believe, but close to the nearly mile-high summit, it rains more than 80 inches a year—enough to qualify as a rain forest. The Molokai Forest, as it was historically known, is the source of 60% of Molokai's water. Nearly 3,000 acres from the summit to the lowland forests of eucalyptus and pine are now held in preserve by the Nature Conservancy, which has identified 219 Hawaiian plants that grow here exclusively. The preserve is also the last stand of the endangered Molokai Thrush (*olomao*) and Molokai Creeper (*kawawahie*).

To get to this Nature Conservancy preserve, take the Forest Reserve jeep road from Kaunakakai. It's a 45-minute, four-wheel drive on a dirt trail to Waikolu Lookout Campground; from there, you can venture into the wilderness preserve on foot across a boardwalk on a 1½-hour hike (see "Hiking Molokai's Pepeopae Trail," above). For more information, contact **The Nature Conservancy** at ☎ **808/ 553-5236.**

EN ROUTE TO HALAWA VALLEY

No visit to Molokai is complete without at least a passing glance at the island's **ancient fishponds,** a singular achievement in Pacific aquaculture. With a hunger for fresh fish and a lack of ice or refrigeration, Hawaiians perfected aquaculture in 1400, before Christopher Columbus "discovered" America. They built gated, U-shaped stone and coral walls on the shore to catch fish on the incoming tide; they would then raise them in captivity. The result: a constant ready supply of fresh fish.

The ponds stretch for 20 miles along Molokai's south shore and are visible from Kamehameha V Highway (Hi. 450). Molokai's fishponds offer a clue to the island's ancient population. It took something like a thousand people to tend a single fishpond, and more than 60 ponds once existed on this coast. All of the fishponds are named; a few are privately owned. Some are silted in by red-dirt runoff from south coast gulches. Others have been revived by folks who raise fish and seaweed.

The largest, 54-acre **Keawa Nui Pond,** is surrounded by a 3-foot-high, 2,000-foot-long stone wall. **Ali'i Fishpond,** reserved for kings, is visible through the coconut groves at One Ali'i Beach Park (see "Beaches," above). You can see **Kalokoeli Pond,** 6 miles east of Kaunakakai on the highway, from the road.

Our Lady of Sorrows Catholic Church, one of five churches built by Father Damien on Molokai and the first outside Kalaupapa, sits across the highway from a fishpond. Park in the church lot (except on Sundays) for a closer look.

St. Joseph's Catholic Church. King Kamehameha V Hwy. (Hi. 450), just after mile marker 10.

The afternoon sun strikes St. Joseph's Church with such a bold ray of light that it's as if God is about to perform a miracle. The stunning brightness compels you to stop and visit the little 1876 wood-frame church, one of four that Father Damien built "topside" on Molokai. Restored in 1971, the church stands beside a seaside cemetery, where feral cats play under the gaze of a Damien statue amid gravestones decorated with flower leis.

Smith Bronte Landing Site. King Kamehameha V Hwy. (Hi. 450), at mile marker 11, on the makai side.

In 1927, Charles Lindbergh soloed the Atlantic Ocean in a plane called *The Spirit of St. Louis* and became an American hero. That same year, Ernie Smith and

Emory B. Bronte took off from Oakland, California, on July 14 in a single-engine Travelair aircraft named *The City of Oakland*, setting out 2,397 miles across the Pacific Ocean for Honolulu. The next day, after running out of fuel, they crash-landed upside-down in a kiawe thicket on Molokai but emerged unhurt to become the first civilians to fly to Hawaii from the U.S. mainland. The 25-hour, 2-minute flight landed Smith and Bronte a place in aviation history—and on a roadside marker on Molokai.

Mapulehu Glass House. King Kamehameha V Hwy. (Hi. 450), at mile marker 15. ☎ **808/558-8160.** Mon–Fri 7am–noon, or by appointment. Free guided tour at 10:30am.

This 1920s-era glass house, the biggest in Hawaii, stands in a garden that in itself is worth a visit, to see the exotic tropicals that Ellen Osborne ships to the mainland (see "Shops & Galleries," below). The tour takes in both the house and the 9-acre cut-flower farm.

HALAWA VALLEY

Of the five great valleys of Molokai, only Halawa, with its two waterfalls, golden beach, sleepy lagoon, great surf, and offshore island, is easily accessible. But now, even that has changed.

No longer can you take Molokai's most popular hike, to 250-foot Moaula Falls, or enjoy this serene wilderness, a fertile valley that was inhabited for centuries. In a kind of 20th-century kapu, the private landowner, worried about slip-and-fall lawsuits, has, on the advice of lawyers, closed the trail to the falls. NO TRESPASSING signs are posted, and folks have been turned away by security guards. *No aloha, here, brah.*

Once the agricultural center of Molokai, the valley was planted in taro as far as the eye could see as recently as the 19th century. A visitor noted in 1877 that "it is a very fertile valley with wild fruits, mountain shrimps, and much water in the streams, most of the land is covered with taro. . . . They totaled a thousand and 32 patches." In 1946, a tidal wave scoured the valley and turned the "velvet taro in sweet mud"—salty ponds of brittle leaf. A second tsunami doomed agriculture there in 1957, and the valley became a natural garden of earthly delights, including escaped mango, papaya, and bananas, all of which attract clouds of dreaded medflies.

The beach is still open for swimming and picnicking (see "Beaches," above), but the falls and the magnificent valley, with its 11 heiau ruins and fish shrines dating from A.D. 650, are off-limits. Offshore, the turtle-shaped island of Mokuhooniki, used by the U.S. Navy for target practice during World War II, is once again a seabird preserve.

While you're on Molokai, check with the **Visitors Bureau** (☎ 808/553-3876) to see if the trail has opened again. If the kapu is lifted and you're permitted to take the hike to Halawa Valley, forget your white tennies and shorts. Beautiful from a distance for its variety of shades of green (there's a scenic lookout on the highway), the valley up close is a fecund jungle of primal ooze; it's like being in a heady perfumed steam bath full of voracious mosquitoes. The trail is always wet and often sloppy; sometimes you might be in ankle-deep muck, but the reward for the tough 2-hour slog is an icy cold, 40-foot-wide pool refreshed by the splashy tail of Moaula Falls.

To get to Halawa Valley, drive north from Kaunakakai on Hi. 450 for 30 miles along the coast to the end of the road, which descends into the valley past Jersalema Hou Church, where the trail begins. If you'd just like a glimpse of the valley on your way to the beach, there's a scenic overlook along the road: after Puuo Hoku Ranch at mile marker 25, the narrow two-lane road widens at a hairpin curve, and you'll find the overlook on your right; it's 2 miles more to the valley floor.

11 Shops & Galleries

by Jocelyn Fujii

KAUNAKAKAI

Seaside Place, Molokai Surf, Molokai Imports, and **Lourdes** are clothing and gift shops in close proximity to each other in downtown Kaunakakai, where most of the retail shops sell T-shirts, muumuus, surf wear, and informal apparel. For food shopping, there are several good alternatives. Since many visitors to the island stay in condominiums, knowing where the grocery stores are on this island is especially important. Other than that, serious shoppers will be disappointed, unless they love kites or native wood vessels. The following are Kaunakakai's notables.

Imamura Store. ☎ **808/553-5615.**

Wilfred Imamura, whose mother founded the store (she died in 1992 at age 97), recalls the old railroad track that stretched from the pier to a spot across the street. "We brought our household things from the pier on a hand-pumped vehicle," he recalls. His store, appropriately, is a leap into the past, a marvelous amalgam of precious old-fashioned things. Rubber boots, Hawaiian-print tablecloths, Japanese tea plates, ukulele cases, plastic slippers, and even coconut bikini tops line the shelves. But it's not all nostalgia. The Molokai T-shirts, jeans, and palaka shorts are of good quality and inexpensive, and the pareu fabrics are a find.

Molokai Drugs. In the Kamoi Professional Center. ☎ **808/553-5313.**

David Mikami, whose father-in-law founded the pharmacy in 1935, has made this more than a drugstore: it's a gleaming, friendly stop full of life's basic necessities, with generous amenities such as a phone and a rest room for passersby (!). You'll find the best selection of guidebooks, books about Molokai, and maps here, as well as greeting cards, paperbacks, party favors, cassette players, flip-flops, and every imaginable essential.

When Mikami's daughter, Kelly, became a pharmacist in 1995, she was the fourth in the family. The Mikamis are a household name on the island not only because of their pharmacy, but also because the family has shown exceptional kindness to the often economically strapped Molokaians.

Molokai Fish & Dive. ☎ **808/553-5926.**

The island's largest selection of T-shirts and souvenirs shares space with fishing, snorkeling, and outdoor gear for rent and sale. Wend your way among the fishnets, boogie boards, diving equipment, bamboo rakes, juices and soft drinks, disposable cameras, and other miscellany of this chockablock store. One entire wall is lined with T-shirts.

Take's Variety Store. ☎ **808/553-5442.**

If you need luggage tags, buzz saws, toys, candy, cloth dolls, canned goods, canteens, camping equipment, hardware, pipe fittings, fishing supplies—whew!—and other products for work and play, this 50-year-old variety store might be your answer. You might suffer from claustrophobia in the crowded, dusty aisles, but Take's carries everything—if you can find it. If you can't, the staff is friendly and helpful.

EDIBLES

Friendly Market Center. ☎ 808/553-5595.

You can't miss this salmon-colored wooden storefront on the main drag of "downtown" Kaunakakai, where multigeneration stores are the norm rather than the exception. It's friendly! We like all the old mom-and-pop stores, but Friendly's is one store that has an especially good selection of produce and healthy foods. (The other is Outpost Natural Foods.) Blue-corn tortilla chips, soy milk, and Kumu Farms macadamia-nut pesto, the island's stellar gourmet foods, are among the items that surpass standard grocery-store fare. The meats are fresh and of good quality, and the selection is democratic, encompassing everything from prime cuts to fresh fish and sashimi fillets.

Misaki's Grocery and Dry Goods. ☎ 808/553-5505.

Established in 1922, this third-generation local legend is one of Kaunakakai's two grocery stores, as essential as the Molokai air. Some surprises lurk on the shelves, such as chopped garlic from Gilroy, California (the garlic capital of the world), but the stock mostly consists of meats, produce, baking products, and a humongous array of soft drinks. Liquor, stationery, candies, and paper products round out the selection.

Molokai Ice House. At the end of Kaunakakai Wharf Rd. ☎ 808/553-3054.

A fishermen's co-op established in 1988 opened its retail doors as a fish market in 1994—and it's a find. Gathered daily from the fishing boats at the wharf, the seafood comes in all forms—sashimi, poke (the seasoned raw fish), lomi (mixed, seasoned, and worked with the fingers) salmon and squid, oysters, seaweed, teriyaki marlin fillets. It can't come any fresher, and it's all skillfully seasoned and reasonably priced. Locals come here for their fresh fish, whole or in fillets. The *lomi 'o'io* and the *lomi ahi* (yellowfin tuna) might look like mashed raw fish to the uninitiated, but with perfectly balanced seasonings of green onions, a pungent type of seaweed (*limukohu*), and roasted kukui nut (*inamona*), they're delicacies sought by Molokaians and neighbor islanders. Various seasoned shrimp and octopus dishes, and frequent surprise catches that catch the fancy of the chef, make this an ever-changing adventure. Best of all, the Molokai prices are kind and unchanging, even during the winter when fresh-fish prices notoriously skyrocket. The prepared foods are perfect for no-fuss cooking or a quiet lunch at the wharf. This fish market is a find for kamaaina and malihini in terms of quality, freshness, pricing, and heart—and, in true Hawaiian spirit, they sell poi to go with the fish!

Molokai Wines & Spirits. ☎ 808/553-5009.

This isn't an Epicurean's cave, but it's your best bet on the island for a decent bottle of wine. The shop offers 200 labels, including Caymus, Silver Oak, Joseph Phelps, Heitz, and a carefully culled European selection. *Wine Spectator* reviews are tacked to some of the selections, which always helps, and the snack selection shows at least some glimmers of mercy: Cambozola gourmet cheeses, salami, and Carr's biscuits. For those who like the effortless frozen burritos, canned tuna, chips, and prepackaged nibbles, they're on the shelves, too.

EN ROUTE TO THE NORTH COAST

Coffees of Hawaii Plantation Store. Kualapuu. ☎ 808/567-9023.

This is a fairly slick—for Molokai—combination coffee bar, store, and gallery for more than 30 artists and craftspeople from Molokai, Maui, and the Big Island.

Sold here are the Malulani Estate and Muleskinner coffees, grown, processed, and packed on the 500-acre plantation surrounding the shop. (A tour of the plantation is offered weekdays at 10am and 1pm, and, upon special request, Saturdays at 10am; it's $14 for adults and $7 for kids.) You might find better prices on coffee at other retail outlets, but the gift items are worth a look: pikake and plumeria soaps from Kauai; perfumes and pure beeswax candles from Maui; koa bookmarks and hair sticks; pottery, woods, and baskets.

Molokai Museum Gift Shop. At the old R. W. Meyer Sugar Mill, Kalae. ☎ **808/567-6436.**

The restored 1878 sugar mill sits 1,500 feet above the town of Kualapuu (see "Seeing the Sights," earlier in this chapter). It's a drive from town, definitely, but a good cause for those who'd like to support the museum and the handful of local artisans who sell their crafts, fabrics, cookbooks, quilt sets, and other gift items in its tiny shop. Modest selections of cards, T-shirts, coloring books, and, at Christmas, handmade ornaments of lauhala and koa are sprinkled throughout.

EDIBLES
Kualapuu Market. Kualapuu. ☎ **808/567-6243.**

This market, in its third generation, is a stone's throw from the new Coffees of Hawaii Store. It's a scaled-down, one-stop shop with wine, food, and necessities—and a surprisingly presentable, albeit small, assortment of produce, from Molokai sweet potatoes to Ka'u navel oranges in season. The shelves are filled with canned goods, propane, rope, hoses, paper products, and baking goods, reflecting the uncomplicated rural lifestyle of the area.

THE WEST END
MAUNALOA
Big Wind Kite Factory & the Plantation Gallery. Maunaloa. ☎ **808/552-2634.**

Jonathan and Daphne Socher, kite designers and inveterate Bali-philes, have combined their interests in a kite factory/import shop that dominates the commercial landscape of Maunaloa, the reconstituted plantation town. Maunaloa's naturally windy conditions make it ideal for kite-flying classes, which are offered free when conditions are right. The adjoining Plantation Gallery features local handicrafts such as milo-wood bowls, locally made T-shirts, Hawaii-themed sandblasted glassware, baskets of lauhala and other fibers, and Hawaiian-music CDs. There are many Balinese handicrafts, from jewelry to clothing and fabrics.

Maunaloa General Store. ☎ **808/552-2346.**

Maunaloa's only general store sells everything from paper products to batteries and socks, dairy products, frozen and fresh meats, wine, canned goods, visors, and a cross-section of necessities.

THE EAST END
EDIBLES
The Neighborhood Store 'N Counter. Pukoo. ☎ **808/554-8498.**

With the closing of the Wavecrest, the Neighborhood Store is the only grocery on the East End. In addition to the breakfast and lunch counter, the store sells batteries, film, aspirin, cookies, beer, Molokai produce, candies, paper products, and other sundries for travelers and residents.

12 Molokai After Dark

by Jocelyn Fujii

The big news is that the movies have come to Molokai. **Maunaloa Cinemas** (☎ **808/552-2707**) is a tri-plex theater that shows first-run movies in the middle of Maunaloa town—four screenings a day at each of the three theaters, beginning with the matinee. Otherwise, Molokai nightlife is an oxymoron. Aside from the Ohia Lodge at the Kaluakoi Resort, which features live entertainment on Friday and Saturday nights, the only other spot for after-dark socializing is the Pau Hana Inn in Kaunakakai (☎ **808/553-5342**). Call the Pau Hana before going over, however. At this writing, its future is uncertain.

Lanai: A Different Kind of Paradise

13

Lanai is not an easy place to get to. There are no direct flights from the mainland, and most air carriers route flights onto the island from Honolulu. It is almost as if this quiet, gentle oasis that's known, paradoxically, for both its small-town feel and its celebrity appeal, demands that its visitors go to great lengths to get here to ensure that those who come will appreciate it.

Lanai (pronounced *lah nigh ee*), Hawaii's sixth-largest island and the nation's biggest defunct pineapple patch, now claims to be one of the world's top tropical destinations. It's a bold claim, since so little is here: no stoplights, barely 30 miles of paved road, no fast-food joints, no strip malls, no taxis—in short, none of what you usually find in a vacation destination. Instead, what you have here is something quite rare: an almost virgin island, unspoiled by what passes for progress, except for a tiny 1920s-era plantation village—and, of course, its fancy new neighbors, two first-class luxury hotels where room rates hover around $400 a night.

As soon as you arrive, the blanket of coziness of a small town is felt: people wave to every car, residents stop to "talk story" with their friends, taking time to fish or work in the garden is considered a priority in life, and leaving the keys in your car's ignition is standard practice.

For generations, Lanai was little more than a small village, owned and operated by the pineapple company, surrounded by acres of pineapple. The few visitors to the island were either relatives of the mainly Filipino residents or occasional weekend hunters. Life in the 1960s was pretty much the same as in the 1930s.

But all that changed in 1990, when The Lodge at Koele, a 102-room hotel resembling an opulent English Tudor mansion, opened its doors, followed a year later by the 250-room Manele Bay Hotel, a Mediterranean-style luxury resort overlooking Hulopoe Bay. Overnight, the isolated island was transformed: corporate jets streamed into the tiny Lanai Airport; former pineapple plantation workers were retrained in the art of serving gourmet meals; and the population of 2,500 swelled with transient visitors and outsiders coming to work in the island's new hospitality industry. Microsoft millionaire Bill Gates chose the island for his lavish wedding, buying up all of its hotel rooms to fend off the press—and uncomplicated Lanai went on the map as a place where the rich and powerful vacation.

But it's also a place where people come looking for dramatic beauty, quiet, solitude, and an experience with nature away from the bright lights of Waikiki, the publicity of Maui, and the hoopla surrounding most resorts. The sojourners who find their way to Lanai come seeking the melodramatic views, the tropical fusion of stars at night, and the chance to be alone with the elements.

They also come for the wealth of activities: snorkeling and swimming in the sapphire waters of the marine life conservation district of Hulopoe Bay; hiking on a hundred miles of remote trails that canvass the 141-square-mile island; talking story with the friendly locals; and beachcombing and whale watching along a stretch of otherwise deserted sand. For the adventurous, there's horseback riding in the mist of the forest, scuba diving in caves, playing golf next to scenic ocean views, shooting sporting clays, or renting a four-wheel-drive jeep for the day and discovering wild plains where spotted deer run free and a rich cultural history comes alive in the ruins of a once-vibrant village.

In a single decade, a plain red-dirt pineapple patch has become one of Hawaii's most unusual fantasy destinations. The people cultivate vacationers here now, not pineapples. But the real Lanai is a multifaceted place that's so much more than its newfound status as a luxury resort—and it's the traveler who comes to discover the island's natural wonders, local lifestyle, and other inherent joys who's bound to have the most genuine island experience.

A BRIEF LOOK AT AN UNUSUAL PAST
THE PINEAPPLE ISLAND

This old shield volcano in the rain shadow of Maui has a history of resisting change in a big way. Early Polynesians, fierce Hawaiian kings, European explorers, 20th-century farmers—it has seen them all and sent most of them packing, empty-handed and broken. The ancient Hawaiians believed that the island was haunted by spirits so wily and vicious that no human could survive there. The "cannibal spirits" were finally driven off around A.D. 1400, and people settled in.

But those spirits never really went away, it seems. In 1778, just before Captain Cook "discovered" Hawaii, the King of the Big Island invaded Lanai in what was called "the war of loose bowels." His men slaughtered every warrior, cut down trees, and set fire to all that was left except a bitter fern whose roots gave them all dysentery.

In 1802, Wu Tsin made the first attempt to harvest on the island, but he ultimately abandoned his cane fields and went away. Charles Gay acquired 600 acres at public auction to experiment with pineapple as a crop, but a 3-year drought left him bankrupt. Others tried in vain to grow cotton, sisal, and sugar beets; they started a dairy and a piggery, and raised sheep for wool. But all enterprises failed, mostly for lack of water.

Harry Baldwin, a missionary's grandson and Massachusetts Institute of Technology grad, was the first to do OK for himself. He bought Lanai for $588,000 in 1917, developed a 20-mile water pipeline between Koele and Manele, and sold the island 5 years later to Jim Dole for $1.1 million.

Dole planted and irrigated 18,000 acres of pineapple, built Lanai City, blasted out a harbor, and turned the island into a fancy fruit plantation. For a half-century, he enjoyed great success. Even Dole was ultimately vanquished, however; cheaper pineapple production in Asia brought an end to Lanai's heyday.

The island still resembles old photographs taken in the glory days of Dole. Any minute now, you half expect to look up and see old Jim Dole himself rattling up the road in a Model-T truck with a load of fresh-picked pineapples. Only now, there's a new lord of the manor, and his name is David Murdock.

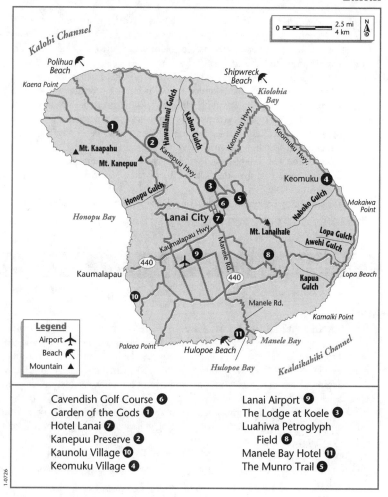

Cavendish Golf Course **6**
Garden of the Gods **1**
Hotel Lanai **7**
Kanepuu Preserve **2**
Kaunolu Village **10**
Keomuku Village **4**

Lanai Airport **9**
The Lodge at Koele **3**
Luahiwa Petroglyph
Field **8**
Manele Bay Hotel **11**
The Munro Trail **5**

A NEW KING—AND A REINVENTED ISLAND

Of all who have looked at Lanai with a gleam in their eye, nobody has succeeded quite like David Murdock, a self-made billionaire who acquired Hawaii's sixth-largest island in a merger more than a decade ago. About 97% of it is now his private holding.

After declaring Lanai's plantation era over, he spent $400 million to build two grand hotels on the island: The Lodge at Koele, which resembles an English country retreat, and the Manele Bay Hotel, a green tile–roofed Mediterranean palazzo by the sea. Murdock recycled the former field hands into waitstaff, even summoning a London butler to school the natives in the fine art of service, and carved a pair of daunting golf courses out of the island's interior and along the wave-lashed coast. He then set out to attract tourists by touting Lanai as "the private island."

He's now trying to make all this pay for itself by selling vacation homes and condos next door to the two resorts. Hardly Thoreau's cabin in the woods, the homes and condos start at around $500,000 and carry an upward price tag of $3 million.

The redevelopment of this tiny rock should have been a pushover for the big-time tycoon, but island-style politics have continually thwarted his schemes. GO SLOW, a sun-faded sign at Dole's old maintenance shed once said. Murdock might have heeded the warning, because his grandiose plans are taking twice as long to accomplish as he'd expected. Every permit he's sought has stuck in the tropic heat like a damp cotton shirt. Lanai is under the political thumb of many who believe that the island's precious water supply shouldn't all be diverted to championship golf courses and Jacuzzis; and there remains opposition from Lanaians For Sensible Growth, who advocate affordable housing, alternative water systems, and civic improvements that benefit residents.

Lanai residents, who might have lived in a rural setting, certainly haven't been isolated. Having watched the other islands in Hawaii attempt the balancing act of economic growth and the maintenance of an island lifestyle, the residents of Lanai are cautiously welcoming visitors, but at a pace that is still easy for this former plantation community to digest.

—Jeanette Foster

1 Orientation

by Jeanette Foster

ARRIVING

BY PLANE   From Maui, you'll have to make a connection in Honolulu, where you can easily catch a small plane for the 25-minute flight to Lanai's new $4 million airport. Jet service to Lanai is now available, but only on **Hawaiian Airlines** (☎ 800/367-5320 or 808/565-6977), which offers one flight a day. Twin-engine planes take longer and are sometimes bumpier, but they offer great views since they fly lower. **Island Air** (☎ 800/652-6541 or 808/565-6744) offers 9 to 12 flights a day. For more details on these airlines—including details on how to get the cheapest fares—see "Getting There & Getting Around" and "Money-Saving Package Deals," in chapter 3.

Prop or jet, you'll touch down in Puuwai Basin, once the world's largest pineapple plantation; it's about 10 minutes by car to Lanai City and 25 minutes to Manele Bay.

BY BOAT   A round-trip on **Expeditions Lahaina/Lanai Passenger Ferry** (☎ 808/661-3756) takes you between Maui and Lanai for $50. The ferry service runs five times a day, 365 days a year, between Lahaina and Lanai's Manele Bay harbor. The ferry leaves Lahaina at 6:45am, 9:15am, 12:45pm, 3:15pm, and 5:45pm; the return ferry from Lanai's Manele Bay Harbor leaves at 8am, 10:30am, 2pm, 4:30pm, and 6:45pm. The 9-mile channel crossing takes 45 minutes to an hour, depending on sea conditions. Reservations are strongly recommended. Baggage is limited to two checked bags and one carry-on.

VISITOR INFORMATION

Destination Lanai (☎ 800/947-4774 or 808/565-7600; fax 808/565-9316) and the **Hawaii Visitors and Convention Bureau** (☎ 800/GO-HAWAII or 808/923-1811; www.gohawaii.com) will both provide you with brochures, maps, and island guides. For a free Road and Site Map of hikes, archaeological sites, and other sights, contact **The Lanai Company,** P.O. Box 310, Lanai, HI 96763 (☎ 808/565-3812).

THE ISLAND IN BRIEF

Inhabited Lanai is divided into three parts—Lanai City, Koele, and Manele—and two distinct climate zones: hot and dry, and cool and misty.

Lanai City (population 2,800) sits at the heart of the island at 1,645 feet above sea level. This is the only place on the island where you'll find services. Built in 1924, this plantation village is a tidy grid of quaint tin-roofed cottages in bright pastels, with roosters penned in tropical gardens of bananas, lilikoi, and papaya. Many of the residents are Filipino immigrants who worked the pineapple fields and imported the art, culture, language, food, and lifestyle of the Philippines. Their clapboard homes, now worth $250,000 or more, are an excellent example of historic preservation; the whole town looks like it's been preserved under a bell jar, or like a Guy Buffet painting of an upscale Southern Philippines *barangay* (village) come to life.

Around Dole Park Square, a charming village square lined with towering Norfolk and Cook Island pines, plantation buildings house general stores with basic necessities: a U.S. post office (where people stop to chat), two banks, and a police station with a jail that consists of three bright, blue-and-white wooden outhouse-sized cells with padlocks.

In the nearby cool upland district of **Koele** is The Lodge at Koele, standing by itself on a knoll overlooking pastures and the sea at the edge of a pine forest, like a grand European manor or a British colonial hill station. The other bastion of indulgence, the Manele Bay Hotel, is on the sunny southwestern tip of the island at **Manele.** You'll get more of what you expect from Hawaii here—beaches, swaying palms, Mai Tais, and the like.

2 Getting Around

by Jeanette Foster

With so few paved roads, you'll need a four-wheel-drive vehicle if you plan on exploring the island's remote shores, its interior, or the summit of Mount Lanaihale. Even if you have only 1 day on Lanai, rent one and see the island. We recommend calling **Red Rover,** P.O. Box 464 (located across the street from the island's only gas station, Lanai City Service), Lanai City, HI 96763 (☎ **808/565-7722;** fax 808/6322). It has a fleet of 10 Land Rover vehicles (which carry from two to nine passengers each), ranging in price from $119 to $159 a day. Staffers will deliver the car to you free anywhere on Lanai. Each vehicle comes equipped with CB radios and cell phone (if you get stuck, they'll come and get you) and winches and tool kits. In addition, as part of the rental fee, they'll supply you with all the beach gear you need (mask, fins, snorkels, towels, sunscreen, boogie boards, even fishing rod and reel) and provide a map of the best off-road trips.

A small fleet of rental vehicles is available at the **Dollar Rent-A-Car** desk at Lanai City Service, 10-36 Lanai Ave. (☎ **800/800-4000** for Dollar reservations; 808/244-9538 or 808/565-7227 for Lanai City Service). Dollar has both cars and four-wheel-drive vehicles. Expect to pay about $60 a day for the cheapest car available, a Dodge Neon (the rate is 30% cheaper if you rent for a week or more), and $119 a day for a four-wheel-drive jeep (the rate drops 34% if you rent for a week or more).

Be warned: Gas is expensive on Lanai. At press time, it was $2.30 a gallon (versus $1.90 in Kona and $1.55 in Honolulu)—and those jeeps don't get good gas mileage. Since everything in Lanai City is within walking distance, it makes sense to just rent a jeep for the day (or days) that you want to explore the island. (The two big resort hotels run shuttle vans around the island, but you can use them only if you're staying at one of the hotels.) **Lanai City Service** (☎ **808/565-7227**) will provide taxi service from the airport to Lanai City for $5 per person and will also transport you from Lanai City to Hulopoe Beach for $10 per person one-way.

Whether or not you rent a car, sooner or later you'll find yourself at Lanai City Service, the glorified name for the only gas station in town. The all-in-one grocery store, coffee bar, rental-car agency, and souvenir shop serves as the island's Grand Central Station; you can pick up information, directions, maps, and all the local gossip.

FAST FACTS: Lanai

Dentists   For emergency dental care, call Dr. Nick's Family Dentistry at ☎ **808/565-7801.**

Doctors   Call Lanai Family Health Center at ☎ **808/565-6423** or the Lanai Community Hospital at ☎ **808/565-6411.**

Emergencies   Call ☎ **911** for police, fire, and ambulance. For non-emergencies, call the Lanai police at ☎ **808/565-6428.**

Poison Control Center   In an emergency, call ☎ **800/362-3585.**

Weather Reports   Call the National Weather Service at ☎ **808/565-6033.**

3 Accommodations

by Jeanette Foster

The majority of the accommodations are located "in the village," as residents call Lanai City. Down the hill at Huelopoe Bay there are two options: the luxurious Manele Bay Hotel or tent camping under the stars at the park.

In addition to the choices listed below, also consider the B&B accommodations offered by Delores Fabrao (☎ **808/565-6134**), who has two guest rooms in her home: a double with a shared bathroom, and a family room with private bathroom that sleeps up to six ($55 double, $100 for four); she doesn't provide breakfast, but you'll have the run of the entire house, including kitchen. At **Hale Moe** (☎ **808/565-9520**), host and Lanai native Momi Suzuki makes two bedrooms in her Lanai City home available to guests; both have private bathrooms, and guests are welcome to use the entertainment center, the large deck, and Momi's two bicycles ($60 to $70 double). For a fully equipped, two-bedroom vacation rental that sleeps up to six, call **Hale O Lanai** in Lanai City (☎ **808/247-3637**); rates range from $95 to $125.

Don't forget to add 10.17% in taxes to all accommodation bills.

VERY EXPENSIVE

✪ **The Lodge at Koele.** P.O. Box 310, Lanai City, HI 96793. ☎ **800/321-4666** or 808/565-7300. Fax 808/565-3868. 107 units. A/C MINIBAR TV TEL. $325–$485 double, $600–$1,500 suite. AE, CB, DC, MC, V.

This is the place to stay for a quiet, relaxing vacation in the cool mist of the mountains. The atmosphere is informal during the day, more formal after sunset (jackets required in main dining room). The Lodge, as folks here call it, stands in a 21-acre grove of Norfolk Island pines at 1,700 feet above sea level, 8 miles inland from any beach—a locus that flies in the face of conventional wisdom, which dictated for more than a century that the beach was the only place for a Hawaii vacation hotel.

The 102-room resort resembles a grand English country estate. Inside, heavy timbers, beamed ceilings, and the two huge stone fireplaces of the "Great Hall" complete the look. Overstuffed furniture sits invitingly around the fireplaces, and all the coffee-table books on Hawaii that you've ever wanted to read are scattered on the tables around you. Richly patterned rugs adorn the floor, and museum-quality art hangs on the walls. Cushioned wicker chairs on the long porches are perfect for a long afternoon with a good book.

The guest rooms continue the English theme with four-poster beds, sitting areas (complete with window seats for reading), flowery wallpaper, formal writing desks, and luxury bathrooms with oversized tubs and just about every amenity imaginable.

There are plenty of activities here and at the sister resort down the hill, Manele Bay, so you'll have the best of both hotels. Most guests who stay at The Lodge are looking for a slightly less frenzied vacation: relaxing out on the porch, reading or watching the turkeys mosey across the manicured lawns; strolling through the Japanese hillside garden; or watching the sun sink into the Pacific and the stars light up at night.

Dining/Diversions: A formal dining room serves dinner; a less formal interior terrace is open all day. Both utilize local island ingredients. Entertainment is limited to quiet live music and hula and periodic guest appearances by celebrities who chat informally in a drawing-room setting about their work (see the box "'Talk Story' with the Greats: Lanai's Visiting Artists Program," below).

Amenities: Complimentary shuttle service to airport, beach, and Manele Bay Hotel. Complimentary coffee and tea in lobby and formal tea every afternoon. Twice-daily maid service, turndowns, some rooms with butler service. Golf at the 18-hole championship Greg Norman/Ted Robinson–designed course, the Experience at Koele; croquet lawns, stables, tennis, bikes, rental jeeps, executive putting green, pool, upcountry hiking trails, extensive lawns, and garden walks. Library, game room, bar, and music room. Guests have access to the Manele Bay facilities as well.

✪ **Manele Bay Hotel.** P.O. Box 310, Lanai City, HI 96793. ☎ **800/321-4666** or 808/565-7700. 250 units. A/C MINIBAR TV TEL. $275–$525 double; $725–$2,000 suite. AE, CB, DC, MC, V.

If you want to stay at the beach, come to this sun-washed southern bluff overlooking Hulopoe Beach, one of Hawaii's best stretches of golden sand. The U-shaped hotel steps down the hillside to the pool and that great beach, then fans out in oceanfront wings separated by gardens with lush flora, man-made waterfalls, lotus ponds, and streams. Bordered on the other side by golf greens on a hillside of dry land scrub, the hotel is a real oasis against the dry Arizona-like heat of Lanai's arid south coast.

This is a traditional luxury beachfront hotel: open, airy, and situated so that every room has a peek of the big blue Pacific. The lobby is filled with murals depicting scenes from Hawaiian history, sea charts, potted palms, soft camel-hued club chairs, and handwoven kilim rugs. The oversized guest rooms resemble an English country house on the beach: sunny chintz fabrics, mahogany furniture, Audubon prints, huge marble bathrooms, and semiprivate lanais.

This resort is much less formal than The Lodge up the hill. Its proximity to the beach attracts more families, and because it's warmer here, people wander through the lobby in shorts and T-shirts. This is perfect for a beach vacation, with a few forays up to The Lodge and Lanai City to enjoy the mountain activities.

Dining/Diversions: Hulopoe Court features innovative Hawaii Regional Cuisine and ocean views; do not miss Chef Philippe Padovani's creations in the Ihilani, the specialty dining room (see "Dining," below). Entertainment is limited to quiet live music and hula and periodic guest-lecture appearances by celebrities.

Amenities: Complimentary shuttle service to the airport, The Lodge at Koele, and Manele Boat Harbor. Twice-daily maid service, turndown, 13 butlered suites. Jack Nicklaus–designed Challenge at Manele adds 18 more holes to play, a seaside layout in nice contrast to the upland Experience (see "The Lodge at Koele," above). Water sports at the neighboring beach; plus pool, tennis, bicycling, game room, library, spa, historic tours, and jeep tours. Guests can also enjoy the amenities at The Lodge at Koele.

INEXPENSIVE

✪ **Dreams Come True.** 547 12th St. (P.O. Box 525), Lanai City, HI 96763. ☎ **800/565-6961** or 808/565-6961. E-mail: hunters@aloha.net. 3 units. $75 double. Rates include continental breakfast. Extra person $20. AE, DC, DISC, MC, V.

Your dreams just might come true in this quaint plantation house, tucked away among papaya, banana, lemon, and avocado trees in the heart of Lanai City, at 1,620 feet. Hosts Susan and Michael Hunter have filled their house with Southeast Asian antiques collected on their travels. Both are jewelers, and they operate a working studio on the premises. All three bedrooms have private bathrooms; two feature a four-poster canopied bed, with an additional single bed (perfect for a small family), and the third room has just one queen bed. The common area looks out on the garden and is equipped with both TV and VCR. Breakfast usually consists of freshly baked bread with homemade jellies and jams, tropical fruit, juice, and coffee. The Hunters rent a nearby three-bedroom/two-bathroom house to families for $190 a night.

✪ **Hotel Lanai.** 828 Lanai Ave. (P.O. Box 520), Lanai City, HI 96763. ☎ **800/795-7211** or 808/565-7211. Fax 808/565-6450. 11 units. $95–$105 double, $135 cottage double. Rates include continental breakfast. Extra person $10. AE, MC, V. Airport shuttle $5 round-trip.

This is the perfect place for families and other vacationers who can't afford to spend $300 to $400 a night for a hotel room but still want to enjoy the atmosphere and activities of Lanai. Just a few years ago, the Hotel Lanai, on a rise overlooking Lanai City, was the only place to stay and eat unless you knew someone who lived on the island. Built in the 1920s for VIP plantation guests, this clapboard plantation-era relic has retained its quaint character, and it lives on as a country lodge. Soon after the resorts opened, the owners of the Hotel Lanai gave their rustic hotel a $450,000 facelift and repositioned it as a B&B. In August 1996, a well-known chef from Maui, Henry Clay Richardson (formerly of the Kapalua Bay Hotel & Villas, David Paul's Lahaina Grill, and Gerard's Restaurant), became the inn's new owner and executive chef in the dining room.

The one-story wooden building is bordered by a verdant lawn, bright flowers, and a stalwart stand of pines. The rooms are small, clean, and newly decorated, plantation style, with Hawaiian quilts, wood furniture, and ceiling fans. The standard hotel rooms are extremely small but have private bathrooms (shower only), a double bed or two twin beds, and little else. The garden rooms, which are the largest, feature king beds and private bathrooms. The most popular are the lanai rooms, which feature a shared lanai with the room next door. They are smaller than the garden rooms and have queen beds, but the lanai is a great spot to sit and watch the sunset. The small one-bedroom cottage on the property is perfect for a family of three or four adults. All rooms have phones, ceiling fans, and bathrooms with shower only. Only the cottage has a TV and bathtub.

The hotel serves as a down-home crossroads where total strangers meet local folks on the lanai to drink iced beer and talk story or play the ukulele and sing into the dark tropic night. Often, a curious visitor in search of an authentic experience will join the party and discover Lanai's very Hawaiian heart. A restaurant is open for continental breakfast for guests only and open to the public for dinner daily.

4 Dining

by Jocelyn Fujii

Dining on Lanai is uncomplicated and extreme. On this island of three hotels, five stores, and fewer than 3,000 residents, you can go from a greasy-spoon breakfast to a five-star dinner in less than a mile and a few hundred feet in altitude. When The Lodge at Koele and the Manele Bay Hotel opened their doors in 1990 and 1991, Lanai went from "Pineapple Island" to luxury resort—and it did so with a vengeance, quickly transforming its agricultural renown into a fine-dining cachet that immediately won top placement in the diner-rated Zagat Hawaii Restaurant Survey.

You can dine like a sultan on this island, but be prepared for high prices. The tony hotel restaurants require deep pockets (or bottomless expense accounts), and there are only a handful of other options. Because there are so few eateries on this island, they're simply listed alphabetically rather than in categories or by price range.

Blue Ginger Cafe. 409 Seventh St., Lanai City. ☎ **808/565-7016.** Most items under $12. No credit cards. Daily 6am–9pm. COFFEE SHOP.

This is a very local, very casual, and moderately priced alternative to Lanai's fancy hotel restaurants. The four tables on the front porch face the cool Norfolk pines of Dole Park and are always filled with locals who talk story from morning to night. The tiny cafe is often jammed from 6 to 7am with construction workers on their way to work. The offerings are solid, no-nonsense everyday fare: fried saimin (no MSG, a plus), the very popular hamburgers on homemade buns, and the mahimahi with capers in a white-wine sauce. Blue Ginger also serves a tasty $1.75 French toast of homemade bread, a vegetable *lumpia* (Filipino version of a spring roll), and a homemade omelet for less than $5 that's reportedly luring Lodge guests away from their $20 breakfasts up the hill.

✪ **Formal Dining Room.** The Lodge at Koele. ☎ **808/565-4580.** Reservations required. Jackets required. Main courses $32–$40. AE, DC, DISC, JCB, MC, V. Daily 6–9:30pm. AMERICAN.

Chef Edwin Goto's menu is a stroke of genius in this grand atmosphere of soaring ceilings, splendid fireplaces, and cheek-reddening upcountry chill. What else but American classics would suffice in a hotel with game rooms, pigskin chairs, and the elusive scent of pipe smoke wafting across wide verandas and wainscoted rooms? The octagonally shaped dining room is elegant yet intimate, with a menu that has earned its rightful place in Hawaii's culinary hierarchy.

Roast rack of lamb and Lanai venison top the list for game lovers, the lamb served with a goat-cheese potato cake and chopped black olives, and the venison in a sour cherry–red wine reduction, served with grilled sweet potatoes and vegetables. The fish au courant, moi, is also an attraction, served braised with oven-dried tomato and crisp pancetta. And in the marinated and grilled quail, the hotel's famous pineapple cider has found its place in American cuisine. The Dining Room is known for its use of fresh herbs, vegetables, and fruit grown on the island, harvested just minutes away, and for its lodge-friendly cuisine—soups both hearty and elegant, and wintry delights of wild mushrooms, buttery squashes, local game, and elegant meats. Although pricey, for most visitors it remains an unavoidable indulgence. The menu changes seasonally and always features a fresh seafood selection.

Henry Clay's Rotisserie. In the Hotel Lanai. 828 Lanai Ave., Lanai City. ☎ **808/565-4700.** Main courses $8.50–$17.95. JCB, MC, V. Daily 5:30–9pm. AMERICAN.

Henry Clay Richardson, a New Orleans native, has made some considerable changes in what used to be the local hangout for hearty, country-style breakfasts. New additions include a cappuccino machine, a sound system, and a glass-enclosed viewing kitchen with rotisserie. The menu focuses on American country cuisine: fresh meats, seafood, and local produce. The meats, which could be rabbit, quail, venison, osso bucco, and plain old beef and chicken, are spit-roasted on the rotisserie. Appetizers such as Cajun shrimp and steamed manila clams reflect regional and international influences. From the rotisserie comes herb-marinated half chicken and Louisiana-style pork ribs; gourmet pizzas and salads occupy the lighter end of the spectrum. The two fireplaces and pine-paneled walls add to the coziness of this old Lanai favorite.

Hulopoe Court. Manele Bay Hotel. ☎ **808/565-7700.** Reservations recommended. Collared shirt required. Main courses $26–$32. AE, DC, DISC, JCB, MC, V. Daily 6–9:30am, 7–11pm. HAWAII REGIONAL.

Hulopoe is casual compared to the hotel's fine dining room, Ihilani, but formal compared to the Pool Grille, the lunchtime oasis for Manele Bay guests. The 17th-century palanquin in the adjoining lower lobby, the Asian accents, the tropical murals by gifted Lanai artists, and the high vaulted ceilings add up to an eclectic, elegant ambiance, with the view of Hulopoe Bay the crowning glory. There are some stunning entrees: taro-crusted ono (with ginger-chive mashed potatoes); steamed onaga with shiitake mushrooms; guava-glazed chicken breast with Molokai sweet potato; and memorable starters that include shrimp summer rolls, seared ahi, and hearts of palm salad.

Ihilani. The Manele Bay Hotel. ☎ **808/565-2290.** Reservations required. Jackets recommended. Main courses $32–$45; set menu $105 without wine, $145 with wine. AE, DC, DISC, JCB, MC, V. Daily 6–9:30pm. FRENCH-MEDITERRANEAN.

The Manele Bay's formal dining room sits across the lobby from Hulopoe Court; its lower ceilings (beautifully painted with bird-of-paradise murals) and pleasing design permit an ocean view and a clubby, darker, more intimate ambiance. There are three sections to the split-level dining room: the terrace, overlooking the ocean and pool; the indoor middle area next to the terrace; and the elevated dining area with banquettes and private niches. The inner area, with its rich, warm ambers and mauves and luscious teak gong and Queen Anne console, suits the Mediterranean fare best.

The menu will likely change with the arrival of a new chef (Philippe Padovani has left for Oahu). As of this writing, the choices are every bit as inviting as the ambiance, including pan-fried *opakapaka* (pink snapper); roasted lamb loins in fresh truffle sauce and artichoke mousseline; and a dessert selection that is simply staggering—particularly the Hawaiian Vintage Chocolate desserts and the cheese tray with walnut bread.

Pele's Other Garden. On Dole Park, 81 Houston St. ☎ **808/565-9628.** Most items under $6. AE, DISC, MC, V. Mon–Thurs 11am–7pm, Fri–Sat 9am–9pm. DELI/PIZZERIA/JUICE BAR.

Healthy, tasty eats come streaming across the counter at this New York–style deli that breaks all the rules: it's healthy *and* delicious, and it's not expensive. Sandwiches, daily soup and menu specials, salads, pizza, fresh organic produce, fresh juices, and special touches such as top-quality roasted red peppers and free-range turkey are some of the features that make Pele's Other Garden a Lanai City must. Mostly it's takeout, but there are a couple of tables on the veranda, facing the tree-shaded square. All menu items are made from natural and organic ingredients.

Pool Grille. Manele Bay Hotel. ☎ **808/565-7700.** Main courses $6–$16. AE, DC, DISC, JCB, MC, V. Daily 11am–5pm. ECLECTIC.

The sybarite's world you've agreed to enter extends poolside as well as in the formal restaurants. At this, the most casual of the hotel's restaurants, you'll dine on $10 hamburgers (homemade bun, of course) and gourmet salads under beach umbrellas, in weather that can be sweltering during the summer and fall months. The salads ($9 to $16) are perfect for the weather and location—cool, light, and sumptuous, as in marinated grilled vegetables with Big Island goat cheese, spicy chicken-breast salad, poached chicken salad with avocado, tabbouleh, Caesar with shrimp, and others. The grilled ahi sandwich and tuna pita are highly recommended.

Tanigawa's. 419 Seventh St., Lanai City. ☎ **808/565-6537.** Reservations not accepted. Main courses under $7. No credit cards. Thurs–Tues 6:30am–1pm. HAMBURGERS.

Formerly S. T. Properties, famous for its hamburgers, Tanigawa's has changed its name but remains the landmark that it's been since the 1920s. In those days, the tiny storefront sold canned goods and cigarettes; the 10 tables, hamburgers, and Filipino food came later. Jerry Tanigawa has kept his hole-in-the-wall a local institution, whose homemade hamburgers and bento lunches (rice with meat or fish, a plantation legacy) have fed two generations of Lanai residents. The fare—saimin, pork teriyaki, beef stew, and omelets—is a nod to sentiment, more greasy spoon than gourmet, and friendliest above all to the pocketbook.

The Terrace. The Lodge at Koele. ☎ **808/565-4580.** Reservations recommended. Breakfast main courses $7.25–$14.50, lunch main courses $9.75–$14, dinner main courses $16–$27. AE, DC, DISC, JCB, MC, V. Daily 6am–9:30pm. AMERICAN.

Located next to the Formal Dining Room, between the 35-foot-high Great Hall and a wall of glass looking out over prim English gardens, The Terrace is far from your typical hotel dining room. The food is fancy for comfort food, but it does, indeed, comfort. Hearty breakfasts of wild-rice waffles and warm cinnamon bread pudding, lunch of seared chicken-breast-and-potato sandwich with red-onion gravy, and grilled artichoke and crisp potatoes with garlic chive aioli: these are some of the reasons everyone remembers The Terrace. In the evening, seafood, osso bucco, New York steak, barbecued Lanai venison meatloaf, and polenta with eggplant, leeks, portobello mushroom, and goat cheese help to satiate the upcountry hunger. In many other places, The Terrace would serve as the fine-dining room instead of a full-service restaurant—but here, all standards are broken.

5 Beaches

by Jeanette Foster

If you like big, wide, empty golden sands and crystal-clear, cobalt-blue water full of bright tropical fish—and who doesn't?—go to Lanai. With 18 miles of sandy shoreline, Lanai has some of Hawaii's least-crowded and most-interesting beaches. One spot in particular is perfect for swimming, snorkeling, and watching spinner dolphins play: Hulopoe Beach, Lanai's best.

✪ HULOPOE BEACH

In 1997, Stephen Leatherman, of the University of Maryland, ranked Hulopoe the best beach in the United States. Leatherman, who compiles an annual ranking, considers 50 standards (including sand and waves, water quality, human use, lifeguard protection, noise, and so on) in judging some 650 public beaches every year. It's easy to see why he said this is the best: the bay at the foot of the Manele Bay Hotel is a protected marine preserve, and the schools of colorful fish know it. So do the spinner dolphins who come here to play, and the Pacific humpback whales who cruise by in winter (that's when the mercury drops below 80°). This palm-fringed, gold-sand beach is bordered by black-lava fingers, protecting swimmers from the serious ocean currents that sweep around Lanai. In summer, Hulopoe is perfect for swimming, snorkeling, or just lolling about; the water temperature is usually in the mid-70s. The protected bay is usually safe, except when swells kick up in the winter. Hulopoe is also Lanai's premier beach park, with a grassy lawn, picnic tables, barbecue grills, rest rooms, showers, and ample parking.

Hulopoe's Tide Pools   Some of the best lava-rock tide pools in Hawaii are found along the south shore of Hulopoe Bay. These miniature Sea Worlds are full of strange creatures: asteroids (sea stars) and holothurians (sea cucumbers), not to mention spaghetti worms, Barber Pole shrimp, and Hawaii's favorite local delicacy, the opihi, a tasty morsel also known as the limpet. Youngsters enjoy swimming in the enlarged tide pool at the eastern edge of the bay.

When you explore tide pools, do it at low tide. Never turn your back on the waves. Wear tennis shoes or reef walkers, because wet rocks are slippery. There's a kapu against collecting specimens in this marine preserve, so don't take any souvenirs home.

SHIPWRECK BEACH

This 8-mile-long windswept strand from Polihua Beach to Kahokunui—named for the rusty ship, *Liberty,* stuck on the coral reef—is a sailor's nightmare and a beachcomber's dream. The strong currents yield all sorts of flotsam, from Japanese handblown glass fish floats and rare pelagic paper Nautilus shells to lots of junk. This is also a great place to spot whales from December to April, when the Pacific humpbacks cruise in from Alaska to winter in the calm offshore waters. The road to the beach is paved most of the way, but you really need four-wheel drive to get down here.

POLIHUA BEACH

So many sea turtles once hauled themselves out of the water to lay their eggs in the sunbaked sand on Lanai's northwestern shore that Hawaiians named the beach there Polihua, or "egg nest." Although Hawaii's endangered green sea turtles are making a comeback, they're seldom seen here now. You're more likely to spot an

☻ Frommer's Favorite Lanai Experiences

Snorkel Hulopoe Beach. Crystal-clear water teems with brilliant tropical fish off a postcard-perfect beach that's one of Hawaii's best. There are tide pools to explore, waves to play in, and other surprises—like a pod of spinner dolphins that often makes a splashy entrance.

Explore the Garden of the Gods. Eroded by wind, rain, and time, this geologic badlands is worth visiting at sunrise or sunset, when the low light plays tricks on the land—and your mind.

Hike the Munro Trail. The 11-mile Munro Trail is a lofty, rigorous hike along the rim of an old volcano, across a razorback ridge through a cloud forest, that offers big views of the nearby islands. Some hike the ridge to see the rain forest; others take a four-wheel-drive vehicle to spend more time on top of the island, where you might catch a rare five-island view.

Four-Wheel It. Four-wheeling is a way of life on Lanai, since there's only 30 miles of pavement. Plenty of rugged trails lead to deserted beaches, abandoned villages, and wild game–filled valleys. No other island offers off-road adventures like this one.

Camp Under the Stars. The campsites at Hulope Beach Park are about as close to the heavens as you can get. The sound of the crashing surf will lull you to sleep at night, and the sound of chirping birds will wake you in the morning. If you're into roughing it, this is the most affordable way to experience Lanai.

Beachcomb at Shipwreck Beach. This 8-mile stretch along the northeastern shore is a great place to dig up treasures of the sea, or perhaps to pick up a new pair of slippers: you might notice that some Lanai residents wear two different slippers, usually because they've found a perfectly good, though unmatched, pair on a recent beachcombing trip. Occasionally, a glass ball from a Japanese fishing boat will float in—in Hawaii, this is considered the greatest beachcombing treasure you can find.

Watch the Whales at Polihua Beach. Located on the northern coast, this beach—which gets its name from the turtles that nest here—is a great place to spend the day scanning the ocean for whales during the winter months.

offshore whale (in season), or the perennial litter that washes up onto this deserted north shore beach, at the end of Polihua Road, a 4-mile jeep trail. There are no facilities except fishermen's huts and driftwood shelters. Bring water and sunscreen. Beware the strong currents, which make the water unsafe for swimming. This strand's really ideal for beachcombing (those little green glass Japanese fishing-net floats often show up here), fishing, or just being alone.

6 Hitting the Water

by Jeanette Foster

Lanai actually has Hawaii's best water clarity, because it lacks major development and has low rainfall and runoff, and its coast is washed clean daily by the sea current known as "The Way to Tahiti." But the strong sea currents pose a threat to swimmers, and there are few good surf breaks. Most of the aquatic adventures—swimming, snorkeling, scuba diving—are centered on the somewhat protected south shore, around Hulopoe Bay.

When traveling to Lanai, bring your own snorkel gear (or boogie board or surfboard), because there are no equipment rentals on the island. Snorkel Bob's, on Maui, Oahu, Kauai, and the Big Island, allows you to rent equipment on one island and return it on another. For details on the other activities listed below, see "The Active Vacation Planner," in chapter 3.

BODYBOARDING (BOOGIE BOARDING), BODYSURFING & BOARD SURFING

When the surf's up on Lanai, it's a real treat. Under the right conditions, Hulopoe and Polihua are both great for catching waves. You've got to bring your own board, because the beach shack at Hulopoe Beach has complimentary boogie boards for hotel guests (Manele Bay and The Lodge at Koele) only. Or you can rent a 4-wheel Land Rover with **Red Rover,** P.O. Box 464 (located across the street from the island's only gas station, Lanai City Service), Lanai City, HI 96763 (☎ 808/565-7722; fax 808/6322). Red Rover provides free boogie boards with every rental.

DEEP-SEA FISHING

Jeff Menze, a Lanai resident, will take you out on the 28-foot Omega boat, *Spinning Dolphin* (☎ 808/565-6613). His 4-hour fishing charters cost $400 for six people, or $600 for six people for 8 hours. He also has exclusive 3-hour whale-watching charters, which are $300 for six passengers.

SCUBA DIVING

Two of Hawaii's best-known dive spots are found in Lanai's clear waters, just off the south shore: **Cathedrals I and II,** so named because the sun lights up the underwater grotto like a magnificent church. **Trilogy Excursion** (☎ 800/TRI-COON or 808/565-2274); www.maui.net/~trilogy; e-mail trilogy@maui.net) offers sailing, diving, and snorkeling trips on a trimaran. The cost is $85 for snorkelers and $120 for certified scuba divers for a one-tank dive. The trip, from 9am to 1pm, includes continental breakfast, lunch, and all snorkeling and diving equipment.

SNORKELING

Hulopoe is Lanai's best snorkeling spot. Fish are abundant and friendly in the marine-life conservation area. Try the lava rock points at either end of the beach and around the lava pools. Snorkel gear is free to guests of the two resorts. No snorkel rentals are available, so bring your own if you're not staying at one of the big two resorts; or call **Red Rover** (☎ 808/565-7722), which provides free snorkeling gear with each 4-wheel Land Rover rental.

7 Hiking & Camping

by Jeanette Foster

ENJOYING A LEISURELY MORNING HIKE

The 3-hour **Koele Nature Hike** starts by the reflecting pool in the backyard of The Lodge at Koele and takes you on a 5-mile loop trail through a cathedral of Norfolk Island pines, into Hulopoe Valley past wild ginger, and up to Koloiki Ridge, with its panoramic view of Maunalei Valley and Molokai and Maui in the distance. You're welcome to take the hike even if you're not a guest at The Lodge. The trailhead isn't obvious—just keep going toward the trees—and the path isn't clearly marked, but the concierge will give you a free map.

HIKING THE CHALLENGING MUNRO TRAIL

This tough, 11-mile (round-trip) uphill climb through the groves of Norfolk pines is a lung-buster, but you'll get a bonus if you reach the top: that breathtaking view of Molokai, Maui, Kahoolawe, the peaks of the Big Island, and—on a really clear day—Oahu in the distance. Figure on 7 hours. The trail begins at Lanai Cemetery along Keomoku Road (Highway 44) and follows Lanai's ancient caldera rim, ending up at the island's highest point, Lanaihale. Go in the morning for the best visibility. After 4 miles, you'll get a view of Lanai City. The weary retrace their steps from there, whereas those determined to see "the view" go the last 1⅓ miles to the top. Diehards go down Lanai's steep south crater rim to join the highway to Manele Bay.

For more details on the Munro Trail—including details on four-wheel-driving it to the top—see "Seeing the Sights," below.

WALKING A SELF-GUIDED NATURE TRAIL

In 1997, with the help of some 40 volunteers, Nature Conservancy of Hawaii completed a self-guided nature trail open to the public in the Kanepuu Preserve. The trailhead is clearly marked on the Polihua Road on the way to the Garden of the Gods. The trail is about a 10- to 15-minute walk through eight stations, with interpretive signs explaining the natural or cultural significance of the area. Kanepuu is one of the last remaining examples of the type of forest that once covered the dry lowlands throughout the state. Here there are some 49 plant species that are found only in Hawaii (such as sandalwood and Hawaiian gardenia, both listed as endangered species). The Nature Conservancy conducts guided hikes every month; call ☎ **808/565-7430.**

CAMPING AT HULOPOE BEACH PARK

There is only one place to "legally" camp on Lanai: Hulopoe Beach Park, which is owned by The Lanai Company. To camp in this exquisite beach park, with its crescent-shaped, white-sand beach bordered by kiawe trees, contact the **Lanai Company,** P.O. Box 310, Lanai City, HI 96763 (☎ **808/565-3982**). There is a $5 registration fee, plus $5 per person, per night. Hulopoe has six campsites, each of which can accommodate up to six people. Facilities include rest rooms, running water, showers, barbecue areas, and picnic tables.

Bring your own camping equipment, because there is nowhere to rent gear on Lanai. The Lanai Company recommends a tent (rain can be expected year-round), a cooking stove or hibachi (the number of barbecues is limited), and insect repellent (mosquitoes are plentiful).

8 Other Outdoor Activities: Golf, Horseback Riding & Tennis

by Jeanette Foster

GOLF

The Challenge at Manele. P.O. Box L, Lanai City, HI 96763. ☎ **808/565-2222.** Located next to the Manele Bay Hotel in Hulopoe Bay.

This target-style, desert-links course, designed by Jack Nicklaus, is one of the most "challenging" courses in the state. First of all, check out the local rules: "No retrieving golf balls from the 150-foot cliffs on the ocean holes 12, 13 or 17," and "All whales, axis deer, and other wild animals are considered immovable obstructions." That's just a hint of the uniqueness of this course routed among lava outcroppings, archaeological sites, kiawe groves, and ilima trees. Two of the more challenging holes of this 7,039-yard, par-72 course are the signature 12th hole, where you simply tee off a couple of hundred yards across the Pacific Ocean 150 yards below (bring extra balls) and the par-4 17th, where you tee off on the ocean cliff across a ravine to a sloping, narrow, downhill fairway (shoot long). The five sets of staggered tees give everyone from the casual golfer to the pro a challenging game. Rates are $100 for guests of Manele Bay Hotel or Koele Lodge and $150 for nonguests. You can get a rate for play at both this course and The Experience at Koele for $150 for hotel guests and $225 for nonguests, plus $22 for the cart rental for the second round. Facilities include clubhouse, pro shop, rentals, practice area, lockers, and showers.

The Experience at Koele. P.O. Box L, Lanai City, HI 96763. ☎ **808/565-4653.** Located next to The Lodge at Koele in Lanai City.

When this par-72 uplands course opened in 1991, it was voted "Best New Golf Course" by *Fortune* magazine and one of 1991's "Top Ten New Resort Courses" by *Golf* magazine. This traditional course, designed by Greg Norman with fairway architecture by Ted Robinson, has very different front and back nine holes. You start off on a high plateau at nearly 2,000 feet, where Mother Nature reigns: Cook Island and Norfolk pines, indigenous plants, and water—lots of water, including seven lakes, flowing streams, cascading waterfalls, and one green (the 17th) completely surrounded by a lake. All goes well until you hit the signature hole, number 8, where you tee off from a 250-foot elevated tee to a fairway bordered by a lake on the right and trees and dense shrubs on the left. After you have recovered, the back nine holes drop dramatically through ravines filled with pine, koa, and eucalyptus trees. The grand finale, the 18th, a par 5, features a green rimmed by waterfalls that flow into a lake on the left side. To give golfers a break, Norman and Robinson have added four different sets of tees to level the playing field. Rates are $100 for guests of Manele Bay Hotel or Koele Lodge and $150 for nonguests. You can get a rate for play at both this course and The Challenge at Manele for $150 for hotel guests and $225 for nonguests, plus $22 for the cart rental for the second round. Facilities include clubhouse, pro shop, rentals, practice area, lockers, and showers.

Cavendish Golf Course. (no phone). Located next to The Lodge at Koele in Lanai City.

It's a quirky par-36, nine-hole public course with not only no clubhouse or club pros, but also no tee times, score cards, or club rentals. To play, just show up, put a donation ($5 to 10 would be nice) into the little wooden box next to the first tee, and hit away. The 3,071-yard, E. B. Cavendish–designed course was built by the Dole plantation in 1947 for its employees. The greens are a bit bumpy—nothing will roll straight here—but the views of Lanai are great, and the temperatures are usually quite mild.

HORSEBACK RIDING

A great way to explore Lanai's unique landscape is by horse. You can venture up wooded upland areas that are impossible to get to, even in a four-wheel-drive vehicle. **The Stables at Koele** (☎ 808/565-4424) offers various rides, starting at $35 for a 1-hour trip. We recommend the 2-hour **Paniolo Trail Ride,** in which you can escape into the hills surrounding Koele. Meander through guava groves and patches of ironwood trees, with glimpses of axis deer, quail, wild turkeys, and Santa

Getrudis cattle, and end with panoramic views of Maui and Lanai. The cost is $65. Long pants and shoes are required; safety helmets are provided. Carry a jacket, because the weather is chilly and rain is frequent. Children must be at least 9 years old and 4 feet tall. Maximum weight limit is 250 pounds.

TENNIS

Public courts, lit for night play as well as day, are available in Lanai City at no charge; call ☎ **808/565-6979** for reservations. Guests staying at The Lodge at Koele or the Manele Bay Hotel have complimentary tennis privileges either at the Tennis Center at Manele, with its six Plexi-pave courts, a fully-equipped pro shop and tournament facilities, or at the courts at Koele. Instruction is available for a fee. For information, call ☎ **808/565-2072.**

9 Seeing the Sights

by Jeanette Foster

You'll need a four-wheel-drive vehicle to reach all of the sights listed below. Renting a jeep is an expensive proposition on Lanai—about $120 a day—so we suggest that you rent one just for the day (or days) you plan on sightseeing; otherwise, it's easy enough to get to the beach and around Lanai City without your own wheels. For details on how to rent a jeep, see "Getting Around," above.

✪ GARDEN OF THE GODS

A dirt Jeep road leads out of Lanai City, through the now-uncultivated pineapple fields, and past the Kanepuu Preserve (a dry-land forest preserve teeming with rare plant and animal life) to the so-called Garden of the Gods, out on Lanai's north shore. This place has little to do with gods, Hawaiian or otherwise. It is, however, the ultimate rock garden: a rugged, barren, beautiful place full of rocks strewn by volcanic forces and shaped by the elements into an infinite variety of shapes and colors: brilliant reds, oranges, ochres, and yellows.

Scientists have numerous explanations for how these boulders got here: some claim it's an "ongoing post-erosional event," whereas others say it's a "plain and simple badlands." However, ancient Hawaiians considered this desolate, windswept place an entirely supernatural phenomenon. Take a four-wheel-drive ride out here and decide for yourself which explanation you accept.

Go early in the morning or just before sunset, when the light casts eerie shadows on the mysterious lava formations that dot the amber- and ocher-colored ground. Drive west from The Lodge on Polihua Road; in about 2 miles, you'll see a hand-painted sign that'll point you in the right direction, left down a one-lane, red-dirt road through a kiawe forest and past sisal and scrub to the site.

✪ FIVE ISLANDS AT A SINGLE GLANCE: THE MUNRO TRAIL

In the first golden rays of dawn, when lone owls swoop low over abandoned pineapple fields, hop into your rented Jeep and head out on the two-lane blacktop toward Mt. Lanaihale, the 3,370-foot summit of Lanai. Your destination is the Munro Trail, the narrow winding ridge trail that runs across Lanai's razorback spine to the summit. From here, hopefully you will be able to see a rare Hawaii treat: five islands at once. On a clear day, you can see all of the main islands in the Hawaiian chain except Kauai.

Lanai's chief arboreal feature isn't the palm tree, the usual tropical icon of Hawaii, but two other interesting Pacific trees: the Norfolk Island and the Cook Island pines, so symmetrical that they look like artificial silk trees made in China. They're everywhere—on ridge lines, in the town square, and on the summit, where they do more than look picturesque: moisture-laden clouds get snagged on the sharp boughs of the summit trees and shed welcome rain on the island, which receives a precious 37 inches a year. (Oahu's Manoa Valley, by comparison, gets 158 inches a year.) New Zealander George Campbell Munro, who came to Hawaii in 1909 to collect birds, was first to figure out this rainmaking technique, which involves hydraulics far too complex to be explained fully here. He planted the pines on horseback, dropping seeds wherever he went to both promote rain and check erosion. The summit trail is named in his memory.

When it rains, the Munro Trail becomes slick and boggy with major washouts. Rainy-day excursions often end with a rental Jeep on the hook of the island's lone tow truck—and a $150 tow charge. You could even slide off into a major gulch and never be found, so don't try it. But in late August and September, when trade winds stop and the air over the islands stalls in what is called a *kona* condition, Mt. Lanai-hale's suddenly visible peak becomes an irresistible attraction.

When you're on Lanai, look to the summit. If it's clear in the morning, get a four-wheel-drive vehicle and take the Munro Trail to the top. Look for a red-dirt road off Manele Road (Highway 440), about 5 miles south of Lanai City; turn left and head up the ridge line. No sign marks the peak. Nothing says, "Summit 3,370 feet," so you have to keep an eye out. Look for a wide spot in the road and a clearing that falls sharply to the sea.

The islands stand in order on the flat blue sea, just like a real-life topographic map: Kahoolawe. Maui. The Big Island of Hawaii. Even Molokini's tiny crescent. Even the summits show. You can see the silver domes of Space City on Haleakala; Puu Moaulanui, the tongue-twisting summit of Kahoolawe; and, looming like the mighty sea mountain it is, Mauna Kea peering above the clouds. At another clearing further along the thickly forested ridge, all of Molokai, including the 4,961-foot summit of Kamakou, and the faint outline of Oahu (more than 30 miles across the sea) are visible. You actually can't see all five in a single glance anymore, because George Munro's thriving pine forest blocks the view. The old forester would have been delighted.

For details on hiking the trail, see "Hiking & Camping," above.

LUAHIWA PETROGLYPH FIELD

With more than 450 known petrogylphs in Hawaii at 23 sites, Lanai is second only to the Big Island in its wealth of prehistoric rock art, but you'll have to search a little to find them. Some of the best are on the outskirts of Lanai City, on a hillside site known as Luahiwa Petroglyph Field. The characters you'll see incised on 13 boulders in this grassy 3-acre knoll include a running man, a deer, a turtle, a bird, a goat, and even a rare, curly-tailed Polynesian dog (some latter-day wag has put a leash on him—some joke).

How to Find Luahiwa   On the road to Hulopoe Beach, about 2 miles out of Lanai City, look to the left, up on the slopes of the crater, for a cluster of reddish-tan boulders (which ancients believed formed a rain heiau, or shrine, where people called up gods Ku and Hina to nourish their crops). A cluster of spiky century plants marks the spot. Take any dirt road that veers across the abandoned pineapple fields to the boulders. Go between 3pm and sunset for ideal viewing and photo ops.

KAUNOLU VILLAGE

Out on Lanai's nearly vertical Gibraltar-like sea cliffs is an old royal compound and fishing village. Now a national historic landmark and one of Hawaii's most treasured ruins, it's believed to have been inhabited by King Kamehameha the Great and hundreds of his closest followers about 200 years ago.

Ruins of 86 house platforms and 35 stone shelters have been identified on both sides of Kaunolu Gulch. The residential complex also includes the Halulu Heiau temple, named after a mythical man-eating bird. His Majesty's royal retreat is thought to have stood on the eastern edge of Kaunolu Gulch, overlooking the rocky shore facing Kahekili's Leap, a 62-foot-high bluff named for the mighty Maui chief who leaped off cliffs as a show of bravado. Nearby are burial caves, a fishing shrine, a lookout tower, and many warrior-like stick figures carved on boulders. Just offshore stands the telltale fin of little Shark Island, a popular dive spot that teems with bright tropical fish and, frequently, sharks.

Excavations are underway to discover more about how ancient Hawaiians lived, worked, and worshipped on Lanai's leeward coast. Who knows? The royal fishing village might yet yield the bones of King Kamehameha. His burial site, according to legend, is known only to the moon and the stars.

It's a hot, dry, dusty, slow-going 3-mile Jeep drive from Lanai City to Kaunolu, but the mini-expedition is worth it. Take plenty of water, don a hat to protect against the sun, and wear sturdy shoes.

KANEPUU PRESERVE

Don't expect giant sequoias big enough to drive a car through; this ancient forest on the island's western plateau is so fragile you can visit only once a month. Kanepuu, which has 48 species of plants unique to Hawaii, including the endangered Hawaiian gardenia (*na'u*) and the once-plentiful sandalwood (*iliahi*), survives under the Nature Conservancy's protective wing. Botanists say the 590-acre forest is the last dry lowland forest in Hawaii; the others have all vanished, trashed by Axis deer, agriculture, or "progress."

Among the botanical marvels of this dry forest are the remains of *olopua* (native olive), *lama* (native ebony), *mau hau hele* (a native hibiscus), and the rare *'aiea* trees, which were used for canoe parts.

Due to the forest's fragile nature, guided hikes are led only 12 times a year, on a monthly, reservations-only basis. Contact the **Nature Conservancy Oahu Land Preserve** manager at 1116 Smith St., Suite 201, Honolulu, HI 96817 (☎ **808/537-4508**), to reserve.

OFF THE TOURIST TRAIL: KEOMOKU VILLAGE

If you have absolutely nothing better to do, are sunburned lobster red, have read all the books you brought, and are starting to get island fever, take a little drive to Keomoku Village, on Lanai's east coast.

You're really off the tourist trail now. All that's in Keomoku, a ghost town since the mid-1950s, is a 1903 clapboard church in disrepair, an overgrown graveyard, an excellent view across the 9-mile Auau Channel to Maui's crowded Kaanapali Beach, and some really empty beaches that are perfect for a picnic or a snorkel. This former ranching and fishing village of 2,000 was the first non-Hawaiian settlement on Lanai, but it dried up after drought killed off the Maunalei Sugar Company. The village, such as it is, is a great little escape from Lanai City. Follow Keomoku Road for 8 miles to the coast, turn right on the sandy road, and keep going for 5.7 miles.

Adventures for Kids—and Kids at Heart

Explore Hulopoe Tide Pools   An entire world of marine life lives in the tide pools on the eastern side of Hulopoe Bay. Not only are there tiny fish swimming around, but everything in the waters is small—kid-size. After examining the wonders of the tide pool, check out the larger swimming holes in the lava rock, perfect for keiki swimming.

Hunt for Petroglyphs   The Luahiwa Petroglyphs Field, located just outside Lanai City, is spread out over 3 acres. Make it a game: whoever finds the most petroglyphs gets ice cream from the Pine Isle Market.

Storytelling at the Lanai Library   Check with the Lanai Library (Fraser Avenue, near Fifth Street, Lanai City, ☎ 808/565-6996) to see if any storytelling or other activities for children are scheduled. The events are usually free and open to everyone.

Run with the Wind   Or play Hide and Seek or any other game in the town square, Dole Park (bordered by Fraser Avenue, Lanai Avenue, Seventh Street, and Eighth Street), which has plenty of room for active children to run to their heart's content.

10 Shops & Galleries

by Jocelyn Fujii

Akamai Trading. 408 Eighth St. ☎ **808/565-6587.**

Located between Richard's and Pine Isle on Dole Park, Akamai sells newspapers and magazines, cappuccino, soft-serve ice cream, fresh pastries and bagels, Lanai T-shirts, inexpensive Island gifts, and souvenir items. Same-day film processing appeals to visitors.

Gifts With Aloha. On Dole Park, at Eighth and Houston sts. ☎ **808/565-6589.**

Phoenix and Kimberly Dupree decided to open a store with their favorite things, and that meant gift items by Hawaii artists, children's books and toys, select jams and jellies, and Hawaiian quilt pillows and kits. And aloha shirts too. Handmade earrings, Raku vessels, gourmet teas, hand-poured candles, and aloha wear serve equally well as souvenirs to go or items for life on Lanai.

International Food & Clothing. 833 Ilima Ave. ☎ **808/565-6433.**

Old-timers still call it the "Dela Cruz" store, after the family who opened it in 1952. Again, the basics: groceries, a few housewares, T-shirts, hunting and fishing supplies, over-the-counter drugs, paper goods, and hardware.

Lanai Art Program. 339 Seventh St. ☎ **808/565-7503.**

This is the retail space for a nonprofit arts program that supports and showcases Lanai artists and shares their work in classes for adults and children. Located between the Laundromat and the community college office, Lanai Art Program displays and sells jewelry, ceramics, watercolors, wood works, and other two- and three-dimensional pieces. Fifteen artists, all from this island, participate in the program. Classes are offered in the schools and at this center, where the artists share their skills in a pottery barn, glass shop, wood shop, and lead classes in painting, wood crafts, and sculpting.

Lanai Marketplace. Dole Square.

Everyone on Lanai, it seems, is a backyard farmer; from 8am to noon on Saturday, they all throng to the square to sell their dewy-fresh produce, home-baked breads, plate lunches, and handicrafts. This is Lanai's version of the green market: petite in scale, like the Island, but charming and unpretentious, especially in the shade of the sky-high pine trees that line the park.

Dolores Fabrao's jams and jellies, under the Fabrao House label (☎ 808/565-6134, if you want to special-order) are a big seller at the market and at the resort gift shops where they're sold. The seven exotic flavors include pineapple-coconut, pineapple-mango, papaya, guaivi (strawberry guava), poha (gooseberry) in season, passion fruit, surinam cherry, and the very tart karamay jelly. All fruits are grown on the Island; gift packs and bags are available.

Pele's Garden Health Food Store. 811 Houston St. ☎ **808/565-9629.**

Lanai residents have embraced Beverly Zigmond's 500-square-foot store with open arms. Tucked around the corner from Dole Park, it opened in July 1995 with an assortment of vitamins, herbs, homeopathics, and supplements, as well as a complete line of natural and organic groceries, including baby food, natural pet products, nondairy items, free-range chicken, turkey products, and health and beauty aids.

Pine Isle Market. 356 Eighth St. ☎ **808/565-6047.**

A two-generation local landmark, Pine Isle specializes in locally caught fresh fish when it's available. Akule (big-eyed scad), opelu (mackerel scad), onaga (ruby snapper), opakapaka (pink snapper), mahimahi (dolphin fish), ahi (tuna), and other fish from local waters make their way to the seafood counter soon after being caught. You can also shop here for fresh herbs and spices from Pete Felipe's garden, fishing gear, canned goods, electronic games, and the basic essentials of work and play.

Richard's Shopping Center. 434 Eighth St.

The Tamashiros' family business has been on the square since 1946, and except for the merchandise, not much has changed. The "shopping center" is in fact a general store that sells groceries, paper products, ethnic foods, meats (mostly frozen), a few pieces of clothing, liquor, film, sunscreens and other recreational needs, and sundries. Until recently, you could still unearth some pre–World War II items in the far niches (I still treasure my wooden ginger grater found there years ago), but these days, the merchandise reflects the wants and needs of the island's modern mix—more visitors and a declining number of plantation workers.

11 Lanai After Dark

by Jocelyn Fujii

Once, when I inquired about nightlife on Lanai, an island woman I had just met raised her eyebrows in mock umbrage. "Oh," she said, "that's personal."

Except for special programs such as the annual **Pineapple Festival** in May, when some of Hawaii's best musicians arrive to show their support for Lanai (see "Maui Calendar of Events," in chapter 3), the only regular nightlife venues are the **Lanai Playhouse,** at the corner of Seventh and Lanai avenues, and the two resorts, The Lodge at Koele and Manele Bay Hotel.

The theater is a historic 1920s building that has received awards for its renovations. When it opened in 1993, the 150-seat venue stunned residents by offering

"Talk Story" with the Greats: Lanai's Visiting Artists Program

Not so very long ago, before CNN, e-mail, faxes, and modems, the word spread in person, on the lips of those who chanced by these remote islands, the most distant populated place on earth. Visitors were always welcome, especially if they had a good story to tell. The *tusitala,* or storyteller, was always held in high regard; Hawaii's kings invited them to the grass palace to discuss topics of contemporary life. Maybe you've seen the pictures in history books: King Kalakaua and Robert Louis Stevenson sitting on the beach at Waikiki, the famous author regaling His Majesty with bons mots. Or jaunty Jack London describing the voyage of his Snark to Queen Liliuokalani. In Hawaiian pidgin, it's called "talk story."

Hawaii grew up with this grand tradition of welcoming performing artists from every corner of the globe. Sooner or later, everyone from Kwame Ture to Tab Hunter seems to wash ashore like a note in a bottle. It's amazing, really. You never know who's going to drop in on Hawaii. Islanders might live apart from the continental drift of history, but such brief intense visits illuminate the lives of these insular folks. Joan Didion once remarked that Honolulu without visitors "would be Racine, Wisconsin, Saturday night," a fate presumably worse than death.

It doesn't just happen in Honolulu. When The Lodge at Koele opened, David Murdock invited a few friends over. The "friends" just happened to be the late Henry Mancini, Sidney Sheldon, and Michael York, and they all had a fabulous time in the Great Hall, singing, playing the piano, and reciting poetry. Kurt Matsumoto, general manager at The Lodge, liked what he saw and scheduled more informal gatherings of creative people. "We never had anything like this on this island before," said Matsumoto, born and reared on Lanai, where the only "live" entertainment in plantation days was chicken fights.

In December 1992, the two resorts began the Lanai Visiting Artists Program. To this former black hole of art and culture come the literati of America, in a new version of talk story. On any given weekend, you might find yourself in the company of poets, musicians, writers, actors, filmmakers, chefs, and other creative types. You can plan your vacation with, say, classical pianist André Watts, humorist Calvin Trillin, author John McPhee, "A Prairie Home Companion" host Garrison Keillor, jazz legend Cleo Laine, chef Larry Forgione (of New York's An American Place), *In the Name of the Father* screenwriter Terry George, award-winning short-story author David Wong Louie, best-selling novelist and screenwriter Susan Isaacs, or who knows which Pulitzer Prize or Academy Award winner, each sharing his or her talent and insights in a casual living-room atmosphere.

Now, with the Lanai Visiting Artists Program, even this little island is no Racine, Wisconsin.

The program is free and open to everyone, so call **The Lodge at Koele** at ☎ **808/565-7300** to see who's visiting while you're on Lanai.

first-run movies with Dolby sound—quite contemporary for anachronistic Lanai. Except for epics (such as *Titanic*), when only one screening is given, Lanai Playhouse usually shows two movies each evening from Friday to Monday, at 6:30 and 8:30pm. Tickets are $6 for adults and $3.50 for kids, and five "movie bucks" accumulated on Sundays get you one free ticket. On Tuesday and Wednesday nights, the only show, at 7pm, costs $3.50.

The Hotel Lanai has discontinued its weekend program of live music, but The Lodge at Koele has stepped up its live entertainment. In the Lodge's Great Hall, in front of its manorial fireplaces, visiting artists from Oahu or Maui bring contemporary Hawaiian, jazz, Broadway, classical, and other genres to listeners who sip port and fine liqueurs while sinking into plush chairs. The special programs are on weekends, but throughout the week, some form of nightly entertainment takes place in the Great Hall from 7 to 10pm. In the lounge area near the main lobby of the Manele Bay Hotel, above Ihilani, a pianist plays nightly from 7 to 10pm.

Both The Lodge at Koele and Manele Bay Hotel are known for their Visiting Artists Program (see above), which brings acclaimed literary and performing artists from across the country to this tiny island. These are scheduled throughout the year, usually on a monthly or bimonthly basis.

Other than that, what happens after dark is really up to you. Dinner becomes leisurely extended entertainment. You can repair to your room with that book you've been meaning to read. You can find an after-dinner crowd in the Tea Room at Koele or a game of billiards at Manele, the local folks out on the veranda of the Hotel Lanai will be happy to welcome you, and there's always a TV set somewhere to remind you of the great world beyond.

Index

See also separate Accommodations index, below.
Page numbers in italics refer to maps.

FROMMER'S® COMPLETE TRAVEL GUIDES
(Comprehensive guides with selections in all price ranges—from deluxe to budget)

Alaska
Amsterdam
Arizona
Atlanta
Australia
Austria
Bahamas
Barcelona, Madrid & Seville
Belgium, Holland &
   Luxembourg
Bermuda
Boston
Budapest & the Best of
   Hungary
California
Canada
Cancún, Cozumel & the
   Yucatán
Cape Cod, Nantucket &
   Martha's Vineyard
Caribbean
Caribbean Cruises &
   Ports of Call
Caribbean Ports of Call
Carolinas & Georgia
Chicago
China
Colorado
Costa Rica
Denver, Boulder &
   Colorado Springs
England
Europe
Florida

France
Germany
Greece
Hawaii
Hong Kong
Honolulu, Waikiki & Oahu
Ireland
Israel
Italy
Jamaica & Barbados
Japan
Las Vegas
London
Los Angeles
Maryland & Delaware
Maui
Mexico
Miami & the Keys
Montana & Wyoming
Montréal & Québec City
Munich & the Bavarian Alps
Nashville & Memphis
Nepal
New England
New Mexico
New Orleans
New York City
Nova Scotia, New
   Brunswick &
   Prince Edward Island
Oregon
Paris
Philadelphia & the Amish
   Country

Portugal
Prague & the Best of the
   Czech Republic
Provence & the Riviera
Puerto Rico
Rome
San Antonio & Austin
San Diego
San Francisco
Santa Fe, Taos &
   Albuquerque
Scandinavia
Scotland
Seattle & Portland
Singapore & Malaysia
South Pacific
Spain
Switzerland
Thailand
Tokyo
Toronto
Tuscany & Umbria
USA
Utah
Vancouver & Victoria
Vermont, New Hampshire &
   Maine
Vienna & the Danube Valley
Virgin Islands
Virginia
Walt Disney World &
   Orlando
Washington, D.C.
Washington State

FROMMER'S® DOLLAR-A-DAY GUIDES
(The ultimate guides to comfortable low-cost travel)

Australia from $50 a Day
California from $60 a Day
Caribbean from $60 a Day
England from $60 a Day
Europe from $50 a Day
Florida from $60 a Day
Greece from $50 a Day
Hawaii from $60 a Day
Ireland from $50 a Day

Israel from $45 a Day
Italy from $50 a Day
London from $70 a Day
New York from $75 a Day
New Zealand from $50 a Day
Paris from $70 a Day
San Francisco from $60 a Day
Washington, D.C., from
   $60 a Day

FROMMER'S® MEMORABLE WALKS

Chicago
London

New York
Paris

San Francisco

YOU TRAVEL, HELP IS NEVER FAR AWAY.

From planning your trip to

providing travel assistance along

the way, American Express®

Travel Service Offices are

always there to help.

American Express Travel Service
Offices are found in central locations
throughout Maui.

Travel

http://www.americanexpress.com/travel